# Lecture Notes in Computer Science 13375

More information about this series at https://link.springer.com/bookseries/558

Osvaldo Gervasi · Beniamino Murgante ·
Eligius M. T. Hendrix · David Taniar ·
Bernady O. Apduhan (Eds.)

# Computational Science and Its Applications – ICCSA 2022

22nd International Conference
Malaga, Spain, July 4–7, 2022
Proceedings, Part I

 Springer

*Editors*
Osvaldo Gervasi (iD)
University of Perugia
Perugia, Italy

Beniamino Murgante (iD)
University of Basilicata
Potenza, Potenza, Italy

Eligius M. T. Hendrix (iD)
Universidad de Málaga
Malaga, Spain

David Taniar
Monash University
Clayton, VIC, Australia

Bernady O. Apduhan
Kyushu Sangyo University
Fukuoka, Japan

ISSN 0302-9743          ISSN 1611-3349   (electronic)
Lecture Notes in Computer Science
ISBN 978-3-031-10521-0       ISBN 978-3-031-10522-7   (eBook)
https://doi.org/10.1007/978-3-031-10522-7

# Preface

These two volumes (LNCS 13375–13376) consist of the peer-reviewed papers from the main tracks at the 22nd International Conference on Computational Science and Its Applications (ICCSA 2022), which took place during July 4–7, 2022. The peer-reviewed papers of the workshops are published in a separate set consisting of six volumes (LNCS 13377–13382).

This year, we again decided to organize a hybrid conference, with some of the delegates attending in person and others taking part online. Despite the enormous benefits achieved by the intensive vaccination campaigns in many countries, at the crucial moment of organizing the event, there was no certainty about the evolution of COVID-19. Fortunately, more and more researchers were able to attend the event in person, foreshadowing a slow but gradual exit from the pandemic and the limitations that have weighed so heavily on the lives of all citizens over the past three years.

ICCSA 2022 was another successful event in the International Conference on Computational Science and Its Applications (ICCSA) series. Last year, the conference was held as a hybrid event in Cagliari, Italy, and in 2020 it was organized as virtual event, whilst earlier editions took place in Saint Petersburg, Russia (2019), Melbourne, Australia (2018), Trieste, Italy (2017), Beijing, China (2016), Banff, Canada (2015), Guimaraes, Portugal (2014), Ho Chi Minh City, Vietnam (2013), Salvador, Brazil (2012), Santander, Spain (2011), Fukuoka, Japan (2010), Suwon, South Korea (2009), Perugia, Italy (2008), Kuala Lumpur, Malaysia (2007), Glasgow, UK (2006), Singapore (2005), Assisi, Italy (2004), Montreal, Canada (2003), and (as ICCS) Amsterdam, The Netherlands (2002) and San Francisco, USA (2001).

Computational science is the main pillar of most of the present research, and industrial and commercial applications, and plays a unique role in exploiting ICT innovative technologies. The ICCSA conference series provides a venue to researchers and industry practitioners to discuss new ideas, to share complex problems and their solutions, and to shape new trends in computational science.

Apart from the six main tracks, ICCSA 2022 also included 52 workshops on topics ranging from computational science technologies and application in many fields to specific areas of computational sciences, such as software engineering, security, machine learning and artificial intelligence, and blockchain technologies. For the main conference tracks we accepted 57 papers and 24 short papers out of 279 submissions (an acceptance rate of 29%). For the workshops we accepted 285 papers. We would like to express our appreciation to the workshops chairs and co-chairs for their hard work and dedication.

The success of the ICCSA conference series in general, and of ICCSA 2022 in particular, vitally depends on the support of many people: authors, presenters, participants, keynote speakers, workshop chairs, session chairs, organizing committee members, student volunteers, Program Committee members, advisory committee members, international liaison chairs, reviewers, and others in various roles. We take this opportunity to wholehartedly thank them all.

We also wish to thank our publisher, Springer, for their acceptance to publish the proceedings, for sponsoring some of the best papers awards, and for their kind assistance and cooperation during the editing process.

We cordially invite you to visit the ICCSA website https://iccsa.org where you can find all the relevant information about this interesting and exciting event.

July 2022

Osvaldo Gervasi
Beniamino Murgante
Bernady O. Apduhan

# Welcome Message from Organizers

The ICCSA 2021 conference in the Mediterranean city of Cagliari provided us with inspiration to offer the ICCSA 2022 conference in the Mediterranean city of Málaga, Spain. The additional considerations due to the COVID-19 pandemic, which necessitated a hybrid conference, also stimulated the idea to use the School of Informatics of the University of Málaga. It has an open structure where we could take lunch and coffee outdoors and the lecture halls have open windows on two sides providing optimal conditions for meeting more safely.

The school is connected to the center of the old town via a metro system, for which we offered cards to the participants. This provided the opportunity to stay in lodgings in the old town close to the beach because, at the end of the day, that is the place to be to exchange ideas with your fellow scientists. The social program allowed us to enjoy the history of Malaga from its founding by the Phoenicians...

In order to provoke as much scientific interaction as possible we organized online sessions that could easily be followed by all participants from their own devices. We tried to ensure that participants from Asia could participate in morning sessions and those from the Americas in evening sessions. On-site sessions could be followed and debated on-site and discussed online using a chat system. To realize this, we relied on the developed technological infrastructure based on open source software, with the addition of streaming channels on YouTube. The implementation of the software infrastructure and the technical coordination of the volunteers were carried out by Damiano Perri and Marco Simonetti. Nine student volunteers from the universities of Málaga, Minho, Almeria, and Helsinki provided technical support and ensured smooth interaction during the conference.

A big thank you goes to all of the participants willing to exchange their ideas during their daytime. Participants of ICCSA 2022 came from 58 countries scattered over many time zones of the globe. Very interesting keynote talks were provided by well-known international scientists who provided us with more ideas to reflect upon, and we are grateful for their insights.

Eligius M. T. Hendrix

# Organization

ICCSA 2022 was organized by the University of Malaga (Spain), the University of Perugia (Italy), the University of Cagliari (Italy), the University of Basilicata (Italy), Monash University (Australia), Kyushu Sangyo University (Japan), and the University of Minho, (Portugal).

## Honorary General Chairs

| | |
|---|---|
| Norio Shiratori | Chuo University, Japan |
| Kenneth C. J. Tan | Sardina Systems, UK |

## General Chairs

| | |
|---|---|
| Osvaldo Gervasi | University of Perugia, Italy |
| Eligius Hendrix | University of Malaga, Italy |
| Bernady O. Apduhan | Kyushu Sangyo University, Japan |

## Program Committee Chairs

| | |
|---|---|
| Beniamino Murgante | University of Basilicata, Italy |
| Inmaculada Garcia Fernandez | University of Malaga, Spain |
| Ana Maria A. C. Rocha | University of Minho, Portugal |
| David Taniar | Monash University, Australia |

## International Advisory Committee

| | |
|---|---|
| Jemal Abawajy | Deakin University, Australia |
| Dharma P. Agarwal | University of Cincinnati, USA |
| Rajkumar Buyya | Melbourne University, Australia |
| Claudia Bauzer Medeiros | University of Campinas, Brazil |
| Manfred M. Fisher | Vienna University of Economics and Business, Austria |
| Marina L. Gavrilova | University of Calgary, Canada |
| Sumi Helal | University of Florida, USA, and University of Lancaster, UK |
| Yee Leung | Chinese University of Hong Kong, China |

## International Liaison Chairs

| | |
|---|---|
| Ivan Blečić | University of Cagliari, Italy |
| Giuseppe Borruso | University of Trieste, Italy |

| | |
|---|---|
| Elise De Donker | Western Michigan University, USA |
| Maria Irene Falcão | University of Minho, Portugal |
| Robert C. H. Hsu | Chung Hua University, Taiwan |
| Tai-Hoon Kim | Beijing Jiaotong University, China |
| Vladimir Korkhov | St Petersburg University, Russia |
| Sanjay Misra | Østfold University College, Norway |
| Takashi Naka | Kyushu Sangyo University, Japan |
| Rafael D. C. Santos | National Institute for Space Research, Brazil |
| Maribel Yasmina Santos | University of Minho, Portugal |
| Elena Stankova | St Petersburg University, Russia |

## Workshop and Session Organizing Chairs

| | |
|---|---|
| Beniamino Murgante | University of Basilicata, Italy |
| Chiara Garau | University of Cagliari, Italy |
| Sanjay Misra | Ostfold University College, Norway |

## Award Chair

| | |
|---|---|
| Wenny Rahayu | La Trobe University, Australia |

## Publicity Committee Chairs

| | |
|---|---|
| Elmer Dadios | De La Salle University, Philippines |
| Nataliia Kulabukhova | St Petersburg University, Russia |
| Daisuke Takahashi | Tsukuba University, Japan |
| Shangwang Wang | Beijing University of Posts and Telecommunications, China |

## Local Arrangement Chairs

| | |
|---|---|
| Eligius Hendrix | University of Malaga, Spain |
| Inmaculada Garcia Fernandez | University of Malaga, Spain |
| Salvador Merino Cordoba | University of Malaga, Spain |
| Pablo Guerrero-García | University of Malaga, Spain |

## Technology Chairs

| | |
|---|---|
| Damiano Perri | University of Florence, Italy |
| Marco Simonetti | University of Florence, Italy |

## Program Committee

| | |
|---|---|
| Vera Afreixo | University of Aveiro, Portugal |
| Filipe Alvelos | University of Minho, Portugal |

| | |
|---|---|
| Raffaele Garrisi | Polizia di Stato, Italy |
| Jerome Gensel | LSR-IMAG, France |
| Maria Giaoutzi | National Technical University of Athens, Greece |
| Arminda Manuela Andrade Pereira Gonçalves | University of Minho, Portugal |
| Andrzej M. Goscinski | Deakin University, Australia |
| Sevin Gümgüm | Izmir University of Economics, Turkey |
| Alex Hagen-Zanker | University of Cambridge, UK |
| Shanmugasundaram Hariharan | B.S. Abdur Rahman Crescent Institute of Science and Technology, India |
| Eligius M. T. Hendrix | University of Malaga, Spain and Wageningen University, The Netherlands |
| Hisamoto Hiyoshi | Gunma University, Japan |
| Mustafa Inceoglu | Ege University, Turkey |
| Peter Jimack | University of Leeds, UK |
| Qun Jin | Waseda University, Japan |
| Yeliz Karaca | UMass Chan Medical School, USA |
| Farid Karimipour | Vienna University of Technology, Austria |
| Baris Kazar | Oracle Corp., USA |
| Maulana Adhinugraha Kiki | Telkom University, Indonesia |
| DongSeong Kim | University of Canterbury, New Zealand |
| Taihoon Kim | Hannam University, South Korea |
| Ivana Kolingerova | University of West Bohemia, Czech Republic |
| Nataliia Kulabukhova | St. Petersburg University, Russia |
| Vladimir Korkhov | St. Petersburg University, Russia |
| Rosa Lasaponara | National Research Council, Italy |
| Maurizio Lazzari | National Research Council, Italy |
| Cheng Siong Lee | Monash University, Australia |
| Sangyoun Lee | Yonsei University, South Korea |
| Jongchan Lee | Kunsan National University, South Korea |
| Chendong Li | University of Connecticut, USA |
| Gang Li | Deakin University, Australia |
| Fang (Cherry) Liu | Ames Laboratory, USA |
| Xin Liu | University of Calgary, Canada |
| Andrea Lombardi | University of Perugia, Italy |
| Savino Longo | University of Bari, Italy |
| Tinghuai Ma | Nanjing University of Information Science and Technology, China |
| Ernesto Marcheggiani | Katholieke Universiteit Leuven, Belgium |
| Antonino Marvuglia | Public Research Centre Henri Tudor, Luxembourg |
| Nicola Masini | National Research Council, Italy |
| Ilaria Matteucci | National Research Council, Italy |
| Nirvana Meratnia | University of Twente, The Netherlands |
| Fernando Miranda | University of Minho, Portugal |
| Giuseppe Modica | University of Reggio Calabria, Italy |
| Josè Luis Montaña | University of Cantabria, Spain |

| | |
|---|---|
| Maria Filipa Mourão | Instituto Politécnico de Viana do Castelo, Portugal |
| Louiza de Macedo Mourelle | State University of Rio de Janeiro, Brazil |
| Nadia Nedjah | State University of Rio de Janeiro, Brazil |
| Laszlo Neumann | University of Girona, Spain |
| Kok-Leong Ong | Deakin University, Australia |
| Belen Palop | Universidad de Valladolid, Spain |
| Marcin Paprzycki | Polish Academy of Sciences, Poland |
| Eric Pardede | La Trobe University, Australia |
| Kwangjin Park | Wonkwang University, South Korea |
| Ana Isabel Pereira | Polytechnic Institute of Bragança, Portugal |
| Massimiliano Petri | University of Pisa, Italy |
| Telmo Pinto | University of Coimbra, Portugal |
| Maurizio Pollino | Italian National Agency for New Technologies, Energy and Sustainable Economic Development, Italy |
| Alenka Poplin | University of Hamburg, Germany |
| Vidyasagar Potdar | Curtin University of Technology, Australia |
| David C. Prosperi | Florida Atlantic University, USA |
| Wenny Rahayu | La Trobe University, Australia |
| Jerzy Respondek | Silesian University of Technology, Poland |
| Humberto Rocha | INESC-Coimbra, Portugal |
| Jon Rokne | University of Calgary, Canada |
| Octavio Roncero | CSIC, Spain |
| Maytham Safar | Kuwait University, Kuwait |
| Chiara Saracino | A.O. Ospedale Niguarda Ca' Granda, Italy |
| Marco Paulo Seabra dos Reis | University of Coimbra, Portugal |
| Jie Shen | University of Michigan, USA |
| Qi Shi | Liverpool John Moores University, UK |
| Dale Shires | U.S. Army Research Laboratory, USA |
| Inês Soares | University of Coimbra, Portugal |
| Elena Stankova | St Petersburg University, Russia |
| Takuo Suganuma | Tohoku University, Japan |
| Eufemia Tarantino | Polytechnic Universiy of Bari, Italy |
| Sergio Tasso | University of Perugia, Italy |
| Ana Paula Teixeira | University of Trás-os-Montes and Alto Douro, Portugal |
| M. Filomena Teodoro | Portuguese Naval Academy and University of Lisbon, Portugal |
| Parimala Thulasiraman | University of Manitoba, Canada |
| Carmelo Torre | Polytechnic University of Bari, Italy |
| Javier Martinez Torres | Centro Universitario de la Defensa Zaragoza, Spain |
| Giuseppe A. Trunfio | University of Sassari, Italy |
| Pablo Vanegas | University of Cuenca, Equador |
| Marco Vizzari | University of Perugia, Italy |
| Varun Vohra | Merck Inc., USA |
| Koichi Wada | University of Tsukuba, Japan |
| Krzysztof Walkowiak | Wroclaw University of Technology, Poland |

| Zequn Wang | Intelligent Automation Inc, USA |
| Robert Weibel | University of Zurich, Switzerland |
| Frank Westad | Norwegian University of Science and Technology, Norway |
| Roland Wismüller | Universität Siegen, Germany |
| Mudasser Wyne | National University, USA |
| Chung-Huang Yang | National Kaohsiung Normal University, Taiwan |
| Xin-She Yang | National Physical Laboratory, UK |
| Salim Zabir | France Telecom Japan Co., Japan |
| Haifeng Zhao | University of California, Davis, USA |
| Fabiana Zollo | Ca' Foscari University of Venice, Italy |
| Albert Y. Zomaya | University of Sydney, Australia |

## Workshop Organizers

## International Workshop on Advances in Artificial Intelligence Learning Technologies: Blended Learning, STEM, Computational Thinking and Coding (AAILT 2022)

| Alfredo Milani | University of Perugia, Italy |
| Valentina Franzoni | University of Perugia, Italy |
| Osvaldo Gervasi | University of Perugia, Italy |

## International Workshop on Advancements in Applied Machine-Learning and Data Analytics (AAMDA 2022)

| Alessandro Costantini | INFN, Italy |
| Davide Salomoni | INFN, Italy |
| Doina Cristina Duma | INFN, Italy |
| Daniele Cesini | INFN, Italy |

## International Workshop on Advances in Information Systems and Technologies for Emergency Management, Risk Assessment and Mitigation Based on the Resilience (ASTER 2022)

| Maurizio Pollino | ENEA, Italy |
| Marco Vona | University of Basilicata, Italy |
| Sonia Giovinazzi | ENEA, Italy |
| Benedetto Manganelli | University of Basilicata, Italy |
| Beniamino Murgante | University of Basilicata, Italy |

## International Workshop on Advances in Web Based Learning (AWBL 2022)

Birol Ciloglugil          Ege University, Turkey
Mustafa Inceoglu          Ege University, Turkey

## International Workshop on Blockchain and Distributed Ledgers: Technologies and Applications (BDLTA 2022)

Vladimir Korkhov          St Petersburg State University, Russia
Elena Stankova            St Petersburg State University, Russia
Nataliia Kulabukhova      St Petersburg State University, Russia

## International Workshop on Bio and Neuro Inspired Computing and Applications (BIONCA 2022)

Nadia Nedjah              State University of Rio De Janeiro, Brazil
Luiza De Macedo Mourelle  State University of Rio De Janeiro, Brazil

## International Workshop on Configurational Analysis For Cities (CA CITIES 2022)

Claudia Yamu              Oslo Metropolitan University, Norway
Valerio Cutini            Università di Pisa, Italy
Beniamino Murgante        University of Basilicata, Italy
Chiara Garau              Dicaar, University of Cagliari, Italy

## International Workshop on Computational and Applied Mathematics (CAM 2022)

Maria Irene Falcão        University of Minho, Portugal
Fernando Miranda          University of Minho, Portugal

## International Workshop on Computational and Applied Statistics (CAS 2022)

Ana Cristina Braga        University of Minho, Portugal

## International Workshop on Computational Mathematics, Statistics and Information Management (CMSIM 2022)

Maria Filomena Teodoro    University of Lisbon and Portuguese Naval Academy, Portugal

## International Workshop on Computational Optimization and Applications (COA 2022)

| | |
|---|---|
| Ana Maria A. C. Rocha | University of Minho, Portugal |
| Humberto Rocha | University of Coimbra, Portugal |

## International Workshop on Computational Astrochemistry (CompAstro 2022)

| | |
|---|---|
| Marzio Rosi | University of Perugia, Italy |
| Nadia Balucani | University of Perugia, Italy |
| Cecilia Ceccarelli | Université Grenoble Alpes, France |
| Stefano Falcinelli | University of Perugia, Italy |

## International Workshop on Computational Methods for Porous Geomaterials (CompPor 2022)

| | |
|---|---|
| Vadim Lisitsa | Sobolev Institute of Mathematics, Russia |
| Evgeniy Romenski | Sobolev Institute of Mathematics, Russia |

## International Workshop on Computational Approaches for Smart, Conscious Cities (CASCC 2022)

| | |
|---|---|
| Andreas Fricke | University of Potsdam, Germany |
| Juergen Doellner | University of Potsdam, Germany |
| Salvador Merino | University of Malaga, Spain |
| Jürgen Bund | Graphics Vision AI Association, Germany/Portugal |
| Markus Jobst | Federal Office of Metrology and Surveying, Austria |
| Francisco Guzman | University of Malaga, Spain |

## International Workshop on Computational Science and HPC (CSHPC 2022)

| | |
|---|---|
| Elise De Doncker | Western Michigan University, USA |
| Fukuko Yuasa | High Energy Accelerator Research Organization (KEK), Japan |
| Hideo Matsufuru | High Energy Accelerator Research Organization (KEK), Japan |

## International Workshop on Cities, Technologies and Planning (CTP 2022)

| | |
|---|---|
| Giuseppe Borruso | University of Trieste, Italy |
| Malgorzata Hanzl | Lodz University of Technology, Poland |
| Beniamino Murgante | University of Basilicata, Italy |

Anastasia Stratigea            National Technical University of Athens, Grece
Ginevra Balletto               University of Cagliari, Italy
Ljiljana Zivkovic              Republic Geodetic Authority, Serbia

## International Workshop on Digital Sustainability and Circular Economy (DiSCE 2022)

Giuseppe Borruso               University of Trieste, Italy
Stefano Epifani                Digital Sustainability Institute, Italy
Ginevra Balletto               University of Cagliari, Italy
Luigi Mundula                  University of Cagliari, Italy
Alessandra Milesi              University of Cagliari, Italy
Mara Ladu                      University of Cagliari, Italy
Stefano De Nicolai             University of Pavia, Italy
Tu Anh Trinh                   University of Economics Ho Chi Minh City, Vietnam

## International Workshop on Econometrics and Multidimensional Evaluation in Urban Environment (EMEUE 2022)

Carmelo Maria Torre            Polytechnic University of Bari, Italy
Maria Cerreta                  University of Naples Federico II, Italy
Pierluigi Morano               Polytechnic University of Bari, Italy
Giuliano Poli                  University of Naples Federico II, Italy
Marco Locurcio                 Polytechnic University of Bari, Italy
Francesco Tajani               Sapienza University of Rome, Italy

## International Workshop on Ethical AI Applications for a Human-Centered Cyber Society (EthicAI 2022)

Valentina Franzoni             University of Perugia, Italy
Alfredo Milani                 University of Perugia, Italy

## International Workshop on Future Computing System Technologies and Applications (FiSTA 2022)

Bernady Apduhan                Kyushu Sangyo University, Japan
Rafael Santos                  INPE, Brazil

## International Workshop on Geodesign in Decision Making: Meta Planning and Collaborative Design for Sustainable and Inclusive Development (GDM 2022)

Francesco Scorza               University of Basilicata, Italy
Michele Campagna               University of Cagliari, Italy
Ana Clara Mourão Moura         Federal University of Minas Gerais, Brazil

## International Workshop on Geomatics in Agriculture and Forestry: New Advances and Perspectives (GeoForAgr 2022)

| | |
|---|---|
| Maurizio Pollino | ENEA, Italy |
| Giuseppe Modica | University of Reggio Calabria, Italy |
| Marco Vizzari | University of Perugia, Italy |

## International Workshop on Geographical Analysis, Urban Modeling, Spatial Statistics (Geog-An-Mod 2022)

| | |
|---|---|
| Giuseppe Borruso | University of Trieste, Italy |
| Beniamino Murgante | University of Basilicata, Italy |
| Harmut Asche | Hasso-Plattner-Institut für Digital Engineering gGmbH, Germany |

## International Workshop on Geomatics for Resource Monitoring and Management (GRMM 2022)

| | |
|---|---|
| Alessandra Capolupo | Polytechnic of Bari, Italy |
| Eufemia Tarantino | Polytechnic of Bari, Italy |
| Enrico Borgogno Mondino | University of Turin, Italy |

## International Workshop on Information and Knowledge in the Internet of Things (IKIT 2022)

| | |
|---|---|
| Teresa Guarda | State University of Santa Elena Peninsula, Ecuador |
| Filipe Portela | University of Minho, Portugal |
| Maria Fernanda Augusto | Bitrum Research Center, Spain |

## 13th International Symposium on Software Quality (ISSQ 2022)

| | |
|---|---|
| Sanjay Misra | Østfold University College, Norway |

## International Workshop on Machine Learning for Space and Earth Observation Data (MALSEOD 2022)

| | |
|---|---|
| Rafael Santos | INPE, Brazil |
| Karine Reis Ferreira Gomes | INPE, Brazil |

## International Workshop on Building Multi-dimensional Models for Assessing Complex Environmental Systems (MES 2022)

| | |
|---|---|
| Vanessa Assumma | Politecnico di Torino, Italy |
| Caterina Caprioli | Politecnico di Torino, Italy |
| Giulia Datola | Politecnico di Torino, Italy |

| Federico Dell'Anna | Politecnico di Torino, Italy |
| Marta Dell'Ovo | Politecnico di Milano, Italy |

## International Workshop on Models and Indicators for Assessing and Measuring the Urban Settlement Development in the View of ZERO Net Land Take by 2050 (MOVEto0 2022)

| Lucia Saganeiti | University of L'Aquila, Italy |
| Lorena Fiorini | University of L'aquila, Italy |
| Angela Pilogallo | University of Basilicata, Italy |
| Alessandro Marucci | University of L'Aquila, Italy |
| Francesco Zullo | University of L'Aquila, Italy |

## International Workshop on Modelling Post-Covid Cities (MPCC 2022)

| Beniamino Murgante | University of Basilicata, Italy |
| Ginevra Balletto | University of Cagliari, Italy |
| Giuseppe Borruso | University of Trieste, Italy |
| Marco Dettori | Università degli Studi di Sassari, Italy |
| Lucia Saganeiti | University of L'Aquila, Italy |

## International Workshop on Ecosystem Services: Nature's Contribution to People in Practice. Assessment Frameworks, Models, Mapping, and Implications (NC2P 2022)

| Francesco Scorza | University of Basilicata, Italy |
| Sabrina Lai | University of Cagliari, Italy |
| Silvia Ronchi | University of Cagliari, Italy |
| Dani Broitman | Israel Institute of Technology, Israel |
| Ana Clara Mourão Moura | Federal University of Minas Gerais, Brazil |
| Corrado Zoppi | University of Cagliari, Italy |

## International Workshop on New Mobility Choices for Sustainable and Alternative Scenarios (NEWMOB 2022)

| Tiziana Campisi | University of Enna Kore, Italy |
| Socrates Basbas | Aristotle University of Thessaloniki, Greece |
| Aleksandra Deluka T. | University of Rijeka, Croatia |
| Alexandros Nikitas | University of Huddersfield, UK |
| Ioannis Politis | Aristotle University of Thessaloniki, Greece |
| Georgios Georgiadis | Aristotle University of Thessaloniki, Greece |
| Irena Ištoka Otković | University of Osijek, Croatia |
| Sanja Surdonja | University of Rijeka, Croatia |

## International Workshop on Privacy in the Cloud/Edge/IoT World (PCEIoT 2022)

| | |
|---|---|
| Michele Mastroianni | University of Campania Luigi Vanvitelli, Italy |
| Lelio Campanile | University of Campania Luigi Vanvitelli, Italy |
| Mauro Iacono | University of Campania Luigi Vanvitelli, Italy |

## International Workshop on Psycho-Social Analysis of Sustainable Mobility in the Pre- and Post-Pandemic Phase (PSYCHE 2022)

| | |
|---|---|
| Tiziana Campisi | University of Enna Kore, Italy |
| Socrates Basbas | Aristotle University of Thessaloniki, Greece |
| Dilum Dissanayake | Newcastle University, UK |
| Nurten Akgün Tanbay | Bursa Technical University, Turkey |
| Elena Cocuzza | University of Catania, Italy |
| Nazam Ali | University of Management and Technology, Pakistan |
| Vincenza Torrisi | University of Catania, Italy |

## International Workshop on Processes, Methods and Tools Towards Resilient Cities and Cultural Heritage Prone to SOD and ROD Disasters (RES 2022)

| | |
|---|---|
| Elena Cantatore | Polytechnic University of Bari, Italy |
| Alberico Sonnessa | Polytechnic University of Bari, Italy |
| Dario Esposito | Polytechnic University of Bari, Italy |

## International Workshop on Scientific Computing Infrastructure (SCI 2022)

| | |
|---|---|
| Elena Stankova | St Petersburg University, Russia |
| Vladimir Korkhov | St Petersburg University, Russia |

## International Workshop on Socio-Economic and Environmental Models for Land Use Management (SEMLUM 2022)

| | |
|---|---|
| Debora Anelli | Polytechnic University of Bari, Italy |
| Pierluigi Morano | Polytechnic University of Bari, Italy |
| Francesco Tajani | Sapienza University of Rome, Italy |
| Marco Locurcio | Polytechnic University of Bari, Italy |
| Paola Amoruso | LUM University, Italy |

## 14th International Symposium on Software Engineering Processes and Applications (SEPA 2022)

| | |
|---|---|
| Sanjay Misra | Østfold University College, Norway |

## International Workshop on Ports of the Future – Smartness and Sustainability (SmartPorts 2022)

| | |
|---|---|
| Giuseppe Borruso | University of Trieste, Italy |
| Gianfranco Fancello | University of Cagliari, Italy |
| Ginevra Balletto | University of Cagliari, Italy |
| Patrizia Serra | University of Cagliari, Italy |
| Maria del Mar Munoz Leonisio | University of Cadiz, Spain |
| Marco Mazzarino | University of Venice, Italy |
| Marcello Tadini | Università del Piemonte Orientale, Italy |

## International Workshop on Smart Tourism (SmartTourism 2022)

| | |
|---|---|
| Giuseppe Borruso | University of Trieste, Italy |
| Silvia Battino | University of Sassari, Italy |
| Ainhoa Amaro Garcia | Universidad de Alcalà and Universidad de Las Palmas, Spain |
| Maria del Mar Munoz Leonisio | University of Cadiz, Spain |
| Carlo Donato | University of Sassari, Italy |
| Francesca Krasna | University of Trieste, Italy |
| Ginevra Balletto | University of Cagliari, Italy |

## International Workshop on Sustainability Performance Assessment: Models, Approaches and Applications Toward Interdisciplinary and Integrated Solutions (SPA 2022)

| | |
|---|---|
| Francesco Scorza | University of Basilicata, Italy |
| Sabrina Lai | University of Cagliari, Italy |
| Jolanta Dvarioniene | Kaunas University of Technology, Lithuania |
| Iole Cerminara | University of Basilicata, Italy |
| Georgia Pozoukidou | Aristotle University of Thessaloniki, Greece |
| Valentin Grecu | Lucian Blaga University of Sibiu, Romania |
| Corrado Zoppi | University of Cagliari, Italy |

## International Workshop on Specifics of Smart Cities Development in Europe (SPEED 2022)

| | |
|---|---|
| Chiara Garau | University of Cagliari, Italy |
| Katarína Vitálišová | Matej Bel University, Slovakia |
| Paolo Nesi | University of Florence, Italy |
| Anna Vanova | Matej Bel University, Slovakia |
| Kamila Borsekova | Matej Bel University, Slovakia |
| Paola Zamperlin | University of Pisa, Italy |

Federico Cugurullo                Trinity College Dublin, Ireland
Gerardo Carpentieri              University of Naples Federico II, Italy

## International Workshop on Smart and Sustainable Island Communities (SSIC 2022)

Chiara Garau                     University of Cagliari, Italy
Anastasia Stratigea              National Technical University of Athens, Greece
Paola Zamperlin                  University of Pisa, Italy
Francesco Scorza                 University of Basilicata, Italy

## International Workshop on Theoretical and Computational Chemistry and Its Applications (TCCMA 2022)

Noelia Faginas-Lago              University of Perugia, Italy
Andrea Lombardi                  University of Perugia, Italy

## International Workshop on Transport Infrastructures for Smart Cities (TISC 2022)

Francesca Maltinti               University of Cagliari, Italy
Mauro Coni                       University of Cagliari, Italy
Francesco Pinna                  University of Cagliari, Italy
Chiara Garau                     University of Cagliari, Italy
Nicoletta Rassu                  Univesity of Cagliari, Italy
James Rombi                      University of Cagliari, Italy
Benedetto Barabino               University of Brescia, Italy

## 14th International Workshop on Tools and Techniques in Software Development Process (TTSDP 2022)

Sanjay Misra                     Østfold University College, Norway

## International Workshop on Urban Form Studies (UForm 2022)

Malgorzata Hanzl                 Lodz University of Technology, Poland
Beniamino Murgante               University of Basilicata, Italy
Alessandro Camiz                 Özyeğin University, Turkey
Tomasz Bradecki                  Silesian University of Technology, Poland

## International Workshop on Urban Regeneration: Innovative Tools and Evaluation Model (URITEM 2022)

Fabrizio Battisti                University of Florence, Italy
Laura Ricci                      Sapienza University of Rome, Italy
Orazio Campo                     Sapienza University of Rome, Italy

## International Workshop on Urban Space Accessibility and Mobilities (USAM 2022)

| | |
|---|---|
| Chiara Garau | University of Cagliari, Italy |
| Matteo Ignaccolo | University of Catania, Italy |
| Enrica Papa | University of Westminster, UK |
| Francesco Pinna | University of Cagliari, Italy |
| Silvia Rossetti | University of Parma, Italy |
| Wendy Tan | Wageningen University and Research, The Netherlands |
| Michela Tiboni | University of Brescia, Italy |
| Vincenza Torrisi | University of Catania, Italy |

## International Workshop on Virtual Reality and Augmented Reality and Applications (VRA 2022)

| | |
|---|---|
| Osvaldo Gervasi | University of Perugia, Italy |
| Damiano Perri | University of Florence, Italy |
| Marco Simonetti | University of Florence, Italy |
| Sergio Tasso | University of Perugia, Italy |

## International Workshop on Advanced and Computational Methods for Earth Science Applications (WACM4ES 2022)

| | |
|---|---|
| Luca Piroddi | University of Cagliari, Italy |
| Sebastiano Damico | University of Malta, Malta |

## International Workshop on Advanced Mathematics and Computing Methods in Complex Computational Systems (WAMCM 2022)

| | |
|---|---|
| Yeliz Karaca | UMass Chan Medical School, USA |
| Dumitru Baleanu | Cankaya University, Turkey |
| Osvaldo Gervasi | University of Perugia, Italy |
| Yudong Zhang | University of Leicester, UK |
| Majaz Moonis | UMass Chan Medical School, USA |

## Additional Reviewers

| | |
|---|---|
| Akshat Agrawal | Amity University, Haryana, India |
| Waseem Ahmad | National Institute of Technology Karnataka, India |
| Vladimir Alarcon | Universidad Diego Portales, Chile |
| Oylum Alatlı | Ege University, Turkey |
| Raffaele Albano | University of Basilicata, Italy |
| Abraham Alfa | FUT Minna, Nigeria |
| Diego Altafini | Università di Pisa, Italy |
| Filipe Alvelos | Universidade do Minho, Portugal |

| | |
|---|---|
| Marina Alexandra Pedro Andrade | ISCTE-IUL, Portugal |
| Debora Anelli | Polytechnic University of Bari, Italy |
| Gennaro Angiello | AlmavivA de Belgique, Belgium |
| Alfonso Annunziata | Università di Cagliari, Italy |
| Bernady Apduhan | Kyushu Sangyo University, Japan |
| Daniela Ascenzi | Università degli Studi di Trento, Italy |
| Burak Galip Aslan | Izmir Insitute of Technology, Turkey |
| Vanessa Assumma | Politecnico di Torino, Italy |
| Daniel Atzberger | Hasso-Plattner-Institute für Digital Engineering gGmbH, Germany |
| Dominique Aury | École Polytechnique Fédérale de Lausanne, Switzerland |
| Joseph Awotumde | University of Alcala, Spain |
| Birim Balci | Celal Bayar University, Turkey |
| Juliana Balera | INPE, Brazil |
| Ginevra Balletto | University of Cagliari, Italy |
| Benedetto Barabino | University of Brescia, Italy |
| Kaushik Barik | University of Alcala, Spain |
| Carlo Barletta | Politecnico di Bari, Italy |
| Socrates Basbas | Aristotle University of Thessaloniki, Greece |
| Rosaria Battarra | ISMed-CNR, Italy |
| Silvia Battino | University of Sassari, Italy |
| Chiara Bedan | University of Trieste, Italy |
| Ranjan Kumar Behera | National Institute of Technology Rourkela, India |
| Gulmira Bekmanova | L.N. Gumilyov Eurasian National University, Kazakhstan |
| Mario Bentivenga | University of Basilicata, Italy |
| Asrat Mulatu Beyene | Addis Ababa Science and Technology University, Ethiopia |
| Tiziana Binda | Politecnico di Torino, Italy |
| Giulio Biondi | University of Firenze, Italy |
| Alexander Bogdanov | St Petersburg University, Russia |
| Costanza Borghesi | University of Perugia, Italy |
| Giuseppe Borruso | University of Trieste, Italy |
| Marilisa Botte | University of Naples Federico II, Italy |
| Tomasz Bradecki | Silesian University of Technology, Poland |
| Ana Cristina Braga | University of Minho, Portugal |
| Luca Braidotti | University of Trieste, Italy |
| Bazon Brock | University of Wuppertal, Germany |
| Dani Broitman | Israel Institute of Technology, Israel |
| Maria Antonia Brovelli | Politecnico di Milano, Italy |
| Jorge Buele | Universidad Tecnológica Indoamérica, Ecuador |
| Isabel Cacao | University of Aveiro, Portugal |
| Federica Cadamuro Morgante | Politecnico di Milano, Italy |

| | |
|---|---|
| Rogerio Calazan | IEAPM, Brazil |
| Michele Campagna | University of Cagliari, Italy |
| Lelio Campanile | Università degli Studi della Campania Luigi Vanvitelli, Italy |
| Tiziana Campisi | University of Enna Kore, Italy |
| Antonino Canale | University of Enna Kore, Italy |
| Elena Cantatore | Polytechnic University of Bari, Italy |
| Patrizia Capizzi | Univerity of Palermo, Italy |
| Alessandra Capolupo | Polytechnic University of Bari, Italy |
| Giacomo Caporusso | Politecnico di Bari, Italy |
| Caterina Caprioli | Politecnico di Torino, Italy |
| Gerardo Carpentieri | University of Naples Federico II, Italy |
| Martina Carra | University of Brescia, Italy |
| Pedro Carrasqueira | INESC Coimbra, Portugal |
| Barbara Caselli | Università degli Studi di Parma, Italy |
| Cecilia Castro | University of Minho, Portugal |
| Giulio Cavana | Politecnico di Torino, Italy |
| Iole Cerminara | University of Basilicata, Italy |
| Maria Cerreta | University of Naples Federico II, Italy |
| Daniele Cesini | INFN, Italy |
| Jabed Chowdhury | La Trobe University, Australia |
| Birol Ciloglugil | Ege University, Turkey |
| Elena Cocuzza | Univesity of Catania, Italy |
| Emanuele Colica | University of Malta, Malta |
| Mauro Coni | University of Cagliari, Italy |
| Elisete Correia | Universidade de Trás-os-Montes e Alto Douro, Portugal |
| Florbela Correia | Polytechnic Institute of Viana do Castelo, Portugal |
| Paulo Cortez | University of Minho, Portugal |
| Lino Costa | Universidade do Minho, Portugal |
| Alessandro Costantini | INFN, Italy |
| Marilena Cozzolino | Università del Molise, Italy |
| Alfredo Cuzzocrea | University of Calabria, Italy |
| Sebastiano D'amico | University of Malta, Malta |
| Gianni D'Angelo | University of Salerno, Italy |
| Tijana Dabovic | University of Belgrade, Serbia |
| Hiroshi Daisaka | Hitotsubashi University, Japan |
| Giulia Datola | Politecnico di Torino, Italy |
| Regina De Almeida | University of Trás-os-Montes and Alto Douro, Portugal |
| Maria Stella De Biase | Università della Campania Luigi Vanvitelli, Italy |
| Elise De Doncker | Western Michigan University, USA |
| Itamir De Morais Barroca Filho | Federal University of Rio Grande do Norte, Brazil |
| Samuele De Petris | University of Turin, Italy |
| Alan De Sá | Marinha do Brasil, Brazil |
| Alexander Degtyarev | St Petersburg University, Russia |

| | |
|---|---|
| Federico Dell'Anna | Politecnico di Torino, Italy |
| Marta Dell'Ovo | Politecnico di Milano, Italy |
| Ahu Dereli Dursun | Istanbul Commerce University, Turkey |
| Giulia Desogus | University of Cagliari, Italy |
| Piero Di Bonito | Università degli Studi della Campania, Italia |
| Paolino Di Felice | University of L'Aquila, Italy |
| Felicia Di Liddo | Polytechnic University of Bari, Italy |
| Isabel Dimas | University of Coimbra, Portugal |
| Doina Cristina Duma | INFN, Italy |
| Aziz Dursun | Virginia Tech University, USA |
| Jaroslav Dvořak | Klaipėda University, Lithuania |
| Dario Esposito | Polytechnic University of Bari, Italy |
| M. Noelia Faginas-Lago | University of Perugia, Italy |
| Stefano Falcinelli | University of Perugia, Italy |
| Falcone Giacomo | University of Reggio Calabria, Italy |
| Maria Irene Falcão | University of Minho, Portugal |
| Stefano Federico | CNR-ISAC, Italy |
| Marcin Feltynowski | University of Lodz, Poland |
| António Fernandes | Instituto Politécnico de Bragança, Portugal |
| Florbela Fernandes | Instituto Politecnico de Braganca, Portugal |
| Paula Odete Fernandes | Instituto Politécnico de Bragança, Portugal |
| Luis Fernandez-Sanz | University of Alcala, Spain |
| Luís Ferrás | University of Minho, Portugal |
| Ângela Ferreira | Instituto Politécnico de Bragança, Portugal |
| Lorena Fiorini | University of L'Aquila, Italy |
| Hector Florez | Universidad Distrital Francisco Jose de Caldas, Colombia |
| Stefano Franco | LUISS Guido Carli, Italy |
| Valentina Franzoni | Perugia University, Italy |
| Adelaide Freitas | University of Aveiro, Portugal |
| Andreas Fricke | Hasso Plattner Institute, Germany |
| Junpei Fujimoto | KEK, Japan |
| Federica Gaglione | Università del Sannio, Italy |
| Andrea Gallo | Università degli Studi di Trieste, Italy |
| Luciano Galone | University of Malta, Malta |
| Adam Galuszka | Silesian University of Technology, Poland |
| Chiara Garau | University of Cagliari, Italy |
| Ernesto Garcia Para | Universidad del País Vasco, Spain |
| Aniket A. Gaurav | Østfold University College, Norway |
| Marina Gavrilova | University of Calgary, Canada |
| Osvaldo Gervasi | University of Perugia, Italy |
| Andrea Ghirardi | Università di Brescia, Italy |
| Andrea Gioia | Politecnico di Bari, Italy |
| Giacomo Giorgi | Università degli Studi di Perugia, Italy |
| Stanislav Glubokovskikh | Lawrence Berkeley National Laboratory, USA |
| A. Manuela Gonçalves | University of Minho, Portugal |

| | |
|---|---|
| Leocadio González Casado | University of Almería, Spain |
| Angela Gorgoglione | Universidad de la República Uruguay, Uruguay |
| Yusuke Gotoh | Okayama University, Japan |
| Daniele Granata | Università degli Studi della Campania, Italy |
| Christian Grévisse | University of Luxembourg, Luxembourg |
| Silvana Grillo | University of Cagliari, Italy |
| Teresa Guarda | State University of Santa Elena Peninsula, Ecuador |
| Carmen Guida | Università degli Studi di Napoli Federico II, Italy |
| Kemal Güven Gülen | Namık Kemal University, Turkey |
| Ipek Guler | Leuven Biostatistics and Statistical Bioinformatics Centre, Belgium |
| Sevin Gumgum | Izmir University of Economics, Turkey |
| Martina Halásková | VSB Technical University in Ostrava, Czech Republic |
| Peter Hegedus | University of Szeged, Hungary |
| Eligius M. T. Hendrix | Universidad de Málaga, Spain |
| Mauro Iacono | Università degli Studi della Campania, Italy |
| Oleg Iakushkin | St Petersburg University, Russia |
| Matteo Ignaccolo | University of Catania, Italy |
| Mustafa Inceoglu | Ege University, Turkey |
| Markus Jobst | Federal Office of Metrology and Surveying, Austria |
| Issaku Kanamori | RIKEN Center for Computational Science, Japan |
| Yeliz Karaca | UMass Chan Medical School, USA |
| Aarti Karande | Sardar Patel Institute of Technology, India |
| András Kicsi | University of Szeged, Hungary |
| Vladimir Korkhov | St Petersburg University, Russia |
| Nataliia Kulabukhova | St Petersburg University, Russia |
| Claudio Ladisa | Politecnico di Bari, Italy |
| Mara Ladu | University of Cagliari, Italy |
| Sabrina Lai | University of Cagliari, Italy |
| Mark Lajko | University of Szeged, Hungary |
| Giuseppe Francesco Cesare Lama | University of Napoli Federico II, Italy |
| Vincenzo Laporta | CNR, Italy |
| Margherita Lasorella | Politecnico di Bari, Italy |
| Francesca Leccis | Università di Cagliari, Italy |
| Federica Leone | University of Cagliari, Italy |
| Chien-sing Lee | Sunway University, Malaysia |
| Marco Locurcio | Polytechnic University of Bari, Italy |
| Francesco Loddo | Henge S.r.l., Italy |
| Andrea Lombardi | Università di Perugia, Italy |
| Isabel Lopes | Instituto Politécnico de Bragança, Portugal |
| Fernando Lopez Gayarre | University of Oviedo, Spain |
| Vanda Lourenço | Universidade Nova de Lisboa, Portugal |
| Jing Ma | Luleå University of Technology, Sweden |
| Helmuth Malonek | University of Aveiro, Portugal |
| Francesca Maltinti | University of Cagliari, Italy |

| | |
|---|---|
| Benedetto Manganelli | Università degli Studi della Basilicata, Italy |
| Krassimir Markov | Institute of Electric Engineering and Informatics, Bulgaria |
| Alessandro Marucci | University of L'Aquila, Italy |
| Alessandra Mascitelli | Italian Civil Protection Department and ISAC-CNR, Italy |
| Michele Mastroianni | University of Campania Luigi Vanvitelli, Italy |
| Hideo Matsufuru | High Energy Accelerator Research Organization (KEK), Japan |
| Chiara Mazzarella | University of Naples Federico II, Italy |
| Marco Mazzarino | University of Venice, Italy |
| Paolo Mengoni | University of Florence, Italy |
| Alfredo Milani | University of Perugia, Italy |
| Fernando Miranda | Universidade do Minho, Portugal |
| Augusto Montisci | Università degli Studi di Cagliari, Italy |
| Ricardo Moura | New University of Lisbon, Portugal |
| Ana Clara Mourao Moura | Federal University of Minas Gerais, Brazil |
| Maria Mourao | Polytechnic Institute of Viana do Castelo, Portugal |
| Eugenio Muccio | University of Naples Federico II, Italy |
| Beniamino Murgante | University of Basilicata, Italy |
| Giuseppe Musolino | University of Reggio Calabria, Italy |
| Stefano Naitza | Università di Cagliari, Italy |
| Naohito Nakasato | University of Aizu, Japan |
| Roberto Nardone | University of Reggio Calabria, Italy |
| Nadia Nedjah | State University of Rio de Janeiro, Brazil |
| Juraj Nemec | Masaryk University in Brno, Czech Republic |
| Keigo Nitadori | RIKEN R-CCS, Japan |
| Roseline Ogundokun | Kaunas University of Technology, Lithuania |
| Francisco Henrique De Oliveira | Santa Catarina State University, Brazil |
| Irene Oliveira | Univesidade Trás-os-Montes e Alto Douro, Portugal |
| Samson Oruma | Østfold University College, Norway |
| Antonio Pala | University of Cagliari, Italy |
| Simona Panaro | University of Porstmouth, UK |
| Dimos Pantazis | University of West Attica, Greece |
| Giovanni Paragliola | ICAR-CNR, Italy |
| Eric Pardede | La Trobe University, Australia |
| Marco Parriani | University of Perugia, Italy |
| Paola Perchinunno | Uniersity of Bari, Italy |
| Ana Pereira | Polytechnic Institute of Bragança, Portugal |
| Damiano Perri | University of Perugia, Italy |
| Marco Petrelli | Roma Tre University, Italy |
| Camilla Pezzica | University of Pisa, Italy |
| Angela Pilogallo | University of Basilicata, Italy |
| Francesco Pinna | University of Cagliari, Italy |
| Telmo Pinto | University of Coimbra, Portugal |

| | |
|---|---|
| Fernando Pirani | University of Perugia, Italy |
| Luca Piroddi | University of Cagliari, Italy |
| Bojana Pjanović | University of Belgrade, Serbia |
| Giuliano Poli | University of Naples Federico II, Italy |
| Maurizio Pollino | ENEA, Italy |
| Salvatore Praticò | University of Reggio Calabria, Italy |
| Zbigniew Przygodzki | University of Lodz, Poland |
| Carlotta Quagliolo | Politecnico di Torino, Italy |
| Raffaele Garrisi | Polizia Postale e delle Comunicazioni, Italy |
| Mariapia Raimondo | Università della Campania Luigi Vanvitelli, Italy |
| Deep Raj | IIIT Naya Raipur, India |
| Buna Ramos | Universidade Lusíada Norte, Portugal |
| Nicoletta Rassu | Univesity of Cagliari, Italy |
| Michela Ravanelli | Sapienza Università di Roma, Italy |
| Roberta Ravanelli | Sapienza Università di Roma, Italy |
| Pier Francesco Recchi | University of Naples Federico II, Italy |
| Stefania Regalbuto | University of Naples Federico II, Italy |
| Marco Reis | University of Coimbra, Portugal |
| Maria Reitano | University of Naples Federico II, Italy |
| Anatoly Resnyansky | Defence Science and Technology Group, Australia |
| Jerzy Respondek | Silesian University of Technology, Poland |
| Isabel Ribeiro | Instituto Politécnico Bragança, Portugal |
| Albert Rimola | Universitat Autònoma de Barcelona, Spain |
| Corrado Rindone | University of Reggio Calabria, Italy |
| Ana Maria A. C. Rocha | University of Minho, Portugal |
| Humberto Rocha | University of Coimbra, Portugal |
| Maria Clara Rocha | Instituto Politécnico de Coimbra, Portugal |
| James Rombi | University of Cagliari, Italy |
| Elisabetta Ronchieri | INFN, Italy |
| Marzio Rosi | University of Perugia, Italy |
| Silvia Rossetti | Università degli Studi di Parma, Italy |
| Marco Rossitti | Politecnico di Milano, Italy |
| Mária Rostašová | Universtiy of Žilina, Slovakia |
| Lucia Saganeiti | University of L'Aquila, Italy |
| Giovanni Salzillo | Università degli Studi della Campania, Italy |
| Valentina Santarsiero | University of Basilicata, Italy |
| Luigi Santopietro | University of Basilicata, Italy |
| Stefania Santoro | Politecnico di Bari, Italy |
| Rafael Santos | INPE, Brazil |
| Valentino Santucci | Università per Stranieri di Perugia, Italy |
| Mirko Saponaro | Polytechnic University of Bari, Italy |
| Filippo Sarvia | University of Turin, Italy |
| Andrea Scianna | ICAR-CNR, Italy |
| Francesco Scorza | University of Basilicata, Italy |
| Ester Scotto Di Perta | University of Naples Federico II, Italy |
| Ricardo Severino | University of Minho, Portugal |

| | |
|---|---|
| Jie Shen | University of Michigan, USA |
| Luneque Silva Junior | Universidade Federal do ABC, Brazil |
| Carina Silva | Instituto Politécnico de Lisboa, Portugal |
| Joao Carlos Silva | Polytechnic Institute of Cavado and Ave, Portugal |
| Ilya Silvestrov | Saudi Aramco, Saudi Arabia |
| Marco Simonetti | University of Florence, Italy |
| Maria Joana Soares | University of Minho, Portugal |
| Michel Soares | Federal University of Sergipe, Brazil |
| Alberico Sonnessa | Politecnico di Bari, Italy |
| Lisete Sousa | University of Lisbon, Portugal |
| Elena Stankova | St Petersburg University, Russia |
| Jan Stejskal | University of Pardubice, Czech Republic |
| Silvia Stranieri | University of Naples Federico II, Italy |
| Anastasia Stratigea | National Technical University of Athens, Greece |
| Yue Sun | European XFEL GmbH, Germany |
| Anthony Suppa | Politecnico di Torino, Italy |
| Kirill Sviatov | Ulyanovsk State Technical University, Russia |
| David Taniar | Monash University, Australia |
| Rodrigo Tapia-McClung | Centro de Investigación en Ciencias de Información Geoespacial, Mexico |
| Eufemia Tarantino | Politecnico di Bari, Italy |
| Sergio Tasso | University of Perugia, Italy |
| Vladimir Tcheverda | Institute of Petroleum Geology and Geophysics, SB RAS, Russia |
| Ana Paula Teixeira | Universidade de Trás-os-Montes e Alto Douro, Portugal |
| Tengku Adil Tengku Izhar | Universiti Teknologi MARA, Malaysia |
| Maria Filomena Teodoro | University of Lisbon and Portuguese Naval Academy, Portugal |
| Yiota Theodora | National Technical University of Athens, Greece |
| Graça Tomaz | Instituto Politécnico da Guarda, Portugal |
| Gokchan Tonbul | Atilim University, Turkey |
| Rosa Claudia Torcasio | CNR-ISAC, Italy |
| Carmelo Maria Torre | Polytechnic University of Bari, Italy |
| Vincenza Torrisi | University of Catania, Italy |
| Vincenzo Totaro | Politecnico di Bari, Italy |
| Pham Trung | HCMUT, Vietnam |
| Po-yu Tsai | National Chung Hsing University, Taiwan |
| Dimitrios Tsoukalas | Centre of Research and Technology Hellas, Greece |
| Toshihiro Uchibayashi | Kyushu University, Japan |
| Takahiro Ueda | Seikei University, Japan |
| Piero Ugliengo | Università degli Studi di Torino, Italy |
| Gianmarco Vanuzzo | University of Perugia, Italy |
| Clara Vaz | Instituto Politécnico de Bragança, Portugal |
| Laura Verde | University of Campania Luigi Vanvitelli, Italy |
| Katarína Vitálišová | Matej Bel University, Slovakia |

| Daniel Mark Vitiello | University of Cagliari, Italy |
| Marco Vizzari | University of Perugia, Italy |
| Alexander Vodyaho | St. Petersburg State Electrotechnical University "LETI", Russia |
| Agustinus Borgy Waluyo | Monash University, Australia |
| Chao Wang | USTC, China |
| Marcin Wozniak | Silesian University of Technology, Poland |
| Jitao Yang | Beijing Language and Culture University, China |
| Fenghui Yao | Tennessee State University, USA |
| Fukuko Yuasa | KEK, Japan |
| Paola Zamperlin | University of Pisa, Italy |
| Michal Žemlička | Charles University, Czech Republic |
| Nataly Zhukova | ITMO University, Russia |
| Alcinia Zita Sampaio | University of Lisbon, Portugal |
| Ljiljana Zivkovic | Republic Geodetic Authority, Serbia |
| Floriana Zucaro | University of Naples Federico II, Italy |
| Marco Zucca | Politecnico di Milano, Italy |
| Camila Zyngier | Ibmec, Belo Horizonte, Brazil |

## Sponsoring Organizations

ICCSA 2022 would not have been possible without tremendous support of many organizations and institutions, for which all organizers and participants of ICCSA 2022 express their sincere gratitude:

 Springer

Springer International Publishing AG, Germany (https://www.springer.com)

 *computers*

Computers Open Access Journal (https://www.mdpi.com/journal/computers)

 *computation*
an Open Access Journal by MDPI

Computation Open Access Journal (https://www.mdpi.com/journal/computation)

University of Malaga, Spain (https://www.uma.es/)

University of Perugia, Italy
(https://www.unipg.it)

University of Basilicata, Italy
(http://www.unibas.it)

Monash University, Australia
(https://www.monash.edu/)

Kyushu Sangyo University, Japan
(https://www.kyusan-u.ac.jp/)

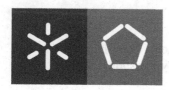

University of Minho, Portugal
(https://www.uminho.pt/)

**Universidade do Minho**
Escola de Engenharia

# Contents – Part I

**High Performance Computing and Networks**

**Information Systems and Technologies**

# Contents – Part II

# Computational Methods, Algorithms and Scientific Applications

Computational Methods, Algorithms
and Scientific Applications

# Effects of Noise on Leaky Integrate-and-Fire Neuron Models for Neuromorphic Computing Applications

Thi Kim Thoa Thieu[1(✉)] and Roderick Melnik[1,2]

[1] MS2Discovery Interdisciplinary Research Institute, Wilfrid Laurier University, 75 University Ave W, Waterloo, ON N2L 3C5, Canada
{tthieu,rmelnik}@wlu.ca
[2] BCAM - Basque Center for Applied Mathematics, Bilbao, Spain

**Abstract.** Artificial neural networks (ANNs) have been extensively used for the description of problems arising from biological systems and for constructing neuromorphic computing models. The third generation of ANNs, namely, spiking neural networks (SNNs), inspired by biological neurons enable a more realistic mimicry of the human brain. A large class of the problems from these domains is characterized by the necessity to deal with the combination of neurons, spikes and synapses via integrate-and-fire neuron models. Motivated by important applications of the integrate-and-fire of neurons in neuromorphic computing for biomedical studies, the main focus of the present work is on the analysis of the effects of additive and multiplicative types of random input currents together with a random refractory period on a leaky integrate-and-fire (LIF) synaptic conductance neuron model. Our analysis is carried out via Langevin stochastic dynamics in a numerical setting describing a cell membrane potential. We provide the details of the model, as well as representative numerical examples, and discuss the effects of noise on the time evolution of the membrane potential as well as the spiking activities of neurons in the LIF synaptic conductance model scrutinized here. Furthermore, our numerical results demonstrate that the presence of a random refractory period in the LIF synaptic conductance system may substantially influence an increased irregularity of spike trains of the output neuron.

**Keywords:** ANNs · SNNs · LIF · Langevin stochastic models · Neuromorphic computing · Random input currents · Synaptic conductances · Neuron spiking activities · Uncertainty factors · Membrane and action potentials · Neuron refractory periods

## 1 Introduction

In recent years, the modelling with artificial neural networks (ANNs) offers many challenging questions to some of the most advanced areas of science and technology [7]. The progress in ANNs has led to improvements in various cognitive

O. Gervasi et al. (Eds.): ICCSA 2022, LNCS 13375, pp. 3–18, 2022.
https://doi.org/10.1007/978-3-031-10522-7_1

tasks and tools for vision, language, behavior and so on. Moreover, some ANN models together with the numerical algorithms bring the outcome achievements at the human-level performance. In general, biological neurons in the human brain transmit information by generating spikes. To improve the biological plausibility of the existing ANNs, spiking neural networks (SNNs) are known as the third generation of ANNs. SNNs play an important role in the modelling of important systems in neuroscience since SNNs more realistically mimic the activity of biological neurons by the combination of neurons and synapses [6]. In particular, neurons in the SNNs transmit information only when a membrane potential, i.e. an intrinsic quality of the neuron related to its membrane electrical charge, reaches a specific threshold value. The neuron fires, and generates a signal that travels to other neurons when the membrane reaches its threshold. Hence, a neuron that fires in a membrane potential model at the moment of threshold crossing is called a spiking neuron. Many models have been proposed to describe the spiking activities of neurons in different scenarios. One of the simplest models, providing a foundation for many neuromorphic applications, is a leaky integrate-and-fire (LIF) neuron model [18, 24, 31]. The LIF model mimics the dynamics of the cell membrane in the biological system [5, 20] and provides a suitable compromise between complexity and analytical tractability when implemented for large neural networks. Recent works have demonstrated the importance of the LIF model that has become one of the most popular neuron models in neuromorphic computing [2, 10, 12, 15, 16, 28]. However, ANNs are intensively computed and often deal with many challenges from severe accuracy degradation if the testing data is corrupted with noise [7, 17], which may not be seen during training. Uncertainties coming from different sources [11], e.g. inputs, devices, chemical reactions, etc. would need to be accounted for. Furthermore, the presence of fluctuations can effect on the transmission of a signal in nonlinear systems [3, 4]. Recent results provided in [1] have shown that multiplicative noise is beneficial for the transmission of sensory signals in simple neuron models. To get closer to the real scenarios in biological systems as well as in their computational studies, we are interested in evaluating the contribution of uncertainty factors arising in LIF systems. In particular, we investigate the effects of the additive and multiplicative noise input currents together with the random refractory period on the dynamics of a LIF synaptic conductance system. A better understanding of random input factors in LIF synaptic conductance models would allow for a more efficient usage of smart SNNs and/or ANNs systems in such fields as biomedicine and other applications [7, 32].

Motivated by LIF models and their applications in SNNs and ANNs subjected to natural random factors in the description of biological systems, we develop a LIF synaptic conductance model of neuronal dynamics to study the effects of additive and multiplicative types of random external current inputs together with a random refractory period on the spiking activities of neurons in a cell membrane potential setting. Our analysis focuses on considering a Langevin stochastic equation in a numerical setting for a cell membrane potential with random inputs. We provide numerical examples and discuss the effects of random inputs on the time evolution of the membrane potential as well as the spiking activities of neurons in our model. Furthermore, the model of LIF synaptic conductances is examined on the data from dynamic clamping (see, e.g., [20, 30, 32]) in the Poissonian input spike train setting.

## 2 Random Factors and a LIF Synaptic Conductance Neuron Model

### 2.1 SNN Algorithm and a LIF Synaptic Conductance Neuron Model

Let us recall the SNN algorithm, presented schematically in Fig. 1 (see, e.g., [10]). At the first step, pre-synaptic neuronal drivers provide the input voltage spikes. Then, we convert the input driver for spikes to a gently varying current signal proportional to the synaptic weights $w_1$ and $w_2$. Next, the synaptic current response is summed into the input of LIF neuron $N_3$. Then, the LIF neuron integrates the input current across a capacitor, which raises its potential. After that, $N_3$ resets immediately (i.e. loses stored charge) once the potential reaches/exceeds a threshold. Finally, every time $N_3$ reaches the threshold, a driver neuron D3 produces a spike.

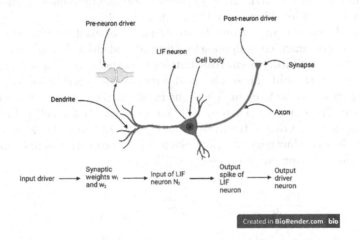

**Fig. 1.** Sketch of SNN algorithm. (Color figure online)

In general, the biological neuronal network is related to the SNN algorithm. Moreover, the main role of SNNs is to understand and mimic human brain functionalities since SNNs enable to approximate efficient learning and recognition tasks in neuro-biology. Hence, to have a better implementation of SNNs in hardware, it would be necessary to describe an efficient analog of the biological neuron. Therefore, in what follows, we are interested in the SNN algorithm starting from the third step, where the synaptic current response is summed into the input of LIF neuron, to the last step of the SNN algorithm. In particular, at the third step of SNN algorithm, it is assumed that the summation of synaptic current responses can be a constant, in a deterministic form or can be even represented by a random type of current. To get closer to the real scenarios of neuronal models, we should also account for the existence of random fluctuations in the systems. Specifically, the random inputs arise primarily through sensory fluctuations, brainstem discharges and thermal energy (random fluctuations at a microscopic level, such as Brownian motions of ions). The stochasticity can arise even from the devices which are used for medical treatments, e.g. devices for injection currents into the neuronal systems. For simplicity, we consider a LIF synaptic conductance model with additive and multiplicative noise input currents in presence of a random refractory period.

In biological systems such as brain networks, instead of physically joined neurons, a spike in the presynaptic cell causes a chemical, or a neurotransmitter, to be released into a small space between the neurons called the synaptic cleft [14]. Therefore, in what follows, we will focus on investigating chemical synaptic transmission and study how excitation and inhibition affect the patterns in the neurons' spiking output. In this section, we consider a model of synaptic conductance dynamics. In particular, neurons receive a myriad of excitatory and inhibitory synaptic inputs at dendrites. To better understand the mechanisms of synaptic conductance dynamics, we investigate the dynamics of the random excitatiory (E) and inhibitory inputs to a neuron [21].

In general, synaptic inputs are the combination of excitatory neurotransmitters. Such neurotransmitters depolarize the cell and drive it towards the spike threshold, while inhibitory neurotransmitters hyperpolarize it and drive it away from the spike threshold. These chemical factors cause specific ion channels on the postsynaptic neuron to open. Then, the results make a change in the neuron's conductance. Therefore, the current will flow in or out of the cell [14].

For simplicity, we define transmitter-activated ion channels as an explicitly time-dependent conductivity $(g_{\mathrm{syn}}(t))$. Such conductance transients can be generated by the following equation (see, e.g., [9,14]):

$$\frac{dg_{\mathrm{syn}}(t)}{dt} = -\bar{g}_{\mathrm{syn}} \sum_k \delta(t - t_k) - \frac{g_{\mathrm{syn}}(t)}{\tau_{\mathrm{syn}}}, \tag{1}$$

where $\bar{g}_{\mathrm{syn}}$ (synaptic weight) is the maximum conductance elicited by each incoming spike, while $\tau_{\mathrm{syn}}$ is the synaptic time constant and $\delta(\cdot)$ is the Dirac delta function. Note that the summation runs over all spikes received by the neuron at time $t_k$. Using Ohm's law, we have the following formula for converting conductance changes to the current:

$$I_{\mathrm{syn}}(t) = g_{\mathrm{syn}}(t)(V(t) - E_{\mathrm{syn}}), \tag{2}$$

where $E_{\mathrm{syn}}$ represents the direction of current flow and the excitatory or inhibitory nature of the synapse.

In general, the total synaptic input current $I_{\text{syn}}$ is the sum of both excitatory and inhibitory inputs. We assume that the total excitatory and inhibitory conductances received at time $t$ are $g_E(t)$ and $g_I(t)$, and their corresponding reversal potentials are $E_E$ and $E_I$, respectively. We define the total synaptic current by the following equation:

$$I_{\text{syn}}(V(t), t) = -g_E(t)(V - E_E) - g_I(t)(V - E_I). \tag{3}$$

Therefore, the corresponding membrane potential dynamics of the LIF neuron under synaptic current (see, e.g., [21]) can be described as follows:

$$\tau_m \frac{d}{dt} V(t) = -(V(t) - E_L) - \frac{g_E(t)}{g_L}(V(t) - E_E) - \frac{g_I(t)}{g_L}(V(t) - E_I) + \frac{I_{\text{inj}}}{g_L}, \tag{4}$$

where $V$ is the membrane potential, $I_{\text{inj}}$ is the external input current, while $\tau_m$ is the membrane time constant. We consider the membrane potential model where a spike takes place whenever $V(t)$ crosses $V_{\text{th}}$. Here, $V_{\text{th}}$ denotes the membrane potential threshold to fire an action potential. In that case, a spike is recorded and $V(t)$ resets to $V_{\text{reset}}$ value. This is summarized in the reset condition $V(t) = V_{\text{reset}}$ if $V(t) \geq V_{\text{th}}$. We define the following LIF model with and a reset condition:

$$\tau_m \frac{d}{dt} V(t) = -(V(t) - E_L) - \frac{g_E(t)}{g_L}(V(t) - E_E) - \frac{g_I(t)}{g_L}(V(t) - E_I)$$

$$+ \frac{I_{\text{inj}}}{g_L} \quad \text{if } V(t) \leq V_{\text{th}}, \tag{5}$$

$$V(t) = V_{\text{reset}} \quad \text{otherwise}, \tag{6}$$

In this model, we consider a random synaptic input by introducing the following random input current (additive noise) $I_{\text{inj}} = I_0 + \sigma_1 \eta(t)$, where $\eta$ is the zero-mean Gaussian white noise with unit variance. For the multiplicative noise case, the applied current is set to $I_{\text{inj}} = V(t)(I_0 + \sigma_2 \eta(t))$. Here, $\sigma_1, \sigma_2$ denote the standard deviations of these random components to the inputs. When considering such random input currents, the equation (4) can be considered as the following Langevin stochastic equation (see, e.g., [25]):

$$\tau_m \frac{d}{dt} V(t) = -(V(t) - E_L) - \frac{g_E(t)}{g_L}(V(t) - E_E) - \frac{g_I(t)}{g_L}(V(t) - E_I)$$

$$+ \begin{cases} \frac{1}{g_L}(I_0 + \sigma_1 \eta(t)) \\ \frac{1}{g_L} V(t)(I_0 + \sigma_2 \eta(t)) \end{cases} \quad \text{if } V(t) \leq V_{\text{th}}. \tag{7}$$

In our model, we use the simplest input spikes with Poisson process which provide a suitable approximation to stochastic neuronal firings [29]. This input spikes will be added in the quantity $\sum_k \delta(t-t_k)$ in the equation (1). In particular, the input spikes are given when every input spike arrives independently of other spikes. For designing a spike generator of spike train, let us call the probability of firing a spike within a short interval (see, e.g. [9]) $P(1 \text{ spike during } \Delta t) = r_j \Delta t$, where $j = e, i$ with $r_e, r_i$ representing the instantaneous excitatory and inhibitory firing rates, respectively. This expression is designed to generate a Poisson spike train by first subdividing time into a group of short intervals through small time steps $\Delta t$. At each time step, we define a random variable $x_{\text{rand}}$ with uniform distribution over the range between 0 and 1. Then, we compare this with the probability of firing a spike, which is described as follows:

$$\begin{cases} r_j \Delta t > x_{\text{rand}}, & \text{generates a spike,} \\ r_j \Delta t \leq x_{\text{rand}}, & \text{no spike is generated.} \end{cases} \qquad (8)$$

In this work, we also investigate the effects of random refractory periods [22]. We define the random refractory periods $t_{\text{ref}}$ as $t_{\text{ref}} = \mu_{\text{ref}} + \sigma_{\text{ref}}\tilde{\eta}(t)$, where $\tilde{\eta}(t) \sim \mathcal{N}(0,1)$.

## 2.2  Firing Rate and Spike Time Irregularity

In general, the irregularity of spike trains can provide information about stimulating activities in a neuron. A LIF synaptic conductance neuron with multiple inputs and coefficient of variation (CV) of the inter-spike-interval (ISI) can bring an output decoded neuron. In this work, we show that the increase $\sigma_{\text{ref}}$ can lead to an increase in the irregularity of the spike trains (see also [13]).

We define the spike regularity via coefficient of variation of the inter-spike-interval (see, e.g., [8,13]) as follows:

$$CV_{\text{ISI}} = \frac{\sigma_{\text{ISI}}}{\mu_{\text{ISI}}},$$

where $\sigma_{\text{ISI}}$ is the standard deviation and $\mu_{\text{ISI}}$ is the mean of the ISI of an individual neuron.

In the next section, we consider the output firing rate as a function of Gaussian white noise mean or direct current value, known as the input-output transfer function of the neuron.

## 3  Numerical Results for the LIF Synaptic Conductance Model

In this subsection, we take a single neuron at the dendrite and study how the neuron behaves when it is bombarded with both excitatory and inhibitory spike trains (see, e.g., [20,21]).

The simulations this section have been carried out by using by a discrete-time integration based on the Euler method inplemented in Python.

In the simulations, we choose the parameter set as follows: $E_E = 70$ (mV), $E_L = -60$ (mV), $E_I = -10$ (mV), $V_{th} = -55$ (mV), $V_{reset} = -70$ (mV), $\Delta t = 0.1$, $\tau_m = 10$ (ms), $\tau_E = 20$ (ms), $\tau_I = 100$ (ms), $\bar{g}_E = 4.8$ (nS), $\bar{g}_I = 6.4$(nS), $r_e = 10$, $r_i = 10$, $n_E = 80$ spikes, $n_I = 20$ spikes. Here, $n_E$ and $n_I$ represent the number of excitatory and inhibitory presynaptic spike trains, respectively. These parameters have also been used in [20,21] for dynamic clamp experiments and we take them for our model validation. In this subsection, we use the excitatory and inhibitory conductances provided in Fig. 2 for all of our simulations.

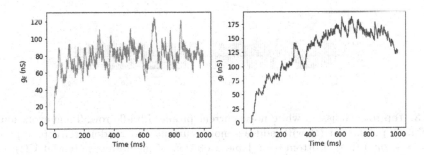

**Fig. 2.** Left: Excitatory conductances profile. Right: Inhibitory conductances profile. (Color figure online)

The main numerical results of our analysis here are shown in Figs. 3, 4, 5, 6 and 11, where we have plotted the time evolution of the membrane potential calculated based on model (4), the distribution of the ISI and the corresponding spike irregularity profile. We investigate the effects of additive and multiplicative types of random input currents inpresence of a random refractory period on a LIF neuron under synaptic conductance dynamics. Under a Poissonian spike input, the random external currents and random refractory period influence the spiking activity of a neuron in the cell membrane potential.

### 3.1 Additive Noise

In Fig. 3, we have plotted the Gaussian white noise current profile, the time evolution of the membrane potential $V(t)$ with Gaussian white noise input current ($I_{inj} = 200 + \eta(t)$ (pA)) and direct input current ($I_{inj} = I_{dc} = 200$ (pA)). In this case, we fix the value of $t_{ref} = 8 + 2\tilde{\eta}(t)$ (ms). We observe that the time evolution of the membrane potential looks quite similar in the two cases. Note that a burst occurred when a neuron spiked more than once within 25 (ms) (see, e.g., [26]). In this case, when considering the presence of random input current and random refractory period in the system, we observe there exist bursts in the case presented in the second row of Fig. 3.

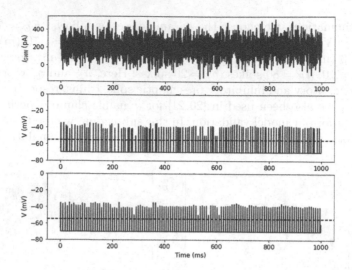

**Fig. 3.** Top row: Gaussian white noise current profile. Middle row: Time evolution of membrane potential $V(t)$ with additive noise current and random refractory period $t_{\text{ref}} = 8 + 2\tilde{\eta}(t)$ (ms). Bottom row: Time evolution of membrane potential $V(t)$ with direct input current and direct refractory period $t_{\text{ref}} = 8$ (ms). The dash line represents the spike threshold $V_{\text{th}} = -55$ (mV). (Color figure online)

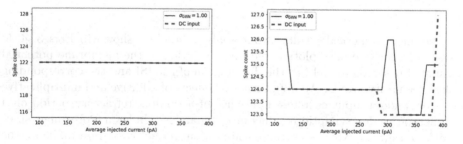

**Fig. 4.** The input-output transfer function of the neuron, output firing rate as a function of input mean for the case with additive noise input current ($\sigma_{\text{Inj}} = 1$). Left: direct time refractory period $t_{\text{ref}} = 8$ (ms). Right: random refractory period $t_{\text{ref}} = 8 + 2\tilde{\eta}(t)$ (ms). (Color figure online)

We look also at the input-output transfer function of the neuron, the output firing as a function of average injected current in Fig. 4. In particular, we see that the spike count values are slightly fluctuating when we add the random refractory period into the system (in the right panel of Fig. 4). Moreover, in the averaged injected current intervals $[130; 290]$ (pA) and $[320; 360]$ (pA), the spike count value is the same in both cases: the Gaussian white noise and direct currents in the right panel of Fig. 4. We have seen this phenomenon for $I_{\text{inj}} = 200$ (pA) also in the Fig. 3.

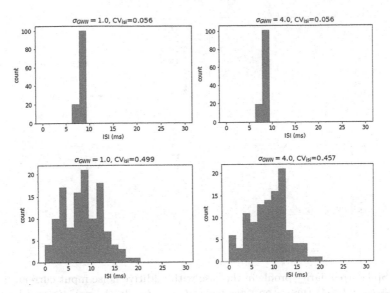

**Fig. 5.** ISI histogram distributions for the case with additive noise input current. First row: $t_{ref} = 8 + 0.5\tilde{\eta}(t)$ (ms). Second row: $t_{ref} = 8 + 4\tilde{\eta}(t)$ (ms). (Color figure online)

In Fig. 5, we have plotted the spike count distribution as a function of ISI. We observe that the coefficient $CV_{isi}$ increases when we increase the value of $\sigma_{ref}$. The spikes are distributed almost entirely in the ISI interval from 6 to 9 (ms) in the first row, while the spikes are distributed mostly in from 0 to 21 (ms) in the second row of Fig. 5. The ISI distribution presented in the first row of Fig. 5 reflects bursting moods. To understand better such phenomenon let us look at the following spike irregularity profile in Fig. 6. In Fig. 6, we look at the corresponding spike irregularity profile of the spike count in Figs. 5 and 6. In this plot, we fix the external current $I_{inj} = 200 + \eta(t)$ (pA) together with considering different values of $\sigma_{ref}$. We observe that when we increase the value of $\sigma_{ref}$ the coefficient $CV_{isi}$ increases. In general, when we increase the mean of the Gaussian white noise, at some point, the effective input means are above the spike threshold and then the neuron operates in the so-called mean-driven regime. Hence, as the input is sufficiently high, the neuron is charged up to the spike threshold and then it is reset. This essentially gives an almost regular spiking. However, in our case, by considering various values of the random refractory period, we see that $CV_{isi}$ increases when we increase the values of $\sigma_{ref}$. This is visible in Fig. 6, $CV_{isi}$ increases from 0.1 to 0.6 when $\sigma_{ref}$ increases from 1 to 6. Note that an increased ISI regularity could result in bursting [23]. Moreover, the spike trains are substantially more regular with a range $CV_{ISI} \in (0; 0.5)$, and more irregular when $CV_{ISI} > 0.5$ [27]. Therefore, in some cases, the presence of random input current with oscillations could lead to the burst discharge.

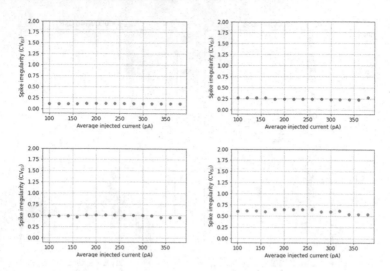

**Fig. 6.** Spike irregularity profile in the case with additive noise input current. Top left panel: $t_{\text{ref}} = 8 + \tilde{\eta}(t)$ (ms). Top right panel: $t_{\text{ref}} = 8 + 2\tilde{\eta}(t)$ (ms). Bottom left panel: $t_{\text{ref}} = 8 + 4\tilde{\eta}(t)$ (ms). Bottom right panel: $t_{\text{ref}} = 8 + 6\tilde{\eta}(t)$ (ms). (Color figure online)

## 3.2  Multiplicative Noise

In Fig. 7, we have plotted the Gaussian white noise current profile, the time evolution of the membrane potential $V(t)$ with multiplicative noise input current ($I_{\text{inj}} = V(t)(200 + \eta(t))$ (pA)) and direct input current ($I_{\text{inj}} = I_{\text{dc}} = 200V(t)$ (pA)). In this case, we fix the value of $t_{\text{ref}} = 8 + \eta(t)$ (ms). There are bursting moods in the membrane potential in both two cases. This is due to the presence of $V(t)$ in the input current together with the random refractory period in the system. However, when we increase the leak conductance from $g_L = 20$ (nS) to $g_L = 200$ (nS), the burst discharges are dramatically reduced in the case with multiplicative noise in Fig. 8. In particular, we observe fluctuations in the membrane potential in the second row of Fig. 8. There is an increase in the time interval between two nearest neighbor spikes in both cases. In order to understand better such phenomena, let us look at the following plots. From now on, we will use the parameter $g_L = 200$ (nS) for cases in Figs. 9, 10 and 11.

In Fig. 9, we look at the input-output transfer function of the neuron, output firing rate as a function of input means. We observe that the input-output transfer function looks quite similar in both cases: direct and random refractory periods. There are slight fluctuations in the spike count profile in the case with random refractory period. It is clear that the presence of multiplicative noise strongly affects the spiking activity in our system compared to the case with additive noise. The spiking activity of the neuron dramatically reduces in presence of the multiplicative noise in the system.

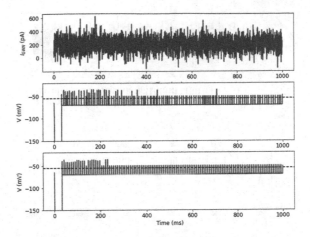

**Fig. 7.** Top row: Gaussian white noise current profile. Middle row: Time evolution of membrane potential $V(t)$ with multiplicative noise current and random refractory period $t_{\mathrm{ref}} = 8 + 2\bar{\eta}(t)$ (ms). Bottom row: Time evolution of membrane potential $V(t)$ with direct input current and direct refractory period $t_{\mathrm{ref}} = 8$ (ms). The dash line represents the spike threshold $V_{\mathrm{th}} = -55$ (mV). (Color figure online)

In Fig. 10, we have plotted the spike distribution as a function of ISI. In the first row of Fig. 10, we see that the spikes are distributed almost entirely in the ISI interval [9;18] (ms). Moreover, when we increase the value of $\sigma_{\mathrm{ref}}$ from 0.5 to 4 the spike irregularity values increase. In addition, they are distributed almost entirely in the ISI interval [1;25] (ms) in the second row of Fig. 10. To understand better such phenomenon we look at the spike irregularity profile of our system in presence of multiplicative noise and random refractory period in Fig. 11. In particular, we observe that the spike irregularity $CV_{\mathrm{ISI}}$ increases when we increase the values of $\sigma_{\mathrm{ref}}$ similar to the case of additive noise. Furthermore, we see that the larger injected currents are, the higher are the values of $CV_{\mathrm{ISI}}$.

Additionally, we notice that the presence of the random refractory period increases the spiking activity of the neuron. The presence of additive and multiplicative noise causes burst discharges in the system. However, when we increase the value of leak conductance, the burst discharges are strongly reduced in the case with multiplicative noise. Under suitable values of average injected current as well as the values of random input current and random refractory period, the irregularity of spike trains increases. The presence of additive noise could lead to the occurrence of bursts, while the presence of multiplicative noise with random refractory period could reduce the burst discharges in some cases. This effect may lead to an improvement in the carrying of information about stimulating activities in the neuron [1]. Moreover, the study of random factors in

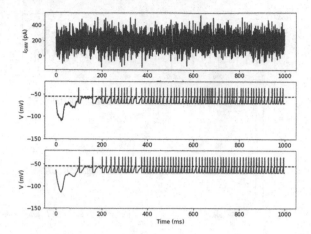

**Fig. 8.** Top row: Gaussian white noise current profile. Middle row: Time evolution of membrane potential $V(t)$ with multiplicative noise current and random refractory period $t_{\text{ref}} = 8 + 2\tilde{\eta}(t)$ (ms). Bottom row: Time evolution of membrane potential $V(t)$ with direct input current and direct refractory period $t_{\text{ref}} = 8$ (ms). The dash line represents the spike threshold $V_{\text{th}} = -55$ (mV). (Color figure online)

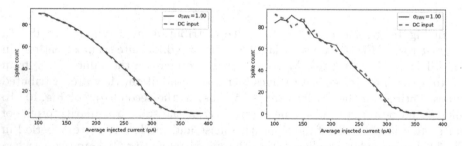

**Fig. 9.** The input-output transfer function of the neuron, output firing rate as a function of input mean for the case with multiplicative noise input current ($\sigma_{\text{Inj}} = 1$). Left: direct time refractory period $t_{\text{ref}} = 8$ (ms). Right: random refractory period $t_{\text{ref}} = 8 + 4\tilde{\eta}(t)$ (ms). (Color figure online)

the LIF conductance model would potentially contribute to further progress in addressing the challenge of how the active membrane currents generating bursts of action potentials affect neural coding and computation [19]. Finally, we remark that noise may come from different sources, e.g., devices, environment, chemical reactions. Moreover, as such, noise is not always a problem for neurons, it can also bring benefits to nervous systems [1, 11].

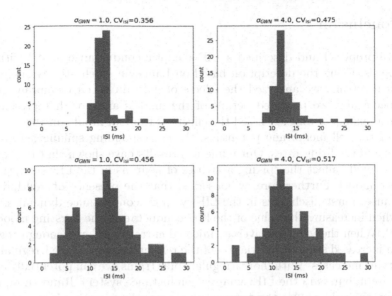

**Fig. 10.** ISI histogram distributions for the case with multiplicative noise input current. $t_{\text{ref}} = 8 + 0.5\tilde{\eta}(t)$ (ms). Second row: $t_{\text{ref}} = 8 + 4\tilde{\eta}(t)$ (ms). (Color figure online)

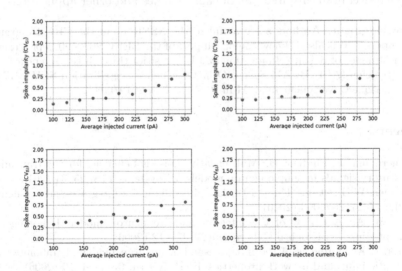

**Fig. 11.** Spike irregularity profile in the case with multiplicative noise input current. Top left panel: $t_{\text{ref}} = 8 + \tilde{\eta}(t)$ (ms). Top right panel: $t_{\text{ref}} = 8 + 2\tilde{\eta}(t)$ (ms). Bottom left panel: $t_{\text{ref}} = 8 + 4\tilde{\eta}(t)$ (ms). Bottom right panel: $t_{\text{ref}} = 8 + 6\tilde{\eta}(t)$ (ms). (Color figure online)

# 4  Conclusion

We have proposed and described a LIF synaptic conductance model with random inputs. Using the description based on Langevin stochastic dynamics in a numerical setting, we analyzed the effects of noise in a cell membrane potential. Specifically, we provided details of the models along with representative numerical examples and discussed the effects of random inputs on the time evolution of the cell membrane potentials, the corresponding spiking activities of neurons and the firing rates. Our numerical results have shown that the random inputs strongly affect the spiking activities of neurons in the LIF synaptic conductance model. Furthermore, we observed that the presence of multiplicative noise causes burst discharges in the LIF synaptic conductance dynamics. However, when increasing the value of the leak conductance, the bursting moods are reduced. When the values of average injected current are large enough together with an increased standard deviation of the refractory period, the irregularity of spike trains increases. With more irregular spike trains, we can potentially expect a decrease in bursts in the LIF synaptic conductance system. Random inputs in LIF neurons could reduce the response of the neuron to each stimulus in SNNs and/or ANNs systems. A better understanding of uncertainty factors in neural network systems could contribute to further developments of SNN algorithms for higher-level brain-inspired functionality studies and other applications.

**Acknowledgment.** Authors are grateful to the NSERC and the CRC Program for their support. RM is also acknowledging support of the BERC 2022–2025 program and Spanish Ministry of Science, Innovation and Universities through the Agencia Estatal de Investigacion (AEI) BCAM Severo Ochoa excellence accreditation SEV-2017-0718 and the Basque Government fund AI in BCAM EXP. 2019/00432.

# References

1. Bauermann, J., Lindner, B.: Multiplicative noise is beneficial for the transmission of sensory signals in simple neuron models. Biosystems **178**, 25–31 (2019)
2. Brigner, W.H., et al.: Three artificial spintronic leaky integrate-and-fire neurons. SPIN **10**(2), 2040003 (2020)
3. Burkitt, A.: A review of the integrate-and-fire neuron model: I. homogeneous synaptic input. Biological Cybern. **95**(2), 97–112 (2006)
4. Burkitt, A.: A review of the integrate-and-fire neuron model: II. inhomogeneous synaptic input and network properties. Biol. Cybern. **95**(1), 1–19 (2006)
5. Cavallari, S., Panzeri, S., Mazzoni, A.: Comparison of the dynamics of neural interactions between current-based and conductance-based integrate-and-fire recurrent networks. Front. Neural Circuits **8**, 12 (2014)
6. Chen, X., Yajima, T., Inoue, I.H., Iizuka, T.: An ultra-compact leaky integrate-and-fire neuron with long and tunable time constant utilizing pseudo resistors for spiking neural networks. J. Appl. Phys. **61**, SC1051 (2021). Accepted for publication in Japanese
7. Chowdhury, S.S., Lee, C., Roy, K.: Towards understanding the effect of leak in spiking neural networks. Neurocomputing **464**, 83–94 (2021)

8. Christodoulou, C., Bugmann, G.: Coefficient of variation vs. mean interspike interval curves: What do they tell us about the brain? Neurocomputing 38–40, 1141–1149 (2001)
9. Dayan, P., Abbott, L.F.: Theoretical Neuroscience. The MIT Press, Massachusetts (2005)
10. Dutta, S., Kumar, V., Shukla, A., Mohapatra, N.R., Ganguly, U.: Leaky integrate and fire neuron by charge-discharge dynamics in floating-body mosfet. Sci. Rep. 7(8257), 8257 (2017)
11. Faisal, A.D., Selen, L.P.J., Wolpert, D.M.: Noise in the nervous system. Nat. Rev. Neurosci. 9, 292–303 (2008)
12. Fardet, T., Levina, A.: Simple models including energy and spike constraints reproduce complex activity patterns and metabolic disruptions. PLoS Comput. Biol. 16(12), e1008503 (2020)
13. Gallinaro, J.V., Clopath, C.: Memories in a network with excitatory and inhibitory plasticity are encoded in the spiking irregularity. PLoS Comput. Biol. 17(11), e1009593 (2021)
14. Gerstner, W., Kistler, W.M., Naud, R., Paninski, L.: Neuronal Dynamics: from single neurons to networks and models of cognition. Cambridge University Press (2014)
15. Gerum, R.C., Schilling, A.: Integration of leaky-integrate-and-fire neurons in standard machine learning architectures to generate hybrid networks: A surrogate gradient approach. Neural Comput. 33, 2827–2852 (2021)
16. Guo, T., Pan, K., Sun, B., Wei, L., Y., Zhou, Y.N., W, Y.A.: Adjustable leaky-integrate-and-fire neurons based on memristor coupled capacitors. Materials Today Advances 12, 100192 (2021)
17. Hendrycks, D., Dietterich, T.: Benchmarking neural network robustness to common corruptions and perturbations. In: International Conference on Learning (2019)
18. Jaras, I., Harada, T., Orchard, M.E., Maldonado, P.E., Vergara, R.C.: Extending the integrate-and-fire model to account for metabolic dependencies. Eur. J. Neurosci. 54(3), 5249–5260 (2021)
19. Kepecs, A., Lisman, J.: Information encoding and computation with spikes and bursts. Network: Comput. Neural Syst. 14, 103–118 (2003)
20. Latimer, K.W., Rieke, F., Pillow, J.W.: Inferring synaptic inputs from spikes with a conductance-based neural encoding model. eLife 8(e47012) (2019)
21. Li, S., Liu, N., Yao, L., Zhang, X., Zhou, D., Cai, D.: Determination of effective synaptic conductances using somatic voltage clamp. PLoS Comput. Biol. 15(3), e1006871 (2019)
22. Mahdi, A., Sturdy, J., Ottesen, J.T., Olufsen, M.S.: Modeling the afferent dynamics of the baroreflex control system. PLoS Comput. Biol. 9(12), e1003384 (2013)
23. Maimon, G., Assad, J.A.: Beyond Poisson: Increased spike-time regularity across primate parietal cortex. Neuron 62(3), 426–440 (2009)
24. Nandakumar, S.R., Boybat, I., Gallo, M.L., Eleftheriou, E., Sebastian, A., Rajendran, B.: Experimental demonstration of supervised learning in spiking neural networks with phase change memory synapses. Sci. Rep. 10(8080), 1–11 (2020)
25. Roberts, J.A., Friston, K.J., Breakspear, M.: Clinical applications of stochastic dynamic models of the brain, part i: a primer. Biol. Psychiatry: Cogn. Neuroscience Neuroimaging 2, 216–224 (2017)
26. So, R.Q., Kent, A.R., Grill, W.M.: Relative contributions of local cell and passing fiber activation and silencing to changes in thalamic fidelity during deep brain stimulation and lesioning: a computational modeling study. J. Comput. Neurosci. 32, 499–519 (2012)

27. Stiefel, K.M., Englitz, B., Sejnowski, T.J.: Origin of intrinsic irregular firing in cortical interneurons. PNAS **110**(19), 7886–7891 (2013)
28. Teeter, C., et al.: Generalized leaky integrate-and-fire models classify multiple neuron types. Nature Commun. **9**(709), 1–15 (2018)
29. Teka, W., Marinov, T.M., Santamaria, F.: Neuronal integration of synaptic input in the fluctuation-driven regime. J. Neurosci. **24**(10), 2345–2356 (2004)
30. Teka, W., Marinov, T.M., Santamaria, F.: Neuronal spike timing adaptation described with a fractional leaky integrate-and-fire model. PLoS Comput. Biol. **10**(3), e1003526 (2014)
31. Van Pottelbergh, T., Drion, G., Sepulchre, R.: From biophysical to integrate-and-fire modeling. Neural Comput. **33**(3), 563–589 (2021)
32. Woo, J., Kim, S.H., Han, K., Choi, M.: Characterization of dynamics and information processing of integrate-and-fire neuron models. J. Phys. A Math. Theor. **54**, 445601 (2021)

# Network Size Reduction Preserving Optimal Modularity and Clique Partition

Alexander Belyi[1]([✉])(iD) and Stanislav Sobolevsky[1,2](iD)

[1] Department of Mathematics and Statistics, Faculty of Science,
Masaryk University, Brno, Czech Republic
{bely,sobolevsky}@math.muni.cz
[2] Center for Urban Science and Progress, New York University, Brooklyn, NY, USA

**Abstract.** Graph clustering and community detection are significant and actively developing topics in network science. Uncovering community structure can provide essential information about the underlying system. In this work, we consider two closely related graph clustering problems. One is the clique partitioning problem, and the other is the maximization of partition quality function called modularity. We are interested in the exact solution. However, both problems are NP-hard. Thus the computational complexity of any existing algorithm makes it impossible to solve the problems exactly for the networks larger than several hundreds of nodes. That is why even a small reduction of network size can significantly improve the speed of finding the solution to these problems. We propose a new method for reducing the network size that preserves the optimal partition in terms of modularity score or the clique partitioning objective function. Furthermore, we prove that the optimal partition of the reduced network has the same quality as the optimal partition of the initial network. We also address the cases where a previously proposed method could provide incorrect results. Finally, we evaluate our method by finding the optimal partitions for two sets of networks. Our results show that the proposed method reduces the network size by 40% on average, decreasing the computation time by about 54%.

**Keywords:** Network size reduction · Clustering · Community detection · Modularity · Clique partitioning problem · Exact solution

## 1 Introduction

Data clustering is a common problem in machine learning and data science [20]. Since many real-world systems are naturally represented as networks or graphs (we use these terms interchangeably as synonyms), the task of clustering network nodes also frequently arises [7] and has applications ranging from group technology [27,31], biology [15], and biochemistry [17], to the transportation [10], geoinformatics [4], tourism management [32] and the study of social networks [14]. It is a particular interest of many researchers because most real-world networks possess a community or modular structure [26], which provides essential insights into the underlying system's properties and dynamics. Community detection in complex networks became a broad and actively developing field of network science dedicated entirely to the problem of network partitioning [12,21].

Proper clustering could mean different things depending on a network and a particular goal. Intuitively, a community in a network is a group of similar or closely related nodes. One common approach to formulating the clustering problem is to define a function that measures the quality of a partition. Then clustering could be done by finding the best partition according to this quality, that is, by maximizing partition quality as an objective function.

Consider a system represented as a complete directed graph $G = (V, E, W)$, where $E = V \times V$ and $W = \{w_{ij} \in \mathbb{R} \mid (i,j) \in E\}$. Individual objects correspond to vertices $V$, and every ordered pair of objects is represented as an arc (or directed edge) with weight $w_{ij}$. If arc weights of graph $G$ represent similarity or dissimilarity between objects, and these weights can be positive or negative, then one way to obtain a meaningful partition could be to group together similar vertices connected with positive arcs while keeping dissimilar vertices in different clusters. In other words, the best partition will be the one that maximizes the sum of arc weights that fall within clusters. This intuitive approach could be mathematically formalized as follows: for the graph $G$, the best partition $C$ (represented as a mapping from vertices to corresponding cluster labels, $C(i) = c_i, i \in V, c_i \in \mathbb{N}$) is the one where the sum $\sum_{i,j|c_i=c_j} w_{ij}$ is maximal. The problem of finding such partition is called the clique partitioning problem (CPP), and it is NP-hard if there are edges of both signs [30].

However, in many real-world systems, the similarity between objects is unknown or not quantified. Moreover, we would often like clustering to reflect something different, for example, close connections or frequent interactions between objects. In such networks, edges could represent various relations and often are unweighted, or their weights have the same (usually positive) sign. In such cases, a good partition would put apart nodes that are not connected or have weaker connections and group together densely connected nodes. The problem of clustering such networks is known as the community detection problem, and there are many approaches to address it. [13].

One widely adopted way to detect communities is to first replace the original network $G$ with a new network $G' = (V, E' = V \times V, W')$ having the same set of vertices $V$ but new edge weights $W' = \{q_{ij} \in \mathbb{R} \mid (i,j) \in E'\}$, and then cluster network $G'$. Every new weight $q_{ij}$ indicates how different the original weight $w_{ij}$ was from the weight edge $(i,j)$ would have in a null model, i.e., if weights were assigned randomly, preserving nodes' incoming and outgoing strengths $s_i^{in} = \sum_j w_{ji}$ and $s_i^{out} = \sum_j w_{ij}$. The expected edge weight in this model could be approximated by $\frac{s_i^{in} s_j^{out}}{S}$, where $S = \sum_{i,j} w_{ij}$. Then the new edge weight is calculated as

$$q_{ij} = \frac{1}{S}\left(w_{ij} - \frac{s_i^{in} s_j^{out}}{S}\right).$$

The weights are normalized by $S$ so that the sum of all weights cannot get larger than 1. These weights can be positive or negative. Larger values of $q$ indicate that the connection between corresponding nodes is stronger than one would expect in a random graph, meaning that it must be an important connection, and the nodes should be grouped. Analogously, a larger absolute value of a negative weight means that corresponding nodes should be assigned to different groups. This way, we arrived at the clique partitioning problem: the best partition into communities is the one that maximizes the sum of weights $q$ within communities. This sum is called a modularity function. It was proposed by Girvan and Newman [14] and is usually denoted as

$$Q = \sum_{i,j|c_i=c_j} q_{ij}.$$

Note that $q_{ij}$ and $q_{ji}$ contribute or do not contribute to the sum together, and values $q_{ii}$ contribute to the sum independently of partition $C$. Therefore, if we define $D = \sum_i q_{ii}$ and redefine $q_{ij}$ as $q_{ij} := q_{ji} := (q_{ij} + q_{ji})/2$, we can rewrite $Q$ as follows:

$$Q = 2 \sum_{i<j|c_i=c_j} q_{ij} + D.$$

To unify our reasoning in the rest of the paper, even if we consider the clique partitioning problem for the original graph $G$, we will refer to the individual edge weights as $q$ and assume $q_{ij} = q_{ji}$.

Even though modularity scores are not arbitrary and have some structure that could be exploited when maximizing $Q$, the problem of finding the exact maximum is still NP-hard [9]. That is why most researchers develop heuristics to quickly find high-quality partitions [8,18,23,29], while only a few methods guarantee to find the exact maximum [2,24].

## 2    Exact Solution of the CPP and Modularity Maximization

While a couple of approaches rely on the branch-and-bound technique [5,6,19], most of the exact methods for solving the CPP employ integer linear programming (ILP) formulation of the problem initially proposed in the seminal works of Grötschel and Wakabayashi [15,16] and later applied to modularity maximization by Agarwal and Kempe [1]. In addition, recent works showed how standard optimization packages could be successfully applied to solving the CPP [11,22,24].

To formulate the ILP problem, for every edge $(i,j)$, define a binary variable $x_{ij}$ that equals 1 when the edge falls within a community and 0 otherwise. Then the objective of the CPP is to

$$\text{maximize:} \quad Q = 2 \cdot \sum_{i<j} q_{ij} \cdot x_{ij} + D,$$

subject to:

$$x_{ij} + x_{jk} - x_{ik} \leq 1, \quad \text{for all } 1 \leq i < j < k \leq n \qquad (1)$$
$$x_{ij} - x_{jk} + x_{ik} \leq 1, \quad \text{for all } 1 \leq i < j < k \leq n$$
$$-x_{ij} + x_{jk} + x_{ik} \leq 1, \quad \text{for all } 1 \leq i < j < k \leq n$$
$$x_{ij} \in \{0,1\}, \quad \text{for all } 1 \leq i < j \leq n.$$

Constraints are called *triangle inequalities* and ensure consistency of partition, i.e., if both edges $(i,j)$ and $(j,k)$ connect nodes from the same cluster, then edge $(i,k)$ does too. Grötschel and Wakabayashi [15] empirically showed that there are many redundant constraints in (1). More recently, Miyauchi and Sukegawa [25] proved that it is sufficient to include only inequalities where at least one of the edges corresponding to two positive terms has non-negative weight. So, the problem can be rewritten as:

$$\text{maximize} \quad Q = 2 \cdot \sum_{i<j} q_{ij} \cdot x_{ij} + D,$$

subject to:

$$x_{ij} + x_{jk} - x_{ik} \leq 1, \quad \forall 1 \leq i < j < k \leq n, q_{ij} \geq 0 \vee q_{jk} \geq 0 \qquad (2)$$
$$x_{ij} - x_{jk} + x_{ik} \leq 1, \quad \forall 1 \leq i < j < k \leq n, q_{ij} \geq 0 \vee q_{ik} \geq 0$$
$$-x_{ij} + x_{jk} + x_{ik} \leq 1, \quad \forall 1 \leq i < j < k \leq n, q_{jk} \geq 0 \vee q_{ik} \geq 0$$
$$x_{ij} \in \{0,1\}, \quad \forall 1 \leq i < j \leq n.$$

Standard optimization packages can be directly applied to this problem. However, the problem size grows very quickly with the size of the network, so the exact solution is only feasible for networks with up to several hundreds of vertices.

## 3   Network Size Reduction

The number of variables in the ILP formulation (2) of the CPP is quadratic, and the number of constraints is cubic in the number of graph vertices, while the computational time needed to solve the problem is not bounded by a polynomial. Thus, even a modest reduction in the number of graph vertices can significantly improve our ability to solve the CPP exactly.

Two studies were dedicated to network size reduction aiming to speed up community detection algorithms [3,22]. However, we are not aware of any methods of graph size reduction preserving the CPP objective function. In what follows, first, we discuss known size reduction methods preserving modularity and then describe our generalization and extension for the general case of the CPP.

Arenas et al. [3] derived conditions when nodes with only one connection (which they call *hairs*, see Fig. 1a) could be merged with their neighbors, preserving the

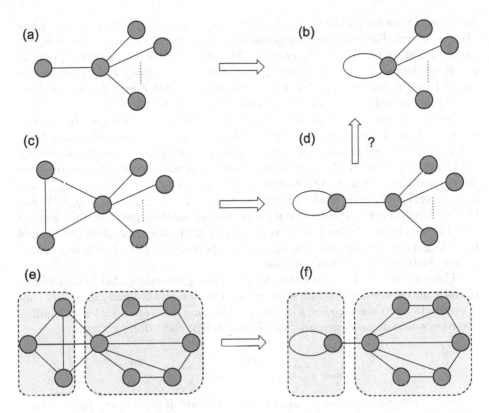

**Fig. 1.** Examples of network size reduction: $a$ to $b$ (*hair*) and $c$ to $d$ (*triangular hair*) were proposed by Arenas et al. [3], $e$ to $f$ (*peripheral clique*) was proposed by Lorena et al. [22]. In figures $e$ and $f$, the partition of optimal modularity for the shown graph is highlighted. It must be noted that in figure $f$, the node on the left falls in its own community separate from other nodes.

optimal partition's modularity. Such merging involves replacing two connected nodes with one node and a loop edge, so a graph from Fig. 1a becomes a graph from Fig. 1b. The authors also showed when two connected nodes with one common neighbor and no other neighbors (*triangular hairs*, see Fig. 1c) could be merged into one node, becoming a hair with a self-loop (Fig. 1d), and then possibly (under some conditions on the weights of connecting edge and self-loop) merged with its neighbor (so, in Fig. 1, graph $c$ becomes graph $d$, and then in some cases – graph $b$). They showed that this approach considerably reduced their modularity optimization heuristic's running time and improved obtained modularity scores. They also argued that their approach would allow the merging of 40 to 83% of nodes in scale-free networks and networks with exponential degree distribution.

In recent work, Lorena et al. [22] extended the work of Arenas et al. They hypothesized that any *peripheral clique* could be merged into one node (in Fig. 1, that corresponds to reducing graph $e$ to graph $b$). While this is often the case, and it was true for all the networks they used in their experiments, this is not always correct. For example, the graph from Fig. 1e can only be reduced to the graph in Fig. 1f and not to the graph in Fig. 1b, which agrees with the previous result of Arenas et al. As we will prove next, any *peripheral clique* could be merged into a *hair* with a loop edge, but merging this *hair* with its neighbor could be done only under some conditions that must be checked.

Let us now consider a general CPP and two nodes, $i$ and $j$. We start by describing what it means to merge $i$ and $j$, preserving objective function and optimal partition. When we merge $i$ and $j$, we replace the initial network $G$ with a new network $G^*$ identical to $G$ except that nodes $i$ and $j$ and all their adjacent edges are replaced by a new node $i^*$ connected to itself with a loop edge $q_{i^*i^*} = q_{ii} + q_{jj} + q_{ij} + q_{ji}$, and to every other node $k$ with an edge of weight $q_{ki^*} = q_{i^*k} = q_{ik} + q_{jk}$. We say that such merging preserves objective function because any partition of $G$ where $i$ and $j$ belong to one cluster has the same quality as the corresponding partition of $G^*$. Merging two nodes preserves the optimal partition if these two nodes belong to one cluster in the optimal partition.

There are at least two cases when we can quickly determine that $i$ and $j$ will be in the same cluster in the optimal partition. The first one is when $i$ and $j$ are connected with a very strong edge, so strong that keeping them apart and not including the edge would worsen any partition. The sufficient condition for this is

$$q_{ij} \geq \sum_{k \in V \setminus \{i,j\} | q_{ik} > 0} q_{ik} - \sum_{k \in V \setminus \{i,j\} | q_{ik} < 0} q_{ik}. \tag{3}$$

Indeed, in any partition where $i$ and $j$ are kept apart, if (3) is true, then moving $i$ to the cluster of $j$ increases the value of the objective function. A pair of *strongly connected* nodes $i, j$ that satisfies (3) covers the case of a *hair* node in modularity maximization: Arenas et al. [3] showed that if $i$ is a *hair* connected only to $j$ and does not have a self-loop, inequality (3) holds.

The following theorem describes the second case when two nodes can be merged, preserving optimal partition.

**Theorem 1.** *Nodes $i$ and $j$ with a non-negative edge between them ($q_{ij} \geq 0$), identically connected to every other node in $G$ (i.e., with edges of the same weight $q_{ik} = q_{jk}$ for all $k \in V \setminus \{i,j\}$), will appear in the same cluster in the optimal partition.*

*Proof.* Consider a partition where nodes $i$ and $j$ belong to different communities $c_i \neq c_j$. If we move node $i$ from $c_i$ to $c_j$, the objective function will change by the value

$$\Delta Q_{i \to j} = q_{ij} + \sum_{k \neq j | c_j = c_k} q_{ik} - \sum_{k \neq i | c_i = c_k} q_{ik},$$

and if we move $j$ from $c_j$ to $c_i$, then $Q$ will change by

$$\Delta Q_{j \to i} = q_{ij} + \sum_{k \neq i | c_i = c_k} q_{jk} - \sum_{k \neq j | c_j = c_k} q_{jk}.$$

Since in the sums, all $q_{ik} = q_{jk}$,

$$\Delta Q_{i \rightarrow j} + \Delta Q_{j \rightarrow i} = 2q_{ij} \geq 0.$$

It follows then that either $\Delta Q_{i \rightarrow j} \geq 0$ or $\Delta Q_{j \rightarrow i} \geq 0$, which means that overall partition quality $Q$ could be improved (or at least will not decrease) either by moving $i$ to the community of $j$ or by moving $j$ to the community of $i$.     $\Box$

The conditions described in Theorem 1 are satisfied, for example, by the nodes in a *peripheral clique*: the modularity score of every edge within such a clique is the same and positive, and every node is connected to the same set of nodes. It follows then that each pair of nodes from the clique will be in the same cluster in the optimal partition, so they can be merged into one node, as shown in Fig. 1e–f. With a correction regarding the articulation point connecting the clique to the rest of the graph, Theorem 1 proves what Lorana et al. [22] showed empirically, that a *peripheral clique* could be merged into one node, preserving modularity. However, Theorem 1 allows the merging of other nodes too. The following section describes algorithms that implement finding and merging nodes satisfying inequality (3) or Theorem 1.

## 4  Nodes Merging Algorithms

First, we introduce an auxiliary procedure to merge two nodes, preserving objective function and optimal partition. It formalizes the steps described in the previous section.

---

**Algorithm 1:** Merge two nodes

---

**input** : Graph $G = (V, E = V \times V, W = \{q_{ij}\})$, nodes $u$ and $v$ to be merged

**output:** New graph $G^*$

1 define node $w$ that will represent merged nodes $u$ and $v$ in $G^*$;
2 $G^* = \left( V^* = \{w\} \cup V \setminus \{u, v\}, E^* = V^* \times V^*, W^* = \{q_{ij}^*\} \right);$
3 $q_{ww}^* = q_{uu} + q_{vv} + 2 \cdot q_{uv};$
4 **foreach** *node* $i \in V \setminus \{u, v\}$ **do**
5 $\quad q_{wi}^* = q_{iw}^* = q_{ui} + q_{vi};$
6 $\quad$ **foreach** *node* $j \in V \setminus \{u, v\}$ **do**
7 $\quad\quad q_{ij}^* = q_{ij}$ ; // All other weights remain the same

8 **return** $G^*;$

---

Theorem 1 defines an equivalence relation on the set of nodes $V$. To reduce network $G$, we first compare each node to all other nodes, assign it to the corresponding equivalence class, and then merge the nodes of each class into one node representing it. Algorithm 2 formalizes this procedure.

---

**Algorithm 2:** Find and merge *identically connected* nodes

---

**input**  : Graph $G = (V, E = V \times V, W = \{q_{ij}\})$
**output:** Updated graph $G$

1  assign each node to represent its own equivalence class: $classes(i) = i$;
2  **foreach** *node* $i \in V$ **do**
3       **foreach** *node* $j \in V \setminus \{i\}$ **do**
4           **if** $q_{ij} \geq 0$ *and* $q_{ik} == q_{jk}$ *for* $\forall k \in V \setminus \{i, j\}$ **then**
5               $classes(i) = classes(j) = \min\left(classes(i), classes(j)\right)$;

6  **foreach** *node* $i \in V$ **do**
7       **if** $i \neq classes(i)$ **then**
8           $G = \texttt{MergeTwoNodes}(G, i, classes(i))$ ; // Algorithm 1

9  **return** $G$;

---

When $G$ is a complete graph, Algorithm 2 uses tree nested for-loops twice: to find identically connected nodes and merge them. Therefore, it has time complexity $O(n^3)$, where $n = |V|$ is the size of the graph.

Next, we provide an algorithm that finds and merges the nodes satisfying inequality (3).

---

**Algorithm 3:** Find and merge *strongly connected* nodes

---

**input**  : Graph $G = (V, E = V \times V, W = \{q_{ij}\})$
**output:** Updated graph $G$

1  **foreach** *node* $i \in V$ **do**
2       $sum\_positive = \sum_{j \in V \setminus \{i\} | q_{ij} > 0} q_{ij}$;
3       $sum\_negative = \sum_{j \in V \setminus \{i\} | q_{ij} < 0} q_{ij}$;
4       $max\_q = \max_{j \in V \setminus \{i\}} q_{ij}$;
5       $j = \arg\max_{j \in V \setminus \{i\}} q_{ij}$;
6       **if** $max\_q \geq sum\_positive - max\_q - sum\_negative$ **then**
7           $G = \texttt{MergeTwoNodes}(G, i, j)$ ; // Algorithm 1

8  **return** $G$;

---

Algorithm 3 might merge almost all nodes, spending $O(n^2)$ operations on each merge. Hence its time complexity is also $O(n^3)$.

Applying Algorithm 2 can produce new *strongly connected* and *identically connected* nodes, as well as applying Algorithm 3 can produce new *identically connected* and new *strongly connected* nodes (see Fig. 2 for some examples). So, to decrease the graph size as much as possible, we apply Algorithms 2 and 3 in turn as long as at least one of them reduces the graph. Since the size of the graph decreases on each iteration, there are no more than $n$ steps, and the overall time complexity of our size reduction procedure is $O(n^4)$. Nevertheless, our experiments show that actual execution time is still negligible for the networks where the CPP can be solved exactly.

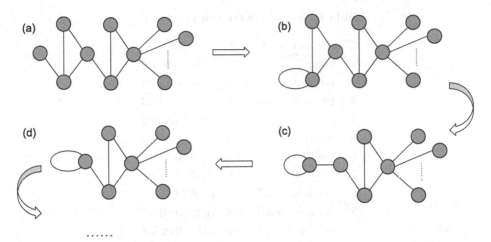

**Fig. 2.** An example of network size reduction iterations: after merging two *strongly connected* nodes (*a* to *b*), a new pair of *identically connected* nodes appeared and was merged (*b* to *c*), which in turn created a pair of *strongly connected* nodes, which were merged (*c* to *d*), creating another pair of *strongly connected* nodes, and so on. The weights of shown positive and omitted negative edges could be easily adjusted to satisfy all necessary conditions and are not shown in the figure to preserve clarity.

## 5    Evaluation and Results

To evaluate our approach, we wrote a program that loads networks, applies Algorithms 2 and 3 to reduce network sizes, creates the ILP problem (2) for the CPP or modularity maximization, and uses the commercial solver IBM ILOG CPLEX 20.1.0 to solve the ILP models obtaining the optimal partition. We implemented our algorithms in C++, compiled the program using Clang 12.0.5, and ran the experiments on a laptop with a 3.2 GHz CPU and 16 GB RAM. We tested our method on two sets of real-world networks previously used in the literature on the exact solution of the modularity maximization problem and the CPP. All our codes and the datasets analyzed in this work are freely available on GitHub[1].

First, we focused on the modularity maximization problem. To compare our results with the results from [22], we mostly followed their evaluation strategy and used the same set of networks. All the networks were downloaded from the Network Repository website [28]. Each network was treated as unweighted and undirected, and only the giant components of the networks were used in the experiments. Table 1 provides a summary of this benchmark. Each network was assigned an ID shown in the first column. The second column shows the network's name on the Network Repository website, $n$ indicates the number of nodes, $m$ is the number of edges, and $Q$ is the modularity of the optimal partition.

---

[1] https://github.com/Alexander-Belyi/best-partition.

**Table 1.** Networks in the first benchmark.

| ID | Network name | $n$ | $m$ | $Q$ |
|---|---|---|---|---|
| 1 | lesmis | 77 | 254 | 0.56001 |
| 2 | GD00-A | 83 | 125 | 0.53091 |
| 3 | ca-sandi-auths | 86 | 124 | 0.73683 |
| 4 | rt-retweet | 96 | 177 | 0.67967 |
| 5 | netscience | 379 | 914 | 0.84859 |
| 6 | bio-DM-LC | 483 | 997 | 0.77870 |
| 7 | power-494-bus | 494 | 586 | 0.85999 |
| 8 | bio-diseasome | 516 | 1188 | 0.83200 |
| 9 | bio-grid-mouse | 791 | 1098 | 0.80101 |
| 10 | ca-CSphd | 1025 | 1043 | 0.92558 |

Table 2 shows how our size reduction algorithms shrink the network sizes in terms of the number of nodes. This decrement in the network sizes corresponds to a significant reduction in the number of variables and the number of constraints in the ILP problem (2), as seen from the corresponding columns. Here and in the next table, we denote values obtained by Lorena et al. [22] with the prime symbol ($'$), and values obtained using our method – with an asterisk (*). As seen from the table, our method reduces the problem further for six networks out of ten. In the network bio-grid-mouse, our algorithm merged two nodes differently, reducing only the number of constraints. However, for one network, our method does not merge two nodes that the algorithm from [22] merges. That is because inequality (3) is not satisfied for these two nodes, and it is not known apriori that these *hairs* belong to the communities of their neighbors in the optimal partition.

**Table 2.** Network and ILP problem size reduction.

| ID | $n$ | $n'$ | $n^*$ | $n^*/n$ | $n^*/n'$ | Var | Var.$'$ | Var.* | Constr | Constr.$'$ | Constr.* |
|---|---|---|---|---|---|---|---|---|---|---|---|
| 1 | 77 | 58 | **46** | 59.74 % | 79.31 % | 2926 | 1653 | **1035** | 34685 | 23110 | **11817** |
| 2 | 83 | 64 | 64 | 77.11 % | 100.00 % | 3403 | 2016 | 2016 | 18434 | 11581 | 11581 |
| 3 | 86 | 57 | **52** | 60.47 % | 91.23 % | 3655 | 1176 | **1326** | 20369 | 7085 | **7267** |
| 4 | 96 | 43 | 43 | 44.79 % | 100.00 % | 4560 | 903 | 903 | 21511 | 4954 | 4954 |
| 5 | 379 | 286 | **254** | 67.02 % | 88.81 % | 71631 | 40755 | **32131** | 682739 | 428071 | **262472** |
| 6 | 483 | 340 | **328** | 67.91 % | 96.47 % | 116403 | 57630 | **53628** | 946606 | 566353 | **525236** |
| 7 | 494 | 344 | *346* | 70.04 % | 100.58 % | 121771 | 58996 | *59685* | 575323 | 295959 | *299067* |
| 8 | 516 | 326 | **287** | 55.62 % | 88.04 % | 132870 | 52975 | **41041** | 1211786 | 578838 | **324517** |
| 9 | 791 | *380* | *380* | 48.04 % | 100.00 % | 312445 | 72010 | 72010 | 1716725 | 510436 | **506702** |
| 10 | 1025 | 332 | 332 | 32.39 % | 100.00 % | 524800 | 54946 | 54946 | 2128786 | 230136 | 230136 |

**Table 3.** Execution time.

| ID | Network name | $t$ (s) | $T$ (s) | $T'$ (s) | $T^*$ (s) | $T^*/T$ | $T^*/T$ |
|---|---|---|---|---|---|---|---|
| 1 | lesmis | 0.00031 | 0.61 | 0.42 | **0.21** | 34.43 % | 50.00 % |
| 2 | GD00-A | 0.00024 | 2.23 | **1.46** | 3.61 | 161.88 % | 247.26 % |
| 3 | ca-sandi-auths | 0.00039 | 0.41 | 0.15 | **0.13** | 31.71 % | 86.67 % |
| 4 | rt-retweet | 0.00059 | 0.64 | 0.18 | **0.11** | 17.19 % | 61.11 % |
| 5 | netscience | 0.01457 | 43.40 | 20.67 | **7.20** | 16.59 % | 34.83 % |
| 6 | bio-DM-LC | 0.02719 | 5315.57 | 1692.86 | **985.47** | 18.54 % | 58.21 % |
| 7 | power-494-bus | 0.02814 | 90419.51 | **17586.84** | 166681.31 | 184.34 % | 947.76 % |
| 8 | bio-diseasome | 0.04083 | 22966.99 | 3046.39 | **480.13** | 2.09 % | 15.76 % |
| 9 | bio-grid-mouse | 0.14692 | 26551.02 | 390.40 | **307.46** | 1.16 % | 78.76 % |
| 10 | ca-CSphd | 0.33687 | 2512.05 | 86.39 | **41.23** | 1.64 % | 47.73 % |

Finally, in Table 3, we report the execution time (in seconds) of our size reduction algorithms $(t)$ and the total time to solve the ILP problems for the initial and reduced networks ($T$, $T'$, and $T^*$, respectively). The execution times $T$ and $T'$ are taken from [22]. Provided values show that the time spent on the size reduction is negligible compared to the total time required to solve the problem. For almost all networks, size reduction leads to a significant decrease in the execution time. For some networks, observed improvements reach more than 98% compared to the initial network and up to 84% compared to the method from [22]. For two networks, the time to solve the ILP problem was higher than the time reported in [22]. The reason could be the solver's different version or parameter settings. This possibility is supported by the fact that in our experiment, the time to solve the full GD00-A network was 6.98 s, and for the power-494-bus network, the solver did not find a solution after 200,000 s. We also note here that it is not guaranteed that the smaller size of the problem

**Table 4.** Results for the networks in the second benchmark.

| Network | $n$ | $n^*$ | $n^*/n$ | Var | Var.* | Constr | Constr.* | $t$ | $T$ | $T^*$ | $T^*/T$ | $Q$ |
|---|---|---|---|---|---|---|---|---|---|---|---|---|
| Wild cats | 30 | **25** | 83% | 435 | **300** | 10043 | **5531** | 0.00004 | 0.14 | **0.08** | 57% | 1 304 |
| Cars | 33 | **31** | 93% | 528 | **465** | 14708 | **12027** | 0.00003 | 0.22 | **0.18** | 82% | 1 501 |
| Workers | 34 | 34 | 100% | 561 | 561 | 14605 | 14605 | 0.00001 | 0.24 | 0.24 | 100% | 964 |
| Cetacea | 36 | **35** | 97% | 630 | **595** | 9798 | **9207** | 0.00002 | 0.13 | **0.12** | 92% | 967 |
| Micro | 40 | 40 | 100% | 780 | 780 | 22201 | 22201 | 0.00002 | 0.32 | 0.32 | 100% | 1 034 |
| UNO | 54 | **16** | 29% | 1431 | **120** | 45756 | **606** | 0.00019 | 0.71 | **0.01** | 1% | 798 |
| UNO 1a | 158 | **19** | 12% | 12403 | **171** | 1161623 | **999** | 0.00228 | 40.78 | **0.01** | 0% | 12 197 |
| UNO 1b | 139 | **10** | 7% | 9591 | **45** | 910908 | **172** | 0.00165 | 28.93 | **0.00** | 0% | 11 775 |
| UNO 2a | 158 | **75** | 47% | 12403 | **2775** | 1542583 | **160952** | 0.00195 | 35.50 | **2.12** | 6% | 72 820 |
| UNO 2b | 145 | **73** | 50% | 10440 | **2628** | 1310497 | **152675** | 0.00151 | 27.63 | **1.98** | 7% | 71 818 |

makes it easier to solve, and in some cases, a smaller problem could be much harder than a larger one.

After applying our method in the setting of modularity maximization, we tested it in the setting of the CPP. To that end, we used a well-known set of real-world networks representing similarities between different objects. It was compiled by Grötschel and Wakabayashi [15] and later reused in several studies [11,19]. Table 4 presents the networks in this benchmark and summarizes the results. From it, one can see that the two networks were not reduced while the size of some other networks was reduced by more than ten times, and the computational time decreased by more than 90%, from seconds to milliseconds. All the networks in this set are relatively easy to solve even without reduction, although a recent study by Du et al. [11] reported the execution time of two minutes for some of the networks using CPLEX. Here we showed that applying a simple and fast preprocessing reduces the total time needed to solve the CPP by orders of magnitude.

## 6   Conclusion

Network clustering is an important and well-studied problem in network science. It gives rise to the clique partitioning problem (CPP) that can be used as a stand-alone clustering method or appear in community detection via modularity maximization. However, the computational complexity of the CPP is in the non-deterministic polynomial-time hard (NP-hard) class. Therefore, finding the exact solution of the CPP is only possible for networks of a small to moderate size. Usually, it is done by solving a corresponding integer linear programming (ILP) problem using one of the specialized solvers.

In this work, we proposed a new method for reducing the size of the network while preserving its optimal partition into clusters according to the CPP criterion. Our work extends two previous efforts in this direction applied to the modularity maximization problem [3,22], but we generalized our approach for the broader class of the CPP. Furthermore, by theoretically proving the correctness of our methods, we also proved the correct part of the approach proposed by Lorena et al. [22], which was validated only empirically. Moreover, we also pointed out that their approach was incorrect in the general case and showed how to address it. Even though their method removed some of the nodes that could not have been removed, our approach decreased the number of nodes by another 6% on average.

We proposed two algorithms implementing our method to identify and merge the appropriate vertices. Our experiments showed that for the networks of the size where an exact solution is possible, the total preprocessing time required by the algorithms is negligible compared to the expected time needed to solve the resulting ILP problem.

To evaluate our methods, we chose two sets of real-world networks previously used in the literature to evaluate algorithms for solving the CPP and modularity maximization exactly. Our experiments showed that our method considerably decreases the size of many real-world networks. On average, the network size is reduced by about 40% for two datasets, and in some cases, we observe a reduction of more than 90%. Correspondingly, the size of the ILP problem was reduced substantially, which significantly reduced the time and memory consumption required to solve the problem exactly. The average time reduction was about 55% in both datasets we used. Such improvements in time efficiency allow the application of the exact solution methods to more extensive networks. One of the possible directions for future work is to apply and evaluate the utility of proposed methods to improve the performance of heuristics that do not find the exact solution but still could benefit from the smaller size of the problem.

**Acknowledgement.** This research was supported by the MUNI Award in Science and Humanities (MASH) of the Grant Agency of Masaryk University under the Digital City project (MUNI/J/0008/2021).

# References

1. Agarwal, G., Kempe, D.: Modularity-maximizing graph communities via mathematical programming. Eur. Phys. J. B **66**(3), 409–418 (2008). https://doi.org/10.1140/epjb/e2008-00425-1
2. Aloise, D., Cafieri, S., Caporossi, G., Hansen, P., Perron, S., Liberti, L.: Column generation algorithms for exact modularity maximization in networks. Phys. Rev. E **82**(4), 46112 (2010). https://doi.org/10.1103/PhysRevE.82.046112
3. Arenas, A., Duch, J., Fernández, A., Gómez, S.: Size reduction of complex networks preserving modularity. New J. Phys. **9**(6), 176–176 (2007). https://doi.org/10.1088/1367-2630/9/6/176
4. Belyi, A., Bojic, I., Sobolevsky, S., Sitko, I., Hawelka, B., Rudikova, L., Kurbatski, A., Ratti, C.: Global multi-layer network of human mobility. Int. J. Geogr. Inf. Sci. **31**(7), 1381–1402 (2017). https://doi.org/10.1080/13658816.2017.1301455
5. Belyi, A., Sobolevsky, S., Kurbatski, A., Ratti, C.: Subnetwork constraints for tighter upper bounds and exact solution of the clique partitioning problem. arXiv preprint arXiv:2110.05627 (2021)
6. Belyi, A.B., Sobolevsky, S.L., Kurbatski, A.N., Ratti, C.: Improved upper bounds in clique partitioning problem. J. Belarusian State Univ. Math. Informatics **2019**(3), 93–104 (2019). https://doi.org/10.33581/2520-6508-2019-3-93-104
7. Benati, S., Puerto, J., Rodríguez-Chía, A.M.: Clustering data that are graph connected. Eur. J. Oper. Res. **261**(1), 43–53 (2017). https://doi.org/10.1016/j.ejor.2017.02.009
8. Blondel, V.D., Guillaume, J.L., Lambiotte, R., Lefebvre, E.: Fast unfolding of communities in large networks. J. Stat. Mech. Theory Exp. **2008**(10), P10008 (2008). https://doi.org/10.1088/1742-5468/2008/10/p10008
9. Brandes, U., Delling, D., Gaertler, M., Gorke, R., Hoefer, M., Nikoloski, Z., Wagner, D.: On modularity clustering. IEEE Trans. Knowl. Data Eng. **20**(2), 172–188 (2008). https://doi.org/10.1109/TKDE.2007.190689
10. Dorndorf, U., Jaehn, F., Pesch, E.: Modelling robust flight-gate scheduling as a clique partitioning problem. Transp. Sci. **42**(3), 292–301 (2008). https://doi.org/10.1287/trsc.1070.0211

11. Du, Y., Kochenberger, G., Glover, F., Wang, H., Lewis, M., Xie, W., Tsuyuguchi, T.: Solving clique partitioning problems: a comparison of models and commercial solvers. Int. J. Inf. Technol. Decis. Mak. **21**(01), 59–81 (2022). https://doi.org/10.1142/S0219622021500504
12. Fortunato, S.: Community detection in graphs. Phys. Rep. **486**, 75–174 (2010). https://doi.org/10.1016/j.physrep.2009.11.002
13. Fortunato, S., Hric, D.: Community detection in networks: a user guide. Phys. Rep. **659**, 1–44 (2016). https://doi.org/10.1016/j.physrep.2016.09.002
14. Girvan, M., Newman, M.E.J.: Community structure in social and biological networks. Proc. Natl. Acad. Sci. **99**(12), 7821–7826 (2002). https://doi.org/10.1073/pnas.122653799
15. Grötschel, M., Wakabayashi, Y.: A cutting plane algorithm for a clustering problem. Math. Program. **45**(1), 59–96 (1989). https://doi.org/10.1007/BF01589097
16. Grötschel, M., Wakabayashi, Y.: Facets of the clique partitioning polytope. Math. Program. **47**(1), 367–387 (1990). https://doi.org/10.1007/BF01580870
17. Guimerà, R., Nunes Amaral, L.A.: Functional cartography of complex metabolic networks. Nature **433**(7028), 895–900 (2005). https://doi.org/10.1038/nature03288
18. Hu, S., Wu, X., Liu, H., Li, R., Yin, M.: A novel two-model local search algorithm with a self-adaptive parameter for clique partitioning problem. Neural Comput. Appl. **33**(10), 4929–4944 (2020). https://doi.org/10.1007/s00521-020-05289-5
19. Jaehn, F., Pesch, E.: New bounds and constraint propagation techniques for the clique partitioning. Discret. Appl. Math. **161**(13), 2025–2037 (2013). https://doi.org/10.1016/j.dam.2013.02.011
20. Jain, A.K., Murty, M.N., Flynn, P.J.: Data clustering: a review. ACM Comput. Surv. **31**(3), 264–323 (1999). https://doi.org/10.1145/331499.331504
21. Javed, M.A., Younis, M.S., Latif, S., Qadir, J., Baig, A.: Community detection in networks: a multidisciplinary review. J. Netw. Comput. Appl. **108**, 87–111 (2018). https://doi.org/10.1016/j.jnca.2018.02.011
22. Lorena, L.H.N., Quiles, M.G., Lorena, L.A.N.: Improving the performance of an integer linear programming community detection algorithm through clique filtering. In: Misra, S., Gervasi, O., Murgante, B., Stankova, E., Korkhov, V., Torre, C., Rocha, A.M.A.C., Taniar, D., Apduhan, B.O., Tarantino, E. (eds.) Improving the Performance of an Integer Linear Programming Community Detection Algorithm Through Clique Filtering. LNCS, vol. 11619, pp. 757–769. Springer, Cham (2019). https://doi.org/10.1007/978-3-030-24289-3_56
23. Lu, Z., Zhou, Y., Hao, J.K.: A hybrid evolutionary algorithm for the clique partitioning problem. IEEE Trans. Cybern., 1–13 (2021). https://doi.org/10.1109/TCYB.2021.3051243
24. Miyauchi, A., Sonobe, T., Sukegawa, N.: Exact Clustering via Integer Programming and Maximum Satisfiability. Proc. AAAI Conf. Artif. Intell. **32**(1) (2018)
25. Miyauchi, A., Sukegawa, N.: Redundant constraints in the standard formulation for the clique partitioning problem. Optim. Lett. **9**(1), 199–207 (2014). https://doi.org/10.1007/s11590-014-0754-6
26. Newman, M.E.J.: The structure and function of complex networks. SIAM Rev. **45**(2), 167–256 (2003). https://doi.org/10.1137/S003614450342480
27. Oosten, M., Rutten, J.H.G.C., Spieksma, F.C.R.: The clique partitioning problem: facets and patching facets. Networks **38**(4), 209–226 (2001). https://doi.org/10.1002/net.10004
28. Rossi, R.A., Ahmed, N.K.: The network data repository with interactive graph analytics and visualization. In: AAAI (2015). http://networkrepository.com

29. Sobolevsky, S., Campari, R., Belyi, A., Ratti, C.: General optimization technique for high-quality community detection in complex networks. Phys. Rev. E - Stat. Nonlinear, Soft Matter Phys. **90**(1) (2014). https://doi.org/10.1103/PhysRevE.90.012811
30. Wakabayashi, Y.: Aggregation of binary relations: algorithmic and polyhedral investigations. Ph.D. thesis, Doctoral Dissertation. University of Augsburg (1986)
31. Wang, H., Alidaee, B., Glover, F., Kochenberger, G.: Solving group technology problems via clique partitioning. Int. J. Flex. Manuf. Syst. **18**(2), 77–97 (2006). https://doi.org/10.1007/s10696-006-9011-3
32. Xu, Y., Li, J., Belyi, A., Park, S.: Characterizing destination networks through mobility traces of international tourists - a case study using a nationwide mobile positioning dataset. Tour. Manag. **82** (2021). https://doi.org/10.1016/j.tourman.2020.104195

# Interval Approximation of the Discrete Helmholtz Propagator for the Radio-Wave Propagation Along the Earth's Surface

Mikhail S. Lytaev[✉][iD]

St. Petersburg Federal Research Center of the Russian Academy of Sciences,
14-th Linia, V.I., No. 39, Saint Petersburg 199178, Russia
mikelytaev@gmail.com

**Abstract.** A new finite-difference approximation of the two-dimensional parabolic equation is proposed in this paper. The specifics of the tropospheric radio-wave propagation problem are taken into account. Rational approximation of the discrete in both dimensions propagation operator is considered. The method of rational interpolation is used instead of local Padé approximation. The results of numerical modeling confirm the advantages of the proposed approach.

**Keywords:** Parabolic equation · Helmholtz equation · Rational interpolation · Radio-wave propagation · Finite-difference methods

## 1  Introduction

Starting with the research of Leontovich and Fock [8], the problem of tropospheric radio-wave propagation modeling by the parabolic equation (PE) method remains relevant to this day [4,10,20,22,23]. Bearing in mind the works on the generalization of the PE method [6], further in this paper PE and one-way Helmholtz equation are considered as synonyms.

There are two effective numerical methods for solving PE: split-step Fourier (SSF) method [18] and finite-difference (FD) approximations [13]. SSF method is somewhat more efficient in terms of computational speed, but it has problems with lower [21] and upper [16] boundary conditions modeling. FD methods enable efficient and reliable modeling of boundary conditions but require more computational resources. However, as will be shown in this paper, their potential has not yet been exhausted.

Keeping in mind the steady increase in the operating frequency of the modern radio systems, the problem of improving the computational speed of both PE numerical methods is urgent. This can be achieved primarily by using more efficient approximations. In particular, the method of wavelet transformations as a kind of generalization of the SSF method is rapidly developing [4,24].

O. Gervasi et al. (Eds.): ICCSA 2022, LNCS 13375, pp. 34–46, 2022.
https://doi.org/10.1007/978-3-031-10522-7_3

It was previously shown [15] that the semi-discrete propagation operator as a function of the vertical diffraction operator can be effectively approximated using an interval approximation, rather than a local one. This made it possible to increase the grid step along the longitudinal coordinate, but a dense grid is still required along the transversal coordinate. To deal with this problem, it was suggested to use a local Padé approximation of the fully discrete propagation operator [5,14]. In this paper, it is proposed to use interval approximation of the fully discrete propagation operator which will allow using an even more sparse grid and obtaining faster numerical solutions.

## 2   Approximation of the Propagator

Step-by-step solution of the one-way Helmholtz equation is written as follows [15]

$$u^{n+1} = Pu^n, \tag{1}$$

$$P = \exp\left(ik\Delta x \left(\sqrt{1 + \frac{1}{k^2}\frac{\partial^2 u}{\partial z^2} + (m^2 - 1)} - 1\right)\right),$$

where $u(x,z)$ is the complex-valued electromagnetic wave component, $u_j^n = u(n\Delta x, j\Delta z)$ is its discrete analogue, $P$ is the semi-discrete propagation operator, $k = 2\pi/\lambda$ is the wavenumber, $\lambda$ is the wavelength, $m^2(x,z)$ is the tropospheric refractive index. The schematic description of the considered problem is depicted in Fig. 1.

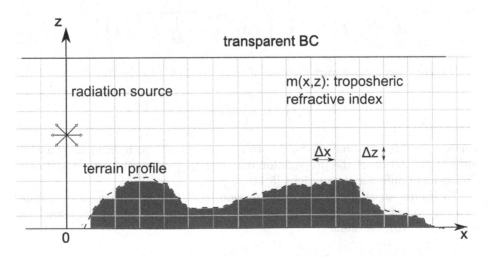

**Fig. 1.** Schematic description of the considered problem.

Operator $P$ can be approximately split into two [9]

$$P \approx P_1 P_2, \tag{2}$$

$$P_1 = \exp\left(ik\Delta x\left(n(x,z) - 1\right)\right),$$

$$P_2 = \exp\left(ik\Delta x\left(\sqrt{1 + \frac{1}{k^2}\frac{\partial^2 u}{\partial z^2}} - 1\right)\right). \tag{3}$$

Operator $P_1$ corresponds to refraction, $P_2$ corresponds to propagation and diffraction. In the case of a homogeneous medium ($m \equiv 1$) operator $P_1$ turns into identical and approximate equality turns into exact one. It should be noted that such an approximation is also used in the derivation of the SSF method, and thus its adequacy has been confirmed by a huge number of experiments.

Action of operator $P_1$ is calculated directly, thus, it remains to construct a numerical approximation of $P_2$. Express the second differential operator in terms of the second difference operator $\delta^2$ [7]

$$\frac{\partial^2 u}{\partial z^2} = g(\delta^2)u, \tag{4}$$

$$g(\xi) = -\frac{1}{\Delta z^2}\ln^2\left(1 + \frac{\xi}{2} + \sqrt{\left(1 + \frac{\xi}{2}\right)^2 - 1}\right),$$

$$\delta^2 u = u_{j-1} - 2u_j + u_{j+1}.$$

Substitution (4) into (3) gives a fully discrete version of operator $P_2$ as a function of $\delta^2$

$$P_2\left(\delta^2\right) = f\left(\delta^2\right) = \exp\left(ik\Delta x\left(\sqrt{1 + \frac{1}{k^2}g\left(\delta^2\right)} - 1\right)\right).$$

We are seeking an approximation of function $f\left(\delta^2\right)$ in the form

$$f\left(\xi\right)u \approx \prod_{l=1}^{p}\frac{1 + a_l\xi}{1 + b_l\xi}u, \tag{5}$$

where $a_l$ and $b_l$ are some coefficients to be determined. Such an approximation reduces the action of the propagation operator to a sequential solution of one-dimensional differential equations [5, 14].

To choose an appropriate approximation, it is first necessary to determine what is meant by an operator function. Consider the definition, based on Cauchy's integral formula

$$f\left(\delta^2\right) = \frac{1}{2\pi i}\oint_{\Gamma} f\left(\xi\right)\left(\xi I - \delta^2\right)^{-1}d\xi,$$

where $\Gamma$ encloses all eigenvalues of operator $\delta^2$. The solution of the eigenvalue problem $\delta^2 u = \omega u$ is written as follows

$$\omega = -4\sin^2\left(\frac{k_z\Delta z}{2}\right), \, u(z) = \exp\left(ik_z z\right).$$

Function $u$ has the physical meaning of a plane wave, where $k_z = k\sin\theta$ is a vertical wavenumber, $\theta$ is a propagation angle. Thus, we have established the relationship between argument $\xi$, transversal grid step $\Delta z$ and propagation angle $\theta$. A good coincidence between function $f$ and its approximation (5) is required only for the desired propagation angles. In is common to use the Padé approximation [3,5] at point $\xi = 0$ to calculate the coefficients of rational approximation (5). Padé approximation is local, i.e. it gives excellent accuracy for small propagation angles, but its accuracy monotonically decreases with increasing $\xi$.

However, in some cases, it is necessary to provide a certain accuracy for a pre-known range of propagation angles [15]. For example, it is a propagation over irregular terrain, where the maximum propagation angle can be estimated from the geometry of the problem. Instead of using a local approximation, in this paper it is proposed to use a rational approximation on a segment. Rational interpolation in Chebyshev roots [19] is used as an approximation method in this research.

The desired approximation interval for function $f$ is expressed as follows

$$\xi \in \left[-4\sin^2\left(\frac{k\sin\theta_{max}\Delta z}{2}\right), 0\right],$$

where $\theta_{max}$ is the maximum propagation angle of interest.

Figure 2 demonstrates the dependence of the approximation error on the value of $\xi$. It is clearly seen that Padé approximation gives excessive accuracy for small values of $\xi$, but the accuracy monotonically decreases with increasing $\xi$. At the same time, the rational interpolation calculated based on the maximum propagation angle of 22° gives a more uniform distribution of the error on the segment of interest.

## 3   Analysis of the Numerical Results

This section presents the numerical results, obtained by several approaches. The following methods are used: the proposed method of rational interpolation of the discrete propagation operator, Padé approximation of the discrete propagation operator [14], Padé approximation of the semi-discrete propagation operator with 2nd [16] and 4th [17] order approximation of the transversal operator, and SSF method. The implementation of the rational interpolation method from Chebfun library [1] (*ratinterp* function) was used. The proposed method is implemented as a Python 3 library and is freely available [11].

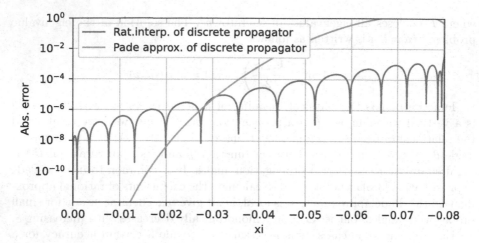

**Fig. 2.** Dependence of the approximation error of the discrete propagator on the value of $\xi$ for Padé approximation and rational interpolation. $\Delta x = 50\lambda$, $\Delta z = 1.1\lambda$, rational approximation order is equal to [7/8].

## 3.1  Wedge Diffraction

The advantages of the proposed method for propagation over irregular terrain will be shown on the wedge diffraction problem. The radiation source is located at an altitude of 100 m and emits a harmonic signal at a frequency of 3 GHz. The wedge is located at a distance of 2 km from the source. Rational interpolation is calculated based on the maximum propagation angle of 22°. The order of rational approximation is equal to [7/8], $\Delta x = 50\lambda$, $\Delta z = 1.1\lambda$. The wedge is modeled using a staircase approximation.

Figure 3 demonstrates the dependence of the absolute error of the discrete horizontal wavenumber $\tilde{k}_x$ [12] on the propagation angle for FD approximations under consideration. It is clearly seen that the proposed method gives the best approximation on the considered interval. For the stability of the numerical scheme, it is required that $\mathrm{Im}\left(\tilde{k}_x\right) > 0$ outside the desired interval. This will guarantee the attenuation of waves propagating at irrelevant propagation angles and evanescent waves. It is clearly seen from Fig. 4 that this condition is satisfied for all FD schemes under consideration.

Figure 5 depicts the two-dimensional distribution of the electromagnetic field amplitude, computed by the proposed method. We verify the result with the SSF method. The two-dimensional distribution of the error between the results, obtained by the proposed method and SSF, is depicted in Fig. 6. Both methods used the same computational grid. It can be seen that both methods yield indistinguishable results for the desired range of propagation angles. In particular, the proposed method with the selected computational parameters correctly calculates the field in the diffraction zone behind the obstacle.

Now let's analyze the results obtained using Padé approximation for the same computational grid and approximation order. Figures 7 and 8 depict the spatial distribution of the error for two variants of Padé approximation. As it was predicted theoretically using discrete wavenumber, Padé approximation, all other things being equal, allows for smaller propagation angles than the rational interpolation method. In this example, both variants of Padé approximation yield a significant underestimation of the filed in the diffraction zone. Of course, reducing the size of the computational grid cells and increasing the approximation order allows one to increase the accuracy of Padé approximation and expand the maximum propagation angle, but at the same time, it will increase the computational costs. Namely, Fig. 9 depicts the spatial distribution of the error for the Padé approximation of the fully-discrete propagator with the reduced longitudinal grid step. One can see that Padé method requires a three times thicker computational grid for achieving an acceptable accuracy. Thus, the proposed method is three times more computationally effective in this example.

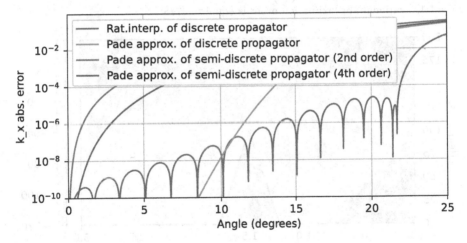

**Fig. 3.** The dependence of the absolute error of the discrete horizontal wavenumber on the propagation angle. In all cases $\Delta x = 50\lambda$, $\Delta z = 1.1\lambda$, rational approximation order is equal to [7/8].

## 3.2 Propagation in a Surface Duct

The purpose of this example is to demonstrate the possibility of inhomogeneous tropospheric refraction index modeling within the proposed method. Propagation in a 150 m high surface waveguide [9] is considered. The source is located at an altitude of 200 m and emits a 3 GHz harmonic signal. Figure 10 depicts the spatial distribution of the field amplitude, computed by the proposed method. Since there are no horizontal obstacles in this example and propagation occurs at small angles to the horizon, it is advisable to reduce the desired angle range to $[0, 5°]$. This, in turn, allows us to increase the grid step along the longitudinal coordinate to $300\lambda$. The comparison is carried out with Padé approximation

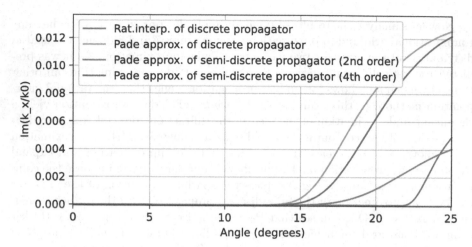

**Fig. 4.** The dependence of $\text{Im}\left(\tilde{k}_x\right)$ on propagation angle. In all cases $\Delta x = 50\lambda$, $\Delta z = 1.1\lambda$, rational approximation order is equal to [7/8].

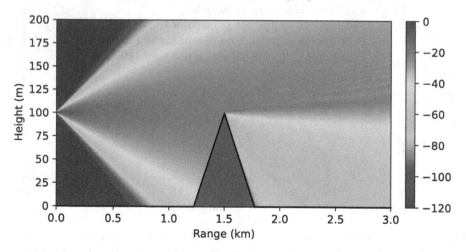

**Fig. 5.** Diffraction on the impenetrable wedge. Spatial distribution of the field amplitude $(20\log|u(x,z)|)$, computed by the ratinterp-[7/8] approximation. $\Delta x = 50\lambda$, $\Delta z = 1.1\lambda$.

of the semi-discrete propagation operator, since it does not contain operator splitting approximation (2). It is clearly seen from Fig. 11, that both methods produce indistinguishable results.

Finally, we will demonstrate the advantages of the FD approximation over the SSF method associated with the upper transparent boundary condition modeling. Figure 12 demonstrates the effect of false reflections from the upper boundary of the computational domain. Errors are especially clearly visible in the shadow zones. Note that by increasing the height of the computational domain

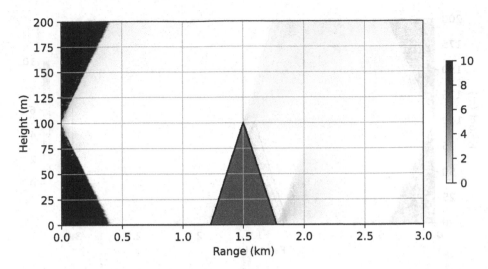

**Fig. 6.** Diffraction on the impenetrable wedge. Spatial distribution of the absolute error ($|20 \log |u_{ri}| - 20 \log |u_{ssf}||$) between the results, obtained by the ratinterp-[7/8] scheme ($u_{ri}$) and SSF method ($u_{ssf}$). $\Delta x = 50\lambda$, $\Delta z = 1.1\lambda$.

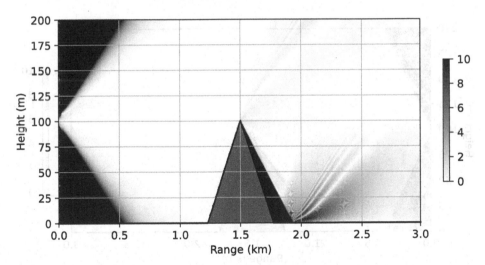

**Fig. 7.** Diffraction on the impenetrable wedge. Spatial distribution of the absolute error ($|20 \log |u_{Pade}| - 20 \log |u_{ssf}||$) between the results, obtained by Padé-[7/8] approximation of the semi-discrete propagator with with 4th order approximation of the vertical operator ($u_{Pade}$) and SSF method ($u_{ssf}$). $\Delta x = 50\lambda$, $\Delta z = 1.1\lambda$.

and the absorbing layer, it is always possible to achieve a coincidence of results between FD approximations and SSF method, but this will require an extra computational costs. In addition, there are no straightforward methods for getting rid of such errors within the SSF method, which somewhat complicates its

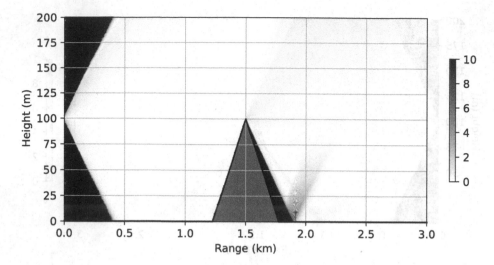

**Fig. 8.** Diffraction on the impenetrable wedge. Spatial distribution of the absolute error ($|20 \log |u_{Pade}| - 20 \log |u_{ssf}||$) between the results, obtained by Padé-[7/8] approximation of the fully discrete propagator ($u_{Pade}$) and SSF method ($u_{ssf}$). $\Delta x = 50\lambda$, $\Delta z = 1.1\lambda$.

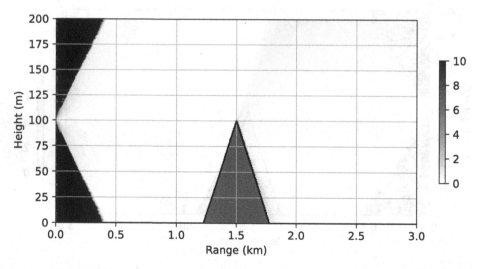

**Fig. 9.** Diffraction on the impenetrable wedge. Spatial distribution of the absolute error ($|20 \log |u_{Pade}| - 20 \log |u_{ssf}||$) between the results, obtained by Padé-[7/8] approximation of the fully discrete propagator ($u_{Pade}$) and SSF method ($u_{ssf}$). $\Delta x = 15\lambda$, $\Delta z = 1.1\lambda$.

practical use. For the FD approximation method, discrete nonlocal boundary conditions [2, 16] were used in all the examples presented, allowing for accurate modeling of the transparent boundary.

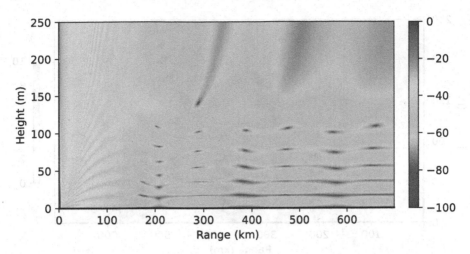

**Fig. 10.** Propagation in the duct. Spatial distribution of the field amplitude ($20 \log |u(x, z)|$), computed by the ratinterp-[7/8] approximation. $\Delta x = 300\lambda$, $\Delta z = \lambda$.

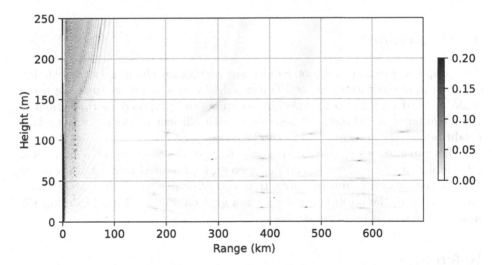

**Fig. 11.** Propagation in the duct. Spatial distribution of the absolute error ($|20 \log |u_{ri}| - 20 \log |u_{Pade}||$) between the results, obtained by Padé-[7/8] scheme ($u_{Pade}$) and ratinterp-[7/8] scheme ($u_{ri}$). $\Delta x = 300\lambda$, $\Delta z = \lambda$.

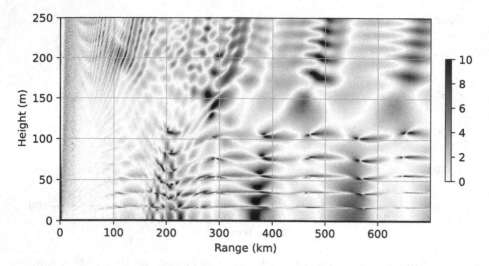

**Fig. 12.** Propagation in the duct. Spatial distribution of the absolute error $(|20\log|u_{ri}| - 20\log|u_{ssf}||)$ between the results, obtained by ratinterp-[7/8] scheme $(u_{ri})$ and SSF method $(u_{ssf})$. $\Delta x = 300\lambda$, $\Delta z = \lambda$.

## 4    Conclusion

The proposed method does not require any significant changes in the existing program implementations of the FD methods, because it differs from the usual Padé method only in coefficients. In addition, the proposed method inherits the advantages of FD methods associated with efficient modeling of boundary conditions.

The paper shows a constructive way to test the stability of a numerical scheme for specific computational parameters. It is desired to establish a priori stability conditions in future works. It is also advisable to conduct a comparative analysis of the optimal computational grid parameters for all existing PE numerical methods in future studies.

## References

1. Chebfun (2020). https://www.chebfun.org/
2. Arnold, A., Ehrhardt, M.: Discrete transparent boundary conditions for wide angle parabolic equations in underwater acoustics. J. Comput. Phys. **145**(2), 611–638 (1998)
3. Baker, G.A., Graves-Morris, P.: Pade Approximants, vol. 59. Cambridge University Press, New York (1996)
4. Bonnafont, T., Douvenot, R., Chabory, A.: A local split-step wavelet method for the long range propagation simulation in 2D. Radio Sci. **56**(2), 1–11 (2021)
5. Collins, M.D.: A split-step Pade solution for the parabolic equation method. J. Acoust. Soc. Am. **93**(4), 1736–1742 (1993)

6. Fishman, L., McCoy, J.J.: Derivation and application of extended parabolic wave theories. I. The factorized Helmholtz equation. J. Math. Phys. **25**(2), 285–296 (1984)
7. Lee, D., Schultz, M.H.: Numerical Ocean Acoustic Propagation in Three Dimensions. World Scientific, Singapore (1995)
8. Leontovich, M.A., Fock, V.A.: Solution of the problem of propagation of electromagnetic waves along the earth's surface by the method of parabolic equation. J. Phys. USSR **10**(1), 13–23 (1946)
9. Levy, M.F.: Parabolic Equation Methods for Electromagnetic Wave Propagation. The Institution of Electrical Engineers, Hertfordshire (2000)
10. Ligny, L., El Ahdab, Z., Douvenot, R.: A phase correction for long distance propagation using split-step methods in non-rectangular domains. IEEE Antennas Wirel. Propag. Lett. **20**(12), 2476–2480 (2021)
11. Lytaev, M.S.: Python wave proragation library (2021). https://github.com/mikelytaev/wave-propagation
12. Lytaev, M.S.: Automated selection of the computational parameters for the higher-order parabolic equation numerical methods. In: Gervasi, O., et al. (eds.) ICCSA 2020. LNCS, vol. 12249, pp. 296–311. Springer, Cham (2020). https://doi.org/10.1007/978-3-030-58799-4_22
13. Lytaev, M.S.: Chebyshev-Type rational approximations of the one-way Helmholtz equation for solving a class of wave propagation problems. In: Paszynski, M., Kranzlmüller, D., Krzhizhanovskaya, V.V., Dongarra, J.J., Sloot, P.M.A. (eds.) ICCS 2021. LNCS, vol. 12742, pp. 422–435. Springer, Cham (2021). https://doi.org/10.1007/978-3-030-77961-0_35
14. Lytaev, M.S.: An improved accuracy split-step Padé parabolic equation for tropospheric radio-wave propagation. In: Gervasi, O., et al. (eds.) ICCSA 2021. LNCS, vol. 12949, pp. 418–433. Springer, Cham (2021). https://doi.org/10.1007/978-3-030-86653-2_31
15. Lytaev, M.S.: Rational interpolation of the one-way Helmholtz propagator. J. Comput. Sci. **58**, 101536 (2022)
16. Lytaev, M.S.: Nonlocal boundary conditions for split-step Padé approximations of the Helmholtz equation with modified refractive index. IEEE Antennas Wirel. Propag. Lett. **17**(8), 1561–1565 (2018)
17. Lytaev, M.S.: Numerov-Pade scheme for the one-way Helmholtz equation in tropospheric radio-wave propagation. IEEE Antenna Wirel. Propag. Lett. **19**(12), 2167–2171 (2020)
18. Ozgun, O., et al.: PETOOL v2.0: parabolic equation toolbox with evaporation duct models and real environment data. Comput. Phys. Commun. **256**, 107454 (2020)
19. Pachón, R., Gonnet, P., Van Deun, J.: Fast and stable rational interpolation in roots of unity and Chebyshev points. SIAM J. Numer. Anal. **50**(3), 1713–1734 (2012)
20. Qin, H., Zhang, X.: Efficient modeling of radio wave propagation in tunnels for 5G and beyond using a split-step parabolic equation method. In: 2021 XXXIVth General Assembly and Scientific Symposium of the International Union of Radio Science (URSI GASS), pp. 1–3. IEEE
21. Sprouse, C.R., Awadallah, R.S.: An angle-dependent impedance boundary condition for the split-step parabolic equation method. IEEE Trans. Antennas Propag. **60**(2), 964–970 (2012)
22. Telescope, R.E., et al.: Modeling in-ice radio propagation with parabolic equation methods. Phys. Rev. D **103**(10), 103007 (2021)

23. Yardim, C., Mukherjee, S., Compaleo, J.: Parabolic wave equation model for ducted environments. In: 2021 XXXIVth General Assembly and Scientific Symposium of the International Union of Radio Science (URSI GASS), pp. 1–4. IEEE
24. Zhou, H., Chabory, A., Douvenot, R.: A fast wavelet-to-wavelet propagation method for the simulation of long-range propagation in low troposphere. IEEE Trans. Antennas Propag. **70**(3), 2137–2148 (2021)

# On the Solution of Time-Fractional Diffusion Models

Angelamaria Cardone$^{(\boxtimes)}$ and Gianluca Frasca-Caccia

Department of Mathematics, University of Salerno,
Via Giovanni Paolo II n. 132, 84084 Fisciano, SA, Italy
{ancardone,gfrascacaccia}@unisa.it

**Abstract.** In many situations, the analysis of viscoelastic materials, like polymers, takes benefit from the introduction of fractional operators in the mathematical formalization. In addition, fractional differential models have been applied in a wide variety of fields, from biology to thermodynamics, from diffusion of information to dehydration/rehydration of food. Thus, a great interest is paid both in the analytical and in the numerical solution of fractional differential problems. The present paper considers a class of time-fractional diffusion problems with Dirichlet boundary conditions. Using Duhamel's principle, the analytical solution is found. As usual in this context, the solution is given in series form and depends on the Mittag-Leffler function. We suggest a computational procedure to evaluate the solution with high accuracy, in a computing environment. Some test examples are presented both in the subdiffusion and in the superdiffusion case, to illustrate the behavior of the solution for different values of the fractional index. Test cases have been carried out in MATLAB.

**Keywords:** Anomalous diffusion · Fractional differential equations · Analytical solution · Dirichlet boundary conditions

## 1 Introduction

The modelling of materials by fractional calculus leads to an accurate description of the experimental data and to reliable predictions of the phenomena in many cases where classical models provide unsatisfactory results. As a matter of fact, the fractional derivative of a function, depends on its past history, therefore fractional operators are specially suitable to model phenomena with memory. Typical examples of fractional models regard viscoelastic materials, which have a hereditary nature, like polymers, epoxy resins, fruit and vegetables (compare [13,14,18,28,30] and references therein). Another field where the memory effects may be well described by fractional operators is heat conduction, giving rise to fractional thermo-elasticity [32], fractional thermo-viscoelasticity [36], fractional electro-thermoelasticity [17]. A special mention is also due to the heat conduction near a crack [40]. The anomalous diffusion, which is observed in many

© The Author(s), under exclusive license to Springer Nature Switzerland AG 2022
O. Gervasi et al. (Eds.): ICCSA 2022, LNCS 13375, pp. 47–60, 2022.
https://doi.org/10.1007/978-3-031-10522-7_4

processes and in particular in the transport through heterogeneous media, is well described by fractional models. In particular, time-fractional operators are able to catch the slow decay of initial conditions and memory effects in subdiffusion of complex systems, like proteins (see references cited in [1]). Anomalous diffusion is observed in dehydration and rehydration processes of food [24, 37], in the diffusion of drugs through skin, in the atrial tissue [35]. Moreover, the anomalous diffusion and its fractional modelling have been considered also in other situations, like the diffusion of information in social networks [20].

The great interest towards the fractional diffusion models led to the development of both analytical and numerical tools. Some important references on the analytical solutions are [2, 25, 26, 34, 39]. A wide literature is available in the numerical approximation, by linear multistep methods, collocation methods, spectral methods and many other approaches [1, 3–12, 15, 16, 19, 22, 29, 41].

In this paper, we provide the analytical solution of the time-fractional diffusion equation

$$D_t^\alpha u = c u_{xx}, \qquad p - 1 < \alpha < p, \qquad x \in [0, L], \qquad t \geq 0, \qquad p \in \mathbb{N} \qquad (1)$$

where $c$ is a constant diffusion coefficient, with null initial conditions, and Dirichlet boundary conditions:

$$D_t^k u(x, 0) = 0, \qquad k = 0, \ldots, p-1, \qquad u(0, t) = \gamma_0(t), \qquad u(L, t) = \gamma_1(t). \quad (2)$$

Here $D_t^\alpha$ is the fractional derivative, in the Riemann-Liouville or in the Caputo sense [31]. Equations of type (1) cover a general class of problems, e.g. [20, 24, 33, 37, 40]. The solution $u$ may represent the temperature field in heat conduction or the concentration of a substance in diffusion processes. Some existence and uniqueness results, for the subdiffusion case $0 < \alpha < 1$, may be found in [2, 25, 26]. For the theory on the more general case $0 < \alpha < 2$, compare [27] and references therein.

We derive the analytical solution by means of Duhamel's principle [34, 38, 39]. Although the solution is given in a series form, it may be accurately evaluated in common computing environments, like Mathematica, MATLAB or Python, thanks to a suitable truncation of the series, as we will show in the numerical examples. Secondly, any a priori knowledge on the analytical solution is a fundamental starting point to obtain reliable and efficient numerical methods, by suggesting the function basis to approximate the solution.

The paper is organized as follows. Some basic notions on fractional calculus are included in Sect. 2. In Sect. 3 we derive the analytical solution of problem (1)–(2). In Sect. 4 we show some examples of solutions in the subdiffusion and superdiffusion case.

## 2   Basic Mathematic Material

In this section we introduce some preliminary material on fractional calculus. For further details compare [31]. Fractional differential equations are defined by establishing a relation between a function and its fractional derivatives (that can also be the standard derivatives of integer order).

The definition of fractional derivative is not unique. The most popular ones are the Riemann-Liouville fractional derivative,

$$^{\mathrm{RL}}D_t^\alpha f = D_t^p(I_t^{p-\alpha} f), \tag{3}$$

and the Caputo fractional derivative,

$$D_t^\alpha f = I_t^{p-\alpha}(D_t^p(f)), \tag{4}$$

where in both cases,

$$I_t^{p-\alpha} f = \frac{1}{\Gamma(p-\alpha)} \int_0^t \frac{f(\tau, x)}{(t-\tau)^{1-p+\alpha}} \, \mathrm{d}\tau \tag{5}$$

is the Riemann-Liouville integral and $\Gamma(z)$ is the Gamma function.

The two definitions (3) and (4) are related by

$$D_t^\alpha f = {}^{\mathrm{RL}}D_t^\alpha f - {}^{\mathrm{RL}}D_t^\alpha \left( \sum_{k=0}^{p-1} \frac{t^k}{k!} f^{(k)}(0) \right), \tag{6}$$

and so they coincide if and only if the function $f$ is such that

$$f^{(k)}(0) = 0, \qquad k = 0, \dots, p-1.$$

In the field of Ordinary Differential Equations (ODEs), the exponential function $y(z) = \mathrm{e}^z$ solves the problem

$$y'(z) = y(z), \qquad y(0) = 1.$$

In the context of fractional ODEs, the solution of the analogue problem

$$D_z^\alpha y(z) = y(z), \qquad y(0) = 1,$$

is $E_\alpha(t^\alpha)$, where $E_\alpha$ is known as the Mittag-Leffler function, defined as

$$E_\alpha(z) = \sum_{k=0}^\infty \frac{z^k}{\Gamma(\alpha k + 1)}.$$

Note that, as expected, $E_1(z) = \mathrm{e}^z$, so the Mittag-Leffler function can be seen as a generalization of the exponential function.

A further generalization is the Mittag-Leffler function with two arguments,

$$E_{\alpha,\beta}(z) = \sum_{k=0}^\infty \frac{z^k}{\Gamma(\alpha k + \beta)}. \tag{7}$$

Setting $\beta = 1$, the function (7) reduces to the Mittag-Leffler function with one argument, i.e., $E_\alpha = E_{\alpha,1}$.

In the next sections we will make use of the following relations that hold true for any $\alpha > 0$, $\beta > 0$, $k$ integer, and $\gamma$ and $\lambda$ real numbers [31]

$$^{\mathrm{RL}} D_t^\gamma \left( t^{\alpha k+\beta-1} E_{\alpha,\beta}^{(k)}(\lambda t^\alpha) \right) = t^{\alpha k+\beta-\gamma-1} E_{\alpha,\beta-\gamma}^{(k)}(\lambda t^\alpha), \tag{8}$$

$$\int_0^t (t-\tau)^{\gamma-1} E_{\alpha,\beta}(\lambda \tau^\alpha) \tau^{\beta-1} \, d\tau = \Gamma(\gamma) t^{\beta+\gamma-1} E_{\alpha,\beta+\gamma}(\lambda t^\alpha). \tag{9}$$

## 3   The Solution of the Time-Fractional Diffusion Problem

We consider the time-fractional diffusion equation (1) with initial and boundary conditions (2).

We assume that the initial data and the boundary conditions are compatible, and therefore

$$D_t^k \gamma_0(0) = D_t^k \gamma_1(0) = 0, \qquad k = 0, \dots, p-1. \tag{10}$$

The symbol $D_t^\alpha$ denotes here the Caputo fractional derivative. However, as the initial condition is of total rest, for this problem this is equivalent to the Riemann-Liouville fractional derivative.

We introduce the auxiliary function

$$h(x,t) = \frac{x}{L}(\gamma_0(t) - \gamma_1(t)) - \gamma_0(t). \tag{11}$$

The variable

$$v(x,t) = u(x,t) + h(x,t) \tag{12}$$

is the solution of

$$D_t^\alpha v = c v_{xx} + D_t^\alpha h \tag{13}$$

that satisfies zero initial and boundary conditions,

$$D_t^k v(x,0) = 0, \qquad k = 0, \dots, p-1, \qquad v(0,t) = 0, \qquad v(L,t) = 0, \tag{14}$$

as a consequence of (10) and (11). We assume that the boundary conditions are regular enough such that $h$ there exists

$$\varphi(x,t) = D_t^p h(x,t). \tag{15}$$

Then,

$$D_t^\alpha h = I_t^{p-\alpha} \varphi(x,t).$$

Note that this fractional derivative can be computed as $h$ is known.

In order to find $v$, we recur to the following fractional Duhamel's principle.

**Theorem 1 (Duhamel's principle [34,38,39]).** *Let be $w(x,t)$ the solution of the unforced fractional problem*

$$D_t^\alpha w(x,t;\tau) = c w_{xx}(x,t;\tau), \tag{16}$$

*with initial and boundary conditions*

$$D_t^k w(x,0;\tau) = 0, \quad k = 0,\ldots,p-1, \qquad D_t^{p-1} w(x,0;\tau) = \varphi(x,\tau),$$
$$w(0,t;\tau) = w(L,t;\tau) = 0. \tag{17}$$

*The solution of the forced problem* (13) *with homogeneous initial and boundary conditions* (14) *is*

$$v(x,t) = \int_0^t w(x,t-\tau;\tau)\,d\tau, \tag{18}$$

The following theorem gives the solution of problem (16)–(17) in closed form for any fractional value of $\alpha$.

**Theorem 2.** *The solution of problem* (16)–(17) *is*

$$w(x,t;\tau) = \sum_{n=1}^{\infty} t^{p-1}\varphi_n(\tau)E_{\alpha,p}(-c\lambda_n^2 t^\alpha)\sin(\lambda_n x), \tag{19}$$

*where* $\lambda_n = n\pi/L$, *and* $\varphi_n(t)$ *is the n-th coefficient of the sine-expansion of* $\varphi(x,t)$ *in space,*

$$\varphi_n(t) = \frac{2}{L}\int_0^L \varphi(x,t)\sin(\lambda_n x)\,dx. \tag{20}$$

*Proof. Evaluating* $w(x,t;\tau)$ *at* $x=0$ *and* $x=L$, *we immediately find that the boundary conditions in* (17) *are satisfied.*
    *Considering that*

$$D_t^k(t^{p-1}E_{\alpha,p}(-c\lambda_n^2 t^\alpha)) - \sum_{j=0}^{k}\binom{k}{j}D_t^j t^{p-1}D_t^{k-j}E_{\alpha,p}(\ c\lambda_n^2 t^\alpha),$$

*then*

$$D_t^k(t^{p-1}E_{\alpha,p}(-c\lambda_n^2 t^\alpha))\big|_{t=0} = 0, \qquad k = 0,\ldots,p-2, \tag{21}$$
$$D_t^{p-1}(t^{p-1}E_{\alpha,p}(-c\lambda_n^2 t^\alpha))\big|_{t=0} = (p-1)!E_{\alpha,p}(0) = 1. \tag{22}$$

*Therefore,*

$$D_t^k w(x,0;\tau) = \sum_{n=1}^{\infty}\varphi_n(\tau)\sin(\lambda_n x)D_t^k(t^{p-1}E_{\alpha,p}(-c\lambda_n^2 t^\alpha))\big|_{t=0} = 0,$$

*for* $k = 0,\ldots,p-2$, *and*

$$D_t^{p-1}w(x,0;\tau) = \sum_{n=1}^{\infty}\varphi_n(\tau)\sin(\lambda_n x)D_t^{p-1}(t^{p-1}E_{\alpha,p}(-c\lambda_n^2 t^\alpha))\big|_{t=0}$$
$$= \sum_{n=1}^{\infty}\varphi_n(\tau)\sin(\lambda_n x) = \varphi(\tau).$$

*Hence, $w(x,t;\tau)$ satisfies also the initial conditions in (17).*
*Finally, we evaluate*

$$w_{xx}(x,t;\tau) = -\sum_{n=1}^{\infty} \lambda_n^2 t^{p-1} \varphi_n(\tau) E_{\alpha,p}(-c\lambda_n^2 t^\alpha) \sin(\lambda_n x),$$

*and*

$$D_t^\alpha w(x,t;\tau) = \sum_{n=1}^{\infty} \varphi_n(\tau) \sin(\lambda_n x) D_t^\alpha (t^{p-1} E_{\alpha,p}(-\lambda_n^2 t^\alpha)). \tag{23}$$

*Considering Eq. (6) and substituting (21) and (22), Eq. (23) is equivalent to*

$$D_t^\alpha w(x,t;\tau) = \sum_{n=1}^{\infty} \varphi_n(\tau) \sin(\lambda_n x) \left( {}^{RL}D_t^\alpha (t^{p-1} E_{\alpha,p}(-c\lambda_n^2 t^\alpha)) - {}^{RL}D_t^\alpha \left( \frac{t^{p-1}}{(p-1)!} \right) \right)$$

$$= \sum_{n=1}^{\infty} \varphi_n(\tau) \sin(\lambda_n x) \left( {}^{RL}D_t^\alpha (t^{p-1} E_{\alpha,p}(-c\lambda_n^2 t^\alpha)) - \frac{t^{p-1-\alpha}}{\Gamma(p-\alpha)} \right). \tag{24}$$

*Moreover, applying formula (8) with $k=0$, $\gamma=\alpha$, $\beta=p$, and $\lambda = -c\lambda_n^2$, yields*

$$^{RL}D_t^\alpha (t^{p-1} E_{\alpha,p}(-c\lambda_n^2 t^\alpha)) = t^{p-\alpha-1} E_{\alpha,p-\alpha}(-c\lambda_n^2 t^\alpha) = t^{p-\alpha-1} \sum_{k=0}^{\infty} \frac{(-c\lambda_n^2 t^\alpha)^k}{\Gamma(\alpha(k-1)+p)}$$

$$= -c\lambda_n^2 t^{p-1} \sum_{k=0}^{\infty} \frac{(-c\lambda_n^2 t^\alpha)^{k-1}}{\Gamma(\alpha(k-1)+p)}$$

$$= -c\lambda_n^2 t^{p-1} \left( \frac{1}{(-c\lambda_n^2 t^\alpha)\Gamma(p-\alpha)} + \sum_{k=0}^{\infty} \frac{(-c\lambda_n^2 t^\alpha)^k}{\Gamma(\alpha k+p)} \right)$$

$$= \frac{t^{p-1-\alpha}}{\Gamma(p-\alpha)} - c\lambda_n^2 t^{p-1} E_{\alpha,p}(-c\lambda_n^2 t^\alpha).$$

*Substituting in formula (24), gives*

$$D_t^\alpha w(x,t;\tau) = -c\sum_{n=1}^{\infty} \lambda_n^2 t^{p-1} \varphi_n(\tau) E_{\alpha,p}(-c\lambda_n^2 t^\alpha) \sin(\lambda_n x) = c w_{xx}(x,t;\tau),$$

*that completes the proof.*

**Theorem 3.** *The solution of problem (1)–(2) is*

$$u(x,t) = \int_0^t \sum_{n=1}^{\infty} (t-\tau)^{p-1} \varphi_n(\tau) E_{\alpha,p}(-c\lambda_n^2 (t-\tau)^\alpha) \sin(\lambda_n x) \, d\tau - h(x,t), \tag{25}$$

*where $\varphi_n$ has been defined in (20).*

*Proof. According to Theorem 1, the solution $v(x,t)$ of problem (13)–(14) is obtained by evaluating $w(x,t-\tau;\tau)$ and substituting in (18). Substituting $v(x,t)$ in (12), we obtain that the solution of (1)–(2) is given by (25).*

## 4    Test Examples

We propose here numerical results for some of the most popular examples of anomalous diffusion modelled by Eq. (1), that are those of subdiffusion, i.e. $0 < \alpha < 1$, and of superdiffusion with $1 < \alpha < 2$. We used MATLAB R2020a to compute and plot the solution.

In order to reproduce numerical results, we need first to set up a grid of nodes on which the solutions are evaluated. We denote with $\mathbf{x}$ and $\mathbf{t}$ the vectors of the nodes in space and time, respectively, i.e.:

$$x_m = m\Delta x, \ m = 0,\ldots,M, \quad t_j = j\Delta t, \ j = 0,\ldots,J,$$

$\Delta x = L/M, \ \Delta t = T/J$.

All the analytical solutions obtained in this paper are in the form of a series:

$$\sum_{n=1}^{\infty} a_n(x,t).$$

Thus, the infinite sum needs to be truncated. The solution at the grid nodes is approximated as

$$\sum_{n=1}^{N} a_n(\mathbf{x},\mathbf{t}), \tag{26}$$

where $a_n(\mathbf{x},\mathbf{t})$ is the matrix of the values of $a_n$ at the grid points, and $N$ is the smallest integer such that $\|a_N(\mathbf{x},\mathbf{t})\| < \text{tol} = 10^{-12}$, with $\|\cdot\|$ denoting the spectral norm, i.e.,

$$\|a_N\| = \sqrt{\lambda_{\max}},$$

and $\lambda_{\max}$ is the maximum eigenvalue of the matrix $a_N^T a_N$.

Secondly, we computed the Mittag-Leffler function by the MATLAB routine ml [21, 23].

### Subdiffusion

Let us consider Eq. (1) with $0 < \alpha < 1$, $c = 1$, $(x,t) \in (0,1) \times (0,2)$, and boundary conditions,

$$u(0,t) = u(1,t) = t.$$

Therefore, Eq. (11) and (15), yield

$$h(x,t) = -t,$$

and

$$\varphi(x,t) = D_t h(x,t) = -1,$$

respectively. Moreover,

$$\varphi_n(t) = -\frac{2}{L} \int_0^L \sin(\lambda_n x) \, dx = \frac{2((-1)^n - 1)}{n\pi}, \tag{27}$$

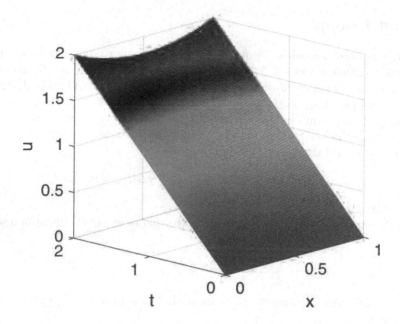

**Fig. 1.** Solution of the subdiffusion problem with $\alpha = 0.5$.

and since for $n$ even $\varphi_n = 0$, the solution (25) reduces to

$$u(x,t) = \int_0^t \sum_{n=1}^\infty \frac{-4}{(2n-1)\pi} E_\alpha(-\lambda_{2n-1}^2(t-\tau)^\alpha) \sin(\lambda_{2n-1}x) \, d\tau + t$$

$$= \sum_{n=1}^\infty \frac{-4}{(2n-1)\pi} \sin(\lambda_{2n-1}x) \int_0^t E_\alpha(-\lambda_{2n-1}^2\tau^\alpha) \, d\tau + t$$

$$= \sum_{n=1}^\infty \frac{-4t}{(2n-1)\pi} \sin(\lambda_{2n-1}x) E_{\alpha,2}(-\lambda_{2n-1}^2t^\alpha) + t$$

where, after a change of variable, we have used formula (9) with $\beta = \gamma = 1$ and $\lambda = -\lambda_{2n-1}^2$.

In Fig. 1 we show, as an example, the solution obtained with the intermediate value $\alpha = 0.5$ and evaluated on a grid with 200 equispaced nodes in space and 100 equispaced points in time. The infinite sum is truncated according to (26), and in this case $N = 12232$. It is visible that starting from a configuration of rest, the heat/substance spreads more uniformly at the beginning, whereas for larger times the temperature/amount of substance is visibly higher at the boundary and lower at the center.

In Fig. 2 we compare the solutions obtained for different values of $\alpha$ uniformly spread in the interval $(0,1)$. Note that when $\alpha = 0$, problem (1)–(2) reduces to a boundary value problem for an ODE. The results obtained highlight that for any fractional value of $\alpha$ corresponds an intermediate configuration of the solution

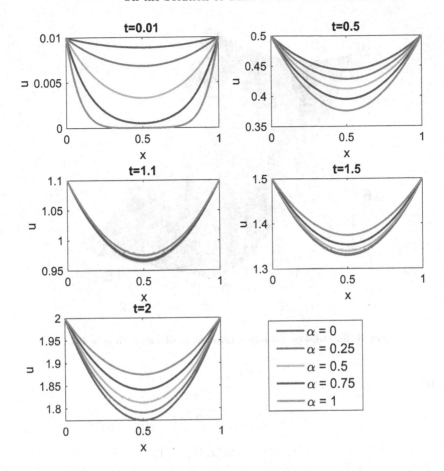

**Fig. 2.** Subdiffusion problem: Solution for different values of $\alpha$ at different times.

between those obtained in the two integer cases, $\alpha = 0$ and $\alpha = 1$. These two extreme configurations are approached continuously and monotonically as $\alpha$ approaches 0 or 1, respectively.

The comparisons show that at the beginning the diffusion from the boundary source to the center of the one dimensional domain is faster for smaller values of $\alpha$. However, there exists a critical time, around $t = 1.1$ where this trend is inverted. After this time, the spread is faster for higher values of $\alpha$.

### Superdiffusion

We consider now Eq. (1) with $1 < \alpha < 2$, again with $c = 1$, $(x,t) \in (0,1) \times (0,2)$ and boundary conditions,

$$u(0,t) = u(1,t) = \frac{t^2}{2}.$$

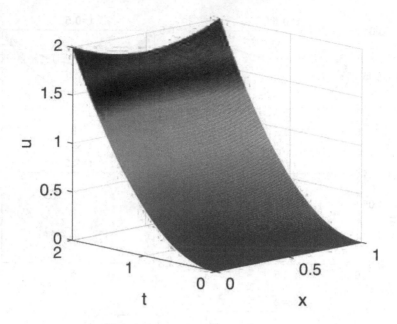

**Fig. 3.** Solution of the superdiffusion problem with $\alpha = 1.5$.

Therefore,

$$h(x,t) = -\frac{t^2}{2},$$

and

$$\varphi(x,t) = D_t^2 h(x,t) = -1,$$

so, also in this case, the coefficients $\varphi_n$ are defined by Eq. (27). Substituting in Eq. (25), gives the following infinite expansion of the solution:

$$
\begin{aligned}
u(x,t) &= \int_0^t \sum_{n=1}^{\infty} \frac{-4(t-\tau)}{(2n-1)\pi} E_{\alpha,2}(-\lambda_{2n-1}^2 (t-\tau)^\alpha) \sin(\lambda_{2n-1} x)\, d\tau + \frac{t^2}{2} \\
&= \sum_{n=1}^{\infty} \frac{-4}{(2n-1)\pi} \sin(\lambda_{2n-1} x) \int_0^t \tau E_{\alpha,2}(-\lambda_{2n-1}^2 \tau^\alpha)\, d\tau + \frac{t^2}{2}, \\
&= \sum_{n=1}^{\infty} \frac{-4t^2}{(2n-1)\pi} \sin(\lambda_{2n-1} x) E_{\alpha,3}(-\lambda_{2n-1}^2 t^\alpha) + \frac{t^2}{2},
\end{aligned}
$$

where we have used (9) with $\gamma = 1$, $\beta = 2$ and $\lambda = -\lambda_{2n-1}$.

As an example, we consider the solution obtained with $\alpha = 1.5$ and truncate the infinite sum after the first $N = 12232$ terms (also in this case the next terms are smaller than the chosen tolerance value). A graph of the solution on the same grid of Fig. 1 is shown in Fig. 3. Similarly as in the case of subdiffusion, starting with an initial condition of total rest the diffusion is more uniform along

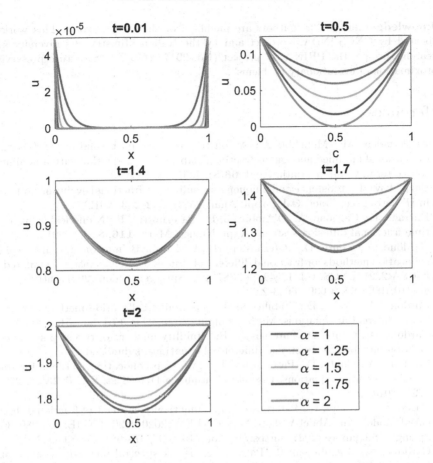

**Fig. 4.** Subdiffusion problem: Solution for different values of $\alpha$ at different times.

the domain for the smallest values of $t$, whereas a clear difference between the boundary and the center is visible for larger values of the boundary source as time increases.

In Fig. 4 we compare the solutions obtained with different values of $\alpha$ chosen uniformly in the interval $(1, 2)$. When $\alpha = 1$, the problem is solved imposing a single initial condition $u(x, 0) = 0$.

As before, the solutions obtained for non integer values of $\alpha \in (1, 2)$ have a configuration that is always intermediate between that of the solutions of the PDEs of integer order. These are approached smoothly for $\alpha$ tending to 1 or to 2, respectively.

At the beginning the diffusion is very slow for the largest values of $\alpha$, and faster as $\alpha$ approaches 1. After a critical time, around $t = 1.4$, this trend is inverted and the diffusion from the boundary source toward the center is faster for higher values of $\alpha$.

**Acknowledgements.** The authors are members of the GNCS group. This work is supported by GNCS-INDAM project and by the Italian Ministry of University and Research, through the PRIN 2017 project (No. 2017JYCLSF) "Structure preserving approximation of evolutionary problems".

# References

1. Abbaszadeh, M., Mohebbi, A.: A fourth-order compact solution of the two-dimensional modified anomalous fractional sub-diffusion equation with a nonlinear source term. Comput. Math. Appl. **66**(8), 1345–1359 (2013)
2. Bazhlekova, E.: Existence and uniqueness results for a fractional evolution equation in Hilbert space. Fract. Calc. Appl. Anal. **15**(2), 232–243 (2012)
3. Burrage, K., Cardone, A., D'Ambrosio, R., Paternoster, B.: Numerical solution of time fractional diffusion systems. Appl. Numer. Math. **116**, 82–94 (2017)
4. Cardone, A., Conte, D., Paternoster, B.: A MATLAB implementation of spline collocation methods for fractional differential equations. In: Gervasi, O., et al. (eds.) ICCSA 2021. LNCS, vol. 12949, pp. 387–401. Springer, Cham (2021). https://doi.org/10.1007/978-3-030-86653-2_29
5. Cardone, A., Conte, D.: Stability analysis of spline collocation methods for fractional differential equations. Math. Comput. Simulation **178**, 501–514 (2020)
6. Cardone, A., Conte, D., Paternoster, B.: Stability analysis of two-step spline collocation methods for fractional differential equations, submitted
7. Cardone, A., Conte, D., Paternoster, B.: Two-step collocation methods for fractional differential equations. Discrete Continuous Dyn. Syst. Ser. B **23**(7), 2709–2725 (2018)
8. Cardone, A., Conte, D., Paternoster, B.: Numerical treatment of fractional differential models. In: Abdel Wahab, M. (ed.) FFW 2020 2020. LNME, pp. 289–302. Springer, Singapore (2021). https://doi.org/10.1007/978-981-15-9893-7_21
9. Cardone, A., D'Ambrosio, R., Paternoster, B.: A spectral method for stochastic fractional differential equations. Appl. Numer. Math. **139**, 115–119 (2019)
10. Cardone, A., Frasca-Caccia, G.: Numerical conservation laws of time fractional diffusion PDEs. Fract. Calc. Appl. Anal. (2022). https://doi.org/10.1007/s13540-022-00059-7
11. Conte, D., Farsimadan, E., Moradi, L., Palmieri, F., Paternoster, B.: Time-delay fractional optimal control problems: a survey based on methodology. Lect. Notes Mech. Eng. pp. 325–337 (2021)
12. Daftardar-Gejji, V., Jafari, H.: Adomian decomposition: a tool for solving a system of fractional differential equations. J. Math. Anal. Appl. **301**(2), 508–518 (2005)
13. Di Paola, M., Fiore, V., Pinnola, F., Valenza, A.: On the influence of the initial ramp for a correct definition of the parameters of fractional viscoelastic materials. Mech. Mater. **69**(1), 63–70 (2014)
14. Di Paola, M., Pirrotta, A., Valenza, A.: Visco-elastic behavior through fractional calculus: An easier method for best fitting experimental results. Mech. Mater. **43**(12), 799–806 (2011)
15. Diethelm, K., Ford, N., Freed, A.: Detailed error analysis for a fractional Adams method. Numer. Algorithms **36**(1), 31–52 (2004)
16. Diethelm, K., Freed, A.: The fracPECE subroutine for the numerical solution of differential equations of fractional order. In: Forschung und wissenschaftliches Rechnen, 1999. pp. 57–71. Göttingen (1998)

17. Ezzat, M., El-Bary, A.: Unified GN model of electro-thermoelasticity theories with fractional order of heat transfer. Microsyst. Technol. **24**(12), 4965–4979 (2018)
18. Failla, G., Zingales, M.: Advanced materials modelling via fractional calculus: challenges and perspectives. Philo. Trans. R. Soc. A **378**(2172), article no. 20200050 (2020). https://doi.org/10.1098/rsta.2020.0050
19. Farsimadan, E., Moradi, L., Conte, D., Paternoster, B., Palmieri, F.: Comparison between protein-protein interaction networks CD4$^{+}$T and CD8$^{+}$T and a numerical approach for fractional hiv infection of CD4$^{+}$T cells. Lect. Notes Comput. Sci. **12949**, 78–94 (2021)
20. Foroozani, A., Ebrahimi, M.: Nonlinear anomalous information diffusion model in social networks. Commun. Nonlinear Sci. Numer. Simul. 103, Paper No. 106019, 18 (2021)
21. Garrappa, R.: The Mittag-Leffler function, March 2015. (http://www.mathworks.com/matlabcentral/fileexchange/48154-the-mittag-leffler-function),    MATLAB Central File Exchange. Accessed February 24, 2022
22. Garrappa, R.: On linear stability of predictor-corrector algorithms for fractional differential equations. Int. J. Comput. Math. **87**(10), 2281–2290 (2010)
23. Garrappa, R.: Numerical evaluation of two and three parameter Mittag-Leffler functions. SIAM J. Numer. Anal. **53**(3), 1350–1369 (2015). https://doi.org/10.1137/140971191
24. Lemus-Mondaca, R., Nuñez, H., Jaques, A., Ramírez, C., Simpson, R.: The anomalous diffusion model based on a fractional calculus approach applied to describe the rehydration process of dried vegetal food matrices. J. Food Process Eng. **44**(9), e13773 (2021)
25. Luchko, Y.: Initial-boundary-value problems for the one-dimensional time-fractional diffusion equation. Fract. Calc. Appl. Anal. **15**(1), 141–160 (2012)
26. Luchko, Y.: Some uniqueness and existence results for the initial-boundary-value problems for the generalized time-fractional diffusion equation. Comput. Math. Appl. **59**(5), 1766–1772 (2010)
27. Mainardi, F.: Fractional calculus. In: Carpinteri, A., Mainardi, F. (eds.) Fractals and Fractional Calculus in Continuum Mechanics. ICMS, vol. 378, pp. 291–348. Springer, Vienna (1997). https://doi.org/10.1007/978-3-7091-2664-6_7
28. Mainardi, F.: Fractional Calculus and Waves in Linear Viscoelasticity: An Introduction to Mathematical Models. World Scientific (2010)
29. Moradi, L., Conte, D., Farsimadan, E., Palmieri, F., Paternoster, B.: Optimal control of system governed by nonlinear Volterra integral and fractional derivative equations. Comput. Appl. Math. **40**(4), Paper No. 157, 15 (2021)
30. Nigmatullin, R., Nelson, S.: Recognition of the "fractional" kinetics in complex systems: Dielectric properties of fresh fruits and vegetables from 0.01 to 1.8 GHz. Signal Process. **86**(10), 2744–2759 (2006)
31. Podlubny, I.: Fractional differential equations, Mathematics in Science and Engineering, vol. 198. Academic Press Inc, San Diego (1999)
32. Povstenko, Y.: Fractional Thermoelasticity. SMIA, vol. 219. Springer, Cham (2015). https://doi.org/10.1007/978-3-319-15335-3
33. Povstenko, Y.: Time-fractional thermoelasticity problem for a sphere subjected to the heat flux. Appl. Math. Comput. **257**, 327–334 (2015)
34. Seemab, A., ur Rehman, M.: A note on fractional Duhamel's principle and its application to a class of fractional partial differential equations. Appl. Math. Lett. **64**, 8–14 (2017)
35. Shen, J., Li, C., Wu, H., Kalantari, M.: Fractional order viscoelasticity in characterization for atrial tissue. Korea Aust. Rheol. J. **25**(2), 87–93 (2013)

36. Sherief, H.H., El-Hagary, M.A.: Fractional order theory of thermo-viscoelasticity and application. Mech. Time Depend. Mater. **24**(2), 179–195 (2019). https://doi.org/10.1007/s11043-019-09415-2
37. Simpson, R., Ramírez, C., Nuñez, H., Jaques, A., Almonacid, S.: Understanding the success of page's model and related empirical equations in fitting experimental data of diffusion phenomena in food matrices. Trends Food Sci. Technol. **62**, 194–201 (2017)
38. Umarov, S.: On fractional Duhamel's principle and its applications. J. Differ. Eq. **252**(10), 5217–5234 (2012)
39. Umarov, S., Saydamatov, E.: A fractional analog of the Duhamel principle. Fract. Calc. Appl. Anal. **9**(1), 57–70 (2006)
40. Yang, W., Chen, Z.: Fractional single-phase lag heat conduction and transient thermal fracture in cracked viscoelastic materials. Acta Mech. **230**(10), 3723–3740 (2019). https://doi.org/10.1007/s00707-019-02474-z
41. Zayernouri, M., Karniadakis, G.E.: Fractional spectral collocation method. SIAM J. Sci. Comput. **36**(1), A40–A62 (2014)

# Prediction of the Impact of the End of year Festivities on the Local Epidemiology of COVID-19 Using Agent-Based Simulation with Hidden Markov Models

Camila Engler[1]([✉]) [iD], Carlos Marcelo Pais[1] [iD], Silvina Saavedra[2],
Emanuel Juarez[1] [iD], and Hugo Leonardo Rufiner[1,3]

[1] Facultad de Ingeniería, Universidad Nacional de Entre Ríos (UNER), Route Prov. 11, Km 10, ciudad de Oro Verde, Provincia de Entre Ríos, Argentina
cami.engler.1@gmail.com, {carlos.pais, emanuel.juarez}@uner.edu.ar, lrufiner@sinc.unl.edu.ar
[2] Subsecretaría de Salud, Municipalidad de Paraná, Provincia de Entre Ríos, Argentina
[3] Instituto de Investigación en Señales, Sistemas E Inteligencia Computacional (Sinc(I)), Universidad Nacional del Litoral (UNL) - Consejo Nacional de Investigaciones Científicas Y Técnicas (CONICET), Parana, Argentina

**Abstract.** Towards the end of 2020, as people changed their usual behavior due to end of year festivities, increasing the frequency of meetings and the number of people who attended them, the COVID-19 local epidemic's dynamic changed. Since the beginnings of this pandemic, we have been developing, calibrating and validating a local agent-based model (AbcSim) that can predict intensive care unit and deaths' evolution from data contained in the state electronic medical records and sociological, climatic, health and geographic information from public sources. In addition, daily symptomatic and asymptomatic cases and other epidemiological variables of interest disaggregated by age group can be forecast. Through a set of Hidden Markov Models, AbcSim reproduces the transmission of the virus associated with the movements and activities of people in this city, considering the behavioral changes typical of local holidays. The calibration and validation were performed based on official data from La Rioja city in Argentina. With the results obtained, it was possible to demonstrate the usefulness of these models to predict possible outbreaks, so that decision-makers can implement the necessary policies to avoid the collapse of the health system.

**Keywords:** Agent-based models · Hidden Markov models · COVID-19 · Epidemiology · Virus transmission · Holyday behavior

## 1 Introduction

In late 2019, a new coronavirus variant, Sars-Cov-2, was identified and the pathology it caused was named Covid-19. Due to the rapid spread of the virus, a pandemic was

© The Author(s) 2022
O. Gervasi et al. (Eds.): ICCSA 2022, LNCS 13375, pp. 61–75, 2022.
https://doi.org/10.1007/978-3-031-10522-7_5

declared in March 2020 and since then, more than 200 million cases and 4 million deaths have been reported [1, 2].

Various outbreaks of this disease in different regions of the world have been studied and their epidemiological analysis has been useful to develop models, mainly mathematical, intending to track and predict the spread of epidemics [3–6]. In this context, the present work is conceived to provide an alternative that includes some realistic factors and predicts the effects of various social and health policies.

This pandemic has some specific characteristics that differentiate itself from others, such as a high basic reproduction number (R0) of up to 2.79 [7], the seasonality [8] and the asymptomatic infectious [9]. Besides, age range, comorbidities and other variables affect the probability of becoming infected, going to ICU (intensive care units) or dying [10–12]. Furthermore, local climate, social behaviour, and health habits have been demonstrated to affect the dynamics of the epidemic [13–15].

Therefore, this work proposes a new approach, more complex and realistic than the traditional mathematical model, by considering the multiplicity of factors. An agent-based model (ABM) is used to incorporate local information and specific characteristics for each area of study, namely social, cultural, geographical and climatological variables related to the dynamics of COVID-19 [16–18]. Moreover, ABM allows taking into account the intrinsic randomness of the system and monitoring the space-time characteristics of the simulation runs, even though this kind of model is more computationally expensive and requires more data [19].

The newly developed model is called the Agent-based local model for COVID19 Simulation or AbCSim [20] and allows modelling groups of people with COVID19, either symptomatic or asymptomatic, together with those considered susceptible or cured. The model also considers the complexity of pathology dynamics and the interpersonal relationships within the populations, along with geographical and climatological information relevant to the pandemic [21]. Additionally, it implements a host transmission block based on a set of Hidden Markov Models (HMMs), which reflect the main aspects of agents´ mobility and social activities [22–24].

Access to local specific population information from La Rioja is provided by the Argentinian Public Health Research on Data Science and Artificial Intelligence for Epidemic Prevention (ARPHAI) [25]. This is a project whose main objective is to develop technological tools based on artificial intelligence and data science applied to electronic health records (EHRs). Information extracted from the Acuario database of La Rioja medical records, among other public information, was used.

This work presents a case study, allowing the evaluation of the dynamics for festive dates to make possible the prediction of the effect of gatherings and parties. Therefore decision-makers can implement relevant health and social policies based on this information.

This document is organized as follows: material and methods are presented in Sect. 2, followed by a brief description of the model in Sect. 3. Section 4 details the case study. The results and discussion are shown in Sect. 5. Finally, Sect. 6 includes the conclusions and future work.

## 2   Material and Methods

### 2.1   The Agent-Based Model

Agent-based modelling (ABM) is a knowledge-based modelling technique and a useful method for representing biological systems that are irreducibly heterogeneous, where randomness plays a major role and which contain numerous interactions between component subsystems and with the environment [26, 27].

One of the reasons why ABM became popular is because it can simulate and help analyze complex organizations or self-organizing systems. This means that the ABM paradigm can represent "large" systems, which are produced by the interaction of many "small" sub-systems (or agents) that can learn or change their behaviour over time [28].

These characteristics of ABMs make them very versatile and have made them impactful in many areas, including epidemiology. Some of the first works that employed ABMs in public health were used to address infectious diseases. However, over time its uses have expanded to other areas such as chronic disease research and social epidemiology. The use of ABMs has been greatly favoured by the ease with which this modelling strategy allows the integration of individual behaviour into frameworks that view health as the product of the interaction of biological, social and environmental factors [29, 30].

In this work, the AbCSim model [20] is used to predict how social behaviours related to end of year festivities impact the epidemiology of COVID-19.

### 2.2   Markov Models in AbCSim

Hidden Markov Models (HMMs) are a proper foundation for creating probabilistic models of linear sequence labelling problems. They deliver a conceptual toolkit for complicated models from a simple intuitive graphical representation. They are at the heart of a diverse range of programs, widely used in the biological field [31].

HMMs have been used in many areas, such as automatic speech recognition [32], analysis of electrocardiographic signals [33], analysis of epileptic seizure frequency [34], and DNA sequence analysis and alignment [35]. Some investigations apply this model to different distributions of epidemiological data (binomial, Gaussian, Poisson) and particularly in the analysis of population surveillance [36, 37].

In AbCSim people's mobility events are modelled in discrete time steps with transition probabilities from one state to another that occur during the day in uniform time periods. A transition probability depends only on the state in which the individual is at a given time. There is a particular HMM for each human agent Ha, based on age range (e), neighbourhood (l) and the time slot (h) corresponding to simulation time. As shown in the state graph in Fig. 1, all these HMMs have four states. Each state represents a different type of location or activity, namely: Home (C), Work (T), Leisure (E) and Others (O). In turn, each HMM has its own transition matrix, which represents state change probabilities, that is, to move from one type of location (j) to another (i); a matrix showing output probabilities for each state (for the k possible places where Ha could go in the state j) and a vector of initial location probabilities. Vector is always (1, 0, 0, 0) for the beginning of the day, as it is assumed that all citizens start the day at home.

In another way, a Markov model applied to the progression of the illness in a host (within-host progression), can be defined as a stochastic model in which the patient is assumed to be always in one of a finite number of health states (called Markov states), which must be exhaustive (i.e., all possible) and mutually exclusive (an individual cannot be in two states at the same time) [38]. In this way, popular epidemiological compartmental models first formulated by Kermak & Mac Kendrik [39] can be seen as Markov chain models, as well. As can be seen in Fig. 2, in AbCSim a modification of the compartmental model proposed by Arenas [40] is used to simulate the in-host virus propagation dynamics.

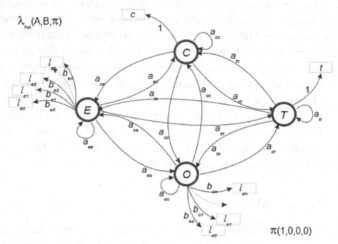

**Fig. 1.** State graph of a Hidden Markov sub-model. The four states circled, represent C: House; T: Work; E: Leisure; O: Others. Rectangular blocks show possible outputs for each state, i.e., each waypoint. States C and T have only one possible output (defined in the attributes of each human agent, see [21]), therefore, that output has a probability 1 of being chosen. States E and O have different possible outputs selected from a list with locations that depend on the human agent's neighbourhood.

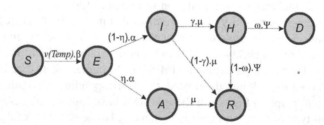

**Fig. 2.** Spread sub-model with seven states: S: susceptible; E: latent or exposed; I: symptomatic infectious; A: asymptomatic infectious; R: recovered; D: dead, and H: hospitalized. Modified from Arenas et al. [40]

## 2.3  Data Sources

The model takes information from several data sources. The first source was Acuario [41], the informatics system used in the province of La Rioja for the registration of outpatient care. It has a relational database with more than 200 tables that gather information on 268,000 individuals treated in the province's public health system. The information used from Acuario was mainly three variables: the initial number of people infected, the proportion of people in each age range, and comorbidities in the population. Also, sociological data [42–47], such as the unsatisfied basic needs index and the existence of a drinking water network were used to characterize the different neighbourhoods that are represented in the model.

The data used were de-identified before leaving state headquarters and were stored and processed at the Centre for High-Performance Computing (CCAD) under strict security and access rules. In addition, all data handlers were required to present the Good Clinical Research Practices certification issued by the National Institute on Drug Abuse (NIDA) in collaboration with the Center for Clinical Trials (CCTN), as well as an individual confidentiality commitment.

On the other hand, several public sources were consulted for different purposes, such as: Google Mobility [48]; Google Maps [49]; Google Places [50]; National Weather Service (SMN) [51]; official government pages [52] and different local demographical literature.

## 3  Model Description

AbCSim is implemented in Java and runs on the computational simulation platform: Repast [53]. This is a platform with a set of open-source modelling and simulation tools based on agents, that runs on different operating systems.

The general scheme of the model is presented in Fig. 3, where its different blocks and implementation levels are identified. The top-level shows the model in its most abstract stage, as a black box, indicating the initial conditions, inputs and outputs. The intermediate level shows the two main blocks that make up the model: one block dedicated to the simulation of the spread of the virus within each host and another dedicated to the transmission of the disease between hosts. Finally, at the lower level, the different sub-models are indicated with their own parameters (Infectivity, Epidemiological characterization, Interpersonal contact, Location and Mobility/Activity, Transport and Infectious trail). In the following sections, they will be properly characterized and detailed individually (together with their contributing modules).

As an agent-based model, a fundamental part of the system is the implementation of human agents (Ha), which possess specific characteristics and attributes of risk factors and co-morbidities. In addition, they can contract and transmit the virus, change their health status and symptoms, and modify their behaviour accordingly.

The relationship between the different human agents with each other and with the environment is also depicted, as the distance between agents, the use of masks, the respect for the place's capacity and the different rules and protocols, are key in modelling the transmission of the virus.

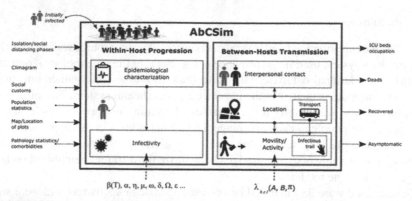

**Fig. 3.** AbCSim block diagram: General model (black block) with inputs, outputs (horizontal solid line arrows) and initial conditions (curved arrows); main functional blocks (blue left and right-side blocks) and the corresponding sub-models for each block (green and magenta blocks). Vertical solid line arrows represent the relationships between various model elements, and vertical dotted line arrows, the corresponding parameters [21]. (Color figure online)

The behaviour of each agent depends on their age group, habits and the neighbourhood where they live, which are randomly assigned at the beginning of the simulation according to the population statistics of La Rioja city.

The mobility of each agent is linked to the transition states matrices (activities/places) implemented by means of a set of HMMs (see Sect. 2.2). Each of the HMMs corresponds to an area where the agent lives, the age group to which it belongs and the time zone in which it is at the time of the simulation.

As already mentioned, AbCSim has two main blocks, the first one is about virus propagation within the host, and includes the infectivity sub-model, considering epidemiological characterization (see Sect. 2.2). The second one is about host-to-host transmission and covers the different virus transmission mechanisms between hosts (infectious trail, direct contact or droplet-to-face) in different spaces (home, office, recreation, public transport), and specific circumstances (place's capacity, ventilation, temperature).

Due to the stochastic nature of the epidemiological phenomenon and the model used to try to reproduce it, several "complete" runs must be carried out to obtain the final results, requiring the use of a computer cluster.

## 4   Case Study: End of Year Festivities

At the end of the year festivities, people tend to get together for dinner and celebrations, and young people go out partying, increasing the number of personal contacts. A particular analysis of this situation is carried out in this work. Parameters of AbCSim were established to reflect the local characteristics of the city of La Rioja and its inhabitants. For more details, including parameters setting and estimation methodology, the reader is referred to [21].

In order to use the AbCSim as a what-if model, different scenarios were proposed, where the regulatory force varied from minor to major. Based on the impact the different scenarios would have on the number of ICU beds, health decision-makers can establish the level of regulation to implement.

For this, some aspects were considered, on the one hand, dinners were represented for the nights of December 24 and 31, where families are considered to gather to celebrate. The duration and attendance of dinners were varied for the different scenarios. In addition, parties attended mainly by young people were also considered. Finally, since on festive dates people visit stores and entertainment venues frequently, the capacity of these places was varied, with differences among the tested scenarios.

Three scenarios were proposed and analyzed:

- **High Regulated**: due to regulatory constraints that would be proposed, it is assumed that 70% of the population would meet at Christmas and New Year's Eve, in gatherings of 10 people for a period of two hours. Additionally, 20% of young people go out partying, both indoors and outdoors. Also, the minimum distance between people of one and a half meters is respected in every place.
- **Medium Regulated**: it is assumed that 80% of the population would gather at Christmas and New Year's Eve, in meetings of 15 people each for a period of two hours. In addition, 20% of young people would go out partying afterwards, both indoors and outdoors. Finally, the minimum distance between people of one and a half meters would not be respected in shops.
- **Low Regulated**: it is assumed that 90% of the population would meet at Christmas and New Year's Eve, in gatherings of 20 people for a period of two hours and a 40% of young people go out partying also, both indoors and outdoors. In addition, the minimum distance between people of one and a half meters would not be respected in shops, leisure and other venues.

## 5 Results and Discussion

For each scenario, bed occupancy (Fig. 4), number of symptomatic cases (Fig. 5) and number of accumulated deaths per Covid-19 (Fig. 6) until the end of February were analyzed. In addition, the number of symptomatic versus non-symptomatic cases was compared (Fig. 7).

It can be seen from the results presented that in the low regulated scenario, where there are more meetings than in the other scenarios, there is a relative increase in cases, ICU bed occupancy and deaths due to Covid-19, from January 20th onwards.

This is in line with expectations, as the effect is not immediate, but due to the in-host illnesses and contagion progression, the impact is expected to be seen two to three weeks after the festivities. Also, it can be seen comparing the subplots in Fig. 4 that as much more gatherings are attended, the effect of the festivities generates a stronger impact on ICU bed occupancy. A similar phenomenon can be seen in the number of daily cases and accumulated deaths.

There is no field data available for the analysis of symptomatic versus non-symptomatic patients. However, AbCSim shows that in the low regulated scenario, where there were more contacts with young people who went partying, and therefore more contagion, the number of asymptomatic patients increased, if it is compared to

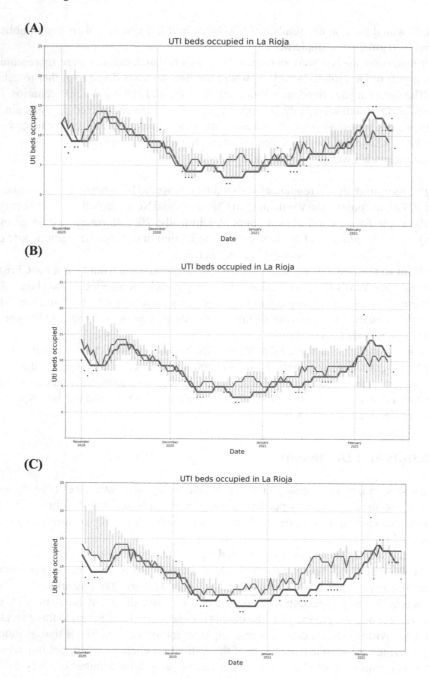

**Fig. 4.** ICU beds occupied by positive COVID-19 patients in the period under study: (A) corresponds to the High Regulated scenario; (B) corresponds to the Medium Regulated scenario and (C) corresponds to the Low Regulated scenario. ICU beds for Covid-19 + surveyed by the official data are shown in black, with the interpolation from field data in green, the dispersion of the corresponding model output in light blue; and in blue its central tendency.

**(A)**

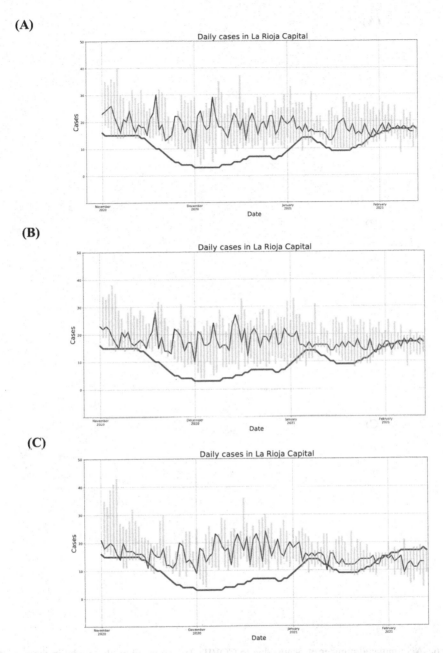

**(B)**

**(C)**

**Fig. 5.** Daily COVID-19 cases (symptomatic + asymptomatic) estimated by the model in the period under study: (A) corresponds to the High Regulated scenario; (B) corresponds to the Medium Regulated scenario and (C) corresponds to the Low Regulated scenario. Light blue shows the dispersion of the model output and blue, its central tendency. The interpolation from field data is shown in green. (Color figure online)

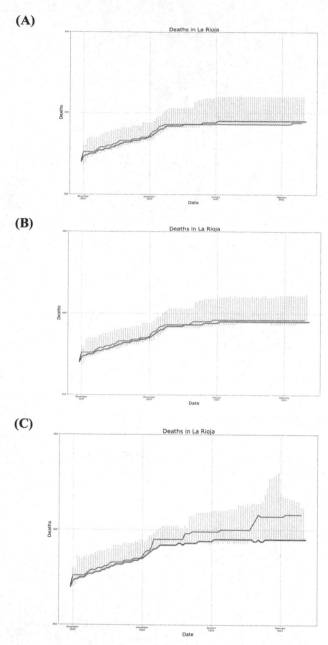

**Fig. 6.** Accumulated number of deaths due to COVID-19 estimated by the model in the period under study: (A) corresponds to High Regulated scenario; (B) corresponds to the Medium Regulated scenario and (C) corresponds to the Low Regulated scenario. Light blue shows the dispersion of the model output and blue its central tendency. The interpolation from field data is shown in green. (Color figure online)

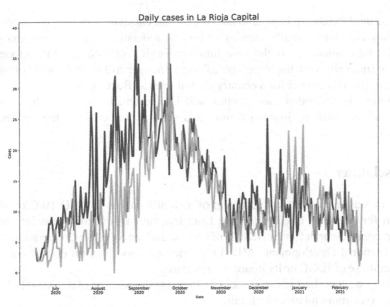

**Fig. 7.** Daily COVID-19 cases estimated by the model in the period under study for the low regulated scenario. Symptomatic cases are in purple and asymptomatic cases are in red. (Color figure online)

previous months. This may be because most of the contacts are among young people, and due to their age range, they tend not to show symptoms.

A detail to be considered when interpreting these results is that at that time only alpha and delta variants were circulating, and mass vaccination had not yet begun in Argentina country. In addition, the model contemplates the ventilation of homes and buildings, which reduces the rate of contagion, because during the holidays it is summer in the southern hemisphere.

Finally, in retrospect and qualitatively compared with the field data, it is considered that the high regulated scenario is the most representative of what really happened in La Rioja city. This is a good corollary since this scenario is precisely the one that the government proposed for the end of the year festivities. Although it is an a posteriori analysis, it makes it clear that the tool offers the possibility of using the information provided by the simulations to propose some type of restriction, contemplating how much impact it would have, for example, on the increase in ICU beds, compared to the cost of implementing these restrictions.

## 6  Conclusion and Future Works

In this work, the impact of the end of year festivities on the local epidemiology of COVID-19 was predicted and analyzed using agent-based model simulations with AbCSim. It can be concluded that AbCSim works well as a "what-if model", allowing the analysis of different scenarios and providing decision-makers with a useful tool to properly select the social and health policies they implement.

These models require large amounts of data and calculation power, but on the other hand, they are almost totally explicit and allow a detailed proposal and analysis of particular local situations. In this case for example, it is expected that the model for a relatively small city with this geographical location, such as La Rioja, will behave very differently from the model for a country capital such as Buenos Aires.

In future works, other case studies will be presented, including the impact of ventilation, vaccination, immunity time and school protocols on the dynamics of Covid-19.

# 7  Disclaimer

This work was carried out with the help of a grant from the COVID-19 Global South Program for Artificial Intelligence and Data Innovation, funded by the International Development Research Center (IDRC) of Canada and the Swedish Cooperation Agency for International Development (AIDS) Opinions expressed herein do not necessarily represent those of IDRC or its Board of Governors.

In the same way, the document does not represent the position of the ARPHAI project or of the consortium member institutions.

**Acknowledgments.** The authors thank Dr Abelardo Del Prado for his collaboration in sociological aspects; Programmer Matías Godano for his contribution through the countless lines of code that implement the program resulting from this model.

This work has been funded by International Development Research Center (IDRC) and Sweden's government agency for development cooperation (SIDA) in the context of ARPHAI project. Also, it has been funded by the Agencia Nacional de Promoción de la Investigación, el Desarrollo y la Innovación (National Agency for the Promotion of Research, Development and Innovation), part of the Ministry of Science and Technology of Argentina through project IP 362 of the Coronavirus Priority line.

# References

1. Singhal, T.: A review of coronavirus disease-2019 (COVID-19). Indian J. Pediatr. **87**, 281–286 (2020). https://doi.org/10.1007/s12098-020-03263-6
2. Our World in Data: Coronavirus (COVID-19) - Google News. https://news.google.com/covid19/map?hl=es-419&gl=US&ceid=US%3Aes-419
3. Tchepmo Djomegni, P.M., Haggar, M.S.D., Adigo, W.T.: Mathematical model for Covid-19 with protected susceptible in the post-lockdown era. Alexandria Eng. J. **60**, 527–535 (2021). https://doi.org/10.1016/j.aej.2020.09.028
4. Gozzi, N.O., et al.: Estimating the spreading and dominance of SARS-CoV-2 VOC 202012/01 (lineage B.1.1.7) across Europe. medRxiv. 2021.02.22.21252235 (2021)
5. Cacciapaglia, G., Cot, C., Sannino, F.: Second wave COVID-19 pandemics in Europe: a temporal playbook. Sci. Rep. **10**, 1–8 (2020). https://doi.org/10.1038/s41598-020-72611-5
6. Kucharski, et al.: Early dynamics of transmission and control of COVID-19: a mathematical modelling study. Lancet Infect. Dis. 3099, 1–7 (2020).https://doi.org/10.1016/S1473-3099(20)30144-4

7. Liu, Y., Gayle, A., Wilder-Smith, A., Rocklöv, J.: The reproductive number of COVID-19 is higher compared to SARS coronavirus. J. Travel Med. 4–10 (2020)
8. Huang, X., Wei, F., Hu, L., Wen, L., Chen, K.: Epidemiology and clinical characteristics of COVID-19. Arch. Iran. Med. **23**, 268–271 (2020). https://doi.org/10.34172/aim.2020.09
9. Hellewell, J., et al.: Feasibility of controlling COVID-19 outbreaks by isolation of cases and contacts. Lancet Glob. Heal. **8**, e488–e496 (2020). https://doi.org/10.1016/S2214-109 X(20)30074-7
10. Hinch, R., et al.: OpenABM-Covid19 - An agent-based model for non-pharmaceutical interventions against COVID-19 including contact tracing. PLoS Comput. Biol. **17**(7), e1009146 (2020)
11. Health, E. for public, Istituto Superiore di Sanità: Characteristics of SARS-CoV-2 patients dying in Italy Report., Trento and Bozen (2020)
12. Deiana, G., et al.: Deaths in SARS-CoV-2 positive patients in Italy: the influence of underlying health conditions on lethality. Int. J. Environ. Res. Public Health. **17**(12), 4450 (2020). https://doi.org/10.3390/ijerph17124450
13. Sajadi, M.M., Habibzadeh, P., Vintzileos, A., Shokouhi, S., Miralles-Wilhelm, F., Amoroso, A.: Temperature, humidity, and latitude analysis to estimate potential spread and seasonality of coronavirus disease 2019 (COVID-19). JAMA Netw. open. **3**, e2011834, (2020). https://doi.org/10.1001/jamanetworkopen.2020.11834
14. Wang, Y., Li, B., Gouripeddi, R., Facelli, J.C.: Human activity pattern implications for modeling SARS-CoV-2 transmission. Comput. Meth. Prog. Biomed. **199**, 105896, (2021). https://doi.org/10.1016/j.cmpb.2020.105896
15. Gwizdałła, T.: Viral disease spreading in grouped population. Comput. Meth. Prog. Biomed. **197**, 105715 (2020). https://doi.org/10.1016/j.cmpb.2020.105715
16. Abar, S., Theodoropoulos, G.K., Lemarinier, P., O'Hare, G.M.P.: Agent Based Modelling and Simulation tools: a review of the state-of-art software. Comput. Sci. Rev. **24**, 13–33 (2017). https://doi.org/10.1016/j.cosrev.2017.03.001
17. Auchincloss, A.H., Diez Roux, A.V.: A new tool for epidemiology: the use-fulness of dynamic-agent models in understanding place effects on health. Am. J. Epidemiol. **168**, 1–8 (2008). https://doi.org/10.1093/aje/kwn118
18. Bian, L.: Spatial approaches to modeling dispersion of communicable diseases - a review. Trans. GIS. **17**, 1–17 (2013). https://doi.org/10.1111/j.1467-9671.2012.01329.x
19. Cuevas, E.: An agent-based model to evaluate the COVID-19 transmission risks in facilities. Comput. Biol. Med. **121**, 103827 (2020). https://doi.org/10.1016/j.compbiomed.2020.103827
20. Pais, C.M., Godano, M.I., Engler, C., del Prado, A., Manresa, J.B., Rufiner, H.L.: City-scale model for COVID-19 epidemiology with mobility and social activities represented by a set of hidden Markov models. SSRN Electron. J. (2021). https://doi.org/10.1590/SciELOPrepri nts.2654
21. Danchin, A., Ng, T.W.P., Turinici, G.: A new transmission route for the propagation of the SARS-CoV-2 coronavirus. medRxiv (2020). https://doi.org/10.1101/2020.02.14.20022939
22. Banisch, S.: Agent-based models as Markov chains. In: Markov Chain Aggregation for Agent-Based Models. UCS, pp. 35–55. Springer, Cham (2016). https://doi.org/10.1007/978-3-319-24877-6_3
23. Brémaud, P.: Markov Chains : Gibbs Fields, Monte Carlo Simulation, and Queues (1999)
24. Gambs, S., Killijian, M.-O., Cortez, M.N. del P.: Towards temporal mobility markov chains. In: 1st International Workshop on Dynamicity Collocated with OPODIS 2011, Toulouse, France (2012)
25. ARPHAI – CIECTI. http://www.ciecti.org.ar/arphai/
26. Bonabeau, E.: Agent-based modeling: Methods and techniques for simulating human systems. Proc. Natl. Acad. Sci. U.S.A. **99**(SUPPL. 3), 7280–7287 (2002). https://doi.org/10.1073/pnas.082080899

27. Galea S., Hall, C., Kaplan G.A.: Social epidemiology and complex system dynamic modelling as applied to health behaviour and drug use research. Int. J. Drug Policy **20**(3), 209–216 (2009)
28. Smallman-Raynor, M., Cliff, A.: Epidemiological spaces: the use of multidi-mensional scaling to identify cholera diffusion processes in wake of the Philippines insurrection, 1899–1902. Trans. Inst. Br. Geogr. **26**(3), 288–305 (2001). https://doi.org/10.1111/1475-5661.00023
29. Zhang, J.J., et al.: Cyber-physical-social systems: the state of the art and perspectives. IEEE Trans. Comput. Soc. Syst. **5**, 829–840 (2018). https://doi.org/10.1109/TCSS.2018.2861224
30. López, L., Fernández, M.A., Gómez, A., Giovanini, L.L.: An influenza epidemic model with dynamic social networks of agents with individual behavior. Ecol. Complex. **41**, (2020). https://doi.org/10.1016/J.ECOCOM.2020.100810
31. Eddy, S.R.: What is a hidden Markov model? Nat. Biotechnol **22**, 1315–1316 (2004). https://doi.org/10.1038/nbt1004-1315
32. Hamidi, M., Satori, H., Zealouk, O., Satori, K., Laaidi, N.: Interactive voice response server voice network administration using hidden Markov model speech recognition system. In: Proceedings of the 2nd World Conference on Smart Trends in Systems, Security and Sustainability, WorldS4 2018, pp. 238–245, (2018). https://doi.org/10.1109/WorldS4.2018.861 1591
33. Cheng, W.T., Chan, K.L.: Classification of electrocardiogram using hidden Markov models, 143–146, (2002). https://doi.org/10.1109/iembs.1998.745850
34. Berg, A.T., Lin, J., Ebrahimi, N., Testa, F.M., Levy, S.R., Shinnar, S.: Modeling remission and relapse in pediatric epilepsy: application of a Markov process. Epilepsy Res. **60**(1), 31–40 (2004). https://doi.org/10.1016/j.eplepsyres.2004.05.002
35. Loytynoja, A., Milinkovitch, M.C.: A hidden Markov model for progressive multiple alignment. Bioinformatics **19**(12), 1505–1513 (2003). https://doi.org/10.1093/bioinformatics/btg193
36. Marshall, A.W., Goldhamer, H.: An application of markov processes to the study of the epidemiology of mental disease. J. Am. Stat. Assoc. **50**(269), 99–129 (1955). https://doi.org/10.1080/01621459.1955.10501253
37. Nucita, A., et al.: A markov chain based model to predict HIV/AIDS epidemiological trends. In: Cuzzocrea, A., Maabout, S. (eds.) MEDI 2013. LNCS, vol. 8216, pp. 225–236. Springer, Heidelberg (2013). https://doi.org/10.1007/978-3-642-41366-7_19
38. Le Strat, Y., Carrat, F.: Monitoring epidemiologic surveillance data using hidden Markov models. Stat. Med. **18**(24), 3463–3478 (1999). https://doi.org/10.1002/(SICI)1097-0258(199 91230)18:24%3c3463::AID-SIM409%3e3.0.CO;2-I
39. Kermack, W.O., McKendrick, A.G.: A contribution to the mathematical theory of epidemics. Proc. R. Soc. London. Ser. Contain. Pap. Math. Phys. Char. **115**, 772, 700–721, (1927). https://doi.org/10.1098/rspa.1927.0118
40. Arenas, A., et al.: A mathematical model for the spatiotemporal epidemic spreading of COVID19. medRxiv (2020). https://doi.org/10.1101/2020.03.21.20040022
41. Acuario Salud | Un sistema para la gestión integral de la salud. http://acuario-salud.com
42. Barrios - La Rioja - Argentina - uMap. http://umap.openstreet-map.fr/es/map/barrios-la-rioja-argentina_248636#16/-29.4149/-66.8611
43. Cr Casas G., et al.: autoridades punto focal ministerio de planeamiento e indus-tria, informe provincial ODS (2019)
44. Ministerio De Hacienda, La Rioja informe sintético de caracterización socio-productiva (2018)
45. DINREP, Subsecretaría de Relaciones con Provincias, Ministerio de Economía y Finanzas Públicas de la Nación, "Necesidades Básicas Insatisfechas (NBI) (2014)
46. Economía Riojana, En el segundo semestre del 2020 la pobreza en la ciudad de La Rioja llegó al 35,3%. https://economiariojana.com.ar/nota/en-el-segundo-semestre-del-2020-la-pobreza-en-la-ciudad-de-la-rioja-llego-al-35-3

47. Zhaoyang, R., Sliwinski, M.J., Martire, L.M., Smyth, J. M.: Age differences in adults' daily social interactions: an ecological momentary assessment study. Psychol. Aging, 33, 4, 607 (2018). https://doi.org/10.1037/PAG0000242
48. Descripción general - Ayuda de Informes de Movilidad Local. https://support.google.com/covid19-mobility/answer/9824897?hl=es&ref_to-pic=9822927
49. Maps G.: Ayuda de Google Maps. https://support.google.com/maps/?hl=es-419#topic=3092425
50. Places, G.: Google Mi Negocio. https://www.google.com/busi-ness/faq/?gmbsrc=us-en-ha-se-z-gmb-s-z-h~bk%3B
51. Nuestro Plan Estratégico | Argentina.gob.ar. https://www.argen-tina.gob.ar/smn/institucional/plan-estrategico
52. Plan Nacional de Vacunación: Se lanza el registro de datos abiertos para seguir on line las dosis aplicadas contra el COVID-19 en todo el país | Argen-tina.gob.ar. https://www.argentina.gob.ar/noticias/plan-nacional-de-vacuna-cion-se-lanza-el-registro-de-datos-abiertos-para-seguir-line-las
53. Informes covid. https://salud.larioja.gob.ar/web/index.php/informes-covid-link
54. Repast Suite Documentation. https://repast.github.io/

# Color-Spanning Problem for Line Segments

Sukanya Maji[✉] and Sanjib Sadhu

Department of CSE, National Institute of Technology Durgapur, Durgapur, India
sm.20cs1102@phd.nitdgp.ac.in, sanjib.sadhu@cse.nitdgp.ac.in

**Abstract.** The color-spanning problem for a given set of colored geometric objects finds a region that contains at least one object of each color. This paper studies the color-spanning problem for a given set of colored line segments $\mathcal{L}$ lying in $\mathbb{R}^2$. For $n$ line segments, each associated with any of $m$ colors ($3 \leq m < n$), we compute (i) one (resp. two congruent disjoint) color-spanning vertical strip (resp. strips) of minimum width in $O(n)$ time after $O(n \log n)$ preprocessing task, (ii) one (resp. two congruent disjoint) color-spanning axis parallel square (resp. squares) of minimum perimeter in $O(n(n-m))$ (resp. $O(n^3)$) time. The same results also exist if the inputs to the aforesaid problems are $n$ simple polygons or disks. Our algorithm improved the time complexity of finding the minimum perimeter color-spanning square problem for the segments [1] by $\log n$ factor. Finally, we show the $\sqrt{2}$ approximation algorithm for computing one (resp. two congruent disjoint) color-spanning disk (resp. disks) of minimum radius for $\mathcal{L}$.

**Keywords:** Computational geometry · Color-spanning objects · Line sweeping · Approximation algorithm

## 1 Introduction

We are given $m$ different types (e.g. hospitals, post-offices, schools, shopping malls, fire-stations etc.) of $n$ resources, where $3 \leq m < n$. These resources are generally represented by geometric objects e.g. points, line segments, simple polygons, circular disks etc. in $\mathbb{R}^2$. The same (resp. different) types of resources are identified by assigning the same (resp. different) colors to them. A color-spanning region contains at least one resource of each color, where the region may be of an unbounded (e.g. a strip) or bounded (e.g. a disk, rectangle, square etc.) types. The *color-spanning problem* computes the smallest color-spanning region for the given set of resources and it was first introduced in 2001 [2], where only colored points were considered as input. The color-spanning problem for points has grown a lot of interest to the researchers due to its huge applications in the facility location problem [2], pattern recognition [4], database queries [10] etc.

© The Author(s), under exclusive license to Springer Nature Switzerland AG 2022
O. Gervasi et al. (Eds.): ICCSA 2022, LNCS 13375, pp. 76–89, 2022.
https://doi.org/10.1007/978-3-031-10522-7_6

**Related Work:** A lot of research works have been done on a set of colored points. Huttenlocher et al. [1] computed the smallest color-spanning circle for a given set of $n$ points with $m$ colors in $O(mn \log n)$ time. Abellanas et al. [2] first computed the color-spanning axis-parallel rectangle for point set in $O(n(n - m) \log^2 m)$. The smallest color-spanning strip and rectangle of arbitrary orientation for a given set of points can be computed in $O(n^2 \log n)$ and $O(n^3 \log m)$ time [3], respectively. The color-spanning axis-parallel square and axis-parallel equilateral triangle can be determined in $O(n \log^2 n)$ [5] and $O(n \log n)$ [6] time, respectively. Acharyya et al. [11] identified the smallest color-spanning axis-parallel square, rectangle and circle for a point set that must contain also a given query point $q$. The minimum width color-spanning circular annulus, and axis-parallel rectangular annulus and axis-parallel square annulus for a set of points can be computed in $O(n^3 \log n)$, $O(n^4)$ and $O(n^3 + n^2 m \log m)$ time [9], respectively. Sang Won Bae [7] also computed the minimum width color-spanning axis-parallel rectangular annulus in $O((n - m)^3 n \log n)$ time. Most of the research works on color-spanning problem deal with only point set as input. However, in real perspective it is not always reasonable to represent each facility by point only. Rather, depending on the size and shape of the facilities, they are represented more precisely by the line segments, simple polygons or disks instead of points. So, in this paper we are interested in the color-spanning objects which cover a set of line segments, simple polygons or disks. Also, the solution to the color-spanning problem for point set cannot be applied to the color-spanning problem for line segments. To the best of our knowledge, there exists one work on color-spanning problem for line segments by Huttenlocher et al. [1], where they first computed the upper envelope of the Voronoi surfaces of the line segments and using that envelope, they shown how to compute the smallest color-spanning axis-parallel square (resp. disk) of the line segments, in $O(n^2 \log n)$ (resp. $O(n^2 \alpha(n) \log n)$) time. In our work, we have improved the time complexity of finding the color-spanning axis-parallel square [1] by $\log n$ factor using the line sweeping technique. We have also studied the color-spanning problem where colored segments are covered by two congruent disjoint strips or squares of minimum size. This is motivated by a variation of color-spanning problem, where for a given set of resources (colored points or segments), $k$ congruent color-spanning objects of minimum size is to be determined, with the constraint that each resource $r_i$ can support at most $f(r_i)$ demand points (centers of the color-spanning regions). For simplicity, we have taken $k = 2$ and $f(r_i) = 1$ for each resource $r_i$.

**Our Contributions:** We propose algorithm(s) to compute color-spanning vertical strip(s) or axis parallel square(s) of minimum size for $n$ line segments or polygons or disks in $\mathbb{R}^2$.

| Color-spanning problems for line segments | Time | Space | Exact/Approx |
|---|---|---|---|
| One color-spanning vertical strip of minimum width | $O(n)$ with $O(n \log n)$ preprocessing | $O(n)$ | Exact |
| Two congruent color-spanning disjoint vertical strips of minimum width | $O(n)$ with $O(n \log n)$ preprocessing | $O(n)$ | Exact |
| One color-spanning axis-parallel square of minimum perimeter | $O(n(n - m))$ | $O(n)$ | Exact |
| Two congruent disjoint color-spanning axis-parallel squares of minimum perimeter | $O(n^3)$ | $O(n^2)$ | Exact |
| One color-spanning disk of minimum radius | $O(n(n - m))$ | $O(n)$ | $\sqrt{2}$-factor approximation |
| Two congruent disjoint color-spanning disks of minimum radius | $O(n^3)$ | $O(n^2)$ | $\sqrt{2}$-factor approximation |

## 2   Preliminaries and Notations

**Definition 1 (Covering).** *A geometric object in $\mathbb{R}^2$ is said to be covered by a region on that plane, if each point of that object lies inside or on the boundary of the region.*

**Definition 2 (Color-spanning region).** *Let there be $n$ geometric objects e.g. points, line segments in $\mathbb{R}^2$, where each object is associated with one of the $m$ distinct colors ($3 \leq m < n$). A region in $\mathbb{R}^2$ is said to be color-spanning, if it covers at least one object of each color.*

**Definition 3 (Vertical strip).** *A vertical strip $V$ is an unbounded region enclosed by two vertical lines, $left(V)$ and $right(V)$ which are the left and right boundaries of $V$, respectively.*

The x-coordinate and y-coordinate of a point $p$ are denoted by $x(p)$ and $y(p)$, respectively. The width of a vertical strip $V$ is determined by the distance between its two boundaries. The given set of line segments are denoted by $\mathcal{L} = \{\ell_1, \ell_2, \ldots, \ell_n\}$. We use four arrays $\mathcal{L}_\ell, \mathcal{L}_r, \mathcal{L}_t$ and $\mathcal{L}_b$, each with the members in $\mathcal{L} = \{\ell_1, \ell_2, \ldots, \ell_n\}$ sorted with respect to their left, right, top, and bottom endpoints, respectively. Each element $\ell_i \in \mathcal{L}$ maintains four pointers to the corresponding element in $\mathcal{L}_\ell, \mathcal{L}_r, \mathcal{L}_t$ and $\mathcal{L}_b$. Also, each element of $\mathcal{L}_i$, $i = \ell, r, t, b$ points to the corresponding segment $\ell_i \in \mathcal{L}$. The arrays $\mathcal{L}_i$, $i = l, r, t, b$ can be created in $O(n \log n)$ time and will be stored using $O(n)$ space. We also maintain another array $\mathcal{C} = (c_1, c_2, \ldots, c_m)$ for $m$ distinct colors to keep the count of segments of each color, where $c_i \in \mathbb{Z}^+$ for each $1 \leq i \leq m$. The array $\mathcal{C}$ is initialized with zero. Each color is also represented by distinct integer $w \in \{1, 2, \ldots, m\}$.

# 3  Color-Spanning Vertical Strip

In this section, three problems are discussed depending on the number (one or two) of color-spanning regions and type of inputs (line segments, simple polygons and disks).

## 3.1  Color-Spanning Problem Using One Vertical Strip

**Problem 1.** *Given a set of n line segments $\mathcal{L} = \{\ell_1, \ell_2, \ldots, \ell_n\}$ in $\mathbb{R}^2$ and m distinct colors (3 $\leq m < n$), where each line segment is associated with one of such m colors. The objective is to compute a color-spanning vertical strip V of minimum width.*

**Definition 4 (*minimal-CSVS*).** *A color-spanning vertical strip that cannot be shrunk further without violating the definition of color-spanning region, is said to be minimal width color-spanning vertical strip (**minimal-CSVS**).*

**Definition 5 (*minimum-CSVS*).** *There may exist more than one minimal-CSVS for a set of segments in $\mathcal{L}$. The one having minimum width among all such minimal-CSVSs is said to be minimum width color-spanning vertical strip (**minimum-CSVS**).*

**Observation 1.** *For any minimal-CSVS, say V, its left(V) (resp. right(V)) must pass through the left endpoint (resp. right endpoint) of a segment, say $\ell_i$ (resp. $\ell_j$). We call $\ell_i$ and $\ell_j$ as the defining segments for the left(V) and right(V) of the strip V, respectively.*

**Property 1 (Property of *minimal-CSVS*).** *Suppose V is a minimal-CSVS. The color of the line segments that define the left(V) and right(V) of the strip V, must be different and unique among the segments lying inside the V, otherwise, V will contain another minimal-CSVS inside it as a proper subset contradicting the assumption that V is a minimal-CSVS.*

**Algorithm:** We compute all possible *minimal-CSVS*s by sweeping two vertical lines $L_1$ and $L_2$ from left to right through the left endpoint and right endpoint of the segments in the arrays $\mathcal{L}_\ell$ and $\mathcal{L}_r$, respectively (see Observation 1), as follows:

First, we set $L_1$ and $L_2$ to the left endpoint and right endpoint of the first segment in array $\mathcal{L}_\ell$ and $\mathcal{L}_r$, respectively. Then sequentially move $L_2$ rightward as mentioned above. As the sweep lines move, we update the array $\mathcal{C}$ to reflect the color of the segments lying within the strip bounded by $L_1$ and $L_2$. The $L_2$ stops when the value of each member of array $\mathcal{C}$ becomes at least 1. Now, if the color of the segment defining $L_1$ repeats more than once within the strip bounded by $L_1$ and $L_2$, then we shift $L_1$ rightward until the Property 1 of a *minimal-CSVS* is satisfied, and compute the width of this strip. We repeat the above procedure by shifting $L_1$ rightward to its next segment to obtain a new *minimal-CSVS*. This process is continued until $L_1$ reaches to the $(n-m)^{th}$ segment, since a minimal-$CSVS$ will cover at least $m$ segments. We compute all such *minimal-$CSVS$s*, and finally report the one with smallest width as *minimum-$CSVS$*. We need linear sized arrays $\mathcal{C}$, $\mathcal{L}_\ell$, $\mathcal{L}_r$ to compute the *minimum-$CSVS$*. In each step of the above procedure, either $L_1$ or $L_2$ moves rightward and one segment is processed in each step. Thus we obtain the following result.

**Theorem 1.** *We can compute the minimum-$CSVS$ of a set of $n$ line segments in $O(n)$ time and $O(n)$ space, after $O(n \log n)$ preprocessing task.*

## 3.2   Color-Spanning Problem Using Two Vertical Strips

**Problem 2.** *Given a set of $n$ line segments $\mathcal{L} = \{\ell_1, \ell_2, \ldots, \ell_n\}$ in $\mathbb{R}^2$, where each segment $\ell_i$ is associated with one of the $m$ distinct colors ($3 \le m < n$). The objective is to compute two congruent color-spanning disjoint vertical strips $V_1$ and $V_2$ of minimum width.*

This problem is equivalent to compute a pair of *minimal-$CSVS$* $(V_1, V_2)$ so that the width of its larger strip is minimized among the larger strips of all possible pair of *minimal-$CSVS$s*. For each *minimal-$CSVS$* $V_1$ of the line segments in $\mathcal{L}$, we choose the *minimum-$CSVS$* $V_2$ of the segments that lie to the right of $V_1$, as follows:

We compute all the *minimal-$CSVS$s* of the segments in $\mathcal{L}$ by sweeping $L_1$ and $L_2$ from right to left, i.e. in the reverse order as described in the Sect. 3.1 for the Problem 1. We also assign a strip-id to each of such strip sequentially starting with 1 in the order of their computations i.e. the strip-id of the rightmost *minimal-$CSVS$* is 1. We construct two arrays $BOUNDARY$ and $STRIP$, while computing these *minimal-$CSVS$s*.

(i) The array $BOUNDARY$ has three fields - $left\_boundary$, $size$ and $strip\_id$. If a *minimal-$CSVS$* $V$ is also a *minimum-$CSVS$* for the segments that lie to the right of $left(V)$, then we store the $left(V)$ in the $left\_boundary$ field of the array $BOUNDARY$. The size and the strip-id of this *minimum-$CSVS$* are stored in the fields $size$ and $strip\_id$ of the array $BOUNDARY$, respectively. The first entry of the array $BOUNDARY$ stores the information for the rightmost *minimal-$CSVS$*.

(ii) The array $STRIP$ has 3 fields: $left\_boundary$, $right\_boundary$ and $strip\_id$ which stores the $left\_boundary$, $right\_boundary$ and the $strip\_id$ of each *minimal-$CSVS$*, respectively.

The information of all the *minimal-$CSVS$s* are inserted sequentially into the array $STRIP$ as they are computed, i.e. the first entry (resp. last entry) in the array $STRIP$ corresponds to the leftmost (resp. rightmost) *minimal-$CSVS$*. However, in case of array $BOUNDARY$, while computing the $i^{th}$ *minimal-$CSVS$* (i.e. with $strip\_id$ $i$), we append its $left\_boundary$, $size$, and $strip\_id$ in the array $BOUNDARY$, provided its width, say $w'$, is less than the width, say $w$, of the *minimum-$CSVS$* obtained so far. Here the $w$ can be obtained from the last row (inserted so far) of the array $BOUNDARY$.

It is to be noted that the rows in the array $BOUNDARY$ are inserted in the descending order with respect to the x-coordinate of the $left\_boundary$ field. For each $minimal\text{-}CSVS$, say $V_i$, stored in the array $STRIP$, we need to search the array $BOUNDARY$ for the $minimum\text{-}CSVS$ that lie to the right of $V_i$. To accomplish this, we search both these arrays in upward direction starting from their bottom row as follows:

In each iteration, for a strip with $strip\_id$, say $V_i$, stored in the array $STRIP$, we search the array $BOUNDARY$ in upward direction, until we get a strip, say $V_j$, so that $left(V_j) \geq right(V_i)$, and then we stop to get a pair $(V_i, V_j)$. Note that the $V_j$ is the $minimum\text{-}CSVS$ for the segments lying to the right of $minimal\text{-}CSVS$ $V_i$. In the next iteration, we consider the strip with $strip\_id$ $V_{i-1}$ stored in the previous row of the array $STRIP$. Now, we find the $minimum\text{-}CSVS$ for the segments lying to the right of $V_{i-1}$ and we search the array $BOUNDARY$ from the row where searching was stopped in previous iteration. We repeat the above steps to compute all possible pairs $(V_i, V_j)$ in linear amount of (amortized) time, where $V_j$ is the $minimum\text{-}CSVS$ for the segments that lie to the right of the $minimal\text{-}CSVS$ $V_i$. We compare the size of the larger strips of each pair $(V_i, V_j)$ to choose the minimum one and report that pair. If there are no such pair of disjoint $minimal\text{-}CSVS$s for the given segments in $\mathcal{L}$, then also we can report it in $O(n)$ time. In this case, for the leftmost $CSVS$, say $V$, there does not exist a $minimum\text{-}CSVS$ to the right of $right(V)$. Thus we obtain the following result.

**Theorem 2.** *For a given set of $n$ line segments in $\mathbb{R}^2$, we can compute two congruent color-spanning vertical strips of the minimum width, if such a pair exists, otherwise we report that no such pair exists in $O(n)$ time and $O(n)$ space, after $O(n \log n)$ preprocessing.*

### 3.3  Color-Spanning Vertical Strip for a Set of Simple Polygons or Disks

If the inputs to the Problem 1 and Problem 2 are colored simple polygons or disks (instead of line segments), then to determine the color-spanning vertical strip(s) of minimum width for these objects, we replace each of these simple polygons (resp. disks) with the line segments (i.e. each polygon/disk corresponds to a segment) in such a way that if a vertical strip exactly[1] covers, $k$ (say) such line segments, then that vertical strip also covers exactly their corresponding $k$ polygons (resp. disks) and vice versa. The color of these line segments are kept same as that of the given simple polygons or disks. We do this as follows:

If the inputs is a simple polygon, we replace it by a segment that connects its extreme leftmost and rightmost vertices, whereas for disk, we replace it by its horizontal diameter. Afterwards, we apply the algorithm of the Problem 1 and Problem 2 to solve the respective color-spanning problem for simple polygons or disks. So, we get the following result.

---

[1] A polygon is said to be exactly covered by a region, if we reduce the size of the region then at least one point of the polygon will lie outside the region.

**Theorem 3.** *For a given set of $n$ simple polygons/disks, we can compute one (resp. two congruent) color-spanning vertical strip (resp. disjoint strips) of minimum width in $O(n)$ time and $O(n)$ space after $O(n \log n)$ preprocessing task.*

# 4 Color-Spanning Axis-Parallel Square

In this section, we discuss the color-spanning problem for the line segments where the color-spanning region is axis-parallel square. Unless otherwise stated, we use square to imply axis-parallel square throughout the paper. We abbreviate color spanning square by $CSS$. The *size* of a square is defined by its perimeter. We consider three problems in this Section.

## 4.1 Color-Spanning Problem Using One Axis-Parallel Square

**Problem 3.** *Given a set of $n$ line segments $\mathcal{L} = \{\ell_1, \ell_2, \ldots, \ell_n\}$ in $\mathbb{R}^2$ and $m$ distinct colors $(3 \leq m < n)$, where each line segment is associated with one of such $m$ colors. The objective is to compute a minimum sized color-spanning square $\mathcal{S}$.*

**Definition 6 (minimal-CSS).** *A color-spanning square $\mathcal{S}$ for a given set of line segments, is said to be minimal if $\mathcal{S}$ cannot be shrunk without violating the color-spanning property. This is denoted by **minimal-CSS**.*

**Definition 7 (minimum-CSS).** *Among all possible minimal-CSS for $\mathcal{L}$, the one with smallest size is called minimum color-spanning square and is denoted by **minimum-CSS**.*

**Fact 1.** *A square $\mathcal{S}$ can be uniquely defined by three points that lie on any three sides of it. However, as a special case, the square $\mathcal{S}$ may also be uniquely identified by two points that are the two endpoints of a diagonal of it.*

We generate the squares with the endpoints of the segments in $\mathcal{L}$. The segments whose endpoint define a square $\mathcal{S}$ uniquely (see Fact 1) are called the "defining segments" for $\mathcal{S}$.

**Fact 2.** *If $\ell_i \in \mathcal{L}$ defines the left (resp. right) side of a square $\mathcal{S}$, then the left (resp. right) endpoint of $\ell_i$ lies on that side of $\mathcal{S}$. Similarly, if $\ell_i$ defines the top (resp. bottom) side of $\mathcal{S}$, then the top (resp. bottom) endpoint of $\ell_i$ lies on that side of $\mathcal{S}$.*

Depending on the three sides of the square $\mathcal{S}$ on which the endpoint of its defining segments lies, we classify the squares into 4 types: (i) (Left, Top, Right), (ii) (Left, Bottom, Right), (iii) (Left, Top, Bottom) and (iv) (Right, Top, Bottom), where the terms "Left", "Top", "Right" and "Bottom" denote the side of the square $\mathcal{S}$ on which an endpoint of the respective defining segment of $\mathcal{S}$ lies. We first generate all possible squares whose left side are defined by a segment, say $\ell_i \in \mathcal{L}$ (see Fact 2). In other words, we compute the squares of types (i), (ii) and (iii) as mentioned above, with $\ell_i$ as the defining segment of their left side. These types of squares are generated using a sweep line $L$, and two sweep rays $\mathcal{R}_1$ and $\mathcal{R}_2$, as follows:

(i) The line $L$ is vertical that sweeps rightwards through its event points that are the left endpoints of the segments stored in the sorted array $\mathcal{L}_\ell$ (defined in Sect. 2).

(ii) The sweep ray $\mathcal{R}_1$ (resp. $\mathcal{R}_2$) is a transverse ray of positive (resp. negative) unit slope directed towards north-east (resp. south-east), and it will move vertically downwards (resp. upwards) through its discrete event points (to be discussed later) on the line $L$. The ray $\mathcal{R}_1$ (resp. $\mathcal{R}_2$) is the locus of the top-right (resp. bottom-right) corner of the squares whose left side and bottom (resp. top) side are defined by the segment $\ell_i \in \mathcal{L}$ and $\ell_j \in \mathcal{L}$, respectively.

Suppose the sweep line $L$ passes through the left endpoint, say $q_1$, of a segment $\ell_i \in \mathcal{L}$ (see Fig. 1(a)). Consider each segment $\ell_j \in \mathcal{L}$ that lie completely to the right of $L$. If bottom (resp. top) endpoint of such segments lie below (resp. above) $q_1$, then from that endpoint take a horizontal projection on the line $L$, which will be the event point for the sweep ray $\mathcal{R}_1$ (resp. $\mathcal{R}_2$) on $L$. Note that if slope of $\ell_i$ is positive (resp. negative), then we take the endpoint $q_1$ also as an event point for $\mathcal{R}_1$ (resp. $\mathcal{R}_2$). The sorted list of the event points of $\mathcal{R}_1$ (resp. $\mathcal{R}_2$) on $L$ can be generated from the sorted array $\mathcal{L}_b$ (resp. $\mathcal{L}_t$) in $O(n)$ time.

For each different positions (i.e. event points) of $L$, there is an event point of $\mathcal{R}_1$ (resp. $\mathcal{R}_2$) on $L$, known as its *"first event point"* from which the ray $\mathcal{R}_1$ (resp. $\mathcal{R}_2$) starts sweeping downwards (resp. upwards). We denote this event point by $d$ whose $y$-coordinate is largest (resp. smallest) among all the event points of $\mathcal{R}_1$ (resp. $\mathcal{R}_2$) on the line $L$. The sweep ray $\mathcal{R}_1$ (resp. $\mathcal{R}_2$) emanating from its event point, say $p$, is represented by $\mathcal{R}_1(p)$ (resp. $\mathcal{R}_2(p)$). We generate the event points of other segments on the ray $\mathcal{R}_1(d)$ (resp. $\mathcal{R}_2(d)$), where these event points indicate the top-right (resp. bottom-right) corner of the squares $S$ whose bottom-left (resp. top-left) corner is at $d$.

**Computation of Event Points on $\mathcal{R}_1(d)$ and $\mathcal{R}_2(d)$:** We denote the two endpoints of a segment $\ell_k \in \mathcal{L}$ by $\ell_k.1$ and $\ell_k.2$. For each segment $\ell_k \in \mathcal{L}$ lying to the right of $L$, we create an event point $e_k$ on the sweep ray $\mathcal{R}_1(d)$, where $e_k$ satisfies the equation of the ray $\mathcal{R}_1(d)$: $y = x + y(d) - x(d)$. Depending on position of $\ell_k$, the events $e_k$ are generated as follows:

(i) $\ell_k$ lies above $\mathcal{R}_1(d)$: Here $y(e_k) = \max(y(\ell_k.1), y(\ell_k.2))$ (e.g. $e_5$ due to $\ell_5$ in Fig. 1(a)).

(ii) $\ell_k$ lies below $\mathcal{R}_1(d)$: Here $x(e_k) = \max(x(\ell_k.1), x(\ell_k.2))$ (e.g. $e_4$ due to $\ell_4$ in Fig. 1(a)).

(iii) $\ell_k$ intersects with $\mathcal{R}_1(d)$: Let the endpoints of $\ell_k$ lying above and below $\mathcal{R}_1(d)$ be $\ell_k.1$ and $\ell_k.2$, respectively. We take the horizontal (resp. vertical) projection, say $p$ (resp. $q$) of $\ell_k.1$ (resp. $\ell_k.2$) on $\mathcal{R}_1(d)$. If $q$ lies above $p$ on $\mathcal{R}_1(d)$, then $e_k = q$ (e.g. $e_2$ due to $\ell_2$ in Fig. 1(a)), otherwise $e_k = p$ (e.g. $e_3$ due to $\ell_3$ in Fig. 1(a)).

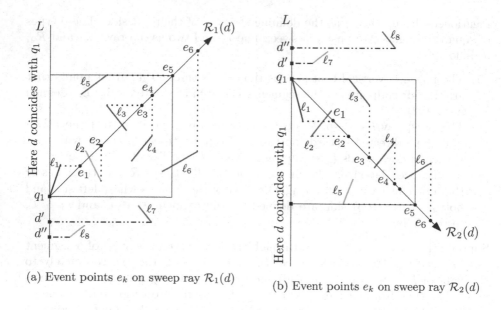

(a) Event points $e_k$ on sweep ray $\mathcal{R}_1(d)$

(b) Event points $e_k$ on sweep ray $\mathcal{R}_2(d)$

**Fig. 1.** Generation of event points on the sweep rays $\mathcal{R}_1$ and $\mathcal{R}_2$

In each of the aforesaid cases, once we compute $x(e_k)$ (resp. $y(e_k)$), the corresponding $y(e_k)$ (resp. $x(e_k)$) can be obtained from the equation of $\mathcal{R}_1(d)$ stated above.

Similarly, for each segment $\ell_k \in \mathcal{L}$, we create an event point $e_k$ on the sweep ray $\mathcal{R}_2(d)$ satisfying the equation: $y + x = y(d) + x(d)$ as shown in Fig. 1(b). We denote the color of a line segment $\ell_k \in \mathcal{L}$ by $color(\ell_k)$. We maintain an array $ACTIVE$, each with the members in $\mathcal{L}$, that keeps track of the segments completely covered by the square generated at each event point of $\mathcal{R}_1$ (resp. $\mathcal{R}_2$) on $L$. We put 1 (resp. 0) to $ACTIVE[k]$, if the segment $\ell_k$ is covered (resp. not covered) by the square. As mentioned in the Sect. 2, the array $\mathcal{C}$ of size $m$ keeps records of the number of different colors of the line segments that are being covered by the square with its bottom-left (resp. top-left) corner at each event point of $\mathcal{R}_1$ (resp. $\mathcal{R}_2$) on $L$. Both these arrays are initialized to zeros. To keep track of the number of colors of the segments that are missing inside a square, we take a variable $\#missing\_color$ which is initialized to $m$. For a color-spanning square, $\#missing\_color$ is 0. A segment lying inside a square $\mathcal{S}$ is said to be *essential*, if it is the only segment with its color inside $\mathcal{S}$. We also take two variables *topmost* and *rightmost*, where *topmost* (resp. *rightmost*) points to a segment whose top (resp. right) endpoint has largest $y$-coordinate (resp. $x$-coordinate) among the other segments lying inside $\mathcal{S}$. As the sweep ray $\mathcal{R}_1$ (resp. $\mathcal{R}_2$) moves down (resp. up) the arrays $ACTIVE$ and $\mathcal{C}$ are dynamically updated.

We denote a square by $S(d, z)$, where $d$ and $z$ are its bottom-left (resp. top-left) corner and top-right (resp. bottom-right) corner, respectively. We first consider ray $R_1(d)$, where $d$ is the *"first event point"* of $R_1$ on $L$. We compare all the event points $e_k$ generated on $R_1(d)$ by the segments $l_k$ (discussed earlier) and choose the one with smallest $x$-coordinate, say $z = e_z$, such that the square $S(d, z)$ is a $CSS$. Obviously, this $S(d, z)$ is of minimum sized among all possible $CSS$ with the bottom-left corner at $d$. The segments lying inside the square $S(d, z)$, and their colors are used to update the arrays $ACTIVE$ and $C$, respectively. Then the sweep ray $R_1(d)$ moves downward to its next event point, say $d'$, on $L$ and we denote the ray by $R_1(d')$. Now construct a square $S(d', z')$, where the point $z'$ on $R_1(d')$ is vertically below the point $z$. So, the square $S(d', z')$ is a congruent to $S(d, z)$ and lies vertically below it. Suppose the segment $\ell'_j$ generated the event $d'$ on $L$. If an endpoint of $\ell'_j$ lies outside $S(d', z')$, then we discard $R_1(d')$, and move $R_1$ to the next event point, say $d''$ on $L$ since the $CSS$ with bottom-left corner at $d'$ will be larger than $S(d, z)$; otherwise, we update the array $ACTIVE$ by (i) inserting $\ell'_j$ and (ii) deleting the segments from $S(d, z)$ whose at least one endpoint lies outside $S(d', z')$. This deletion is done sequentially from $S(d, z)$ in the decreasing order with respect to their top endpoint. During such insertion and deletion operations, we update (if required) both *topmost* and *rightmost* variable after each such operation. During the deletion operation, if we encounter the segment $\ell_i$, we can not delete it, since we are generating the squares whose left side is to be defined by $\ell_i$. In that case, we stop and return the square $S(d, z)$ as a *minimal-CSS* for all the event points of $R_1$ lying on $L$. At each operation of insertion and deletion, we update the $C$ array also as follows:

While deleting (resp. inserting) the segment $\ell_k$ from (resp. into) the array $ACTIVE$, we decrease (resp. increase) the value of $C[color(\ell_k)]$ by 1. If the value of an index of $C$ array changes from 1 (resp. 0) to 0 (resp. 1), we increase (resp. decrease) the variable $\#missing\_color$ by 1. While generating the square at $R_1(d)$, if $\#missing\_color > 0$ after the completion of the aforesaid update operation, then the square $S(d', z')$ is not a $CSS$ and we do not compute the *minimal-CSS* for $R_1(d')$ as it would be larger than the already computed $CSS$ $S(d, z)$. Hence, $R_1(d')$ moves downward to its next event point, say $d''$ on $L$. On the other hand, if $\#missing\_color$ is zero, then $S(d', z')$ is a $CSS$ whose size can be reduced further, provided $z'$ is not the event point of the *topmost* segment or *rightmost* segment of $S(d', z')$ on $R_1(d')$. In such case, we compare the two event points on $R_1(d')$ which are generated by the topmost segment and rightmost segment, and then we choose that segment, say $\ell$, which generates event with larger $x$-coordinate. If $C[color(\ell)] > 1$, the segment $\ell$ is not *essential* and we delete it, and update the arrays $ACTIVE$, $C$ and the variables *topmost*, *rightmost*. We keep on updating the topmost and rightmost variables until one of them becomes an *essential* one, i.e. $C[color(\ell)] = 1$. In that case, we cannot delete any segment further and we get a *minimal-CSS* with its top-right corner defined by the event point, say $e$, of that segment $\ell$ on $R_1(d')$. The size of this $CSS$ is less than the $CSS$ $S(d, z)$. So, we update $z$ with $e$ and $d$ with $d'$, and then shift the sweep ray $\mathcal{R}_1$ downwards to its next event. This process is continued until all the event points of $\mathcal{R}_1$ lying on $L$ are processed and we update the *minimal-CSS*, say $\mathcal{S}_1$ accordingly.

Similarly, we move the sweep ray $\mathcal{R}_2$ upwards from its first event point to last event point on $L$ and compute the *minimal-CSS*, say $\mathcal{S}_2$. Finally, from the two squares $\mathcal{S}_1$ and $\mathcal{S}_2$, we choose the one with minimum size, and this one will be the *minimum-CSS* among all the squares whose left side is defined by $\ell_i$. Next the sweep line $L$ moves rightward through its event points which are the left endpoints of the line segments stored in the array $\mathcal{L}_\ell$. Since a color-spanning square covers at least $m$ different colored segments inside it, we follow the aforesaid procedures only for the first $(n-m)$ event points of $L$ to compute the *minimal-CSS*s whose left sides are defined by those event points of $L$. All these $CSS$ generated by the aforesaid method are of types (i), (ii) and (iii), as mentioned earlier. Similarly, to generate *minimum-CSS* of type (iv), we sweep the line $L$ from right to left through the last $(n-m)$ sorted right endpoints of the segments that are stored in the sorted array $\mathcal{L}_r$. In these cases, the sweep ray $\mathcal{R}_1$ (resp. $\mathcal{R}_2$) is directed towards south-west (resp. north-west). The event points of $\mathcal{R}_1$ (resp. $\mathcal{R}_2$) on $L$ along with the event points $e_k$ of other segments on $\mathcal{R}_1$ (resp. $\mathcal{R}_2$) are generated in the similar way as that of generating the square of types (i), (ii) and (iii) and we follow the same technique to compute the *minimal-CSS* of type (iv) for $(n-m)$ event points of $L$. Finally, we choose the $CSS$ of minimum size among all possible *minimal-CSS* of type (i), (ii), (iii) and (iv), and report it.

**Theorem 4.** *For a given set of $n$ line segments $\mathcal{L}$, we can compute a minimum sized color-spanning axis-parallel square in $O(n(n-m))$ time and $O(n)$ space.*

*Proof.* Our algorithm computes the minimum $CSS$ for all possible positions (i.e. the event points) of the sweep line $L$, and among all such squares, we choose the minimum one as the *minimum-CSS* for $\mathcal{L}$. The line $L$ sweeps through $(n-m)$ event points in both forward and backward direction. For each fixed position (i.e. event point) of $L$, we first compute the *minimal-CSS* at the "*first event point*" of $\mathcal{R}_1$ on $L$ in $O(n)$ time and then we compute the *minimum-CSS* on that position of $L$ by inserting and deleting segments where each line segment in $\mathcal{L}$ is inserted at most once and deleted at most once. Hence this computation needs $O(n)$ time (amortized). To compute *minimum-CSS*, two linear sized arrays $\mathcal{C}$ and $ACTIVE$ are reused at different position of $L$. Hence this proves the result. □

## 4.2  Color-Spanning Problem Using Two Axis-Parallel Squares

**Problem 4.** *Given a set of $n$ line segments $\mathcal{L} = \{\ell_1, \ell_2, \ldots, \ell_n\}$ in $\mathbb{R}^2$, where each $\ell_i$ is associated with one of such $m$ distinct colors $(3 \leq m < n)$. The objective is to compute two congruent CSS $\mathcal{S}_1$ and $\mathcal{S}_2$ of minimum size.*

In this problem, we compute all possible pairs of *minimal-CSS*s and choose that pair for which the size of its larger square is minimized among all other pairs.

For each segment $\ell_i$, we compute all possible *minimal-CSS*s whose left sides are defined by $\ell_i$. All such squares can be determined by computing *minimal-CSS* at each event point $d$ of $\mathcal{R}_1$ (or $\mathcal{R}_2$) on $L$ similar to process described in the Sect. 4.1 for the Problem 3. Similarly, we also compute all possible *minimal-CSS*s whose right sides (resp. top sides and bottom sides) are defined by $\ell_i$. Now consider one of such *minimal-CSS*, say $\mathcal{S}_1$. For this $\mathcal{S}_1$, we must choose its corresponding square $\mathcal{S}_2$ which is *minimum-CSS* for the segments that are not covered by $\mathcal{S}_1$, and $\mathcal{S}_2$ is disjoint[2] with $\mathcal{S}_1$. One of the following statements must be true for $\mathcal{S}_2$.

(i) The square $\mathcal{S}_2$ lies to the right of the vertical line passing through the right side of $\mathcal{S}_1$.

(ii) The square $\mathcal{S}_2$ lies to the left of the vertical line passing through the left side of $\mathcal{S}_1$.

(iii) The square $\mathcal{S}_2$ lies above the horizontal line passing through the top side of $\mathcal{S}_1$.

(iv) The square $\mathcal{S}_2$ lies below the horizontal line passing through the bottom side of $\mathcal{S}_1$.

**Computation of $\mathcal{S}_2$:** We find the *minimum-CSS* whose left side (resp. right side, top side, bottom side) is defined by a segment $\ell_i$. We do this for each $\ell_i \in \mathcal{L}$, and store each such squares in four different arrays, which corresponds to the squares defined by either the left side (resp. right side, top side, bottom side) of each segment $\ell_i$. For any given square $\mathcal{S}_1$, we compute the *minimum-CSS* lying to the left (resp. right, above, below) of it in $O(n)$ time from the aforesaid four different arrays, and choose the minimum one of these four squares as $\mathcal{S}_2$. Considering each *minimal-CSS* as $\mathcal{S}_1$, we compute its corresponding square $\mathcal{S}_2$, and then return the pair having minimum size of larger square. However, if for all *minimal-CSS* $\mathcal{S}_1$, there exists no such $\mathcal{S}_2$ satisfying one of the above mentioned criteria, then no two congruent disjoint *CSS*s are possible for $\mathcal{L}$.

**Theorem 5.** *For a given set of $n$ line segments in $\mathbb{R}^2$, we can compute two congruent color-spanning squares of the minimum size if such a pair exists; otherwise report no such pair exists in $O(n^3)$ time and $O(n^2)$ space.*

*Proof.* Since we consider all possible *minimal-CSS* $\mathcal{S}_1$ along with its corresponding minimized $\mathcal{S}_2$, our algorithm generates correct output. The computation of each *minimal-CSS* needs $O(n)$ times, and there are $O(n^2)$ such *minimal-CSS*s. For each *minimal-CSS* $\mathcal{S}_1$ we can compute its corresponding *mimimum-CSS* $\mathcal{S}_2$, in linear time. So, we need $O(n^3)$ time to determine all possible pairs $(\mathcal{S}_1, \mathcal{S}_2)$ from which we choose the optimal pair. We need $O(n^2)$ space to store all the *minimal-CSS*. Thus the theorem follows.    □

### 4.3  Color-Spanning Square for Simple Polygons or Disks

In this case, the inputs to the Problem 3 and Problem 4 are a set of $n$ simple polygons or circular disks. We cover each such simple polygon (resp. circular

---

[2] Here disjoint means the common area of intersection of $\mathcal{S}_1$ and $\mathcal{S}_2$ is zero.

disk) exactly by an axis-parallel rectangle (resp. square). Next, replace each rectangle (resp. square) by a line segment that corresponds to any one of its diagonals. In this way, the given set of simple polygons and circular disks are mapped to the line segments. The color of these line segments are kept same as that of the given simple polygons or disks. Next, we execute the algorithm for the Problem 3 (resp. Problem 4) to compute one $CSS$ (resp. two congruent disjoint $CSS$) of minimum size for the aforesaid diagonals. Now if a square $S$ (resp. two congruent squares $S_1$ and $S_2$) covers any $k$ such diagonals, then $S$ (resp. $S_1$ and $S_2$) also covers their corresponding $k$ simple polygons or circular disks, and vice versa. Hence, we obtain the following result.

**Theorem 6.** *For a given set of $n$ simple polygons (resp. disks) in $\mathbb{R}^2$, we can compute (i) one minimum sized color-spanning square in $O(n(n-m))$ time and $O(n)$ space, (ii) two congruent color-spanning squares of minimum size in $O(n^3)$ time and $O(n^2)$ space.*

# 5   Color-Spanning Disks

**Problem 5.** *Given a set of $n$ line segments $\mathcal{L} = \{\ell_1, \ell_2, \ldots, \ell_n\}$ in $\mathbb{R}^2$ and $m$ ($3 \le m < n$) distinct colors, where each line segment is associated with one of such $m$ colors. The objective is to compute one (resp. two congruent) color-spanning disk (resp. disks) of minimum radius.*

**Algorithm:** First, we compute a color-spanning square $S$ (resp. two color-spanning squares $S_1$ and $S_2$) of minimum size as described in the Problem 3 (resp. Problem 4). Then, we report the circum-circle (resp. circum-circles) $D$ of $S$ (resp. $D_1$ and $D_2$ of $S_1$ and $S_2$ respectively) as an approximate solution of this problem.

We have the following results for the Problem 5 that follows immediately from the lower bound and approximation result of the two center problem[3] for line segments, by Sadhu et al. [8].

**Lemma 1.** *A lower bound for the optimal radius $r^*$ of one (resp. two congruent disjoint) color-spanning disk (resp. disks) for a set of segments in $\mathcal{L}$ is the radius $r'$ of in-circle of the color-spanning square $S$ (resp. two congruent color-spanning squares $S_1$ and $S_2$) of minimum size for $\mathcal{L}$; i.e. $r' \le r^*$.*

**Theorem 7.** *The algorithm stated above for the Problem 5, generates a $\sqrt{2}$ approximation result for covering the segments in $\mathcal{L}$ by one (resp. two congruent) color-spanning disk (resp. disks) of minimum radius.*

---

[3] In the two center problem for a given line segments $\mathcal{L}$, the objective is to cover $\mathcal{L}$ by two congruent disks of minimum (common) radius.

# 6   Conclusion

In this paper, we proposed a linear time algorithm to compute minimum width color-spanning vertical strip(s) for the for line segments, simple polygons and disks after $O(n \log n)$ preprocessing tasks. For these geometric objects, we also computed one (resp. two congruent disjoint) minimum sized color-spanning square (resp. squares) in $O(n(n - m))$ (resp. $O(n^3)$) time. We improved the time complexity $O(n^2 \log n)$ [1] of finding the minimum sized $CSS$ for $\mathcal{L}$, to $O(n(n - m))$. We also showed a $\sqrt{2}$ approximation result for computing color-spanning disks of minimum radius for the segments. We leave the exact computation of two congruent color-spanning disks of minimum radius as open problem for future work.

# References

1. Huttenlocher, D.P., Kedem, K., Sharir, M.: The upper envelope of Voronoi surfaces and its applications. In:7th Annual Symposium on Computational Geometry, pp. 194–203 (1991)
2. Abellanas, M., et al.: Smallest color-spanning objects. In: European Symposium on Algorithm, pp. 278–289 (2001)
3. Das, S., Goswami, P.P., Nandy, S.C.: Smallest color-spanning object revisited. Int. J.Comput. Geometry Applications, pp. 457–478 (2009)
4. Asano, T., Bhattacharya, B.K., Keil, M., Yao, F.F.: Clustering algorithms based on minimum and maximum spanning trees. In: 4th Annual Symposium on Computational Geometry, pp. 252–257 (1988)
5. Khanteimouri, P., Mohades, A., Abam, M.A., Kazemi, M.R.: Computing the smallest color-spanning axis-parallel square. In: Cai, L., Cheng, S.-W., Lam, T.-W. (eds.) ISAAC 2013. LNCS, vol. 8283, pp. 634–643. Springer, Heidelberg (2013). https://doi.org/10.1007/978-3-642-45030-3_59
6. Hasheminejad, J., Khanteimouri, P., Mohades, A.: Computing the Smallest Color-Spanning Equaliteral Triangle, 31st European Workshop on Computational Geometry, pp. 32–35 (2015)
7. Bae, S.W.: An algorithm for computing a minimum-width color-spanning rectangular annulus. J. Korean Inst. Inf. Sci. Eng. 246–252 (2017)
8. Sadhu, S., Roy, S., Nandy, S.C., Roy, S.: Optimal covering and hitting of line segments by two axis-parallel squares. Int. Comput. Comb. Conf. 457–468 (2017)
9. Acharyya, A., Nandy, S.C., Roy, S.: Minimum width color-spanning annulus. Theor. Comput. Sci. 16–30 (2018)
10. Pruente, J.: Minimum diameter color-spanning sets revisited. Discrete Optim. 100550 (2019)
11. Acharyya, A., Maheshwari, A., Nandy, S.C.: Color-spanning Localized query. Theor. Comput. Sci. 85–101 (2021)

# A Modified SEIR Model: Stiffness Analysis and Application to the Diffusion of Fake News

Raffaele D'Ambrosio[2] , Patricia Díaz de Alba[1(✉)] , Giuseppe Giordano[1] ,
and Beatrice Paternoster[1]

[1] Università degli Studi di Salerno, 84084 Fisciano, Italy
{pdiazdealba,gigiordano,beapat}@unisa.it
[2] Università degli Studi dell'Aquila, 67100 L'Aquila, Italy
raffaele.dambrosio@univaq.it

**Abstract.** In this work we propose a novel and alternative interpretation of the SEIR model, typically used in epidemiology to describe the spread of a disease in a given population, to describe the diffusion of fake information on the web and the consequent truth re-affirmation. We describe the corresponding system of ordinary differential equations, giving a proper definition of the involved parameters and, through a local linearization of the system, we calculate the so-called stiffness ratio, i.e. the ratio between the real parts of the largest and smallest eigenvalues of the Jacobian matrix of the linearized problem. A large gap in the spectrum of such a Jacobian matrix (i.e., a large stiffness ratio) makes the underlying differential problem stiff. So, we study and analyze the stiffness index of the SEIR model and, through selected numerical examples on real datasets, we show that the more the model is stiff, the faster is the transit of fake information in a given population.

**Keywords:** SEIR model · Fake news · Stiffness index

## 1 Introduction

Nowadays, internet is widely used as a primary medium of information all over the world, since it is a rapidly accessible and low cost source. The availability of such a large amount of information makes digital world deeply integrated with the lifestyle habits of our society. Clearly, since veracity is a huge issue in the spread out of online information, the circulation of fake news has been extensively increasing during last years.

The concept of *fake news* concerns with information that does not coincide with the reality, and is usually transmitted through a communication environment, in general for economic and political purposes, or in order to influence public opinion on a specific aspect. Recently, this topic has become very attractive since fake news are spread out much faster than real news on internet, certainly in a more rapid way with respect to traditional media such as radio, television,

O. Gervasi et al. (Eds.): ICCSA 2022, LNCS 13375, pp. 90–103, 2022.
https://doi.org/10.1007/978-3-031-10522-7_7

newspapers, etc. So, internet is the ideal environment encouraging users to share information between individuals (also over long distances), included fake news (see, for instance, [5,15,22,23,27,35,38,46,48,50] and references therein).

On the one hand, one of the most natural questions about fake information is how to deal with its detection. It is an extremely important issue, since the quantity of false news circulating around us, especially online, is increasing very rapidly. Because of this, the mechanism of detection of fake news should be able to predict enough information quickly enough in order to stop the spread of fake news, almost in real time.

On the other hand, the analysis of the spreading of fake news should be addressed taking into account the different types of fake news, its role and purpose, as well as the context in which it can be found. Indeed, fake news can be presented in different ways and for different purposes: for instance, satire or parody, news based on false content for humor purposes, misleading contents, manipulated contents, etc. More details on the topic can be found, for instance, in [17,19,26,33,40,47,52,53] and references therein.

Mathematical models in epidemiology are usually considered to study the diffusion of fake news, because they are able to describe a realistic interaction between the fake information and the people who receive it. In this paper, we focus our attention on a modified version of the classical SEIR model and we apply it to describe the diffusion of fake news. During last years, the classical SEIR model applied in epidemiology has been studied and modified in order to create more realistic mathematical models capable of predicting the spread of diseases. For instance, in [49] a new SEIR model was introduced for the dynamical analysis of the COVID-19 infection in Saudi Arabia and was tested on real data. In that paper, the authors give an expression of the reproduction number and report the stability analysis. The authors of [45] have used mathematical modelling and numerical simulations to describe coronavirus dynamics with data from China, Italy, Iran, and Brazil. In order to study the evolution of COVID-19 in Italy since the beginning of the vaccination process, a new hybrid compartmental model has been introduced in [4]. Other versions of SEIR model are described, for instance, in [3,6,7,9,10,12,20,21,24,25,36,37,39,41,51] and references therein.

More recently, this kind of models have been treated also for the description of the transmission of fake news [8,16,18,30,32,34]. For example, in [16], the authors describe a SEIR rumor spreading model in online social networks, while in [18] the interaction between fake news spreading and competence of individuals has been described by means of kinetic theory arguments.

In this paper, we propose a novel and alternative interpretation of the SEIR model for the spread of fake information in a given country, first of all explaining the proposed meaning of the involved parameters. Then, through a local linearization of the system, we compute the so-called stiffness ratio, defined as the ratio between the real parts of the largest and smallest eigenvalues of the Jacobian matrix of the linearized problem. If the gap in the spectrum of such a Jacobian matrix is large and, as a consequence, the stiffness ratio is large, the underlying differential problem is stiff. As described on a simplified prototypical model (i.e., the SIR model) in [12], we show that the stiffness ratio is related to the diffusion of fake news. More in details, in this paper it is confirmed that the higher the stiffness ratio, the faster the re-establishment of the truth after the diffusion of fake information.

The paper is structured as follows. In Sect. 2, we introduce and formulate the modified SEIR model describing the meaning of the different involved populations and parameters. Section 3 is devoted to the stiffness analysis of the underlying system of ordinary differential equations model, passing through the linearization of the problem and the computation of the stiffness ratio of the problem. Numerical experiments on real data that illustrate the behaviour of the spread of fake news are reported in Sect. 4. Finally, in Sect. 5 some conclusions and possible future developments of this research are discussed.

## 2    Formulation of the Modified SEIR Model

The use of compartmental models technique for modelling an infectious disease was first introduced in the early 20th century; see [28, 29, 42–44].

In this paper, we consider a new formulation of the classical SEIR (Susceptible-Exposed-Infective-Recovered) model, which is a mathematical model based on a system of dynamic ordinary differential equations. It was first introduced to characterize the epidemic dynamics in order to understand the behaviour of transmission of an infectious disease [49]. In this scenario (see Fig. 1), the population is considered to be divided into four sub-populations as follows

- $S(t)$ represents the Susceptible group who are healthy but can contract the disease.
- $E(t)$ acts as the Exposed population who infected but not yet infectious.
- $I(t)$ is dedicated to the people who confirmed infected.
- $R(t)$ collects the individuals who have recovered and cannot contract the disease again,

and the parameters involved are defined as

- $\Lambda$ new add rate to Susceptible population.
- $\beta$ contact rate from Susceptible population $S$ to Infected population $I$.
- $\gamma$ transmission rate of confirmed infected from the Exposed population $E$.
- $\delta$ transmission rate of recovery from the Exposed population $E$.
- $\alpha$ transmission rate of recovery from Infected $I$ to Recovered $R$.

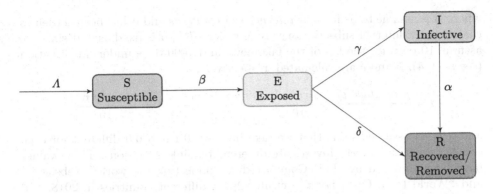

**Fig. 1.** Scheme of the SEIR model.

Taking into account the scheme presented in Fig. 2, the corresponding system of ODEs is then given by

$$\begin{cases} \dfrac{dS(t)}{dt} = \Lambda - \beta \dfrac{S(t)}{N} I(t) \\[2mm] \dfrac{dE(t)}{dt} = \beta \dfrac{S(t)}{N} I(t) - (\gamma + \delta) E(t) \\[2mm] \dfrac{dI(t)}{dt} = \gamma E(t) - \alpha I(t) \\[2mm] \dfrac{dR(t)}{dt} = \alpha I(t) + \delta E(t), \end{cases} \tag{1}$$

where $N$ represents the number of total population and is defined as

$$N = S + E + I + R.$$

In this paper, we adapt the model (1) to the fake news diffusion, where $S(t)$ represents the number of internet users, who are still not aware of the news up to time $t$, $E(t)$ are the users who have been exposed to the item of fake news through the internet and have to decide to spread or not the news, $I(t)$ speaks for the spreader ones, who read and actively disseminate the news, and $R(t)$ are silent ones, individuals who have encountered the news item but choose not to spread it. Regarding the different parameters involved in (1), we take

- $\Lambda$ new add rate to Susceptible population.
- $\beta$ contact rate at which Susceptible population $S$ are aware of the news and becomes infected population $I$.
- $\gamma$ rate at which agents decide to spread the news.
- $\delta$ rate at which agents decide not to spread the news.
- $\alpha$ time life of the fake news measured in days divided by the total number of days under investigation,

where $\Lambda$ is assume to be for *new internet subscriptions* and it has been chosen so that the new internet subscriptions are of order $10^{-5}$, $\alpha$ is fixed as 0.01 since we assume 10 days for the life of the fake news and 1000 days under investigation (see Sect. 4), $\beta$ and $\delta$ are calculated, respectively, as

$$\beta = \frac{percentage\ of\ individuals\ using\ internet}{10}, \quad \delta = \frac{literacy\ rate}{10^3},$$

and $\gamma$ is an assumed value that we take between 0.1 and 0.9 different for each country with the aim to investigate different possible situations. These values have been provided by "ITU Committed to connecting the world" website [1] and "World Bank Open Data" website [2] for different countries in 2018, and are collected in Table 1.

**Table 1.** Values of the parameters for different countries in 2018.

| Country | $\Lambda$ | $\beta$ | $\gamma$ | $\delta$ | $N$ |
|---|---|---|---|---|---|
| Morocco | 2300 | 0.065 | 0.5 | 0.074 | 36029089 |
| Guatemala | 230 | 0.042 | 0.9 | 0.081 | 16346950 |
| Argentina | 2300 | 0.078 | 0.2 | 0.099 | 44494502 |
| Thailand | 2300 | 0.057 | 0.1 | 0.094 | 69428454 |
| Portugal | 230 | 0.075 | 0.7 | 0.096 | 10283822 |

## 3  Stiffness Analysis

In this section we analyze the stiffness ratio of system (1). To do this, let us consider an initial value vector $[S_0, E_0, I_0, R_0]^T = [S(0), E(0), I(0), R(0)]^T$, and let us linearize model (1) around it, obtaining

$$\begin{cases} \dfrac{dS(t)}{dt} = \Lambda + \beta\dfrac{S_0}{N}I_0 - \beta I_0\dfrac{S(t)}{N} - \beta\dfrac{S_0}{N}I(t) + \text{high order terms} \\[2mm] \dfrac{dE(t)}{dt} = -\beta\dfrac{S_0}{N}I_0 + \beta I_0\dfrac{S(t)}{N} + \beta\dfrac{S_0}{N}I(t) - (\gamma + \delta)E(t) + \text{high order terms} \\[2mm] \dfrac{dI(t)}{dt} = \gamma E(t) - \alpha I(t) + \text{high order terms} \\[2mm] \dfrac{dR(t)}{dt} = \alpha I(t) + \delta E(t) + \text{high order terms}. \end{cases}$$

$$(2)$$

The Jacobian matrix associated to the linear part of (2) is defined as

$$
J_{\beta,\gamma,\delta,\alpha}\left(\frac{S_0}{N}, I_0\right) =
\begin{bmatrix}
-\beta\frac{I_0}{N} & 0 & -\beta\frac{S_0}{N} & 0 \\
\beta\frac{I_0}{N} & -(\gamma+\delta) & \beta\frac{S_0}{N} & 0 \\
0 & \gamma & -\alpha & 0 \\
0 & \delta & \alpha & 0
\end{bmatrix}.
\tag{3}
$$

By calculating the eigenvalues of the above matrix, we get one eigenvalue equal to 0 and two real eigenvalues that we use to compute the stiffness ratio (see [14,31]) of the differential equations system as

$$
r_{\beta,\gamma,\delta,\alpha}\left(\frac{S_0}{N}, I_0\right) = \frac{\left|\lambda_{\beta,\gamma,\alpha}^{\max}\left(\frac{S_0}{N}, I_0\right)\right|}{\left|\lambda_{\beta,\gamma,\alpha}^{\min}\left(\frac{S_0}{N}, I_0\right)\right|}.
\tag{4}
$$

## 4   Numerical Experiments

The numerical experiments were performed on a Intel Core i7-8565U CPU @ 1.80 GHz x 8 system with 16Gb RAM, running the Debian GNU/Linux operating system and Matlab 9.9. We consider a different initial data vector for each investigated country and we report them in Table 2. The value of $S_0$ is obtained from [2] as the percentual of the population which has access to internet, while $E_0$, $I_0$, and $R_0$ have been assumed for each country.

**Table 2.** Values of the initial vector for each country.

| Country | $S_0$ | $E_0$ | $I_0$ | $R_0$ |
|---------|-------|-------|-------|-------|
| Morocco | 23059000 | 12941000 | 29089 | 0 |
| Guatemala | 6784000 | 9516000 | 46950 | 0 |
| Argentina | 34572000 | 9900000 | 22502 | 0 |
| Thailand | 39449000 | 29900000 | 79454 | 0 |
| Portugal | 7677900 | 2000000 | 605922 | 0 |

By following the numerical procedure described in Sect. 3 and taking into account the initial vectors in Table 2, we compute the different values of the stiffness ratio from (4) corresponding to the different countries; see Table 3.

Figure 2, 3, 4, 5, 6 contain, on the right, a graph of the behavior of each population involved in our SEIR model obtained by the standard Matlab built-in

**Table 3.** Values of the stiffness ratio for each country and their corresponding parameters.

| Country | $r_{\beta,\gamma,\delta,\alpha}\left(S_0, \dfrac{I_0}{N}\right)$ |
|---|---|
| Morocco | 34.5155 |
| Guatemala | 65.5248 |
| Argentina | 27.2741 |
| Thailand | 14.1569 |
| Portugal | 71.9384 |

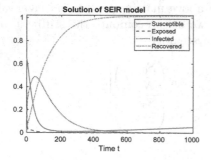
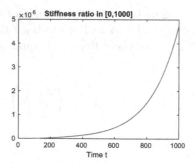

**Fig. 2.** Solution for Morocco to the SEIR model (left) together with the corresponding stiffness ratio (right).

function ode23s. On the left, we have reported the pattern of the ratio $r_{\beta,\gamma,\delta,\alpha}$ at time $t$. For each numerical simulation, we investigate problem (1) on the interval time $[0, 1000]$, where the time unit is measured in days. Each plot confirm that when the stiffness index is higher (see Table 3), the transition of fake news is faster.

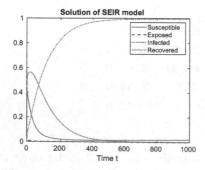
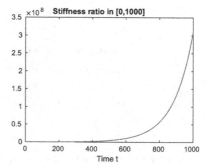

**Fig. 3.** Solution for Guatemala to the SEIR model (left) together with the corresponding stiffness ratio (right).

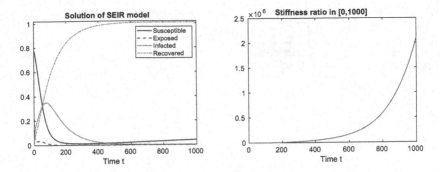

**Fig. 4.** Solution for Argentina to the SEIR model (left) together with the corresponding stiffness ratio (right).

The smaller stiffness ratio corresponds to Thailand (see Table 3), for which we can see in Fig. 5, that maximum value of the Infected population is smaller in comparison with the other cases. Moreover, the width on the curve shape represents the slow transmission of fake news in this country. On the contrary, the countries which have the highest stiffness value are Guatemala and Portugal. For the case of Guatemala we can see in Fig. 3 that the maximum of the Infected population is immediately acceded, while in the case of Portugal, see Fig. 6, even if is the country with the biggest stiffness index, the Infected population reaches the maximum later in time with respect to Guatemala. This could be justified by the literacy rate parameter which is higher for Portugal, which means that the portion of Exposed population that arrives to the Recovered compartment is bigger, and this fact could influence on the behavior of the Infected population.

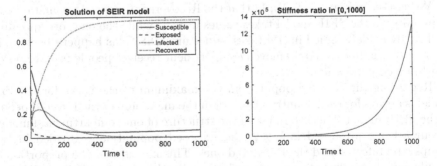

**Fig. 5.** Solution for Thailand to the SEIR model (left) together with the corresponding stiffness ratio (right).

After the obtained numerical results that show the relation between the stiffness index of model (1) and the behavior of the transmission of fake news, we have compared the solution of our SEIR model and the SIR model investigated in [12].

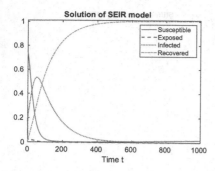
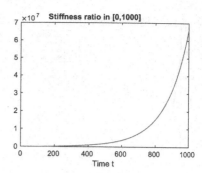

**Fig. 6.** Solution for Portugal to the SEIR model (left) together with the corresponding stiffness ratio (right).

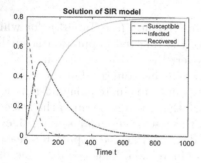
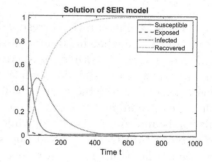

**Fig. 7.** Comparison between the solution of the SIR (left) and the SEIR (right) model for Morocco.

We can see in Fig. 7, 8, 9, 10, 11 that the Recovered/Removed population corresponding to the SEIR model takes values until 1, while the one corresponding to the SIR model studied in [12] takes values until 0.8. This happens because in our model, the Recovered/Removed compartment receives people from Exposed and Infected population.

Regarding the Infected population, the maximum of the curve for the SIR model is always for each country bigger than the maximum of the Infected people in the SEIR model. This is because of the structure of our compartmental model. In our scheme presented in Fig. 2, the Exposed population is divided in two groups, the Infected and the Recovered ones. This means that the proportion of population that arrives to the Infected one is smaller for the SEIR model than for the SIR model.

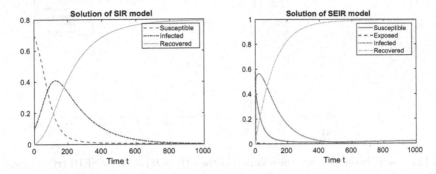

**Fig. 8.** Comparison between the solution of the SIR (left) and the SEIR (right) model for Guatemala.

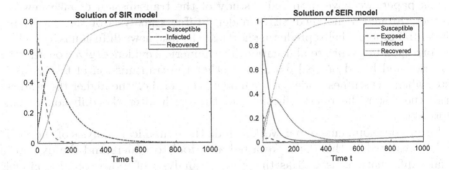

**Fig. 9.** Comparison between the solution of the SIR (left) and the SEIR (right) model for Argentina.

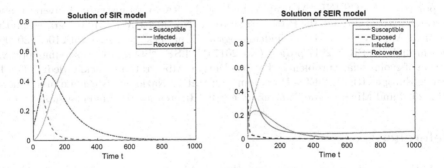

**Fig. 10.** Comparison between the solution of the SIR (left) and the SEIR (right) model for Thailand.

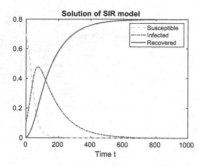 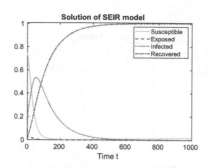

**Fig. 11.** Comparison between the solution of the SIR (left) and the SEIR (right) model for Portugal.

## 5    Conclusions and Future Developments

In this paper, we have proposed a study of the transmission of fake news in internet through a modified SEIR model. Stiffness analysis of the underlying differential problem helps predicting how fast the fake news diffusion is, as well as the corresponding truth re-affirmation. The numerical evidence, given on selected countries and based on real data, shows that the transmission of fake news is faster when the stiffness index of the model is larger, i.e., the higher the stiffness ratio, the faster the re-establishment of the truth after the diffusion of fake information.

Future developments of our work include the dynamical analysis of the SEIR model presented in this paper, recasted as a tool to understand the dynamics of fake information, as well as the stiffness analysis of more complex models which include other populations and parameters. Other challenging features of this problem are the study of sentimental analysis, social network analysis and applications of machine learning techniques; see [11,13].

**Acknowledgements.** The authors are members of the GNCS group. This work was supported by GNCS-INDAM project, and by the Italian Ministry of University and Research (MUR) through the PRIN 2020 project (No. 2020JLWP23) "Integrated Mathematical Approaches to Socio-Epidemiological Dynamics" (CUP: E15F21005420006) and through the PRIN 2017 project (No. 2017JYCLSF) "Structure preserving approximation of evolutionary problems". Patricia Díaz de Alba gratefully acknowledges Fondo Sociale Europeo REACT EU - Programma Operativo Nazionale Ricerca e Innovazione 2014–2020 and Ministero dell'Università e della Ricerca for the financial support.

## References

1. ITU Committed to connecting the world. https://www.itu.int/en/ITU-D/Statistics/Pages/stat/default.aspx. Accessed 31 Mar 2022
2. World Bank Open Data. https://data.worldbank.org/. Accessed 31 Mar 2022

3. Ansumali, S., Kaushal, S., Kumar, A., Prakash, M., Vidyasagar, M.: Modelling a pandemic with asymptomatic patients, impact of lockdown and herd immunity, with applications to SARS-CoV-2. Annu. Rev. Control. **50**, 432–447 (2020). https://doi.org/10.1016/j.arcontrol.2020.10.003
4. Antonelli, E., Piccolomini, E., Zama, F.: Switched forced SEIRDV compartmental models to monitor COVID-19 spread and immunization in Italy. Infect. Dis. Model. **7**, 1–15 (2022). https://doi.org/10.1016/j.idm.2021.11.001
5. Berduygina, O., Vladimirova, T., Chernyaeva, E.: Trends in the spread of fake news in mass media. Media Watch **10**(1), 122–132 (2019). https://doi.org/10.15655/mw/2019/v10i1/49561
6. Brauer, F., Castillo-Chavez, C.: Mathematical Models in Population Biology and Epidemiology. TAM, vol. 40. Springer, New York (2012). https://doi.org/10.1007/978-1-4614-1686-9
7. Brauer, F., van de Driessche, P., Wu, J.: Mathematical Epidemiology. Springer, Heidelberg (2008). https://doi.org/10.1007/978-3-540-78911-6
8. Brody, D., Meier, D.: How to model fake news. arXiv arXiv:1809.00964 (2018)
9. Calvetti, D., Hoover, A., Rose, J., Somersalo, E.: Metapopulation network models for understanding, predicting, and managing the coronavirus disease COVID-19. Front. Phys. **8** (2020). https://doi.org/10.3389/fphy.2020.00261
10. Chowell, G.: Fitting dynamic models to epidemic outbreaks with quantified uncertainty: a primer for parameter uncertainty, identifiability, and forecasts. Infect. Dis. Model. **2**, 379–398 (2017). https://doi.org/10.1016/j.idm.2017.08.001
11. Conte, D., D'Ambrosio, R., Paternoster, B.: Improved theta-methods for stochastic Volterra integral equations. Commun. Nonlinear Sci. Numer. Simul. **93** (2021). https://doi.org/10.1016/j.cnsns.2020.105528. Article no. 105528
12. D'Ambrosio, R., Giordano, G., Mottola, S., Paternoster, B.: Stiffness analysis to predict the spread out of fake news. Future Internet **13**, 222 (2021). https://doi.org/10.3309/fi13090222
13. D'Ambrosio, R., Moccaldi, M., Paternoster, B.: Adapted numerical methods for advection-reaction-diffusion problems generating periodic wavefronts. Comput. Math. Appl. **74**(5), 1029–1042 (2017). https://doi.org/10.1016/j.camwa.2017.04.023
14. D'Ambrosio, R., Paternoster, B.: Multivalue collocation methods free from order reduction. J. Comput. Appl. Math. **387** (2021). https://doi.org/10.1016/j.cam.2019.112515. Article no. 112515
15. Dentith, M.: The problem of fake news. Public Reason **8**(1–2), 65–79 (2016)
16. Dong, S., Deng, Y., Huang, Y.: SEIR model of rumor spreading in online social network with varying total population size. Commun. Theor. Phys. **68**, 545–552 (2017). https://doi.org/10.1088/0253-6102/68/4/545
17. D'Ulizia, A., Caschera, M., Ferri, F., Grifoni, P.: Fake news detection: a survey of evaluation datasets. PeerJ Comput. Sci. **7**, e518 (2021). https://doi.org/10.7717/peerj-cs.518
18. Franceschi, J., Pareschi, L.: Spreading of fake news, competence, and learning: kinetic modeling and numerical approximation. arXiv arXiv:2109.14087 (2021)
19. Giordano, G., Mottola, S., Paternoster, B.: A short review of some mathematical methods to detect fake news. Int. J. Circuits Syst. Signal Process. **14**, 255–265 (2020). https://doi.org/10.46300/9106.2020.14.37
20. Godio, A., Pace, F., Vergnano, A.: SEIR modeling of the Italian epidemic of SARS-CoV-2 using computational swarm intelligence. Int. J. Environ. Res. Public Health **17**(10), 3535 (2020). https://doi.org/10.3390/ijerph17103535

21. Gopal, R., Chandrasekar, V.K., Lakshmanan, M.: Analysis-of-the-second-wave-of-Covid19-in-India-based-on-SEIR-model. Eur. Phys. J. (2022). https://doi.org/10.1140/epjs/s11734-022-00426-8
22. Guo, B., Ding, Y., Sun, Y., Ma, S., Li, K., Yu, Z.: The mass, fake news, and cognition security. Front. Comp. Sci. 15(3), 1–13 (2020). https://doi.org/10.1007/s11704-020-9256-0
23. Guo, B., Ding, Y., Yao, L., Liang, Y., Yu, Z.: The future of false information detection on social media: new perspectives and trends. ACM Comput. Surv. 53(4) (2020). https://doi.org/10.1145/3393880. Article no. 3393880
24. Inthamoussou, F.A., Valenciaga, F., Núñez, S., Garelli, F.: Extended SEIR model for health policies assessment against the COVID-19 pandemic: the case of Argentina. J. Healthcare Inform. Res. 6(1), 91–111 (2021). https://doi.org/10.1007/s41666-021-00110-x
25. Iwata, K., Miyakoshi, C.: A simulation on potential secondary spread of novel coronavirus in an exported country using a stochastic epidemic SEIR model. J. Clin. Med. 944(9) (2020). https://doi.org/10.3390/jcm9040944
26. Kapantai, E., Christopoulou, A., Berberidis, C., Peristeras, V.: A systematic literature review on disinformation: toward a unified taxonomical framework. New Media Soc. 23(5), 1301–1326 (2021). https://doi.org/10.1177/1461444820959296
27. Kelly, D.: Evaluating the news: (mis)perceptions of objectivity and credibility. Polit. Behav. 41(2), 445–471 (2018). https://doi.org/10.1007/s11109-018-9458-4
28. Kendall, D.G.: Deterministic and Stochastic Epidemics in Closed Populations, pp. 149–166. University of California Press (2020). https://doi.org/10.1525/9780520350717-011
29. Kermack, W.O., McKendrick, A.G.: A contribution to the mathematical theory of epidemics. Proc. R. Soc. A 115, 700–721 (1927). https://doi.org/10.1098/rspa.1927.0118
30. Khurana, P., Kumar, D.: Sir model for fake news spreading through Whatsapp. In: Proceedings of 3rd International Conference on Internet of Things and Connected Technologies (2018). https://doi.org/10.2139/ssrn.3166095
31. Lambert, J.: Numerical Methods for Ordinary Differential Systems. Wiley, New York (1992)
32. Mahmoud, H.: A model for the spreading of fake news. J. Appl. Probab. 57(1), 332–342 (2020). https://doi.org/10.1017/jpr.2019.103
33. Murayama, T.: Dataset of fake news detection and fact verification: a survey. arXiv https://arxiv.org/pdf/2111.03299.pdf (2021)
34. Murayama, T., Wakamiya, S., Aramaki, E., Kobayashi, R.: Modeling the spread of fake news on Twitter. PLoS ONE 16(4), e0250419 (2021). https://doi.org/10.1371/journal.pone.0250419
35. O'Connor, C., Weatherall, J.: The Misinformation Age: How False Beliefs Spread. Yale University Press, London (2019)
36. Peng, L., Yang, W., Zhang, D., Zhuge, C., Hong, L.: Epidemic analysis of COVID-19 in China by dynamical modeling (2020). https://www.medrxiv.org/content/10.1101/2020.02.16.20023465v1
37. Pengpeng, S., Shengli, C., Peihua, F.: SEIR transmission dynamics model of 2019 nCoV coronavirus with considering the weak infectious ability and changes in latency duration (2020). https://doi.org/10.1101/2020.02.16.20023655
38. Rider, S., Peters, M.A.: Post-truth, fake news: viral modernity and higher education. In: Peters, M.A., Rider, S., Hyvönen, M., Besley, T. (eds.) Post-Truth, Fake News, pp. 3–12. Springer, Singapore (2018). https://doi.org/10.1007/978-981-10-8013-5_1

39. Piccolomini, E., Zama, F.: Monitoring Italian COVID-19 spread by a forced SEIRD model. PLoS ONE **15**(8), e0237417 (2020). https://doi.org/10.1371/journal.pone.0237417
40. Reyes-Menendez, A., Saura, J., Filipe, F.: The importance of behavioral data to identify online fake reviews for tourism businesses: a systematic review. PeerJ Comput. Sci. **5**, e219 (2019). https://doi.org/10.7717/peerj-cs.219
41. Robinson, M., Stilianakis, N.: A model for the emergence of drug resistance in the presence of asymptomatic infections. Math. Biosci. **243**, 163–177 (2013). https://doi.org/10.1016/j.mbs.2013.03.003
42. Ross, R.: An application of the theory of probabilities to the study of a priori pathometry.-Part I. Proc. R. Soc. A **A92**, 204–230 (1916). https://doi.org/10.1098/rspa.1916.0007
43. Ross, R., Hudson, H.: An application of the theory of probabilities to the study of a priori pathometry.- Part II. Proc. R. Soc. A **A93**, 212–225 (1917). https://doi.org/10.1098/rspa.1917.0014
44. Ross, R., Hudson, H.: An application of the theory of probabilities to the study of a priori pathometry.- Part III. Proc. R. Soc. A **A93**, 225–240 (1917). https://doi.org/10.1098/rspa.1917.0015
45. Savi, P., Savi, M., Borges, B.: A mathematical description of the dynamics of coronavirus disease 2019 (COVID-19): a case study of Brazil. Comput. Math. Methods Med. (2020). https://doi.org/10.1155/2020/9017157
46. Shin, J., Jian, L., Driscoll, K., Bar, F.: The diffusion of misinformation on social media: temporal pattern, message, and source. Comput. Hum. Behav. **83**, 278–287 (2018). https://doi.org/10.1016/j.chb.2018.02.008
47. Tandoc, E.: The facts of fake news: a research review. Sociol. Compass **13**(9) (2019). https://doi.org/10.1111/soc4.12724. Article no. c12724
48. Tandoc, E., Lim, D., Ling, R.: Diffusion of disinformation: how social media users respond to fake news and why. Journalism **21**(3), 381–398 (2020). https://doi.org/10.1177/1464884919868325
49. Youssef, H., Alghamdi, N., Ezzat, M., El-Bary, A., Shawky, A.: A new dynamical modeling SEIR with global analysis applied to the real data of spreading COVID-19 in Saudi Arabia. Math. Biosci. Eng. **17**, 7018–7044 (2020). https://doi.org/10.3934/mbe.2020362
50. Zannettou, S., Sirivianos, M., Blackburn, J., Kourtellis, N.: The web of false information: rumors, fake news, hoaxes, clickbait, and various other shenanigans. J. Data Inf. Qual. **11**(3) (2019). https://doi.org/10.1145/3309699. Article no. 10
51. Zhang, J., Jianquan, L., Zhien, M.: Global dynamics of an SEIR epidemic model with immigration of different compartments. Acta Mathematica Scientia **26B**(3), 551–567 (2006)
52. Zhang, X., Ghorbani, A.: An overview of online fake news: characterization, detection, and discussion. Inf. Process. Manag. **57**(2) (2020). https://doi.org/10.1016/j.ipm.2019.03.004. Article no. 102025
53. Zhou, X., Zafarani, R.: A survey of fake news: fundamental theories, detection methods, and opportunities. ACM Comput. Surv. **53**, 40 (2020). https://doi.org/10.1145/3395046

# Anonymous Trajectory Method
# for Indoor Users for Privacy Protection

Sultan Alamri[✉]

School of Computing and Informatics, Saudi Electronic University,
Riyadh, Saudi Arabia
salamri@seu.edu.sa

**Abstract.** The privacy of the trajectories of indoor space users is just as important as that of the users of outdoor spaces. Many users of indoor spaces consider it very important to maintain the privacy of their movements within buildings and not reveal their visit to a certain room/cell inside buildings. In this paper, we propose a cloaking diversity approach for moving entities in indoor spaces. This new privacy-assurance approach uses the cloaking concept adapted with processing diversity trajectories to safeguard user privacy in an indoor space. Extensive simulations and evaluations have demonstrated that the proposed privacy approach algorithm performs well and at a low cost.

**Keywords:** Indoor space · Privacy · Indoor trajectories · Cloaking

## 1 Introducing

Generally, people spend spent most of their lives in indoor spaces [1–4]. However, little research has been done on securing the privacy of users' trajectories indoors [5–7]. Instead, the focus has been on the privacy of user locations in outdoor space. However, since we spend most of our time indoors, and often in very large buildings, the privacy issue is the same as that related to outdoor privacy. For example, a certain user might like to visit a certain room and keep his/her movements private, as a breach of this privacy could be used for advertising purposes, to spread rumours, or for other unauthorized purposes. Therefore, protecting the users' trajectories in indoor spaces is essential for many users [8–11].

In this paper, we proposed a cloaking diversity approach for moving objects in indoor environments. The algorithm will choose the shortest path for the user which maintain his privacy and allowing him/her to the optional for cloaking a certain cell/room for protecting the user privacy. For user privacy in indoor environments, the new privacy solution adapts the cloaking concept with providing a diversity of trajectories. Here the user will be associated more to dynamic rooms in order to protect his/her privacy. Extensive simulations and tests revealed that the proposed privacy approach algorithm functions well and at a reasonable cost, as well as successfully protecting the user trajectory privacy.

O. Gervasi et al. (Eds.): ICCSA 2022, LNCS 13375, pp. 104–112, 2022.
https://doi.org/10.1007/978-3-031-10522-7_8

This paper is organized as follows. Section 2 gives an overview of previous works on indoor path routing and spatial cloaking. Section 3 describes the system methodology and the cloaking algorithms. Section 4 explains the testing of the system's performance, and presents the analysis of results. Section 5 concludes the paper and indicates future research directions.

## 2    Related Works

In this section, we discuss previous research on indoor routing, and spatial privacy in outdoor spaces.

Many studies have been conducted in order to find the best indoor routing algorithms [6,8,12]. In Tiara, for example, a three-dimensional space implementation of a routing system is proposed. In this study, four algorithms were compared to determine the one that provided the best shortest path in three-dimensional spaces. These algorithms are: Dijkstra algorithm, A* algorithm, Bellman-Ford algorithm, and Floyd-Warshall algorithm. The results indicated that the A* Algorithm performed the best in a three-dimensional setting.

On the other hand, some works saw the mobility of an object in an interior environment being controlled or directed in a way similar to that in an outdoor spatial road network me2. Some works have focused on indoor zoning as a means of controlling social distancing, especially in open indoor spaces where large social, entertainment or sporting events are held [8]. Furthermore, in the presence of crowds, the indoor crowd-aware, fastest-way query finds the path with the shortest travel time, whereas the indoor least-crowded path query identifies the route containing the fewest items [13].

Many works have focused on the privacy of moving objects' trajectories in outdoor space [10,14–16]. For example, spatial cloaking was used in many works as a means of protecting the privacy of the user. For instance, anonymity was achieved by reporting a cloaked area large enough to include the group size required to fulfill the targeted anonymity restriction citation [16]. Figure 1, shows an example of a cloaked zone (region) in an outdoor space. Another study focused on the mixed-one concept [15]. Mix-zones, where the user's disguise is renewed, were proposed. The term 'mix-zones' is derived from the fact that the temporal order in which users enter and exit these zones must be obscured (mixed), otherwise the adversary may be able to link the new disguise to the old one [14].

To the best of our knowledge, we are the first to consider the privacy of trajectories in indoor spaces. Indoor spaces have several features that distinguish them from outdoor spaces such as obstacles (e.g., doors), various structures such as dynamic rooms (corridors), stairs etc. Therefore, this paper focuses on first obtaining the best path for the moving user, and then protecting his/her privacy by concealing the room/cell which is being visited.

## 3    Cloaking Cells Algorithms

In this section, we present and explain in detail the algorithms proposed for protecting the user's privacy in an indoor space.

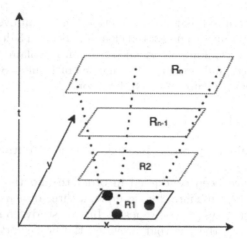

**Fig. 1.** Outdoor cloaked spatial regions $R_1, R_2, ..R_n$

First, we describe the indoor structure on which this algorithm will be based. The basic data structure for the indoor environments will be the indoor space that will be divided into cells (i.e., cellular indoor s pace).

**Definition 1.** Let $P$ be a set of indoor cells $C_1$, $C_2$, $C_3$,..*etc*, where the cells are classified as follows:
$C_i$ is a dynamic cell if it is a connection between other cells such as corridors, pathways, stairs or common paths or stairways. $C_j$ is a static cell if it does not provide a connection between other cells.

The focus here will be on the static cells. These are cells that might be visited by users who want to protect the privacy of their visit, and do not want the locations of the cells to be revealed. The algorithm will start choosing the most suitable path for the user by determining the user's trajectory, using the hop distance approach.

**Definition 2.** The shortest path from cell $C_x$ to $C_y$ is the lowest number of static cells of the trajectory from $C_x$ to $C_y$.

An example of the shortest path is shown in Fig. 2. Here, user $A$ wants to visit *cell*22 and then his last destination was room 18 ($C_{18}$). Based on the adjacent cells, the shortest path will be $C_1 3, C14d, C21, C22, C15a, C15b, C_1 8$ which is a distance of 7 hops. However, with our proposed algorithm intended to ensure privacy protection, we include a greater number of dynamic cells rather than traversing more static cells. In addition, this approach allows users to apply the cloak cell approach by themselves without exposing their exact cell to third parties. The basic idea of the algorithm is to cloak the cell (a specific static cell) of the user while showing a greater number of dynamic cells. The system architecture of the trajectory cloak is shown in Fig. 3.

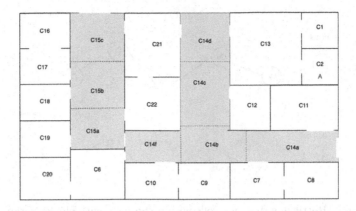

**Fig. 2.** Example of indoor space where blue shading indicates the dynamic cells

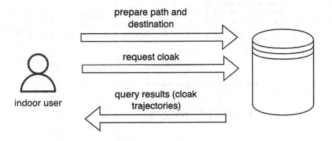

**Fig. 3.** System architecture

Here, when a user requests a cloaking for his trajectory, the algorithm will return the first candidate path to the destination cell, which will include as many dynamic cells as possible, such as one or more corridors and common cells (common rooms). Figure 4, illustrates a requested trajectory with a cloaks option where in (b) the algorithm focuses more on retrieving dynamics cell along the path to the user's destination cell(s).

Figure 5, illustrates the cloak method. When a user determines a destination cell, if the cell is a static cell that for reasons of user privacy should not be disclosed, if the user visits the cell/location ($C_i$) a cloak diversion will be initiated as follows : the destination cell here will be associated with user $A$ and at least one semantically different object in the cell. For example, in the previous example, to achieve l-diversity with l = 3, the server needs to consider three other cells of the designation cell adjacent (from level 1 or the next level) containing different semantic objects, which will contain 3 different trajectories containing the one from user $A$, and two from fake users $A_x$, and $A_y$ located in the other cells. The algorithm will continue building the trajectory until the last destination cell is reached. These trajectories are illustrated in Fig. 8. Note that when the LBS returns all results to the anonymity server, the latter filters out the results for the fake users and returns to the relevant result to the legitimate user.

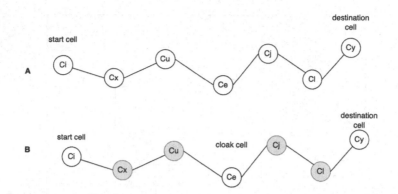

**Fig. 4.** Retrieving dynamic cells within the path with cloaks option

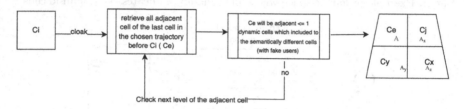

**Fig. 5.** Diversity-cloak method

**Definition 3.** Let $C_e, C_j, C_h, C_t$, be chosen for the cloak diversity of the adjacent cells of $C_i$, if the dynamic cells adjacent $\leq 1$ (e.g. $C_h, C_j$ are dynamic cells).

## 4   Results and Evaluation

In this section, we present the experimental data used to assess the performance of the proposed indoor privacy algorithm. The simulation was carried out on a PC with a 2.60 GHz Intel Core i7-9750H CPU and 16 GB of RAM running 64-bit Windows 10 Enterprise. MATLAB was used to implement the strategy.

In this experiment, we used a synthetic dataset for an indoor environment which was comprised of 25 room/cells. There are 8 dynamic cells which is the common area for the movement between the cells, and 17 regular cells. Note that all the tested paths are assumed based on realistic scenarios. It is worth noting that the processes were carried out eight times before the average was calculated.

We began by measuring the construction cost of the proposed privacy algorithm. Previous cloaking diversity algorithms proposed for the indoor environment used an undirected graph for indoor cells where metric distance was applied. However, we used the hop distances. Figures 6 and 7 show that the proposed algorithm is cost-efficient. The application of the algorithm to two different scenarios yielded an interesting result: when the number of cells increases,

---

**Algorithm 1.** privacy indoor trajectory

---

1: Input: Indoor $S$, objects $O$, indoor cell $C$
2: Output: cloaking indoor cells trajectory for indoor users
3: $s_i$ request shortest path to $c_i$
4: **while** $s_i$ loctaed in $C$ **do**
5:     **if** $s_i$ activate cloak option then **then**
6:         confine the dynamic cell $dc$
7:         confine the static cell $sc$
8:         return candidate path
9:         **if** $dc > sc$ then **then**
10:             return path $p_i$
11:         **end if**
12:         **if** $sc$ is part of $p_i$ then **then**
13:             apply cloak to $sc$
14:         **end if**
15:     **else**
16:         return 1st candidate path to $c_i$
17:     **end if**
18: **end while**

---

the construction cost increases slightly. Figure 6, depict slightly longer paths, whereas Fig. 7 shows the construction costs for scenarios with shorter paths.

We also tested the cost construction of the anonymity server, which basically filters out the results for the fake users and returns to the relevant result to the legitimate user. Figure 9 shows that in all three scenarios comprising different paths, the server filters to their original paths efficiently. Although in path 3 (in all scenarios), there is a relatively larger number of cells, which incurs a small increase in filtering costs, the algorithm still performs efficiently.

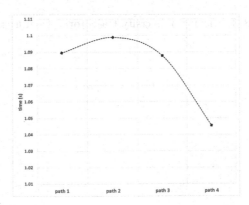

**Fig. 6.** The construction cost of the proposed algorithm in longer paths scenarios

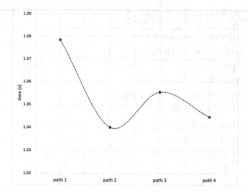

**Fig. 7.** The construction cost of the proposed algorithm in shorter paths scenarios

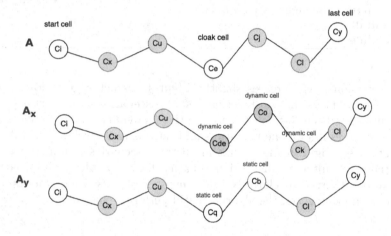

**Fig. 8.** Retrieving 3 diversity trajectories from user $A$

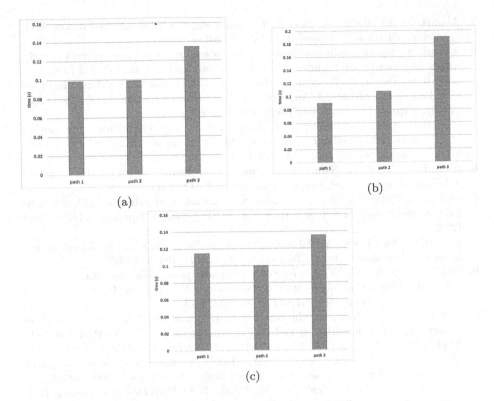

**Fig. 9.** The cost of the filtering the of three different scenarios

## 5   Conclusion

In this paper, we proposed a cloaking diversity approach for moving objects in indoor environments. Since previous research on the privacy of spatial trajectories has been done in the context of outdoor spaces, this work focuses uniquely on the privacy of the indoor spatial trajectories. The algorithm will find the shortest path for the user while maintaining his/her privacy, while giving the user the option to cloak a specific cell/room. For user privacy in indoor environments, the proposed privacy solution uses the cloaking principle with the inclusion of several trajectories. In order to maintain privacy, the user will be more attached to the dynamic rooms. Extensive simulations and tests demonstrated that the proposed privacy approach method works well and is cost-efficient, also successfully safeguarding the privacy of the user's trajectory.

## References

1. Shao, Z., Cheema, M.A., Taniar, D., Lu, H., Yang, S.: Efficiently processing spatial and keyword queries in indoor venues. IEEE Trans. Knowl. Data Eng. **33**(9), 3229–3244 (2021)

2. Alamri, S.: An efficient shortest path routing algorithm for directed indoor environments. ISPRS Int. J. Geo-Inf. **7**(4), 133 (2018)
3. Alamri, S.: Spatial data managements in indoor environments: current trends, limitations and future challenges. Int. J. Web Inf. Syst. **14**(4), 402–422 (2018)
4. Alamri, S., Taniar, D., Nguyen, K., Alamri, A.: C-tree: efficient cell-based indexing of indoor mobile objects. J. Ambient. Intell. Humaniz. Comput. **11**(7), 2841–2857 (2019). https://doi.org/10.1007/s12652-019-01397-w
5. Alamri, S., Taniar, D., Safar, M., Al-Khalidi, H.: A connectivity index for moving objects in an indoor cellular space. Pers. Ubiquit. Comput. **18**(2), 287–301 (2013). https://doi.org/10.1007/s00779-013-0645-3
6. Alamri, S., Taniar, D., Safar, M.: A taxonomy for moving object queries in spatial databases. Future Gener. Compt. Syst. **37**, 232–242 (2014)
7. Fariña, A., Gutiérrez-Asorey, P., Ladra, S., Penabad, M.R., Rodeiro, T.V.: A compact representation of indoor trajectories. IEEE Pervasive Comput. **21**(1), 57–64 (2022)
8. Alamri, S.: An efficient spatial zoning algorithm for maintaining social distancing in open indoor spaces. Int. J. Web Grid Serv. **18**(2), 194–212 (2022)
9. Tan, R., Tao, Y., Si, W., Zhang, Y.-Y.: Privacy preserving semantic trajectory data publishing for mobile location-based services. Wirel. Netw. **26**(8), 5551–5560 (2019). https://doi.org/10.1007/s11276-019-02058-8
10. Sazdar, A.M., Alikhani, N., Ghorashi, S.A., Khonsari, A.: Privacy preserving in indoor fingerprint localization and radio map expansion. Peer-to-Peer Network. Appl. **14**(1), 121–134 (2020). https://doi.org/10.1007/s12083-020-00950-1
11. Zhao, Y., Zhao, X., Chen, S., Zhang, Z., Huang, X.: An indoor crowd movement trajectory benchmark dataset. IEEE Trans. Reliab. **70**(4), 1368–1380 (2021)
12. Mura, C., Pajarola, R., Schindler, K., Mitra, N.J.: Walk2Map: extracting floor plans from indoor walk trajectories. Comput. Graph. Forum **40**(2), 375–388 (2021)
13. Liu, T., et al.: Shortest path queries for indoor venues with temporal variations. In: 2020 IEEE 36th International Conference on Data Engineering (ICDE), pp. 2014–2017 (2020)
14. Sweeney, L.: K-anonymity: a model for protecting privacy. Int. J. Uncertain. Fuzziness Knowl. Based Syst. **10**(5) 557–570 (2002)
15. Chow, C.-Y., Mokbel, M.F.: Trajectory privacy in location-based services and data publication. SIGKDD Explor. Newsl. **13**(1), 19–29 (2011)
16. Khoshgozaran, A., Shahabi, C.: A taxonomy of approaches to preserve location privacy in location-based services. Int. J. Comput. Sci. Eng. **5**(2), 86–96 (2010)

# MIAMI: MIxed Data Augmentation MIxture

Robin Fuchs[1](✉), Denys Pommeret[1,2], and Samuel Stocksieker[2]

[1] Aix Marseille Univ, CNRS, Centrale Marseille, I2M, Marseille, France
{robin.fuchs,denys.pommeret}@univ-amu.fr
[2] Lyon 1 Univ, ISFA, Lab. SAF EA2429, 69366 Lyon, France
samuel.stocksieker@univ-amu.fr

**Abstract.** Performing data augmentation for mixed datasets remains an open challenge. We propose an adaptation of the Mixed Deep Gaussian Mixture Models (MDGMM) to generate such complex data. The MDGMM explicitly handles the different data types and learns a continuous latent representation of the data that captures their dependence structure and can be exploited to conduct data augmentation. We test the ability of our method to simulate crossings of variables that were rarely observed or unobserved during training. The performances are compared with recent competitors relying on Generative Adversarial Networks, Random Forest, Classification And Regression Trees, or Bayesian networks on the UCI Adult dataset.

**Keywords:** Mixed data · Data augmentation · Mixture models · Unbalanced data

## 1 Introduction

Data augmentation is a powerful methodology to deal with unbalanced data, with data containing missing values, as well as to produce synthetic and anonymous datasets. Most data augmentation approaches are designed for a single data type: either continuous or non-continuous, with a particular focus on the continuous case. In the continuous data framework, the main methods are k-nearest neighbors (kNN), perturbation methods adding random noises to the data [13,16], methods based on the dependence structure obtained by modeling joint distribution or copulas [25], Gaussian Mixture Models [24], Generative Adversarial Networks (GAN) [14,22], and Variational Autoencoder (VAE) [17]. For non-continuous data, methods often rely on kNN [7] using adapted metrics, Classification And Regression Trees (CART) or Random Forest [21].

Methods dealing with each data type separately aim at capturing the dependence structure of the observations and using it to generate data. However,

Granted by the Research Chair DIALog under the aegis of the Risk Foundation, an initiative by CNP Assurances.

when the data are mixed, performing data augmentation can be challenging since the approaches have to simultaneously model categorical, binary, ordinal, discrete, and continuous data. These mixed distributions often contain multi-modal marginal densities, non-standard continuous distributions, and unbalanced modalities for the binary, categorical and ordinal variables.

There exist several recent works in the literature dedicated to the problem of mixed data. Some of them are adaptations of the previously cited methods, such as kNN with a specific distance [3], probabilistic models based on conditional copulas as synthetic data generators [10], or conditional GANs [4,27]. This generalization of GANs was introduced to overcome the fact that traditional GANs had difficulties reproducing complex distributions such as multimodal distributions (e.g. mixture distributions) or modeling entire distributions and to keep the full dependence structure of the data [15]. The Bayesian framework also constitutes a powerful family of methods to deal with mixed data. Dirichlet process mixtures can be used as latent spaces to generate data [9,20]. The Bayesian framework can also be combined with Gaussian copulas to generate fully-synthetic mixed data [5]. Yet, one of the main difficulties of Bayesian models remains in the choice of the priors to reflect the underlying model and the complexity of the dependence structure.

In this work, we introduce an approach based on the Mixed Deep Gaussian Mixture Model (MDGMM) [6]. The MDGMM learns a continuous representation of the dataset and can be inverted to generate pseudo-observations. The proposed methodology keeps the dependence structure of mixed datasets in a flexible way considering the flexible parametric distribution of the latent space which relies on Deep Gaussian Mixture Models [26]. Furthermore, all mixed data types are handled explicitly, especially the ordinal data type that is often assimilated to categorical or continuous data by competitor methods. The MDGMM is hence used as a data generator and coupled with an acceptation-rejection procedure to select observations presenting the desired characteristics. Our main objective is here to reconstruct unobserved regions of the mixed multivariate support of the data. We call this complete procedure "MIAMI", standing for "MIxed data Augmentation MIxture".

## 2    MDGMM Brief Presentation

The MDGMM is an unsupervised multi-layer model designed for mixed data clustering introduced by [6]. The mixed data are mapped into a continuous latent space using a Generalized Linear Latent Variable Model (GLLVM) [2,18,19]. The latent space is a Deep Gaussian Mixture Model [26] which enables the latent space to capture a broad range of possible distributions. More formally, denoting $Y = (Y_1, \cdots, Y_n)$ the $n$ observations of dimension $p$, we have for $i \in [1, n]$:

$$\begin{cases} Y_i \rightarrow z_i^{(1)} \text{ through GLLVM link via } (\lambda^{(0)}, \Lambda^{(0)}) \\ z_i^{(1)} = \eta_{k_1}^{(1)} + \Lambda_{k_1}^{(1)} z_i^{(2)} + u_{i,k_1}^{(1)} \text{ with probability } \pi_{k_1}^{(1)} \\ \dots \\ z_i^{(L-1)} = \eta_{k_{L-1}}^{(L-1)} + \Lambda_{k_{L-1}}^{(L-1)} z_i^{(L)} + u_{k_{L-1}}^{(L-1)} \text{ with} \\ \text{probability } \pi_{k_L}^{(L-1)} \\ z_i^{(L)} \sim \mathcal{N}(0, I_{r_L}), \end{cases} \tag{1}$$

where "GLLVM link" refers to the link functions relating the original mixed variable space to the continuous latent space. These link functions $f(Y_i|z_i^{(1)}, \Theta)$ are part of exponential families and the parameters $\Theta$ are learned during training (more details are given in [6]). To illustrate the possible link functions, if the $j$th component of the $i$th observation, $Y_{ij}$, is a count variable, one can choose a Binomial distribution:

$$f(Y_{ij}|z^{(1)}, \Theta) = \binom{n_j}{Y_{ij}} f(z^{(1)})^{Y_{ij}} (1 - f(z^{(1)}))^{n_j - Y_{ij}}, \tag{2}$$

with $n_j$ the upper bound of the count variable support. Other examples of link functions are given in [2].

In the simulations, the ordinal variables are linked to the latent space using ordered multinomial distributions, the categorical variables using unordered multinomial distributions, the count variables using Binomial distributions, the binary variables with Bernoulli distributions, and the continuous variables with Gaussian distributions.

The graphical model of the MDGMM described in (1) is presented in Fig. 1. This architecture was introduced as the M1DGMM in [6]. There exists a second architecture, M2DGMM, which merges the embeddings learned separately on continuous and non-continuous variables. We have chosen a simple one-layer deep M1DGMM architecture with a two-dimensional latent space and $K_1 = 4$ components, which has proven to be the more stable architecture [6] and will ensure to obtain more reproducible results.

## 3   Data Augmentation Procedure

The latent representation of the data is first determined by training the MDGMM on the data $Y$. The parameters learned are hereafter denoted by a tilde. The model is then inverted to generate pseudo-observations and only the observations with the desired characteristics are kept.

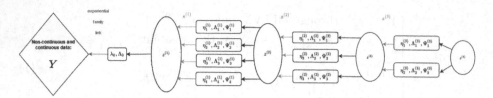

**Fig. 1.** Graphical model of a M1DGMM

Model training is described in the original MDGMM and enables drawing $z^{(1)}$ samples from a $DGMM(\tilde{\Theta})$ distribution. The model is then inverted using Bayes rule:

$$f(Y|\tilde{\Theta}) = \frac{f(\tilde{z}^{(1)}|\tilde{\Theta})f(Y|\tilde{z}^{(1)},\tilde{\Theta})}{f(\tilde{z}^{(1)}|Y,\tilde{\Theta})} \tag{3}$$

$$\propto f(\tilde{z}^{(1)}|\tilde{\Theta}) \prod_{j=1}^{p} f(Y_j|\tilde{z}^{(1)},\tilde{\Theta}). \tag{4}$$

The passage from (3) to (4) comes from the fact that, by construction, there is mutual independence between the original variables given the latent variable. This means that the latent representation captures all the dependence structure existing in the original dataset, which is a suitable feature to perform data augmentation in the mixed data case.

Let $C$ be the set of wanted characteristics, being for example a region of the original variable space, missing crossings of variables, or unbalanced modalities for non-continuous variables. One can simulate the $N^*$ pseudo-observations presenting the characteristics $C$ using the procedure described in Algorithm 1.

---

**Algorithm 1. MIAMI**

---

**Input:** $Y$, $N^*$, $C$, $m_0$, $m_1$.
Initialize $s = 0$.
**repeat**
　　Generate $m_0$ draws of $z^{(1)}$ from $DGMM(\tilde{\Theta})$.
　　Use these draws to sample $m_1$ pseudo-observations from $f(Y^*|\tilde{z}^{(1)},\tilde{\Theta})$ using (4).
　　**for** $i = 1$ to $m_1$ **do**
　　　　**if** $Y_i^*$ satisfies condition $C$ **then**
　　　　　　Add $Y_i^*$ to $Y^*$.
　　　　　　$s = s + 1$.
　　　　**end if**
　　**end for**
**until** $s \geq N^*$
**Output:** $N^*$ draws of $Y^*$.

---

In this algorithm, "$Y^*$ satisfies condition $C$" means that the pseudo-observations $(Y^*)$ present the wanted characteristics $(C)$. In this sense, Algorithm 1 can be viewed as an oversampling method creating pseudo-observations with the desired features. The $N^*$ pseudo-observations can be simulated by changing the number of copies of the latent variables $z^{(1)}$, $m_0$, or the number of pseudo-observations $Y^*$, $m_1$, to draw from each $z^{(1)}$. More $z^{(1)}$ draws ensure better coverage of the latent space while more $Y^*$ draws per $z^{(1)}$ give more information about the link existing between each latent point and the original variable space.

# 4   Numerical Illustration

## 4.1   Competitors

We propose to compare our approach with four recent competitors:

- *CTGAN* [1] is part of the SDV project and relies on a GAN-based Deep Learning data synthesizer to deal with continuous as well as categorical data.
- *Synthpop* proposed in the synthpop package in R [21]. Operating in a non-parametric framework, Synthpop generates the synthetic dataset sequentially by using either a CART procedure or a Random Forest (RF) approach. It is suitable for continuous as well as categorical, ordinal, and binary data. We consider both approaches, namely SynthPop-CART and SynthPop-RF, as competitors.
- *DataSynthesizer* [23] in the DataSynthesizer package in Python captures the underlying correlation structure between the different attributes through a Bayesian network and then draws samples from this model. It is suitable for continuous as well as categorical or binary data.

It is worth pointing out that we had also tested extensions of the SMOTE algorithm [3]: the SMOTE-NC algorithm with the HEOM distance and the so-called Adasyn algorithm [8]. However, these methods obtained much worse results than the other competitors on this dataset. Thus, their results are not shown here.

## 4.2   Evaluation Metrics

The model performances are here evaluated graphically and by using properly defined metrics. First, the dependence structure between couples of variables can be graphically assessed using Associations Matrices (AM) which are a generalization of correlations matrices for mixed data. In AM, the standard correlations are used to compare pairs of ordered variables (continuous, ordinal, and count variables), correlation ratios are used to compare an ordered variable with a non-ordered variable, and the Cramer's V to compare two non-ordered variables.

Secondly, the performances are also measured by three metrics:

- The association distance which is the Mean Relative Absolute Errors (MRAE) between the test and the generated datasets obtained by summing the absolute relative differences between the values of their association matrices.
- The MAE (Mean Absolute Error) between proportions for binary and categorical variables.
- The Kullback-Liebler divergence between the multivariate continuous distributions of the test and generated datasets.

The association distance hence summarizes how well each method captures the dependence structure, the MAE the quality of the marginal distributions reconstruction for categorical and binary variables, and the Kullback-Liebler a pseudo-distance between the multivariate continuous distributions.
The presented results are obtained over ten runs for each competitor and the formulas of the MAE and Kullback-Liebler divergence are given in Appendix.

### 4.3  Dataset

We test our approach on the Adult Census Income data. This dataset contains weighted census data extracted from the 1994 and 1995 current population surveys conducted by the U.S. Census Bureau [11]. The dataset contains n = 32.561 observations and is composed of three continuous variables, six categorical variables, two binary variables, and three ordinal variables. A detailed list of the variables is given in Appendix according to the UCI documentation.

### 4.4  Experimental Designs

In this work, the ability of the competitor models to generate observations presenting a given combination of two and three variables is tested. This combined modality is either weakly present (10 observations, called "Unbalanced design" hereafter) or completely missing (hereafter "Absent design") in the training set. We have then four designs:

- Absent design for a bivariate modality ("Bivariate Absent"),
- Absent design for a trivariate modality ("Trivariate Absent"),
- Unbalanced design for a bivariate modality ("Bivariate Unbalanced"),
- Unbalanced design for a trivariate modality ("Trivariate Unbalanced").

The bivariate modality is in our case, women of more than 60 years old (age>60 & sex=="Female") and the trivariate modality is widowed women of more than 60 years old (age>60 & sex=="Female" & Marital.status=="Widowed").
    The stability of the methods is evaluated using a 10-fold approach: for each experimental design, ten training sets of 1000 observations are drawn from the original dataset. The test sets are composed of the observations presenting the desired modality and that are not included in the train set. The number of pseudo-observations presenting the desired crossing of variables $N^*$ to draw is 200 for each competitor.

## 4.5  Results Analysis

We restrict our attention here to the most representative results.

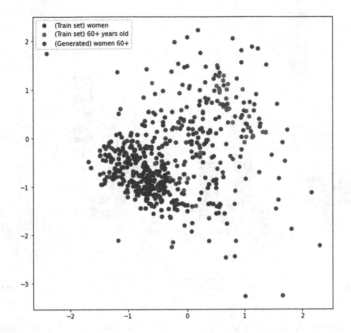

**Fig. 2.** Latent representation of women (in blue) and 60+ years old individuals (in red) coming from the train dataset, and women of 60+ years old generated by MIAMI (in green) in the Absent bivariate design. (Color figure online)

As shown in Fig. 2, the characteristics of the original dataset are well mapped into the latent space $(z^{(1)})$, which is the first layer of the MDGMM as illustrated in Fig. 1. Women and individuals of more than 60 years old are represented in two different and coherent zones. The generated individuals which present both characteristics are mainly generated near these two zones denoting that this global area well encodes the modality crossing.

Concerning the reproduction of the dependence structure through the association distances (Fig. 3), CTGAN generally obtains the best performance followed by MIAMI, DataSynthesizer, and SynthPop-CART. MIAMI is especially competitive on the Absent bivariate and Unbalanced trivariate designs. The SynthPop-RF approach outperforms most methods on trivariate designs but fails to capture the dependence structure of the bivariate designs.

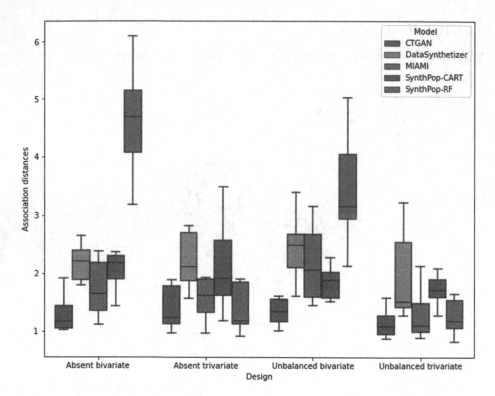

**Fig. 3.** Association distance for the four designs. The lower the distance, the best the dependence structure is reproduced.

CTGAN and MIAMI still obtain the best results for the reconstruction of categorical and binary variables but DataSynthesizer also performs well (Fig. 4(a)). The SynthPop methods present a much higher variance than the other competitors for three designs out of four, while MIAMI and CTGAN obtain comparable variances and DataSynthesizer a much lower variance.

Besides, the continuous variables are best accounted for by SynthPop-RF, MIAMI, and SynthPop-CART (Fig. 4(b)). The distributions generated by CTGAN are furthest from the test ones and show more variability, especially in comparison with DataSynthesizer and MIAMI. This pattern can also be observed in Fig. 5 representing the bivariate distribution of the age and fnwgt variables on the test dataset and for the observations generated by MIAMI and CTGAN. The continuous distributions reconstructed by MIAMI are more concentrated and the density maximum is closest to the one of the test dataset when compared to CTGAN.

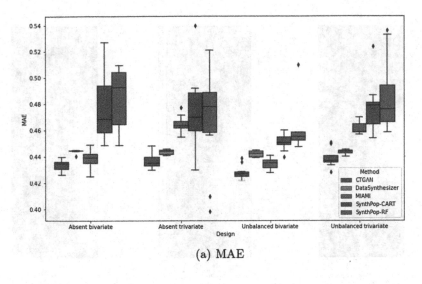

(a) MAE

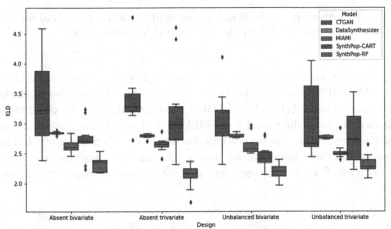

(b) Multivariate Kullback-Liebler

**Fig. 4.** MAE (a) and Kullback-Liebler divergence (b) between the test and the generated datasets for all designs

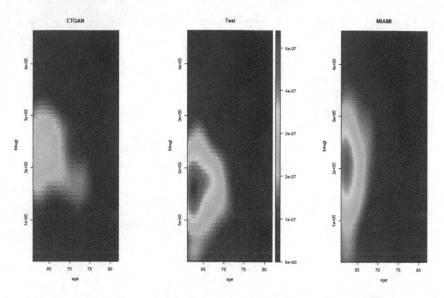

**Fig. 5.** Density estimation of the bivariate distribution (Fnlweight, Age) for CTGAN, on the test set, and for MIAMI for the Unbalanced bivariate design.

Figure 6 gives an illustration of the generation of the seven modalities of the variable "Marital Status" for the Bivariate Unbalanced and Absent designs. It can be seen that only MIAMI and DataSynthesizer manage to generate all the possible modalities in the first design. MIAMI is closest to the observations while DataSynthesizer creates unobserved modalities. CTGAN is concentrated on only one modality. In the Absent design, none of the methods manage to cover all the modalities while DataSynthesizer once again proposes an unobserved modality.

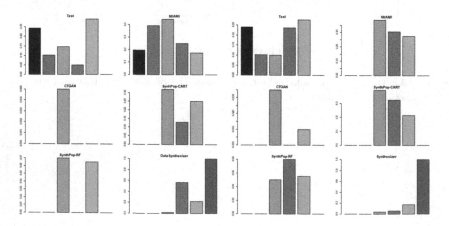

**Fig. 6.** Modality proportions for the Marital-status under the Bivariate Unbalanced design (left) and the Bivariate Absent design (right)

Finally, compared to the competitor methods, MIAMI gives associations close to the true associations existing in the test set but with a slightly lower intensity than in the test set (Fig. 7). The associations between "Education.num" and "Occupation" or the one between the marital status and the "Relationship" variable are captured. These two associations are also well reproduced by SynthPop-CART, which tends however to create nonexistent associations between most variables. CTGAN has more difficulty in reproducing the original patterns. For concision purposes, the results of SynthPop-RF and DataSynthesizer are not presented. Indeed, SynthPop-RF exaggerates the associations existing between variables even more than SynthPop-CART, and DataSynthesizer fails to reproduce the main patterns of the test association matrix.

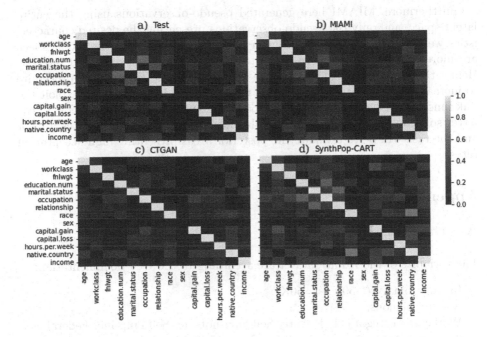

**Fig. 7.** Association matrices for women of more than 60 years old existing in the test set of the Unbalanced bivariate design (a), generated by MIAMI (b), by CTGAN (c) and by SynthPop-CART (d).

The code to reproduce the results is available at https://github.com/RobeeF/M1DGMM.

## 5    Discussion and Perspective

MIAMI is an algorithm dedicated to mixed data which oversamples desired areas of the sampling space while preserving the multivariate dependence structure of the data. Based on our numerical study, we conclude that MIAMI seems to reconstruct well the joint dependence of the mixed data, the univariate non-continuous distributions, and the multivariate continuous distributions. Its major competitor seems to be CTGAN in terms of dependence structure and non-continuous variable, and SynthPop-CART on the multivariate continuous distributions reconstruction.

The flexibility of its latent space enables MIAMI to properly reconstruct areas of high density for continuous variables and to generate a wide range of modalities for non-continuous variables while the other methods often reproduce only the most represented ones (Fig. 6 and Figs. 8 and 9 in Appendix). In this work, the latent space takes the form of a simple one hidden layer architecture. More complex architectures and hyperparameters could be investigated in future works.

Furthermore, MIAMI here generated pseudo-observations using the entire latent space, and only the pseudo-observations presenting the desired characteristics were kept. However, as shown in Fig. 2, some regions of the latent space are more likely than others to generate these pseudo-observations of interest. Hence, the sampling of the latent space could be adapted through the procedure to increase the generation/acceptation ratio. One could for instance exploit the link functions of the MDGMM or rely on Bayesian optimization methods. In the latter solution, the distribution of the latent variable would be taken as a prior and the task will be to estimate the posterior areas presenting high-acceptation rates.

# Appendix

## A    Datasets Details

The variables of the Adult dataset are according to the UCI documentation:

- Income: binary (>50K, <=50K).
- Age: continuous.
- Workclass: categorical (Private, Self-emp-not-inc, Self-emp-inc, Federal-gov, Local-gov, State-gov, Without-pay, Never-worked).
- Fnlwgt: continuous.
- Education-num: ordinal.
- Marital-status: categorical (Married-civ-spouse, Divorced, Never-married, Separated, Widowed, Married-spouse-absent, Married-AF-spouse).
- Occupation: categorical (Tech-support, Craft-repair, Other-service, Sales, Exec-managerial, Prof-specialty, Handlers-cleaners, Machine-op-inspct, Adm-clerical, Farming-fishing, Transport-moving, Priv-house-serv, Protective-serv, Armed-Forces).
- Relationship: categorical (Wife, Own-child, Husband, Not-in-family, Other-relative, Unmarried).
- Race: categorical (White, Asian-Pac-Islander, Amer-Indian-Eskimo, Other, Black).

- Sex: binary (Female, Male).
- Capital-gain: ordinal.
- Capital-loss: ordinal.
- Hours-per-week: continuous.
- Native-country: categorical (United-States, Cambodia, England, Puerto-Rico, Canada, Germany, Outlying-US(Guam-USVI-etc.), India, Japan, Greece, South, China, Cuba, Iran, Honduras, Philippines, Italy, Poland, Jamaica, Vietnam, Mexico, Portugal, Ireland, France, Dominican-Republic, Laos, Ecuador, Taiwan, Haiti, Columbia, Hungary, Guatemala, Nicaragua, Scotland, Thailand, Yugoslavia, El-Salvador, Trinadad&Tobago, Peru, Hong, Holand-Netherlands).

## B   Evaluation Metrics Details

Our overall criterion between a test dataset and a generated dataset is the association distance obtained as follows:

$$DA = \frac{1}{P} \sum_{1 \leq i < j \leq p}^{p} |M_{ij}(test) - M_{ij}(gen)|/M_{ij}(test),$$

where $p$ denotes the number of variables (14 in the Adult dataset), $P = (p^2 - p)/2$, and $M_{ij}(test)$ (resp. $M_{ij}(gen)$) is the $(i,j)$th entry of the test (resp. generated) Association Matrix.

To measure the similarity between the dependence structures of the vectors formed by the three continuous variables (Age, Fnlwgt, and Hours) we used the multivariate Kullback Leibler divergence [12].

For qualitative data, we chose the mean absolute errors (MAE) between proportions. More precisely, for a $k$th intersection of modalities we consider

$$MAE(k) = |p_k(test) - p_k(gen)|,$$

where $p_k(test)$ (resp. $p_k(gen)$) stands for $k$th test (resp. generated) proportion. The final MAE is the mean of all the $MAE(k)$ over all the possibilities.

## C   Additional Results: Unobserved Marginal Density Reconstruction

When it comes to reconstructing univariate densities, MIAMI generates well-identified unimodal densities contrary to DataSynthesizer which generates flat densities, or SynthPop-CART which generates multi-modal densities (Fig. 8). More precisely, Figs. 8 and 9 represent the estimations of the observed density versus the generated one for Age in the case of the Bivariate and Trivariate Unbalanced designs. We observe that MIAMI can recover the right distribution, yet not observed in the training set. It means that MIAMI captures well the dependence structure of such a partially unobserved variable. CTGAN and

SynthPop-RF also seem to work well for both designs. DataSynthesizer shows a larger variance. This illustration shows that we cannot clearly decide between the methods by looking only at the marginal distributions. Only a criterion like the association distance can take into account a more complex multivariate dependence structure.

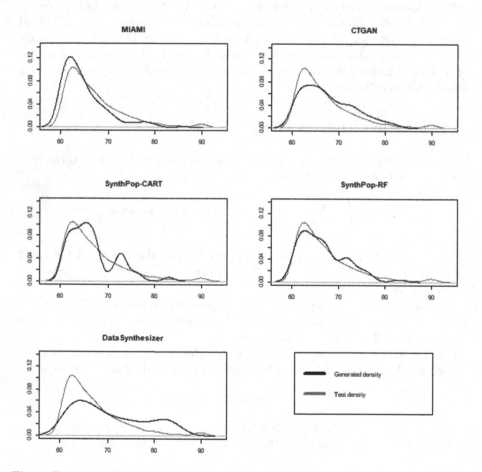

**Fig. 8.** Density estimations for Age based on the test dataset (red) or based on the Bivariate Unbalanced design (black) (Color figure online)

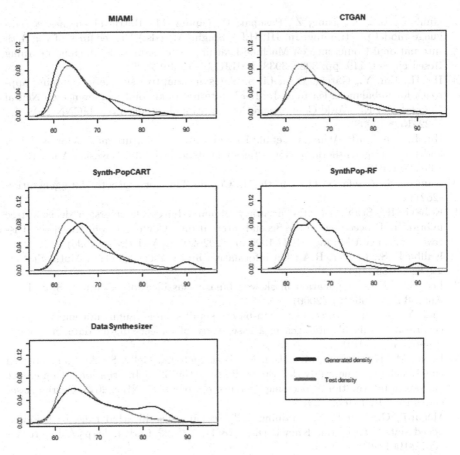

**Fig. 9.** Density estimations for Age based on the test dataset (red) or based on the Trivariate Unbalanced design (black) (Color figure online)

# References

1. Buuren, S.V., Brand, J.P., Groothuis-Oudshoorn, C.G., Rubin, D.B.: Fully conditional specification in multivariate imputation. J. Stat. Comput. Simul. **76**(12), 1049–1064 (2006)
2. Cagnone, S., Viroli, C.: A factor mixture model for analyzing heterogeneity and cognitive structure of dementia. AStA Advances in Statistical Analysis **98**(1), 1–20 (2013). https://doi.org/10.1007/s10182-012-0206-5
3. Chawla, N.V., Bowyer, K.W., Hall, L.O., Kegelmeyer, W.P.: Smote: synthetic minority over-sampling technique. J. Artif. Int. Res. **16**(1), 321–357 (2002)
4. Engelmann, J., Lessmann, S.: Conditional wasserstein gan-based oversampling of tabular data for imbalanced learning. Expert Syst. Appl. **174**, 114582 (2021)
5. Feldman, J., Kowal, D.: A bayesian framework for generation of fully synthetic mixed datasets (2021)
6. Fuchs, R., Pommeret, D., Viroli, C.: Mixed deep gaussian mixture model: a clustering model for mixed datasets. In: Advances in Data Analysis and Classification, pp. 1–23 (2021)

7. Guu, K., Lee, K., Tung, Z., Pasupat, P., Chang, M.: Retrieval augmented language model pre-training. In: III, H.D., Singh, A. (eds.) Proceedings of the 37th International Conference on Machine Learning. Proceedings of Machine Learning Research, vol. 119, pp. 3929–3938. PMLR, 13–18 Jul 2020
8. He, H., Bai, Y., Garcia, E.A., Li, S.: Adasyn: adaptive synthetic sampling approach for imbalanced learning. In: IEEE International Joint Conference on Neural Networks (IEEE World Congress on Computational Intelligence), IJCNN 2008, pp. 1322–1328 (2008)
9. Hu, J., Reiter, J.P., Wang, Q., et al.: Dirichlet process mixture models for modeling and generating synthetic versions of nested categorical data. Bayesian Anal. **13**(1), 183–200 (2018)
10. Kamthe, S., Assefa, S., Deisenroth, M.: Copula flows for synthetic data generation (2021)
11. Kohavi, R.: Scaling up the accuracy of naive-bayes classifiers: a decision-tree hybrid. In: Proceedings of the Second International Conference on Knowledge Discovery and Data Mining, KDD 1996, pp. 202–207. AAAI Press (1996)
12. Kullback, S., Leibler, R.A.: On information and sufficiency. Ann. Math. Statist. **22**(1), 79–86 (1951)
13. Lee, S.S.: Noisy replication in skewed binary classification. Comput. Stat. Data Anal. **34**(2), 165–191 (2000)
14. Liu, Y., et al.: Wasserstein gan-based small-sample augmentation for new-generation artificial intelligence: a case study of cancer-staging data in biology. Engineering (2019)
15. Lucic, M., Kurach, K., Michalski, M., Bousquet, O., Gelly, S.: Are gans created equal? a large-scale study. In: Proceedings of the 32nd International Conference on Neural Information Processing Systems, pp. 698–707. NIPS 2018, Curran Associates Inc., Red Hook (2018)
16. Menardi, G., Torelli, N.: Training and assessing classification rules with imbalanced data. Data Min. Knowl. Disc. **28**(1), 92–122 (2012). https://doi.org/10.1007/s10618-012-0295-5
17. Moreno-Barea, F.J., Jerez, J.M., Franco, L.: Improving classification accuracy using data augmentation on small data sets. Expert Syst. Appl. **161**, 113696 (2020)
18. Moustaki, I.: A general class of latent variable models for ordinal manifest variables with covariate effects on the manifest and latent variables. Br. J. Math. Stat. Psychol. **56**(2), 337–357 (2003)
19. Moustaki, I., Knott, M.: Generalized latent trait models. Psychometrika **65**(3), 391–411 (2000)
20. Murray, J.S., Reiter, J.P.: Multiple imputation of missing categorical and continuous values via bayesian mixture models with local dependence. J. Am. Stat. Assoc. **111**(516), 1466–1479 (2016)
21. Nowok, B., Raab, G.M., Dibben, C.: Synthpop: bespoke creation of synthetic data in R. J. Stat. Soft. **74**(11), 1–26 (2016). https://doi.org/10.18637/jss.v074.i11
22. Park, N., Mohammadi, M., Gorde, K., Jajodia, S., Park, H., Kim, Y.: Data synthesis based on generative adversarial networks. Proc. VLDB Endow. **11**(10), 1071–1083 (2018)
23. Ping, H., Stoyanovich, J., Howe, B.: Datasynthesizer: privacy-preserving synthetic datasets. In: Proceedings of the 29th International Conference on Scientific and Statistical Database Management, SSDBM 2017, Association for Computing Machinery, New York (2017)

24. Richardson, E., Weiss, Y.: On gans and gmms. In: Bengio, S., Wallach, H., Larochelle, H., Grauman, K., Cesa-Bianchi, N., Garnett, R. (eds.) Advances in Neural Information Processing Systems, vol. 31. Curran Associates, Inc. (2018)
25. Sun, Y., Cuesta-Infante, A., Veeramachaneni, K.: Learning vine copula models for synthetic data generation. In: AAAI (2019)
26. Viroli, C., McLachlan, G.J.: Deep gaussian mixture models. Stat. Comput. **29**(1), 43–51 (2019)
27. Xu, L., Skoularidou, M., Cuesta-Infante, A., Veeramachaneni, K.: Modeling tabular data using conditional gan. In: NeurIPS (2019)

# A Galerkin Approach for Fractional Delay Differential Equations Using Hybrid Chelyshkov Basis Functions

Dajana Conte⬥, Eslam Farsimadan⬥, Leila Moradi^(✉)⬥,
Francesco Palmieri⬥, and Beatrice Paternoster⬥

University of Salerno, 84084 Fisciano, Italy
{dajconte,efarsimadan,lmoradi,fpalmieri,beapat}@unisa.it

**Abstract.** This study proposes a numerical technique based on a hybrid of block-pulse functions and Chelyshkov polynomials to solve fractional delay differential equations. The Galerkin approach transforms the solution of fractional delay differential equations into a system of algebraic equations using the fractional operational matrix of integration for these hybrid functions. The suggested method's accuracy and efficiency are demonstrated using numerical examples.

**Keywords:** Chelyshkov polynomials · Block-pulse functions · Hybrid functions · Fractional delay differential equations · Operational matrix

## 1 Introduction

Fractional calculus is a fascinating topic that piques the interest of a significant number of researchers. G.W. Leibniz (1695, 1697) and Leonhard Euler (1730) initiated the construction of the fractional calculus, which has been carried on up until the present day [1].

The applications of fractional calculus in fields such as physics, engineering, and others have piqued the interest of scientists in recent decades [2–12]. Nowadays, more proceedings and special issues in journals refer to fractional calculus applications in numerous scientific domains, such as special functions, control theory, chemical physics, stochastic processes, anomalous diffusion, and rheology, etc. See [13].

Fractional derivatives and integrals have been practical tools for characterizing memory and hereditary properties in various materials and processes. For instance, fractional differential equations are employed to explain a range of natural phenomena in physics, chemistry, fluid mechanics, and mathematics [14].

In contradiction to Ordinary Differential Equations (ODEs), Delay Differential Equations (DDEs) incorporate addition derivatives from earlier-time, making the mathematical model closer to the real-world occurrence. Biology, economics, medicine, chemistry, control, and electrodynamics are only a few of the topics where delay differential equations have been widely used for analysis and prediction [15,16]. As a generalization, Fractional Delay Differential Equations (FDDEs) deal with differential equations governed by fractional differential operators. In the last two decades, numerical approaches based on orthogonal polynomials have been commonly used to approximate the solution of fractional differential and integral equations. The primary characteristic of these methods is that they convert fractional problems to a system of algebraic equations that can be solved more conveniently using the orthogonal properties of polynomials and typical spectral methods.

Several numerical methods have been applied to solve DDEs. For instance, Chebyshev polynomials [17], Bernoulli polynomials [18], variational iteration method [19], one-leg $\theta$-method [20], Adomian decomposition method [21], hybrid of block-pulse functions and Taylor series [22], Legendre wavelet [23], etc. However, not many studies focus on finding numerical solutions to FDDEs. Some of these works are Hermite wavelet method [24], spectral-collocation method [25], Legendre pseudospectral method [26], Adams-Bashforth-Moulton method, and the linear interpolation method [27], finite difference method [28] and Bernoulli wavelets method [36].

This research came up with a novel idea for an efficient numerical method to approximate the solution to the FDDEs presented below, using a combination of block-pulse functions and Chelyshkov polynomials. Consider

$$\begin{cases} D^\alpha q(t) = p(t, q(t), q(t - \tau)), & 0 \le t \le 1, r - 1 < \alpha \le r, 0 < \tau < 1, \\ q^{(i)}(0) = \lambda_i, & i = 0, 1, ..., r - 1, \\ q(t) = \xi(t), & t < 0. \end{cases} \tag{1}$$

$$\begin{cases} D^\alpha q(t) = p(t, q(t), q(t\tau)), & 0 \le t \le 1, r - 1 < \alpha \le r, 0 < \tau < 1, \\ q^{(i)}(0) = \mu_i, & i = 0, 1, ..., r - 1, \end{cases} \tag{2}$$

where $p$ is an analytical function, $\tau$ is delay, $\lambda_i, \mu_i, i = 0, 1, ..., r - 1$, are real constants, $\xi(t)$ is an arbitrary known function, $q$ is the solution to be determined, and $D^\alpha, (r - 1 < \alpha \le r)$ is the fractional derivative in the Caputo sense [36,38]. The goal of this work is to get a direct numerical method that is based on hybrid Chelyshkov orthogonal polynomials for solving a system of FDDEs (1) and (2).

Initially, to solve FDDEs, we shall discuss hybrid Chelyshkov polynomials and the properties of these polynomials. After that, the Galerkin method was applied to solve FDDEs utilizing the fractional integration operational matrix of the hybrid Chelyshkov polynomials. The most notable benefit of using hybrid Chelyshkov orthogonal polynomials and the Galerkin technique for the problem of solving FDDEs is the ability to convert the problem to a set of algebraic equations with unknown coefficients. Numerical examples demonstrate that the provided numerical method is accurate and efficient.

The components of this work are organized as follows: In Sect. 2, we discuss the definitions of fractional derivatives and integrals and their properties. In Sect. 3, an overview of the hybrid Chelyshkov polynomial is presented, including a description of the polynomial and its history. Three subsections make up Sect. 3. In the first, we are given an overview of the definition of Chelyshkov polynomials. The second is linked to the hybrid Chelyshkov functions (HCFs) and the transformation and fractional operational matrices for HCFs. A numerical method for solving FDDEs will be presented in Sect. 4, and it will be based on HCFs and the operational matrices of the problem. In Sect. 5, the approach based on HCFs that was proposed is applied to the resolution of specific numerical cases. In Sect. 6, we will provide some concluding remarks.

## 2    Fractional Calculus: Definition and Properties

Fractional calculus has been acknowledged as an indispensable tool for dealing with various processes. This section will cover the principles of fractional calculus shortly and concisely. Multiple definitions exist for variable-order fractional derivatives, including the Riemann-Liouville sense and the Caputo sense. In this paper, the definition in Caputo's sense is examined. For additional information, please see [1, 38].

**Definition 1.** *The formula that defines the Caputo fractional derivative of order* $\alpha$ *is as follows:*

$$\mathcal{D}^\alpha p(t) = \frac{1}{\Gamma(n-\alpha)} \int_0^t (t-u)^{n-\alpha-1} \frac{d^n}{du^n} p(u) du, \quad n-1 < \alpha \le n, \, t > 0, \quad (3)$$

*where n is the upper limit of* $\alpha$.

This operator $\mathcal{D}^\alpha$ is defined to have the following properties:

$$\mathcal{D}^\alpha c = 0, \tag{4}$$

where $c$ is a constant.

$$\mathcal{D}^\alpha t^\beta = \frac{\Gamma(\beta+1)}{\Gamma(\beta+1-\alpha)} t^{\beta-\alpha} \tag{5}$$

and

$$\mathcal{D}^\alpha(\lambda p(t) + \mu q(t)) = \lambda \mathcal{D}^\alpha p(t) + \mu \mathcal{D}^\alpha q(t). \tag{6}$$

**Definition 2.** *According to Riemann-Liouville, the formula for the fractional integral of order* $\alpha \ge 0$ *can be written as follows:*

$$\mathcal{I}^\alpha p(t) = \frac{1}{\Gamma(\alpha)} \int_0^x (t-u)^{\alpha-1} p(u) du, \quad \alpha > 0, \, t > 0. \tag{7}$$

This form of the fractional integral possesses the following fundamental characteristics:

$$\mathcal{I}^0 p(t) = p(t), \tag{8}$$

$$\mathcal{I}^\alpha \mathcal{I}^\delta p(t) = \mathcal{I}^{\alpha+\delta} p(t), \tag{9}$$

$$\mathcal{I}^\alpha \mathcal{I}^\delta p(t) = \mathcal{I}^\delta \mathcal{I}^\alpha p(t), \tag{10}$$

Riemann-Liouville integrals also have additional properties:

$$\mathcal{I}^\alpha t^\beta = \frac{\Gamma(\beta+1)}{\Gamma(\beta+1+\alpha)} t^{\beta+\alpha}. \tag{11}$$

Here, by Definitions 1 and 2, we can get the following formula:

$$\mathcal{I}^\alpha \mathcal{D}^\alpha p(t) = p(t) - \sum_{t=0}^{m-1} p^{(i)}(0) \frac{t^i}{i!}. \tag{12}$$

## 3   Chelyshkov Functions

Vladimir. S. Chelyshkov [39] developed one of the most recent classes of orthogonal polynomials, the Chelyshkov polynomials. These polynomials are defined explicitly by

$$\rho_{N,k}(t) = \sum_{j=k}^{N} \mathbf{z}_{k,j}^N t^j, \quad k = 0, 1, ...N, \quad \mathbf{z}_{k,j}^N = (-1)^{j-k} \binom{N-k}{j-n} \binom{N+j+1}{N-k} \tag{13}$$

### Orthogonality

The Chelyshkov polynomials satisfy the orthogonality condition in terms of the weight function $w(t) = 1$ in the range $[0, 1]$, and their orthogonality requirement is:

$$\int_0^1 \rho_{N,i}(t)\rho_{N,j}(t) = \frac{\delta_{ij}}{i+j+1}. \tag{14}$$

### 3.1   Hybrid of the Chelyshkov Polynomials and Block-Pulse Functions

This section will focus on the fundamental definition of HCFs and some of the aspects associated with them. The Chelyshkov orthogonal polynomials are very significant in the performance of HCFs. Following the introduction of the Chelyshkov orthogonal polynomials, HCFs will be built by mixing these orthogonal polynomials with block-pulse functions [40].

The hybrid of Chelyshkov polynomials and block pulse functions, $\phi_{nm}(t)$, $n = 1, 2, ..., N$, $m = 0, 1, 2, ..., M$ are defined on the interval $[0, 1]$ as

$$\phi_{nm}(t) = \begin{cases} \sqrt{N}\rho_{N,m}(Nt - n + 1) & t \in [\frac{n-1}{N}, \frac{n}{N}] \\ 0 & otherwise, \end{cases} \tag{15}$$

where $\rho_{N,m}$ denotes the Chelyshkov polynomials of degree m defined in (13).

## Function Approximation

The set of $\{\phi_{nm}(t), n = 1, 2, ..., N, m = 0, 1, 2, ..., M\}$ constitutes an orthogonal basis over $[0, 1)$ and every square inegrable function $p(t)$ in interval $[0, 1)$ may be enlarged as

$$p(t) \simeq \sum_{n=1}^{N} \sum_{m=0}^{M} c_{nm}\phi_{nm}(t) = C^T \Phi(t) \tag{16}$$

where

$$\Phi(t) = \left[\phi_{10}(t), \phi_{20}(t), ..., \phi_{N0}(t), \phi_{11}(t), \phi_{21}(t), ..., \phi_{N1}(t), ..., \phi_{1M}(t),\right.$$
$$\left.\phi_{2M}(t), ..., \phi_{NM}(t)\right]^T, \tag{17}$$

$$C = [c_{10}, c_{20}, ..., c_{N0}, c_{11}, c_{21}, ..., c_{N1}, ..., c_{1M}, c_{2M}, ..., c_{NM}]^T. \tag{18}$$

The vectors $\Phi(t)$ and $C$ in series (16) can be rewritten as

$$p(t) \simeq \sum_{i=1}^{\hat{m}} c_i \phi_{nm}(t) = C^T \Phi(t), \tag{19}$$

where $\Phi(t) = [\phi_1(t), \phi_2(t), ..., \phi_{\hat{m}}(t)]$, and $C = [c_1, c_2, ..., c_{\hat{m}}]$. Also $c_i = c_{nm}$, $\phi_i(t) = \phi_{nm}(t)$, $i = (n-1)(M+1) + m + 1$, $\hat{m} = (M+1)N$.

## 3.2  Operational Matrix

The solution of variable-order fractional differential or integral equations is accomplished using an operational matrix technique. The primary idea behind this part is to generate the operational integration matrix using hybrid Chelyshkov functions.

**Theorem 1.** *[29–31] Given that $\Psi(t)$ represents the Chelshkov polynomial vectors, the Riemann-Liouville fractional integral of order $\alpha$ of the Chelshkov polynomial vector can be expressed as:*

$$\mathcal{I}^{\alpha}\Psi(t) = \Theta^{(\alpha)}\Psi(t), \tag{20}$$

*where $\Theta^{(\alpha)}$ indicates the fractional integral matrix of order $\alpha$ and has the dimensions $(M+1) \times (M+1)$. The $(i,j)$-th element of this matrix is generated by the following operations:*

$$\Theta_{i,j}^{(\alpha)} = \sum_{j=i}^{M} \sum_{s=j}^{M} \frac{\mathbf{z}_{j,s}\mathbf{z}_{i,j}\Gamma(j+1)(2j+1)}{\Gamma(j+\nu+1)(j+s+1)}, \quad i, j = 1, 2, ..., M+1.$$

**Lemma 1.** *[29–31] The $\hat{m}$ HCFs vector $\Phi(t)$ can be convert into the $(M+1)$ Chelyshkov polynomials vector $\Psi(t)$ by expanding as follows:*

$$\Phi(t) = \Lambda\Psi(t), \tag{21}$$

*where $\Lambda$ is a $\hat{m} \times (M+1)$ matrix,*

$$\Lambda_{ij} = (2j+1)\sum_{r=j}^{M}\sum_{s=m}^{M}\sum_{k=0}^{r}\frac{\binom{r}{k}(n-1)^{r-k}N^{-\frac{1}{2}-r}\mathbf{z}_{r,j}\mathbf{z}_{s,m}}{r+s+1},$$

*and $i = 1, ..., \hat{m}, \ j = 1, ..., M+1$.*

**Theorem 2.** *[29–31] Consider the $(M+1)$ Chelyshkov polynomials vector to be denoted by $Psi(t)$. Then, the HCFs representation of $Psi(x)$ can be developed as follows:*

$$\Psi(t) = \Pi\Phi(t), \tag{22}$$

*where $\Pi$ is $(M+1) \times \hat{m}$ matrix and*

$$\Pi_{i,j} = \sum_{r=i-1}^{M}\sum_{s=m}^{M}\sum_{k=0}^{r}\frac{\mathbf{z}_{r,i-1}\mathbf{z}_{s,m}N^{-\frac{1}{2}-r}\binom{r}{k}(n-1)^{r-k}}{k+s+1}.$$

**Theorem 3.** *[29–31] Using $\Phi(t)$ as the HCFs vector, the fractional integration of order $\alpha$ for this vector can be written as:*

$$\mathcal{I}^{\alpha}\Phi(t) = \mathcal{P}^{(\alpha)}\Phi(t), \tag{23}$$

*where $\mathcal{P}^{(\alpha)} = \Lambda\Theta^{(\alpha)}\Pi$ is a $\hat{m} \times \hat{m}$ matrix, and $\Lambda$ and $\Pi$ are transformation matrices derived in Eqs. (21) and (22), respectively. In addition, $\Theta^{\nu}$ is operational matrix of fractional integration for HCFs vector $\Phi(t)$.*

## 4    Problem Statement and Approximation Scheme

In this part, we solve FDDEs (1) and (2) by employing the Galerkin method and the fractional integration operational matrices of the HCFs.

**Problem(1)**

Consider the FDDEs (1). To solve this problem, we approximate $D^{\alpha}q(t)$ via HCFs basis $\phi_i(t), i = 0, 1, 2, ..., \hat{m}$, as

$$D^{\alpha}q(t) = C^{T}\Phi(t), \tag{24}$$

where $C$ is an unknown vector that can be acquired. By utilizing (20), we obtain:

$$q(t) \simeq I^\alpha \left( C^T \varPhi(t) \right) + \sum_{i=0}^{r-1} \frac{\lambda_i}{i!} t^i = C^T \mathcal{P}^{(\alpha)} \varPhi(t) + d^T \varPhi(t). \qquad (25)$$

In other words, for the problem (1), we get:

$$q(t-\tau) = \begin{cases} \xi(t-\tau), & 0 \le t \le \tau \\ C^T \mathcal{P}^{(\alpha)} \varPhi(t-\tau) + d^T \varPhi(t-\tau), & \tau \le t \le 1 \end{cases} = C_\tau^T \varPhi(t). \qquad (26)$$

We can obtain the following residual function by substituting Eqs. (24)–(26) for the original equations in problem (1).

$$R(t) = C^T \varPhi(t) - p\left(t, C^T \mathcal{P}^{(\alpha)} \varPhi(t) + d^T \varPhi(t), C_\tau^T \varPhi(t)\right). \qquad (27)$$

To obtain the answer $q(t)$, we must first identify the residual $R(t)$ at the $\hat{m}+1$ points. As demonstrated below, we use the roots of shifted Chebyshev polynomials to determine appropriate collocates.

$$R(t_j) = 0, j = 1, 2, ...\hat{m}+1. \qquad (28)$$

It is possible to find the solution to this problem using the vector $C$ coefficients that are unknown. As a direct consequence of this, we can obtain the numerical solution by substituting the resulting vector $C$ into the Eq. (25).

## Problem(2)

We use a method that was employed for the previous problem (1) to solve the FDDEs (2). Replacing Eqs. (24) and (25) in (2), we have the following residual function:

$$R(t) = C^T \varPhi(t) - p\left(t, C^T \mathcal{P}^{(\alpha)} \varPhi(t) + d^T \varPhi(t), C^T \mathcal{P}^{(\alpha)} \varPhi(\tau t) + d^T \varPhi(\tau t)\right). \quad (29)$$

As shown follows, we then compute the residual value $R(t)$ at the $\hat{m}+1$ roots of the shifted Chebyshev polynomials.

$$R(t_j) = 0, \quad j = 1, 2, ...\hat{m}+1. \qquad (30)$$

These equations are then solved for unknown coefficients of the vector $C$. As a result, by solving these systems by determining $C$, we obtain the numerical solution to this problem (2).

# 5    Numerical Results

This section will examine three different example scenarios to highlight the usefulness and advantages of the proposed technique.

*Example 1.* Consider the FDDEs

$$\begin{cases} D^\alpha q(t) = q(t-\tau) - q(t) + \frac{2t^{2-\alpha}}{\Gamma(3-\alpha)} - \frac{t^{1-\alpha}}{\Gamma(2-\alpha)} + 2t\tau - \tau^2 - \tau, \ 0 \le t \le 1, \ 0 < \alpha \le 1, \\ q(t) = 0, \hspace{7.5cm} t \le 0. \end{cases}$$

In the case where $\alpha = 1$, the exact solution to this system is $q(t) = t^2 - t$. The approximate solutions for several different values of $\alpha$ and the absolute error for $\alpha = 1$ are displayed in Fig. 1 for the case in which $M = 2$, $N = 2$, and $\tau = 0.01$ are the input values. When utilizing the current approach with $\hat{m} = 6$, the RMSE for various values of $t$ is displayed in the table referenced by the Table 1. As anticipated, the outcomes of this example get closer and closer to the exact solution as the fractional order $\alpha$ approaches 1.

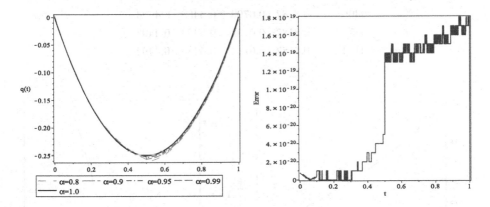

**Fig. 1.** The approximate solution for various values of $\alpha$ (Left) and absolute error for $\alpha = 1$ (Right).

**Table 1.** The RMSE ($\|q - \tilde{q}\|_2$) for different values of t (Example 1).

| Methods | $t = 0.2$ | $t = 0.4$ | $t = 0.6$ | $t = 0.8$ |
|---|---|---|---|---|
| [32] | $3.46 \times 10^{-16}$ | $2.35 \times 10^{-16}$ | $3.46 \times 10^{-16}$ | $9.69 \times 10^{-17}$ |
| [33] | $1.19 \times 10^{-14}$ | $1.63 \times 10^{-15}$ | $7.29 \times 10^{-15}$ | $4.64 \times 10^{-15}$ |
| [34] | $7.58 \times 10^{-14}$ | $3.90 \times 10^{-14}$ | $1.45 \times 10^{-14}$ | $7.96 \times 10^{-14}$ |
| [36] | $0$ | $1.11 \times 10^{-16}$ | $3.15 \times 10^{-14}$ | $3.23 \times 10^{-14}$ |
| HCFs | $0$ | $2.00 \times 10^{-16}$ | $1.00 \times 10^{-16}$ | $0$ |

*Example 2.* Consider the following FDDEs

$$\begin{cases} D^\alpha q(t) = -q(t - 0.3) - q(t) + e^{-t+0.3}, & 0 \le t \le 1, \quad 2 < \alpha \le 3 \\ q(0) = 1, \quad q'(0) = -1, \quad q''(0) = 1, \\ q(t) = e^{-t}, t < 0. \end{cases}$$

$q(t) = e^{-t}$ that provides an exact solution for the present test problem for $\alpha = 3$. The approximate solutions for several different values of $\alpha$ and the absolute error for $\alpha = 3$ are displayed in Fig. 2, when $M = 8, N = 2$, and $\tau = 0.3$ are the input variables. The approximate solutions obtained by applying the current approach with $\hat{m} = 14$ are displayed in the Table 2. As the fractional-order $\alpha$ approaches 3, these results demonstrate that the approximate solutions converge to the precise solution.

**Table 2.** The approximate solutions for different values of t (Example 2).

| Methods | $t = 0.2$ | $t = 0.4$ | $t = 0.6$ | $t = 0.8$ |
|---------|-----------|-----------|-----------|-----------|
| [35]    | 0.8187    | 0.6703    | 0.5488    | 0.4494    |
| [36]    | 0.8187    | 0.6703    | 0.5488    | 0.4494    |
| [37]    | 0.8187    | 0.6703    | 0.5488    | 0.4493    |
| HCFs    | 0.8187    | 0.6703    | 0.5488    | 0.4494    |

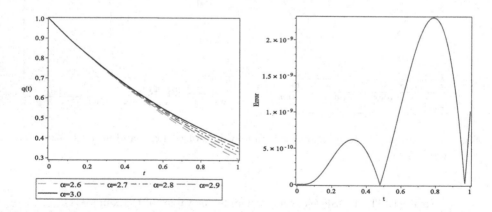

**Fig. 2.** The approximate solution for various values of $\alpha$ (Left) and absolute error for $\alpha = 3$ (Right).

*Example 3.* Consider the following FDDEs

$$\begin{cases} D^\alpha q(t) = 1 - 2 q^2(\frac{1}{2}t), & 0 \le t \le 1, \quad 1 < \alpha \le 2, \\ q(0) = 1, \quad q'(0) = 0. \end{cases}$$

In this example, the exact solution is $q(t) = \cos(t)$ when $\alpha = 2$. The approximate solutions for several different values of $\alpha$ and the absolute error for $\alpha = 2$ are displayed in Fig. 3 for the case when $M = 6$ and $N = 2$. The RMSE is shown for different values of $t$ in Table 3, which uses the current approach and has $\hat{m} = 14$. Based on the information obtained, we can derive the following conclusion: the approximate solution will eventually converge to the exact solution as the fractional order $\alpha$ goes closer and closer to 2.

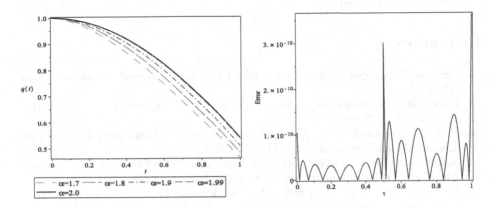

**Fig. 3.** The approximate solution for various values of $\alpha$ (Left) and absolute error for $\alpha = 2$ (Right).

**Table 3.** The RMSE ($\|q - \tilde{q}\|_2$) for different values of t and N (Example 3).

| Methods | $t = 0.2$ | $t = 0.4$ | $t = 0.6$ | $t = 0.8$ |
|---------|-----------|-----------|-----------|-----------|
| [36] | $3.21 \times 10^{-11}$ | $3.81 \times 10^{-11}$ | $1.31 \times 10^{-06}$ | $1.82 \times 10^{-06}$ |
| HCFs | $3.20 \times 10^{-11}$ | $3.81 \times 10^{-11}$ | $8.90 \times 10^{-11}$ | $6.21 \times 10^{-11}$ |

## 6   Conclusion

This research presented a new and effective method for performing the numerical technique on hybrid Chelyshkov orthogonal polynomials. In the HCFs strategy, the operational matrix of fractional integration for HCFs is the first and most significant aspect of solving the system of FDDEs that we experience, as we have seen in Sect. 2, these matrices were derived. To solve FDDEs, these matrices, in addition to the Galerkin method, are utilized. As in the final step of the procedure, the robustness and efficiency of the suggested method are evaluated using some numerical examples of FFDEs.

**Acknowledgment.** Authors Dajana Conte, Leila Moradi, and Beatrice Paternoster are GNCS-INDAM members. This work is supported by the GNCS-INDAM project and by the Italian Ministry University and Research (MUR) through the PRIN 2017 project (No. 2017JYCLSF) Structure preserving approximation of volutionary problems, and the PRIN 2020 project (No. 2020JLWP23) Integrated Mathematical Approaches to SocioEpidemiological Dynamics (CUP: E15F21005420006). The authors would like to thank the anonymous referee who provided useful and detailed comments to improve the quality of the publication.

# References

1. Oldham, K.B., Spanier, J.: The Fractional Calculus. Academic Press, New York (1974)
2. Baillie, R.T.: Long memory processes and fractional integration in econometrics. J. Econ. **73**, 5–59 (1996)
3. Hall, M.G., Barrick, T.R.: From diffusion-weighted MRI to anomalous diffusion imaging. Magn. Reson. Med. **59**, 447–455 (2008)
4. Mandelbrot, B.: Some noises with $\frac{1}{f}$ spectrum, a bridge between direct current and white noise. IEEE Trans. Inform. Theory **13**, 289–298 (1967)
5. Povstenko, Y.Z.: Signaling problem for time-fractional diffusion-wave equation in a half-space in the case of angular symmetry. Nonlinear Dyn. **55**, 593–605 (2010)
6. Engheta, N.: On fractional calculus and fractional multipoles in electromagnetism. IEEE Trans. Antennas Propag. **44**, 554–566 (1996)
7. Oldham, K.B.: Fractional differential equations in electrochemistry. Adv. Eng. Soft. **41**, 9–12 (2010)
8. Lederman, C., Roquejoffre, J.M., Wolanski, N.: Mathematical justification of a nonlinear integrodifferential equation for the propagation of spherical flames. Annali di Matematica **183**, 173–239 (2004)
9. Mainardi, F.: Fractional calculus. In: Carpinteri, A., Mainardi, F. (eds.) Fractals and Fractional Calculus in Continuum Mechanics. ICMS, vol. 378, pp. 291–348. Springer, Vienna (1997). https://doi.org/10.1007/978-3-7091-2664-6_7
10. Rossikhin, Y.A., Shitikova, M.V.: Applications of fractional calculus to dynamic problems of linear and nonlinear hereditary mechanics of solids. Appl. Mech. Rev. **50**, 15–67 (1997)
11. He, J.H.: Some applications of nonlinear fractional differential equations and their approximations. Bull. Sci. Technol. **15**, 86–90 (1999)
12. He, J.H.: Approximate analytical solution for seepage flow with fractional derivatives in porous media. Comput. Methods Appl. Mech. Eng. **167**, 57–68 (1998)
13. Oldham, K., Spanier, J.: The Fractional Calculus Theory and Applications of Differentiation and Integration to Arbitrary Order, vol. 111. Elsevier, Academic Press, New York (1974)
14. Podlubny, I.: Fractional Differential Equations: An Introduction to Fractional Derivatives, Fractional Differential Equations, to Methods of Their Solution And Some of Their Applications, vol. 198. Academic Press, New York (1998)
15. Ockendon, J.R., Tayler, A.B.: The dynamics of a current collection system for an electric locomotive. Proc. R. Soc. Lond. Ser. A **322**, 447–468 (1971)
16. Ajello, W.G., Freedman, H.I., Wu, J.: A model of stage structured population growth with density depended time delay. SIAM J. Appl. Math. **52**, 855–869 (1992)

17. Sedaghat, S., Ordokhani, Y., Dehghan, M.: Numerical solution of the delay differential equations of pantograph type via Chebyshev polynomials. Commun. Nonlinear Sci. Numer. Simul. **17**, 4815–4830 (2012)
18. Tohidi, E., Bhrawy, A.H., Erfani, K.: A collocation method based on Bernoulli operational matrix for numerical solution of generalized pantograph equation. Appl. Math. Model. **37**, 4283–4294 (2012)
19. Yu, Z.H.: Variational iteration method for solving the multi-pantograph delay equation. Phys. Lett. A **372**, 6475–6479 (2008)
20. Wang, W.S., Li, S.F.: On the one-leg $\theta$ method for solving nonlinear neutral functional differential equations. Appl. Math. Comput. **193**, 285–301 (2007)
21. Evans, D.J., Raslan, K.R.: The Adomian decomposition method for solving delay differential equation. Int. J. Comput. Math. **82**, 49–54 (2005)
22. Marzban, H.R., Razzaghi, M.: Solution of multi-delay systems using hybrid of block-pulse functions and Taylor series. Sound Vib. **292**, 954–963 (2006)
23. Sadeghi Hafshejani, M., Karimi Vanani, S., Sedighi Hafshejani, J.: Numerical solution of delay differential equations using Legendre wavelet method. World Appl. Sci. **13**, 27–33 (2011)
24. Saeed, U., Rehman, M.U.: Hermite wavelet method for fractional delay differential equations. J. Diff. Equ. **2014**, 1–8 (2014)
25. Yang, Y., Huang, Y.: Spectral-collocation methods for fractional pantograph delay-integro differential equations. Adv. Math. Phys. **2013**, 1–14 (2013)
26. Khader, M.M., Hendy, A.S.: The approximate and exact solutions of the fractional-order delay differential equations using Legendre seudospectral method. Int. J. Pure Appl. Math. **74**, 287–297 (2012)
27. Wang, Z.: A numerical method for delayed fractional-order differential equations. J. Appl. Math. **2013**, 1–7 (2013)
28. Moghaddam, B.P., Mostaghim, Z.S.: A numerical method based on finite difference for solving fractional delay differential equations. J. Taibah Univ. Sci. **7**, 120–127 (2013)
29. Conte, D., Farsimadan, E., Moradi, L., Palmieri, F., Paternoster, B.: Time-delay fractional optimal control problems: a survey based on methodology. In: Abdel Wahab, M. (ed.) FFW 2020 2020. LNME, pp. 325–337. Springer, Singapore (2021). https://doi.org/10.1007/978-981-15-9893-7_23
30. Moradi, L., Conte, D., Farsimadan, E., Palmieri, F., Paternoster, B.: Optimal control of system governed by nonlinear Volterra integral and fractional derivative equations. Comput. Appl. Math. **40**(4), 1–15 (2021). https://doi.org/10.1007/s40314-021-01541-3
31. Farsimadan, E., Moradi, L., Conte, D., Paternoster, B., Palmieri, F.: Comparison between protein-protein interaction networks $CD4^+T$ and $CD8^+T$ and a numerical approach for fractional HIV infection of $CD4^+T$ cells. In: Gervasi, O., et al. (eds.) ICCSA 2021. LNCS, vol. 12949, pp. 78–94. Springer, Cham (2021). https://doi.org/10.1007/978-3-030-86653-2_6
32. Ibrahim, A.: Numerical simulation of fractional delay differential equations using the operational matrix of fractional integration for fractional-order Taylor basis. Fractal Fractional **6**, 1–10 (2022). https://doi.org/10.3390/fractalfract6010010
33. Singh, H.: Numerical simulation for fractional delay differential equations. Int. J. Dyn. Control **9**(2), 463–474 (2020). https://doi.org/10.1007/s40435-020-00671-6
34. Ali, K.K., El Salam, M.A.A., Mohamed, E.M.: Chebyshev operational matrix for solving fractional order delay-differential equations using spectral collocation method. Arab. J. Basic Appl. Sci. **26**, 342–353 (2019)

35. Srivastava, H.M., Daba, M., Gusu, P.O., Mohammed, G.W., Kamsing, N., Hamed, Y.S.: Solutions of general fractional-order differential equations by using the spectral Tau method. Fractal Fractional **6**, 1–7 (2022). https://doi.org/10.3390/fractalfract6010007
36. Rahimkhani, P., Ordokhani, Y., Babolian, E.: A new operational matrix based on Bernoulli wavelets for solving fractional delay differential equations. Numer. Algorithms **74**(1), 223–245 (2016). https://doi.org/10.1007/s11075-016-0146-3
37. Jing Du, M.: A specific method for solving fractional delay differential equation via fraction Taylor's series. Math. Probl. Eng. **2022**, 1–6 (2022). https://doi.org/10.1155/2022/4044039
38. Samko, S.G., Kilbas, A.A., Marichev, O.I.: Fractional Integrals and Derivatives: Theory and Applications. Gordon and Breach, Langhorne (1993)
39. Chelyshkov, V.S.: Alternative orthogonal polynomials and quadratures. Electron. Trans. Numer. Anal. **25**(7), 17–26 (2006)
40. Mashayekhi, S., Ordokhani, Y., Razzaghi, M.: Hybrid functions approach for nonlinear constrained optimal control problems. Commun. Nonlinear Sci. Numer. Simul. **17**, 1831–1843 (2012)

# Full Waveform Inversion of the Scattered Component of the Wavefield: Resolution Analysis

Kirill Gadylshin[✉] and Maxim Protasov

Institute of Petroleum Geology and Geophysics, SB RAS, Novosibirsk, Russia
GadylshinKG@ipgg.sbras.ru

**Abstract.** The paper considers the influence of the scattered component of the wavefield on the full waveform inversion results. Utilizing the one step of the quasi-Newton method, we demonstrate that scattered wavefields bring helpful information in the context of the solution of the inverse dynamical problem. Theoretically, usage of the scattered waves should increase the resolution of the method. For different scenarios, the contribution of scattered waves is investigated numerically. We investigate the influence of scattered components only by using singular value decomposition of the linearized inverse problem operator. The numerical experiments are performed for the well-known Marmousi2 model.

**Keywords:** Scattering · FWI · SVD · Hessian pseudo-inversion

## 1 Introduction

The solution to an inverse dynamic seismic problem, the purpose of which is to restore the parameters of a geological section from a complete set of recorded seismograms, has long attracted the attention of researchers. In the mid-1980s, a practical approach to solving the inverse dynamic problem was proposed [1, 2]. The inverse problem was posed as the problem of minimizing the target functional characterizing (in a particular norm) the discrepancies of seismograms recorded in the field and synthetic ones, i.e., calculated seismograms. Synthetic seismograms are computed using some algorithm for modeling waveforms within the framework of the selected mathematical model, which describes the physical processes of seismic wave propagation in the medium with varying degrees of certainty. The appearance of the first works on this topic caused great enthusiasm among seismic prospectors. The term "Full Waveform Inversion" (FWI) was firmly entrenched in the professional community, which in the mathematical sense implies the solution of the inverse dynamic seismic problem.

FWI is a procedure for constructing high-resolution deep velocity models [3]. It is based on fitting the modeled seismic data with the raw field data by introducing a misfit functional with the subsequent application of local optimization

Supported by RSF grant 21-71-20002.

O. Gervasi et al. (Eds.): ICCSA 2022, LNCS 13375, pp. 143–157, 2022.
https://doi.org/10.1007/978-3-031-10522-7_11

techniques. The algorithm starts with the best guess of the subsurface Earth model, which is then enhanced using the iterations of linearized local inversion for solving a nonlinear problem [4].

Experiments on real seismic data have shown that FWI does not achieve satisfactory results without setting an excellent initial medium model. It was shown that the initial model should correctly describe the behavior of the low-frequency (in space) components of the characteristics of the geological section, the so-called macro velocity model of the medium, which represents the propagation times of waves. Thus, a paradox arose since the macro model is of the most significant interest for constructing deep seismological sections, and it was the most challenging part of the inverse problem. The first reason was the absence in the recorded data of low frequencies (<7–10 Hz), which are most sensitive to disturbances of the macro model. This limitation was caused by the technical characteristics of the seismic data acquisition equipment that existed at that time. Currently, the acquisition tools allow to quite confidently register the low-frequency component of useful signals starting 3 Hz. The second reason, which is a consequence of the first, is the low sensitivity of the high-frequency components of the spectrum of the reflected wavefield to smooth variations in the velocity model of the medium. It was shown in [5, 6] that the use of refracted waves makes it possible to significantly increase the sensitivity of the misfit functional to the macro velocity model and thereby fill in the missing information about the low-frequency component.

With standard seismic data processing, the obtained depth-velocity model focuses on the qualitative result of the migration of reflected waves. At the same time, the image result of scattered waves in such a model is not sufficiently focused. Therefore, to improve the quality of diffraction images, it is necessary to refine the migration model for which FWI is supposed to be used.

Theoretically [7], the resolution of the method when using scattered waves should be higher. In recent work [8], using a simple model example, it was shown that diffracted waves increase the resolution of the method. However, the influence of the scattered component of the wavefield on the inversion result has been poorly studied. In this work, we aim to assess the influence of the scattered component of the full waveform on the quality of the inverse dynamic problem solution.

## 2   Method

We assume that the wave process under study is described by the scalar Helmholtz Eq. (1) for a two-dimensionally inhomogeneous medium. Let $c(x, z)$ be the wave propagation speed in a two-dimensional medium. In what follows, it will be convenient to use the value $m = c^{-2}(x, z)$ (the squared slowness) for the solution of the inverse problem. We will call $m$ a model and write $m \in M$, meaning by $M$ some space of models. Let the function $u(x, z; \omega)$ (full waveform in the time-frequency domain) satisfy the Helmholtz equation:

$$(\Delta + \omega^2 m)u = -f, \tag{1}$$

with the right-hand side $f(x, z)$ and angular frequency $\omega$. The principle of limiting absorption determines the behavior at infinity of this solution:

$$u = \lim_{s \to +0} u_s;$$

$$(\Delta + (\omega + i\epsilon)^2 \, m) u_s = -g; \tag{2}$$

$$u_s \to 0, \quad \sqrt{x^2 + z^2} \to \infty.$$

By operator of the forward problem $\mathcal{F}_f(m; \omega)$ we mean a mapping that assigns a function $m(x, z)$ to a solution of Eq. (1). When the right-hand side of this equation has the form $g(x, z; \omega) = f(\omega)\delta(x - x_s)\delta(z - z_s)$, the corresponding operator will be denoted by $\mathcal{F}_{x_s}(m; \omega)$. One should note that the result of the action of this operator coincides with the product of the spectral characteristic of source signature $f(\omega)$ and the Green's function $G(x, x_s, z, z_s; m; \omega)$. The waveform in the time-frequency domain is a complex function of the position of the point $(x, z)$ and the frequency $\omega$. The inverse problem is to determine the velocity model of the medium from the wavefield recorded at a finite number of points in $R^2$ where the geophones are located. Let us introduce a linear operator that calculated the trace of the full wavefield from one point source for a fixed time frequency at the points corresponding to the location of the receivers:

$$P : U \to C^{NR}, \tag{3}$$

where $NR$ is the number of receivers. If all $NS$ sources with coordinates $(x_i, z_i)$ are used, then the data space for each of them at a fixed frequency $\omega_j$ is determined by the action of the following operator, which transfers an element m from the model space to a vector from the space $C^{NR}$:

$$F_i^j(m) = P \cdot \mathcal{F}_{x_i}(m; \omega_j). \tag{4}$$

In what follows, we will also use a compact notation:

$$F(m) = \begin{pmatrix} F^1(m) \\ \vdots \\ F^{NF}(m) \end{pmatrix}, \tag{5}$$

where $F^j : M \to C^{NS \times NR}$ such that:

$$F^j(m) = \begin{pmatrix} F_1^j(m) \\ \vdots \\ F_{NS}^1(m) \end{pmatrix}. \tag{6}$$

Finally, we obtain the following forward modeling operator:

$$F : M \to D, \tag{7}$$

where the data space $D = C^{Nf \times NS \times NR}$. In this notation, the inverse dynamical problem of constructing a velocity model from seismic data is reduced to solving a nonlinear operator equation:

$$d^{obs} = F(m_{true}), \tag{8}$$

here $d^{obs}$ – is the observed data and $m_{true}$ – the "true" velocity model. The Full Waveform Inversion (FWI) applies a nonlinear least-squares method to Eq. (8). The general FWI formulation is to find the minimum point of the misfit functional characterizing the mean square deviation of the recorder data from those calculated for the current velocity model:

$$m_* = arg(\min_{m \in M} ||F(m) - d||_D^2). \tag{9}$$

## 3  Numerical Experiments

### 3.1  Marmousi2 Synthetic Model

We carry out all considerations using the synthetic velocity model shown in Fig. 1: a modified Marmousi2 $P$-wave velocity model [9]. We perform the seismic full waveform modeling using the finite-difference solver in the time-frequency domain for Eq. (1) for the following source-receiver acquisition geometry: 320 volumetric point sources were at line $z = 0$ m starting at $x = 500$ m with equal step 50 m. We use the geometry of the receiver (one measures the pressure) with a regular step of 25 m, and the maximum source-receiver offset equals 6000 m. For forward modeling, we exclude all effects associated with the presence of multiple waves caused by a free surface in the medium by introducing the absorbing layers around the numerical domain [10].

### 3.2  Diffraction FWI Resolution Analysis

Let us introduce the following notation:

- $m^*$ – is the Marmousi2 model after addition the depth point diffractors (Fig. 2 A);
- $m_0$ – is the starting model for the inversion (Fig. 2 B);
- $dm1$ – is the desired velocity perturbation we wish to recover using FWI (Fig. 2 C);
- $dm_{diff}$ – are depth point diffractors (Fig. 2 D).

In this notation, the full model $m^*$ is represented as follows:

$$m^* = m_0 + dm1 + dm_{diff}. \tag{10}$$

Consider the original statement of the inverse dynamic seismic problem $d^{obs} = F(m_{true})$. Using the notation introduced above, we have:

$$d^{obs} = F(m^*) = F(m_0 + dm1 + dm_{diff}) =$$
$$F(m_0 + dm_{diff}) + \frac{\delta F}{\delta m}(m_0 + dm_{diff})dm1 +$$
$$o(||dm1||_M) =$$
$$F(m_0) + \frac{\delta F}{\delta m}(m_0)dm_{diff} + \frac{\delta F}{\delta m}(m_0 + dm_{diff})dm1 +$$
$$o(||dm1||_M) + o(||dm_{diff}||_M).$$

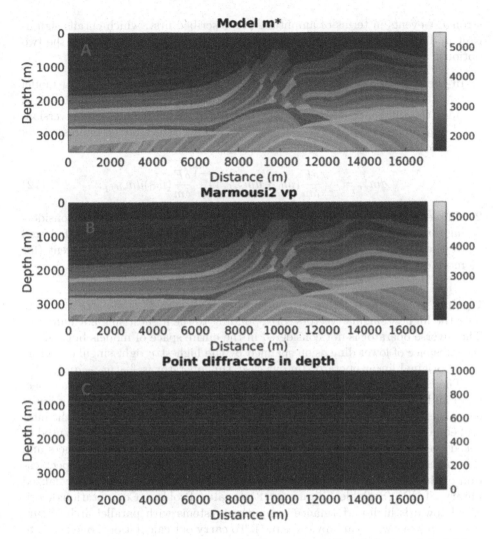

**Fig. 1.** The model Marmousi2 with point diffractors at 3100 m (A), the original Marmousi2 model (B), and the difference between (A) and (B).

The last expression can be rewritten as:

$$\frac{\delta F}{\delta m}(m_0 + dm_{diff})dm1 \approx d^{obs} - F(m_0) - \frac{\delta F}{\delta m}(m_0)dm_{diff}. \qquad (11)$$

Based on this expression, there is a clear connection between the model perturbation and the corresponding perturbation in the data. The scattered component of the wavefield associated with the presence of deep point diffractors (3100 m) is a very small order of magnitude (the norm $\|dm_{diff}\|_M$ is an order of magnitude smaller than the norm of the desired perturbation $\|dm1\|_M$). This explains such behavior of the FWI procedure in the standard formulation. The strongest events in terms of amplitude are described first, which entails significant updates to the velocity model. How can this be bypassed? We see the two options:

1. In the first option all considerations are carried out for the starting model $m_0$. It is proposed in formula (11) to neglect intense events on the right side (the difference $d^{obs} - F(m_0)$), and try to make a linearized inversion: $\frac{\delta F}{\delta m}(m_0 + dm_{diff})dm1 = -\frac{\delta F}{\delta m}(m_0)dm_{diff}$ The latter can be expressed via regularized solution ($r$-Solution, see [12]):

$$dm1_r = -\left(\frac{\delta F}{\delta m}(m_0 + dm_{diff})\right)_r^{-1} \frac{\delta F}{\delta m}(m_0)dm_{diff}. \qquad (12)$$

2. The second option inspires more confidence in success. It is based on considering an approximate calculation of the Hessian, its pseudo-inversion, followed by the action on the gradient, built only on the diffraction component (for more details, see below).

**Option 1.** To construct an $r$-pseudoinverse operator, it suffices to calculate only the highest singular vectors corresponding to the highest singular numbers. The inverse operator is not considered in the entire space of models but only in the subspace of lower dimension spanned by the highest $r$ right singular vectors of the original linear operator (in our case, this operator is $\frac{\delta F}{\delta m}(m_0 + dm_{diff})$).

The choice of the parameter $r$ depends on the behavior of the singular spectrum and the condition number of the corresponding truncated system of linear equations obtained after performing a finite-difference approximation of the integral equation of the first kind (see [14]). An iterative Arnoldi method was used to speed up numerical calculations to construct the highest singular numbers and the corresponding singular vectors, which does not require an explicit specification of the matrix [15]. Its implementation was performed using the specialized library SLEPc (Scalable Library for Eigenvalue Problem Computations), oriented towards high-performance computing systems with parallel architecture (see: http://www.grycap.upv.es/slepc/). To carry out calculations, one needs to set the parameter $r$, i.e., the dimension of stable space, and have a subroutine that calculates the action of a matrix on an arbitrary vector. Such a subroutine was created based on a finite-difference solution of the Helmholtz equation. In this case, an LU-decomposition of the matrix is constructed for each frequency from a given range. The matrix is determined by a finite-dimensional approximation of the Helmholtz operator. After obtaining the LU-factors for all frequencies, the iterative finding of eigenvectors is reduced to a specific set of forward and backward substitutions. Now let us return to the parameters of the numerical experiment. Since the calculation of singular value decomposition (SVD) is a very resource-intensive task, and on most computing clusters, the calculation time is limited to 24 h, it is necessary to choose the calculation parameters carefully. By running a series of test runs (trial and error), we settled on the following parameters:

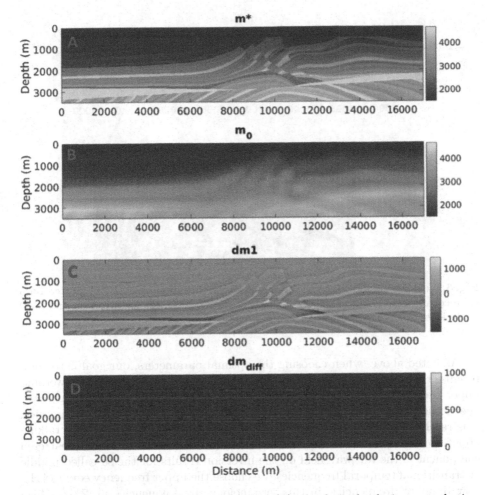

**Fig. 2.** Velocity model $m^*$ (A), starting model (B), the desired velocity perturbation (C), and depth point diffractors (D).

- calculation grid with steps $dx = dz = 15$ m;
- the target area has a size of $147 \times 400$ pixels (see Fig. 3);
- the step by sources had to be thinned and made equal to $100$ m (total $160$ sources of the expansion point type);
- the number of frequencies for an inversion - 4: $\{5, 7, 10, 14\}$ Hz (what causes this choice, we will describe below).

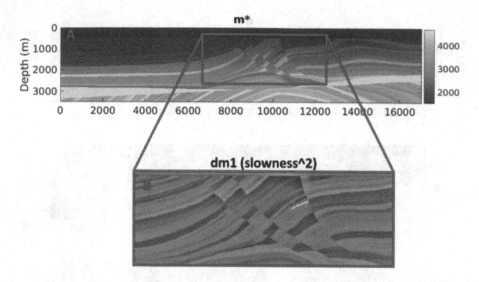

**Fig. 3.** Velocity model $m^*$ (A). The unknown perturbation $dm1$ (B) is plotted on a scale corresponding to the square of slowness. The target area for inversion and SVD analysis is depicted in red. (Color figure online)

As noted above, when choosing the optimal parameters, our goal is to compromise the resolution of the problem and the computation time. The lower and upper timing frequencies 5 Hz and 14 Hz, respectively. The choice of the lower one is due to strict requirements for the quality of input data – in practice, it is rarely possible to find informative frequencies 5 Hz, even if we are talking about marine data. Since we plan to investigate the influence of the scattered component of the full wavefield on the inversion results for the so-called middle or transitional temporal frequencies, we choose the upper frequency equal 14 Hz. Low temporal frequencies, in this terminology, are frequencies up 2 Hz, which are necessary for the stable reconstruction of a smooth model or a model that is kinematically equivalent to the true one. Our starting model is good enough not to need the lower time frequencies in this experiment. High frequencies are the frequencies responsible mainly for the reflected component of the wavefield. The choice of the target area is because this part of the model is complex and is of the greatest interest for inversion (Fig. 3). It is also worth noting that we get a complete observation system with this choice of the target area (there are no edge effects associated with poor illumination).

A source step of 100 m is sufficient for the inversion, at least for a qualitative assessment of the result. By choosing a step of 100 m instead of 50 m, forward and backward substitutions are sped up by about two times. As a result, the entire SVD calculation time is sped up by two times. Let us describe in more detail the choice of time frequencies for inversion. On the one hand, each temporal frequency is considered independently and in parallel, and the calculation of the action of the matrix on the vector should not change significantly. The more

time frequencies we consider, the slower the singular spectrum of the operator
decreases (the same one can say about the number of sources, the fewer there
are, the faster the spectrum decreases, but this dependence is not linear). The
optimal set of frequencies will be carried out following the work [16]. For our
observation system, the maximum offset is 6000 m, while the depth of the target
area is less than 3000 m. Therefore $\alpha_{min} = \frac{1}{\sqrt{2}}$, $f_0 = 5$ Hz, $f_1 = \frac{f_0}{\alpha_{min}} \approx 7$ Hz,
$f_2 = \frac{f_1}{\alpha_{min}} \approx 10$ Hz, and $f_3 = \frac{f_2}{\alpha_{min}} \approx 14$ Hz. It is argued that this choice of
temporal frequencies provides continuous coverage of spatial frequencies in the
reconstructed model during FWI in the range [5, 14] Hz for a given observation
system.

Singular spectra (first 768 values) for operators $\frac{\delta F}{\delta m}(m_0 + dm_{diff})$ and $\frac{\delta F}{\delta m}(m_0)$
are presented in Fig. 4.

As one may observe, they are almost indistinguishable. If we take the ratio
of these values (Fig. 4 C), we can see that this value is nearly equal to 1. From
this, we can conclude that these operators are almost indistinguishable from
solving the inverse problem. In confirmation of this, we present several random
comparisons of the right singular vectors of these operators corresponding to the
same singular numbers. Such a comparison is shown in Fig. 5.

**Option 2.** Consider the objective function of the standard FWI method:

$$E(m) = \|F(m) - d^{obs}\|_D^2. \tag{13}$$

Assume that we have the operator for extracting the scattered component of the
wavefield:

$$P_{diff} : D \to D, \tag{14}$$

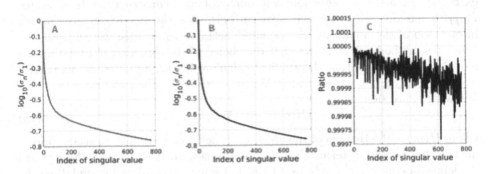

**Fig. 4.** Singular spectrum of $\frac{\delta F}{\delta m}(m_0)$ operator (A), $\frac{\delta F}{\delta m}(m_0 + dm_{diff})$ operator (B),
and their ratio (C).

for simplicity, we assume that this operator is linear and self-adjoint. Then the changed formulation of the FWI oriented on the use of the scattered component have the following objective function:

$$\widetilde{E}(m) = \|P_{diff}F(m) - P_{diff}d^{obs}\|_D^2. \tag{15}$$

Then the modified objective functional gradient $\nabla \widetilde{E}(m)$ will take the form:

$$\nabla \widetilde{E}(m) = -Re\left(\frac{\delta F}{\delta m}^*(m)P_{diff}^*\Delta d\right), \tag{16}$$

where $\Delta d = P_{diff}F(m) - P_{diff}d^{obs}$. Under our assumption that $P_{diff}$ is linear and self-adjoint, finally (16) will take the form:

$$\nabla \widetilde{E}(m) = -Re\left(\frac{\delta F}{\delta m}^*(m)(P_{diff}F(m) - P_{diff}d^{obs})\right). \tag{17}$$

We have carried out two numerical experiments. In each experiment, we assumed that the correct velocity model was obtained by adding a finite number of point diffractors (Figs. 6 C, 6 D) to the model shown in Fig. 6 A. Thus, the scattered component of the full waveform is the difference between the solutions of the wave equation calculated in the model with diffractors and in the model without them (see Fig. 7). In terms of solving the inverse problem, we can assume that at the first step of inversion, the residual $P_{diff}F(m) - P_{diff}d^{obs}$ is built without any explicit statement of the operator. Indeed, we have no point diffractors in the starting model, therefore $P_{diff}F(m_0) = 0$. $P_{diff}d^{obs}$ could be obtained as follows: $P_{diff}d^{obs} = F(m_0 + dm1 + dm_{diff}) - F(m_0 + dm1)$ since this difference is due only to the presence of the point diffractors. It is worth noting here that after the first inversion step, it will no longer be possible to extract the scattered component without explicitly constructing the operator $P_{diff}$. Therefore, we will concentrate on obtaining the maximum information in one step of the nonlinear least-squares method. To do this, we will resort to Newton's method, which states that the choice of the direction of updating the model should be such that the gradient calculated in the updated model is zero, we have reached the extreme value: $\nabla \widetilde{E}(m + dm) = 0$. The last brings us to the following expression:

$$H(m)dm = -\nabla \widetilde{E}(m), \tag{18}$$

where $H(m)$ is the Hessian of the objective functional (15). The Hessian approximation by neglecting terms that include the second derivative of the forward modeling operator [13] leads us to the following expression for updating the model:

$$dm_r = -\left(\frac{\delta F}{\delta m}(m)\frac{\delta F}{\delta m}^*(m)\right)_r^{-1}\nabla \widetilde{E}(m) \tag{19}$$

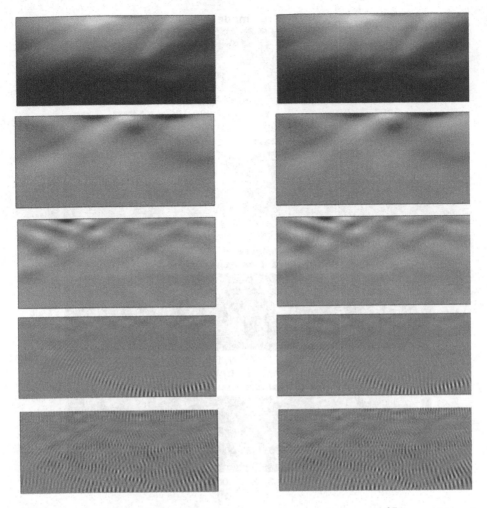

**Fig. 5.** The comparison of the right singular vectors of the operator $\frac{\delta F}{\delta m}(m_0 + dm_{diff})$ – left column, and $\frac{\delta F}{\delta m}(m_0)$ – right column. From top to bottom, different random indexes of the corresponding singular vectors.

here $-\left(\frac{\delta F}{\delta m}(m)\frac{\delta F}{\delta m}^*(m)\right)_r^{-1}$ $r$-pseudoinverse operator, whose action we will calculate through the singular value decomposition of the first Fréchet derivative $\frac{\delta F}{\delta m}(m)$ [14].

The solution to the inverse problem within the framework of the modified Newton method was constructed for a group of time frequencies [5, 7, 10, 14] Hz. The parametrization of the velocity model is the value equal to the square of the slowness. In the first experiment, the effect of only depth point diffractors was investigated (Fig. 6 C). In contrast, point scatterers were added to the entire model (except for the upper 500 m thick water layer). The models restored by

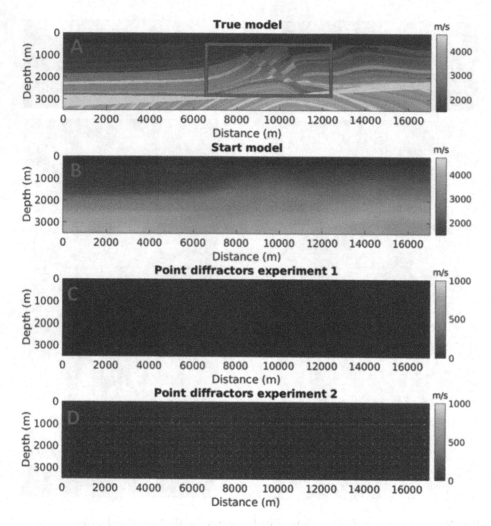

**Fig. 6.** The Marmousi2 velocity model (A), the starting model for performing the FWI (B), and two scenarios for point diffractors locations: depth point diffractors at the depth 3100 m (C) and uniformly spaced point diffractors throughout the velocity model (D). The target area for the inversion is shown as a red rectangle. (Color figure online)

formula (19) are shown in Fig. 8. As can be seen, even involving only the scattered component in the inversion process carries information about the structure of the medium. When one uses only depth point diffractors the result has a poor resolution. While using a larger number of scatterers increases the quality of the solution to the inverse problem.

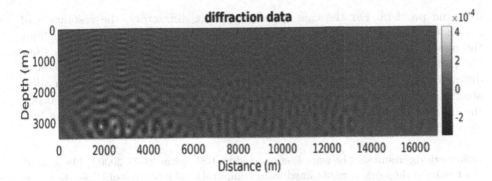

**Fig. 7.** Scattered component of the full wavefield for a frequency 10 Hz in the modified Marmousi2 model, associated with the presence of point diffractors located at a depth of 3100 m (see Fig. 5C). The source is located at the point x = 2800 m.

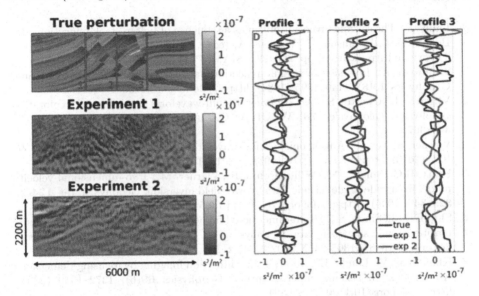

**Fig. 8.** Desired perturbation of the model (A), inversion results for Experiment 1 (B) and Experiment 2 (C). On the right (D), vertical profiles are shown corresponding to the positions marked with red lines on the graph on the left (A): black is the desired perturbation, blue and red are the reconstructed perturbations in experiments 1 and 2, respectively. (Color figure online)

## 4    Conclusions

The influence of the scattered component on the results of the FWI method has been studied. We enhance the inversion workflow by incorporating the $r$-pseudo-inverse approximate Hessian operator into the inversion process. We investigate one step of the nonlinear least-squares method. For two inversion scenarios, we demonstrate the contribution of scattered waves to the solution of the inverse dynamic problem. For the case with deep point diffractors, the resolution of the method is low. When point scatterers are evenly distributed throughout the model, the resolution of the method increases. The last experiments show the possibility of improving the velocity model via full-waveform inversion of diffracted/scattered waves. Finally, we conclude one needs to construct an operator to extract the scattered component of the wavefield and enforce it inside the nonlinear inversion iteration process to provide an algorithm for the full-waveform inversion of diffracted/scattered waves.

**Acknowledgements.** The work is supported by RSF grant 21-71-20002. The numerical results of the work were obtained using computational resources of Peter the Great Saint-Petersburg Polytechnic University Supercomputing Center (scc.spbstu.ru).

# References

1. Lailly, P.: The seismic inverse problem as a sequence of before stack migrations. In: Bednar, J.B., Robinson, E., Weglein, A. (eds.) Conference on Inverse Scattering-Theory and Application, pp. 206–220. SIAM, Philadelphia (1983)
2. Tarantola, A.: Inversion of seismic reflection data in the acoustic approximation. Geophysics **49**(8), 1140–1395 (1984). https://doi.org/10.1190/1.1441754
3. Virieux, J., Operto, S.: An overview of full-waveform inversion in exploration geophysics. Geophysics **78**, WCC1–WCC26 (2009). https://doi.org/10.1190/1.3238367
4. Warner, M., et al.: Anisotropic 3D full-waveform inversion. Geophysics **78**, R59–R80 (2013). https://doi.org/10.1190/geo2012-0338.1
5. Pratt, R.G., Song, Z.M., Williamson, P.R., Warner, M.: Two-dimensional velocity model from wide-angle seismic data by wavefield inversion. Geophys. J. Int. **124**(2), 323–340 (1996). https://doi.org/10.1111/j.1365-246X.1996.tb07023.x
6. Shipp, R.M., Singh, S.C.: Two-dimensional full wavefield inversion of wide-aperture marine seismic streamer data. Geophys. J. Int. **151**(2), 325–344 (2002). https://doi.org/10.1046/j.1365-246X.2002.01645.x
7. Khaidukov, V., Landa, E., Moser, T.J.: Diffraction imaging by focusing-defocusing: An outlook on seismic superresolution. Geophysics **69**(6), 1372–1570 (2004). https://doi.org/10.1190/1.1836821
8. Dell, S., Abakumov, I., Znak, P., Gajewski, D., Kashtan, B., Ponomarenko, A.: On the role of diffractions in velocity model building: a full-waveform inversion example. Stud. Geophys. Geod. **63**(4), 538–553 (2019). https://doi.org/10.1007/s11200-019-0733-6
9. Martin, G.S., Wiley, R., Marfurt, K.J.: Marmousi2: an elastic upgrade for Marmousi. Lead. Edge **25**(2), 156–166 (2006). https://doi.org/10.1190/1.2172306
10. Grote, M., Sim, I. : Efficient PML for the wave equation. Report arXiv:1001.0319 (2010). https://arxiv.org/abs/1001.0319
11. Protasov, M., Tcheverda, V.: True/preserving amplitude seismic imaging based on Gaussian beams application. In: SEG Technical Program Expanded Abstracts 2006, pp. 2126–2130 (2006). https://doi.org/10.1190/1.2369957
12. Cheverda, V.A., Kostin, V.I.: R-pseudoinverses for compact operators in Hilbert spaces: existence and stability. J. Inverse Ill-Posed Probl. **3**(2), 131–148 (1995). https://doi.org/10.1515/jiip.1995.3.2.131

13. Pratt, R.G., Shin, Ch., Hick, G.J.: Gauss-Newton and full Newton methods in frequency-space seismic waveform inversion. Geophys. J. Int. **133**(2), 341–362 (1998). https://doi.org/10.1046/j.1365-246X.1998.00498.x
14. Gadylshin, K., Bakulin, A., Dmitriev, M., Golikov, P., Neklyudov, D., Tcheverda, V.: Effect of free-surface related multiples on near surface velocity reconstruction with acoustic frequency domain. In: Proceedings 76th EAGE Conference and Exhibition 2014, LNCS, vol. 2014, pp. 1–5. European Association of Geoscientists & Engineers (2014). https://doi.org/10.3997/2214-4609.20141410
15. Hernandez, V., Roman, J.E., Tomas, A.: Parallel Arnoldi Eigensolvers with enhanced scalability via global communications rearrangement. Parallel Comput. **33**(7–8), 521–540 (2007). https://doi.org/10.1016/j.parco.2007.04.004
16. Sirgue, L., Pratt, R.G.: Efficient waveform inversion and imaging: a strategy for selecting temporal frequencies. Geophysics **69**(1), 231–248 (2004). https://doi.org/10.1190/1.1649391

# Differential Kinematics
# of a Multisection–Robot

Fabian C. Castro[1]([✉]), Nicolás J. Walteros Vergara[2], Cesar A. Cardenas[1],
Juan C. Amaya[1], Emiro-De-la-Hoz-Franco[3], Paola A. Colpas[3],
and Carlos A. Collazos[1]([✉])

[1] Vicerrectoria de investigación, Universidad Manuela Beltrán, Bogotá, Colombia
{fabian.castro,carlos.collazos}@docentes.umb.edu.co
[2] Departamento de matematicas, Universidad Distrital, Bogotá, Colombia
[3] Departamento de Ciencias de la Computación y Electrónica, Universidad de la
Costa, Barranquilla, Colombia

**Abstract.** The multi-section robots also  called variable geometry
robots (VGT), are formed by different modules and have multiple degrees
of freedom (DOF); These robots are a new class that can be defined as
systems adaptable to different environments, unlike conventional robots,
multi-section robots allow greater flexibility and adaptability to carry out
tasks with restricted space conditions, their locomotion has a high degree
of manipulation and dexterity in environments with difficult access and
very closed spaces where maneuverability must be high, these characteristics are very similar to those exhibited by the movements of snakes,
elephant trunks, and octopus tentacles, capabilities beyond them reach
of traditional handlers of rigid link, multi-link robots can adapt their
shape to navigate through complex environments. In this work, we show
the implementation of the Lie Matrix Theory of the rigid movements
of a body in a multi-link Robot so that through kinematics and with
the planning of trajectories through third-order polynomials this resem-
bles curves smoothed by Bezier to generate different deformations in the
robot in such a way that its movements elude obstacles in a given one
within the workspace. The developed algorithm was implemented on a
simulated virtual platform in a robotics environment. The motivation
of the work was to be able to demonstrate a planning of robot trajectories with multiple degrees of freedom using deterministic algorithms
and not focused on computational intelligence such as neural networks
or reinforced learning.

**Keywords:** Multi-section robot · Screw transformation · Path
planning · Curvature discretization

## 1 Introduction

In recent years, a growing interest in bio-inspired robotics has emerged, currently
great advances have been made in numerous applications at an industrial level

O. Gervasi et al. (Eds.): ICCSA 2022, LNCS 13375, pp. 158–172, 2022.
https://doi.org/10.1007/978-3-031-10522-7_12

and in the field of medicine, continuous and multi section robots inspired by biological tubes, tentacles and snakes, can vary Its curvature, a feature called VGT (Variable Geometry Truss), has recently seen an increase in efforts aimed at taking advantage of these qualities to improve frontiers in the field of medicine mainly in minimally invasive surgical interventions. Several designs have now been commercialized, which are inspiring and allow a traditional change from the traditional robot that is in greater demand in today's market, however surgical approaches towards flexible access routes, for example, through natural orifices such as the nose, where The multi-section robots can easily access.

The main objective of this work is to introduce some mathematical - analytical concepts applied to model the kinematics of a particular case of Multisection Robot and a simulation that involves the ROS, MATLAB and GAZEBO computational environments, in such a way as to show the advantages of the implemented mathematical model. and visualize in 3d a construction of a robot with 20 cylindrical links 15 cm long and 1.5 cm in diameter with ball-type joints.

Exponential and its multiplications can parameters angles present in each joint of the device of this paper, the design here has a nice approach taking into account product of $4 \times 4$ square matrices at most. Bezier curves and splines are introduced to describe paths in the Multi section-Robot.

## 2   Rigid Body Movements

Rigid motions in the space are modeled in a efficient way using *Twist theory*. An affiance map $T : \mathbb{R}^3 \to \mathbb{R}^3$ is called a *Rigid motion* if: (1) preserve distances, and (2) preserve orientations (in the sense that, the map $T$ preserves cross product [1,2]. Given $O$ a non-empty subset of the space $\mathbb{R}^3$, the set of all rigid motions restricted on $O$ are rotations followed by translations such that conforms the 6-dimensional Lie group: *the 3-Special Euclidean group* SE(3), where its Lie algebra vectors are named *Twists*. Let SO(3) the Lie group of rotations that preserve lengths in $\mathbb{R}^3$ named 3-*Special Orthogonal group*, *Chasles' theorem* means that all rigid motions can be viewed like a composition between a rotation and a translation about a fixed axis, hence, in symbols, the 3-Special Euclidean group is the semi direct product [3]

$$SE(3) = SO(3) \times R^3.$$

### 2.1   Twists Lie's Theory

Is straightforward that, each element of SO(3) is a rigid motion in the space. An important strategy here is introducing all element of SO(3) by pick a rotation axis and a measure of an angle. To give an adequate usage for coordinates, the first one step is fix an inertial frame and next, fix other positive oriented reference system about the rigid body with an axis parallel to the rotation axis, where, if $p$ is an arbitrary point of a rigid body $O$ rotated since a point $p(0)$ by a matrix $R_{IO}$, suppose $p_I$ the coordinates of the point $p$ respect to the inertial frame and

$p_O$ the coordinates of $p$ respect to the body frame [4]. The relation between the coordinates are given by the following formula

$$p_I = R_{IO}p_O.$$

Let $\mathfrak{so}(3)$ the Lie algebra of $SO(3)$ which is re presentable by the skew-symmetric matrices with Lie bracket the commutator such that is isomorphic to the natural Lie algebra structure of $\mathbb{R}^3$ with cross product operation. An identification Isomorphic between the Lie's algebras $\mathbb{R}^3$ and $\mathfrak{so}(3)$ is given in the following way

$$w := \begin{pmatrix} w_1 \\ w_2 \\ w_3 \end{pmatrix} \to \hat{w} := \begin{bmatrix} 0 & -w_3 & w_2 \\ w_3 & 0 & -w_1 \\ -w_2 & w_1 & 0 \end{bmatrix} \tag{1}$$

Also, for each pair $\omega = [\omega_1, \omega_2, \omega_3]^T$ and $\nu = [\nu_1, \nu_2, \nu_3]^T$ then $\omega \times \nu = \hat{\omega}\nu$. In all cases, $\omega \in \mathfrak{so}(3)$ will give the direction of a rotation fixing a measure of an angle, choosing $|\omega| = 1$ by the magnitude of angular spatial velocity, *Rodrigues' formula* says that the relation

$$e^{\hat{\omega}\theta} = I + \sin\theta\hat{\omega} + (1 - \cos\theta)\hat{\omega}^2 \tag{2}$$

gives rotations around the axis described by $\hat{\omega}$ with a measure $\theta$, indeed; giving an arbitrary point $p = p(0)$ in a rigid body $O$ and a parametrization for determinate rotation of $t$ radians, is generated the following differential equation

$$\dot{p}(t) = \hat{\omega}p(t) \tag{3}$$

where, the solution is given by $p(t) = e^{\hat{\omega}t}p(0)$ (here, $\omega \times p(t) = \hat{\omega}p(t)$). Because exponential map $\exp : \mathfrak{so}(3) \to SO(3)$ is surjective [2,9] all rotation matrix is the exponential of a skew-symmetric matrix.

Onwards, we denote the Lie algebra of $SE(3)$ by $\mathfrak{se}(3)$. Twists give a way to parametrize motions of the joints in the Multi–section Robot of this paper (our Robot are a set of links and joints that form a kinematical chain: an assembly of rigid bodies connected by joints to provide motion that is the mathematical model for the mechanical system). Robot modeled here looks like a hypnotized cobra that eludes obstacles by motions of its links product of setting adequate configurations of its joints.

## 2.2   Screw Theory

One of the multiple ways to introduce twists is representing elements by matrices $6 \times 1$ in the form $\left[v^T, \omega^T\right]^T$, where $v$ denotes linear velocity and $\omega$ spatial angular velocity. Another way consists in the following, let $\omega \in \mathbb{R}^3$ the vector that describes the direction of the axis of rotation with $|\omega| = 1$, and $q \in \mathbb{R}^3$ a point on the axis [5]. Assuming that the link rotates with unit velocity, then the velocity of a point $p(t)$ in a rigid body $O$, is

$$\dot{p}(t) = \omega \times (p(t) - q). \tag{4}$$

This equation allows representing each element $\xi \in \mathfrak{so}(3)$ in homogeneous coordinates by defining the $4 \times 4$ matrix

$$\hat{\xi} := \begin{bmatrix} \hat{w} & v \\ 0 & 0 \end{bmatrix} \tag{5}$$

where $v = -\omega \times q$. Since that the exponential map $\exp : \mathfrak{se}(3) \to \mathrm{SE}(3)$ can work in matricial sense by the information given above, $e^{\hat{\xi}\theta} \in \mathrm{SE}(3)$ produces rotations followed by translations in both cases of magnitude $\theta$ radians (translations parallel to the rotation axis scaled by $\omega$), *Chasles' theorem* says that, *all rigid motion can split by a rotation following by a translation*. There are available computational advantages by using in this way twist's techniques, as optimize the computational cost in contrast to *Denavid–Hatenberg's Algorithm*.

A geometric approach to twists is given by *Screws*. A *Screw* is a triple $(l, h, \theta)$ where $l$ denotes an axis, $h$ the pitch, and $\theta$ the magnitude of angle around of $l$. A screw motion represents a rigid bdy motion by a magnitude of rotation about the axis $l$ followed by translation by an amount $h\theta$ parallel to the axis $l$. If $h = \infty$ then the corresponding screw motion consists of a pure translation along the axis of the screw by a distance $\theta$. In other words, in the case that the pitch $h < \infty$ the motion of rotation and translation (could be a pure rotation around the axis when $h = 0$) is named *finite*. When $h = \infty$ the motion is named *infinite* or *prismatic*. Other important facts about Screws are: (1) Rigid motions associated with screws are in surjective correspondence with motions generated by twists, and (2) exponential map $\exp : \mathfrak{so}(3) \to \mathrm{SO}(3)$ is a surjective map.

To can change coordinates in a twist, there exists a map called *Adjoint Representation* denoted by Ad. In general, suppose $G$ is a Lie group, $C_g : G \to G$ *the inner automorphism of* $g \in G$, $\mathfrak{g}$ the Lie algebra of $G$ and $\mathrm{GL}(\mathfrak{g})$ *the general linear group of* $\mathfrak{g}$ (i.e. group of linear automorphism of $\mathfrak{g}$). Suppose that $g \in G$, adjoint representation is defined as

$$\mathrm{Ad} : G \longrightarrow \mathrm{GL}(\mathfrak{g})$$
$$g \longmapsto dC_g.$$

In this particular case, making identifications, for each $g \in \mathrm{SE}(3)$ with a twist $\xi$, occurs that $\mathrm{Ad}_g = g\xi g^{-1}$ is a *twist change of coordinates of* $\xi$.

## 2.3 Product of Exponential Formula

The manipulator described here is a sequence of links and joints such that, they go out of a device setting its joints for eluding obstacles. Until passing an obstacle, the manipulator takes a determinate sequence of configurations to avoid. Election of pure rotational motions induces a restriction to a subgroup of associated screws in $\mathrm{SE}(3)$, in this case, joints are named *Spherical* or of *Socket Ball Joint*. The forward kinematics here is based in achieve different configurations for each joint to can describe the configuration of the last link of the sequence of joints, in this last join, is installed a camera that visualizes the locally available motion space to can elude obstacles, and the initial part emerges from a device that puts out a determinate number of links and above is located a camera that maps globally around the manipulator. More precisely, let $I$ the inertial reference frame, and given a sequence of $n + 1$ links, then are $n$ joints, hence; for the $i$ joint $(1 \leq i \leq n)$, $i$ should denote the joint that lie between the $i - 1$-nth and $i$-nth link. Then, the relationship that involves the configuration with the initial joint and the configuration of the nth joint is [5]

$$g_{I,n}(\theta) = g_{I,1}(\theta_1)g_{1,2}(\theta_2)...g_{n,n+1}(\theta_n) \tag{6}$$

where $\theta_1, \theta_2, ..., \theta_n$ are the sequence of the amounts of the rotations. We can construct recursively that in this case

$$g_{I,n+1}(\theta) = e^{\hat{\xi}_1\theta_1}e^{\hat{\xi}_{1,2}\theta_2}...e^{\hat{\xi}_{n,n+1}\theta_n}g_{I,n+1}(0) \tag{7}$$

Choosing an adequate reference frame, is possible pick $g_{n,n+1}(0) = Id$. Using adjoint representation is possible to prove that $\hat{\xi}_i$ is the twist that corresponds to the $i$-nth joint $(1 \leq i \leq n)$.

An important step to modeling the manipulator of this paper is, given a determined net configuration, gives each rotation involved in the motion, for this objective, we apply *Paden-Kahan subproblems* to design the inverse kinematic by focus in Rotation about two subsequent axes [6–8].

## 3   Path Planning

It is a path where certain time distributions are specified, for example in terms of speeds and accelerations at each of the different points. Thus, a trajectory is related to the time in which each part of the path is completed, so depending on the speed with which it is carried out, the trajectory will change. The different trajectories are selected considering the physical restrictions of the drives, as well as certain criteria path quality such as precision and smoothness.

This path planning is made using the point to point method, also using third degree polynomial for control the position and velocities. To carry out the planning process it is necessary that the inverse kinematics of the robot have been designed. I also know must implement a path generation method as point-to-point movement, sequence movement points, among others.

For this movement a third degree polynomial equation is used, this together with a set of parameters is performed to obtain the position and acceleration of the links. These parameters were chosen in a way that the user can modify both the position and the speed that he expects the actuator to have. This path planning is made using the point to point method, also using third degree polynomial for control the position and velocities. To carry out the planning process it is necessary that the inverse kinematics of the robot have been designed. I also know must implement a path generation method as point-to-point movement, sequence movement points, among others.

For this movement a third degree polynomial equation is used, this together with a set of parameters is performed to obtain the position and acceleration of the links. These parameters were chosen in a way that the user can modify both the position and the speed that he expects the actuator to have.

## 3.1  Path Point to Point

This is a movement method where the manipulator must move from an initial position ($\theta_0$) to a final position ($\theta_n$) in a time ($t_f$). For this case the path of the effector is not taken into account. For this movement a third degree polynomial equation is used, this together with a set of parameters is performed to obtain the position and acceleration of the links. These parameters were chosen in which you can modify both the position and the speed that you expect the actuator to have.

Parameters for positions:

$$\theta(0) = \theta_0 \,|rad|$$
$$\theta(T_f) = \theta_f \,|rad| \tag{8}$$

Parameters for speeds:

$$\dot\theta(0) = \dot\theta_0 \,|rad/s|$$
$$\dot\theta(T_f) = \dot\theta_f \,|rad/s| \tag{9}$$

Polynomial for position:

$$\theta(0) = a_0 + a_1 t + a_2 t^2 + a_3 t^3 \tag{10}$$

Deriving Eq. 10 gives the speed polynomial:

$$\dot\theta(0) = a_1 + 2a_2 t + 3a_3 t^2 \tag{11}$$

Deriving Eq. 11 the acceleration polynomial:

$$\ddot\theta(0) = 2a_2 + 6a_3 t \tag{12}$$

For the initial time $t_0 = 0$, substituting in 10, 11 obtain $a_0 = \theta_0$ and $a_1 = \dot\theta_0$ Replacing $t = T_f$ in to find the parameters $a_2$ and $a_2$ arises the following equations.

$$a_2 = \frac{\dot\theta_f - \dot\theta_o}{2} - \frac{3}{2}a_3 t \tag{13}$$

$$a_3 = \frac{2}{t^3}(\theta_f - \theta_0) + \frac{2}{t^2}\dot\theta_0 + \frac{1}{t}(\dot\theta_f - \dot\theta_0) \tag{14}$$

164     F. C. Castro et al.

Equations can be summarized

$$\begin{cases} a_0 = \theta_0 \\ a_1 = \dot{\theta}_0 \\ a_2 = \left(\frac{\dot{\theta}_f - \dot{\theta}_0}{2}\right) t - \frac{3}{t^2}(\theta_f - \theta_0) + \frac{2}{t}\dot{\theta}_0 + \left(\dot{\theta}_f - \dot{\theta}_0\right) \\ a_3 = \frac{2}{t^3}(\theta_f - \theta_0) + \frac{2}{t^2}\dot{\theta}_0 + \frac{1}{t}\left(\dot{\theta}_f - \dot{\theta}_0\right) \end{cases} \quad (15)$$

In the Fig. 1 the $q_i$ that represent the angles of the rotational joints and the $P_x$, $P_y$, $P_z$ are the points respectively in the Cartesian Plane

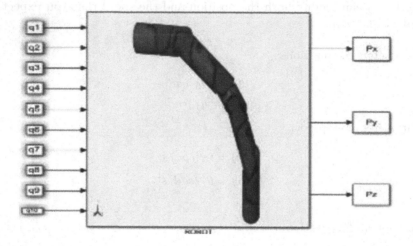

**Fig. 1.** Diagram of a servant robot with 10 degrees of freedom

## 3.2 Implemented Points

A servant-type multi section robot with 10 degrees of freedom was generated. As a first measure, a simplification of the robot's block diagram was carried out where the direct kinematics equations were implemented.

– Goal points
  - $P_{01} = (0, 0.6750, 0)$
  - $P_{02} = (0, 0.1219, -0.0646)$
  - $P_{03} = (0.43, 0.2464, 0.3)$
  - $P_{04} = (-0.3, 0.53, 0.1)$

In Fig. 2 you can see the goal points in three-dimensional space.

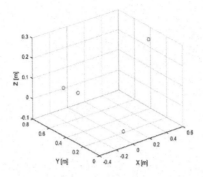

**Fig. 2.** Goal points

With the target points defined, the following is to calculate the inverse kinematics to know which points the obtained angles will reach, and a comparison was made of the angles found using the Paden-Kahan sub problem algorithm and the real angles of the robot. See Table 1.

**Table 1.** Position error for each target point

| Goal point | Point kinematic direct | Error |
|---|---|---|
| 0, 0.6750, 0 | −0.0038, 0.6421, 0.111 | 0.11% |
| 0, 0.1219, −0.0649 | 0.0195, 0.4422, −0.2484 | 36.98% |
| 0.4300, 0.2464, 0.3 | 0.4190, 0.0083, −0.1589 | 27.70% |
| −0.3, 0.53, 0.010 | −0.2752, 0.5743, −0.0320 | 8.49% |

In Fig. 3 you can see the difference between the desired target point (blue circle) with respect to the point obtained with the inverse kinematics with Paden-Kahan (red circle).

It is important to take into account the angles with which they were achieved, for this it presents Table 2, where you can see all the angles for the desired trajectories, in this table you can see the number of articulation and the objective angles of this for each point, with which it will go from angle $P_0$ to angle $P_1$ a if until reaching $P_4$,

As previously described for point-to-point movement, it is necessary that the trajectory is defined in a period of time . Table 3 shows the selected time for each way point.

However, this is not the only parameter that must be taken into account. In addition, all the initial and final speeds were assigned a zero range, with which the robot will have an infinitesimal time in which it will not move.

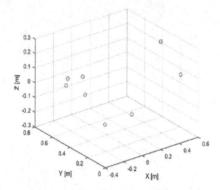

**Fig. 3.** Goal point and obtained point (Color figure online)

**Table 2.** Joint movement for all trajectories

| Joint | $P_1$ | $P_2$ | $P_3$ | $P_4$ |
|---|---|---|---|---|
| 1 | −0.0740 | 0.4118 | 0.4569 | 0.1549 |
| 2 | 0.22633 | −0.0740 | −0.8782 | 0.2470 |
| 3 | 0.0445 | −0.3343 | 0.1862 | −0.251 |
| 4 | 0.0538 | 0.2459 | −0.8732 | 0.0538 |
| 5 | −0.2660 | −0.6566 | 0.7926 | 0.1135 |
| 6 | −0.0740 | 0.4118 | 0.4569 | 0.1549 |
| 7 | −0.4281 | −08652 | −0.1151 | 0.1096 |
| 8 | −0.0824 | −0.2602 | 0.0724 | 0.3057 |
| 9 | 0.0751 | 0.0913 | −0.9756 | 0.0167 |
| 10 | −0.1827 | 0.1072 8 | −0.1373 | −0.2001 |

**Table 3.** Times for each trajectory

| | $P_1$ | $P_2$ | $P_3$ | $P_4$ |
|---|---|---|---|---|
| T(S) | 0 | 3 | 4 | 10 |

# 4  Architecture System and Algorithms Implemented and Simulation

The environment is developed in GAZEBO and integrated with ROS *(Robot Operating System)* and MATLAB. For the generation in the world, the robot has been designed as a chain of links taking into account a dynamic (i,e inertia, friction, and mass), each actuator has a servomotor. This means that the position and speed of each of them can be used by a PID, the final effector has a camera that allows determining the correct distance. The virtual environment receives the angles of each link generated by a twist.

To avoid obstacles in a static environment was used the *algorithm $A*$* or *Astar type search of graphs*. The algorithm uses an evaluation function, where represents the heuristic value within a point in the work-space (*C-space*) evaluate from the $n$ step and the end, the real cost of the path traveled to reach the goal $n$ from the initial point. Algorithm $A^*$ uses an evaluation function, where $f(n) = g(n) + h'(n)$ Thus $h'(n)$ represents the heuristic value of the node to be evaluated from the current one $n$ $g(n)$ the actual cost of the path to reach that node, until the end. The Fig. 2 and Fig. 3 we show the algorithm implemented in Matlab for different pathways with restrictions given an initial and final point. Thus Fig. 2 you can see a trajectory with little deformation since the points are very close, but unlike figure ?? the trajectory needs deformation due to the restrictions and distance of the points.

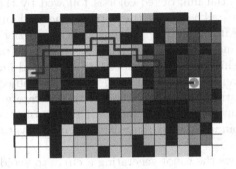

**Fig. 4.** Path planning using A*

For softening the trajectory the Bezier curves algorithm is used in a polynomial way of order 3. The idea of geometrically defining the shapes is not too complex: a point on the plane can be defined by coordinates. For example, an initial point $P_o$ has some coordinates $(x_1, y_1)$ and a final point $P_f$ corresponds to it $(x_2, y_2)$. To draw a curve between both, it is enough to know its position and the essential elements of a Bezier curve; the points are called "reference points" or "nodes". $P_r$. The shape of the curve is defined by invisible points in the plane, called "control points", "handlers" or "hands".

The generalization would become the curves called "Spline", that is, the Bezier curve is a third-degree Spline. The Bezier curve of degree $n$ can be generalized as follows. Given the points $P_0$, $P_1, ..., P_n$, the Bezier curve is of the type:

$$B(t) = \sum_{i=0}^{n} \binom{n}{i} P_i (1-t)^{n-i} t^i, t \in [0,1]$$

In Fig. 4 we show how the curve softens after applying the algorithm $A$, according to the deformations found, the nodal points are produced which control the curvature in the robot with the previous expressions, we easily obtain the positions in which we must place the 3 additional vertices to achieve specific initial conditions, depending on the position of the point and the first and second discrete derivatives in it, for each component (in the flat, $x$ and $y$).

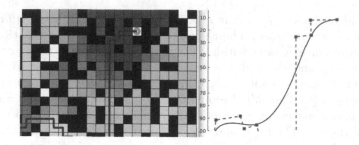

**Fig. 5.** Spline curve softens after applying the algorithm A*

For the simulation of the robot, cylindrical links are connected through revolution joints, the initial link of red color is followed by the blue cylinders, in the end effector is located a camera, this corrects the final angles that the Bezier algorithm delivers. After the curve is found with the Bezier algorithm, we proceed by inverse kinematics to find the angles that will be the control variables for each twist. The simulation here has twenty connected links. The simulation is tested with two events, the first one step is with two objects as obstacles and several zones of constraints forcing the robot to generate an s, the second one generates a virtual environment of a house where the robot searches for the exit for this test. Environments were controlled, giving curvature parameters and restriction zones.

The Fig. 6(a) shows the robot generating a curve to avoid different obstacles and 6(b) generating a curve to embroider an area.

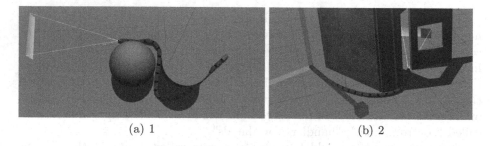

(a) 1                                          (b) 2

**Fig. 6.** curvature of the robot in the virtual world

## 5   Results

In the first trajectory, it was calculated for the links outside the point $P_1$ to $P_n$ Table 2, this movement was carried out in time shown in Table 3 In the Fig. 7(a) you can see the movement in three-dimensional space the from movement $P_1$ to $P_2$ in 7(b) we can see all the complete routes (the sum of all the routes), since This mode made the robot move from the starting point. $P_1$ to the end point $P_4$ passing through the intermediate points $P_2$ and $P_3$. It can also be seen that the curves are made with a smooth movement, this is due to combining it with a bezier allowing the robot not to generate sudden movements, protecting the actuators.

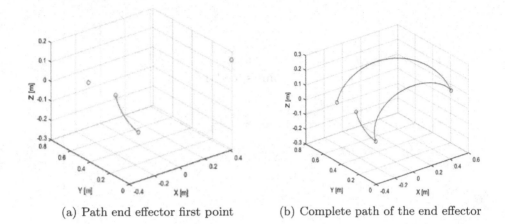

(a) Path end effector first point      (b) Complete path of the end effector

**Fig. 7.** Path end effector

In the Fig. 8 see the position of joints with respect to time, in each of these figures it can be seen that the primary requirement of having a smooth movement in each joint was met, in addition to this, the desired parameter of the initial and final velocity was met, since it starts at $0\ rad/s$ and ends in $0\ rad/s$. In the Fig. 9 see the velocity of joints with respect to time, in each of these figures, it is important to observe the behavior of the velocity, this tells us that it stops when it reaches the point end. It can also be observed that a straight path was not made between point and point, since there were no intermediate points between these points. Now, if you want to improve this implementation, you should generate a trajectory with more intermediate points. From Fig. 10 the total movement of each of the links can be observed, in these figures it can be observed how, by modifying the time in which the task is required to be carried out, the speed is modified, making the robot have more abrupt movements.

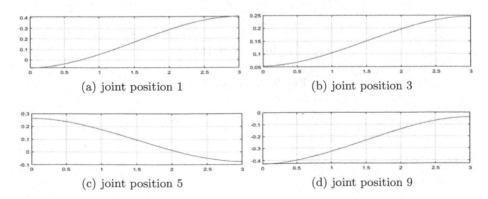

(a) joint position 1                    (b) joint position 3

(c) joint position 5                    (d) joint position 9

**Fig. 8.** Joint positions

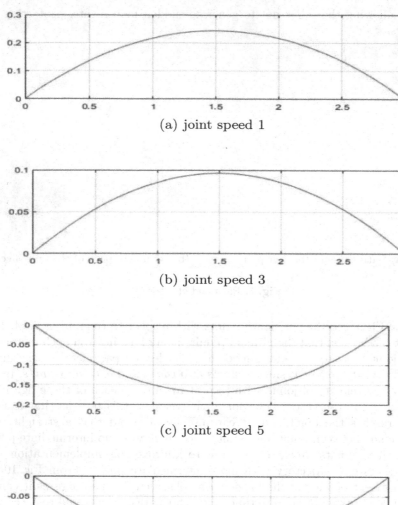

(a) joint speed 1

(b) joint speed 3

(c) joint speed 5

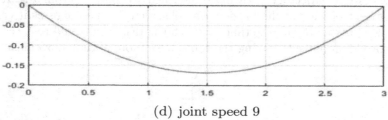

(d) joint speed 9

**Fig. 9.** Joint speeds

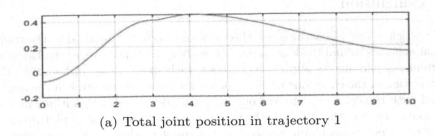

(a) Total joint position in trajectory 1

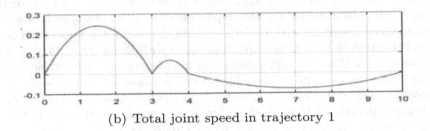

(b) Total joint speed in trajectory 1

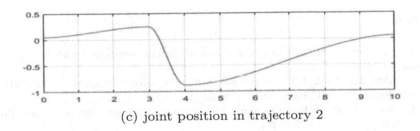

(c) joint position in trajectory 2

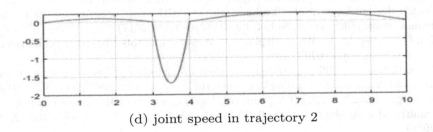

(d) joint speed in trajectory 2

**Fig. 10.** Joint speeds

# 6   Conclusion

This article showed how the screw theory is an alternative method to the traditional methods to find the kinematics of a robbery, as is the case of the Denavit-Hartenberg parameters applied to a robot with many links, although in the clarification of the equations inverse kinematics there was an error in the angles found with respect to the desired ones. We integrate several algorithms including route planning that controls the rotation smoothness of each link through a third order polynomial, you can see how the robot reaches the inverse kinematics point in the desired time, for each link it is necessary to find a Polynomial control global path planning was also implemented to avoid obstacles in a static environment and together with Bezier's suvizdo algorithm it is possible to generate a curve that the robot can copy. A problem with this methodology is that you have to know the work environment and the obstacles must be static, without the ability to navigate in an unknown environment for future work, it is proposed to work with more recent methods in the field of artificial intelligence as a learner. Reinforced to teach the robot how to move according to different obstacles and see the behaviors in a dynamic environment.

# References

1. Denavit, J., Hartenberg, R.S.: A kinematic notation for lower-pair mechanisms based on matrices (1955)
2. Duistermaat, J.J., Kolk, J.A.: Lie groups. Springer Science & Business Media (2012). https://doi.org/10.1007/978-1-4614-8024-2
3. Featherstone, R.: Rigid Body Dynamics Algorithms. Springer (2014). https://doi.org/10.1007/978-1-4899-7560-7
4. Kim, Y., Cheng, S.S., Diakite, M., Gullapalli, R.P., Simard, J.M., Desai, J.P.: Toward the development of a flexible mesoscale MRI-compatible neurosurgical continuum robot. IEEE Trans. Robot. **33**(6), 1386–1397 (2017)
5. Niu, G., Zhang, Y., Li, W.: Path planning of continuum robot based on path fitting. J. Control Sci. Eng. 2020 (2020)
6. Oliver-Butler, K., Till, J., Rucker, C.: Continuum robot stiffness under external loads and prescribed tendon displacements. IEEE Trans. Rob. **35**(2), 403–419 (2019)
7. Ouyang, B., Liu, Y., Tam, H.Y., Sun, D.: Design of an interactive control system for a multisection continuum robot. IEEE/ASME Trans. Mechatron. **23**(5), 2379–2389 (2018)
8. Paden, B., Sastry, S.: Optimal kinematic design of 6R manipulators. Int. J. Robot. Res. **7**(2), 43–61 (1988)
9. Vergara, N.J.W., et al.: Un ejemplo de aplicación momento en dimensión infinita. Master's thesis, Uniandes

# Seismic Inversion After Depth Migration

Maxim Protasov[✉] and Danil Dmitrachkov

Institute of Petroleum Geology and Geophysics, Novosibirsk 630090, Russia
protasovmi@ipgg.sbras.ru, d.dmitrachkov@g.nsu.ru

**Abstract.** Seismic inversion is used in practice as a tool for predicting reservoir properties. It allows one to extract a model with a high level of detail from seismic data, i.e. high-frequency component of the model. In this case, the input data are the time processing results, and the issues related to the low-frequency component of the model are not considered usually. This work describes the implementation of a model-based seismic inversion algorithm. The input data for the inversion are the depth image results in true amplitudes and the depth migration velocity model. The possibilities of seismic inversion are numerically investigated to refine the low-frequency component of the model. Experiments were carried out using synthetic seismic data got for realistic Sigsbee model.

**Keywords:** Seismic inversion · Depth migration · Low-frequency model

## 1 Introduction

Seismic inversion has become a standard procedure, which most times is mandatory for predicting reservoir properties. Traditionally, people consider seismic inversion as an algorithm that provides conversion of a time or migrated time seismic section into an acoustic impedance section [1, 2]. Usually, the input data for inversion result from time processing of seismic data, both pre-stack and post-stack [3, 4].

However, depth processing is often necessary, and seismic inversion is desirable based on the results of the depth processing. There are approaches to perform seismic inversion directly in the depth domain after migration [5], but they are computationally expensive. A simpler approach, when the image after depth migration is transformed into the time domain and standard inversion algorithms based on one-dimensional convolutional modeling, gives reasonable results, and it is this one that is used in practice.

The major result of the standard use of seismic inversion is a detailed model of the elastic properties of the geological environment, which makes it possible to predict the properties of reservoirs [6]. The inversion provides restoring the high-frequency component of the model. However, the low-frequency component "remains in the shadows", although the logic of the inversion operation points out that this part of the model should also be refined. If this is the case, then depth-processing inversion can refine the low-frequency component of the model.

O. Gervasi et al. (Eds.): ICCSA 2022, LNCS 13375, pp. 173–183, 2022.
https://doi.org/10.1007/978-3-031-10522-7_13

Therefore, within the framework of this work, we investigate seismic inversion in order to determine its capabilities for reconstructing the low-frequency component of the model. We implement model-based seismic inversion algorithm, where we use the migration model as the initial approximation. We provide the study using synthetic data and the Sigsbee model. This paper is organized as follows. First, we present model based seismic inversion, next, we describe briefly the procedure for seismic depth imaging. Then we provide numerical experiments, and we finalize with the conclusion.

## 2  Model Based Seismic Inversion

Acoustic seismic inversion is based on a one-dimensional convolutional model [2, 3, 7]:

$$S(t) = w(t) * R(t). \tag{1}$$

Here $S(t)$ – seismic trace, $R(t)$ – reflection coefficients, $w(t)$ – seismic impulse. When discretized, Eq. (1) takes the following form:

$$S = \begin{bmatrix} S_1 \\ S_2 \\ \vdots \\ S_N \end{bmatrix} = \begin{bmatrix} w_1 & 0 & 0 & \\ w_2 & w_1 & 0 & \cdots \\ w_3 & w_2 & w_1 & \\ \vdots & & & \ddots \end{bmatrix} \cdot \begin{bmatrix} R_1 \\ R_2 \\ \vdots \\ R_N \end{bmatrix} = WR. \tag{2}$$

Here $W$ – convolution matrix, $w_i$, $S_i$,$R_i$ –discrete values of momentum, trace and reflection coefficients, respectively. The model-based inversion algorithm uses a low-contrast approximation [3, 4, 7]:

$$R_i \approx \frac{1}{2}(\ln Z_{i+1} - \ln Z_i). \tag{3}$$

Here $Z_i$ – acoustic impedance. In matrix form, expression (3) looks like this:

$$R = \frac{1}{2}Dx - \frac{1}{2}\hat{L}. \tag{4}$$

$D - N$- dimensional matrix, a $x, \hat{L} - N$- dimensional vectors:

$$D = \begin{bmatrix} 1 & 0 & 0 & & 0 & 0 \\ -1 & 1 & 0 & \cdots & 0 & 0 \\ 0 & -1 & 1 & & 0 & 0 \\ & \vdots & & \ddots & & \vdots \\ 0 & 0 & 0 & & 1 & 0 \\ 0 & 0 & 0 & \cdots & -1 & 1 \end{bmatrix}, \quad x = \begin{bmatrix} \ln Z_2 \\ \ln Z_3 \\ \vdots \\ \ln Z_{N+1} \end{bmatrix}, \quad \hat{L} = \begin{bmatrix} \ln \hat{Z}_1 \\ 0 \\ \vdots \\ 0 \end{bmatrix}. \tag{5}$$

We assume in the upper layer the acoustic impedance $\widehat{Z}_1$ to be known. Let us write the system of Eqs. (2) with respect to the vector $x$ (the logarithm of acoustic impedances), substituting expression (4) for the reflection coefficients into it:

$$\frac{1}{2}WDx = S + \frac{1}{2}W\widehat{L}. \tag{6}$$

Then we introduce definitions:

$$C = \frac{1}{2}WD, A = C^T C, b = C^T\left(S + \frac{1}{2}W\widehat{L}\right). \tag{7}$$

Multiplying both parts of the system of Eqs. (6) by the matrix $C^T$, we arrive at a system of linear algebraic equations (SLAE):

$$Ax = b. \tag{8}$$

The matrices $W$ and $D$ are $N \times N$ square and nonsingular, therefore the matrix $A = C^T C$ is symmetric and positive definite. Therefore, we solve the system (8) by using the conjugate gradient method. To do this, we need an initial approximation - an a priori model of acoustic impedances. Hence the name of this type of inversion, i.e. model-based inversion when it needs some initial model. In the practice, when solving geological problems by seismic inversion, the interpolation of smoothed logging data along the traced horizons provides the initial model.

There is noise in the observed data, and in order to suppress its influence and get an adequate solution, we use regularization. One of the popular approaches is the Tikhonov regularization [8, 9]. It means to move from solving SLAE (8) to the problem of minimizing the parametric functional:

$$\Psi(x, \alpha) = \|Ax - b\|_2^2 + \alpha\|x\|_2^2. \tag{9}$$

Here $\alpha > 0$ and is called the regularization parameter. Too small values of the regularization parameter lead to the original ill-posed problem, and too large values give solutions that have little in common with the original system. Therefore, the choice of the regularization parameter is critically important. One of the most popular approaches for automatic selection of the regularization parameter is the residual principle [10]. It boils down to the fact that, for a noise level $\varepsilon$, the regularization parameter $\alpha$ is the solution of the equation:

$$\|Ax_\alpha - b\|_2 = \|\varepsilon\|_2. \tag{10}$$

This establishes an explicit relationship between the regularization parameter and the errors in the observed data. The efficiency of the method depends on the accuracy of noise estimation. For a seismic inversion problem, this information is usually got from well data.

In order to obtain smooth solutions, the regularization method needs to be changed. To do this, the functional of the form is minimized:

$$\Psi(x, \alpha) = \|Ax - b\|_2^2 + \alpha \|x - x_0\|_2^2. \tag{11}$$

The form of the second term imposes on the solution the requirement of proximity to the initial approximation $x_0$. Further, it is required that the solution be smooth. We do this using the second-order gradient [8, 11], which in matrix form has the form:

$$D = \begin{bmatrix} -1 & 1 & 0 & \cdots & \cdots & 0 \\ -1 & 2 & -1 & 0 & \cdots & 0 \\ 0 & -1 & 2 & -1 & \ddots & 0 \\ \vdots & \ddots & \ddots & \ddots & \ddots & \cdots \\ \vdots & 0 & 0 & -1 & 2 & -1 \\ 0 & \cdots & \cdots & 0 & -1 & 1 \end{bmatrix}. \tag{12}$$

Then the problem comes to minimizing the functional of the form:

$$\Phi(x, \alpha) = \|Ax - b\|_2^2 + \alpha \|D(x - x_0)\|_2^2. \tag{13}$$

In the work, we implement and use two regularization methods described above. To distinguish between them, the first method, corresponding to the minimization of the functional (11), is conditionally called the "standard" regularization, and the second method, corresponding to the minimization of the functional (13), is called the "maximum smoothness" regularization.

## 3 Seismic Imaging

For seismic image construction, the Gaussian beam based true amplitude imaging is used [12, 13]:

$$I(\bar{x}; \alpha, \beta) = \int T_p^s(x_s; \bar{x}; \alpha, \beta; \omega) \cdot T_p^r(x_r; \bar{x}; \alpha, \beta; \omega) \cdot d(x_r; x_s; \omega) dx_r dx_s d\omega d\alpha. \tag{14}$$

Here $d$ is the seismic data, $x_r/x_s$ is the source/receiver coordinate, $\omega$ is the frequency, $\alpha, \beta$ are the dip and opening angles, $T_p^{s(r)}$ are the source (receiver) Gaussian beam stacking weights.

This procedure allows one to build images of target objects with high resolution and signal-to-noise ratio. Tracing Gaussian beams from the image points to the observation system is used to achieve such results. We choose beams as the most narrowly focused at the image points. Also, we choose identical Gaussian beams at the image points. Therefore, we provide the uniformity of the resolution throughout the imaging area. However, these Gaussian beams are different depending on the depth and angles on the observation surface. We achieve the maximum image resolution because of the minimization of the Gaussian beam width at the image points. Such a Gaussian imaging algorithm selects coherent events. It focuses the energy on the image point, and therefore it provides Gaussian beam images with high resolution and signal-to-noise ratio.

## 4   Numerical Examples

To test the developed inversion algorithm, we create a model identical to the one presented in [7]. Then, we calculate the ideal seismic trace by convolving the corresponding model reflection coefficients and the seismic wavelet according to (1). Here, we use a Ricker pulse with a dominant frequency of 20 Hz. Next, we apply seismic inversion using data without noise, but we change the regularization parameter. The results show that as the parameter $\alpha$ increases; the solution becomes smoother (Fig. 1a, 1b). We carried the next series of calculations out for data with the Gaussian noise. The residual principle provides the regularization parameter automatically in this case (Fig. 1c). We note that in the specific case, when the noise level is 15%, the result (Fig. 1c) visually does not differ from the result of similar calculations presented in [7]. The repeatability of the result on identical data shows that the developed algorithms work correctly.

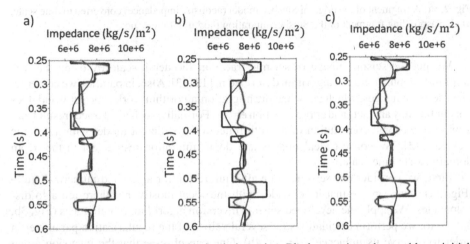

**Fig. 1.** The result of the model based seismic inversion. Black - true impedances, blue - initial model, red - inversion result: a) data without noise, "standard" regularization parameter $\alpha = 1$; b) data without noise, $\alpha = 20$; c) data with a noise of 15%, with the selection of a parameter according to the residual principle $\alpha = 2.71$. (Color figure online)

In the next series of numerical experiments, we apply the developed model based seismic inversion algorithm to the results of depth seismic migration in true amplitudes. Since both the migration velocity model and the migration result are specified on a depth scale, and seismic inversion works on a time scale, we use the depth-to-time transform [14]. For its implementation, we use migration velocity model. Thus, through this transformation, we get the original and migration Sigsbee models in a time scale and further converted into acoustic impedance values (Fig. 2).

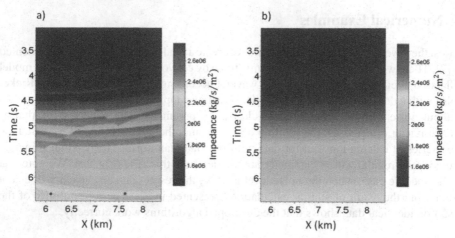

**Fig. 2.** a) A fragment of the original Sigsbee model (acoustic impedance) converted to time scale. b) Corresponding fragment of the Sigsbee migration model in time scale.

We get the seismic image or seismic traces at the depth scale by using the true amplitude depth migration algorithm described in [12, 13]. Also, in parallel, we construct ideal seismic images, which get when the migration algorithm works correctly and does not contain any artifacts and approximation errors. Formally, such ideal traces result from a two-dimensional convolution of a depth reflection coefficient model with a seismic wavelet [13]. We convert ideal images and depth migration results got in the depth domain to the time scale.

First, we consider one seismic trace after migration for a detailed numerical study (Fig. 3a). One can see that it coincides with the ideal mostly, but there are also discrepancies. We apply the developed seismic inversion algorithm to both traces (Fig. 3b, 3c). Also, we perform calculations for several values of the regularization parameter in order to observe its influence (Fig. 4a, 4b). One can observe that the inversion along the ideal path gives a result that coincides with the true solution with high accuracy (Fig. 3b). However, the result of the inversion of the seismic trace after migration is less accurate, which is a consequence of the difference between the migrated trace and the ideal one (Fig. 3c). One can see that the reconstructed impedance model "captures" many jumps in true impedances, and inaccuracies appear mainly inside the reservoirs. This behavior is partly because of regularization. With an increase in the "standard" regularization parameter, the inversion result is closer to the initial model (Fig. 4a, 4b). One can observe that the "standard" regularization parameter makes it possible to balance between a more accurate description of abrupt changes in the model and more correct values within the layers. To improve this situation, we change the regularization in the inversion. The algorithm uses the "maximum smoothness" regularization (Fig. 4c). One can see that this solution describes the true impedances more accurately than the solution constructed using the "standard" regularization.

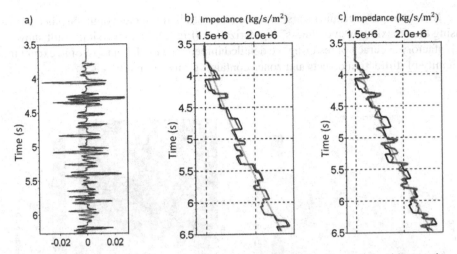

**Fig. 3.** a) Ideal seismic trace – black, seismic trace after running the migration algorithm – red, x = 6705 m. b) and c) Inversion results of the ideal seismic trace and the seismic trace after migration, respectively, x = 6705 m. Black – true acoustic impedances, turquoise – initial background model, red – inversion result at $\alpha = 0.01$ with "standard" regularization. (Color figure online)

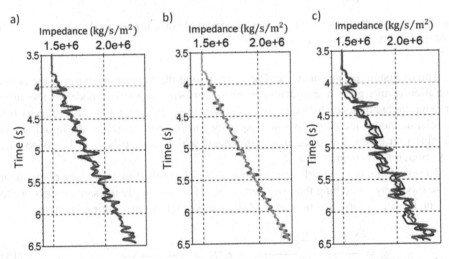

**Fig. 4.** Seismic inversion results after migration, x = 6705 m. a) Inversion result with "standard" regularization at $\alpha = 0.001$ - blue, at $\alpha = 0.01$ - red, initial model – turquoise. b) The inversion result with "standard" regularization at $\alpha = 0.1$ - violet, at $\alpha = 1.0$ - orange, initial model – turquoise. c) The inversion result with "standard" regularization at $\alpha = 0.01$ - blue, the inversion result with "maximum smoothness" regularization at $\alpha = 0.01$ - red, true acoustic impedances - black. (Color figure online)

Next, we apply seismic inversion to the entire studied fragment of the Sigsbee model using the "maximum smoothness" regularization (Fig. 5). The inversion result shows a satisfactory accuracy of restoring the detailed impedance model in most of it, except the vicinity of diffraction objects and zones containing migration artifacts.

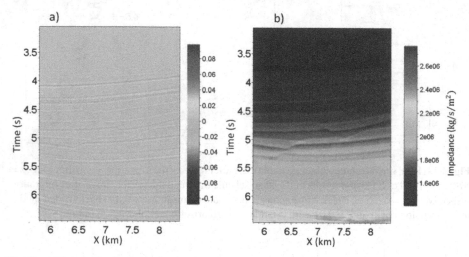

**Fig. 5.** a) The result of seismic depth migration converted to a time scale. b) Corresponding result of seismic inversion.

The inversion results got above (Fig. 5) show that the seismic inversion of the depth migration results gives a satisfactory result of restoring a detailed model of the environment, including its high-frequency component. One can see that this result describes the seismic model, including the low-frequency component. Of course, the initial model contains part of the low-frequency component, which is used both in inversion and migration, but it is being refined.

To reveal this more clearly, we propose to highlight the low-frequency component of the model by smoothing the inversion result. Here, we apply the same procedure to the true model. We use function with a Gaussian kernel as a smoothing operator:

$$\tilde{y}_i = \frac{\sum_{j=1}^{n} K\left(\frac{x_i - x_j}{b}\right) \cdot y_j}{\sum_{j=1}^{n} K\left(\frac{x_i - x_j}{b}\right)}, \qquad K(t) = \frac{1}{\sqrt{2\pi}(0.37)} e^{-\frac{t^2}{2 \cdot (0.37)^2}}. \tag{15}$$

Here $x_i$ – these are the nodes of the grid, and $y_i$ and $\tilde{y}_i$ are the values of the original and smoothed functions on this grid, $b$ is the parameter that controls the smoothness of the resulting function. Next, we provide various low-frequency components of the true model and the result of the inversion by smoothing with different values of the parameter $b$

(Fig. 6). For large values of $b$, for example $b = 0.8$, the result of smoothing the true model becomes close to the initial inversion model (Fig. 6a). For small values of $b$, for example $b = 0.05$, the smoothing result differs little from the true model (Fig. 6a). However, between these values, for example $b = 0.3$, rather smooth solutions are obtained, which differ markedly from the initial model for inversion (Fig. 6a). One can get similar results when smoothing the model got by seismic inversion (Fig. 6b). Comparison of the low-frequency components of the true model, the result of the inversion of "ideal traces" and the traces after migration shows that the inversion determines these components with high accuracy (Fig. 7). Relative root-mean-square error of the trace inversion result after migration (Fig. 8) relative to the true model for the components obtained by smoothing using the parameter $b = 0.3$, equals to 1.35%. When using the parameter $b = 0.1$, the error is 1.78%. Based on these results, we can conclude that the inversion really determines the low-frequency component of the model, while restoring it with a fairly high accuracy.

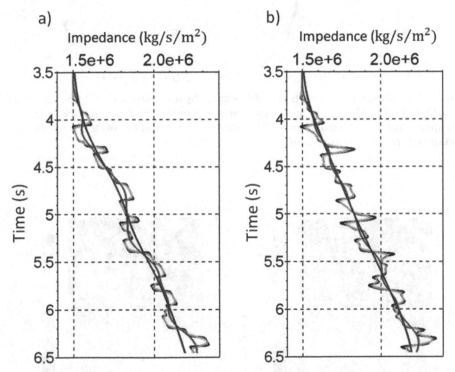

**Fig. 6.** a) The original model - black, and its smooth components at x = 6705 m: smoothing parameter b = 0.05 - green, b = 0.3 - red, b = 0.8 - blue; b) model obtained by inversion after migration - black, and its smooth components at x = 6705 m: smoothing parameter b = 0.05 - green, b = 0.3 - red, b = 0.8 - blue. (Color figure online)

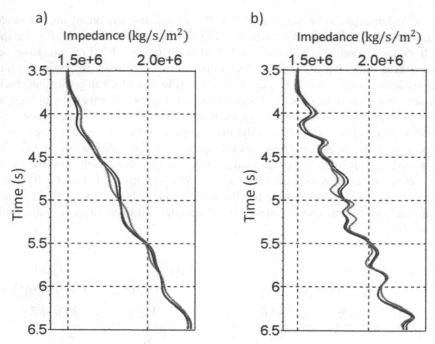

**Fig. 7.** Low-frequency components of models obtained by smoothing at x = 6705 m: a) parameter b = 0.3; b) b = 0.1. The smooth component of the true acoustic impedances is black, the result of the inversion of the ideal seismic trace is blue, the result of the inversion of the seismic trace after migration is red. (Color figure online)

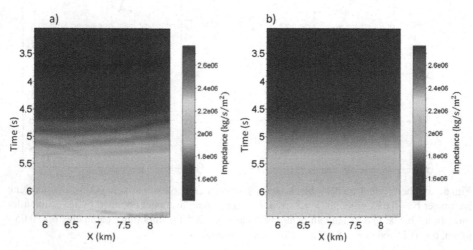

**Fig. 8.** Low-frequency components of the seismic inversion result after depth migration, obtained by smoothing with the parameter: a) b = 0.1; b) b = 0.3.

## 5  Conclusions

The paper presents an algorithm of seismic inversion after depth migration. It provides a study of the influence of the regularization parameter on the result of the inversion, as well as the influence of the regularization method itself. We extract low-frequency components from the impedance model and inversion results of ideal seismic traces and seismic traces after migration. We show model based seismic inversion of the depth seismic migration result reconstructs the high-frequency component of the model with acceptable quality. It is consistent with the standard application of seismic inversion to time processing results. By comparative analysis of the low-frequency components of the original model and the results of the inversion, we show that seismic inversion can recover the smooth component of the model. Such circumstances create prerequisites for using seismic inversion as a tool for refining the depth migration model.

**Acknowledgments.** The reported study was funded by RFBR and GACR, project number 20–55-26003.

## References

1. Russell, B.H.: Introduction to Seismic Inversion Methods. Course Notes Series, pp. 80–101. Society of Exploration Geophysicists, Houston (1988)
2. Ampilov, Y., Barkov, A., Yakovlev, I.V., Filippova, K.E., Priezzhev, I.I.: Almost everything is about seismic inversion. Part 1. Seism. Technol. **4**, 3–16 (2009)
3. Russell, B.H., Hampson, D.P.: Comparison of poststack seismic inversion methods. In: SEG Technical Program Expanded Abstracts, pp. 876–878 (1991)
4. Hampson, D.P., Russell, B.H., Bankhead, B.: Simultaneous inversion of pre-stack seismic data. In: SEG Technical Program Expanded Abstracts, pp. 1633–1637 (2005)
5. Fletcher, R., Archer, S., Nichols, D., Mao, W.: Inversion after depth imaging. In: SEG Technical Program Expanded Abstracts, pp. 1–5 (2012)
6. Yakovlev, I.V., Ampilov, Y., Filippova, K.E.: Almost everything is about seismic inversion. Part 2. Seism. Technol. **1**, 5–15 (2011)
7. Li, Ts.: Development of noise-immune algorithms for dynamic inversion of seismic data. Ph.D. thesis (2017)
8. Tikhonov, A.N.: On ill-posed problems in linear algebra and a stable method for their solution. DAN SSSR **163**, 591–594 (1965)
9. Tikhonov, A.N., Arsenin, V.: Methods for Solving Ill-Posed Problems. Nauka, Moscow (1986)
10. Morozov, V.A.: On the regularization of ill-posed problems and the choice of the regularization parameter. J. Comput. Math. Math. Phys. **6**, 170–175 (1966)
11. Zhdanov, M.S.: Theory of Inverse Problems and Regularization in Geophysics. Nauchnyy Mir, Moscow (2007)
12. Protasov, M.I., Tcheverda, V.A.: True amplitude imaging. Dokl. Earth Sci. **407**, 441–445 (2006)
13. Protasov, M., Tcheverda, V.: True amplitude imaging by inverse generalized Radon transform based on Gaussian beam decomposition of the acoustic Green's function. Geophys. Prospect. **59**, 197–209 (2011)
14. Robein, E.: Seismic Imaging. EAGE Publications, Houten (2010)

# Dispersion Analysis of Smoothed Particle Hydrodynamics to Study Convergence and Numerical Phenomena at Coarse Resolution

Olga Stoyanovskaya[1] , Vadim Lisitsa[2][(✉)] , Sergey Anoshin[3],
and Tamara Markelova[1]

[1] Boreskov Institute of Catalysis SB RAS, Lavrentiev Ave. 5,
Novosibirsk 630090, Russia
[2] Institute of Mathematics SB RAS, Koptug Ave. 4, Novosibirsk 630090, Russia
lisitsavv@ipgg.sbras.ru
[3] Novosibirsk State University, Pirogova, 2, Novosibirsk 630090, Russia
s.anoshin@g.nsu.ru

**Abstract.** The Smoothed Particle Hydrodynamics (SPH) method is a meshless Lagrangian method widely used in continuum mechanics simulation. Despite its wide application, theoretical issues of SPH approximation, stability, and convergence are among the unsolved problems of computational mathematics. In this paper, we present the application of dispersion analysis to the SPH approximation of one-dimensional gas dynamics equations to study numerical phenomena that appeared in practice. We confirmed that SPH converges only if the number of particles per wavelength increases while smoothing length decreases. At the same time, reduction of the smoothing length when keeping the number of particles in the kernel fixed (typical convergence results for finite differences and finite elements) does not guarantee the convergence of the numerical solution to the analytical one. We indicate the particular regimes with pronounced irreducible numerical dispersion. For coarse resolution, our theoretical findings are confirmed in simulations.

**Keywords:** Smoothed particles hydrodynamics (SPH) · Numerical dispersion · Convergence analysis

## 1  Introduction

The SPH method is a meshless Lagrangian method for solving continuum mechanics problems or systems of partial differential equations written in the

V.L. did the dispersion analysis under the support of Russian Science Foundation grant no. 21-71-20003, O.S. performed numerical experiments, and T.M. did the asymptotic analysis; O.S. and T.M. work were founded by Russian Science Foundation grant no 21-19-00429, S.A. visualized the results.

divergence-free form. The SPH method was suggested in [7,12] and is used in astrophysics, ballistics, volcanology, oceanography, and many other applications nowadays [15]. It synergetically couples with other numerical techniques, e.g., particle-in-cell approaches for solving stiff problems [23,24]. Several multiphysics commercial [28] and freeware codes [8,9,19,22,26] have been developed on its basis. In the SPH method, a continuous medium is replaced by a discrete set of particles. These particles are moving interpolation nodes for spatial derivatives computation. The spatial derivatives of a function given at moving nodes irregularly located nodes are calculated using a smooth non-linear function (kernel). The kernel is nonzero in a bounded region called the kernel support domain. The accuracy of the spatial derivative computation is determined by two numerical parameters - the average distance between the interpolation nodes and the average size of the support domain or the smoothing length. Due to the irregular distribution of model particles in space and the non-linearity of the kernel, it is challenging to study the properties of the SPH method theoretically. Therefore, the theoretical issues of approximation, stability, and convergence are among the unsolved problems of the SPH method [25].

Dispersion analysis is a powerful tool that allows directly estimating the convergence of the numerical solution to a plane wave solution admitted by the original system of hyperbolic differential equations [5]. This approach is widely used in seismic modeling to choose appropriate grid steps or to construct dispersion suppressing schemes which can be used with extremely coarse discretizations (close to 2.5 points per wavelength) [11]. If applied to finite elements [17], discontinuous Galerkin [2,10], or spectral elements [13] dispersion allows estimating the convergence rate of the numerical solution, studying the artificial modes, and also performing the stability analysis. Analysis of the numerical dispersion caused by SPH approximation was also reported in [4,6,14–16,20] Dispersion analysis of SPH is based on the assumption of a liner small-amplitude wave propagation. Thus, the particles are supposed to oscillate near a fixed position, and the problem can be linearized, and relative phase velocity error can be estimated depending on the distance between the particles and the kernel size.

This paper presents the dispersion analysis of the SPH approximation of one-dimensional gas dynamics equations. First, we consider the basic classical form of the SPH (1) with a constant smoothing length, (2) with guaranteed mass and momentum conservation in the whole computational domain, (3) without artificial viscosity. Then, we provide the formula for the numerical velocity of propagation of a sound wave, which is a function of three independent variables: wavelength, the distance between the unperturbed particles, and the kernel length. Finally, we prove that the phase velocity of the SPH plane-wave solution converges to that of the solution of the differential equations; both kernel length and the inter-particle distance tend to zero simultaneously, which confirms the results of [6,20,21,27]. However, if the distance between the particles tends to zero with a fixed kernel length, the dispersion error may not converge to zero, resulting in irreducible phase error.

The paper has the following structure. We formulate the problem in Sect. 2. Construction of the phase velocity of the numerical solution is presented in Sect. 3. Numerical experiments are provided in Sect. 4.

## 2    Statement of the Problem

### 2.1    System of Gas Dynamics

Consider system of equations describing dynamics of viscous compressible gas

$$\frac{\partial \rho_g}{\partial t} + \vec{v} \cdot \nabla \rho_g = -\rho_g \nabla \cdot \vec{v},$$
$$\frac{\partial \vec{v}}{\partial t} + \vec{v} \cdot \nabla \vec{v} = -\frac{1}{\rho_g} \nabla p, \tag{1}$$
$$p = c_s^2 \rho_g,$$

where $\rho_g$ is the gas mass density, $\vec{v}$ is the gas velocity, $p$ is pressure, $c_s$ is the speed of sound.

We consider a small perturbation of the solution in the vicinity of the stationary mode; that is $\rho_g = \rho^0 + \delta\rho$ and $\vec{v} = \delta\vec{v}$. Thus the system can be linearized as

$$\frac{\partial \delta\rho_g}{\partial t} + \rho_g^0 \nabla \cdot \delta\vec{v} = 0, \quad \rho_g^0 \frac{\partial \delta\vec{v}}{\partial t} + c_s^2 \nabla \delta\rho_g = 0, \tag{2}$$

where $\delta\rho_g$ is the density perturbation, $\delta\vec{v}$ is the velocity perturbation. In our further considerations we will deal with 1D statements; thus, system (2) can be rewritten as

$$\frac{\partial \delta\rho_g}{\partial t} + \rho_g^0 \frac{\partial \delta v}{\partial x} = 0, \quad \rho_g^0 \frac{\partial \delta\vec{v}}{\partial t} + c_s^2 \frac{\partial \delta\rho_g}{\partial x} = 0. \tag{3}$$

System (3) admits a plane-wave solution of the form

$$\begin{pmatrix} \delta\rho \\ \delta v \end{pmatrix} = \begin{pmatrix} \tilde{\rho} \\ \tilde{v} \end{pmatrix} e^{i(kx - \omega t)}.$$

if time-frequency $\omega$ and wavenumber $k$ satisfy the dispersion relation

$$\omega^2 - c_s^2 k^2 = 0.$$

In these notations $(\tilde{\rho}, \tilde{v})^T$ is the polarization vector which is nonzero. Using the definition of the phase velocity, one gets

$$c \equiv \frac{\omega}{\|k\|} = \pm c_s.$$

and corresponding polarization vectors are:

$$\begin{pmatrix} \tilde{\rho} \\ \tilde{v} \end{pmatrix} = \begin{pmatrix} \rho_g^0 \\ \pm c_s \end{pmatrix}$$

In our study, we focus on the phase velocity and the error in the phase velocity induced by the SPH approximation of Eq. 1).

## 2.2   Smoothed Particle Hydrodynamics Method

Following [15,18] semi-discrete formulation of smooth particle hydrodynamics method applied to 1D case of system (1) can be written as

$$
\frac{dx_a}{dt} = v_a,
$$
$$
\rho_a = M \sum_{b=a-B}^{a+B} W_{a,b},
$$
$$
\frac{dv_a}{dt} = -M \sum_{b=a-B}^{a+B} \left( \frac{P_a}{\rho_a^2} + \frac{P_b}{\rho_b^2} \right) \frac{\partial W_{a,b}}{\partial x_a},
$$
$$
P_a = c_s^2 \rho_a,
$$

(4)

where $x_a$ is the particle coordinate, $x_b$ are coordinates of the neighbour particles which are involved in the local stencil, $\rho_a$ and $v_a$ are mass density and velocity of the $a$-th particle, $M$ is a particle mass (same for all particles), $B$ is the half of the number of neighbours (for equally spaced particles). Function $W_{a,b} = W(x_a - x_b, H)$ is the kernel function, which defines the properties of particular SPH approximation. The kernel is even function with respect to $x_a$; which is $W_{a,b} = W(x_a - x_b, H) = W(x_b - x_a, H) = W_{b,a}$. It is finite function with limited support and it is smooth enough. Moreover, $W_{a,b}$ tends to Dirac delta function as $x_b - x_a$ tends to zero.

In this study we consider the kernel function based on the cubic splines interpolation:

$$
W_{a,b} = \frac{2}{3H} \begin{cases} 1 - \frac{3}{2}\left(\frac{|x_a - x_b|}{H}\right)^2 + \frac{3}{4}\left(\frac{|x_a - x_b|}{H}\right)^3, & \frac{|x_a - x_b|}{H} \in [0,1], \\ \frac{1}{4}\left(2 - \frac{|x_a - x_b|}{H}\right)^3, & \frac{|x_a - x_b|}{H} \in [1,2], \\ 0, & \frac{|x_a - x_b|}{H} > 2. \end{cases}
$$

(5)

## 3   Numerical Dispersion

Numerical dispersion measures the error caused by the numerical method in the phase velocity of a plane wave solution. On the other hand, it can be considered as a direct method to estimate the convergence of the numerical solution to the plane wave solution [1,3,5,10]. To estimate the numerical dispersion, one needs to construct the plane wave solution of the linearized system (4).

To construct a plane-wave solution of system (4) we follow the approach of [4]. Assume that we seek for the small perturbation of the solution of the form:

$$
x_a = a\Delta x + X e^{i(kx_a - \omega t)},
$$
$$
\rho_a = \rho_0 + R e^{i(kx_a - \omega t)},
$$
$$
v_a = V e^{i(kx_a - \omega t)}.
$$

(6)

where $\Delta x$ is the unperturbed distance between the particles, $X$, $R$, and $V$ are the unknown components of the polarization vector.

Substituting relations (6) into the system (4) and neglecting the high-order terms one gets the system of linear equations with respect to the polarization vector components:

$$i\omega X + V = 0,$$

$$R = MX \sum_{b=a-B}^{a+B} (1 - e^{ik(x_b - x_a)}) \frac{\partial W_{a,b}}{\partial x_a},$$

$$V = \frac{M}{i\omega} \frac{c_s^2}{\rho_0} \sum_{c=a-B}^{a+B} \left( -\frac{R}{\rho_0}(1 + e^{ik(x_c - x_a)}) \frac{\partial W_{a,c}}{\partial x_a} + 2X(1 - e^{ik(x_c - x_a)}) \frac{\partial^2 W_{a,c}}{\partial x_a^2} \right).$$

If one requires the system to posses nontrivial solution; thus, the determinant to be equal to zero one may construct the dispersion relation:

$$\omega^2 - 8M \frac{c_s^2}{\rho_0} \sum_{b=0}^{B} \sin^2(kr_b/2) \frac{\partial^2 W_{a,b}}{\partial r_b^2} + 4M^2 \frac{c_s^2}{\rho_0^2} \left[ \sum_{b=0}^{B} \sin(kr_b) \frac{\partial W_{a,b}}{\partial r_b} \right]^2 = 0. \quad (7)$$

where $r_b = x_b - x_a = (b - a)\Delta x$. Using the definition of the phase velocity one gets:

$$c_s^{SPH} = \pm c_s \sqrt{\frac{8M}{k^2 \rho_0} \sum_{b=0}^{B} \sin^2(kr_b/2) \frac{\partial^2 W_{a,b}}{\partial r_b^2} - \frac{4M^2}{k^2 \rho_0^2} \left[ \sum_{b=0}^{B} \sin(kr_b) \frac{\partial W_{a,b}}{\partial r_b} \right]^2} = 0.$$

$$(8)$$

## 3.1   Asymptotic Analysis

The first step in the dispersion analysis of the SPH should be consideration of the limiting case of $\Delta x \to 0$.

Consider

$$\lim_{\Delta x \to 0} (c_s^{SPH})^2 = -c_s^2 \left( \int_{-\infty}^{+\infty} \frac{\sin(kr)}{k} \frac{\partial W}{\partial r} dr \right)^2 + c_s^2 \int_{-\infty}^{+\infty} \frac{\sin^2(\frac{kr}{2})}{(\frac{k}{2})^2} \frac{\partial^2 W}{\partial r^2} dr \quad (9)$$

$$= c_s^2 \mathcal{F}[W] (2 - \mathcal{F}[W])$$

where $\mathcal{F}[W](k)$ is the Fourier transform of the kernel function. For the cubic spline kernel, provided by Eq. 5) the Fourier transform is known (see e.g. [18]) and the limit can be represented as:

$$\lim_{\Delta x \to 0} \frac{\omega_{SPH}^2}{k^2} = c_s^2 \frac{\sin^4(\frac{kH}{2})}{(\frac{kH}{2})^4} \left( 2 - \frac{\sin^4(\frac{kH}{2})}{(\frac{kH}{2})^4} \right) \quad (10)$$

Thus, it is seen that when $\Delta x$ tends to zero simultaneously with $kH$ tends to zero, $c_s^{SPH}$ tends to $c_s$, and convergence of the numerical solution to analytical one takes place. However, any fixed $H$ SPH possesses irreducible error even if $\Delta x$ tends to zero. Moreover, this error has a pronounced impact when $kH > 10$. Below we study the irreducible error in detail.

## 3.2   Dimensionless Variables

We consider the linear wave propagation process; thus, it is convenient to introduce the dimensionless variables, describing the discretization. Originally, defining SPH approximation, two variables were introduced. They are the distance between the particles $\Delta x$ and the smoothing length $H$, considered as the stencil length in analogy with finite differences. However, the number of grid points per wavelength is typically used for the dispersion analysis. It is defined as $N = \dfrac{\lambda}{\Delta x} = \dfrac{2\pi}{k\Delta x}$, where $\lambda$ is the wavelength. The other parameter which is convenient for the SPH method is the number of kernels per wavelength $K = \dfrac{2\pi}{kH}$. In addition, we introduce the parameter $\varphi = \dfrac{\Delta x}{H}$ representing the number of neighbors or points in a stencil. These three parameters are dependent, so we will deal with the pairs of $(N, \varphi)$ or $(K, \varphi)$ to characterize the discretization. It is clear that $K = \varphi N$.

Using these notations the phase velocity can be rewritten as

$$c_s^{SPH}(N, \varphi) = \frac{c_s N \varphi}{\pi} \sqrt{2\varphi \sum_{j=0}^{[2/\varphi]} \sin^2\left(j\frac{\pi}{N}\right) \tilde{W}_2(j\varphi) - \varphi^2 \left[\sum_{j=0}^{[2/\varphi]} \sin\left(j\frac{2\pi}{N}\right) \tilde{W}_1(j\varphi)\right]^2}, \quad (11)$$

or

$$c_s^{SPH}(K, \varphi) = \frac{c_s K}{\pi} \sqrt{2\varphi \sum_{j=0}^{[2/\varphi]} \sin^2\left(j\varphi\frac{\pi}{K}\right) \tilde{W}_2(j\varphi) - \varphi^2 \left[\sum_{j=0}^{[2/\varphi]} \sin\left(j\varphi\frac{2\pi}{K}\right) \tilde{W}_1(j\varphi)\right]^2}, \quad (12)$$

where

$$\tilde{W}_1(j\varphi) = H^2 \frac{\partial W(r, H)}{\partial r}(j\Delta x, H) = \frac{2}{3} \begin{cases} -3j\varphi + \dfrac{9}{4}(j\varphi)^2, \ j\varphi \in [0, 1], \\ -\dfrac{3}{4}(2 - j\varphi)^2, \quad j\varphi \in [1, 2], \\ 0, \qquad\qquad\quad j\varphi > 2. \end{cases}$$

$$\tilde{W}_2(j\varphi) = H^3 \frac{\partial^2 W(r, H)}{\partial r^2}(j\Delta x, H) = \frac{2}{3} \begin{cases} -3 + \dfrac{9}{2}j\varphi, \ j\varphi \in [0, 1], \\ \dfrac{3}{2}(2 - j\varphi), \ j\varphi \in [1, 2], \\ 0, \qquad\qquad j\varphi > 2. \end{cases}$$

Using formulae (11) and (12) one may estimate the phase velocities of the numerical solutions for working (coarse enough) discretizations, even if the asymptotic regime is not achieved.

## 4   Numerical Experiments

### 4.1   Numerical Analysis of the Dispersion Relations

First, we need to study the derived estimation of the phase velocities. We considered the linearized problem (3) with $c_s = 1$ and $\rho_g^0 = 1$. Thus, the exact phase velocity of the plane-wave solution of the differential equation equals one. Next, we computed phase velocity of the plane-wave solution of SPH problem (9), according to formulae (11) and (12). We assumed that parameter $\varphi = \Delta x/H \in [0,1]$. The case of $\varphi \to 0$ corresponds to a fixed kernel length, but the distance between the particles tending to zero, which is $\Delta x \to 0$ for $H = const$. The case of $\varphi = 1$ corresponds to $\Delta x = H$, which means that the kernel includes only one neighboring point. This case is physically meaningless, but it allows illustrating the main problems of SPH approximation. Arbitrary fixed value of $\varphi$ means that we fix the ratio $\Delta x/H$ or we fix the stencil to make the analysis close to that of finite differences or finite elements [1, 10]. Parameters $N$ and $K$ representing the number of particles per wavelength and number of stencils per wavelength, respectively, may vary between 1 and $\infty$. The higher their values are, the fine the discretization is. In Fig. 1 we provide the plots of $c_s^{SPH}$ as function of two variables, both $(\varphi, N)$ and $(\varphi, K)$. Note that phase velocity is a monotonous function of $N$ or $K$, whereas its behavior as a function of $\varphi$ is complex and requires detailed study. In addition, even for high values of $N$ and $K$, phase velocity may strongly variate from one, i.e., from the correct value. Moreover, the velocity plot as a function of $(\varphi, N)$ illustrates that for fixed $N$ and low values of $\varphi$, velocity tends to zero, leading to 100% error. This case corresponds to the fixed distance between the particles $\Delta x$ but reduces $\Delta x/H$. Thus, $H$ increases and exceeds a wavelength, which causes the loss of any approximation. This effect is also observed in [21]. This effect can be seen in Fig. 2 where the phase velocity is provided as a function of $\varphi$ for fixed $N = 100$ and $K = 100$. The plots illustrate the complex dependence of the phase velocity (relative error) on $\varphi = \Delta x/H$. It is not monotonous; moreover, it is not a smooth function. If a fixed $N$ with $\varphi \to 0$ is considered, the error tends to be 100%, as discussed above.

The main effect that can be observed in Fig. 2 is the lack of convergence in the SPH method when $\varphi$ is fixed. Indeed, the plots illustrate that for fine enough discretizations $K = 100$; which is 100 kernels per wavelength, and reasonable $\varphi \in [\varepsilon, 1]$ phase velocity error tends to be a constant different from zero. This leads to irreducible error in numerical solution; i.e., the plane wave propagates with an incorrect velocity which could not be corrected by mesh refinement with a fixed stencil or fixed number of neighbors. There are a set of local maximums where the error is close to zero; they are $\varphi = 1/P$, where $P$ is an integer. The other local maximums $\varphi = 2/(2P + 1)$, where $P$ is an integer. The error values in these points strongly deviate from zero, thus causing the irreducible error. To illustrate the influence of $\varphi$ on error, we considered relative error as a

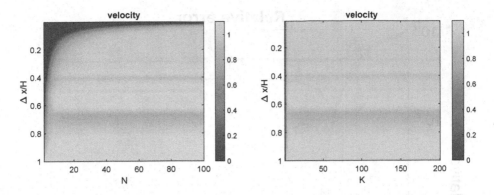

**Fig. 1.** Phase velocity of the SPH method as function of $(\varphi, N)$ - left and $(\varphi, K)$ - right.

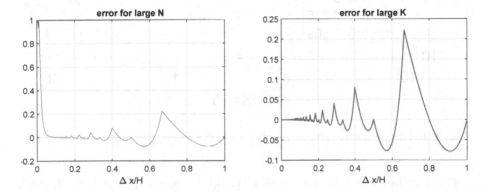

**Fig. 2.** Relative velocity error as function of $\varphi = \Delta x / H$ for fixed $N = 100$ - left, and $K = 100$ - right.

function of $K$ for several fixed values of $\varphi$. In particular, we considered $\varphi = 0.5$ which corresponds to a local maximum, where the error tends to zero for large $K$; $\varphi = 2/3$ corresponding to local maximum deviating from zero; $\varphi = 0.569$ corresponding to one of the local minimums also deviating from zero, and $\varphi = 0.625$ corresponding to a point where the error is close to zero (not a local minimum). According to the presented results (Fig. 3), SPH converges with the second order, if $\varphi = 1/P$, where $P$ is integer. However, for other values of $\varphi$, the error tends to some values, different from zero. These asymptotic are reached rather fast; i.e., for $K < 100$ and further mesh refinement does not improve the accuracy.

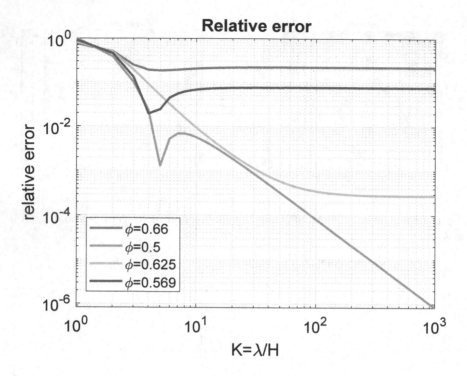

**Fig. 3.** Relative velocity error as function of $K$ for fixed $\varphi$ (in logarithmic scale).

The last but not least case which should be considered is fixed $K$ with decreasing $\varphi$. It corresponds to the situation when the smoothing length $H$ is fixed, but the distance between the particles $\Delta x$ is refined. According to the plot in Fig. 2 convergence of the relative error is expected, however, in a non-monotonous way. To estimate the convergence rate, we considered relative error in local maximums $\varphi = 2/(2P + 1)$, where $P$ is integer, as presented in Fig. 4. The results illustrate the second order of the maximum error reduction if $\varphi \to 0$. Additionally, we provide the plots of the relative error with respect to $K$ for several values of $\varphi$ corresponding to the local maximums (5). One may observe the reduction of the asymptotic error; moreover, the error converges to asymptotic with the second order with respect to $K$.

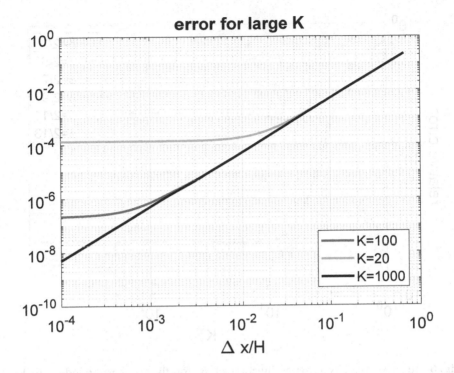

**Fig. 4.** Relative velocity error at local maximums $\varphi = 2/(2P + 1)$, where $P$ is integer for fixed $K$ (in logarithmic scale).

## 4.2   Effect of Numerical Dispersion on Propagating Impulse

To illustrate the effect of the numerical dispersion of the solution, we simulated propagation of the Ricker wavelet

$$f(t) = (1 - 2\pi^2\nu_0^2 t^2)e^{-\pi^2\nu_0^2 t^2},$$

if the propagation velocity is constant and frequency-independent the solution propagates unperturbed along the characteristics; i.e., $u(t, x) = f(t - x/c_s)$. However, if the sound speed depends on the frequency, the pulse will be destructed, and the solution should be constructed as:

$$\tilde{f}(t - x/\hat{c}_g(\omega)) = \mathcal{F}^{-1}\left[ e^{i\omega(t - x/\hat{c}_g(\omega))}\mathcal{F}[f(t)] \right],$$

where $\mathcal{F}$ is the Fourier transform with respect to time, and $c(\omega)$ is the phase velocity obtained from the dispersion analysis, $\hat{c}_g(\omega)$ is the frequency-dependent phase velocity. Ricker pulse is defined by its central frequency $\nu_0 = \frac{\omega_0}{2\pi}$, so that its spectra can be considered finite $\omega \in 2\pi[\nu_0/2, 2\nu_2]$. It means that if we fix the discretization with respect to the central frequency, the discretization will be coarser for high-frequency modes, and it will be finer for low-frequency models presented in the pulse.

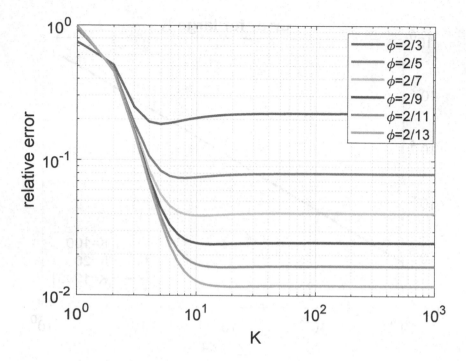

**Fig. 5.** Relative velocity error as function of $K$ for fixed $\varphi$ corresponding to local maximums (in logarithmic scale).

We considered the impulse propagated ten wavelengths (measured according to central frequency). We chose three discretizations $N = 50$ for all experiments, whereas $\varphi$ varied. In particular Fig. 6 corresponds to $\varphi = 0.19$, Fig. 7 corresponds to $\varphi = 0.25$, and Fig. 8 corresponds to $\varphi = 0.2875$. In the first case, we observe significant dispersion in the signal because the phase velocity error tends to almost zero for $\varphi = 0.19$, but it still strongly depends on the discretization for $N \in [25, 100]$. Point $\varphi = 0.25$ corresponds to the local maximum of the error function, which equals zero. As a result, the numerical dispersion is small, and the impulse is almost not distorted. The last case of $\varphi = 0.2875$ corresponds to high irreducible phase velocity error. Moreover, the error is almost achieved its limit for the considered discretizations $N \in [25, 100]$. Thus, we observed almost no impulse distortion, but it propagated with incorrect velocity.

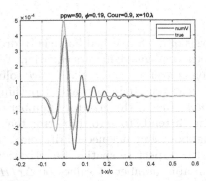
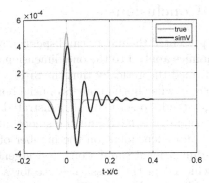

**Fig. 6.** Original impulse (red) and distortion of the impulse due to numerical dispersion. Left plot represents theoretical prediction, right plot represents numerical simulation results. Discretization was $N = 50$ and $\varphi = 0.19$. (Color figure online)

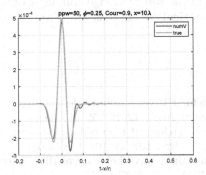
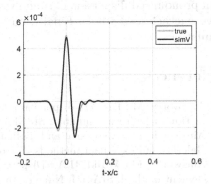

**Fig. 7.** Original impulse (red) and distortion of the impulse due to numerical dispersion. Left plot represents theoretical prediction, right plot represents numerical simulation results. Discretization was $N = 50$ and $\varphi = 0.25$. (Color figure online)

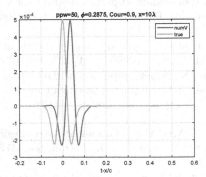
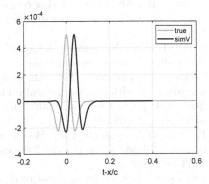

**Fig. 8.** Original impulse (red) and distortion of the impulse due to numerical dispersion. Left plot represents theoretical prediction, right plot represents numerical simulation results. Discretization was $N = 50$ and $\varphi = 0.2875$. (Color figure online)

## 5    Conclusions

We presented the numerical dispersion analysis of the Smoothed Particle Hydrodynamics applied to the one-dimensional isothermal gas dynamics equation. We confirmed theoretically that the SPH solution converges to the plane wave solution only when both numbers of neighbor particles tend to infinity and smoothing length tends to zero. We demonstrated visually that if the arbitrary number of the neighbor is fixed and the smoothing length tends to zero, the error tends to a value dependent on the number of neighbors, but not necessarily zero. In one-dimensional simulations, convergence with respect to spatial discretization is achieved in the classical sense for a countable number of values of $\Delta x/H$. According to the numerical analysis, if the method converges, it possesses the second order of convergence with respect to grid step (stencil length).

Moreover, we demonstrated the ability of dispersion analysis to explain some numerical artifacts of SPH with coarse resolution. In particular, we found regimes with pronounced dispersion of sound waves in the wave package and delay of the wave package as a whole. Finally, our theoretical predictions are confirmed in simulations.

## References

1. Ainsworth, M.: Discrete dispersion relation for HP-version finite element approximation at high wave number. SIAM J. Numer. Anal. **42**(2), 553–575 (2004)
2. Ainsworth, M.: Dispersive and dissipative behaviour of high order discontinuous Galerkin finite element methods. J. Comput. Phys. **198**(1), 106–130 (2004)
3. Ainsworth, M., Wajid, H.A.: Dispersive and dissipative behavior of the spectral element method. SIAM J. Numer. Anal. **47**(5), 3910–3937 (2009)
4. Cha, S.-H., Whitworth, A.P.: Implementations and tests of Godunov-type particle hydrodynamics. Mon. Not. R. Astron. Soc. **340**, 73–90 (2003)
5. Cohen, G. (ed.): Metodes numeriques d'ordre eleve pour les ondes en regime transitoire. INRIA (1994). (in French)
6. Dehnen, W., Aly, H.: Improving convergence in smoothed particle hydrodynamics simulations without pairing instability. Mon. Not. R. Astron. Soc. **425**, 1068–1082 (2012)
7. Gingold, R.A., Monaghan, J.J.: Smoothed particle hydrodynamics: theory and application to non-spherical stars. Mon. Not. R. Astron. Soc. **181**, 375–89 (1977)
8. Grigoryev, V., Stoyanovskaya, O., Snytnikov, N.: Supercomputer model of dynamical dusty gas with intense momentum transfer between phases based on OpenFPM library. J. Phys: Conf. Ser. **2099**, 012056 (2021). https://doi.org/10.1088/1742-6596/2099/1/012056
9. Hubber, D.A., Rosotti, G.P., Booth, R.A.: GANDALF - Graphical Astrophysics code for N-body dynamics and Lagrangian fluids. Mon. Not. R. Astron. Soc. **473**, 1603–1632 (2018)
10. Lisitsa, V.: Dispersion analysis of discontinuous Galerkin method on triangular mesh for elastic wave equation. Appl. Math. Model. **40**, 5077–5095 (2016). https://doi.org/10.1016/j.apm.2015.12.039
11. Liu, Y.: Optimal staggered-grid finite-difference schemes based on least-squares for wave equation modelling. Geophys. J. Int. **197**(2), 1033–1047 (2014)

12. Lucy, L.B.: A numerical approach to the testing of the fission hypothesis. Astron. J. **82**, 1013–24 (1977)
13. Mazzieri, I., Rapetti, F.: Dispersion analysis of triangle-based spectral element methods for elastic wave propagation. Numer. Algorithms **60**(4), 631–650 (2012)
14. Monaghan, J.J.: On the problem of penetration in particle methods. J. Comput. Phys. **82**(1), 1–15 (1989)
15. Monaghan, J.J.: Smoothed particle hydrodynamics. Rep. Prog. Phys. **68**, 1703–1759 (2005). https://doi.org/10.1088/0034-4885/68/8/R01
16. Morris, J.P.: A study of the stability properties of smooth particle hydrodynamics. Publ. Astron. Soc. Austral. **13**(1), 97–102 (1996)
17. Mulder, W.A.: Spurious modes in finite-element discretizations of the wave equation may not be all that bad. Appl. Numer. Math. **30**(4), 425–445 (1999)
18. Price, D.J.: Smoothed particle hydrodynamics and magnetohydrodynamics. J. Comput. Phys. **231**(3), 759–794 (2012)
19. Price, D., et al.: Phantom: a smoothed particle hydrodynamics and magnetohydrodynamics code for astrophysics. Publ. Astron. Soc. Austral. **35**, e031 (2020)
20. Rasio, F.A.: Particle methods in astrophysical fluid dynamics. Prog. Theor. Phys. Suppl. **138**, 609–621 (2000)
21. Quinlan, N.J., Basa, M., Lastiwka, M.: Truncation error in mesh-free particle methods. International journal for numerical methods in engineering Int. J. Numer. Meth. Eng. **66**, 2064–2085 (2006)
22. Springel, V.: The cosmological simulation code gadget-2. Mon. Not. R. Astron. Soc. **364**(4), 1105–1134 (2005)
23. Stoyanovskaya, O.P., Glushko, T.A., Snytnikov, N.V., Snytnikov, V.N.: Two-fluid dusty gas in smoothed particle hydrodynamics: fast and implicit algorithm for stiff linear drag. Astron. Comp. **25**, 25–37 (2018)
24. Stoyanovskaya, O.P., Davydov, M., Arendarenko, M., Isaenko, E., Markelova, T., Snytnikov, V.: Fast method to simulate dynamics of two-phase medium with intense interaction between phases by smoothed particle hydrodynamics: gas-dust mixture with polydisperse particles, linear drag, one-dimensional tests. J. Comp. Phys. **430**, 110035 (2021)
25. Vacondio, R., et al.: Grand challenges for smoothed particle hydrodynamics numerical schemes. Comput. Particle Mech. **8**(3), 575–588 (2020). https://doi.org/10.1007/s40571-020-00354-1
26. Zhang, C., et al.: SPHinXsys: an open-source meshless, multi-resolution and multiphysics library. Softw. Impacts **6**, 100033 (2020)
27. Zhu, Q., Hernquist, L., Li, Y.: Numerical convergence in smoothed particle hydrodynamics. Astrophys. J. **800**, Number 1 (2015)
28. LS-DYNA Homepage. https://www.lstc.com/products/ls-dyna. Accessed 2 Mar 2022

# Algorithms for Design of Robust Stabilization Systems

Olha Sushchenko[1](✉) [iD], Yuliya Averyanova[1] [iD], Ivan Ostroumov[1] [iD],
Nataliia Kuzmenko[1] [iD], Maksym Zaliskyi[1] [iD], Oleksandr Solomentsev[1] [iD],
Borys Kuznetsov[2], Tatyana Nikitina[3] [iD], Olena Havrylenko[4] [iD], Anatoliy Popov[4] [iD],
Valerii Volosyuk[4] [iD], Oleksandr Shmatko[4] [iD], Nikolay Ruzhentsev[4] [iD],
Simeon Zhyla[4] [iD], Vladimir Pavlikov[4] [iD], Kostiantyn Dergachov[4] [iD],
and Eduard Tserne[4] [iD]

[1] National Aviation University, Kyiv, Ukraine
{sushoa,ostroumovv,nataliiakuzmenko,maximus2812,
avsolomentsev}@ukr.net, ayua@nau.edu.ua
[2] A. Pidhornyi Institute of Mechanical Engineering Problems of the National Academy of
Sciences of Ukraine, Kharkiv, Ukraine
[3] Educational scientific professional pedagogical Institute Ukrainian Engineering Pedagogical
Academy, Bakhmut, Ukraine
[4] National Aerospace University H.E. Zhukovsky "Kharkiv Aviation Institute", Kharkiv,
Ukraine
{o.havrylenko,a.v.popov,v.volosyuk,o.shmatko,s.zhyla,v.pavlikov,
k.dergachov,e.tserne}@khai.edu

**Abstract.** Accuracy of measuring and observation processes depends greatly on
the stabilization of the appropriate equipment located on moving vehicles. We
propose to design stabilization systems based on robust control that can ensure
the required accuracy in difficult conditions of real operation. The main issue of
the research is the development of numerical algorithms for designing robust stabilization systems assigned for control of inertial platforms motion. The analysis
of applications and classification of inertially stabilized platforms is given. The
block diagram of the algorithm of the robust parametrical optimization is represented. Features of this numerical algorithm are discussed including forming
the optimization criterion and implementation of the optimization procedure. The
block diagram of the robust structural synthesis is represented. Features of forming
the function of mixed sensitivity are given. Results of simulation for the inertially
stabilized platforms assigned for the operation of the ground moving vehicles are
shown.

**Keywords:** Robust control · Inertially stabilized platforms · Numerical
algorithms · Robust parametrical optimization · Robust structural synthesis ·
Minimum realization · Balanced realization · Function of mixed sensitivity ·
Weighting functions

O. Gervasi et al. (Eds.): ICCSA 2022, LNCS 13375, pp. 198–213, 2022.
https://doi.org/10.1007/978-3-031-10522-7_15

# 1  Introduction

The topicality of developing numerical algorithms for design of inerially stabilized plat-forms (ISPs) is explained by the necessity to satisfy the high requirements for stabiliza-tion and tracking accuracy. Nowadays, there are two basic groups of the above-mentioned problems [1]:

1)  precision stabilization of inertial sensors in gimballed inertial navigation systems;
2)  stabilization and tracking of measuring devices and equipment for different purposes;
3)  combined stabilization of inertial sensors and measuring devices.

To solve the problem of the inertial stabilization, it is necessary to take into con-sideration the Earth and moving vehicle motions including the translational speed, and translational and Coriolis accelerations [1, 2]. These factors are taken into account in operating algorithms of gimballed inertial navigation systems. The inertial stabilization of measuring devices and equipment for different purposes requires correction from the inertial navigation systems. Otherwise, this stabilization is considered to be inertial at some approximation.

The block diagrams of the gimballed inertial navigation system and ISP with payload are represented in Figs. 1, 2 [2].

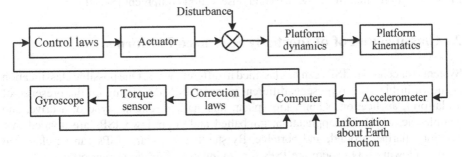

**Fig. 1.** The block diagram of the gimballed inertial navigation system.

The inertial navigation can be realized by means of both gimballed and strap-down systems [3]. It should be noted that such factors as the drastic progress of inertial sensors (laser, fiber-optic, and MEMS gyroscopes) and computing techniques have been led to the wide application of strap-down inertial navigation systems. This trend was accelerated with arising the possibility to correct inertial navigation systems from Global Positioning System (GPS) [4]. Nowadays, high-precision gimballed inertial stabilization systems are mostly used in strategic applications [3]. On contrary, gimballed systems are important for the stabilization of measuring devices and equipment operated on moving vehicles. Strap-down systems are used in this area only in applications with rigid restrictions on dimensions and low requirements for accuracy [5]. This trend will be kept in the future as efforts directed to the development of measuring devices and observation equipment of high accuracy could be useless without their stabilization [6, 7].

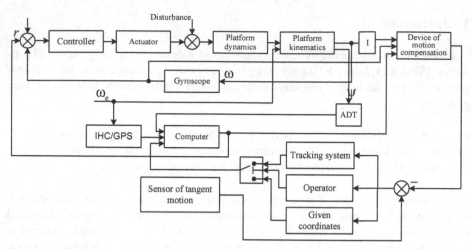

**Fig. 2.** Block diagram of the inertially stabilized platform: I is the integrator; ADT is the angle-data-transmitter.

Hence, the modern trend of developing ISPs changes accents on types of stabilization systems. Earlier, great attention was paid to the stabilization of inertial sensors. Now, the most topical is the problem of inertial stabilization and controlling orientation by lines-of-sight for measuring devices and observation equipment [8–10].

## 2   Classification of of Inertially Stabilized Platforms

Systems for control of ISPs can be classified in different ways. One possible classification is shown in Fig. 3. It represents different types of ISPs depending on the presence of a platform, application, stabilization plant, kinematical scheme, type of a drive, and completeness [11]. By application, gimballed and strap-down ISPs are divided into aviation, marine, ground, and portable. By stabilization plant, ISPs can be classified in the following way. There are ISPs for equipment of different purposes, sensors of precision navigation systems, optic sensors, mobile antennas. Depending on the type of the kinematical diagram, ISPs can be one-axis, two-axis, three-axis, and multi-axis. Inertially stabilized platforms can be divided also by the type of drive depending on the presence of the reducer. Features of ISPs for equipment of different purposes depend on payload dimensions, which could vary in the wide range. This factor influences on design and dimensions of the platform and gimbals, and also on the realization of control loops. The typical ISP includes the electro-mechanical unit, which ensures the physical interface between the observation equipment and moving vehicle, stabilization system, and the system of tracking by the line-of-sight of the observation equipment.

An autonomous precision inertial navigation system includes the inertial measuring unit located on the gimballed platform and the computing device. The inertial measuring unit consists of three accelerometers with measuring axes oriented along the platform's axes, and gyroscopic devices, which ensure determining the attitude of the moving vehicle in the inertial space.

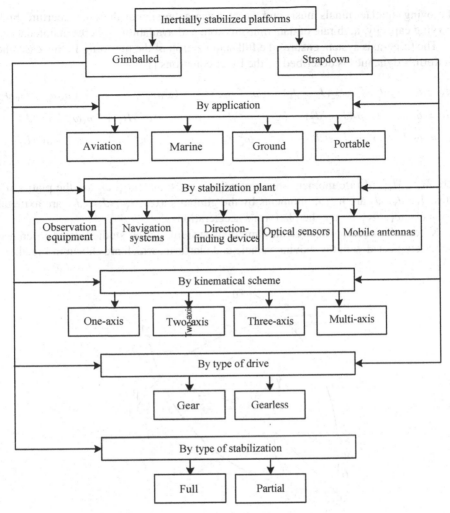

**Fig. 3.** Classification of inertially stabilized platforms.

The high precision stabilization of optical sensors including television and infra-red cameras can be achieved only if the line-of-sight is controlled [12]. This problem is complicated in conditions of operation of sensors on the moving vehicle or motion of the observation object. Most practical applications of optical sensors in these conditions require stabilization by two axes [1].

Perspective applications of ISPs are control systems of mobile antennas of satellite communication [4]. Nowadays, mobile communication covers practically all the world, but the transmission rate for some applications is not sufficiently high. The increasing rate of data transmission and decreasing cost are possible in conditions of using new satellites able to ensure functioning small satellite terminals. Antennas of satellite communication of moving small terminals must combine such characteristics as the small aperture, high carrying capacity, high rate of data transmission, and availability by cost maintenance.

The three-axis system ensures the full stabilization of the platform. In this case, the platform's dynamics is described by the Euler equations [13].

$$M_x = \dot{\omega} \rightarrow_x J_x + \omega_y \omega_z (J_z - J_y) - (\omega_y^2 - \omega_z^2)J_{yz} - (\omega_x \omega_y + \dot{\omega}_z)J_{xz} + (\omega_x \omega_z - \dot{\omega}_y)J_{xy},$$
$$M_y = \dot{\omega}_y J_y + \omega_x \omega_z (J_x - J_z) - (\omega_z^2 - \omega_x^2)J_{xz} - (\omega_z \omega_y + \dot{\omega}_x)J_{xy} + (\omega_x \omega_y - \dot{\omega}_z)J_{xz},$$
$$M_z = \dot{\omega}_z J_z + \omega_x \omega_y (J_y - J_x) - (\omega_x^2 - \omega_y^2)J_{xy} - (\omega_x \omega_z + \dot{\omega}_y)J_{yz} + (\omega_x \omega_z - \dot{\omega}_x)J_{xz},$$

$$(1)$$

here $M_x$, $M_y$, $M_z$ are moments by the gimbal's axes; $\omega_x$, $\omega_y$, $\omega_z$ are the platform's rates; $J_x$, $J_y$, $J_z$ are inertia moments by the gimbal's axes; $J_{yz}$, $J_{xz}$, $J_{xy}$ are axifugal moments; $\dot{\omega}_x$, $\dot{\omega}_y$, $\dot{\omega}_z$ are the platform's accelerations.

Kinematics relationships of the three-axis system can be studied using reference frames connected with the moving vehicle and platform, which are shown in Fig. 4.

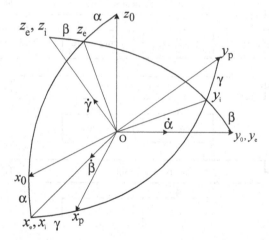

**Fig. 4.** The mutual position of reference frames connected with the moving vehicle and platform: $Ox_0y_0z_0$ is the reference frame connected with the moving vehicle; $Ox_p y_p z_p$ is the reference frame connected with the platform; $Ox_e y_e z_e$ is the reference frame connected with the external gimbal, and $Ox_i y_i z_i$ is the reference frame connected with the internal gimbals.

The main tasks solved by ISP operated on moving vehicles include:

1) stabilization of observation equipment in the vertical, horizontal, and lateral planes during angular motion of the vehicle;
2) tracking of the line-of-sight of the observation equipment for both immovable and moving reference points;
3) combination of two previous tasks.

In accordance with Fig. 4, expressions for determining the platform's angle rates may be represented in the following way [13]

$$\omega_x = \dot{\beta} \cos \gamma + \dot{\alpha} \cos \beta \sin \gamma,$$
$$\omega_y = \dot{\alpha} \cos \beta \cos \gamma - \dot{\beta} \sin \gamma, \tag{2}$$
$$\omega_z = \dot{\gamma} - \dot{\alpha} \sin \beta,$$

here $\alpha$, $\beta$, $\gamma$ are angles of the deviations from the horizontal plane and the vertical axis respectively.

Based on expressions (2), differential equations, which characterize changing angular rates of the platform, become

$$\dot{\alpha} = (\omega_x \sin \gamma + \omega_y \cos \gamma) / \cos \beta,$$
$$\dot{\beta} = \omega_x \cos \gamma - \omega_y \sin \gamma, \tag{3}$$
$$\dot{\gamma} = \omega_z + \mathrm{tg}\beta(\omega_x \sin \gamma + \omega_y \cos \gamma).$$

Hence, Eqs. (2), (3) describe the kinematics of ISPs.

Four-axis ISPs are used when it is necessary to eliminate the effect of the lock of frames. Such a situation arises if at least two angles of the stabilized platform turns vary in the wide range.

The best results in the accuracy of observation equipment could be achieved by the combination of precision stabilization, improving the accuracy of inertial measuring units, and processing of measuring information [14–16].

## 3  Algorithm of Robust Parametrical Optimization

It is necessary to develop space-state models for the robust parametrical optimization. Based on these models and model of the controller, we can derive a set of matrices A,B,C,D of the closed-loop system necessary for the synthesis and analysis of the control laws.

The robust parametrical optimization requires using both nominal and parametrically disturbed models. Solutions taking into account maximum and minimum parameters are true for any values, which belong to the range of permissible parameters. This assertion is true for the detectable and stabilizable systems. This situation takes place in most practical applications [17]. Usage of parametrically disturbed models allows us to take into account uncertainties in the mathematical description. These uncertainties are caused by changing parameters of the real system in some bounds and the impossibility to represent all the features of the real system in a mathematical way. Commonly, such uncertainties are separated into two types as parametrical structured and unstructured (unmodelled dynamics [18]). For the parametric optimization, it is easiest to take into account parametric structured disturbances. Block diagrams of deterministic and stochastic models are shown in Fig. 5.

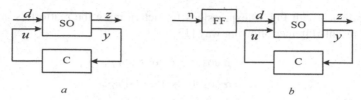

**Fig. 5.** Deterministic (*a*) and stochastic (*b*) models: SO is the stabilization object; C is the controller; FF is the forming filter; $d$ is the signal of input; $z$ is the signal of observation; $u$ is the signal of control; $y$ is the signal of output; $\eta$ is a disturbance.

It is possible to increase the efficiency of the robust optimization using the mixed $H_2/H_\infty$ approach [19]. The combination of $H_2$ and $H_\infty$ optimizations allows us to state the task of designing optimal stabilization systems on the basis of the quadratic criterion while maintaining its properties under the influence of disturbances [80]. In this case, the optimal synthesis should be carried out using a combined optimization criterion taking into account both the quality and the robustness of ISP [20].

Such a criterion is determined on the basis of $H_2$, $H_\infty$ norms. The influence of each component can be regulated by weighting coefficients, which depend on the characteristics and features of the system. For designing robust systems, it is advantageous to apply the complex criterion founded on accuracy indices of nominal and perturbed systems. In this case, the parametric structured perturbations are taken into account. Hence, the complex objective function takes the form [11, 20]

$$
\begin{aligned}
J_{H_2/H_\infty} &= \lambda_2^{\text{nom d}}||\Phi(K,x,u,j\omega)||_2^{\text{nom d}} + \lambda_2^{\text{nom s}}||\Phi(K,x,u,j\omega)||_2^{\text{nom s}}+ \\
&+\lambda_\infty^{\text{nom}}||\Phi(K,x,u,j\omega)||_\infty^{\text{nom}} + \sum_{i=1}^{n} \lambda_{2_i}^{\text{par d}}||\Phi(K,x,u,j\omega)||_{2_i}^{\text{par d}}+ \\
&+\sum_{i=1}^{n} \lambda_{2_i}^{\text{par s}}||\Phi(K,x,u,j\omega)||_{2_i}^{\text{par s}} + \sum_{i=1}^{n} \lambda_{\infty i}^{\text{par}}||\Phi(K,x,u,j\omega)||_{\infty i}^{\text{par}} + PF,
\end{aligned}
\tag{4}
$$

here $||\cdot||_2^{\text{nom d}}$, $||\cdot||_2^{\text{nom s}}$, $||\cdot||_{2_i}^{\text{par d}}$, $||\cdot||_{2_i}^{\text{par s}}$ are $H_2$-norms of transfer functions of the deterministic and stochastic systems with nominal and parametrically disturbing parameters, $||\cdot||_\infty^{\text{nom}}$, $||\cdot||_{\infty i}^{\text{par}}$ are $H_\infty$-norms of transfer functions of the nominal and parametrically disturbed systems, $\lambda_2^{\text{nom d}}$, $\lambda_2^{\text{nom s}}$, $\lambda_\infty^{\text{nom}}$, $\lambda_{2_i}^{\text{par d}}$, $\lambda_{2_i}^{\text{par s}}$, $\lambda_{\infty i}^{\text{par}}$ are weighting coefficients of appropriate norms, $n$ is the number of the system's models, $PF$ is the penalty function that ensures fulfillment of a system's stability conditions at the time of the optimization procedure, K is a vector of optimized parameters.

Consider constituents of the objective function (4). The weight coefficients in the deterministic case are calculated on the ground of Gramian of controllability. Usage of $H_\infty$-norms of models with parametrically disturbed parameters in the objective function ensures a certain insensitivity of the synthesized system to changing parameters in the range of the acceptable values. It is common knowledge [17, 20] that requirements for performance and robustness are mutually contradictory. Hence, the problem of the $H_2/H_\infty$ synthesis of the stabilization system asserts in searching for a compromise between performance and robustness. This compromise can be ensured through the use of the combined objective function with changing weight coefficients (4). Such technique permits a researcher to decrease or increase the level of performance or robustness during design of the system.

The search for a solution requires the multiple minimizations of the objective function (4) using one of the well-known techniques. For control or stabilization systems, it is expedient to use the non-strict Nelder-Mead method or the genetic algorithm [21]. The preference of the latter algorithm asserts the possibility to obtain the global minimum in contrast to the Nelder-Mead method.

The heuristic procedure of robust optimization is carried out in two phases.

Solutions admissible in the view of technical performances are determined at the first phase. At this phase, constituents of the vector $\Lambda$ are considered to be units. For some given values of matrices Q and R, it is necessary to implement minimization of the criterion (4). After fulfillment the optimization procedure, it is necessary to check functional constraints. If these constraints are not satisfied, it is necessary to increase weight coefficients $q_i$ (for condition $x_i > x_{i0}$) and $r_j$ (for condition $u_j > u_{j0}$). The optimization procedure is repeated until the functional constraints will be satisfied. The obtained solutions are permissible from the point of view fulfillment requirements that are given to control systems.

At the second phase, elements of matrices Q and R are believed to be fixed. And weighting coefficients (vector $\Lambda$) are varied.

It should be noted that both phases are implemented in the interactive mode.

A compromise between indices of accuracy and robustness is defined by a researcher, which could give a preference one of the criteria depending on operation conditions and constructive features of the designed system. For example, the preference must be given to the component $J_{H_2}^s$ for the influence of intense random external disturbances. In conditions of significant parametric disturbances, it is advisable to decrease the objective function $J_\infty$.

Based on the results of practical applications, we can say that some cycles of the above-mentioned optimization procedure ensure a desired compromise.

It is worth considering that the described approach is characterized by a heuristic nature. There is no way to prove it convergence in an analytical way. But its efficiency is proved by the great quantity of the practical applications.

The block diagram of the algorithm of designing a stabilization system based on the parametrical robust optimization is represented in Fig. 7.

The algorithm of robust parametrical optimization is characterized by some features. It should be noted that a model of the control system can have non-controlled and non-observable parts. In this case, it is necessary to simplify the model that is to determine its minimum realization. There are two approaches to the implementation of the minimum realization [22].

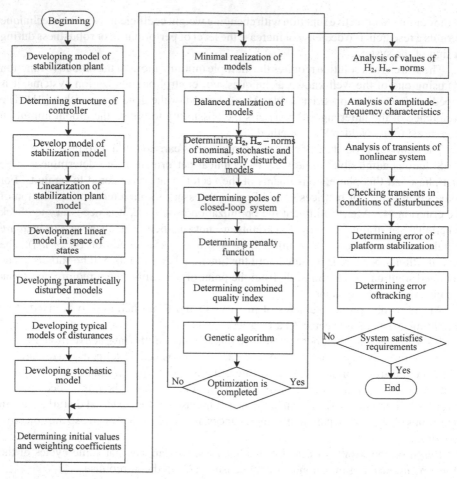

**Fig. 6.** The algorithm of designing inertially stabilized platform using the robust parametrical optimization.

The first approach is based on using non-minimum realization in the space of states, which is formed on the basis of the model, which corresponds to the real system. Further, the obtained model is reduced to observable and controllable parts.

The second approach is based on using impulse characteristics of the system and obtaining the minimum realization by the transformation of the Hankel matrices. In our situation, it is expedient to use the first approach as impulse characteristics of the system are not always known at beginning of the design process. The review of known algorithms gives grounds to choose the Rosenbrock algorithm. It should be noted that minimum realization can be implemented by MatLab software [23–26].

In some applications, it is expedient to use astatic control systems. In this case, we can use a shift of the matrix of state-space model [25]. In such a way, it is possible to avoid the appearance of the zero poles that is of great importance for astatic systems. The shifted matrix looks like $A_{sh} = A-A_0$, where $A_0$ is the matrix with some small elements. Usage of such an approach leads to to obtaining the balanced realization.

For industrial applications, models of control systems very often are characterized by sufficient dispersion of elements. Usually, the state-space matrices are believed to be ill-conditioned. To eliminate this disadvantage, it is necessary to use scaling. For this, it is possible to use the balanced realization or a realization with equal Gramians of controllability and observability [22].

## 4  Algorithm of Robust Structural Synthesis

The modern approach to designing ISPs foresees usage of robust structural synthesis. One of the widespread methods is $H_\infty$-synthesis, which ensures designing in conditions of uncertainty. It is known, that the designing of real systems must satisfy some conflict purposes. Research of a compromise in this situation can be achieved by the usage function of mixed sensitivity for forming the optimization objective function. It is also convenient to use two control loops by the reference signal and by the disturbance. Such systems are called two-degree-of-freedoms systems. There are different approaches for their designing. The method supposed in [17] is grounded on the robust stabilization and representation of the parametrical disturbances using the normalized co-prime factorization. It is based on loop shaping that is forming the required frequency responses of the designed ISP. After forming the stabilization object with desired characteristics, it is possible to synthesize $H_\infty$-controller, which ensures the robust stability and robust performance of the designed system [27].

The advantages of the above-mentioned approach arc ensuring robust stabilization and taking into account parametrical disturbances. It should be noted, the influence of coordinate perturbations in practical applications is essential. The method of improving the above-mentioned procedure is based on introducing components connected with external disturbances in the optimization criterion, as this has been supposed in [6, 28] – [30]. The optimization criterion for $H_\infty$-synthesis becomes

$$
J = \left\| \begin{array}{cc} -W_1 T_{ref}+ & W_1 G_d (1 + GK_2)^{-1} \\ + W_1 GK_1 (I + GK_2)^{-1} & \\ W_2 K_1 (I + GK_2)^{-1} & -W_2 K_2 G_d (I + GK_2)^{-1} \\ W_3 GK_1 (I + GK_2)^{-1} & W_3 G_d (I + GK_2)^{-1} \end{array} \right\|_\infty , \tag{5}
$$

here $W_1$, $W_2$, $W_3$ and $T_{ref}$ are weighting and reference transfer functions, G, $K_1$, $K_2$, $G_d$ are transfer functions of the plant, controllers, and disturbance.

The models of disturbances were developed after analysis of the features of the system. For example, for the ISPs operated on the ground moving vehicles, it is expedient to take into account the imbalance moment and disturbances caused by the angular rate of the ground moving vehicle [6]. Further, it is necessary to develop the mathematical model of the generalized augmented system taking into account both parallel and serial connections of the system's units [28]. Equations of state and observation become

$$
\begin{aligned}
\dot{x}_G &= A_G x_G - B_G u + B_{G_d} d, \\
\dot{x}_{Tef} &= A_{T_{ref}} x_{Tref} + B_{T_{ref}} r, \\
\dot{x}_{W_1} &= A_{W_1} x_{W_1} - B_{W_1} u + B_{W_1} r, \\
\dot{x}_{W_2} &= A_{W_2} x_{W_2} - B_{W_2} u, \\
\dot{x}_{W_3} &= A_{W_3} x_{W_3} - B_{W_3} u + B_{W_3} r, \\
z_1 &= C_{W_1} x_{W_1} + D_{W_1} r, \\
z_2 &= C_{W_2} x_{W_2} + D_{W_2} u, \\
z_3 &= C_{W_1} x_{W_3} + D_{W_3} u + D_{G_d} d, \\
y_1 &= r, \\
y_2 &= D_G u + D_{G_d} d,
\end{aligned}
\tag{6}
$$

here, x, z, y, u represent signals of state, observation, output, and control; A, B, C, D are matrices of the state, control, observation, and disturbance in the space of states.

The model in the space of states looks like

$$
P =
\begin{bmatrix}
A_G & 0 & 0 & 0 & 0 & 0 & B_{G_d} & B_G \\
0 & A_{T_{ref}} & 0 & 0 & 0 & B_r & 0 & 0 \\
-B_{W_1} & 0 & A_{W_1} & 0 & 0 & B_{W_1} & 0 & -B_{W_1} D_G \\
0 & 0 & 0 & A_{W_2} & 0 & 0 & 0 & B_{W_2} \\
B_{W_3} C_G & 0 & 0 & 0 & A_{W_3} & B_{W_3} & 0 & B_{W_3} D_G \\
-D_{W_1} D_G & 0 & C_{W_1} & 0 & 0 & D_{W_1} & 0 & D_{W_1} D_G \\
0 & 0 & 0 & C_{W_2} & 0 & 0 & 0 & D_{W_2} \\
D_{W_3} C_G & 0 & 0 & 0 & C_{W_3} & 0 & D_{G_d} & D_{W_3} D_G \\
0 & 0 & 0 & 0 & 0 & I & 0 & 0 \\
C_G & 0 & 0 & 0 & 0 & 0 & D_{G_d} & D_G
\end{bmatrix}.
\tag{7}
$$

$H_\infty$-synthesis can be implemented by MatLab software [31, 32]. In contrast to the known approaches, we propose to take into consideration the influence of the external disturbances.

The block diagram of $H_\infty$-synthesis of ISP is represented in Fig. 8. Expressions (5) – (7) are the mathematical grounds of the algorithm.

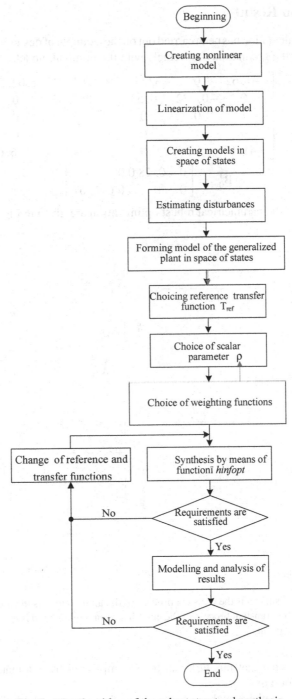

**Fig. 7.** The algorithm of the robust structural synthesis.

## 5 Simulation Results

The numerical calculation has been carried out on the example of designing ISPs assigned for operation on the ground moving vehicle with the nominal model.

$$A_{0g} = \begin{bmatrix} -1,62 & 0 & -3225,37 & -1,64 \cdot 10^6 & 1602,56 \\ 0 & -0,232 & 0,55 & -281,85 & 0 \\ 1 & 0 & 0 & 0 & 0 \\ 0 & 1 & 0 & 0 & 0 \\ -41,67 & 0 & 0 & 0 & -666,67 \end{bmatrix}$$

$$B_{0g}^T = \begin{bmatrix} 0 & -0,28 & 0 & 0 & 0 \\ 0 & 0 & 0 & 0 & 666,67 \end{bmatrix}$$

The results of the parametrical robust optimization are given in Fig. 9.

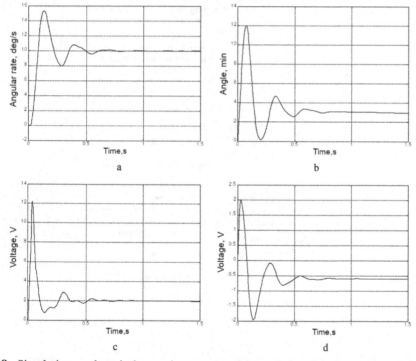

**Fig. 8.** Simulation results: a is the transient process of the angle rate; b is the transient process of angle position; c is the transient process of the electric motor angle rate; d is the transient process of feedback by the current.

It should be noted that this task can be accomplished by automated tools of the Robust Control Toolbox.

Results of $H_\infty$-synthesis of the two-degrees-of-freedom system are shown in Fig. 10. The represented graphs prove the advantages of robust systems in conditions of significant parametric disturbances ($\pm 50\%$).

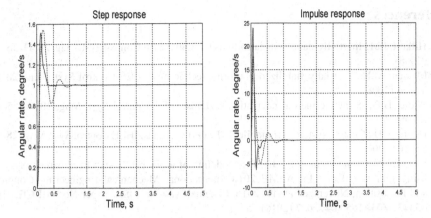

**Fig. 9.** Reaction on the step and impulse signals for increased moment of inertia

# 6  Discussion

Note the important feature of the proposed algorithms for designing stabilization systems, which can successfully function on moving vehicles. The usage of robust control systems has advantages in comparison with adaptive systems of the cost and complexity. The proposed algorithm ensures precision and other operating performances of the stabilization systems during designing in conditions of uncertainties caused by inaccuracies in the mathematical description and the possible influence of coordinate disturbances. The necessity of improving the quality of stabilization processes is mentioned in [33–35]. The important item is the possibility of implementing proposed algorithms by MatLab software.

The main result of the research is the development of the algorithm for designing robust ISP. This algorithm ensures keeping the high precision of stabilization in conditions of real operation, which is accompanied by the influence of the external disturbances. The research improves the quality of stabilization systems operated on vehicles.

# 7  Conclusions

The classification of ISPs is given.

The algorithm of the robust parametrical optimization is represented. The features of this algorithm including the necessity of the minimum and balanced realizations, usage of the genetic algorithm are described.

The numerical algorithm of designing the robust structural system with the two-degrees-of-freedom has been developed. The optimization criterion using the sensitivity function by the external disturbances has been supposed. The expression for the optimization criterion and the model in the space of states are represented.

# References

1. Hilkert, J.M.: Inertially stabilized platform technology. IEEE Control Syst. Mag. **28**(1), 26–46 (2008)
2. Masten, M.K.: Inertially stabilized platforms technology. IEEE Control Syst. Mag. **28**(1), 47–64 (2008)
3. Wang, H.G.: Strategic inertial navigation systems. IEEE Control Syst. Mag. **28**(1), 65–85 (2008)
4. Debruin, D.: Control systems for mobile SATCOM antennas. IEEE Control Syst. Mag. **28**(1), 86–101 (2008)
5. Haggart, G., Nandikolla, V.K., Jia, R.: Modeling of an inertially stabilized camera sysyem using gimbalplatform. In: ASME 2016 International Mechanical Engineering Congress and Exposition, November 11–17, 2016, Phoenix, Arizona, USA, paper No: IMECE2016–65343, V04AT05A047, p. 7 (2016)
6. Sushchenko, O.A.: Robust control of angular motion of platform with payload based on $H_\infty$-synthesis. J. Autom. Inf. Sci. **48**(12), 13–26 (2016)
7. Kuznetsov, B.I., Nikitina, T.B., Bovdui, I.V.: Structural-parametric synthesis of rolling mills multi-motor electric drives. Electr. Eng. Electromech. (5), 25–30 (2020). https://doi.org/10.20998/2074-272X.2020.5.04
8. Ostroumov, I.V., Kuzmenko, N.S.: Risk analysis of positioning by navigational aids. In: Signal Processing Symposium: SPSympo-2019, International Conference of IEEE, pp. 92–95, September 2019
9. Sushchenko, O.A., et al.: Design of robust control system for inertially stabilized platforms of ground vehicles. In: EUROCON 2021 - 19th IEEE International Conference on Smart Technologies, Proceedings, pp. 6–10 (2021)
10. Li, S., Zhong, M., Qin, J.: The internal mode control design of three-axis inertially stabilized platform for airborne remote sensing. In: Proceeding 2012 8th IEEE International Symposium on Instrumentation and Control Technology, London UK, 11–13 July 2012
11. Sushchenko, O.A., Tunik, A.A.: Optimization of inertially stabilized platforms. In: Proceeding IEEE 2nd International Conference on Methods and Systems of Navigation and Motion Control, Kyiv, Ukraine, pp. 101–105, 9–12 October 2012
12. Hurak, Z., Rezac, M.: Image-based pointing and tracking for inertially stabilized airborne camera. IEEE Trans. Control Syst. Technol. **20**(5), 1146–1159 (2012)
13. Lemos, N.A.: Analytical Mechanics. Cambridge University Press, London, p. 470 (2019)
14. Bezkorovainyi, Y.N., Sushchenko, O.A.: Improvement of UAV positioning by information of inertial sensors. In: Proceeding 2018 IEEE 5th International Conference on Methods and Systems of Navigation and Motion Control (MSNMC), October 16–19, Kiev, Ukraine, pp. 123–126 (2018)
15. Chikovani, V., Sushchenko, O., Tsiruk, H.: Redundant information processing techniques comparison for differential vibratory gyroscope. Eastern-Eur. J. Enterprise Technol. **4**(7–82), 45–52 (2016)
16. Sushchenko, O.A., Bezkorovainyi, Y.M., Golytsin, V.O.: Processing of redundant information in airborne electronic systems by means of neural networks. In: Proceeding 2019 IEEE 39th International Conference on Electronics and Nanotechnology, ELNANO-2019, Kyiv, Ukraine, pp. 652–655, 16–18 April 2019
17. Skogestad, S., Postlethwaite, I.: Multivariable Feedback Control, p. 572. Jonh Wiley and Sons, New York (2001)
18. Chapellat, H., Dahlen, M., Bhattacharyya, S.P.: Robust stability under structured and unstructured perturbations. IEEE Trans. Autom. Control, **35**(10), 1100–1107 (1990)
19. Liu, K.Z., Yao, Y.: Robust Control, p. 500. Wiley, Theory and Applications, London (2016)

20. Tunik, A.A., Rye, H., Lee, H.C.: Parametric optimization procedure for robust flight control system design. KSAS Int. J. **2**(2), 95–107 (2001)
21. Buontempo, F.: Genetic algorithms and machine learning for programmers, p. 234 (2019)
22. Schutter, B.: Minimal state-space realization in linear system theory: an overview **121**(1–2), 331–354 (2000)
23. Garcia-Sanz, M.: Robust Control Engineering, CRC Press, p. 578 (2017)
24. Gu, D., Petkov, P., Konstantinov, M.: Robust Control Design with MATLAB, p. 389p. Springer-Verlag, London (2005)
25. Balas, G., Chiang, R., Packard, A., Safononv, M.: Robust Control Toolbox User's Guide, The Math Works Inc. 2005–2008
26. Fortuna, L., Frasca, M.: Optimal and Robust Control: Advanced Topics with MATLAB (2012)
27. Lavretsky, E., Wise, K.A.: Robust and Adaptive Control with Aerospace Applications, Springer (2012)
28. Sushchenko, O.A.: Synthesis of two-degree-of-freedom system for stabilization of information-measuring devices on moving base. In: Proceedings of IEEE 3rd International Conference on Methods and Systems of Navigation and Motion Control, MSNMC 2014, Kyiv, Ukraine, pp. 150–154, 14–17 October 2014
29. Kuznetsov, B.I., Nikitina, T.B., Bovdui, I.V.: "Multiobjective synthesis of two degree of freedom nonlinear robust control by discrete continuous plant", Tekhnichna elektrodynamika. Inst. Electrodyn. Natl. Acad. Sci. Ukraine **5**, 10–14 (2020)
30. Ostroumov, I., Kuzmenko, N.: Risk assessment of mid-air collision based on positioning performance by navigational aids. In: 2020 IEEE 6th International Conference on Methods and Systems of Navigation and Motion Control (MSNMC), KYIV, Ukraine, pp. 34–37 (2020)
31. Li, T., Zhang, B., Zheng, B.: Robust control with engineering applications. Math. Problems Eng. ID567672 (2014)
32. Zhang, Y., Yang, T., Li, C., Liu, S., Du, C., Li, M.: Fuzzy-PID control for the position loop of aerial inertially stabilized platform. Aerospace Sci. Technol. **36**, 21–26 (2014)
33. Ostroumov, I., et al.: Ukrainian navigational aids network configuration estimation. In: 16th International Conference on the Experience of Designing and Application of CAD Systems (CADSM), Lviv, Ukraine, pp. 5–9 (2021). https://doi.org/10.1109/CADSM52681.2021.938 5226
34. Votrubec, R.: Stabilization of platform using gyroscope. Procedia Eng. **69**, 410–414 (2014)
35. Lange, J.: Platform stabilization: an autoethnographic exploration of the multiple relations and role of data behind the interface of online tutoring software. Critical Stud. Educ. **62**(1), 82–96 (2021)

# A Fast Discrete Transform for a Class of Simultaneously Diagonalizable Matrices

Antonio Boccuto[1] , Ivan Gerace[1(✉)] , and Valentina Giorgetti[2]

[1] Dipartimento di Matematica e Informatica, Via Vanvitelli, 1, 06123 Perugia, Italy
{antonio.boccuto,ivan.gerace}@unipg.it
[2] Dipartimento di Matematica e Informatica, viale G. B. Morgagni, 67/A,
50134 Firenze, Italy
valentina.giorgetti@unifi.it

**Abstract.** We introduce a new class of simultaneously diagonalizable real matrices, the $\gamma$-matrices, which include both symmetric circulant matrices and a subclass of the set of all reverse circulant matrices. We define some algorithms for fast computation of the product between a $\gamma$-matrix and a real vector. We proved that the computational cost of a multiplication between a $\gamma$-matrix and a real vector is of at most $\frac{7}{4} n \log_2 n + o(n \log_2 n)$ additions and $\frac{1}{2} n \log_2 n + o(n \log_2 n)$ multiplications. Our algorithm can be used to improve the performance of general discrete transforms for multiplications of real vectors.

**Keywords:** Symmetric circulant matrix · Reverse circulant matrix · Discrete real Fast Fourier transform

## 1 Introduction

Recently, there have been several studies about simultaneously diagonalizable real matrices. In particular, in investigating the preconditioning of Toeplitz matrices (see, e.g., [9]), several matrix algebras are considered, among which the class of all circulant matrices (see, e.g., [7,12]), the family of all $\omega$-circulant matrices (see, e.g., [10]), the set of all $\tau$-matrices (see, e.g., [2]) and the family of all matrices diagonalized by the Hartley transform (see, e.g., [3]).

In this paper we focus on approximation of real symmetric Toeplitz matrices. Thus, the involved data are always *real*, so that it is not advisable to use the classical complex Discrete Fast Fourier Transform. We investigate a particular class of simultaneously diagonalizable real matrices, whose elements we call $\gamma$-*matrices*. Such a class, similarly as that of the matrices diagonalizable by the Hartley transform (see, e.g., [3]) includes symmetric circulant matrices and a subclass of the family of all reverse circulant matrices. Symmetric circulant matrices have several applications to ordinary and partial differential equations (see, e.g., [13]), images and signal restoration (see, e.g., [6]), graph theory (see, e.g., [8]). Reverse circulant matrices have different applications, for instance in exponential data fitting and signal processing (see, e.g., [1]).

Successively, we deal with the problem of real fast transform algorithms (see, e.g., [11, 15]). In particular we define some algorithms for fast computation of the product between a $\gamma$-matrix and a real vector and between two $\gamma$-matrices. We show that the computational cost of a multiplication between a $\gamma$-matrix and a real vector is of at most $\frac{7}{4} n \log_2 n + o(n \log_2 n)$ additions and $\frac{1}{2} n \log_2 n + o(n \log_2 n)$ multiplications. The proposed algorithm can be used to improve the performance of different discrete transforms given for multiplications of real vectors. In [5] it is shown how the $\gamma$-matrices can be suitably used for preconditioning Toeplitz symmetric matrices, which are widely used in several practical problems and applications. Moreover in [4], by means of various experimental results, it is shown how such a matrix class approximates symmetric Toeplitz matrices better than some other classes used in the literature.

The paper is structured as follows. In Sect. 2 we characterize $\gamma$-matrices, in Sect. 3 we define the real fast transforms by means of which it is possible to implement the product between a $\gamma$-matrix and a real vector.

## 2   Spectral Characterization of $\gamma$-matrices

In order to present a new class of simultaneously diagonalizable matrices, we first define the following matrix. Let $n$ be a fixed positive integer, and $Q_n = (q_{k,j}^{(n)})_{k,j}$, $k, j = 0, 1, \ldots, n-1$, where

$$
q_{k,j}^{(n)} = \begin{cases} \alpha_j \cos\left(\dfrac{2\pi\,k\,j}{n}\right) & \text{if } 0 \le j \le \lfloor n/2 \rfloor, \\[2mm] \alpha_j \sin\left(\dfrac{2\pi\,k\,(n-j)}{n}\right) & \text{if } \lfloor n/2 \rfloor \le j \le n-1, \end{cases} \tag{1}
$$

$$
\alpha_j = \begin{cases} \dfrac{1}{\sqrt{n}} = \overline{\alpha} & \text{if } j = 0, \text{ or } j = n/2 \text{ if } n \text{ is even}, \\[2mm] \sqrt{\dfrac{2}{n}} = \widetilde{\alpha} & \text{otherwise}, \end{cases} \tag{2}
$$

and put

$$
Q_n = \left( \mathbf{q}^{(0)} \,\Big|\, \mathbf{q}^{(1)} \,\Big|\, \cdots \,\Big|\, \mathbf{q}^{(\lfloor \frac{n}{2} \rfloor)} \,\Big|\, \mathbf{q}^{(\lfloor \frac{n+1}{2} \rfloor)} \,\Big|\, \cdots \,\Big|\, \mathbf{q}^{(n-2)} \,\Big|\, \mathbf{q}^{(n-1)} \right), \tag{3}
$$

where

$$
\mathbf{q}^{(0)} = \frac{1}{\sqrt{n}} \left( 1\ 1\ \cdots\ 1 \right)^T = \frac{1}{\sqrt{n}}\, \mathbf{u}^{(0)}, \tag{4}
$$

$$\mathbf{q}^{(j)} = \sqrt{\frac{2}{n}} \left( 1 \quad \cos\left(\frac{2\pi j}{n}\right) \quad \cdots \quad \cos\left(\frac{2\pi j(n-1)}{n}\right) \right)^T = \sqrt{\frac{2}{n}} \, \mathbf{u}^{(j)},$$

$$\mathbf{q}^{(n-j)} = \sqrt{\frac{2}{n}} \left( 0 \quad \sin\left(\frac{2\pi j}{n}\right) \quad \cdots \quad \sin\left(\frac{2\pi j(n-1)}{n}\right) \right)^T = \sqrt{\frac{2}{n}} \, \mathbf{v}^{(j)}, \qquad (5)$$

$j = 1, 2, \ldots, \lfloor \frac{n-1}{2} \rfloor$. Moreover, when $n$ is even, set

$$\mathbf{q}^{(n/2)} = \frac{1}{\sqrt{n}} \left( 1 \ -1 \ \ 1 \ -1 \ \cdots \ -1 \right)^T = \frac{1}{\sqrt{n}} \, \mathbf{u}^{(n/2)}. \qquad (6)$$

In [14] it is proved that all columns of $Q_n$ are orthonormal, and thus $Q_n$ is an orthonormal matrix.

Now we define the following function. Given $\boldsymbol{\lambda} \in \mathbb{C}^n$, $\boldsymbol{\lambda} = (\lambda_0 \, \lambda_1 \cdots \lambda_{n-1})^T$, set

$$\mathrm{diag}(\boldsymbol{\lambda}) = \Lambda = \begin{pmatrix} \lambda_0 & 0 & 0 & \ldots & 0 & 0 \\ 0 & \lambda_1 & 0 & \ldots & 0 & 0 \\ 0 & 0 & \lambda_2 & \ldots & 0 & 0 \\ \vdots & \vdots & \vdots & \ddots & \vdots & \vdots \\ 0 & 0 & 0 & \ldots & \lambda_{n-2} & 0 \\ 0 & 0 & 0 & \ldots & 0 & \lambda_{n-1} \end{pmatrix},$$

where $\Lambda \in \mathbb{C}^{n \times n}$ is a diagonal matrix.

A vector $\boldsymbol{\lambda} \in \mathbb{R}^n$, $\boldsymbol{\lambda} = (\lambda_0 \, \lambda_1 \cdots \lambda_{n-1})^T$ is said to be *symmetric* (resp., *asymmetric*) iff $\lambda_j = \lambda_{n-j}$ (resp., $\lambda_j = -\lambda_{n-j}) \in \mathbb{R}$ for every $j = 0, 1, \ldots, \lfloor n/2 \rfloor$.

Let $Q_n$ be as in (3), and $\mathcal{G}_n$ be the space of the matrices *simultaneously diagonalizable* by $Q_n$, that is

$$\mathcal{G}_n = \mathrm{sd}(Q_n) = \{ Q_n \Lambda Q_n^T : \Lambda = \mathrm{diag}(\boldsymbol{\lambda}), \, \boldsymbol{\lambda} \in \mathbb{R}^n \}.$$

A matrix belonging to $\mathcal{G}_n$, $n \in \mathbb{N}$, is called $\gamma$-*matrix*. Moreover, we define the following classes by

$$\mathcal{C}_n = \{ Q_n \Lambda Q_n^T : \Lambda = \mathrm{diag}(\boldsymbol{\lambda}), \, \boldsymbol{\lambda} \in \mathbb{R}^n, \, \boldsymbol{\lambda} \text{ is symmetric} \},$$

$$\mathcal{B}_n = \{ Q_n \Lambda Q_n^T : \Lambda = \mathrm{diag}(\boldsymbol{\lambda}), \, \boldsymbol{\lambda} \in \mathbb{R}^n, \, \boldsymbol{\lambda} \text{ is asymmetric} \}.$$

Note that the class $\mathcal{C}_n$ corresponds to the set of all circulant symmetric matrices, while $\mathcal{B}_n$ is a particular subclass of the set of the reverse circulant matrices. We have the following.

**Theorem 1.** (see [5]) *One has*

$$\mathcal{G}_n = \mathcal{C}_n \oplus \mathcal{B}_n, \qquad (7)$$

*where $\oplus$ is the orthogonal sum.*

Any matrix belonging to the class $\mathcal{G}_n$ will be called $\gamma$-*matrix*.

# 3   Multiplication Between a $\gamma$-matrix and a Real Vector

In this section we deal with the problem of computing the product

$$\mathbf{y} = G\mathbf{x}, \tag{8}$$

where $G \in \mathcal{G}_n$. Since $G$ is a $\gamma$-matrix, there is a diagonal matrix $\Lambda^{(G)} \in \mathbb{R}^{n \times n}$ with $G = Q_n \Lambda^{(G)} Q_n^T$, where $Q_n$ is as in (1). To compute

$$\mathbf{y} = Q_n \Lambda^{(G)} Q_n^T \mathbf{x},$$

we proceed by doing the next operations in the following order:

$$\mathbf{z} = Q_n^T \mathbf{x}; \tag{9}$$

$$\mathbf{t} = \Lambda^{(G)} \mathbf{z}; \tag{10}$$

$$\mathbf{y} = Q_n \mathbf{t}. \tag{11}$$

To compute the product in (9), we define a new fast technique, which we will call *inverse discrete sine-cosine transform* (IDSCT), while to do the operation in (11), we define a new technique, which will be called *discrete sine-cosine transform* (DSCT).

From now on, we assume that the involved vectors $\mathbf{x}$ belong to $\mathbb{R}^n$, where $n = 2^r$, $r \geq 2$, and we put $m = n/2$, $\nu = n/4$.

## 3.1   The IDSCT Technique

In this subsection we present the technique to compute (9). Given $\mathbf{x} \in \mathbb{R}^n$, we denote by

$$\text{IDSCT}(\mathbf{x}) = Q_n^T \mathbf{x} = \begin{pmatrix} \alpha_0 \, C_0(\mathbf{x}) \\ \alpha_1 \, C_1(\mathbf{x}) \\ \vdots \\ \alpha_m \, C_m(\mathbf{x}) \\ \alpha_{m+1} \, S_{m-1}(\mathbf{x}) \\ \vdots \\ \alpha_{n-1} \, S_1(\mathbf{x}) \end{pmatrix}, \tag{12}$$

where $\alpha_j$, $j = 0, 1, \ldots, n-1$, are as in (2),

$$C_j(\mathbf{x}) = \mathbf{x}^T \mathbf{u}^{(j)}, \quad j = 0, 1, \ldots, m, \tag{13}$$

$$S_j(\mathbf{x}) = \mathbf{x}^T \mathbf{v}^{(j)}, \quad j = 1, 2, \ldots, m-1, \tag{14}$$

where $\mathbf{u}^{(j)}$ and $\mathbf{v}^{(j)}$ are as in (4)–(6).

For $\mathbf{x} = (x_0\, x_1\, \cdots x_{n-1})^T \in \mathbb{R}^n$, let $\eta$ (resp., $\zeta$): $\mathbb{R}^n \to \mathbb{R}^m$ be the function which associates to any vector $\mathbf{x} \in \mathbb{R}^n$ the vector consisting of all even (resp., odd) components of $\mathbf{x}$, that is

$$\eta(\mathbf{x}) = \eta\,\mathbf{x} = (x_0'\, x_1'\, \dots\, x_{m-1}'), \text{ where } x_p' = x_{2p}, \ p = 0,1,\dots,m-1;$$
$$\zeta(\mathbf{x}) = \zeta\,\mathbf{x} = (x_0''\, x_1''\, \dots\, x_{m-1}''), \text{ where } x_p'' = x_{2p+1}, \ p = 0,1,\dots,m-1.$$

**Proposition 1.** (see, e.g., [5,12]) *For $k = 0,1,\dots,m$, we have*

$$C_k(\mathbf{x}) = C_k(\eta\,\mathbf{x}) + \cos\left(\frac{\pi k}{m}\right) C_k(\zeta\,\mathbf{x}) - \sin\left(\frac{\pi k}{m}\right) S_k(\zeta\,\mathbf{x}). \tag{15}$$

*Moreover, for $k = 1,2,\dots,\nu$, it is*

$$S_k(\mathbf{x}) = S_k(\eta\,\mathbf{x}) + \cos\left(\frac{\pi k}{m}\right) S_k(\zeta\,\mathbf{x}) + \sin\left(\frac{\pi k}{m}\right) C_k(\zeta\,\mathbf{x}). \tag{16}$$

**Lemma 1.** *For $k = 0,1,\dots,\nu-1$, let $t = m - k$. We have*

$$C_t(\mathbf{x}) = C_k(\eta\,\mathbf{x}) - \cos\left(\frac{\pi k}{m}\right) C_k(\zeta\,\mathbf{x}) + \sin\left(\frac{\pi k}{m}\right) S_k(\zeta\,\mathbf{x}). \tag{17}$$

*Furthermore, for $k = 1,2,\dots,\nu-1$ we get*

$$S_t(\mathbf{x}) = S_k(\eta\,\mathbf{x}) - \cos\left(\frac{\pi k}{m}\right) S_k(\zeta\,\mathbf{x}) + \sin\left(\frac{\pi k}{m}\right) C_k(\zeta\,\mathbf{x}). \tag{18}$$

*Proof.* We begin with (17). For $t = \nu+1, \nu+2, \dots, m$, we have

$$C_t(\mathbf{x}) = \sum_{p=0}^{m-1} x_{2p} \cos\left(\frac{4\pi t p}{n}\right) + \sum_{p=0}^{m-1} x_{2p+1} \cos\left(\frac{2\pi t(2p+1)}{n}\right)$$

$$= \sum_{p=0}^{m-1} x_p' \cos\left(2\pi p - \frac{2\pi k p}{m}\right) + \sum_{p=0}^{m-1} x_p'' \cos\left(\pi(2p+1) - \frac{\pi k(2p+1)}{m}\right)$$

$$= \sum_{p=0}^{m-1} x_p' \cos\left(\frac{2\pi k p}{m}\right) - \cos\left(\frac{\pi k}{m}\right) \sum_{p=0}^{m-1} x_p'' \cos\left(\frac{2\pi k p}{m}\right)$$

$$+ \sin\left(\frac{\pi k}{m}\right) \sum_{p=0}^{m-1} x_p'' \sin\left(\frac{2\pi k p}{m}\right)$$

$$= C_k(\eta\,\mathbf{x}) - \cos\left(\frac{\pi k}{m}\right) C_k(\zeta\,\mathbf{x}) + \sin\left(\frac{\pi k}{m}\right) S_k(\zeta\,\mathbf{x}).$$

Now we turn to (18). For $t = \nu+1, \nu+2, \dots, m-1$, it is

$$S_t(\mathbf{x}) = \sum_{p=0}^{m-1} x_{2p} \sin\left(\frac{4\pi t p}{n}\right) + \sum_{p=0}^{m-1} x_{2p+1} \sin\left(\frac{2\pi t(2p+1)}{n}\right)$$

$$= \sum_{p=0}^{m-1} x_p' \sin\left(2\pi p - \frac{2\pi k p}{m}\right) + \sum_{p=0}^{m-1} x_p'' \sin\left(\pi(2p+1) - \frac{\pi k(2p+1)}{m}\right)$$

$$= -S_k(\eta\,\mathbf{x}) + \sin\left(\frac{\pi k}{m}\right) C_k(\zeta\,\mathbf{x}) + \cos\left(\frac{\pi k}{m}\right) S_k(\zeta\,\mathbf{x}). \qquad \square$$

Note that

$$C_0(\mathbf{x}) = C_0(\eta\,\mathbf{x}) + C_0(\zeta\,\mathbf{x}), \tag{19}$$

$$C_m(\mathbf{x}) = C_0(\eta\,\mathbf{x}) - C_0(\zeta\,\mathbf{x}). \tag{20}$$

Since $S_\nu(\mathbf{x}) = 0$ whenever $\mathbf{x} \in \mathbb{R}^m$, then

$$C_\nu(\mathbf{x}) = C_\nu(\eta\,\mathbf{x}) - S_\nu(\zeta\,\mathbf{x}) = C_\nu(\eta\,\mathbf{x}) \tag{21}$$

and

$$S_\nu(\mathbf{x}) = S_\nu(\eta\,\mathbf{x}) + C_\nu(\zeta\,\mathbf{x}) = C_\nu(\zeta\,\mathbf{x}). \tag{22}$$

We call $\rho : \mathbb{R}^n \to \mathbb{R}^m$ that function which reverses all components of a given vector $\mathbf{x} \in \mathbb{R}^n$ but the 0-th component, and $\sigma$ (resp., $\alpha$): $\mathbb{R}^n \to \mathbb{R}^n$ that function which associates to every vector $\mathbf{x} \in \mathbb{R}^n$ the double of its symmetric (resp., asymmetric) part, namely

$$\rho(\mathbf{x}) = (x_0\,x_{n-1}\,x_{n-2}\cdots x_2\,x_1)^T,$$
$$\sigma(\mathbf{x}) = \sigma\,\mathbf{x} = \mathbf{x} + \rho(\mathbf{x}), \quad \alpha(\mathbf{x}) = \alpha\,\mathbf{x} = \mathbf{x} - \rho(\mathbf{x}).$$

Note that

$$\mathbf{x} = \frac{\sigma\,\mathbf{x} + \alpha\,\mathbf{x}}{2}. \tag{23}$$

Now we state the next technical results.

**Lemma 2.** *Let* $\mathbf{a} = (a_0\,a_1\cdots a_{n-1})^T$, $\mathbf{b} = (b_0\,b_1\cdots b_{n-1})^T \in \mathbb{R}^n$ *be such that* $\mathbf{a}$ *is symmetric and* $\mathbf{b}$ *is asymmetric. Then,* $\mathbf{a}^T\,\mathbf{b} = 0$.

*Proof.* First of all, we observe that $b_0 = b_{n/2} = 0$. So, we have

$$\mathbf{a}^T\,\mathbf{b} = \sum_{j=0}^{n-1} a_j\,b_j = \sum_{j=1}^{n-1} a_j\,b_j = \sum_{j=1}^{n/2-1} a_j\,b_j + a_{n/2}\,b_{n/2} + \sum_{j=n/2+1}^{n} a_j\,b_j$$

$$= \sum_{j=1}^{n/2-1} a_j\,b_j + \sum_{j=1}^{n/2-1} a_{n-j}\,b_{n-j} = \sum_{j=1}^{n/2-1} a_j\,b_j - \sum_{j=1}^{n/2-1} a_j\,b_j = 0. \qquad \square$$

**Corollary 1.** *Let* $\mathbf{x} \in \mathbb{R}^n$ *be a symmetric vector and* $k \in \{0, 1, \ldots, n-1\}$. *Then, we get*

$$S_k(\mathbf{x}) = 0. \tag{24}$$

*Proof.* Note that $S_k(\mathbf{x}) = \mathbf{x}^T\,\mathbf{v}^{(k)}$. The formula (24) follows from Lemma 2, since $\mathbf{x}$ is symmetric and $\mathbf{v}^{(k)}$ is asymmetric. $\qquad \square$

**Corollary 2.** *Let $\mathbf{x} \in \mathbb{R}^n$ be an asymmetric vector and $k \in \{0, 1, \ldots, n-1\}$. Then, we have*

$$C_k(\mathbf{x}) = 0. \tag{25}$$

*Proof.* Observe that $C_k(\mathbf{x}) = \mathbf{x}^T \mathbf{u}^{(k)}$. The formula (25) is a consequence of Lemma 2, because $\mathbf{u}^{(k)}$ is symmetric and $\mathbf{x}$ is asymmetric. □

**Lemma 3.** *Let $\mathbf{x} \in \mathbb{R}^n$ and $k \in \{0, 1, \ldots, m\}$. Then we get*

$$C_k(\sigma \, \mathbf{x}) = 2 \, C_k(\mathbf{x}). \tag{26}$$

*Moreover, if $k \in \{1, 2, \ldots, m-1\}$, then*

$$S_k(\alpha \, \mathbf{x}) = 2 \, S_k(\mathbf{x}). \tag{27}$$

*Proof.* We begin with proving (26). For every $j \in \{0, 1, \ldots, n-1\}$ we have

$$C_k(\sigma \, \mathbf{x}) = 2x_0 + \sum_{j=1}^{n-1} x_j u_j^{(k)} + \sum_{j=1}^{n-1} x_{n-j} u_j^{(k)}$$

$$= 2x_0 + \sum_{j=1}^{n-1} x_j u_j^{(k)} + 2 \sum_{j=1}^{n-1} x_j u_j^{(k)} = 2 \sum_{j=0}^{n-1} x_j u_j^{(k)} = 2 \, C_k(\mathbf{x}).$$

Now we turn to (27). For any $j \in \{0, 1, \ldots, n-1\}$, since $v_0^{(k)} = 0$, we get

$$S_k(\alpha \, \mathbf{x}) = \sum_{j=1}^{n-1} x_j v_j^{(k)} - \sum_{j=1}^{n-1} x_{n-j} v_j^{(k)} = \sum_{j=1}^{n-1} x_j v_j^{(k)} + \sum_{j=1}^{n-1} x_{n-j} v_{n-j}^{(k)}$$

$$= 2 \sum_{j=1}^{n-1} x_j v_j^{(k)} = 2 \sum_{j=0}^{n-1} x_j v_j^{(k)} = 2 \, S_k(\mathbf{x}). \quad \square$$

Observe that from (12), (23), (24) and (25), taking into account that $\sigma \, \mathbf{x}$ is symmetric and $\alpha \, \mathbf{x}$ is asymmetric, we obtain

$$\text{IDSCT}(\mathbf{x}) = Q_n^T \, \mathbf{x} = \begin{pmatrix} \alpha_0 \dfrac{C_0(\sigma \, \mathbf{x})}{2} \\ \alpha_1 \dfrac{C_1(\sigma \, \mathbf{x})}{2} \\ \vdots \\ \alpha_m \dfrac{C_m(\sigma \, \mathbf{x})}{2} \\ \alpha_{m+1} \dfrac{S_{m-1}(\alpha \, \mathbf{x})}{2} \\ \vdots \\ \alpha_{n-1} \dfrac{S_1(\alpha \, \mathbf{x})}{2} \end{pmatrix}. \tag{28}$$

Thus, to compute IDSCT($\mathbf{x}$), we determine the values $C_k(\sigma\mathbf{x})$ for $k = 0, 1, \ldots, m$ and $S_k(\alpha\mathbf{x})$ for $k = 1, 2, \ldots, m-1$, and successively we multiply such values by the constants $\alpha_k/2$, $k = 0, 1, \ldots, n-1$. Now we give the following.

**Lemma 4.** *Let $\mathbf{x} \in \mathbb{R}^n$ be symmetric. Then for $k = 1, 2, \ldots, \nu - 1$ we get*

$$C_k(\mathbf{x}) = C_k(\eta\,\mathbf{x}) + \frac{1}{2\cos\left(\dfrac{\pi k}{m}\right)}\, C_k(\sigma\,\zeta\,\mathbf{x}). \tag{29}$$

*Moreover, if $t = m - k$, then*

$$C_t(\mathbf{x}) = C_k(\eta\,\mathbf{x}) - \frac{1}{2\cos\left(\dfrac{\pi k}{m}\right)}\, C_k(\sigma\,\zeta\,\mathbf{x}). \tag{30}$$

*Proof.* We begin with (29). Since $\mathbf{x}$ is symmetric, we have

$$S_k(\mathbf{x}) = S_k(\eta\,\mathbf{x}) = 0. \tag{31}$$

From (16) and (31) we obtain

$$S_k(\zeta\,\mathbf{x}) = -\frac{\sin\left(\dfrac{\pi k}{m}\right)}{\cos\left(\dfrac{\pi k}{m}\right)}\, C_k(\zeta\,\mathbf{x}). \tag{32}$$

From (15), (26) and (32) we get (29). The equality in (30) follows from (17), (26) and (32). $\qquad\square$

Now we define the following algorithm:

```
1: function CS(x, n)
2: if n = 4 then
3:     c₀ = x₀ + 2x₁ + x₂;
4:     c₁ = x₀ − x₂;
5:     c₂ = x₀ − 2x₁ + x₂;
6: else
7:     c̃ =CS(η x, n/2);
8:     c̄ =CS(σ ζ x, n/2);
9:     for k = 1, 2, … n/4 − 1 do
10:        aux = 1/(2 cos(2 π k/n)) c̄ₖ;
11:        cₖ = c̃ₖ + aux;
12:        c_{n/2−k} = c̃ₖ − aux;
13:    end for
14:    aux = c̄₀/2;
15:    c₀ = c̃₀ + aux;
16:    c_{n/4} = c̃_{n/4};
17:    c_{n/2} = c̃₀ − aux;
18: end if
19: return c
```

**Lemma 5.** *For each symmetric vector* $\mathbf{x} \in \mathbb{R}^n$, *the vector* $\eta\,\mathbf{x} \in \mathbb{R}^m$ *is symmetric.*

*Proof.* Let $\widetilde{\mathbf{x}} = \eta\,\mathbf{x}$, where $\mathbf{x}$ is a symmetric vector. So, we have

$$\widetilde{x}_j = x_{2j} = x_{n-2j} = x_{2(n/2-j)} = \widetilde{x}_{n/2-j}, \quad j = 0, 1, \ldots m. \tag{33}$$

Since $\widetilde{\mathbf{x}} \in \mathbb{R}^m$, from (33) it follows that $\widetilde{\mathbf{x}}$ is symmetric. $\qquad\square$

**Theorem 2.** *Let* $\mathbf{x} \in \mathbb{R}^n$ *be a symmetric vector and* $\mathbf{c} = \mathrm{CS}(\mathbf{x}, n)$. *Then,*

$$c_j = C_j(\mathbf{x}) = \mathbf{x}^T \mathbf{u}^{(j)}, \quad j = 0, 1, \ldots, m.$$

*Proof.* First of all we prove that, when we call the function CS, the first variable is symmetric. Concerning the external call, the vector $\mathbf{x}$ is symmetric in CS. Now we consider the internal calls of CS at lines 7 and 8. By Lemma 5, $\eta\,\mathbf{x}$ is symmetric. Hence, line 7 of our algorithm satisfies the assertion. Furthermore, it is readily seen that the assertion is fulfilled also by line 8.

Now, let us suppose that $n = 4$. Then,

$$c_0 = \mathbf{x}^T \mathbf{u}^{(0)} = x_0 + x_1 + x_2 + x_3.$$

Since $\mathbf{x}$ is even, we get the formula at line 3 of the algorithm CS. Moreover,

$$\mathbf{u}^{(1)} = (1 \quad 0 \ -1 \quad 0)^T,$$

and hence

$$c_1 = \mathbf{x}^T \mathbf{u}^{(1)} = x_0 - x_2,$$

obtaining the formula at line 4 of the algorithm CS. Furthermore,

$$\mathbf{u}^{(2)} = (1 \ -1 \quad 1 \ -1)^T,$$

and thus we have

$$c_2 = \mathbf{x}^T \mathbf{u}^{(2)} = x_0 - 2\,x_1 + x_2,$$

since $\mathbf{x}$ is symmetric. So, we obtain the formula at line 5 of the algorithm CS.

Now we consider the case $n > 4$. Since $\mathbf{x}$ is symmetric, from Lemma 4 we deduce that line 11 of the algorithm CS gives the correct value of $C_k(\mathbf{x})$ for $k = 1, 2, \ldots, \nu - 1$. As $\mathbf{x}$ is symmetric, from Lemma 4 we obtain that line 12 gives the exact value of $C_{m-k}(\mathbf{x})$ for $k = 1, 2, \ldots, \nu - 1$.

From (19) and (26) we deduce that line 15 of the function CS gives the correct value of $C_0(\mathbf{x})$, and by (20) and (26) we obtain that line 17 of the function CS gives the exact value of $C_m(\mathbf{x})$. Furthermore, by virtue of (21), line 16 of the function CS gives the correct value of $C_\nu(\mathbf{x})$. This completes the proof. $\qquad\square$

**Theorem 3.** *Suppose to have a library in which the values $1/(2\cos(2\pi k/n))$ have been stored for $n = 2^r$, $r \in \mathbb{N}$, $r \geq 2$, and $k \in \{0, 1, \ldots, n-1\}$. Then, the computational cost of a call of the function* CS *is given by*

$$A(n) = \frac{3}{4}n \log_2 n - \frac{1}{2}n + 1, \tag{34}$$

$$M(n) = \frac{1}{4}n \log_2 n + \frac{1}{2}n - 2, \tag{35}$$

*where $A(n)$ (resp., $M(n)$) denotes the number of additions (resp., multiplications) requested to compute* CS.

*Proof.* Concerning line 8, we first compute $\sigma \zeta \mathbf{x}$. To do this, $\nu - 1$ sums and 2 multiplications are required. To compute the **for** loop at lines 9–13, $2\nu - 2$ sums and $\nu - 1$ multiplications are necessary. Moreover, to compute lines 14–17, 2 sums and one multiplication are necessary. Thus, the total number of additions is given by

$$A(n) = \frac{3}{4}n - 1 + 2A\left(\frac{n}{2}\right), \tag{36}$$

while the total number of multiplications is

$$M(n) = \frac{1}{4}n + 2 + 2M\left(\frac{n}{2}\right). \tag{37}$$

Concerning the initial case, we have

$$A(4) = 5, \quad M(4) = 2.$$

For every $n = 2^r$, with $r \in \mathbb{N}$, $r \geq 2$, let $A(n)$ be as in (34). We get $A(4) = 6 - 2 + 1 = 5$. Now we claim that the function $A(n)$ defined in (34) satisfies (36). Indeed, we have

$$A\left(\frac{n}{2}\right) = \frac{3}{8}n \left(\log_2 n - 1\right) - \frac{1}{4}n + 1,$$

and hence

$$\frac{3}{4}n - 1 + 2A\left(\frac{n}{2}\right) = \frac{3}{4}n - 1 + \frac{3}{4}n \left(\log_2 n - 1\right) - \frac{1}{2}n + 2 = A(n),$$

getting the claim.

Moreover, for any $n = 2^r$, with $r \in \mathbb{N}$, $r \geq 2$, let $M(n)$ be as in (35). One has $M(4) = 2 + 2 - 2 = 2$. Now we claim that the function $M(n)$ defined in (35) fulfils (37). It is

$$M\left(\frac{n}{2}\right) = \frac{1}{8}n \left(\log_2 n - 1\right) + \frac{1}{4}n - 2,$$

and hence

$$\frac{1}{4}n + 2 + 2M\left(\frac{n}{2}\right) = \frac{1}{4}n + 2 + \frac{1}{4}n \left(\log_2 n - 1\right) + \frac{1}{2}n - 4 = M(n),$$

obtaining the claim. □

**Lemma 6.** *Let* $\mathbf{x} \in \mathbb{R}^n$ *be asymmetric. Then, for* $k = 1, 2, \ldots, \nu - 1$ *it is*

$$S_k(\mathbf{x}) = S_k(\eta\,\mathbf{x}) + \frac{1}{2\cos\left(\dfrac{\pi k}{m}\right)}\,S_k(\alpha\,\zeta\,\mathbf{x}). \tag{38}$$

*Moreover, if* $t = m - k$*, then*

$$S_t(\mathbf{x}) = -S_k(\eta\,\mathbf{x}) + \frac{1}{2\cos\left(\dfrac{\pi k}{m}\right)}\,S_k(\alpha\,\zeta\,\mathbf{x}). \tag{39}$$

*Proof.* We begin with (38). As $\mathbf{x}$ is asymmetric, we have

$$C_k(\mathbf{x}) = C_k(\eta\,\mathbf{x}) = 0. \tag{40}$$

From (15) and (40) we deduce

$$C_k(\zeta\,\mathbf{x}) = \frac{\sin\left(\dfrac{\pi k}{m}\right)}{\cos\left(\dfrac{\pi k}{m}\right)}\,S_k(\zeta\,\mathbf{x}). \tag{41}$$

From (16), (27) and (41) we get (38).
    The relation (39) follows from (18), (27) and (41).     □

Now we define the following algorithm:

```
1: function SN(x, n)
2: if n = 4 then
3:     s₁ = 2 x₁;
4: else
5:     s̃ = SN(η x, n/2);
6:     s̄ = SN(α ζ x, n/2);
7:     for k = 1, 2, ... n/4 − 1 do
8:         aux = 1/(2 cos(2 π k/n)) s̄ₖ;
9:         sₖ = s̃ₖ + aux;
10:        s_{n/2−k} = aux − s̃ₖ;
11:    end for
12:    s_{n/4} = 0;
13:    for j = 0, 2, ..., n/4 − 2 do
14:        s_{n/4} = s_{n/4} + x_{2j+1} − x_{2j+3}
15:    end for
16:    s_{n/4} = 2 s_{n/4}
17: end if
18: return s
```

**Lemma 7.** *For every asymmetric vector* $\mathbf{x} \in \mathbb{R}^n$*, the vector* $\eta\,\mathbf{x} \in \mathbb{R}^m$ *is asymmetric.*

*Proof.* Let $\overline{\mathbf{x}} = \eta \mathbf{x}$, where $\mathbf{x}$ is asymmetric. Then,

$$\overline{x}_j = x_{2j} = -x_{n-2j} = -x_{2(n/2-j)} = -\overline{x}_{n/2-j}, \quad j = 0, 1, \ldots m. \tag{42}$$

Since $\widetilde{\mathbf{x}} \in \mathbb{R}^m$, from (42) it follows that $\overline{\mathbf{x}}$ is asymmetric. $\qquad\square$

**Lemma 8.** *Given any asymmetric vector* $\mathbf{x} \in \mathbb{R}^n$, *set* $\widehat{\mathbf{x}} = \zeta \mathbf{x}$. *Then,*

$$S_\nu(\widehat{\mathbf{x}}) = 2 \sum_{j=0}^{\nu-1} (-1)^j \widehat{x}_{2j+1}. \tag{43}$$

*Proof.* Let $\mathbf{x} \in \mathbb{R}^n$ be any asymmetric vector. Then, $\widehat{\mathbf{x}} = \zeta \mathbf{x} \in \mathbb{R}^m$. It is not difficult to check that

$$\widehat{x}_j = -\widehat{x}_{n-1-j}, \quad j = 0, 1, \ldots n - 1. \tag{44}$$

Since $\mathbf{u}^{(\nu)} = (1 \;\; -1 \;\; \ldots 1 \;\; -1)^T$ whenever $\mathbf{u}^{(\nu)} \in \mathbb{R}^m$, the equality in (43) follows from (22) and (44). $\qquad\square$

**Theorem 4.** *Given an asymmetric vector* $\mathbf{x} \in \mathbb{R}^n$, *let* $\mathbf{s} = \mathrm{SN}(\mathbf{x}, n)$. *We get*

$$s_j = S_j(\mathbf{x}) = \mathbf{x}^T \mathbf{v}^{(j)}, \quad j = 1, 2, \ldots, m - 1.$$

*Proof.* First we prove that, when we call the function SN, the first variable is asymmetric. Concerning the external call, we have that $\mathbf{x}$ is asymmetric. Now we consider the internal calls of SN at lines 5 and 6. By Lemma 7, $\eta \mathbf{x}$ is asymmetric. Therefore, line 5 of our algorithm fulfils the assertion. Moreover, it is easy to see that line 6 satisfies the assertion too.

Now, let us suppose that $n = 4$. We have

$$\mathbf{v}^{(1)} = (0 \;\; 1 \;\; 0 \;\; -1)^T,$$

and hence

$$s_1 = \mathbf{x}^T \mathbf{v}^{(1)} = x_1 - x_3 = 2x_1,$$

because $\mathbf{x}$ is asymmetric. Therefore, we obtain the formula at line 3 of the algorithm SN.

Now we consider the case $n > 4$. As $\mathbf{x}$ is asymmetric, from Lemma 6 we get that line 9 of the function SN gives the right value of $S_k(\mathbf{x})$ for $k = 1, 2, \ldots, \nu-1$. Since $\mathbf{x}$ is asymmetric, from Lemma 6 we obtain that line 10 of the function SN gives the exact value of $S_{m-k}(\mathbf{x})$ for $k = 1, 2, \ldots, \nu-1$. Thanks to Lemma 8 and asymmetry of $\mathbf{x}$, lines 12–16 give the exact value of $S_\nu(\mathbf{x})$. This ends the proof. $\qquad\square$

**Theorem 5.** *Suppose to have a library in which the values* $1/(2\cos(2\pi k/n))$ *have been stored for* $n = 2^r$, $r \in \mathbb{N}$, $r \geq 2$, *and* $k \in \{0, 1, \ldots, n-1\}$. *Then, the computational cost of a call of the function SN is given by*

$$A(n) = n \log_2 n - \frac{11}{4}n + 3, \tag{45}$$

$$M(n) = \frac{1}{4}n \log_2 n - \frac{1}{4}n, \tag{46}$$

where $A(n)$ (resp., $M(n)$) denotes the number of additions (resp., multiplications) required to compute CS.

*Proof.* Concerning line 6, we first compute $\alpha \zeta x$. To do this, $\nu - 1$ sums and no multiplications are required. To compute the **for** loop at lines 7–11, $2\nu - 2$ sums and $\nu - 1$ multiplications are necessary. Concerning the **for** loop at lines 13–15, $\nu$ sums are necessary. Finally, at line 16, one multiplication is necessary. Thus, the total number of additions is

$$A(n) = n - 3 + 2A\left(\frac{n}{2}\right), \tag{47}$$

and the total number of multiplications is

$$M(n) = \frac{1}{4}n + 2M\left(\frac{n}{2}\right). \tag{48}$$

Concerning the initial case, we have

$$A(4) = 0, \quad M(4) = 1.$$

For each $n = 2^r$, with $r \in \mathbb{N}$, $r \geq 2$, let $A(n)$ be as in (45). We get $A(4) = 8 - 11 + 3 = 0$. Now we claim that the function $A(n)$ defined in (45) satisfies (47). Indeed, we have

$$A\left(\frac{n}{2}\right) = -\frac{11}{8}n + \frac{1}{2}n\,(\log_2 n - 1) + 3.$$

Therefore,

$$n - 3 + 2A\left(\frac{n}{2}\right) = n - 3 - \frac{11}{4}n + n\,(\log_2 n - 1) + 6 = A(n),$$

which gives the claim.

Moreover, for every $n = 2^r$, with $r \in \mathbb{N}$, $r \geq 2$, let $M(n)$ be as in (46). One has $M(4) = 2 - 1 = 1$. Now we claim that the function $M(n)$ defined in (46) fulfils (48). Indeed,

$$M\left(\frac{n}{2}\right) = -\frac{1}{8}n + \frac{1}{8}n\,(\log_2 n - 1),$$

and hence

$$\frac{1}{4}n + 2M\left(\frac{n}{2}\right) = \frac{1}{4}n - \frac{1}{4}n + \frac{1}{4}n\,(\log_2 n - 1) = M(n),$$

getting the claim.    □

**Corollary 3.** *Let* $\mathbf{x} \in \mathbb{R}^n$, $\mathbf{y} =\text{IDSCT}(\mathbf{x})$, $\mathbf{c} = \text{CS}(\sigma \mathbf{x}, n)$ *and* $\mathbf{s} = \text{SN}(\alpha \mathbf{x}, n)$. *Then,*

$$
y_j = \begin{cases} \dfrac{\alpha_j\, c_j}{2}, & \text{if } j \leq m; \\[3mm] \dfrac{\alpha_j\, s_{n-j}}{2}, & \text{otherwise.} \end{cases} \tag{49}
$$

*Proof.* Since $\sigma \mathbf{x}$ is symmetric, from Theorem 2 we obtain

$$
c_j = \mathrm{C}_j(\sigma \mathbf{x}), \quad j = 0, 1, \ldots, m.
$$

Moreover, as $\alpha \mathbf{x}$ is asymmetric, from Theorem 4 we get

$$
s_j = \mathrm{S}_j(\alpha \mathbf{x}), \quad j = 1, 2, \ldots, m-1.
$$

Therefore, from (28) we deduce (49).    □

To complete the computation of $\text{IDSCT}(\mathbf{x})$ as in (28), we have to compute $\sigma \mathbf{x}$ and $\alpha \mathbf{x}$ and to multiply every entry of the result of $\text{CS}(\sigma \mathbf{x}, \alpha \mathbf{x}, n)$ by $\alpha_k/2$, $k = 0, 1, \ldots, n-1$. The computational cost of these operations is $O(n)$. Therefore, the total cost for the computation of (9) is $\frac{7}{4} n \log_2 n + o(n \log_2 n)$ additions and $\frac{1}{2} n \log_2 n + o(n \log_2 n)$ multiplications.

## 3.2   Computation of the Eigenvalues of a $\gamma$-Matrix

In this subsection we find an algorithm to compute the expression in (10). We first determine the eigenvalues of the matrix $G$ in (8), in order to know the matrix $\Lambda^{(G)}$ in (10).

Since $G \in \mathcal{G}_n$ and $\mathcal{G}_n = \mathcal{C}_n \oplus \mathcal{B}_n$, we determine two matrices $C \in \mathcal{C}_n$ and $B \in \mathcal{B}_n$, $C =\text{circ}(\mathbf{c})$, $B =\text{rcirc}(\mathbf{b})$. Observe that

$$
\begin{aligned}
g_{0,0} &= c_0 + b_0, & g_{\nu,\nu} &= c_0 + b_m, \\
g_{0,m} &= c_m + b_m, & g_{\nu,m+\nu} &= c_m + b_0.
\end{aligned} \tag{50}
$$

By solving the system in (50), we find $c_0$, $b_0$, $c_m$, $b_m$. Knowing $c_0$, from the principal diagonal of $G$ it is not difficult to determine the numbers $b_{2i}$, $i = 1, 2, \ldots, \nu - 1$. If we know these quantities, it is possible to determine the numbers $c_{2i}$, $i = 1, 2, \ldots, \nu - 1$, from the first row of $G$. Moreover, note that

$$
\begin{aligned}
g_{0,1} &= c_1 + b_1, & g_{1,2} &= c_1 + b_3, \\
g_{0,3} &= c_3 + b_3, & g_{m-1,m+2} &= c_3 + b_1.
\end{aligned} \tag{51}
$$

By solving the system in (51), we obtain $c_1$, $b_1$, $c_3$, $b_3$. If we know $c_1$, then from the first diagonal superior to the principal diagonal of $G$ it is not difficult to determine the numbers $b_{2i+1}$, $i = 2, 3, \ldots, \nu - 1$. Knowing these values, it is not difficult to find the quantities $c_{2i+1}$, $i = 2, 3, \ldots, \nu - 1$, from the first row of

$G$. It is possible to prove that the computational cost of all these operations is $O(n)$. Note that

$$G\mathbf{q}^{(j)} = C\mathbf{q}^{(j)} + B\mathbf{q}^{(j)} = \left(\lambda_j^{(C)} + \lambda_j^{(B)}\right)\mathbf{q}^{(j)}, \quad j = 0, 1, \ldots, n-1, \quad (52)$$

where the $\lambda_j^{(C)}$'s and the $\lambda_j^{(B)}$'s are the $j$-th eigenvalues of $C$ and $B$, and the orders are given by

$$\lambda_j^{(C)} = \mathbf{c}^T\mathbf{u}^{(j)} \quad (53)$$

for $j = 0, 1, \ldots, n-1$, and

$$\lambda_j^{(B)} = \mathbf{b}^T\mathbf{u}^{(j)} \quad (54)$$

for $j = 0, 1, \ldots \lfloor \frac{n-1}{2} \rfloor$. Moreover, for $j = 1, 2, \ldots \lfloor \frac{n-1}{2} \rfloor$, we get

$$\lambda_{n-j}^{(B)} = -\lambda_j^{(B)} \quad (55)$$

(see [5, Theorems 5 and 9]).

**Proposition 2.** *Given two symmetric vectors* $\mathbf{c}, \mathbf{b} \in \mathbb{R}^n$ *such that*

$$\sum_{t=0}^{n-1} b_t = 0 \quad \text{and} \quad \sum_{t=0}^{n-1} (-1)^t b_t = 0,$$

*set* $\mathbf{d}^{(C)} = \mathrm{CS}(\mathbf{c}, n)$ *and* $\mathbf{d}^{(B)} = \mathrm{CS}(\mathbf{b}, n)$. *Then the eigenvalues of* $G = \mathrm{circ}(\mathbf{c}) + \mathrm{rcirc}(\mathbf{b})$ *are given by*

$$\lambda_0^{(G)} = d_0^{(C)}; \quad \lambda_j^{(G)} = d_j^{(C)} + d_j^{(B)}, \quad j = 1, 2, \ldots m - 1; \quad (56)$$
$$\lambda_m^{(G)} = d_m^{(C)}; \quad \lambda_j^{(G)} = d_{n-j}^{(C)} - d_{n-j}^{(B)}, \quad j = m+1, m+2, \ldots n - 1.$$

*Proof.* Since $\mathbf{c}$ and $\mathbf{b}$ are symmetric, from Theorem 2 we obtain

$$d_j^{(C)} = C_j(\mathbf{c}) = \mathbf{c}^T\mathbf{u}^{(j)}, \quad d_j^{(B)} = C_j(\mathbf{b}) = \mathbf{c}^T\mathbf{u}^{(j)}, \quad j = 0, 1, \ldots, m.$$

From (53)–(55) we get that $\lambda_j^{(C)} = d_j^{(C)}$ and $\lambda_j^{(B)} = d_j^{(B)}$ for $j = 0, 1, \ldots, m$, where $\lambda_j^{(C)}$ (resp., $\lambda_j^{(B)}$) are the eigenvalues of $\mathrm{circ}(\mathbf{c})$ (resp., $\mathrm{rcirc}(\mathbf{b})$). From (52)–(55) we obtain (56). □

To complete the computation of (10), we have to multiply the diagonal matrix $\Lambda^{(G)}$ by $\mathbf{z}$. The cost of this operation consists of $n$ multiplications. Thus, by Theorem 3, the total cost to compute (10) is of $\frac{3}{2} n \log_2 n + o(n \log_2 n)$ additions and $\frac{1}{2} n \log_2 n + o(n \log_2 n)$ multiplications.

## 3.3  The DSCT Technique

Now we compute $\mathbf{y} = Q_n\,\mathbf{t} = \mathrm{DSCT}(\mathbf{t})$. Let $\overline{\alpha}$ and $\widetilde{\alpha}$ be as in (2). By (1), for $j = 0, 1, \ldots, m$ it is

$$y_j = \overline{\alpha}\,t_0 + (-1)^j\,\overline{\alpha}\,t_{n/2} + \widetilde{\alpha}\sum_{k=1}^{m-1}\cos\left(\frac{2\,k\,\pi\,j}{n}\right)t_k$$

$$+ \widetilde{\alpha}\sum_{k=1}^{m-1}\sin\left(\frac{2\,k\,\pi\,j}{n}\right)t_{n-k} = \mathrm{DSCT}_j(\mathbf{t}), \tag{57}$$

and for $j = 1, 2, \ldots, m-1$ we have

$$y_{n-j} = \overline{\alpha}\,t_0 + (-1)^j\,\overline{\alpha}\,t_{n/2} + \widetilde{\alpha}\sum_{k=1}^{m-1}\cos\left(\frac{2\,k\,\pi\,(n-j)}{n}\right)t_k$$

$$+ \widetilde{\alpha}\sum_{k=1}^{m-1}\sin\left(\frac{2\,k\,\pi\,(n-j)}{n}\right)t_{n-k} \tag{58}$$

$$= \overline{\alpha}\,t_0 + (-1)^j\,\overline{\alpha}\,t_{n/2} + \widetilde{\alpha}\sum_{k=1}^{m-1}\cos\left(\frac{2\,k\,\pi\,j}{n}\right)t_k$$

$$- \widetilde{\alpha}\sum_{k=1}^{m-1}\sin\left(\frac{2\,k\,\pi\,j}{n}\right)t_{n-k} = \mathrm{DSCT}_{n-j}(\mathbf{t}).$$

Now we define the functions $\varphi,\,\vartheta : \mathbb{R}^n \to \mathbb{R}^n$ by

$$\varphi(\mathbf{t}) = \overline{\mathbf{t}} = (t_0\ t_1\ \ldots t_{m-1}\ t_m\ t_{m-1}\ \cdots\ t_1), \tag{59}$$

$$\vartheta(\mathbf{t}) = \widetilde{\mathbf{t}} = (0\ t_{n-1}\ t_{n-2}\ \ldots t_{m+1}\ 0\ -t_{m+1}\ \cdots\ -t_{n-1}).$$

The following result holds.

**Theorem 6.** *For $j = 1, 2, \ldots, m-1$, it is*

$$\mathrm{DSCT}_j(\mathbf{t}) = \frac{\widetilde{\alpha}}{2}\left(\mathrm{C}_j(\overline{\mathbf{t}}) - t_0 - (-1)^j t_m + \mathrm{S}_j(\widetilde{\mathbf{t}})\right) \tag{60}$$

$$+ \overline{\alpha}\,t_0 + (-1)^j\,\overline{\alpha}\,t_m$$

*and*

$$\mathrm{DSCT}_{n-j}(\mathbf{t}) = \frac{\overline{\alpha}}{2}\left(\mathrm{C}_j(\overline{\mathbf{t}}) - t_0 - (-1)^j t_m - \mathrm{S}_j(\widetilde{\mathbf{t}})\right) \tag{61}$$

$$+ \overline{\alpha}\,t_0 + (-1)^j\,\overline{\alpha}\,t_m.$$

*Moreover, one has*

$$\mathrm{DSCT}_0(\mathbf{t}) = \frac{\widetilde{\alpha}}{2}\left(\mathrm{C}_0(\overline{\mathbf{t}}) - t_0 - t_m\right) + \overline{\alpha}\,t_0 + \overline{\alpha}\,t_m; \tag{62}$$

$$\mathrm{DSCT}_m(\mathbf{t}) = \frac{\widetilde{\alpha}}{2}\left(\mathrm{C}_m(\overline{\mathbf{t}}) - t_0 - t_m\right) + \overline{\alpha}\,t_0 + \overline{\alpha}\,t_m. \tag{63}$$

*Proof.* We have

$$
C_j(\bar{\mathbf{t}}) = \bar{\mathbf{t}}^T \mathbf{u}^{(j)} = \bar{t}_0 + (-1)^j \bar{t}_m + \sum_{k=1}^{m-1} \cos\left(\frac{2\,k\,\pi\,j}{n}\right)\bar{t}_k + \sum_{k=m+1}^{n-1} \cos\left(\frac{2\,k\,\pi\,j}{n}\right)\bar{t}_k
$$

$$
= t_0 + (-1)^j\,t_m + \sum_{k=1}^{m-1} \cos\left(\frac{2\,k\,\pi\,j}{n}\right) t_k + \sum_{k=1}^{m-1} \cos\left(\frac{2\,(n-k)\,\pi\,j}{n}\right)\bar{t}_{n-k}
$$

$$
= t_0 + (-1)^j t_m + \sum_{k=1}^{m-1} \cos\left(\frac{2\,k\,\pi\,j}{n}\right) t_k + \sum_{k=1}^{m-1} \cos\left(\frac{2\,(n-k)\,\pi\,j}{n}\right) t_k \qquad (64)
$$

$$
= t_0 + (-1)^j t_m + 2\sum_{k=1}^{m-1} \cos\left(\frac{2\,k\,\pi\,j}{n}\right) t_k;
$$

$$
S_j(\widetilde{\mathbf{t}}) = \widetilde{\mathbf{t}}^T \mathbf{v}^{(j)} = \sum_{k=1}^{m-1} \sin\left(\frac{2\,k\,\pi\,j}{n}\right)\widetilde{t}_k + \sum_{k=m+1}^{n-1} \sin\left(\frac{2\,k\,\pi\,j}{n}\right)\widetilde{t}_k
$$

$$
= \sum_{k=1}^{m-1} \sin\left(\frac{2\,k\,\pi\,j}{n}\right) t_{n-k} - \sum_{k=1}^{m-1} \sin\left(\frac{2\,(n-k)\,\pi\,j}{n}\right) t_{n-k} \qquad (65)
$$

$$
= 2\sum_{k=1}^{m-1} \sin\left(\frac{2\,k\,\pi\,j}{n}\right) t_{n-k}.
$$

From (57) and (64) we obtain (60), (62) and (63), while from (58) and (65) we get (61).    □

The computational cost of the valuation of the functions $\varphi$ and $\vartheta$ is linear, and the cost of the call of the functions CS and SN to determinate the values $C_j(\bar{\mathbf{t}})$ for $j = 0, 1, \cdots, m$ and $S_j(\widetilde{\mathbf{t}})$ for $j = 1, 2, \cdots, m$ is of $\frac{7}{4} n \log_2 n + o(n \log_2 n)$ additions and $\frac{1}{2} n \log_2 n + o(n \log_2 n)$ multiplications. The remaining computations for $\mathrm{DSCT}(\mathbf{t})$ are of $O(n)$. Thus, the total cost to compute $\mathrm{DSCT}(\mathbf{t})$ is of $\frac{7}{4} n \log_2 n + o(n \log_2 n)$ additions and $\frac{1}{2} n \log_2 n + o(n \log_2 n)$ multiplications. Therefore, the total cost to compute (8) is given by $5\,n \log_2 n + o(n \log_2 n)$ additions and $\frac{3}{2} n \log_2 n + o(n \log_2 n)$ multiplications.    □

## 4    Conclusions

In this article we presented a new class of simultaneously diagonalizable real matrices, which can be expressed as the direct sum between a symmetric circulant matrix and a suitable reverse circulant matrix. Such matrices are used in several applications. We constructed a fast discrete transform in order to implement the multiplication between such a matrix and a real vector. We proved that the computational cost of such a transform is very low, especially in terms of multiplications. Our transform can be used also to compute multiplications between other classes of simultaneously diagonalizable real matrices and real vectors. Thus, our algorithm can be used to improve the performance of various discrete transforms proposed for multiplications of real vectors.

**Acknowledgments.** This work was partially supported by University of Perugia, G.N.A.M.P.A. (Italian National Group of Mathematical Analysis, Probability and Applications) and I.N.d.A.M. (Italian National Institute of Higher Mathematics).

# References

1. Andrecut, M.: Applications of left circulant matrices in signal and image processing. Mod. Phys. Lett. B **22**, 231–241 (2008)
2. Bini, D., Di Benedetto, F.: A new preconditioner for the parallel solution of positive definite Toeplitz systems. In: Second Ann. Symp. Parallel Algorithms and Architecture, Crete, Greece, pp. 220–223 (1990)
3. Bini, D., Favati, P.: On a matrix algebra related to the discrete Hartley transform. SIAM J. Matrix Anal. Appl. **14**, 500–507 (1993)
4. Boccuto, A., Gerace, I., Giorgetti, V.: Image Deblurring: a Class of Matrices Approximating Toeplitz Matrices. viXra 2201.0155 (2022)
5. Boccuto, A., Gerace, I., Giorgetti, V., Greco, F.: $\gamma$-matrices: a new class of simultaneously diagonalizable matrices. arXiv:2107.05890 (2021)
6. Carrasquinha, E., Amado, C., Pires, A.M., Oliveira, L.: Image reconstruction based on circulant matrices. Signal Process. Image Commun. **63**, 72–80 (2018)
7. Chan, R.: The spectrum of a family of circulant preconditioned Toeplitz systems. SIAM J. Numer. Anal. **26**, 503–506 (1989)
8. Codenotti, B., Gerace, I., Vigna, S.: Hardness results and spectral techniques for combinatorial problems on circulant graphs. Linear Algebra Appl. **285**, 123–142 (1998)
9. Di Fiore, C., Zellini, P.: Matrix algebras in optimal preconditioning. Linear Algebra Appl. **335**, 1–54 (2001)
10. Fischer, R., Huckle, T.: Using $\omega$-circulant matrices for the preconditioning of Toeplitz systems. Selçuk J. Appl. Math. **4**, 71–88 (2003)
11. Frigo, M., Johnson, S.G.: A modified split-radix FFT with fewer arithmetic operations. IEEE Trans. Signal Process. **55**(1), 111–119 (2006)
12. Gerace, I., Pucci, P., Ceccarelli, N., Discepoli, M., Mariani, R.: A preconditioned finite element method for the $p$-Laplacian parabolic equation. Appl. Numer. Anal. Comput. Math. **1**, 155–164 (2004)
13. Győri, I., Horváth, L.: Utilization of circulant matrix theory in periodic autonomous difference equations. Int. J. Differ. Equ. **9**, 163–185 (2014)
14. Lei, Y.J., Xu, W.R., Lu, Y., Niu, Y.R., Gu, X.M.: On the symmetric doubly stochastic inverse Eigenvalue problem. Linear Algebra Appl. **445**, 181–205 (2014)
15. Shao, X., Johnson, S.G.: Type-II/III DCT/DST algorithms with reduced number of arithmetic operations. IEEE Signal Process. **88**(6), 1553–1564 (2008)

# Enhancing UAV Communication Performance: Analysis Using Interference Based Geometry Stochastic Model and Successive Interference Cancellation

Emmanuel Ampoma Affum[1]($\boxtimes$)(iD), Matthew O. Adigun[2](iD),
Kofi Anane Boateng[1], Sunday Adeola Ajagbe[3](iD), and Emmanuel Addo[1]

[1] Department of Telecommunication Engineering,
Kwame Nkrumah University of Science and Technology, Kumasi, Ghana
eaffum.coe@knust.edu.gh, kaboateng10@st.knust.edu.gh
[2] Department of Computer Science, University of Zululand,
Richards Bay, South Africa
adigunm@unizulu.ac.za
[3] Computer Engineering Department, Ladoke Akintola University of Technology,
Ogbomoso, Nigeria
saajagbe@pgschool.lautech.edu.ng

**Abstract.** The reliability and transmission quality in any wireless communication network is paramount. Unmanned Aerial Vehicle (UAV) communication networks are no exception to this fact. Hence, the need to investigate various communication technologies that will improve and be able to support the various applications of the UAV communication network. Correlated based stochastic models (CBSM) have been used to assess theoretical performances in UAV communication networks. CBSM has insufficient precision in a practical system. Geometry based stochastic channel models (GBSM) on the other hand, displays realistic channel features. These realistic channel features include pathloss, angle of arrival (AoA), angle of departure (AoD), etc. GBSM is better and ideal for channel modeling. This paper analyses the UAV communication networks in terms of their reliability and quality in transmission. MIMO-OFDM technology has been proposed to improve the UAV communication network. In this UAV network, the transmitters are modeled as cylindrical array (CA) because of its attribute of good regulation in 3-D space among others. A 3-D GBSM is proposed in the analysis. Also, an interference model has been presented in the UAV communication network. Results from this research show that MIMO-OFDM improves the reliability and quality of the UAV communication network. Generally, the capacity and BER increased with increasing number of antennas and SINR. However, beyond SINR of $25dB$, we observed an irreducible error floor, that is, BER remained constant with increasing SINR. Successive Interference Cancellation (SIC) was therefore employed to minimize the irreducible error floor in the UAV communication network. This increased the average capacity and BER to about $25bits/s/Hz$ and $10^{-8}$ respectively.

© The Author(s), under exclusive license to Springer Nature Switzerland AG 2022
O. Gervasi et al. (Eds.): ICCSA 2022, LNCS 13375, pp. 232–245, 2022.
https://doi.org/10.1007/978-3-031-10522-7_17

**Keywords:** UAV communication networks · MIMO-OFDM ·
Cylindrical array · CBSM · GBSM · Successive interference cancellation

# 1  Introduction

Unmanned Aerial Vehicles (UAVs), often known as drones, are airplanes that
do not have any human passengers on board. They are set up to be totally or
partially self-contained. Even though UAVs are classed based on their application and Quality of Service (QoS), they are commonly categorized based on
their altitude and wing type [1–3]. UAV communication network comprises a
drone, a base station, and a communication link between the UAV and the base
station (BS). UAVs have a broad range of applications that include precision
agriculture, disaster management, monitoring and surveillance, aerial photogra-
phy, military applications, telecommunications, delivery of medical supplies, and
rescue operations [4–8].

## 1.1  Related Works

With the broad and diverse applications of UAV communication in our world,
there is the need to ensure efficiency and reliability in the UAV network communication link. This has been the recent focus of researchers regarding UAV
communication networks. Given this, authors in [9,10] presented on Orthogonal
Frequency Division Multiplexing (OFDM)and Single Carrier-Frequency Division
Multiplexing (SC-FDM) in improving the communication link. This is because
of the prominent resilience they have with regards to multipath distortion and
higher throughput and likely data rates as compared to the traditional spread
spectrum technology being currently employed in the UAV communication network. SC-FDM and OFDM improved the UAV communication network. However, in [9,10], correlated based stochastic channel models (CSBM) were used for
the analysis. The accuracy of CSBM is insufficient for practical systems, therefore they are used to analyze theoretical performance. These realistic features
include pathloss, AoA, AoD, etc.

Again, authors in [11–16] have considered Massive Multiple Input Multiple
Output (mMIMO) in the UAV communication network under realistic 3GPP
assumptions. The multi-user mode was compared to the typical single-user mode,
and the multi-user mode significantly increased the channel and control (C&C)
capacity. However, with mMIMO, as the number of transmit antennas increases,
the pilot overhead for channel estimate becomes excessively large, which is an
issue in wireless communication [17]. To reduce the channel estimation overhead, authors in [18] used time division duplex (TDD) communication. Where
the downlink (DL) and channel state information (CSI) can be attained from
that of the uplink (UL) channel by utilizing channel reciprocity. Another way

is to employ frequency division duplex (FDD) which is more efficient compared with TDD. Authors in [19], presented the use of MIMO-OFDM in the UAV communication networks as MIMO will decrease the effect of multipath fading without expanding power, sacrificing bandwidth, and also utilize channel capacity. MIMO can viably defeat issues of limited capacity and low transmission rate of UAV communication [20]. OFDM on the other hand mitigates frequency selective fading [21] which is a problem associated with the MIMO system [22]. MIMO-OFDM improves the capacity and also effectively overcomes frequency selective fading which improves the data transmission quality and reliability [23]. However, in this literature, small antenna scale and a correlated based channel model were considered for analysis.

## 1.2    Motivation

In comparison to prior research on UAV communication networks [9,11,19], having a realistic study that takes into account the diverse uses of UAV communication over a cellular network presents additional challenges. To begin, the channel model between the UAV and the ground station (base station) will no longer follow correlated based stochastic channel models (CBSM) but will instead be geometry based stochastic channel models (GBSM). CBSM analyses are theoretical and offer less precision in a communication system. GBSM on the other hand displays realistic channel features which consider pathloss, AoA, AoD, etc. Despite the additional processing complexity, this is better for channel modeling [24]. Second, because the UAV communication network will be deployed over a shared frequency band with other cellular networks, interference concerns may arise. Previous research on UAV communication networks, such as [11–17], have not considered both the first and second issues. In this literature, we looked into these issues and their trade-offs. This work will, to the best of our knowledge, offer *analysis of the performance of UAV communication in MIMO-OFDM in the presence of interference using GBSM.*

## 1.3    Contribution

The main contribution of this paper is to present and analyze UAV communication regarding GBSM between the UAV and the CA MIMO-OFDM BS. We considered the WINNER+ channel model standard in [25] that follows GBSM and present a new channel realization when the transmitter is modeled as CA. Here, the BS of the UAV communication network is modeled as a cylindrical array (CA). CA is considered because the emitted MIMO signals from these arrays can be well controlled in 3-D space increasing system capacity [26,27]. Additionally, the CA enables the generation of focused beams in any horizontal direction or an omnidirectional pattern in the horizontal plane [28]. Furthermore, the CA can be used to minimize clutter by using scanning acceleration and space-time signal processing [29]. In addition, we investigate the impact of interference on MIMO-OFDM in UAV communication networks. We considered several UAVs that support downlink transmission to several user equipments (UE) and CA MIMO-OFDM base stations. The contributions of this paper have been summarized as follows:

1. We modeled the base station (BS) as a cylindrical array (CA) and presented a new channel model based on GBSM for the MIMO-OFDM system in the UAV communication network.
2. We presented an interference model and incorporated the model into the channel to see the impact of interference on the UAV communication network.
3. We considered successive interference cancellation at the receiver in the proposed UAV communication network. When SIC is used, it enables the user to uniquely decode the data being received with minimal interference and data loss.
4. We present results to show that the capacity and BER generally increase with increase in the number of antennas and SINR. Here, beyond SINR of $25dB$, the BER of the network remains constant with increasing SINR. This is known as the irreducible error floor. We then present on SIC to reduce the irreducible error floor.

## 2   The System Model

### 2.1   Proposed UAV System Model

In this section, we discuss the various aspect of the UAV communication network and how they are linked to form the system model. We considered a circular area with UAVs deployed for an application. For this network, the following scenarios were considered: communication between the user equipment and the UAV, communication between the UAV and base stations, and communication between the base stations and the UEs. All base stations within this network are considered to be MIMO-OFDM transceivers with their antennas modeled as cylindrical array (CA). Here we looked at the downlink scenario. Also, base stations are located at a fixed distance from each other as shown in Fig. 1.

### 2.2   Proposed Interference Model

In this section, we examine the various interference that can be experienced by all the systems within this network considering the downlink scenario. Based on this, an appropriate Signal-to-Interference-plus noise ratio (SINR) was established. As shown in the diagram in Fig. 2, the received signal at the base stations consists of the intended signal from the UAV transmitter as well as interference from other UAVs and MIMO-OFDM transmitters. On the other hand, the UE receives the

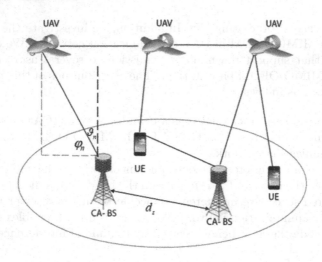

**Fig. 1.** UAV system model including UAVs, UEs, and CA MIMO-OFDM base stations (CA-BS)

intended signal from the UAV but is also subjected to interference from all other MIMO-OFDM transmitters. The interference expression is given as [30]:

$$I = p_i \sum_{i \in k} \xi_i^2 \Upsilon_i^{-v} \tag{1}$$

where $\xi_i$ is the fading amplitude of the $ith$ interfering signal. All interfering signals are considered to be sent at the same power level $p_i$ [30], however, pathloss and fading occur in a mutually independent manner. In addition, it is assumed that the interferers are independent and identically distributed (i.i.d). Also, $\Upsilon_i$ represents the distance between the interfering terminal $i$ and the receiver, while $v$ represents the pathloss exponent in the receiver's environment. The output signal-to-interference-plus-noise ratio (SINR)expression as:

$$\gamma = \frac{p_s \alpha_s^2 d_s^{-v}}{N_o + I} \tag{2}$$

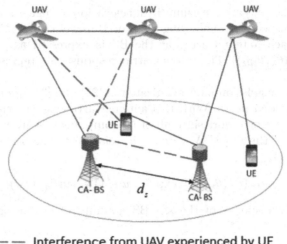

—  —  —  Interference from UAV experienced by UE

—  —  —  Interference from other CA-BS experienced
by CA-BS

—  —  —  Interference from UAV experienced by CA-BS

**Fig. 2.** Interference model showing interference among UAVs, UEs and CA-BSs

where $p_s$ is the transmitting power of the desired signal, $d_s$ is the distance between the transmitter and the receiver, $\alpha_s$ is the Rayleigh-faded amplitude of the desired signal. $I$ represents the interference being experienced by the BS.

### 2.3 The Channel Model

In this section, we examined the GBSM standards and the WINNER+ model in [31] and [32], which follows a GBSM approach and presented a relating channel realization between the BS when modeled as CA and the UAV. We considered these WINNER+ and 3GPP standards because it has a substantial component of energy that is radiated in the elevation according to research. Therefore, in the azimuth, the propagation path does not enhance performance [33]. For the 3D MIMO-OFDM analysis, we represent the BS as CA. However, the UAV is represented by summing contributions of $N$ multiple paths with channel parameters such as delay, power, and both azimuthal and elevation spread. In [25], authors defined the effective channel between the $sth$ transmitting UAV and the $uth$ receiving BS as:

$$[H_{s,u}] = \sum_{n=1}^{N} \alpha_n \sqrt{g_t\left(\phi_n, \theta_n, \theta_{tilt}\right)} \sqrt{g_r\left(\varphi_n, \vartheta_n\right)} \times [\alpha_n\left(\varphi_n, \vartheta_n\right)]_u \times [\alpha_t\left(\phi_n, \theta_n\right)] \qquad (3)$$

where $s = 1, ..., N_{UAV}, u = 1, ..., N_{BS}, \alpha_n$ is the complex amplitude of the $n^{th}$ path, $(\phi_n, \theta_n)$ are the azimuth and the elevation angles-of-departure (AODs) respectively. $(\varphi_n, \vartheta_n)$ are the azimuth and elevation of angles of arrival (AOAs) of the $n^{th}$ path respectively. Following the procedures of ITU and 3GPP standards, the gain of each antenna array at the BS is expressed as $g_t(\phi_n, \theta_n, \theta_{tilt}) \approx g_t, H(\phi_n g_t, v(\theta_n, \theta_{tilt}))$. The antenna array responses are represented by $\alpha_t(\phi, \theta)$ and $\alpha_r(\phi, \theta)$.

Different transmission modes indicated in [27] and [34] are required with the use of CA antenna ports. With this antenna arrangement, each antenna port appears to be a single port since all of its components convey the same signal. The response of the $uth$ UAV antenna in relation to the 3-D channel model is expressed as [34].

$$[\alpha_r(\phi_n, \theta_n)]_s = \exp(ik(u-1)d_r \sin\theta_n \sin\vartheta) \tag{4}$$

Also the array response of the $sth$ BS antenna of CA using Eq. (3) can be expressed as

$$[\alpha_t(\phi_n, \theta_n)]_s = \exp(ik\rho(4\lambda(m-1)/M)\cos(\phi_n - \varphi_s)\sin\theta_n) \tag{5}$$

The resulting 3-D channel realization between the $sth$ transmit antenna of the CA and the single receiving antenna can be expressed as

$$[H_{s,u}]_{CA} = \sum_{n=1}^{N} \alpha_n \sqrt{g_t(\phi_n, \theta_n, \theta_{tilt})} \times \exp(ik\rho(4\lambda(m-1)/M)\cos(\phi_n - \varphi_s)\sin\theta_n)$$

$$\times \sqrt{g_r(\varphi_n, \vartheta_n)} \times \exp(ik(u-1)d_r \sin\theta_n \sin\vartheta) \tag{6}$$

where $k$ is the wave number, $d_r$ is the separation between the receiving antennas, $\rho = 4\lambda/l$ which represents the radius of the cylinder. $m = 1, ..., M$ is the total number of UCA elements within the CA in the z-direction.

## 2.4    The MIMO-OFDM System Model

In this section, we dicuss the MIMO-OFDM system model in the network. Here, we assumed that the system has $N_t$ transmitting antennas and $N_r$ receiving antenna. By transforming serial streams to parallel streams using space-time pre-processing, the serial information bit stream is transformed into $N_t$ sub-data streams. After being OFDM modulated, the sub-data streams are transmitted simultaneously by $N_t$ antennas. If the OFDM system contains $N$ carriers, then there will be a total of $N_t N$ OFDM samples in one OFDM symbol period. The $N_t \times N$ samples sent by the $nth$ OFDM symbol period is represented by $x_n$. Where $x_n$ is an $N_t \cdot N$ dimensional column vector. We represent the received OFDM signal as $y_n$. Where $y_n$ is an $(N + N_g + I) \cdot N_r$ dimensional column vector. Where $N_g$ represent additive white Gaussian noise and $I$ the interference within the channel. The total number of OFDM symbols being transmitted can be expressed as [19]

$$x_n = \left[x_{1,n}^T, x_{2,n}^T, ..., x_{N,n}^T\right]^T \tag{7}$$

with a corresponding received signal expressed as

$$y_n = \left[y_{1,n}^T, y_{2,N}^T, ..., y_{N,n}^T\right]^T \tag{8}$$

When perfect synchronization is achieved at the receiver, the MIMO-OFDM system's input and output relationship may be described in the matrix form below

$$\bar{y} = \bar{H}x + \bar{n} + \bar{I} \tag{9}$$

where $\bar{y}$ is a $N \cdot N_r$ dimensional column vector. $\bar{n}$ is a $N \cdot N_r$ dimensional vector of additive white Gaussian noise. $\bar{I}$ is a $N \cdot N_r$ dimensional vector of interference and $\bar{H}$ is a $(N \cdot N_r) \times (N \cdot N_t)$ dimensional cyclic matrices. The GBSM channel proposed in Eq. 6 can be expressed as

$$\left[\bar{H}_{s,u}\right]_{CA} = \begin{bmatrix} H_{11} & H_{12} & \cdots & H_{1N_t} \\ H_{21} & H_{22} & \cdots & H_{2N_t} \\ \vdots & \vdots & \ddots & \vdots \\ H_{N_r1} & H_{N_r2} & \cdots & H_{N_rN_t} \end{bmatrix} \tag{10}$$

$H_{ij}$ is a $N \times N$ dimensional discrete inverse Fourier Transform sub-matrix in Eq. 11. $H_{s,u}$ is diagonalized in other to obtain independence and maximum capacity for each channel. The diagonal sub-blocks are of $N \times N$ dimensional discrete Fourier Transform matrix in Eq. 12. The block diagonal matrices are shown as follows

$$F^{H(N_t)} = \begin{bmatrix} F_N^H & 0 & \cdots & 0 \\ 0 & F_N^H & \cdots & 0 \\ \vdots & \vdots & \ddots & \vdots \\ 0 & 0 & \cdots & F_N^H \end{bmatrix} \tag{11}$$

and

$$F^{(N_r)} = \begin{bmatrix} F_n & 0 & \cdots & 0 \\ 0 & F_n & \cdots & 0 \\ \vdots & \vdots & \ddots & \vdots \\ 0 & 0 & \cdots & F_n \end{bmatrix} \tag{12}$$

Equation 9 can then be re-written as

$$F^{(N_r)}\bar{y} = F^{(N_r)}\bar{H}x + F^{(N_r)}\bar{n} + F^{(N_r)}\bar{I} \tag{13}$$

and further simplified as

$$Y = F^{(N_r)}\bar{H}F^{H(N_r)}X + Z \tag{14}$$

$Y = \left[ Y_1^T, Y_1^T, ..., Y_{N_r}^T \right]^T$ is a $N_r \cdot N$ dimensional demodulated signal column vector. $X = \left[ X_1^T, X_2^T, ..., X_{N_t}^T \right]^T$ is a $N_t \cdot N$ dimensional original transmitted signal column vector. $Z$ is a combination of the noise vector and the interference. The frequency response of the $k-th$ subcarrier channel between the transmitting antenna $i$ and the receiving antenna $j$ will be $H_{ji}(k)$. The summation of $N_t$ flat fading signals will constitute the demodulation signal on the $k - th$ subcarrier of each receiving antenna $j$ [19].

$$Y_j(k) = \sum_{i=1}^{N_t} H_{ji}(k) \cdot X_i(k) + Z_j(k) \tag{15}$$

## 2.5 Successive Interference Cancellation in UAV Communication Network

In this section, we discuss how the interference within the UAV communication system can be reduced using the concept of successive interference cancellation (SIC). In SIC, a single user, in this example the UAV, is decoded uniquely at the base station, with all other users, such as other UAVs, base stations, and user equipment, being treated as interference. This decision is done by the decision region $\rho$. Single user matching filters are used to make these decisions, which ignores the existence of interference [35]. At the receiver, the interfering signal can be replicated and removed from the received waveform. This process is continued until all of the information streams sent have been demodulated. If the decision made was accurate, this procedure cancels the interfering signal [35]. Figure 3 depicts a two-user SIC being employed by the base station in the downlink scenario.

In Fig. 3, supposing UAV 2 is demodulated by its matched filter:

$$y_2 = sgn(Y_2) \tag{16}$$

The signal of user 2 with $y_2$ is remodulated to obtain $A_2 y_2 s_2(t)$ and then subtracted from the received signal to yield

$$\hat{y}(t) = Y(t) - A_2 y_2 s_2(t) \tag{17}$$

$$= A_1 y_1 s_1(t) + A_2 (\hat{y}_2 - y_2) s_2(t) + n(t) \tag{18}$$

Using the matched filter for $s_1$ to process $\hat{y}$, we obtain

$$y_1 = sgn(\{\hat{y}, s_1\}) \tag{19}$$

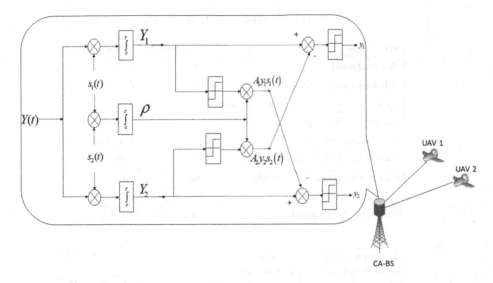

**Fig. 3.** CA-BS performing a two-user SIC

$$= sgn(y_1 - A_2 y_2 \rho) \qquad (20)$$

$$= sgn\left(y_1 - A_2 \rho sgn\left(Y_2\right)\right) \qquad (21)$$

$$= sgn\left(A_1 \hat{y}_1 + A_2\left(\hat{y}_2 - y_2\right)\rho + \sigma\left(n, s_1\right)\right) \qquad (22)$$

## 3  Numerical Results

In this section, we provide the simulated results to evaluate our proposed system for the UAV communication network. The experimental environment of this paper is based on MATLAB 2018a. For this study, we demonstrate how the capacity and BER of a signal are affected in UAV communication networks when MIMO-OFDM together with SIC are employed. Also, SINR will be used to analyze the impact on the performance evaluation metrics. Table 1 shows the simulation parameters used for the experiment.

For the cylindrical array base stations, we considered three circular arrays each in the zenith domain. Where each circular array constitutes two antennas and also an instance where each circular array constitutes four antennas. For the 3-D channel modeling, we set $\theta_{tilt} = 95°$, $\theta = 15°$, and $\phi = 70°$ as described in [32]. The AoA and AoD are drawn from the Laplacian distribution. The results in Fig. 4 shows that an increase in the number of antennas increases the capacity with increasing SINR. With interference within the UAV communication network, the channel capacity reduces generally regardless of the number of antennas used in the UAV communication network. When SIC was used in the communication network, the channel capacity improved as it reduced the

**Table 1.** UAV simulation parameters

| Description | Parameter | Value |
|---|---|---|
| UAV transmit power | $P_s$ | 5 W |
| Path loss exponent | $v$ | 3 |
| Fixed distance between base stations | $d_s$ | 20 m |
| Interfering signal power | $p_i$ | 5 W |
| Modulation scheme | | 16QAM |
| Number of OFDM samples used | $N_s$ | 100000 |
| Downward tilt of the antenna | $\theta_{tilt}$ | 95° |
| Vertical beamwidth | $\theta$ | 15° |
| Horizontal beamwidth | $\phi$ | 70° |

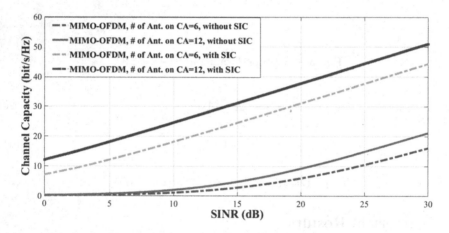

**Fig. 4.** Capacity vs SINR of CA MIMO-OFDM with and without SIC

interference with the network. For the BER analysis, BER in the UAV communication network was improving with a corresponding increase in the number
of antennas used and increasing SINR. However, in Fig. 5 it was observed that
beyond SINR of about 25 dB, it was observed that the BER no longer reduced
with increasing SINR. This is a result of the irreducible error floor due to the
interference. When SIC was employed in the experiment it could be observed
from Fig. 5 that the irreducible error floor had been reduced and that an increase
in SINR continued to give a better BER for our proposed system. Table 2 shows
a comparison of existing literature and our proposed network.

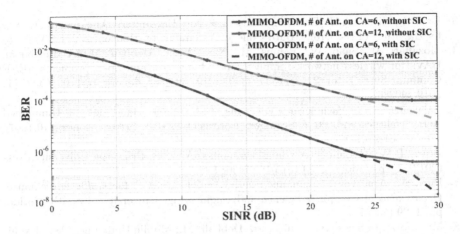

**Fig. 5.** BER vs SINR of CA MIMO-OFDM with and without SIC

**Table 2.** Comparison of prior work and proposed system

| Reference | Channel | Interference | SIC | Capacity(bits/s/Hz) | BER |
|---|---|---|---|---|---|
| [19] | CBSM | No | No | 20 | $10^{-2}$ |
| Proposed system | GBSM | Yes | Yes | 30 | $10^{-4}$ |

## 4   Conclusion

Improving transmission quality in UAV communication networks has been of major concern in UAV communication. In this research, we proposed the use of MIMO-OFDM in UAV communication networks. The antenna of the base stations was modelled as a cylindrical array with the channel GBSM. Also, we presented an interference model in the channel to the impact of interference on the communication system. Results indicated that as the number of antennas increases in the UAV communication network, so does the channel capacity and BER of the network increase with increasing SINR. This trend continues till the irreducible error floor point where an increase in SINR no longer improves the BER. Successive Interference Cancellation (SIC) is introduced such that the interference within the system will be mitigated and reduce the irreducible error floor.

## References

1. Zeng, Y., Zhang, R., Lim, T.J.: Wireless communications with unmanned aerial vehicles: opportunities and challenges. IEEE Commun. Mag. **54**(5), 36–42 (2016). https://doi.org/10.1109/MCOM.2016.7470933
2. Al-Hourani, A., Kandeepan, S., Jamalipour, A.: Modeling air-to-ground path loss for low altitude platforms in urban environments. In: 2014 IEEE Global Communications Conference, pp. 2898–2904 (2014). https://doi.org/10.1109/GLOCOM. 2014.7037248

3. Dan, G., Michel, A.H.: Drone Sightings and Close Encounters: An Analysis. Center for the Study of the Drone, Bard College, Annandale-on-Hudson, NY, USA (2015)
4. Mozaffari, M., Saad, W., Bennis, M., Nam, Y.-H., Debbah, M.: A tutorial on UAVs for wireless networks: applications, challenges, and open problems. IEEE Commun. Surv. Tutor. **21**(3), 2334–2360 (2019). https://doi.org/10.1109/COMST.2019.2902862
5. Valavanis, K.P., VachtsevanosValavanis, G.J. (eds.): Handbook of Unmanned Aerial Vehicles, vol. 2077. Springer, Dordrecht (2015). https://doi.org/10.1007/978-90-481-9707-1
6. Beard, R.W., McLain, T.W.: Small Unmanned Aircraft. Princeton University Press (2012). https://doi.org/10.1515/9781400840601
7. Puri, A.: A survey of unmanned aerial vehicles (UAV) for traffic surveillance. Department of Computer Science and Engineering, University of South Florida, pp. 1–29 (2005)
8. Mozaffari, M., Saad, W., Bennis, M., Debbah, M.: Mobile Unmanned Aerial Vehicles (UAVs) for energy-efficient internet of things communications. IEEE Trans. Wireless Commun. **16**(11), 7574–7589 (2017). https://doi.org/10.1109/TWC.2017.2751045
9. Atoev, S., Kwon, O.H., Lee, S.H., Kwon, K.R.: An efficient SC-FDM modulation technique for a UAV communication link. Electronics **7**(12), 352 (2018)
10. Ehichioya, D., Golriz, A.: Performance comparison of OFDM and DSSS on aeronautical channels. International Foundation for Telemetering (2009)
11. Geraci, G., Garcia-Rodriguez, A., Giordano, L.G., Lopez-Perez, D., Bjoernson, E.: Supporting UAV Cellular Communications through Massive MIMO. In: 2018 IEEE International Conference on Communications Workshops (ICC Workshops), pp. 1–6 (2018). https://doi.org/10.1109/ICCW.2018.8403630
12. Geraci, G., Garcia-Rodriguez, A., Hassan, M., Ding, M.: UAV Cellular Communications: Practical Insights and Future Vision (2018)
13. ENTT DOCOMO Inc., Ericsson. New SID on enhanced support for aerial vehicles. 3GPP RP-170779 RAN#75, Mar., 2017
14. LG Electronics. Interference mitigation for aerial vehicle. 3GPP R1–1718267, # 90bis, October 2017
15. Sony. Height parameter and CRS collision for aerial vehicle. 3GPP R1–1718267, #90bis, October 2017
16. Sequans Communications. Interference mitigation for aerial vehicle. 3GPP R1–1718267 #90bis, August 2017
17. Marzetta, T.L.: Noncooperative cellular wireless with unlimited numbers of base station antennas. IEEE Trans. Wireless Commun. **9**(11), 3590–3600 (2010). https://doi.org/10.1109/TWC.2010.092810.091092
18. Rusek, F., et al.: Scaling Up MIMO: opportunities and challenges with very large arrays. IEEE Signal Process. Mag. **30**(1), 40–60 (2013). https://doi.org/10.1109/MSP.2011.2178495
19. Tan, X., Su, S., Guo, X., Sun, X.: Application of MIMO-OFDM technology in UAV communication network. In: 2020 2nd World Symposium on Artificial Intelligence (WSAI), pp. 1–4 (2020). https://doi.org/10.1109/WSAI49636.2020.9143309
20. Gupta, A.K., Chockalingam, A.: Performance of MIMO modulation schemes with imaging receivers in visible light communication. J. Lightwave Technol. **36**(10), 1912–1927 (2018). https://doi.org/10.1109/JLT.2018.2795698

21. Al-Askery, A.J., Tsimenidis, C.C., Boussakta, S., Chambers, J.A.: Performance analysis of coded massive MIMO-OFDM systems using effective matrix inversion. IEEE Trans. Commun. **65**(12), 5244–5256 (2017). https://doi.org/10.1109/TCOMM.2017.2749370

22. Sun, X., Gao, X., Li, G.Y., Han, W.: Single-site localization based on a new type of fingerprint for massive MIMO-OFDM systems. IEEE Trans. Veh. Technol. **67**(7), 6134–6145 (2018). https://doi.org/10.1109/TVT.2018.2813058

23. Zhang, W., Li, H., Kong, W., Fan, Y., Cheng, W.: Structured compressive sensing based block-sparse channel estimation for MIMO-OFDM systems. Wireless Pers. Commun. **108**(4), 2279–2309 (2019). https://doi.org/10.1007/s11277-019-06522-8

24. Ampoma, A.E., Wen, G., Huang, Y., Gyasi, K.O., Tebe, P.I., Ntiamoah-Sarpong, K.: Spatial correlation models of large-scale antenna topologies using maximum power of offset distribution and its application. IEEE Access **6**, 36295–36304 (2018). https://doi.org/10.1109/ACCESS.2018.2846260

25. Document 3GPP TR 36.873 v12.0.0. Study on 3D channel model for LTE. September 2014

26. Zheng, K., Ou, S., Yin, X.: Massive MIMO channel models: a survey. Int. J. Antennas Propag. **2014** (2014). Article no. 848071

27. Liu, G., Hou, X., Wang, F., Jin, J., Tong, H., Huang, Y.: Achieving 3D-MIMO with massive antennas from theory to practice with evaluation and field trial results. IEEE Syst. J. **11**(1), 62–71 (2017)

28. Sipus, Z., Bosiljevac, M., Skokic, S.: Mutual coupling analysis of cylindrical waveguide arrays using hybrid SD-UTD method. In: Proceedings of the IEEE Antennas Propagation Society International Symposium, vol. 1A, pp. 155–158, July 2005

29. Pluzhnikov, A.D., Pribludova, E.N., Ryndyk, A.G.: Cylindrical array as a means of the clutter suppression via scanning acceleration and spacetime signal processing. In: Proceedings of the 44th European Microwave Conference, pp. 1864–1867, Rome, Italy (2014)

30. Kanatas, A.G., Nikita, K.S., Mathiopoulos, P.: New Direction in Wireless Communications Systems: from mobile to 5G. ISBN: 978-1-4987-8545-7

31. Study on 3D Channel Model for LTE, document 3GPP TR 36.873 V12.0.0, September 2014

32. Nadeem, Q.U.A., Kammoun, A., Debbah, M., Alouini, M.S.: Spatial correlation characterization of a uniform circular array in 3D MIMO systems. In: Proceedings of the 17th International Workshop Signal Process. Advanced Wireless Communication (SPAWC), pp. 1–6, Edinburgh, U.K. (2016)

33. Nadeem, Q.U.A., Kammoun, A., Debbah, M., Alouini, M.S.: 3D massive MIMO systems: modeling and performance analysis. IEEE Trans. Wireless Commun. **14**(12), 6926–6939 (2015)

34. Kammoun, A., Khanfir, H., Altman, Z., Debbah, M., Kamoun, M.: Preliminary results on 3D channel modeling: from theory to standardization. IEEE J. Sel. Areas Commun. **32**(6), 1219–1229 (2014)

35. Verdu, S.: Multiuser detection, pp. 344–368, ISBN:0-521-59373-5 (1998)

# High Performance Computing
# and Networks

# Model Based Migration of Cloud Systems: Review and Roadmap

Jaleleddine Hajlaoui[1]([✉]), Zied Trifa[2], and Zaki Brahmi[3]

[1] MARS Research Laboratory, University of Sousse, Sousse, Tunisia
hajlaouijalel.ig@gmail.com
[2] MIRACL Research Laboratory, University of Sfax, Sfax, Tunisia
trifa.zied@gmail.com
[3] College of Science and Arts at Al-Ola, Taibah University, Madina, Saudi Arabia
eibrahmi@taibahu.edu.sa

**Abstract.** Cloud computing has become a dominating trend in the IT industry and academia. In recent years, many Cloud providers have emerged in the market, each one has proper standards and service interface. Migration of legacy systems and their data to a Cloud platform or moving applications from one Cloud provider to another are complicated and high cost processes. In major legacy on-premise applications, they bring technical and business challenges. The choice of the best migration strategy is a hard task for Small and Medium-Sized Enterprises (SMEs) looking at best price and zero risk. Although guidelines offered by Cloud providers to support their users in migration tasks, the user implication is often mandatory to perform a conclusive migration. In this paper, we provide an overview of contemporary approaches for the model based migration of applications into Cloud computing. We highlight the Pros and Cons of each one and we present a summary comparison of these approaches. As well, we propose a new Cloud migration approach that renders the migration process more straightforward than with existent approaches and guarantees the services and data portability.

**Keywords:** Model based migration · Cloud computing · MDA · Multi-agent systems · Survey

## 1 Introduction

Cloud computing is a fundamental shift in delivering IT services with large impact on organizations. It responds to their requirements in terms of computational power, reduced cost of infrastructure, efficient resource usages and availability of applications. We recognize five main characteristics of Cloud computing namely: on-demand service, broad network access, resource pooling, rapid elasticity, and measured service.

The fast shift of Cloud Computing has contributed to a large market of Cloud services that provide infrastructure, platforms and software for multiple usages. Recently, the paradigm of multi-cloud has imposed itself for several purposes [1]. This paradigm allows, for example, to overcome the problems of elasticity of resources provided by

O. Gervasi et al. (Eds.): ICCSA 2022, LNCS 13375, pp. 249–264, 2022.
https://doi.org/10.1007/978-3-031-10522-7_18

only one Cloud provider. This promotes Cloud user independence to a unique provider (i.e., avoid the vendor lock-in) and offers the opportunity to optimize the quality of the resources offered by providers at a time. However, these providers generally use heterogeneous technologies which constitutes various challenges for the use of a multi-cloud ecosystem. Among the most inherent challenges, we find interoperability and portability of resources. Interoperability is related to the ability to deploy applications to different Cloud vendors. Portability is the ability for a user to easily move their data to another Cloud provider. Otherwise, the heterogeneous characteristics of a multi-cloud ecosystem are at the origin of difficulties of deploying applications in different environments. Heterogeneity can appear between the supported programming languages, libraries, services, and others. To solve these problems, standardization initiatives [2] have emerged including Unified Service Description Language (USDL), Topology and Orchestration Specification for Cloud Applications (TOSCA), Open Cloud Computing Interface (OCCI) Cloud Infrastructure Management Interface (CIMI), Cloud Data Management Interface (CDMI), just to cite some of them.

Cloud benefits like Cost reduction, automatic updates, high availability application attract Small and Medium-Sized Enterprises (SMEs) to move totally or partially their data, applications or other business elements from their onsite computers to the Cloud [3]. This process is known as *Cloud migration* which involves also migration of these elements from one Cloud to another. However, the migration process reveals many challenges: *i*) *Vendor lock-in problem and portability*; *ii*) *Complexity of Cloud deployment iii*) *Gap between Cloud stakeholders; iv*) *Lack of domain concepts and methodologies; vi*) *Choice of migration strategy*. The migration to the Cloud is not always so simple because it entails several interventions and modifications. The passage of the application from its classical architecture to a modern architecture needs in most cases the refactoring of the application [4]. Conversely, before passing to the refactoring, it's necessary to perform detailed feasibility studies in order to define the different constraints (technical, security, financial ...). These studies help to choose the type of migration (partial or total) or the Cloud provider(s) [5].

Several approaches have been proposed to ensure or facilitate application migration into single or multi-cloud environments. They proposed solutions for the different stages of migration processes. In this paper, we perform a deep study of existing approaches and we compare them according to several criteria such as data portability, degree of automation and type of migration. We propose a new Cloud migration approach based on three main blocks (migration strategy, migration execution, monitoring and maintenance). The rest of this paper is organized as follows. Section 2 identifies challenges of the migration process and defines its different steps. Section 3 surveys the contemporary approaches and compare them across identified criteria. Section 4 describes our proposed approach. Section 5 discuss related surveys. Finally, Sect. 6 concludes the paper.

## 2  Background

Migration to the Cloud computing is a critical process since there are many challenges to adopt for Cloud solutions. To migrate application to the Cloud environment, we must plan three steps: migration strategy, migration execution and administration.

## 2.1   Challenges and Motivations

There are many challenges facing Cloud consumer such as:

*Vendor lock-in problem*: this is a major impediment to the adoption of Cloud computing. It's due to the lack of standardization for Cloud Application Programming Interfaces (APIs) and data models. The heterogeneity of Cloud provider interfaces makes it hard to migrate applications between different Cloud providers or combine different offerings [6]. When every Cloud provider uses his own APIs and platforms, the consumer hasn't the ability to adapt an application and/or its components between different platforms with minimal efforts and costs. Without portability, migrating application requires modifications on code which is hard and expensive.

*Complexity of cloud deployment*: the deployment in the Cloud is a cumbersome process considering the numerous tasks unavoidable to get a successful deployment (i.e., pre-migrating tasks, migrating tasks and post-migrating tasks). Moreover, the deployment, management and reconfiguration of sophisticated applications across multiple Clouds is even harder. For instance, after the successful multi-cloud deployment, and execution of different components in different Cloud platforms, we should run a monitoring process to detect possible requirements violations, which may oblige a reconfiguration.

*Gap between cloud stakeholders*: it's important to understand the requirements of diverse stakeholders (providers, developers, administrators, financial managers, etc) and to obtain models at the early stage of development to address their applications concerns [7]. Since variability [8] occurs in all levels of Cloud applications, the configuration and customization of the migrations processes should be considered to fulfill goals and requirements of all tenants. Software Product Line (SPL) and feature modelling [9] can be useful to address engineering complexity and manage variability induced by multi-tenant Cloud migration. In addition, handling security issues and requirements of tenants while defining their migration variants should also be taken into account.

*Lack of domain concepts and methodologies*: developers need to understand the identity of Cloud applications. Cloud applications are composed of a set of interconnected software components [7]. Each component can be deployed and executed on a different Cloud provider in multi-cloud environment. We need a Cloud modeling language that represent a Cloud architecture deployment model for multi-tenant geo-distributed applications.

*Choice of migration strategy*: in the first step of the migration process, it is important to define the different constraints (technical, financial, juridical) and details concerning applications, consumers and companies. In addition, it is fundamental to analyze information collected to make the right decisions. The definition of the migration strategy is considered as a complex optimization problem since it is necessary to satisfy all the requirements of customers and applications with zero risk, zero problem and at low costs.

## 2.2   Migration Steps

### a.   Migration strategy

According to [10], the migration process begins with feasibility and requirements analysis and defining the migration strategy. Basera et al., [5] define the steps to follow to identify the strategy for migration of the legacy application. There are two categories of migration [11],

- Migration to Cloud or modernization of legacy applications: it's the transition of the application from traditional IT environment to the Cloud environment. After satisfying all constraints of the company, we choose the most suitable type of migration and the Cloud providers and we launch the code refactoring. This category contains 4 subcategories [12]:

  - Replace component(s) with Cloud offering: this type of migration requires adaptation and reconfiguration to address the problems of incompatibility between the Cloud service and the rest of the application. Example: using Google App Engine DataStore in the place of the local MySQL database server.
  - Partially migrate some of the application functionalities to the Cloud: this type of migration entails the migration of one or more application layers to the Cloud. Example: use a combination of Amazon SimpleDB and EC2 instance to host the auditing data and business logic.
  - Migrate the whole software stack of the application to the Cloud: this is the classic example of migration. The application is encapsulated in one or more virtual machines which are running in Cloud platforms [13]. For this type of migration, there is no need to make any changes to the application.
  - Cloudify the application: this is the migration of the entire application. All functionalities of the application are implemented as services which run in the Cloud. For this type, the data and the business layers are mondatory.

- The migration from one provider to another: the lack of standardization between Cloud providers represents a real obstacle hindering interoperability and portability. This problem is unfavorable to the desired objectives by companies. For some companies, the most important is insurance of portability services and data from one Cloud platform to another. By cons, others dream to the possibility of harmonizing the handling of different application components and the interoperability [2] in a standard way between different objects through orchestration [14] of Cloud resources distributed across multiple Clouds to ensure good interaction between the components of the application

b. **Migration execution**

This step includes modeling, development, test and validation and deployment of application components to migrate complicated tasks. Several approaches have been proposed in the literature to facilitate developer's jobs. These approaches are based on Model Driven Architecture, Cloud patterns and semantic modeling. They are more detailed in Sect. 3.

c. **Monitoring and maintenance**

This step follows the deployment of the application. Monitoring and maintenance of the application are mondatory and it is recommended to automate them. Mosaic [15] (Cloud agency) is one of the approaches which offers a semi-automatic solution based on the Multi-Agent Systems for the monitoring and administration.

# 3   Literature Review and Comparison

To deal with the above challenges (c.f., previous section), many approaches have been proposed. We propose to classify them as approaches based on: Multi-Agent Systems, Cloud patterns, Semantic Modelling, Model Driven Architecture, Cloud Standards and Software Product Line.

## 3.1   Multi-agent Systems Based Approaches

Multi-Agent Systems (MAS) help to solve complex problems using a system based on a set of smart, interactive, autonomous and dynamic agents. MAS offer techniques to solve problems and improve a number of activities such as brokering, negotiation, management, monitoring and reconfiguration in a multi-Cloud environments [16]. This family of approaches has some boundaries as it does not provide solutions for the step of adaptation and refactoring of application code and data in the migration process. MOSAIC (Cloud Agency) [15] offers a Cloud agency component to deploy and execute application. It helps user to discover and select the best Cloud solution that satisfies applications requirements. During the migration phase, MOSAIC proposes an agnostic interface based on MAS to manage resources of different providers, negotiate with other Cloud providers and reconfigure the MOSAIC application in the new chosen Cloud.

## 3.2   Cloud Patterns Based Approaches

Several alternatives are offered by different providers that help developers to identify the most viable architecture. For this, Cloud providers and researchers define many Cloud patterns that can organize a pre-configured architecture. The concepts of design patterns are used to implement them. These patterns describe proven solutions and the common aspects of Cloud environments. They help developers to understand the application architecture or the necessary changes to the application code for a successful migration. Many Cloud patterns catalogs are offered by researchers and Cloud providers like IBM Virtual Patterns and Azure Cloud Patterns. These catalogs contain general and specific description solutions to recurring problems in the Cloud.

This line of approaches gives developers patterns to facilitate the tasks of development and migration. Nevertheless, it is hard to define a large number of patterns for each provider and each problem especially with the lack of standardization. Also, patterns must be clear and well-detailed to reduce complexity. Moreover, the major problem of this class of approaches is the mapping between the pattern and the real implementation.

Andrikopoulos and al., [12] determine the three layers of application (presentation, business logic and data) and they focus on the two lower layers of the application (business logic and data). Authors identify three categories of Cloud data patterns: *i*) Confidentiality of patterns for data security *ii*) Functional Cloud data patterns (for data manipulation) *iii*) Non-functional Cloud data patterns (to ensure elasticity and scalability). Cai and al., [15] design an approach for code2code transformation to migrate applications in Cloud environment. The approach automatically transforms the source code to the target code using a set of patterns. The proposed approach contains 4 steps: code scanning, pattern matching, template design and code transformation.

### 3.3 Semantic Modelling Based Approaches

To develop a Cloud application, developers must have professional skills and knowledge about different programming models, API and the underlying infrastructure. This is due to the lack of standardization and the differences in the semantics of the resources offered by Cloud providers. In fact, every provider has his own terms and representations of available resources. Besides, all Cloud providers expose their operations via Web services. Conversely, each vendor offers its own service interface. For this, it's essential to create semantic models to have good interoperability between different components. These models are helpful in three aspects: functional and non-functional definitions, data modeling and service description enhancement. Technologies used in semantic Web can be useful to address these three aspects. The proposed approaches in this category focus more on the Cloud API and Cloud resources to provide access to heterogeneous resources. MOSAIC (Ontology) [17] provides an open source platform for developing multi-cloud applications. At design time, the developers use the APIs to create applications in the form of a set of multiple Cloud components. At run time, MOSAIC deploys each component on the Cloud platform that provides the best implementation. Thus, developers can choose on which Cloud provider they want to deploy each component.

### 3.4 MDA Based Approaches

MDA (Model Driven Architecture) is a model based approach for the development of software methodology that focuses on creating models or abstractions. It supports full lifecycle (analysis, design, implementation, deployment, maintenance, etc). The goal of the MDA is *"Design once, build it on any platform"*. MDA defines three main abstraction levels: *i) Computation Independent Model (CIM)* which presents exactly what the system is expected to do, but hides all information technology related specifications to remain independent of how that system will be implemented, *ii) Platform Independent Model (PIM)* is a *"formal"* specification of the structure and function of a system that abstracts away technical details, *iii) Platform Specific Model (PSM)* Specifies how the functionality specified in a PIM is realized on a particular platform.

MDA allows developers to design applications in a Cloud-agnostic way. In fact, it's possible to describe a system as models with high level of abstraction; these models are independent from any platform (PIM Model) of Cloud provider on which we will deploy and run applications. From one PIM model, several PSM models can be generated using model transformation techniques [16], each PSM is specific to a well-defined platform. In fact, the key of MDA's success is the transformation techniques that provides automatic or semi-automatic transformations from a model to another or from a model to code.

The main benefits of MDA for Cloud applications are facility of portability, interoperability and reusability of application components which can be migrated easily from one platform to another [3]. The MDA approach is based on modeling in high level of abstraction and a transformation engine to reduce the complexity of the migration process especially the refactoring and the adaptation. Although the functional method of transformation engine is ambiguous, the degree of automation of this process is not explicit.

MODAClouds [3] provides decision support systems which guide to select Clouds based on cost and requirements. It offers an open source IDE for application design, development and deployment within a run-time environment for the high-level design, early prototyping, the semi-automatic translation of design artifacts into code and automatic deployment of applications on multi-cloud. REMICS (REuse and Migration of legacy applications to Interoperable Cloud Services) [18] provides a series of tools for software modernization using the *Model Driven Modernization* methodology. The process of modernization of legacy software starts with a recover activity to design the application's architecture. The designed architecture helps to analyze the legacy application and identify the best way for the migration to Cloud platforms. The source architecture will be reformed into target architecture. Herein, MDA is used to obtain the Cloud service implementation. In [19], authors argue how to transform the architecture of a legacy application into a Cloud native application architecture earlier than its deployment in a Cloud environment. Based on the concept of smart use case coupled with the *Architecture Driven Modernization* (ADM), they concretize the process of modernizing of legacy applications through transiting to a Cloud environment. The objective of this process is not only to raise the IT agility but also to increase its business agility. The process is pipelined in a semi-automatic manner especially transformation/upgrade and forward engineering stages implemented by dedicated transformation chain for a specific application. [20] focus on the migration of Cloud infrastructure services and develop a *Model-Based Round-Trip Engineering Approach* which combine generation techniques with runtime reflection. This approach deals with differential changes of IaaS models. After specification of a Cloud infrastructure service topology in terms of a *de jure* model, it will be compared with another model coming from the runtime. The interaction between a reflection service with the interfaces of the IaaS provider generates such a *de facto* model. After that, a model containing differences between the two pre-mentioned models is computed and model transformation is executed.

MoDAC-Deploy [21] is an approach designed to simplify Cloud service deployment and migration between different Cloud Service Providers (CSPs) without user interventions. Moreover, this framework is based on generative mechanisms to overcome APIs heterogeneity and avoid the vendor lock-in by providing application portability across multiple Cloud providers. However, this framework is based on a domain specific modeling language and is not aligned with any Cloud standard which limit its reuse and extension.

StratusML (Stratus Modeling Language) [7] is an architectural framework that grants for the Cloud stakeholders a user interface to model multi-cloud and multi-tenant applications, configure them and define its behavior at the run-time and estimate cost under different Cloud platforms. The CloudML language (*Cloud Modeling Language*) [22] aims to facilitate provisioning and adaptation of multi-cloud application. It is based on two concepts DSML (*Domain-Specific Modeling Languages*) and a Model at run-time. DSkyl [23] is a development platform (PaaS) to develop and deploy Cloud application components. It provides a modeling tool editor with application modeler template and deployment template. Recently, a systematic review of Cloud modeling languages and tools is described by [24].

### 3.5 Cloud Standard-Based Approaches

Standardization initiatives have emerged including [2]: USDL (*Unified Service Description Language*) for the (SaaS) Software as a Service which provide a generic description of the business and service-level components to make them exchangeable and consumable in a Cloud environment. TOSCA (*Topology and Orchestration Specification for Cloud Applications*) for (PaaS) Platform as a Service which describe how to define the components of an application and their relationships as a graph topology. Using management plans, these components can be deployed, configured, and managed at a Cloud provider. OCCI (*Open Cloud Computing Interface*) dedicated for the (IaaS) Infrastructure as a Service and provide consistent access to existing IaaS resources. CIMI (*Cloud Infrastructure Management Interface*) looks like OCCI and covers main features of IaaS (deployment and management of virtual machines and other artifacts such as volumes, networks, or monitoring. CDMI (*Cloud Data Management Interface*) that defines the interface to manage Cloud elements from storage.

[25] outlines the integration of configuration management with model-driven Cloud management realized through TOSCA and Chef which is a well-known configuration management tool. The mappings between TOSCA and OCCI are defined in [14] to build a model driven Cloud-provider agnostic Cloud orchestrator leveraging both of them for portable application and resource provisioning and deployment. [25] combines TOSCA and Chef, a popular configuration management tool to ensure portability when migrating services from one Cloud environment to another.

The Model-Driven Configuration Management of Cloud Applications with OCCI (MoDMaCAO) framework is developed by [6] to handle the issues of the current version of OCCI in terms of configuration management of Cloud applications. In this framework, the capabilities of the OCCIware tool chain are used to implement disparate configuration management tools. The proposed framework is illustrated by modeling, deploying and managing four different distributed Cloud applications and generating prototypical implementations for three configuration management tools. In overall, MoDMaCAO is claimed to be an extension of OCCI among others enumerated in [25] where semantic interoperability is achieved in multiclouds through FCLOUDS. This framework can support the Cloud consumer to migrate from one API to another. The illustrative example shows a migration from an OCCI Infrastructure VM (Virtual Machine) to Google Cloud Platform VM.

## 3.6  Software Product Line-Based Approaches

Both PLE (Product Line Engineering) and MDA are combined in several works to perform model based Cloud migration with variability modelling and analysis. PLE supports this by offering choice flexibility in the targeted Cloud environments.

[27] presents a model-driven approach to manage, instantiate configurations and deploy images for Virtual Machine provisioning in Cloud computing. Virtual images are represented as product lines with feature model configurations. Their deployment is automated by model-based techniques in a flexible way. This approach is applied in [28] to minimize the amount of not required software installed in VMIs. This allows to reduce the power consumption of VMI provisioning and the data transfer via network. The approach of [29] aims to find the best Cloud IaaS configuration required to migrate or to optimize the choice for internal systems migration to a Cloud environment. Since authors perceive this need as a variability management and analysis concerns, they are based on FM to design the IaaS variability of the different *Amazon Web Service*[1] virtual machine offerings. Authors claim that their proposal can be generalized to providers other than AWS, like Rackspace/OpenStack or Microsoft.

**Table 1.** Comparison between the proposed approaches

| Approaches | Portability | | Techniques | Degree of automation | Type of migration | | Steps |
|---|---|---|---|---|---|---|---|
| | DL | BL | | | LA | C2C | |
| [12] | – | – | Cloud patterns | Manuel | + | – | Migration execution |
| MOSAIC (Cloud agency) [15] | – | + | MAS | Semi-automatic | + | + | Migration strategy-monitoring & maintenance |
| [15] | – | + | Cloud patterns | Automatic | – | + | Migration execution |
| [23, 30] | – | + | MDA | Manuel | – | + | Migration execution |
| Mosaic ontology methodology and framework [17] | – | + | Semantic modeling | Semi-automatic | – | + | Migration execution |
| MODAClouds [3] | – | + | MDA | Semi-automatic | + | + | Migration strategy-Migration execution-monitoring & maintenance |

*(continued)*

---

[1] http://aws.amazon.com/products/.

**Table 1.** (*continued*)

| Approaches | Portability | | Techniques | Degree of automation | Type of migration | | Steps |
|---|---|---|---|---|---|---|---|
| | DL | BL | | | LA | C2C | |
| Remics [18] | – | – | MDA | Semi-automatic | + | – | Migration execution |
| StratusML [7] | – | + | MDA | Semi-automatic | – | + | Migration execution |
| CloudML [22] | – | + | MDA | Semi-automatic | – | + | Migration execution |
| MLSAC [41] | + | + | MDA | Semi-automatic | + | – | Migration execution |

Azure. However, they counted no less than 1758 possible configurations just for an Amazon instance without considering middleware layer options. In addition, they proceed by matching the searched configurations against all enumerated offered configurations which really time consumable.

In [23, 30], the focus is on facility of migration to multiple Clouds. Indeed, FM are used to conduct the migration planning process considering SLA constraints like VM properties (size of RAM, No of processors, CPU processing speed etc.). In this work, the nodes of a Feature model represent the application components or features, whose edges define the relations between these application components. A model-driven multi-cloud configuration approach is developed by [31]. The implemented framework which is named SALOON combines feature model and ontologies to explicit infrastructure and platform variability, and give semantic descriptions of Cloud applications. SALOON involves four PaaS providers and the authors affirm that it can cover provider models that match the metamodel they design. Nonetheless, this may be not easy since this framework has not standard interfaces or formal specifications.

The above mentioned approaches discuss different aspects. For example, some approaches have focused on SLA negotiation, vendor selection. Other approaches focused on the migration of legacy application. To make a comparison between the different approaches, we choose the following criteria:

- The portability of Data Layer (DL): is the ability to easily transfer data into and out of the Cloud service environment.
- The portability of Business Layer (BL): is the ability to easily transfer an application or application components between Cloud providers.
- Techniques: define the techniques used in the approach such as MAS or MDA.
- Degree of automation: define the degree of automation of the approach (automatic, semi-automatic and manual).
- Type of migration: There are two categories:

- Migration of legacy application (LA): approaches that address the migration of legacy applications.
- Migration from a Cloud to Cloud (C2C): approaches that address the migration of application or application components from Cloud provider to another.

- Steps: define in which steps of the migration process the approach works.

In the Table 1, the majority of approaches involve legacy application migration. The only automatic approach is [15] which only processes the code2code transformation. The unique contribution which present an evaluation process is proposed in [41] to get a feedback from users via reusing through MLSAC metamodel method fragments to ensure the quality of the reengineering process. However, Security is not well considered in the migration process. Data portability issue is still ambiguous and the proposed approaches do not give a clear solution, excluding [41] where data confidentiality and sensitivity requirements are present for simple data structure. It is essential to concentrate on data portability. There are a variety of data storage models of Cloud providers. Each Cloud provider supports its own set of data types.

## 4  Cloud Migration Approach

In this section, we propose a new Cloud migration approach to define the different steps of the migration process. It contains the steps to follow once we decide to migrate an application to or between Cloud providers. Our proposal, also, addresses the steps that follow the moving of the application to the Cloud as the maintenance and the monitoring. It covers the case when the customer wishes to migrate application again to another provider. In all steps of migration process, it is necessary to consider the security aspect.

a. **Migration strategy**

This step is composed of a set of blocks such that its functioning is based on MAS:

- Negotiation block: for the negotiation of SLA (Service Level Agreement)
- Discover services block: to search for the most suitable Cloud service when the user want to replace component(s) with Cloud offering.
- Discover providers block: to find a list of Cloud providers in the market that offers the desired services with the cost estimation.
- Service composition block: to select the best structure of the set of services that build the application and define the services which are interoperable.
- Monitoring reports block: this block is executed from the second iteration of component migration. This block defines the problems encountered and the behavior of service during its execution.

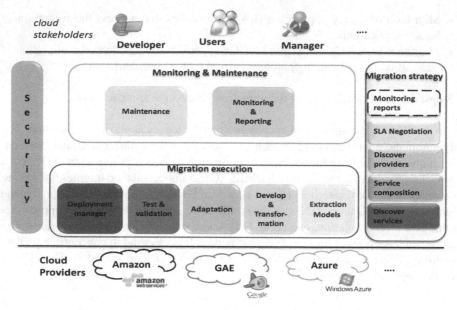

**Fig. 1.** Comprehensive cloud migration approach architecture

b. **Migration execution**

This step is composed of a set of blocks such that its functioning is based on Model Driven Architecture:

- Extraction Model block: extract the model from a piece of code or from a database.
- Develop & transformations block: apply the necessary operations (development, transformation…) in order to obtain the new version of code or data.
- Adaptation block: define the necessary changes to the rest of the application and apply them to ensure interoperability between the new component and the rest of the application.
- Test & validation block: test the application with the new version of the migrated component and validate it.
- Deployment manager block: deploy the migrated component or data in the new Cloud platform.

c. **Monitoring & maintenance**

This step is composed of two blocks:

- Monitoring and reporting block: this block is dedicated to monitor the functioning of the application and generating performance reports.
- Maintenance block: this block is responsible for the maintenance of the application and apply the necessary updates.

# 5   Research Implication

Prior surveys have been devoted to identify taxonomies, examine approaches and reviews tools of Cloud migration. [32] gives a survey about the Cloud architectures and Cloud decision making approaches and frameworks. This work address the steps, key concerns of a Cloud migration decision framework and the key decisions that the system should maintain. Similarly, authors of [33] attempt to distill Cloud migration approaches, identify their common characteristics and their empirical findings. This survey allows to show a global view of the state of the art from the methodological point of view of Cloud migration comprising key concerns, activities, and criteria to be considered. [34] identifies a set of relevant process elements included in the moving legacy systems from on-premise to Cloud platforms. The presented legacy-to-Cloud process model aims to clarify how organizational legacy systems can be transformed by Cloud services. The comparative study between Cloud migration methods given by [35] concentrate especially on those based on MDE (Model Driven Engineering) and takes models in the heart of the software engineering process. It identifies the key factors to evaluate the application in terms of technical and non-technical considerations in pre-migration, migration and post-migration phases. In a very recent survey [36], these phases are discussed from the scope of processes of migration to open source software in the world but without considering Cloud particularities.

Our work highlights a comprehensive taxonomy of Cloud migrations proposals including SPL based approches which offer the customizability of the Cloud migration decisions and the configurability of components. As well, we can argue that Cloud standard based approaches are interesting to promise interoperability and portability across multiple Clouds.

Also, we consider the survey of [37] dealing with security concerns for live virtual machine migration. It confirms the lack of comprehensive approaches for task migrations in mobile Cloud computing aligned with large scale deployment environment. [38] compares different industrial solutions proposed by Cloud vendors while [39] reports a systematic literature review about both academic and industrial tools for different migration types.

[40] scrutinizes aspects of Cloud computing that leads to vendor lock-in and proposed solutions for this issue. Moreover, the literature on proprietary lock-in risks in Cloud computing is explored in terms of its principal causes, consequences, mitigations strategies, and encountered challenges by company stakeholders on their Cloud migration exercises. The proposed taxonomy of Cloud lock-in perspectives is performed at the light of reports about real experiences on migration allowing a good knowledge concerning all Cloud SaaS migration issues. Moreover, authors describe measures to enhance the portability, security and interoperability of Cloud (and on-premise) applications in hybrid environments. In our current survey, we also recognize the vendor lock-in challenge and recapitulate proposed solutions to avoid this pitfall. Being agree with [37] about the lack of migration approaches for mobile Cloud computing, our proposal can be easily extended to ambient systems while benefiting from our previous research. Furthermore, we endeavor to align our proposal with variability concerns and Cloud standards.

# 6    Conclusion

Cloud migration is an interesting topic. Several approaches have been proposed, but there are still other challenges that have not been well treated. There are several obstacles for an easy and successful migration as the Lack of standardization and the choosing of the best migration strategy. In this context, we propose a new Cloud migration approach to describe the different functionality in the migration process, the first step of this process Migration strategy based on MAS techniques and the second step Migration execution based on MDA technologies. The proposed approach is under development. Our approach proposes to automate some features which saves time and effort, and ensures services and data portability between Cloud providers.

# References

1. Ferrer, A.J., Pérez, D.G., González, R.S.: Multi-cloud platform-as-a-service model, functionalities and approaches. Procedia Comput. Sci. **97**, 63–72 (2016)
2. Stravoskoufos, K., Preventis, A., Sotiriadis, S., Petrakis, E.G.: A survey on approaches for interoperability and portability of cloud computing services. In: CLOSER, pp. 112–117, April 2014
3. Cretella, G., Di Martino, B.: An overview of approaches for the migration of applications to the cloud. In: Caporarello, L., Di Martino, B., Martinez, M. (eds.) Smart Organizations and Smart Artifacts. LNISO, vol. 7, pp. 67–75. Springer, Cham (2014). https://doi.org/10.1007/978-3-319-07040-7_8
4. Zhao, J.F., Zhou, J.T.: Strategies and methods for cloud migration. Int. J. Autom. Comput. **11**(2), 143–152 (2014)
5. Beserra, P.V., Camara, A., Ximenes, R., Albuquerque, A.B., Mendonça, N.C.: Cloudstep: a step-by-step decision process to support legacy application migration to the cloud. In: 2012 IEEE 6th International Workshop on the Maintenance and Evolution of Service-Oriented and Cloud-Based Systems (MESOCA), pp. 7–16, September 2012
6. Muñoz, V.M., Ferguson, D., Helfert, M., Pahl, C. (eds.): CLOSER 2018. CCIS, vol. 1073. Springer, Cham (2019). https://doi.org/10.1007/978-3-030-29193-8
7. Hamdaqa, M., Tahvildari, L.: Stratus ML: a layered cloud modeling framework. In: 2015 IEEE International Conference on Cloud Engineering (IC2E), pp. 96–105. IEEE, March 2015
8. Hajlaoui, J.E., Omri, M.N., Benslimane, D.: Multi-tenancy aware configurable service discovery approach in cloud computing. In: 2017 IEEE 26th International Conference on Enabling Technologies: Infrastructure for Collaborative Enterprises (WETICE), pp. 232–237. IEEE, June 2017
9. Jumagaliyev, A., Whittle, J.N.D., Elkhatib, Y.S.S.A.: Evolving multi-tenant SaaS cloud applications using model-driven engineering (2016)
10. Rai, R., Sahoo, G., Mehfuz, S.: Advancements and approaches towards moving from legacy application to cloud. Int. J. Commun. Netw. Distrib. Syst. **16**(2), 114–139 (2016)
11. Dombrowski, S., Ermakova, T., Fabian, B.: Graph-based analysis of cloud connectivity at the internet protocol level. Int. J. Commun. Netw. Distrib. Syst (2018)
12. Andrikopoulos, V., Binz, T., Leymann, F., Strauch, S.: How to adapt applications for the cloud environment. Computing **95**(6), 493–535 (2013)
13. Pahl, C., Xiong, H., Walshe, R.: A comparison of on-premise to cloud migration approaches. In: European Conference on Service-Oriented and Cloud Computing, pp. 212–226. Springer, Berlin, Heidelberg, September 2013

14. Glaser, F., Erbel, J.M., Grabowski, J.: Model driven cloud orchestration by combining TOSCA and OCCI. In: 7th International Conference on Cloud Computing and Services Science (CLOSER), pp. 644–650 (2017)
15. Cai, Z., Zhao, L., Wang, X., Yang, X., Qin, J., Yin, K.: A pattern-based code transformation approach for cloud application migration. In: 2015 IEEE 8th International Conference on Cloud Computing (CLOUD), pp. 33–40. IEEE, June 2015
16. Di Martino, B., Cretella, G., Esposito, A.: Methodologies for cloud portability and interoperability. In: Cloud Portability and Interoperability, pp. 15–44. Springer, Cham (2015)
17. Moscato, F., Di Martino, B., Aversa, R.: Enabling model driven engineering of cloud services by using mosaic ontology. Scalable Comput. Pract. Exp. 13(1), 29–44 (2012)
18. Sadovykh, A., Srirama, S., Jakovits, P., Smialek, M., Nowakowski, W., Ferry, N., Morin, B.: Deliverable D4. 5 REMICS Migrate Principles and Methods (2010)
19. Sabiri, K., Benabbou, F., Khammal, A.: Model driven modernization and cloud migration framework with smart use case. In: Proceedings of the Mediterranean Symposium on Smart City Applications, pp. 17–27. Springer, Cham, October 2017
20. Ta'id, H.: Facilitating migration of cloud infrastructure services: a model-based approach. In: CloudMDE@ MoDELS, pp. 7–12 (2015)
21. Alili, H., Drira, R., Ghezala, H.H.B.: Model driven framework for the configuration and the deployment of applications in the cloud. Cloud Comput. 2016, 73 (2016)
22. Ferry, N., Rossini, A., Chauvel, F., Morin, B., Solberg, A.: Towards model-driven provisioning, deployment, monitoring, and adaptation of multi-cloud systems. In: Cloud Computing (CLOUD), pp. 887–894. IEEE, June 2013
23. Vijaya, A., Neelanarayanan, V.: A model driven framework for portable cloud services: proof of concept implementation. Int. J. Educ. Manag. Eng 4, 27–35 (2015)
24. Bergmayr, A., et al.: A systematic review of cloud modeling languages. ACM Comput. Surv. (CSUR) 51(1), 22 (2018)
25. Wettinger, J., et al.: Integrating configuration management with model-driven cloud management based on TOSCA. In: CLOSER, pp. 437–446, May 2013
26. Challita, S., Zalila, F., Merle, P.: Specifying semantic interoperability between heterogeneous cloud resources with the FCLOUDS formal language. In: CLOUD 2018–11th IEEE International Conference on Cloud Computing, July 2018
27. Le Nhan, T., Sunyé, G., Jézéquel, J.M.: A model-driven approach for virtual machine image provisioning in cloud computing. In: European Conference on Service-Oriented and Cloud Computing, pp. 107–121. Springer, Berlin, Heidelberg, September 2012
28. Le Nhan, T., Sunyé, G., Jézéquel, J.M.: A model-based approach for optimizing power consumption of IaaS. In: Network Cloud Computing and Applications (NCCA), 2012 Second Symposium on 2012 Dec 3, pp. 31–39. IEEE (2012)
29. Ivanov, I.I., van Sinderen, M., Leymann, F., Shan, T. (eds.): CLOSER 2012. CCIS, vol. 367. Springer, Cham (2013). https://doi.org/10.1007/978-3-319-04519-1
30. Vijaya, A., Dash, P., Neelanarayanan, V.: Migration of enterprise software applications to multiple clouds: a feature based approach. Lecture Notes on Software Engineering 3(2), 101 (2015)
31. Quinton, C., Romero, D., Duchien, L.: SALOON: a platform for selecting and configuring cloud environments. Softw. Pract. Exp. 46(1), 55–78 (2016)
32. Wan, Z., Wang, P.: A survey and taxonomy of cloud migration. In: 2014 International Conference on Service Sciences (ICSS), pp. 175–180. IEEE, May 2014
33. Gholami, M.F., Daneshgar, F., Low, G., Beydoun, G.: Cloud migration process—a survey, evaluation framework, and open challenges. J. Syst. Softw. 120, 31–69 (2016)
34. Gholami, M.F., Daneshgar, F., Beydoun, G., Rabhi, F.: Key challenges during legacy software system migration to cloud computing platforms—an empirical study (2017)

35. Akodadi, K.: A survey of cloud migration methods: a comparison and proposition
36. Sobhani, R., Seifzadeh, H., Gandomani, T.J.: A review of migration processes to open source software. Int. J. Open Source Softw. Process. (IJOSSP) **9**(1), 20–31 (2018)
37. Balobaid, A., Debnath, D.: An empirical study of different cloud migration techniques. In: 2017 IEEE International Conference on Smart Cloud (SmartCloud), pp. 60–65. IEEE, November 2017
38. Balobaid, A., Debnath, D.: Cloud migration tools: overview and comparison. In: World Congress on Services, pp. 93–106. Springer, Cham, June 2018
39. Da Silva Filho, H.C., de Figueiredo Carneiro, G., Costa, E.S.M., Monteiro, M.: Tools to support SMEs to migrate to the cloud: opportunities and challenges. In: Information Technology-New Generations, pp. 159–165. Springer, Cham (2018)
40. Opara-Martins, J.: Taxonomy of Cloud Lock-in Challenges (2018)
41. Fahmideh, M., Grundy, J., Beydoun, G., Zowghi, D., Susilo, W., Mougouei, D.: A model-driven approach to reengineering processes in cloud computing. Inf. Softw. Technol. **144**, 106795 (2022)
42. Khemili, W., Hajlaoui, J.E., Omri, M.N.: Energy aware fuzzy approach for placement and consolidation in cloud data centers. J. Parallel Distrib. Comput. **161**, 130–142 (2022)
43. Mokni, M., Yassa, S., Hajlaoui, J.E., Chelouah, R., Omri, M.N.: Cooperative agents-based approach for workflow scheduling on fog-cloud computing. J. Ambient Intell. Human. Comput. 1-20 (2021)
44. Trifa, Z., Hajlaoui, J.E., Khemakhem, M.: Pollution attacks identification in structured P2P overlay networks. In: International Conference on Information and Communications Security, pp. 674–686. Springer, Cham, December 2017

# An Extension of the Babel Protocol to Include Operating Cost: Providing Sustainability in Community Networks

Rodolfo B. S. Carvalho(✉) ⓘ, Carla Merkle Westphall ⓘ,
and Caciano Machado ⓘ

Department of Informatics and Statistics Graduate Program in Computer Science -
PPGCC, Federal University of Santa Catarina, Florianópolis, Brazil
rodolfo.carvalho@posgrad.ufsc.br, carla.merkle.westphall@ufsc.br,
caciano.machado@ufrgs.br

**Abstract.** The expansion of networks worldwide and its benefits allowed the emergence and application of several technologies aimed at exchanging information in a decentralized manner, such as Blockchain, where there is no need for a reliable agent or third party for management. In this context, the emergence of various distributed wireless networks was possible, such as community networks, where large mesh networks composed of hundreds of nodes built by communities seek to solve digital inclusion problems. Wireless mesh networks still present some challenges in their growth. Even with specific protocols like Babel, which optimize its operation, there are problems such as reliability among network members and the correct distribution of resources to encourage its growth. These characteristics prevent wireless mesh networks from developing to reach areas of technology scarcity called the last mile. Thus, this work uses the optimization techniques for WMNs achieved by the Babel protocol and proposes the modification of the original Babel protocol to insert financial incentive mechanisms into the protocol. The article presents the proposed modifications and demonstrates, through simulation tests, the functioning and efficiency of the protocol extensions through the OMNeT++ platform combined with the INET Framework tool.

**Keywords:** Babel · Protocol · Routing · Incentive · Wireless · Mesh · Network

## 1 Introduction

Wireless mesh networks (WMNs) are networks capable of not only providing wireless connectivity to large areas (such as shopping malls and urban centers), but also taking such connectivity to remote locations [2]. There are several

This study was financed in part by the Coordenação de Aperfeiçoamento de Pessoal de Nível Superior - Brasil (CAPES) - Finance Code 001.

O. Gervasi et al. (Eds.): ICCSA 2022, LNCS 13375, pp. 265–282, 2022.
https://doi.org/10.1007/978-3-031-10522-7_19

remote areas without Internet access due to the lack of economic interest from the large telephone operators. This fact motivates the construction of community networks [5,14], which use WMNs and affordable handsets, are relatively easy to deploy and help to solve the last mile problem. An example of this type of infrastructure is the Freifunk network in Germany [9].

The need to carry out many activities online, mainly due to the influence of the pandemic, has revealed shortcomings in making "last mile" connectivity widely accessible. It is necessary to meet the need, for example, 63% of school-age children who do not have access to the Internet [20]. The problems already identified in 2017 [7] continue to exist, and it is necessary: stable access to the network, accessible costs, and incentives for network maintenance and expansion.

Some studies have appeared in the literature in recent years that address the use of financial incentive mechanisms linked to the network [12,13] to guarantee the correct sustainability of the WMNs. The effort and quality of the work developed by the network nodes in incentive mechanisms can be measured with associated routing protocols present in the network layer.

There are several protocols in the literature that are directly associated with WMN environments [16]. Babel and B.A.T.M.A.N. are examples of such protocols that clearly stand out as shown in performance evaluations results [1,15]. This work adopts the Babel protocol due to its broad adoption for routing in WMNs [22], active development and concise documentation [8].

This work incorporates financial incentive metrics to encourage the expansion and operation of WMN infrastructure. The proposal analyzes the Babel protocol's efficiency, benefits, and costs when associated with incentive mechanisms. Tests were performed in laboratory mounted scenarios comparing, through the results obtained, the behavior of the protocol with financial incentive mechanisms with its version without the use of incentive mechanisms. The main aspects analyzed are related to the best selection of routes for traffic on the network, the message exchange mechanisms, and the state maintenance structure of the channels used for communication.

The remainder of this paper is organized as follows: Sect. 2 describes the basic concepts; in Sect. 3, related works are discussed; Sect. 4 presents the proposed solution; the experimental results and evaluation are described in Sect. 5 and, finally, Sect. 6 presents the conclusions of the paper.

## 2   Basic Concepts

WMNs (Wireless mesh networks) are considered Ad Hoc networks enhanced with several features present in mesh networks, allowing a self-organizing and decentralized communication between network participants, thus favoring communication in large areas and the extension of this connectivity to participants neighbors without the need for centralized control or cabling linking each node.

Although Ad Hoc networks have their structure of clients and network routers, mesh Networks incorporate specific structure characteristics to WMNs, basically leading to the existence of two types of devices, mesh clients and mesh

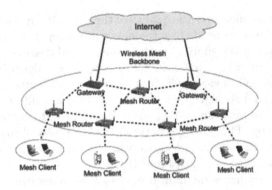

**Fig. 1.** WMN example [23].

routers (Fig. 1). While mesh clients can be both stationary and mobile, being able to receive packets or form a network among themselves and connected to other routers, mesh routers, in turn, have minimal and restricted mobility and are responsible for forming the backbone of WMNs. Arranged in a mesh topology where communication is performed wirelessly in a dynamically self-organizing and self-configuring environment, both mesh clients and mesh routers using the IEEE 802.11 standard, aimed at ensuring maximum stability, mainly due to constant state changes of the links and network connectivity that may occur [2].

The responsibility for managing the links and organizing the routing of packets rests with the protocols that run at the network layer and can be divided in two areas, based on reputation and based on credits. Reputation-based models seek, based on the behavior of network nodes, to punish network elements that act in a way that is harmful to the protocol. On the other hand, the credit-based models use a form of charging linked to the services provided by the elements of the network, providing or withdrawing credits according to harmful or beneficial behavior, respectively, which are identified by the protocol.

Routing protocols within WMNs have peculiar characteristics compared to conventional ones, mainly because they are dealing with *ad hoc* networks. Each existing node has partial or full mobility, being able to change the network topology with a certain frequency, which does not occur in wired connections, thus requiring better management in the definition of routes for the network layer.

## 2.1 Babel Protocol

The Babel protocol is considered a distance-vector routing protocol, and it uses the Bellman-Ford algorithm to discover the best path that each packet must take to reach its destination [10]. Designed to be robust and effective in unstable wireless networks, the Babel protocol adds some modifications to the general working dynamics of distance-vector protocols, which seek to avoid, through preventive refinements, the formation of loops in packet forwarding, and even that these do occur, undoing them in a timely manner and preventing them from forming again. Still, the protocol can also be used within fixed networks.

The protocol also measures the quality of the links. It can use several methods to calculate its routes, as needed by the network manager, and can be based on the packet loss rate or the shortest path to the desired destination. Within these and several other metrics existing in the protocol, the algorithm can adapt to different networks and devices, which, due to their respective limitations, such as a battery or signal strength or location, can take on different characteristics such as time interval between exchanges, that will be different between a mobile device and a desktop. That characteristic allows the protocol to support different types of wifi networks, knowing how to deal with heterogeneous environments, including networks with both IPv4 and IPv6.

The protocol also has some limitations, such as generating traffic to update the routing tables constantly, unlike other protocols such as OSPF and IS-IS that only generate updates when topology changes occur. Another limitation is the time for a participant to be reconnected to the network, when a node quickly disconnects and reconnects, a wait is required (about a few minutes) for it to be recognized again, which can become a limitation in mobile networks with automatic node inclusion.

## 3   Related Works

The related works identified were selected through bibliographic research, carried out and documented through a Systematic Literature Review Protocol, where a search string linked to the study topic was created and applied within 5 databases (IEEE, ACM, Wiley, Springer, Elsevier). A total of 390 studies were identified, which after exclusion by Title and Abstract, full reading of the texts and finally the application of the defined inclusion and exclusion criteria, 7 studies were selected, which cover the use of mechanisms to encourage WMNs and also the protocols most geared towards supporting such networks. At the end of the section, a comparative table of related works is shown about the proposal developed, seeking to combine the most suitable protocol with incentive mechanisms (Table 1).

The work of [4] seeks to explore viable and sustainable alternatives for access to the network that do not involve traditional private cabling companies, creating a sustainable and economically promising environment. Within the possible alternatives, the work focuses on community networks, specifically on one of the largest community networks in the world called Guifi.net. The paper describes how this WMN attaches economic incentives to the network, combined with infrastructure, implementation, and practices, which guarantee its sustainability. The case study shows many benefits of the association of a WMN to incentive mechanisms, association and benefits also applicable to the present paper, but the author of the work [4] does not use a specifically altered protocol to run at the network layer, and also does not perform comparative tests with traditional protocols for WMNs such as Babel.

The work of [17] proposes a new protocol named *Fair*, which seeks to ensure the economic management of the network in an automated way, contrary to the work proposed by [18], where the financial adjustments are performed manually. The main idea of the protocol is based on the more devices a service provider has on the network, the higher the price per MB allocated to it. There is a certain limit to avoid network monopoly, leading one provider to own all nodes and creating possible disadvantages for users. The work adopts incentive mechanisms like the study presented in this paper, but it attributes the incentives for the choice of network bandwidth channels, while the study in this paper attributes the incentive for choosing the neighboring nodes that the packet will pass on routing.

Among the challenges found for the construction, maintenance, and use of WMNs, the work of [22] cites the logistic *last mile* problem, showing the difficulties of taking network connections to distant points in large cities, where for infrastructure, economic and logistical reasons, large operators and ISPs are not interested in taking their services. In order to enable the creation of a connected environment with low operational cost, adequate bandwidth, stable and capable of eliminating the traditional contracts manually made, the study proposes a network architecture called *Althea*. Althea is a network architecture based on distance-vector routing protocols, extending the Babel protocol. It associates the use of Ethereum cryptocurrencies to support its automated payment system, using a PoS-based blockchain (Proof-of-Stake), through the Cosmos platform. The work specifies modifications to the Babel protocol including mechanisms to encourage a functioning network, but does not present performance tests and comparisons with the original form of the Babel protocol or compare with other protocols currently focused on WMNs.

Another study on incentive mechanisms within WMNs [18] is focuses on ensuring the possibility of financial transactions, trust between participants, data immutability, and neutrality in data management. It adopts Blockchain technology as a solution linked to WMNs, using more specifically the structure of permissive Blockchains, which combine the benefits of Blockchain with mechanisms of identity and trust on users. The framework chosen by the article for implementation and testing was the Hyperledger Fabric (HLF) [3], which was evaluated both in production and in simulated laboratory testing environments.

The work of [19] addresses two problems found in multi-channel wireless ad hoc networks: a) the difficulty in correctly assigning channels to their respective interfaces, trying to align the stability of network connectivity to the maximum use of different channels; and b) the various interferences to which these channels are subject, reducing the efficiency of the network. The paper performs an analysis of cognitive mechanisms linked to the context of the network. This mechanism is used as the basis for the proposal of a multi-channel ad hoc network associated with hybrid channels. A responsible, fair rate control algorithm is applied for pricing each channel according to its availability as an incentive, ensuring a quick convergence in simulations carried out.

Within the related works, there are two comparative studies related to the efficiency of protocols aimed at WMNs: [16], and [21]. The work described in [16] test the five most mentioned protocols so far in the literature (AODV,

DYMO, HWMP, OLSR, BATMAN) in order to analyze and compare each one within four aspects: packet loss rate, packet delivery delay time, the average energy consumption of all network nodes and finally the number of collisions that occurred in the network. The study shows a comparison between proactive and reactive protocols, indicating that the proactive protocols, despite the high data overhead and higher energy consumption, have low latency in the delivery of packets and a low rate of packet loss, which is considered extremely positive for WMNs.

Finally, the article by [21] seeks to measure the performance of three routing protocols focused on WMNs (HWMP, BATMAN advanced, and Babel), in network deficiency/disaster environments caused by possible natural disasters, to which the network nodes need to respond quickly and in a coordinated way to restore the network. Both HWMP and BATMAN Advanced stood out within the static network scenario with similar performance. In contrast, only HWMP proved efficient in dealing with dynamic processes for the dynamic network scenario. For the scenario of large networks composed of up to one hundred routers, none of the protocols showed efficiency in dealing with large networks, except for the Babel protocol. New network architecture is proposed to deal with large networks and mitigate its problems. For the scenario of large networks composed of up to one hundred routers, none of the protocols showed efficiency in dealing with large networks. New network architecture is proposed to deal with large networks and mitigate its problems.

The Table 1 shows a summary of the related work compared to this paper, indicating possible gaps to be filled.

The first column of the table indicates the related works, with their respective references and year of publication. The second column identifies the works that added financial incentive mechanisms to the proposed models to sustain the network. The third column indicates the works that included/addressed the Babel and/or BATMAN protocols in their analysis. The fourth column indicates the works that performed virtual and/or real tests on the models proposed as a solution. Finally, the fifth and last column indicates the works that, after testing, showed clear comparisons with other solutions belonging to the same group/category of the study.

As the table shows, it is possible to identify several points that were not covered by related works proposals but aim to be included in this paper. Most of the related works include the application of incentive mechanisms for WMNs [4, 17–19, 22], but only one proposes changes to the protocol [17], creating a new protocol model to be used at the link layer level, but it doesn't include tests with the proposed model and it does not show comparisons with today traditional protocols for WMNs. Two other works [16, 21] show comparisons between protocols for WMNs, the first work [16] evidence the efficiency of proactive protocols in the WMN environment and the second [21] highlighting the Babel protocol for environments of large networks that have suffered some type of disaster. Both solutions ended up not allying any type of incentive mechanism to the mentioned protocols.

**Table 1.** Related works comparison.

| Work | Incentive mechanisms | Babel or BATMAN protocol | Virtual and/or real tests | Comparison group |
|------|------|------|------|------|
| [4], 2016 | O | | | |
| [17], 2019 | O | O | | |
| [22], 2020 | O | | | |
| [18], 2018 | O | | O | |
| [19], 2018 | O | | | |
| [16], 2016 | | O | O | O |
| [21], 2017 | | O | O | O |
| This paper | O | O | O | O |

This paper seeks to integrate such incentive mechanisms with the Babel protocol, combining a protocol aimed at WMN networks with the benefits brought by the incorporation of incentives to the network, demonstrated in related works.

## 4  Proposed Solution

The solution proposed is based on the inclusion of price cost metrics to calculate the selection of ETX (Expected Transmission Count) routes, using for this a fixed cost value to be assigned to each network node, called *tocost* (transmission operational cost), which will be passed on to neighbors through a TLV packet, at the time the IHU ("I Heard You") message exchanges occur.

Inside each TLV packet used, of the IHU type, a new Sub-TLV called OC (Operational Cost) will be added, which will be responsible for transporting the *tocost* value of its origin node to all neighbors so that the cost links is consistent among all nodes in the network.

The *tocost* value assigned to each participant, as it represents the operating cost that each node has to forward packets, will be determined by the user or person responsible for the host belonging and can be represented by any currency or token that can be freely chosen according to the needs of the network. Depending on the location of the node and the costs involved, considering hardware, maintenance, energy, and other expenses, the operating value of the node in a real network will always vary, so the cost is stipulated through a specified integer during node startup.

## 4.1  Routing Metric

The routing metric uses the ETX algorithm plus the cost variable called *tocost*, leading each network node to calculate the cost of a link based on four factors:

1. the *txcost* cost of receiving packets informed by a neighbor;
2. the transmission cost *rxcost* calculated by the node itself;
3. the estimated RTT (round-trip time) delay cost for the link, initially not present in the ETX algorithm but added to identify the best quality networks [11]; and,
4. the transmission operating cost *tocost* representing the incentive mechanism proposed in this paper.

The metric used is based on the sum of each cost variable, allowing the combination of the incentive strategy with others that are necessary for the network environment, without breaking basic rules of the Babel protocol [10], avoiding the possible formation of loops in the route paths and thus maintaining the integrity of the network. The basic rules of the protocol, considered for any change made, are based on three immutable and essential requirements for the operation of the protocol [11]. Starting from a function $M(c, m)$, which represents the Babel cost metric, where $c$ is the calculation of the link's local cost, computed by the node itself, and $m$ is the computed and advertised cost by the neighbor for the same link, by the except the following rules must be complied with:

- If $c$ is infinite, then $M(c,m)$ is also infinite.
- $M$ is strictly monotonic:: $M(c,m) > m$.
- $M$ meets the left distributive property: if $m <= m'$ then $M(c, m) <= M(c, m')$.

The last rule is important because it guarantees that the best global path will be found for the routes. However, the first two rules are responsible for avoiding the formation of routing loops, and their satisfaction is necessary to guarantee the integrity of the network.

The basic conditions cited can be easily met using additive metrics, recommended as the default for a wide variety of cost calculations [11]. All changes made to the code sought to meet these conditions, especially the changes made within the final calculation of the ETX algorithm, as can be seen in the code snippet presented, showing the summation structure of each metric adopted.

**Require:** Neighbor Object
**Ensure:** An integer, indicating the cost to send packets through Neighbor.
  **if** $txcost \geq infinity$ OR $rxcost \geq infinity$ **then**
    return $infinity$
  **end if**
  **if** $txcost \geq 256$ OR $rxcost \geq 256$ **then**
    $cost \leftarrow txcost$
  **else**
    $cost \leftarrow 256/(alpha * betha)$

$$cost \leftarrow cost + rttcost$$
$$cost \leftarrow cost + tocost$$
**end if**

Due to the modular structure of the Babel protocol, it is possible to use different techniques or algorithms for the route selection policy. In all of them, there is the possibility of using the OC operating cost metric, provided that the basic principles specified for the operation of the protocol, thus avoiding the creation of Loops in the routing paths and starvation problems associated with changing the conditions of network sustainability.

### 4.2    Message Exchange

The exchange of messages is carried out constantly by the protocol through the TLV packets, so in order to transmit the new cost variable *tocost*, a sub-TLV called OC (Operational Cost) was added to the end of the existing and standardized TLV IHU (Fig. 2).

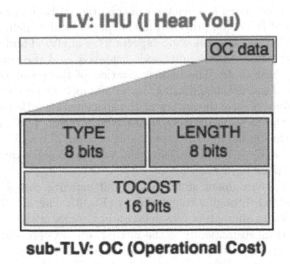

**Fig. 2.** Sub-TLV OC (Operational Cost).

The modular structure of the Babel protocol allows the inclusion of new sub-TLVs as long as they are in the same context as the parent TLV, that is, as both the OC sub-TLV and the IHU TLV are responsible for informing the cost and quality of links to the neighbors, they together allow to optimize the detection of changes in the topology and to reduce the overhead caused in the network, not being necessary the creation of a new TLV.

The sub-TLV OC has a size of 32 bits, which will be added to the end of the IHU message. The initial 16 bits make up its header structure, with 8 bits used for its type and 8 bits for the size. The rest of the 16 bits are used to store the cost variable *tocost* (Fig. 2). The header has fixed values linked to the sub-TLV structure, where the type established for the first 8 bits is defined by a constant with a fixed value of 4 for the extension performed. The size bits are assigned the value 16, referring to the *short* type of *tocost* included in the message body.

The sub-TLV also has the most significant bit of its typing set to zero, therefore considered a non-mandatory bit. The data inserted in the structure can be ignored if a network node does not recognize them, reading the remainder of the TLV, thus maintaining backward compatibility with the Babel protocol.

As a proactive protocol, all route tables seek to keep up-to-date with the best links in terms of QoS and its operating costs, which can be changed at any time through the exchange of IHU messages.

## 5    Experimental Results and Evaluation

We analyzed and compared the behavior of the original Babel protocol with the modified version of Babel [6], proposed in this paper, which includes the operating cost in its behavior. The following aspects were analyzed and compared: the choice of routing paths, throughput levels achieved, and the convergence time for choosing the best route. The implementation of the proposed extension of the Babel protocol was developed using the babeld module (version 1.10), implemented, and maintained by the author of the specifications. Babeld module was integrated with the INET framework tool (stable version 4.2.9) to execute the protocol within the Omnet++ software (stable version 5.7), a discrete event simulator based on the C++ language, using the Wireshark software (version 3.2.3) to record and analyze packets.

The first test environment simulate a small network composed of 5 mesh nodes interconnected through a ring topology (Fig. 3). The second test environment was designed to simulate a real network environment, and is composed of 60 mesh nodes arranged randomly in the virtual test environment, always keeping a minimum distance so that the wireless network reaches at least 2 other nodes.

Ring topology (Fig. 3) allows two paths to be tested between two ends of the network, the first path being shorter and of better quality, but 50% more expensive (red line), and the second path being longer and of lower quality, but at a lower cost. The second mesh topology allows the analysis to be more coherent with the large networks present in real environments, the costs are assigned to each node with the same proportion of values, leading some nodes to be 50% more expensive but that eventually can make part of a lower quality path.

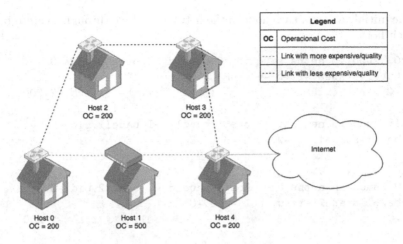

**Fig. 3.** Routing paths (Color figure online)

Packet traffic simulation in both test environments always occurs between two network nodes (Host0 and Host4), where Host4 makes a packet request to Host0 based on the following configuration within the OSI model (Fig. 4).

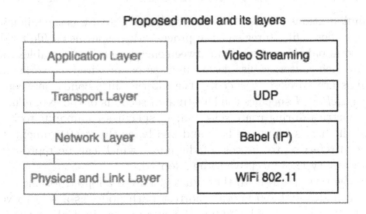

**Fig. 4.** Proposed layers model

The application layer simulates a Video Stream configured within INET through the "UdpBasic" packet. The transport layer is configured to use UDP, which does not guarantee the delivery of packets, with some analysis of throughput and packet loss rates being carried out. The network layer will consist of Babel, responsible for managing the routing and transfer of packets within the IP layer to reach their destination. Finally, the physical layer simulates data traffic through WiFi 802.11 radio signals.

The initialization of each node in the network is done through a call to babeld for each host:

```
Host0$ sudo ip netns exec host0 babeld -I babel0.pid -S
↪  babel-state0 -r -w -h 2 -M 0 -C 'reflect-kernel-metric true'
↪  -C 'interface tap0 channel 1 link-quality false' -Y 200

Host1$ sudo ip netns exec host1 babeld -I babel1.pid -S
↪  babel-state1 -r -w -h 2 -M 0 -C 'reflect-kernel-metric true'
↪  -C 'interface tap1 channel 1 link-quality false' -Y 700

Host2$ sudo ip netns exec host2 babeld -I babel2.pid -S
↪  babel-state2 -r -w -h 2 -M 0 -C 'reflect-kernel-metric true'
↪  -C 'interface tap2 channel 1 link-quality false' -Y 200

Host3$ sudo ip netns exec host3 babeld -I babel3.pid -S
↪  babel-state3 -r -w -h 2 -M 0 -C 'reflect-kernel-metric true'
↪  -C 'interface tap3 channel 1 link-quality false' -Y 200

Host4$ sudo ip netns exec host4 babeld -I babel4.pid -S
↪  babel-state4 -r -w -h 2 -M 0 -C 'reflect-kernel-metric true'
↪  -C 'interface tap4 channel 1 link-quality false' -Y 200
```

The configurations adopted in the execution of Babel was the following arguments: $I$ specifies a file to register the process id; $S$ specifies a file used to preserve long-term babeld information between each execution; $r$ enables random id selection for each router; $w$ disables optimizations for wired networks, assuming that all links are wireless; $h$ specifies the interval in seconds between sending each packet *Hello*; $M$ specifies the half-time in seconds of the exponential decay to smooth metrics during route selection; $C$ specifies commands to be entered directly on the host's command line; and finally, as the last argument, the term $Y$ was added referring to the cost of the node, which can be represented by a currency or any type of incentive to be adopted.

Within the tests performed, the values 200 were adopted for the cost of the longest path nodes and 700 for the shortest path node, as a way to verify the choice of the best routes, as by adding the cost of each host along the path, the longer one will cost 500, and the shortest path will cost 900.

The main aspects analyzed are related to the best selection of routes for network traffic, message exchange mechanisms, and the structure for maintaining the state of the communication channels. The correct routing and choice of the best paths must be maintained, whether due to the cost linked to the participants or the quality of the links.

## 5.1  Simulation Results

The simulation results were obtained by counting UDP packets that ran under the network and were successfully delivered to the destination host and are represented by the red line (Fig. 5), seeking to identify the number of received packets as a function of time. In order to observe the network execution in a mesh network scenario, two tests were carried out, the first simulating the streaming transfer with static participants, and the second simulating the transfer with a member leaving the network and getting back, that is initially used for the path (Host1), demonstrating the convergence time until a new route is defined.

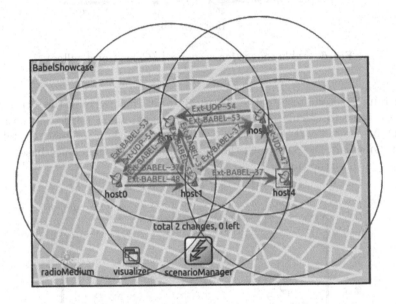

**Fig. 5.** Execution of inet framework. (Color figure online)

In the first analyzed test (Fig. 6), when the operating cost is added to the metric, the protocol achieves good stability in the choice of routes. The application layer starts streaming video at second 15 when UDP packets are sent, and the best route is selected to be used. The added weight (blue line) clarifies that the most interesting route is the longest, as its cost is lower. This guarantees that the protocol in its decisions will be more stable always maintaining the same route at each verification. In the long term it will reach a higher packet transmission rate (second 18 onwards). In its original version (red line), as there are some hops to other routes at times when the connection presents a less advantageous QoS, some transmission delays occur due to the instability of the transmission itself, resulting in a lower packet transmission rate.

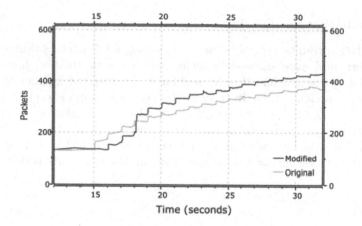

**Fig. 6.** Stable connection scenario 1 (Color figure online)

Within the second test analyzed (Fig. 7), taking into account the introduction of a cost value to calculate the best routing path, when the lowest cost node (Host1) in the network fails (second 14 onwards), there is the possibility of choosing not only the path with the best cost but also the choice based on the best Qos path at the time.

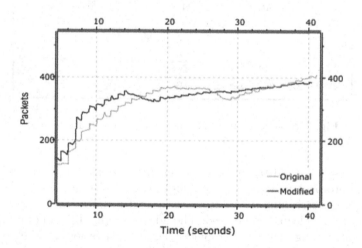

**Fig. 7.** Dropped connection scenario

However, when making a choice, the loss of packets that occurs due to the failure presented is not very significant in the long term, as the stability of the network when added the operating cost variable, leads it to avoid unnecessary hops by other routes at each cost verification.

The third test uses a large mesh network of 60 nodes (Fig. 8), where both the withdrawal of a participant within 15 s and its activation again in the network within 40 s are performed.

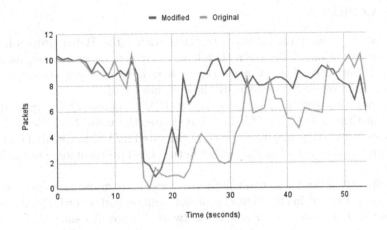

**Fig. 8.** Dropped connection scenario 2

As a node that participates in the route was removed (Fig. 8), the average of successfully transmitted packets drops quickly at 15 s, the network reconvergence mechanisms look for new neighbors to propagate the packet, and the version of modified Babel can return more quickly to the level of transmission prior to the modified crash, taking about 10 s for the packet traffic to normalize to the initial transmission level.

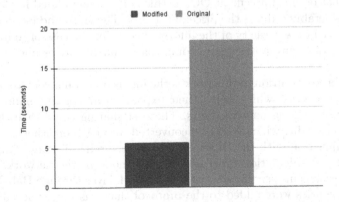

**Fig. 9.** Convergence time comparation

The network convergence time was also analyzed, taking into account the time between the participant leaving, and the time until packets start to be transmitted again to the destination. The graph (Fig. 9) shows that the network with the addition of an incentive mechanism behaves 69% faster to establish a new traffic route, thus reducing interference from node exits or node failures.

## 6  Conclusions

In this work, a modification was presented within the Babel protocol, which allows the inclusion of the operational cost involved in each node, as a form of financial incentive for the network, so that it transmits a packet over the network, such cost is represented by the variable *tocost*.

Modifications were also included in the IHU response TLVs, appending to the end of them a new sub-TLV OC that carries the value *tocost* to neighbors. Neighbors include the variable received in the sub-TLV OC in the final cost of the ETX metric, already used as a standard in the Babel protocol for communication in WMNs.

Modifications carried out in the protocol were put under test and compared with tests carried out in the original protocol (unmodified) in order to analyze the effects on route calculation for a WMN network. The results showed that despite the increase in the size of the IHU messages, which cause a slight overhead, the connections showed greater stability and, consequently, greater throughput. This occurs because cheaper connections are chosen in most calculations, decreasing route changes as there is higher QoS.

In the changes made in the protocol, there are some limitations found. The first one is the overhead caused by the increase in the size of TLV IHU: this traffic overhead could be alleviated by sending the sub-TLV OC only in times of cost change. The second one is interoperability with routers that use the original Babel 1.10 protocol versus the previous ones, which did not implement OC in the metric: the choice of routes, in this case, would always privilege routers with protocols that do not implement OC, as this is not being added in the cost of a link, it considerably reduces the price of the link. The third and last limitation is the confidence in the veracity of the informed cost: for the case of routes without alternatives, the route participants could place abusive prices and still have to be chosen.

The main contribution of this work is the inclusion of an incentive mechanism for WMNs networks, which helps their expansion and maintenance, dividing operating costs among network users. The cost-sharing could take the form of a currency or credit, which could be converted into cash or other benefits, and used in conjunction with the Blockchain to ensure reliability and transparency in the final cost calculation processed by each node in the network. Including incentive mechanisms associated with the network layer through Babel protocol, new functionalities were added to the protocol that was not explored before by the related works [16,21], and through tests on simulated network environments, which also was not included by related works presented [4,17–19,22], it is possible to identify the performance of the modified version of Babel protocol.

For future works, it is possible to incorporate cost management mechanisms between nodes in a decentralized and transparent way, recording and accounting all the resources supplied/consumed by the network, ensuring that costs are correctly distributed according to the work of each node, through a structure allied to the Blockchain. It would also be interesting to test in real environments of WMNs, such as community networks, to analyze and improve the proposal developed in real-use environments. Finally, the modifications to insert operating costs can also be applied in other protocols to guarantee the sustainability and development of the network.

# References

1. Abolhasan, M., Hagelstein, B., Wang, J.C.P.: Real-world performance of current proactive multi-hop mesh protocols. In: 2009 15th Asia-Pacific Conference on Communications, pp. 44–47 (2009). https://doi.org/10.1109/APCC.2009.5375690
2. Akyildiz, I.F., Wang, X., Wang, W.: Wireless mesh networks: a survey. Comput. Netw. **47**(4), 445 – 487 (2005). https://doi.org/10.1016/j.comnet.2004.12.001, http://www.sciencedirect.com/science/article/pii/S1389128604003457
3. Androulaki, E., et al.: Hyperledger fabric: a distributed operating system for permissioned blockchains. In: Proceedings of the Thirteenth EuroSys Conference. EuroSys 2018, New York, NY, USA. Association for Computing Machinery (2018). https://doi.org/10.1145/3190508.3190538, https://doi.org/10.1145/3190508.3190538
4. Baig, R., Dalmau, L., Roca, R., Navarro, L., Freitag, F., Sathiaseelan, A.: Making community networks economically sustainable, the guifi.net experience. In: Proceedings of the 2016 Workshop on Global Access to the Internet for All. GAIA 2016, New York, NY, USA, pp. 31–36. Association for Computing Machinery (2016). https://doi.org/10.1145/2940157.2940163
5. Baig, R., Roca, R., Freitag, F., Navarro, L.: guifi.net, a crowdsourced network infrastructure held in common. Comput. Netw. **90**, 150–165 (2015). https://doi.org/10.1016/j.comnet.2015.07.009, http://www.sciencedirect.com/science/article/pii/S1389128615002327, crowdsourcing
6. Borges, R.: Babeld modified cost protocol (2022). https://www.gitlab.com/rodolfoCarvalho/babeld-cost
7. Brown, K.: 2017 internet society global internet report: Paths to our digital future (2017). Accessed 9 Jun 2018
8. Chroboczek, J.: Extension mechanism for the babel routing protocol (2015). https://tools.ietf.org/html/rfc7557
9. Freifunk.net: Freifunk network (2021). https://freifunk.net
10. Chroboczek, J., Schinazi, D.: The babel routing protocol (2021). https://datatracker.ietf.org/doc/html/rfc8966
11. Jonglez, B., Chroboczek, J.: Delay-based metric extension for the babel routing protocol (2019). https://datatracker.ietf.org/doc/html/draft-ietf-babel-rtt-extension-00
12. Machado, C., dos Santos, R.R.S., Westphall, C.M.: Hop-by-hop accounting and rewards for packet dispatching (2021)
13. Machado, C., Westphall, C.M.: Blockchain incentivized data forwarding in manets: Strategies and challenges. Ad Hoc Networks **110**, 102321 (2021). https://doi.org/10.1016/j.adhoc.2020.102321, https://www.sciencedirect.com/science/article/pii/S1570870520306752

14. Micholia, P., et al.: Community networks and sustainability: a survey of perceptions, practices, and proposed solutions. IEEE Commun. Surv. Tutor. **20**(4), 3581–3606 (2018). https://doi.org/10.1109/COMST.2018.2817686
15. Murray, D., Dixon, M., Koziniec, T.: An experimental comparison of routing protocols in multi hop ad hoc networks. In: 2010 Australasian Telecommunication Networks and Applications Conference, pp. 159–164 (2010). https://doi.org/10.1109/ATNAC.2010.5680190
16. Piechowiak, M., Zwierzykowski, P., Owczarek, P., Wasłowicz, M.: Comparative analysis of routing protocols for wireless mesh networks. In: 2016 10th International Symposium on Communication Systems, Networks and Digital Signal Processing (CSNDSP), pp. 1–5 (7 2016). https://doi.org/10.1109/CSNDSP.2016.7573902
17. San Miguel, E., Timmerman, R., Mosquera, S., Dimogerontakis, E., Freitag, F., Navarro, L.: Blockchain-enabled participatory incentives for crowdsourced mesh networks. In: Djemame, K., Altmann, J., Bañares, J.Á., Agmon Ben-Yehuda, O., Naldi, M. (eds.) GECON 2019. LNCS, vol. 11819, pp. 178–187. Springer, Cham (2019). https://doi.org/10.1007/978-3-030-36027-6_15
18. Selimi, M., Kabbinale, A.R., Ali, A., Navarro, L., Sathiaseelan, A.: Towards blockchain-enabled wireless mesh networks. In: Proceedings of the 1st Workshop on Cryptocurrencies and Blockchains for Distributed Systems. CryBlock 2018, pp. 13–18, New York, NY, USA. Association for Computing Machinery (2018). https://doi.org/10.1145/3211933.3211936, https://doi.org/10.1145/3211933.3211936
19. Singh, M., Kim, S.: Trust bit: reward-based intelligent vehicle commination using blockchain paper. In: 2018 IEEE 4th World Forum on Internet of Things (WF-IoT), pp. 62–67 (2018)
20. Society, I.: 2020 impact report the internet is a lifeline (2020). https://www.internetsociety.org/impact-report/2020/
21. Tchinda, A.P., Frick, G., Trick, U., Lehmann, A., Tchinda, A.P., Ghita, B.: Performance analysis of wmn routing protocols for disaster networks. In: 2017 IEEE Symposium on Communications and Vehicular Technology (SCVT), pp. 1–6 (2017)
22. Tremback, J.: Althea white paper (2020). https://github.com/althea-net/althea-whitepaper/blob/master/whitepaper.pdf
23. Yang, J., Sakai, K., Kim, B., Okada, H., Sun, M.-T.: Cost-aware route selection in wireless mesh networks. In: Cao, J., Stojmenovic, I., Jia, X., Das, S.K. (eds.) MSN 2006. LNCS, vol. 4325, pp. 171–184. Springer, Heidelberg (2006). https://doi.org/10.1007/11943952_15

# Secure East-West Communication to Approve Service Access Continuity for Mobile Devices in a Distributed SDN

Maroua Moatemri[1,2](✉) , Hamdi Eltaief[1,2] , Ali El Kamel[1,2] ,
and Habib Youssef[1,2]

[1] University of Sousse, Khalifa Karoui Street Sahloul 4 Sousse, Sousse, Tunisia
hamdi.eltaief@issatso.rnu.tn, Habib.youssef@fsm.rnu.tn
[2] PRINCE Research Lab. ISITC Hammam Sousse, Sousse, Tunisia
{maroua.moatemri,ali.kamel}@isitc.u-sousse.tn

**Abstract.** In a distributed mobile Software Defined Mobile Network (SDMN), a device is in a continuous movement from one domain to another. Since a different controller is responsible for each domain, the devices' authentication information needs to be communicated between the SDN controllers (this type of communication is called East-West communication) to ensure the continuity access to the used devices services. This paper proposes a new secure East-West communication to approve service access continuity for mobile devices in a Distributed SDN. A comparative study between the VPN based approach and the proposed one is done both analytically and by simulation according to two criteria: the approval access authentication delay and the communication overhead. The results show that the proposed approach provides a secure East-West communication using less communication overhead and decreases the approval access authentication delay of mobile devices in an SDN.

**Keywords:** Service access continuity · SDN · Security · East-west communication · Approval access authentication delay

## 1 Introduction

Software Defined Network is a network paradigm defined by the physical separation of the control plane and the data plane of a network [5]. A distributed SDN is composed with numerous controllers and every controller is responsible of a different domain. To be able to apply the SDN paradigm to wireless mobile networks, SDMN has been defined. In fact, SDMN is an extension due to the addition of mobile networks' special functions [3]. It presents multiple advantages compared to regular mobile network such as flexibility, centralized control and reduction of the backhaul device operating cost [3]. In the recent years, network services are becoming more and more time sensitive. In a distributed SDN, any mobile device must have access to the service while moving from one domain to another. In this context, his authentication information needs to be communicated between the SDN controllers in a minimal time. On the other hand, this information is considered extremely sensitive, so they must be communicated in a secure environment. In this paper, we propose a new secure east-west communication approach to approve service access continuity for mobile devices in a distributed SDN. The proposed solution provides the security basics (confidentiality, integrity, and authentication) in order to protect the users' authentication information communicated between the different controllers. It also minimizes the time needed to approve the continuity of the access to the service in order to not affect the QoS. The rest of this paper is organized as follow. The next section presents a brief overview of the background and related work about multi controller SDN and the protocols that could be used to protect the SDN east-west communications. Section 3 defines the proposed east-west communication approach to approve service access continuity for mobile devices in a distributed SDN. The analytical and experimental evaluations are presented in Sect. 4. Section 5 concludes this paper.

## 2   Background and Related Work

In a traditional SDN, only one controller is used to manage all the network. This will present a limitation in terms of scalability. In fact, with the continuous evolution of the network demands, a single controller will not be able to manage an entire network due to its limited capacity. Another problem that a single controller SDN encounter is the single point of failure. In order to overcome these issues, the use of multi-controller SDN have been proposed [9]. When using a multi-controller SDN, several architectures could be adopted. The first, is the flat architecture, composed with various domains and every controller manages one domain. The second architecture is the hierarchical architecture. It is tree like architecture using different layers of controllers. Most solutions propose a two layer controller architecture. The domain controllers which handle switches in their domains and a root controller that keeps a global view of the network and manage the domain controllers [9]. Another design of architecture that could be adopted is the hybrid architecture [20]. It is a two layer architecture composed with multiple root controllers and each one manages a few domain controllers. To secure the east west communications in a distributed SDN, a few ways have been proposed. Jun-Huy Lam et al. [13] suggest using Identity-Based Cryptography (IBC) for this purpose. IBC protocol has been introduced in 1984 by Adi Shamir [21]. It is based on the generation of the users' private keys through their unique identities via a trusted third party called the Private Key Generator (PKG). However, using this protocol require a secure channel to exchange data between the PKG and the users [2]. Another problem due to the use of the IBC is that if the PKG is compromised then all the messages that had been signed by the keys generated by it are also compromised. In [8], the use of both TLS[19] and IPsec [10–12,15,17] protocols has been proposed to secure SDN's east west communications. With the use of TLS, many problems will be encountered. First, if we have different communication scenarios, which is the case in our scenario, we cannot implement different security policies [18]. Second, TLS is not capable of providing the data origin authentication which will cause problems since it is one of the most important security services to guarantee in a network. As for the IPsec, its first problem is that it needs a lot of communications for the users' authentication. Also, another disadvantage of the IPsec is due to the use of the tunneling mode which will cause bandwidth problems.

## 3    The Proposed Approach to Approve Service Access Continuity for Mobile Devices in a Distributed SDN

### 3.1    Overview and Motivation

The main idea of our approach consists of centralizing the authentication information of all the network users. Thus, when a new mobile device enters in the domain of a foreign controller, it will need his authentication information to authenticate it. To do so, the foreign controller sends the device's authentication information (user profile, attributes, master session key, time stamp...)[1] to the network administrator through the shortest path. If the user is registered, then, the network administrator responds with a confirmation message through the same path. In that case, it will grant its access to the service. Compared to the VPN authentication method, the proposed approach presents several advantages. First, using the VPN based approach requires the use of a new VPN channel for each communication between two controllers. This will make using this method on large scale networks not possible due to the resource limitation. This will as well introduce a heavy network load which will lead to bandwidth problems. Secondly, since the authentication information is centralized, they will not be shared between all the controllers. This will decrease the risk that an intruder steals and uses this critical data. The proposed architecture is presented in Fig. 1.

### 3.2    Security Analysis

Some of the users' authentication information such as the master session key are critical and needs to be protected against some malicious attacks. In our approach, three different communication types are proposed. The first type is the "Controller-Controller" communications. In this type, the authentication information data will only be accessible by the end devices. Thus, the intermediate controllers will only play the simple role of data routing. The second type is the

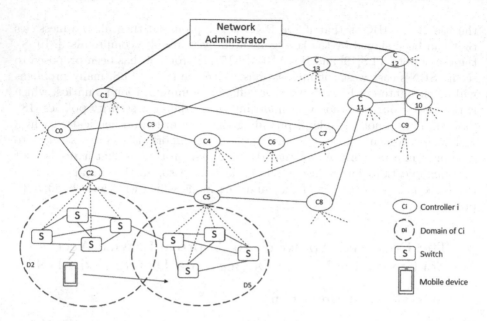

**Fig. 1.** The proposed architecture

communications "Controller-Network administrator". In this type, the authentication information data will pass through an exterior network. In this case, the confidentiality is required so the critical data will not be intercepted. Also, the network administrator must be sure that the message from the controller $C_i$ is authentic, and that the data has not been modified. To ensure that, we must guarantee the source authentication and the data integrity. The last communication type is the "Network administrator-Controller" communication. This communication is nothing more than a simple acknowledgment that will allow the controller to approve service access continuity for the mobile device. In that case, the confidentiality is not required since the data sent is not critical. Contrariwise, the source authentication and the data integrity are very important because the controller must be sure that the response did truly come from the network administrator and that it has not been modified during the data transfer.

### 3.3    Conduct of the Proposed Approach

The proposed approach has two different phases: the first is an offline phase and the second is online.

**The Offline Phase: Pre-Establishment.** This first phase aims to set up the network. Several tasks will take place offline:

*Keys Distribution.* The network administrator and all the controllers will have a public key and a private key. The notation of the different keys is presented in the Table 1.

**Table 1.** Keys' description.

| Notation | Representation |
|---|---|
| $K_{admin}^{-1}$ | The network administrator's private key |
| $K_{admin}$ | The network administrator's public key |
| $K_{Ci}^{-1}$ | The controller i private key |
| $K_{Ci}$ | The controller i public key |

*Keys' Exchange.* The network administrator and the controllers make their public keys available for all the other network elements [7].

*Protocol Hello.* Used by the controllers to discover the network.

*Shortest Path Selection.* The shortest path is used to send the user's authentication information. For this task, the OSPF protocol [16] is used.

*Switches' Establishment.* Using the proposed approach to improve switch-to-controller assignment [4].

*Users' Registration on the Network.* To benefit from a service, the user needs to join the network through a challenge-response authentication [1].

*Send the Users' Authentication Information to the Network Administrator.* Every controller needs to send the authentication information of his users to the network administrator.

**The Online Phase,** Now that the network is set up, it will start functioning. The scenario is as follow: When a mobile device moves from his source domain to foreign domain, the access authentication approval process will star and presented as follow:

*Step 1:* The mobile device asks for approval to access to the service. It sends its authentication information to the foreign controller.
The following notation is used to express the communication between controllers in the next steps.

$M_i$: Plaintext authentication information message sent by the controller $C_i$
$M_s$: Encrypted message
$C_i$ : Foreign controller's identity
admin : Network administrator's identity
N : Sequence number
H : Hash function
m : Plaintext acknowledgement message
admin : Network administrator's identity
N : Sequence number
$m_s$ : Acknowledgement message sent by admin

*Step 2:* The foreign controller sends the authentication information to the network administrator. To ensure the confidentiality of $M_i$, $C_i$ encrypts $M_i$ with the administrator's public key.

$$C_i \rightarrow admin : M_s = \left\{ M_i, N, C_i, admin, \left\{ H\left(M_i, N, C_i, admin\right) \right\}_{K_{Ci}^{-1}} \right\}_{K_{admin}}$$

*Step 3:* The network administrator decrypts the message using its own private key.

$$admin : M_i', N', C_i', admin', \left\{ H\left(M_i, N, C_i, admin\right) \right\}_{K_{Ci}^{-1}} = \left\{ M_s \right\}_{K_{admin}^{-1}}$$

*Step 4:* To ensure the identity and the message are from the claimed controller Ci, the network administrator needs to be able to decrypt the message digest using the controller's public key $(K_{Ci})$.

$$H\left(M_i, N, C_i, admin\right) = \left\{ \left\{ H\left(M_i, N, C_i, admin\right) \right\}_{K_{Ci}^{-1}} \right\}_{K_{Ci}}$$

*Step 5:* To make sure that the message has not been altered, the network administrator computes the received message digest through the same hush function H. If,

$$H\left(M_i', N', C_i', admin'\right) = H\left(M_i, N, C_i, admin\right),$$

then the message has not been altered.

*Step 6:* If the user is subscribed to the service, then the network administrator sends an acknowledgement message to the controller $C_i$ to approve the access.

$$admin \rightarrow C_i : m_s = m, N, admin, C_i, \left\{ H\left(m, N, admin, C_i\right) \right\}_{K_{admin}^{-1}}$$

*Step 7:* The controller decrypts the message digest using the network administrator's public key to ensure the identity and the message are from the claimed network administrator.

$$\left\{ m_s \right\}_{K_{admin}} = \left\{ m, N, admin, C_i, \left\{ H(m, N, admin, C_i) \right\}_{K_{admin}^{-1}} \right\}_{K_{admin}}$$

*Step 8:* The controller computes the received message digest through the same hush function H. If

$$H(m', N', C_i', admin') = H(m, N, C_i, admin),$$

then the message has not been altered.

*Step 9:* The controller saves the information to allow the user to access the service during the intra-domain movement for the same session. These different steps are represented in the diagram of the Fig. 2.

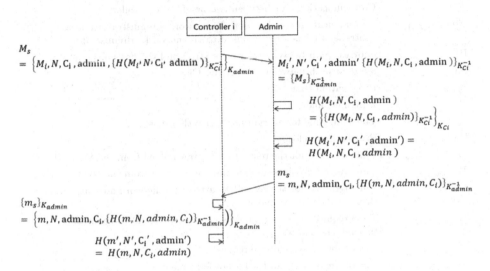

**Fig. 2.** Controller-Network administrator communications

## 4   Evaluation

The proposed approach is evaluated based on an analytical and experimental study according to two criteria: the approval access authentication time and the communication overhead.

### 4.1   Analytical Evaluation

**Notation.** During this section, the notation used is presented in the Table 2.

**Table 2.** Analytical evaluation notation.

| Symbol | Representation |
|---|---|
| HC | Home or source controller |
| VC | Visitor or foreign controller |
| Ck | The border controller (C1 or C12) |
| NA | Network administrator |
| $T^{prop}_{ACAS}(VC, NA)$ | Time to approve the continuity of the access to the service using the proposed method |
| $T^{vpn}_{ACAS}(VC, HC)$ | Time to approve the continuity of the access to the service using the VPN based approach |
| $Com_{(Ci,Cj)}$ | Communication cost between two neighbor controllers |
| $Com_{(Ck,NA)}$ | Communication cost between the network administrator and a controller that is directly linked to the network administrator |
| P | Shortest path between the source (HC) and the destination (VC) |
| Pa | Shortest path between the VC and Ck |
| $T_{prop}$ | Propagation time |
| $T_{em}$ | Emission time |
| $T_{cal}$ | The total time for encryption, decryption, hash, |
| $V_{prop}$ | Propagation velocity |
| $T_{trans(request)}$ | Time required for the request to be transmitted from the VC to the HC |
| $T_{trans(reply)}$ | Time required for the reply to be transmitted from the HC to the VC |
| $T_{request}$ | Time required for the request to attend the network administrator through the shortest path |
| $T_{response}$ | Time required for the acknowledgement to attend the controller through the shortest path |
| $size_{req}$ | Size of the message of the request |
| $size_{reply}$ | Size of the message of the acknowledgement |
| $datarate$ | Transmission speed |

## Analytical Evaluation of the VPN Based Approach

*Approval Access Authentication Delay.* Knowing the source controller, the time to approve the continuity of the access to the service by the foreign controller is expressed using the Eq. 1

$$T^{vpn}_{ACAS}(VC, HC) = T_{trans(request)} + T_{trans(reply)} + T_{Cal} \tag{1}$$

The communication cost between two neighbor controllers Ci and Cj ($Com_{(Ci,Cj)}$) is calculated as follow in the Eq. 2

$$Com_{(Ci,Cj)} = 2 * \frac{(distance(Ci, Cj))}{V_{prop}} + \frac{(size_{req} + size_{reply})}{datarate} + T_{Cal} \tag{2}$$

The total approval access authentication cost is the sum of the costs of all the needed communications.

$$T^{vpn}_{ACAS}(VC, HC) = \sum_{(Ci,Cj)\in P} Com_{(Ci,Cj)} \tag{3}$$

$$T^{vpn}_{ACAS}(VC, HC) = \sum_{(Ci,Cj)\in P} 2*\frac{(distance(Ci,Cj))}{V_{prop}} + \frac{(size_{req} + size_{reply})}{datarate} + T_{Cal} \tag{4}$$

*Communication Overhead.* To protect the sent data, security protocols add to the payload an overhead that will guarantee some security services. The tunnel mode of the ESP mechanism of the IPsec protocol, that will be used to compare our approach, guarantee the following security services:

- Confidentiality: through data encryption
- Integrity and data origin authentication: through hashing and digital signature
- Reply attack protection: through the Nonce

Knowing that the AES-CBC Cipher is used for the authentication and the HMAC-SHA-256 is used for the integrity and authentication, the data packet format and the total communication overhead used are presented in Table 3.

**Analytical Evaluation of the Proposed Approach**

*Approval Access Authentication Delay.* The time to approve the continuity of the access to the service by the foreign controller is expressed using the Eq. 5

$$T^{prop}_{ACAS}(VC, NA) = T_{request} + T_{response} + T_{cal} \tag{5}$$

**Table 3.** Communication overhead for the used VPN based approach.

| Field | Size(Bits) |
|---|---|
| Source address | 32 |
| Destination address | 32 |
| SPI | 32 |
| Sequence number | 32 |
| Padding | 144 |
| Padding length | 8 |
| Next header | 8 |
| Authentication data | 256 |
| Total communication overhead | 544 |

The communication cost between two neighbor controllers Ci and Cj ($Com_{(Ci,Cj)}$) is calculated as in the Eq. 2.

The approval access authentication delay cost is the sum of the cost of all the needed communications to attend the border controller and the cost of the communication to attend the network administrator. This is expressed in the Eq. 6

$$T_{ACAS}^{prop}(VC, NA) = ( \sum_{(Ci,Cj) \in Pa} Com_{(Ci,Cj)}) + Com_{(Ck,NA)} \tag{6}$$

$$T_{ACAS}^{prop}(VC, NA) = ( \sum_{(Ci,Cj) \in Pa} 2 * \frac{(distance(Ci, Cj))}{V_{prop}} + \frac{(size_{req} + size_{reply})}{datarate} +$$

$$T_{Cal}) + 2 * \frac{(distance(Ck, NA))}{V_{prop}} +$$

$$\frac{(size_{req} + size_{reply})}{datarate} + T_{Cal} \tag{7}$$

*Communication Overhead.* In the proposed approach, we propose to add the following data to protect the sent data packets:

– Source Identifier: 32 bits
– Network administrator identifier: 32 bits
– Sequence number: 32 bits
– Authentication data: 256 bits (due to the use of the ECC [14])

The total size of the overhead of the proposed approach is 352 bits. This is less than the overhead added with the VPN based approach, which will generate a bandwidth gain.

## 4.2   Experimentation

To test the proposed approach and compare it with the VPN based approach, the NSFNET [22] network architecture is used. It is composed of 14 nodes and 21 links. The Fig. 3 presents the approximate distances between the nodes in kilometers [6]. We suppose that the network administrator is equidistant from the two controllers it is connected to.

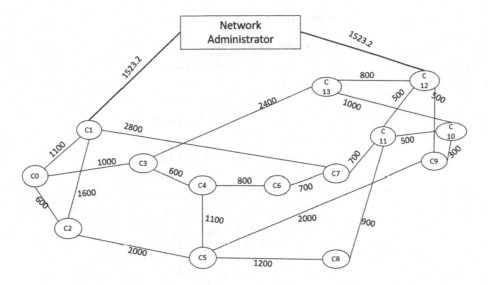

**Fig. 3.** The proposed architecture with approximate distances

The comparison is realized both analytically and with simulation. It is based on the approval access authentication delay using the VPN based approach and the proposed approach. The approval access authentication delay is computed using the Eq. 4 for the used VPN based approach and the Eq. 7 for the proposed approach. The route is composed with the controllers managing the domains that the mobile device visited during his movement. Since one route is composed with various foreign controllers (VCi), we will have an approval access authentication delay for each VCi. Thus, we will compare the average approval access authentication delay computed by the Eq. 8 for the VPN based approach and by the Eq. 9 for the proposed method.

$$Average\ T^{vpn}_{ACAS} = \frac{\sum_{(VCi)\in Route} T^{vpn}_{ACAS}(VCi, HC)}{(number\ of\ VCi \in Route) - 1} \tag{8}$$

$$Average\ T^{prop}_{ACAS} = \frac{\sum_{(VCi)\in Route} T^{prop}_{ACAS}(VCi, NA)}{(number\ of\ VCi \in Route) - 1} \tag{9}$$

The different scenarios are presented in the Table 4. The source node represents the node where the mobile is originally registered.

*Analytical Results.* The results obtained analytically presented in the Fig. 4 prove an improvement of our proposed approach in terms of average approval access authentication delay ($T_{ACAS}$) in most scenarios compared to the VPN based approach. Those improvements are explained by the distance optimization in the proposed approach.

**Table 4.** Different test scenarios.

| Scenario | Source node | Route |
|---|---|---|
| 1 | 11 | 8-5-2-0-1 |
| 2 | 7 | 7-1-0-2 |
| 3 | 9 | 7-1-0-3 |
| 4 | 2 | 8-9-10-13-12 |
| 5 | 13 | 13-1-0-2-5 |
| 6 | 0 | 0-1-7-11-12 |
| 7 | 0 | 0-1-13-12-10 |
| 8 | 3 | 3-13-12-10-9 |
| 9 | 7 | 8-5-2-0-1-7 |
| 10 | 10 | 10-13-3-2-1-0 |
| 11 | 5 | 5-9-10-12-13-1 |
| 12 | 13 | 13-1-0-2-5 |
| 13 | 11 | 8-5-2-0 |
| 14 | 7 | 8-5-2-0-1 |
| 15 | 9 | 9-7-1-0-3 |
| 16 | 8 | 8-11-12-13-1-0 |
| 17 | 13 | 13-1-3-4-5 |

The average delay obtained from the different scenarios in the proposed approach is of 24.18 ms compared to 31.1 ms obtained with the VPN based approach which presents an improvement of 6.9 2 ms.

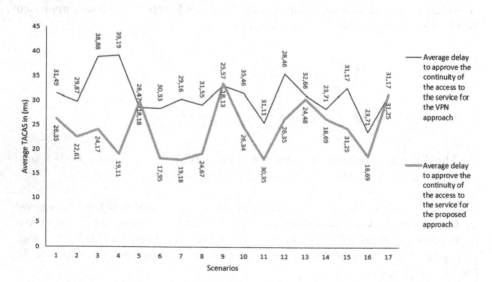

**Fig. 4.** Analytical comparison of the average authentication time

*Experimental Results.* To implement the experimental tests, we used the NS2 for simulating the network and the NAM tool to visualize the network simulations.

The computer used has 4 GB of Ram and 931 GB of hard disk size. Its processor is the Intel® Core™ i3-7020U CPU @ 2.30 GHz.

We simulated the same scenarios as those used with the analytical results. The obtained simulation results presented in the Fig. 5 validate the analytical results. The proposed approach, with an average delay of 24.19 ms generates a 6.91 ms gain compared to 31.1 ms for the classical approach.

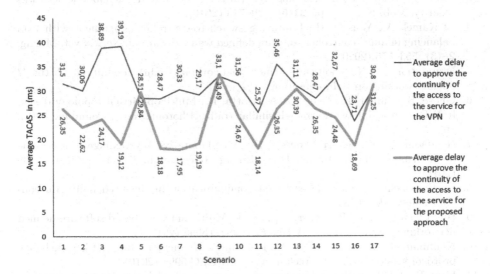

**Fig. 5.** Experimental comparison of the average authentication delay

## 5   Conclusion

The main purpose of this paper is to present a new secure east-west communication approach to approve service access continuity for mobile devices in a distributed Software Defined Network. East-west communication approaches need to provide communications' security to secure the users' authentication information. Another criterion is the approval access authentication delay that should be minimal to not negatively influence the Quality of Service (QoS). For a large scale network, our proposed approach ensure east-west communications' security to secure the users' authentication information generating a lightweight network load. The analytical and the simulation studies prove that the proposed approach presents an improvement in terms of both overhead size and approval access authentication delay compared with the used VPN based approach.

# References

1. Aissaoui, H., Urien, P., Pujolle, G.: Low latency of re-authentication during handover: Re-authentication using a signed token in heterogeneous wireless access networks. In: 2013 International Conference on Wireless Information Networks and Systems (WINSYS), pp. 1–7. IEEE (2013)
2. Anand, D., Khemchandani, V., Sharma, R.K.: Identity-based cryptography techniques and applications (a review). In: 2013 5th International Conference and Computational Intelligence and Communication Networks, pp. 343–348. IEEE (2013)
3. Chen, M., Qian, Y., Mao, S., Tang, W., Yang, X.: Software-defined mobile networks security. Mob. Netw. Appl. **21**(5), 729–743 (2016)
4. El Kamel, A., Youssef, H.: Improving switch-to-controller assignment with load balancing in multi-controller software defined wan (sd-wan). J. Netw. Syst. Manag. **28**(3), 553–575 (2020)
5. Foundation, O.N.: Software-defined networking (sdn) definition. https://opennetworking.org/sdn-definition/
6. Ghose, S., Kumar, R., Banerjee, N., Datta, R.: Multihop virtual topology design in WDM optical networks for self-similar traffic. Photonic Netw. Commun. **10**(2), 199–214 (2005)
7. Hendaoui, F., Eltaief, H., Youssef, H.: A collaborative key management scheme for distributed smart objects. Trans. Emerg. Telecommun. Technol. **29**(6), e3198 (2018)
8. Hettiarachchi, S.: Securing east-west communication in clustered multi-sdn controller network (2018)
9. Hu, T., Guo, Z., Yi, P., Baker, T., Lan, J.: Multi-controller based software-defined networking: a survey. IEEE Access **6**, 15980–15996 (2018)
10. Kaufman, C., Hoffman, P., Nir, Y., Eronen, P., Kivinen, T.: Internet key exchange protocol version 2 (ikev2). Technical report, RFC 5996 (2010)
11. Kent, S., Atkinson, R.: Ip encapsulating security payload (esp): Rfc 4303 (proposed standard) (2005)
12. Kent, S., Header, I.A.: Rfc 4302. IETF (2005)
13. Lam, J.H., Lee, S.G., Lee, H.J., Oktian, Y.E.: Securing distributed SDN with IBC. In: 2015 Seventh International Conference on Ubiquitous and Future Networks, pp. 921–925. IEEE (2015)
14. Langley, A., Hamburg, M., Turner, S.: Elliptic Curves for Security. RFC 7748 (2016). https://doi.org/10.17487/RFC7748, https://rfc-editor.org/rfc/rfc7748.txt
15. Maughan, D., Schertler, M., Schneider, M., Turner, J.: Internet security association and key management protocol (ISAKMP) (1998)
16. Moy, J.: Rfc2328: Ospf version 2 (1998)
17. Orman, H.: The oakley key determination protocol rfc 2412. IETF, Freemont, CA (1998)
18. Qin, H., Wang, N.: A data-origin authentication protocol based on ONOS cluster. In: MATEC Web of Conferences. vol. 56, p. 01006. EDP Sciences (2016)
19. Rescorla, E., Dierks, T.: The transport layer security (TLS) protocol version 1.3 (2018)
20. Sarmiento, D.E., Lebre, A., Nussbaum, L., Chari, A.: Decentralized SDN control plane for a distributed cloud-edge infrastructure: a survey. IEEE Commun. Surv. Tutor. **23**, 256281 (2021)

21. Shamir, A.: Identity-based cryptosystems and signature schemes. In: Blakley, G.R., Chaum, D. (eds.) CRYPTO 1984. LNCS, vol. 196, pp. 47–53. Springer, Heidelberg (1985). https://doi.org/10.1007/3-540-39568-7_5
22. Tomovic, S., Radonjic, M., Radusinovic, I.: Bandwidth-delay constrained routing algorithms for backbone SDN networks. In: 2015 12th International Conference on Telecommunication in Modern Satellite, Cable and Broadcasting Services (TELSIKS), pp. 227–230 (2015). https://doi.org/10.1109/TELSKS.2015.7357775

# High Performance Software Systolic Array Computing of Multi-channel Convolution on a GPU

Kazuya Matsumoto(✉)🆔, Yoichi Tomioka🆔, and Stanislav Sedukhin🆔

The University of Aizu, Aizu-Wakamatsu, Fukushima, Japan
{kazuya-m,ytomioka,c21stans}@u-aizu.ac.jp

**Abstract.** The multi-input/multi-output (MIMO) channel 2D convolution is the most compute-intensive operation in Convolutional Neural Networks (CNNs). This paper presents a high-performance implementation for the MIMO convolution by extending the well-known software systolic array model (SSAM) in which the partially computed results are shifted or shuffled across multiple threads in a CUDA warp to compute the single-input/single-output (SISO) channel convolution. We propose two methods for computing a full MIMO convolution on the GPU system. In the first method, the MIMO convolution is performed by iterations of the multi-input/single-output (MISO) convolution across multiple output channels while the second method iterates the single-input/multi-output (SIMO) convolution across multiple input channels. Both methods systolically shuffle partial results multiple times during the MIMO computing. It is shown that the first method mostly demonstrates a higher performance than the second one, since the first one reuses data effectively on the L1/L2 caches as well as on the register files. We also experimentally demonstrate that a single-precision performance of the directly implemented MIMO convolution is much better than that of the SSAM/SISO-based convolution and a GEMM-based MIMO convolution of the NVIDIA cuDNN library.

**Keywords:** Multi-channel convolution · Software systolic array · GPU

## 1 Introduction

Currently, Convolutional Neural Networks (CNNs) are an effective approach in machine learning to solve many kinds of real world problems. CNNs need a large amount of computations for both the training and inference procedures. CNNs consist of several layers including convolution, activation, fully-connected, and other types of layers. In particular, the convolution layers are the most compute-intensive part in the advanced CNN models. The required multi-channel 2D convolution can be implemented in different ways either by converting it to the General Matrix-matrix Multiplication (GEMM) [2,7], Winograd algorithm [3], Fast Fourier Transform (FFT) [6], or by direct computing [8].

© The Author(s), under exclusive license to Springer Nature Switzerland AG 2022
O. Gervasi et al. (Eds.): ICCSA 2022, LNCS 13375, pp. 298–309, 2022.
https://doi.org/10.1007/978-3-031-10522-7_21

In [1], the authors have demonstrated that an SSAM single-input/single-output channel (SISO)-based direct computing can achieve a much higher performance than deep learning libraries such as cuDNN, ArrayFire and Halide on Graphics Processing Units (GPUs). However, to accelerate deep learning further we need an extension of the SSAM-based approach for the basic multiple-input/multiple-output (MIMO) channels convolution because the convolutional layers of CNNs typically deal with a tensor data with MIMO channels.

The SSAM-based input-stationary approach proposed in [1] realizes a systolic data movement for SISO convolution using CUDA shuffle primitives. The approach reuses the input feature map from caches and intermediate results on the register files more effectively and reduces the time and energy expensive DRAM read/write accesses, which are helpful to extract a higher performance and, at the same time, to reduce energy consumption. However, for the MIMO convolution, we need much more data for computing each output pixel. Therefore, it is essential to effectively use the L1/L2 caches as well as register files to extract the full performance of the SSAM-based approach.

This paper presents a high-performance implementation for the multi-channel convolution computing by extending the SSAM-based convolution kernel. We propose two methods for the multi-channel convolution computing on the GeForce RTX 3090 of the NVIDIA Ampere GPU architecture. The first method conducts iterations of a multi-input/single-output convolution. In the second method, iterations of a single-input/multi-output convolution are conducted by keeping the partial sums during the MIMO computing. This paper presents performance evaluation results by using a profiling tool and describes performance comparison results with the original SSAM/SISO-based convolution kernel and the NVIDIA cuDNN library.

## 2   Convolution Implementations with Software Systolic Array for Multi-input and Multi-output Channels

The terminology used in this paper is described in Table 1. The 2D convolution is expressed as

$$y[i,j] = (x * w)[i,j] = \sum_{s=a_l}^{a_u} \sum_{t=b_l}^{b_u} x[i-s, j-t] \cdot w[s,t],$$

where $*$ is the convolution operation, $\cdot$ is the multiplication operation, $w$ is a filter of the size $M \times N$ ($M = a_u - a_l + 1$ and $N = b_u - b_l + 1$), $x$ is a 2-dimensional input matrix (or image) of the size $H \times W$, and $y$ is a 2-dimensional output matrix of the size $(H + 2pad - M + 1) \times (W + 2pad - N + 1)$ (*pad* is a padding value). The multi-channel convolution with $C$-input channels and $K$-output channels is expressed as

$$y_m[k, i, j] = (x_m * w_m)[k, i, j]$$

$$= \sum_{c=1}^{C} \sum_{s=a_l}^{a_u} \sum_{t=b_l}^{b_u} x_m[c, i - s, j - t] \cdot w_m[k, c, s, t]. \qquad (1)$$

$w_m$ is a filter of the size $K \times C \times M \times N$. $x_m$ is an input tensor of the size $C \times H \times W$. $y_m$ is an output tensor of the size $K \times (H + 2pad - M + 1) \times (W + 2pad - N + 1)$.

**Table 1.** Terminology

| Term | Description |
|------|-------------|
| $H$ | Input image height |
| $W$ | Input image width |
| $M$ | Filter height |
| $N$ | Filter width |
| $C$ | The number of input channels |
| $K$ | The number of output channels |
| $x_m$ | Input tensor |
| $y_m$ | Output tensor |
| $w_m$ | Filter tensor |
| $pad$ | Padding value |
| $BS$ | CUDA thread block size |
| $P$ | Number of rows processed by each thread |

In this study, the given tensor data are stored in KCHW, CHW, and KHW orders for filter, input and output tensors, respectively. For example, in the KCHW order, the $W$ data elements of the same row are continuously stored, the $H \times W$ matrix data for each of $C$ input channels are continuously allocated, and the $C \times H \times W$ tensor data for each of $K$ output channels are continuously stored.

The methods proposed in this paper basically follow the 2D convolution algorithm by the Software Systolic Array Model (SSAM) described in [1]. The software systolic array simulates a mechanism of hardware systolic arrays, and the SSAM is suitable for memory-bound computations with regular memory access patterns. The features of the SSAM-based 2D convolution algorithm are as follows:

– All data of filters are stored into shared memory in the beginning of the CUDA kernel and are reused during the convolution computing.
– Input image data are cached into registers. A sliding window scheme is used for the careful management of the limited number of registers.

- Each thread in a CUDA warp caches $D(= N + P - 1)$ elements of the input image also in the beginning, where $P$ is the number of sliding window steps. Hence, each thread computes the $P$ rows of elements in the image.
- The input data are multiplied with the filter data and the product is accumulated. The computation is conducted by the fused multiply-add (MAD) operation, and the partial sums are transferred to the neighbor threads by the *shuffle* primitive.

CUDA kernels are called with a block dimension (blockDim) and a grid dimension (gridDim) of the 3D arrays. The blockDim denotes the number of threads in a block. The gridDim denotes the number of the blocks in a grid. In this study, the dimensions of the CUDA kernels are given as

$$\text{blockDim} = (BS, 1, 1) \text{ and}$$
$$\text{gridDim} = (\lceil \frac{W + 2pad}{WarpCount \cdot (WarpSize - N + 1)} \rceil, \lceil \frac{H + 2pad}{P} \rceil, 1),$$

where $BS$ is the CUDA thread block size, $WarpSize$ is the CUDA warp size, and $WarpCount = BS/WarpSize$. Threads in a block of the CUDA kernels are in charge of computing a $K \times P \times BS$ sub-tensor of the $K \times (H + 2pad - M + 1) \times (W + 2pad - N + 1)$ output tensor.

In the present study, we have implemented two convolution methods for multi-input and multi-output channels. Listing 1.1 presents iterations across output channels in the outermost loop, while Listing 1.2 shows iterations across input channels in the outermost loop. In the following, Listings 1.1 and 1.2 are called OUT_IN method and IN_OUT method, respectively. In the implementation of both the methods, the filters are accessed in a decremental order and the input images are accessed in an incremental order, whereas each of these is accessed in the opposite order of the Eq. (1).

In the OUT_IN method, the data for the accumulation is initialized to the zero at the beginning of each outermost-loop (Lines 8–9 in Listing 1.1) and the computed results are stored to the destination array at the end of each outermost-loop (Lines 32–33). On the other hand, in the IN_OUT method, the array for the accumulation is initialized before the outermost loop (Lines 7–9 in Listing 1.2) and the results are written out to the destination array after the outermost-loop (Lines 34–37).

For both the methods, the number of required floating-point operations per CUDA thread is $FLOP_{thread} = 2 \cdot K \cdot C \cdot M \cdot N \cdot P$. The output amount to the GPU off-chip memory for both the methods is $K \cdot P \cdot sizeof(dataType)$. The input amount of data from the GPU's off-chip memory for the OUT_IN method is $K \cdot C(P + M - 1 + \lceil M \cdot N/BS \rceil) \cdot sizeof(dataType)$. The IN_OUT method reuses input data in each outermost iteration after reading the data (Lines 11–12 in Listing 1.2), and the input amount from the GPU's off-chip memory for the IN_OUT method is $C(P + M - 1 + \lceil M \cdot N/BS \rceil) \cdot sizeof(dataType)$. This means that the IN_OUT method requires $K$ times less memory accesses for the input tensor than the OUT_IN method. However, the IN_OUT method has to keep $K$ times larger temporary data for the summations of sum_final in a 2D array. Note that the temporary data might be forced out to the off-chip memory if the available number of registers is not enough for keeping the data.

**Listing 1.1.** CUDA kernel of multi-channel SSAM-based convolution (the loop across the output channels is the outermost).

```
1   template<typename T, int BS, int P, int M, int N>
2   __global__ void convolution_OUT_IN(const T *xm, T *ym, const T *wm, const int
        H, const int W, const int C, const int K) {
3     const int D = P + N - 1;
4     T data[D], sum[P];
5     __shared__ T smem[N][M];
6     T *psmem = &smem[0][0];
7     for (int k = 0; k < K; k++) {
8       for (int p = 0; p < P; p++)
9         sum[p] = 0;
10      for (int c = 0; c < C; c++) {
11        __syncthreads();
12        for (int l = threadIdx.x; l < M*N; l += BS)
13          psmem[l] = wm[M*N*(C*k+c)+l];
14        __syncthreads();
15        for (int d = 0; d < D; d++)
16          data[d] = xm[SRC_IDX+H*W*c+W*d];
17        #pragma unroll
18        for (int p = 0; p < P; p++) {
19          T sum_partial = 0;
20          #pragma unroll
21          for (int j = 0; j < N; j++) {
22            if (j >= 1)
23              sum_partial = __shfl_up_sync(0xffffffff, sum_partial, 1);
24            #pragma unroll
25            for (int i = 0; i < M; i++) {
26              sum_partial = MAD(data[p+i], smem[M-1-i][N-1-j], sum_partial);
27            }
28          }
29          sum[p] += sum_partial;
30        }
31      }
32      for (int p = 0; p < P; p++)
33        ym[DST_IDX+(W+2*pad-N+1)*((H+2*pad-M+1)*k+p)] = sum[p];
34    }
35  }
```

**Listing 1.2.** CUDA kernel of multi-channel SSAM-based convolution (the loop across the input channels is the outermost).

```
1   template<typename T, int BS, int P, int M, int N>
2   __global__ void convolution_IN_OUT(const T *xm, T *ym, const T *wm, const int
         H, const int W, const int C, const int K) {
3     const int D = P + N - 1;
4     T data[D], sum[K][P];
5     __shared__ T smem[N][M];
6     T *psmem = &smem[0][0];
7     for (int k = 0; k < K; k++)
8       for (int p = 0; p < P; p++)
9         sum[k][p] = 0;
10    for (int c = 0; c < C; c++) {
11      for (int d = 0; d < D; d++)
12        data[d] = xm[SRC_IDX+H*W*c+W*d];
13      for (int k = 0; k < K; k++) {
14        __syncthreads();
15        for (int l = threadIdx.x; l < M*N; l += BS)
16          psmem[l] = wm[M*N*(C*k+c)+l];
17        __syncthreads();
18        #pragma unroll
19        for (int p = 0; p < P; p++) {
20          T sum_partial = 0;
21          #pragma unroll
22          for (int j = 0; j < N; j++) {
23            if (j >= 1)
24              sum_partial = __shfl_up_sync(0xffffffff, sum_partial, 1);
25            #pragma unroll
26            for (int i = 0; i < M; i++) {
27              sum_partial = MAD(data[p+i], smem[M-1-i][N-1-j], sum_partial);
28            }
29          }
30          sum[k][p] += sum_partial;
31        }
32      }
33    }
34    for (int k = 0; k < K; k++)
35      for (int p = 0; p < P; p++)
36        ym[DST_IDX+(W+2*pad-N+1)*((H+2*pad-M+1)*k+p)] = sum[k][p];
37  }
```

## 3  Performance Evaluation

The specification of the NVIDIA RTX 3090 GPU [5] is shown in Table 2. The used CUDA toolkit version is 11.4 and the GPU driver version is 470.57.02. The operating system of the environment is Ubuntu 20.04.2 LTS with Linux 5.13.0-35-generic kernel. The program codes are compiled by nvcc command with -gencode arch=compute_86,code=sm_86 -fmad true options and the parameter setting[1] of $P = 4$ and $BS = 128$. The performance measurements are conducted with the padding value $pad = 1$. Matrix and tensor data in the program are allocated as single-precision floating-point arrays and single-precision operations are used for computing the multi-channel convolution. CUDA cores of the GPU are utilized and its Tensor Cores are not used in the evaluation.

**Table 2.** Specification of the NVIDIA RTX 3090 GPU. The L1 cache and shared memory use the same 128 KB hardware resources per SM, and the preferred cache configuration can be selected.

| | |
|---|---|
| Number of CUDA/shader cores | 10,496 |
| Number of Streaming Multiprocessors (SMs) | 82 |
| Core base clock speed | 1,395 MHz |
| Theoretical peak single-precision performance | 29,284 Gflop/s |
| Memory type | GDDR6X |
| Memory size | 24 GB |
| Memory base clock speed | 1,219 MHz |
| Memory bus width | 384-bit |
| Memory system bandwidth | 936 GB/s |
| L2 cache size | 6 MB |
| L1 cache size per SM | Up to 96 KB |
| Max 32-bit registers per SM | 65,536 |
| Max 32-bit registers per thread | 255 |
| Warp size | 32 |

Figure 1 shows the performance of the convolution kernel implementation for the $H \times W$ image with $C$-input and $K$-output channels. The Gflop/s performance is calculated by the following formula:

$$\text{Performance [flop/s]} = \frac{2 \cdot H \cdot W \cdot M \cdot N \cdot C \cdot K \text{ [flop]}}{\text{time [second]}}.$$

In the evaluation, each of the convolution CUDA kernels is called 20 times and its average time is used as the computation time. The "Original" in Fig. 1 is the performance of the 2D convolution kernel[2] by Chen et al. [1]. Note that the performance of the "Original" method is almost the same as the performance of the implemented SISO case ($C = K = 1$ case).

---

[1] The parameter setting in the convolution kernels affects its performance. Evaluations of the effects and optimizations of the parameter setting are considered in our future work.

[2] The "Original" kernel implementation was slightly modified for evaluating the performance on the same condition because their kernel supposes that the input matrix size is equal to the output matrix size.

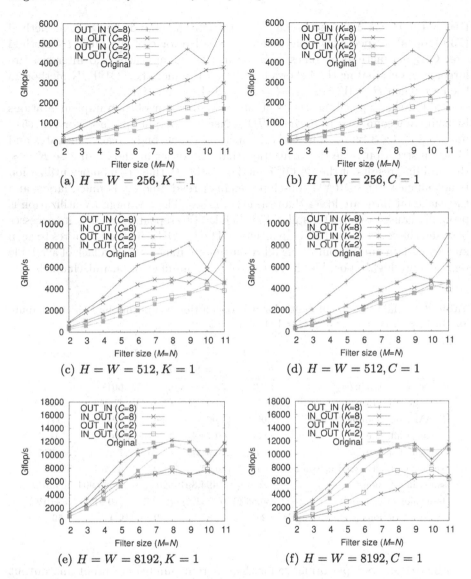

**Fig. 1.** Performance of computing convolution with $C$-input and $K$-output channels for the $H \times W$ image.

As shown in Fig. 1, the performance of the IN_OUT method is higher than the OUT_IN and Original methods in the most cases. For example, in case of the $H = W = 256, K = 1$ (Fig. 1a), the performance of the OUT_IN method with $C = 8$ for $M \times N$ filter is 435 Gflop/s and it is 1.14 and 5.95 times higher than that of the IN_OUT method with $C = 8$ (383 Gflop/s) and the Original method (73 Gflop/s), respectively. The performance advantage of the OUT_IN method over Original method becomes weaker when the image sizes and filter size are larger; the Original method shows higher performance than OUT_IN method in the case when $H = W = 8192, M = N = 10$ (Figs. 1e, 1f).

Table 3 shows profiling results of multi-channel convolution implementations by using ncu command from the NVIDIA Nsight Compute profiler[3] for $512 \times 512$ images and $3 \times 3$ filters. The OUT_IN method shows higher cache hit rates and higher instruction issue slot utilization than the other methods. In case $K = 8$, the profiling results of the IN_OUT method indicate that its memory utilization is not efficient: the DRAM (off-chip memory) read amount is much larger and the cache hit rates are lower than the other cases. The low memory utilization is probably caused by register spills [4], which lead to repeating read-write accesses between the registers and off-chip memory. The IN_OUT method requires to keep sum array data during computing all $K$ output channels; hence, a lack of available registers are highly possible in the case of large number of output channels.

**Table 3.** Profiling results of multi-channel convolution computing by Nsight Compute for the case of $H = W = 512, C = 1, M = N = 3$.

| | OUT_IN | | IN_OUT | | Original |
|---|---|---|---|---|---|
| | $K = 2$ | $K = 8$ | $K = 2$ | $K = 8$ | |
| Performance [Gflop/s] | 1,030 | 2,042 | 665 | 601 | 587 |
| (% to peak performance) | (3.52%) | (6.97%) | (2.27%) | (2.05%) | (2.00%) |
| DRAM read amount [Mbytes] | 1.05 | 1.06 | 1.06 | 12.68 | 1.05 |
| L1 cache hit rate | 52.50% | 69.73% | 59.13% | 39.07% | 27.66% |
| L2 cache hit rate | 75.42% | 90.91% | 89.20% | 72.25% | 65.05% |
| Warp cycles per issued instruction | 11.10 | 10.15 | 21.92 | 61.28 | 15.56 |
| Issued instructions | 952,283 | 3,494,891 | 920,085 | 2,560,904 | 464,372 |
| (Issue slot utilization) | (56.56%) | (63.23%) | (27.56%) | (10.91%) | (39.01%) |
| Issued instuctions per active cycle | 2.26 | 2.53 | 1.10 | 0.44 | 1.56 |

Figure 2 shows a performance for the different numbers of input and output channels, and different sizes of images, and $3 \times 3$ filters. In Fig. 2, the performance of a GEMM-based computing of multi-channel convolution computing in the NVIDIA cuDNN v8.3.1 is also depicted. The cuDNN is a GPU-accelerated library for deep neural networks. The cuDNN supports several algorithms for the convolution foward (cudnnConvolutionForward) function. Figure 2 shows the cuDNN performance of the IMPLICIT_PRECOMP_GEMM algorithm which demonstrates higher performance than other supported algorithms in the most cases for single-precision data. A performance of the cuDNN library modestly increases when the image and the number of channels are increased.

---

[3] https://developer.nvidia.com/nsight-compute.

The OUT_IN implementation shows much higher performance than the cuDNN library. As shown in Fig. 2, increasing the number of channels does not always improve the performance of the OUT_IN implementation. In the case of relatively small image sizes like $H = W = 256$ or $H = W = 512$ (Fig. 2a, b), the performance tends to improve with respect to increasing the number of channels. However, the performance deteriorates when $H = W = 1024, K = 8$ or $K = 32$ (Fig. 2d). Figure 3 shows L1 and L2 cache hit rates of the OUT_IN implementation (the rates are measured also by the Nsight Compute profiler). The L1 hit rates for $128 \times 128$ images do not drop down even when the number of channels increases. On the flip side, the L1/L2 hit rates for $512 \times 512$ or $1024 \times 1024$ images are first decreased and leveled off along with increasing the number of channels. These results of cache hit rates are compiled with the performance tendencies as shown in Fig. 2.

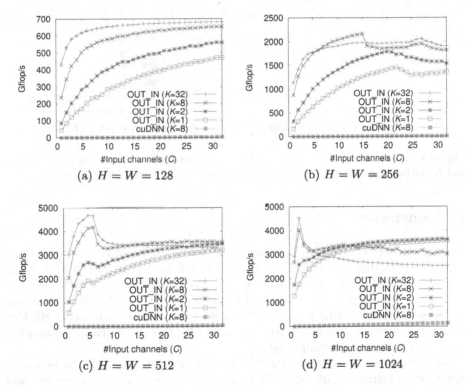

(a) $H = W = 128$

(b) $H = W = 256$

(c) $H = W = 512$

(d) $H = W = 1024$

**Fig. 2.** Performance of convolution computing by the OUT_IN method and cuDNN with $C$-input and $K$-output channels for the $H \times W$ image and $3 \times 3$ filters.

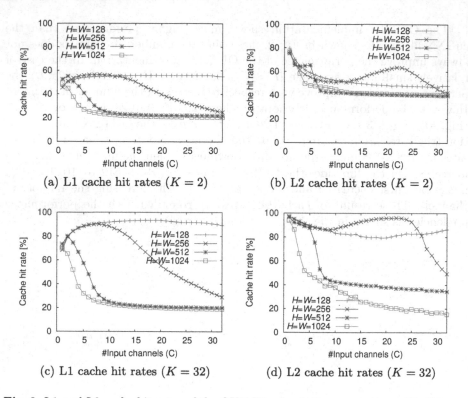

(a) L1 cache hit rates ($K = 2$)    (b) L2 cache hit rates ($K = 2$)

(c) L1 cache hit rates ($K = 32$)    (d) L2 cache hit rates ($K = 32$)

**Fig. 3.** L1 and L2 cache hit rates of the OUT_IN convolution computing with $C$-input and $K$-output channels for the $H \times W$ image and $3 \times 3$ filters.

## 4    Conclusion

We have developed a high-performance kernel for multi-channel convolution computing by extending an existing convolution kernel with a software systolic array model [1]. The implemented multi-channel kernel demonstrates a higher performance than the original single-channel kernel and the GEMM-based computing of cuDNN library. Profiling results of the implemented kernel show that efficient usage of registers and caches is more important for the multi-channel computing than the single-channel computing.

Our future work includes an application of the implemented multi-channel convolution kernel to different CNN models such as VGG, GoogleNet, and ResNet. Another future work is to conduct more detailed performance comparison with other deep learning libraries using Tensor and CUDA Cores of the current and future GPUs.

# References

1. Chen, P., Wahib, M., Takizawa, S., Takano, R., Matsuoka, S.: A versatile software systolic execution model for GPU memory-bound kernels. In: SC 2019: Proceedings of the International Conference for High Performance Computing, Networking, Storage and Analysis, pp. 1–81. ACM (2019). https://doi.org/10.1145/3295500.3356162
2. Jorda, M., Valero-Lara, P., Pena, A.J.: Performance evaluation of cuDNN convolution algorithms on NVIDIA volta GPUs. IEEE Access **7**(1), 70461–70473 (2019). https://doi.org/10.1109/ACCESS.2019.2918851
3. Lavin, A., Gray, S.: Fast algorithms for convolutional neural networks. In: Proceedings of the IEEE Conference on Computer Vision and Pattern Recognition, pp. 4013–4021 (2016)
4. Micikevicius, P.: Local Memory and Register Spilling. NVIDIA Corporation (2011)
5. NVIDIA Corporation: 3090 & 3090 Ti Graphics Cards — NVIDIA GeForce. https://www.nvidia.com/en-us/geforce/graphics-cards/30-series/rtx-3090-3090ti/
6. Podlozhnyuk, V.: FFT-based 2C convolution. NVIDIA White Paper (2007)
7. Vasudevan, A., Anderson, A., Gregg, D.: Parallel multi channel convolution using general matrix multiplication. In: Proceedings of the International Conference on Application-Specific Systems, Architectures and Processors, pp. 19–24 (2017). https://doi.org/10.1109/ASAP.2017.7995254
8. Zhao, Y., Wang, D., Wang, L.: Convolution accelerator designs using fast algorithms. Algorithms **12**(5), 112 (2019). https://doi.org/10.3390/a12050112

# Attacks, Detection Mechanisms and Their Limits in Named Data Networking (NDN)

Abdelhak Hidouri[1], Mohamed Hadded[2(✉)], Haifa Touati[1],
Nasreddine Hajlaoui[1], and Paul Muhlethaler[3]

[1] Hatem Bettaher IResCoMath Lab, University of Gabes, Gabes, Tunisia
haifa.touati@cristal.rnu.tn
[2] IRT SystemX, Palaiseau, France
mohamed.elhadad@irt-systemx.fr
[3] INRIA, Paris, France
paul.muhlethaler@inria.fr

**Abstract.** Proposals for Information Centric Networking (ICN) have recently emerged to rethink the foundations of the Internet and design a native data-oriented network architecture. Among the current ICN projects, Named Data Networking (NDN) is a promising architecture supported by the National Science Foundation (NSF). The NDN communication model is based on the Publish/Subscribe paradigm and focuses on broadcasting and finding content and introduces caching in intermediate routers. Data packets are sent in response to a prior request called an Interest packet and the data are cached along the way to the original requester. Content caching is an essential component of NDN in order to reduce bandwidth consumption and improve data delivery speed, however, this feature allows malicious nodes to perform attacks that are relatively simple to implement but very effective. For that reason, the goal of this paper is to study and classify the types of attacks that can target the NDN architecture such as (Cache Pollution Attack (CPA), Cache Poisoning Attack, Cache Privacy Attack, Interest Flooding Attack (IFA), etc.) according to their consequences in terms of reducing the performance of the network. Moreover, we give an overview about the proposed detection mechanisms and their limitations.

**Keywords:** Named Data Networking · NDN attacks · Attack detection

## 1 Introduction and Motivation

The Internet architecture was developed in the late 70s, when its main goal was only to ensure communication between a limited number of devices. Since the release of the World Wide Web, the original design of the Internet has had to cope with many new requirements such as mobility, security, scarcity of IP addresses, etc. Such requirements pose serious challenges to the traditional TCP/IP architecture. These challenges include the inefficiency of the security model deployed in

O. Gervasi et al. (Eds.): ICCSA 2022, LNCS 13375, pp. 310–323, 2022.
https://doi.org/10.1007/978-3-031-10522-7_22

the TCP/IP architecture to deal with the increasing number of vulnerabilities and attacks that are recorded every day, such as Denial of Service attacks (DoS), Distributed Denial of Service attacks (DDoS), relay attacks, traffic analysis attacks, flooding attacks, etc. Moreover, massive content distribution has changed data communication in recent years. Today's Internet is mostly characterized by the consumption of multimedia material.

Many solutions have been suggested to deal with the vast amount of data traffic, such as Content Delivery Networks (CDN), Peer to Peer (P2P) networks and Distributed Database (DDB) systems [1]. Most of these solutions are based on the deployment of dedicated servers situated in areas close to consumers to hold content replicas and optimize the download experience for consumers. Nonetheless, the widespread adoption of these solutions is far from being an ideal solution for the content delivery issue. These solutions require ISP cooperation and DNS configurations. Furthermore, they impose significant operational and capital costs that can only be afforded by a small number of large commercial companies. Importantly, these solutions are still vulnerable to multiple security issues.

Recently, a new research direction in networking, called Information-Centric Networks (ICN), has been proposed to deal with massive content distribution. The underlying philosophy of ICN is to focus on the content itself and not on its location. Several ICN architectures have been proposed in the literature [2], mainly in the United States and Europe, and include TRIAD, DONA, PSIRP and its successor PURSUIT, CCN and NDN. Among all these projects, the NDN architecture seems to be the most promising.

NDN is an architecture initially proposed by Van Jacobson in 2009 [3] and supported by the National Science Foundation (NSF). It follows a receiver-based communication model and introduces caching in intermediate routers. Data packets are sent in response to a prior request called an Interest packet and the data are cached along the way to the original requester [4]. In other words, the NDN communication model is based on the Publish/Subscribe paradigm and focuses on content distribution and discovery. This receiver-based service model naturally adapts to the data-centric model of several emerging networks, like WSN [5], IoT [7] and VANET [6].

Content caching is an essential component of NDN and serves to reduce bandwidth consumption and improve data delivery speed. Additionally, NDN introduces new content self-certification (signing) features that obviously improve data security and make NDN a security-by-design architecture capable of supporting efficient and effective content distribution, and large-scale security. However, basic NDN security mechanisms, such as signatures and encryption, are not sufficient to ensure the complete security of these networks. Indeed, the availability of data in several network caches allows malicious nodes to carry out attacks that are relatively simple to implement but very effective.

Unlike the traditional Internet where data is centralized on servers and accessible to the public via TCP/IP, in NDN, routers can cache data and reuse it, reducing the number of repeated requests and the resulting overhead for today's Internet services. However, new attacks specific to the NDN architecture have recently been identified in the literature. In particular, these attacks target the new internal structures of routers, such as the table used for pooling requests or the cache. These attacks have not yet been precisely characterized, thus leaving the first NDN networks deployed open to a potential danger.

In this paper, we present the relevant attack models that can threaten the NDN architecture and the impact such attacks may have. Then, we give an overview of recent attack-detection mechanisms, and we point out some of their limitations. The remaining part of this paper is organized as follows. In Sect. 2, we highlight the NDN architecture. In Sect. 3, we give an overview of security attacks on NDN. Section 4 introduces the state of the art regarding the detection mechanisms and in Sect. 5, we discuss their limitations. Finally, the conclusion is given in Sect. 6.

## 2   Overview of the NDN Architecture

In this section we present the main building blocks of the NDN architecture, especially the data structures implemented in each node to manage data dissemination as well as the NDN naming scheme. In NDN, all communications are performed using two distinct types of packets: *Interest* packets and *Data* packets. The node that sends an Interest is called the *Consumer* and the original Data source is called the *Producer*. The Data and Interest packets carry a *name* field, which uniquely identifies a piece of content that can be carried in one Data packet [8]. Each node in NDN implements three components:

- **The Pending Interest Table (PIT):** It contains the interest packet entries and the corresponding list of incoming interfaces and "on hold" Interests that have not yet been satisfied. Multiple incoming interfaces indicate the same Data is requested from multiple downstream users.
- **Forwarding Information Base (FIB):** FIB entries associate prefix names to one or many output interfaces to which the Interest packets should be forwarded.
- **Content Store (CS):** The CS holds a copy of the *Data* packets that have been passed by the NDN router, and this copy will be used to satisfy subsequent interests that request the same content. This caching mechanism speeds up data delivery and decreases the network load.

## 3   Security Threats in the NDN Architecture

As explained in the previous section, most of the attacks in the current TCP/IP model, such as snooping, spoofing, traffic analysis attack, Man In The Middle, SMB attack, relay attack, etc., are no longer effective in the NDN architecture due to its security foundation. This security foundation is based on signing each data packet by the producer.

An attack called "DNSspooq" [9] had a huge impact on TCP/IP architecture, where it leaked plenty of legitimate users' private information. This attack uses the IP addresses of each user to attack the neighbour users. This attack is no longer applicable in NDN, because NDN uses naming instead of IPs and encapsulates a signature field. Moreover, this attack could not be applied because NDN relies only on the interfaces to transmit the Interest and the Data packets.

Despite this solid security base in NDN, this secured by design" architecture still suffers from several vulnerabilities, mainly: Cache Pollution Attack (CPA), Cache Privacy Attack, Cache Poisoning Attack and Interest Flooding attack (see Fig. 1). These attacks affect its essential components, namely the PIT and the CS, which is very critical since content can be spread everywhere through the pervasive caching of NDN.

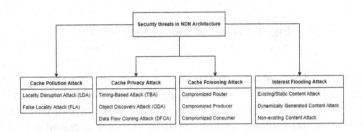

**Fig. 1.** Security threats in NDN Architecture.

## 3.1   Cache Pollution Attack (CPA) and Its Impact

In a Cache Pollution Attack (CPA), the attacker tries to cache unpopular content in the Content Store (CS) in an attempt to make the cache unavailable to legitimate consumers. This attack mostly targets NDN routers Cache Hits.

As shown in (Fig. 2), an *Attacker* node sends interest packets to change the priority of the content stored in the CS of nearby routers. This induces the caching of a large number of malicious packets in the CS of router R1 (malicious contents are represented in red in our example). This behaviour changes the priority of the content and increases the popularity of these malicious content items. As a result, this attack reduces the probability of obtaining legitimate content from the cache by legitimate consumers.

This attack is difficult to detect because it is hard to identify the attacker in the NDN architecture (NDN conserves the privacy of the consumers). In addition, the attacker does not follow a specific pattern, such as the amount of interests sent per second and the hierarchy of prefix naming. Moreover, the time of launching the attack is not stable and, in several cases, follows different strike-timing.

Deng et al. [10] classified CPA into 2 main categories: *Locality Disruption Attack (LDA)* and *False Locality Attack (FLA)*. For LDA, the malicious consumer requests masses of junk content. This type of content gets cached in the CS and this malicious consumer keeps requesting it so as to keep it in the CS.

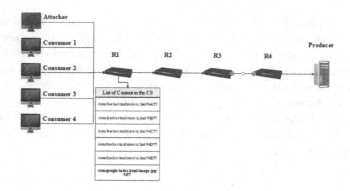

**Fig. 2.** Cache Pollution Attack (CPA).

In the case of FLA, the malicious node requests already existing content with less popularity in order to prevent other legitimate content from getting higher popularity and falsify the priority rules implemented in the caching policies, which forces it to be useless. As explained in [11], CPA essentially affects the Cache Hit Ratio (CHR) by decreasing the hit ratio of legitimate content [12]. Explains that in several cases the CHR of legitimate requests could decrease to 0% in edge routers, i.e. routers that are directly connected to the attackers. CPA attacks also affect the Average Retrieval Delay (ARD), which greatly increases compared to the normal state. This leads to a direct effect on the legitimate consumer and may result in an unnecessary retransmission of the legitimate interest.

## 3.2   Cache Privacy Attack and Its Impact

In a Cache Privacy Attack, the attacker tries to access the cached content present in the CS to find out whether this content has recently been accessed by certain legitimate consumers or not. When the attacker knows the time of the access of such content, the attacker associates this content either to malicious consumers or to different legitimate consumers. This attack breaks the privacy of the legitimate users, and it requires several steps to apply it starting from the "Enumeration" of the content present in the CS and other information like the access time of each content item in the CS cache, then requesting such content by either predicting the next pattern of the interest or requesting the same content.

The authors of [13] studied cache privacy attack for CCN. They identified three types of cache privacy attack, such as a request monitoring attack or Timing-Based Attack (TBA), Object Discovery Attack (ODA) and Data Flow Cloning Attack (DFCA).

In TBA the attacker tries to enumerate the content presented in the CS. The attacker finds the hit time of the cache by requesting the same content twice. The first request caches the content. The second request is satisfied from the cache, as the content has been already cached. The attacker requests the desired content to check whether it remains in the cache or not. If it is cached and the cache hit occurs by legitimate users, the attacker can interpret that the consumer who requested this content is linked to such content.

In ODA the attacker sends an interest that has the root name space "/", then the router responds with a random content from the cache of the nearby router or any other routers by specifying the HopLimit. After that, it constructs the prefix based on the recent result of the enumeration. Taking the example of an attacker who sends an interest with root name space "/", the CS cache responds with "/com/website/www/media/video.mp4/%77", then the attacker changes the prefix into "/com/website/www/media/" to get a list of content in that name space and so on. In DFCA, the attacker tries to use ODA to enumerate the cache content. He targets the ongoing flow interests and predicts the next name space that the legitimate consumer still hasn't requested and sends it to change the ongoing flow interest on his side. This attack is applied, for example, in Voice-over-CCN applications. Globally, a Cache Privacy Attack targets the confidentiality of content in the CS.

### 3.3   Cache Poisoning Attack and Its Impact

A Cache Poisoning Attack mainly aims to inject either fake or corrupted content into the router, which remains in the routers and keeps spreading into the neighbour nodes. Processing a content item in a line speed timing, leads the NDN router to be unable to deeply verify the malicious content [14]. This attack can be performed either by a compromised router which spreads poisoned content in reply to the interest packets. The other neighbour routers will cache this content which will be accessed later by other consumers. The attack is highly dangerous as it can distribute poisoned content through compromised publishers and routers, and spread fake or corrupted content very quickly. The main security concern in a Cache Poisoning Attack is the availability of the content.

### 3.4   Interest Flooding Attack and Its Impact

An Interest Flooding Attack is a type of attack that targets the Pending Interest Table (PIT), and aims to send a huge amount of interests into the desired router, which forces all these routers to create entries in their PIT that remain open during the attack. As a result, the PIT entries will no longer be available for legitimate consumers and keep dropping each packet sent by them [11,14].

Three types of such attacks have been specified: existing or static, dynamically-generated and non-existing attack. For the first type, the attacker sends an interest of an existing content item that will be cached in the CS and this will open a small number of entries in the PIT. The second type is based on dynamically generating different interests with high frequency. This type of attack is more efficient than type 1. For the type 3, the malicious node sends interest packets of non-existing content. This type ensures that the router creates a higher number of PIT entries that remain open until the time-out. This type is more severe than types 1 and 2 because PIT entries remain open for a longer duration. Table 1 summarizes the four attacks introduced in this section, we compare their security goals, the NDN component affected and the potential attacker entity.

**Table 1.** The effects of NDN attacks on the security goals

| Attack | The attacked entity | Target security goal | Target entity |
|---|---|---|---|
| Cache Pollution | Consumer/Producer | Availability | CS |
| Cache Privacy | Consumer | Confidentiality | CS |
| Cache Poisoning | Consumer/Producer | Availability | CS |
| Interest Flooding | Consumer | Availability | PIT |

# 4 Attack Detection Mechanisms in NDN

## 4.1 CPA Detection Mechanisms

The first early mechanism to detect CPA has been proposed by Mengjun Xie et al. in [15] and is called, CacheShield. The main process of this mechanism is based on a shield function which calculates the frequency of receiving a content item and indexing it with each associated content based on its popularity and its naming-prefix, then it verifies if such content is already cashed. If so, it delivers it to the consumer that requests it, otherwise, it stores a slice of this content and resets its frequency counter.

By respecting the chronology, Guo et al. [16] suggested a mechanism based on path diversity. The goal of this mechanism is to base its decision on the collected information related to each data packet stored in the cache of the CS. The collected parameters concisted by the hit time of a content item $o.hit$, the path traversed of a content item $o.PathTracker$, the damage ratios on backbone router, false positive of the decision and false negative error ratios of the decision.

Then this mechanism compares the normal state before the attack and the attack state using a "PathTracker". The authors defined a threshold which is compared with the value obtained. If the value is higher than the predefined threshold, the attack is detected. Kamimoto et al. [17] suggest a different mechanism based on prefix hierarchy and called "Cache Protection Method based on prefix Hierarchy" (CPMH). This mechanism goes through 3 main steps: extracting the malicious nodes' prefixes and saving them on a BlackList. This is done by calculating the Request rate Variation for each prefix (RVP), and to avoid obtaining a false positive, the mechanism also calculates the Weighted Request rate Variation for each prefix (WRVP). The next step is to eliminate the prefixes existing on the BlackList. Finally, each interest that requests a blacklisted prefix will be dropped. Zhang et al. [18] propose a mechanism based on the Coefficient of Variation (CV), where the decision is made based on several parameters, namely: The prefix received $x$, the interface from which the interest is received and the frequency of sending such an interest.

These collected statistics are used to calculate the $CV_i(x)$ of an interest $i$ with prefix $x$, if the value is low, it is more likely that it is from an attacker source, if not, it is suitable to be cached. The decision in this mechanism is made on the data, which means either to cache it or not to cache it. Another CPA detection mechanism has been proposed in [19] and it is based on clustering. Globally, this mechanism collects some information upon the running of the mechanism, for-instance, the number of interests received, the number of interests for the same content and the time interval between two consecutive requests for the same content

Then it classifies the interests into 2 different clusters based on the probability of an interest $i$ appearing and the AVG time interval between two interests requesting the same content. This helps in the final step to determine the type of the attack (LDA or FLA) then each router broadcasts to its neighbours a list of suspicious content items in order to avoid them being cached.

The authors of [20] suggested a detection mechanism called ICAN (Intrusion detection system for CPA attack in NDN architecture) based on metrics of performance including the average cache hit ratio, average interest inter-arrival time, hop count and prefix variation that is basically stands by monitoring dynamically the variation of those metrics to decide the appearance of the attack in different realistic network topologies. This solution demonstrated high efficiency compared to previous mentioned solutions in terms of conserving router resources, the conservation of the user's privacy and the high accuracy of detecting the attack.

Other detection approaches that are Based on Probability Decision (BPD). This approach includes a mechanism called Randomness Check [21]. This solution starts by creating a matrix composed of the names and how many times each content item is received. Upon receiving some content, it increments the value of that content in the matrix. If requested content goes higher than the predefined threshold, it is suspected of being an attack. In the case of an attack, the content is eliminated, otherwise, it stays for future demand.

A detection mechanism called Adaptive Neuro-Fuzzy Inference System (ANFIS) has been proposed by Karami et al. [22], which mainly aims to change the caching replacement policy. The main step in this mechanism starts by collecting data related to each interest which lead to feeding the features of its neurones that are constituted by 5 fuzzy layers, as result a goodness value is collected on each interest. This value is taken into consideration to decide whether to cache the content or remove it from the cache of the CS.

Kumar et al. [23] proposed a mechanism to detect CPA called Interface-Based Popularity Caching (IBPC) which goes through collecting data based on the number of interfaces that receive a content item in a certain period of time. IBPC focuses on calculating the number of users requesting a content item using the Exponentially Weighted Moving Average (EWMA) to define the popularity of the content over a given period of time, considering that the number of attackers is smaller than the number of legitimate consumers. New technique of detecting CPA has been introduced by Lei et al. [24], where this mechanism is relies on collecting information such as, Data validator, Provider CS, Content Name, Task Prefix and Digest Prefix.

By collecting this information, the mechanism constructs blocks on each content item and verifies by comparing it with a predefined threshold to either proceed in caching the content or denying it from being accessed to the cache of the CS.

### 4.2    Cache Privacy Attack Detection Mechanisms

For a Cache Privacy Attack, [25] proposed a mechanism relying on disabling the *scope* and the *exclude* fields because the malicious node is able to perform the attack by utilizing those 2 fields. More precisely, the *exclude* field guarantees that the attacker gets the desired content without getting the same content covered from the first attempt, and the *scope* field allows the attacker to request the root namespace, which makes it easy for him to locate the desired content.

Ntuli et al. [26] suggested checking the interest and the content associated to the same prefix in order to identify the attack probability. The attack is suspected by the increase in the cache hit and the frequency of sending an interest, so it denies such an interest from accessing the content. [27] extended the work presented in [26] by adding other parameters such as repeat requests for multiple content in short period of time. A predefined threshold is used: if the goodness value decreases, an attack is suspected. Kumar et al. [28] proposed to decide either to add a delay on the malicious interest or to let it pass by judging through a static defined prefix hierarchy. This mechanism is applied for a Timing-Based Attack (TBA).

### 4.3    Cache Poisoning Attack Detection Mechanisms

The detection of Cache Poisoning Attack is hard and expensive in terms of the resources of the NDN router, which led Gasti et al. [29] to propose a mechanism based on Self-certifying the data packet and the interest packet. Certain information is collected, including the hash of the content associated by the mechanism by each passing data, the Content Name and the signature of the content.

This makes it possible to compare both the data collected of the interest and the data packet. Kim et al. [30] extended the work by reducing the overload on the NDN routers caused by these extensive verifications. The mechanism mainly aims to verify only the content existing in the cache: in the case of a cache hit, the verification is applied, otherwise, it is not. Ghali et al. [31] investigated the attack by associating each content item in the cache with a rank, this rank is variated by the number of requests for content $x$. The lower the value is, the higher probability there is of an attack.

### 4.4    IFA Detection Mechanisms

In IFA, some mitigation mechanisms have been suggested. In [32], the authors propose using PIT entries as the main parameter when it goes beyond a predefined threshold. Then, the NDN router lists the unwanted interest packets with the longest prefix and sends the associated data packets to the backbone routers which process the interface where this interest comes from. Compagno et al. [33] proposed a mechanism to detect IFA by utilizing the ratio of interests that come from an interface $i$, the ratio of interests that go out from an interface $i^*$ and PIT capacity for each interface $i$.

The mechanism calculates the goodness value using those parameters, if it goes more than a pre-defined threshold, an attack is detected so the NDN router revokes such an interest and a notification message is sent to the neighbour router about the malicious interest. A neural network mechanism has been suggested by [34], the features used in detection are: The number of arriving data packets, the number of arriving interest packets, the number of outgoing data packets, the number of outgoing interest packets, the number of satisfied interest packets and the size of the PIT entries.

This mechanism has been evaluated on the DFN topology and has shown high accuracy compared to recent, previously mentioned mitigation mechanisms.

## 5    Detection Mechanisms Limitations

As shown in Table 2, most of the detection mechanisms presented in the previous section (II) aim to provide a better strategy to prevent the effect of the attacks presented in Section (III) or to limit their impact. These mechanisms present a variety of vulnerabilities that can be exploited by the attackers to exhaust the router resources and expose the end-point node's identity, etc.

An early solution, CacheShield [15] presented several limitations that affect the efficiency of the NDN routers, such as the complexity of the algorithm for detecting the malicious behaviour of CPA. Another limitation is space exhaustion as this mechanism does not consider the limited space that the cache of the CS has, the name placeholder can cause an issue in this point, in which this mechanism keeps storing them continuously. Prefix Hierarchy suggested by [17] solves the problem of exhausting NDN router resources, but still depends on the topology itself. Also, this mechanism has issues when it comes to performing an attack consisting of caching unpopular content of popular prefix in order to confuse the mechanism. The mechanism proposed by Guo et al. [16], has a medium level of memory exhaustion. In addition, this mechanism is not applicable on all types of topology, and it keeps storing the information collected on each interest, which over-consumes the router space resources. The clustering method recommended by Yao et al. [19] has shown good results in classifying different attack models such as LDA and FLA, but it still has a lack of certainty and makes too many false judgements, where in this case the attacker keeps demanding low popularity content to spoil the cache of the CS. ANFIS [22] has been a more reliable suggestion compared to previous mechanisms in terms of accuracy and efficiency. But, this mechanism may fall into two main states:

- The huge exhaustion of the routers resources such as bandwidth, caching resources, etc. because many data packet need to be cached in order to decide the probability of attack.

– The huge rate of false positives, which leads the mechanism to allow content demanded by the malicious node to be cached hindering the storage demanded by legitimate nodes.

On the other hand, Cache privacy Attacks present a challenge for researchers to invent new mechanisms that can resist it, unfortunately those mechanisms still have many limitations that are given below. The authors in [25] suggest disabling two main fields in NDN packet specification in order to mitigate the privacy of the content presented in the cache, such as for *"Paid-Content"*. Thus, by eliminating the scope field from the new packet specification, the *"hop-Limit"* field still can be manipulated as a scope field. As for the mechanisms presented in [26,27] and [28], which propose applying an extra delay on the suspected interest with a specific prefix, this would delay the attack such as in the case of TBA, but it still cant resist if the intruder gets the desired content. In order to mitigate Cache Poisoning Attack accurately, [29] and [30] use a Self-certifying-based method. This method presents several drawbacks that may lead to false positive decisions. Based on this point, these methods are focusing more on static content, which means that the dynamic content can not be detected.

The above mentioned mechanisms suffers from the extreme exhaustion of the NDN router that can cause damage in the main components' functionality. In the case of IFA detection mechanism, the suggestion of [32] presents some limits. By relying on the edge NDN routers, the authors do not take in consideration that those routers may get effected by the malicious nodes. False positive decisions may appear as the legitimate consumers may request unavailable content. The authors of [34] base their solution on a neural network-based detection system, that may cause a huge space exhaustion and overload CPU usage. This mechanism keeps storing the data and the interest related information even in a non attacking state.

**Table 2.** Detection mechanisms limitations

| | Ref | Limitations | | | | | | | | |
|---|---|---|---|---|---|---|---|---|---|---|
| | | Compromisable | Identity leakage | Bandwidth usage | Space storage | CPU Overload | Accuracy | Topology | Complexity | False positive |
| CPA | [15] | | | ✓ | ✓ | ✓ | | | ✓ | |
| | [17] | | | | | | | | | ✓ |
| | [16] | | | ✓ | ✓ | ✓ | ✓ | | | |
| | [19] | ✓ | | | | | | | | ✓ |
| | [22] | ✓ | | ✓ | ✓ | ✓ | | | | ✓ |
| Cache Privacy Attack | [25] | ✓ | ✓ | | | | ✓ | | | |
| | [26] | | ✓ | | | | | ✓ | | ✓ |
| | [27] | ✓ | | | | | ✓ | | | |
| | [28] | ✓ | | | | | | | | |
| Cache Poisoning Attack | [29] | ✓ | | | | | | | | ✓ |
| | [30] | ✓ | | | | ✓ | | | | ✓ |
| IFA | [32] | ✓ | | | | | | | | ✓ |
| | [34] | | | ✓ | ✓ | ✓ | ✓ | | | ✓ |

# 6  Conclusion

The success of NDN has always been based on its security and its high performances, ensuring it a promising future in the network revolution. However, since NDN is not vulnerable to a range of basic attacks that are effective on the TCP/IP model, a number of new attacks have appeared that target NDNs main components. In this paper, we illustrated the potential threats that could affect the NDN architecture. Most of these vulnerabilities result from the availability of the data in the cache of intermediate routers. The most important of these attacks are the Cache Poisoning Attack, the Cache Privacy Attack and the Cache Pollution Attack. Moreover, we provide an overview about new detection mechanisms that have been presented in the literature, together with their limitations.

# References

1. Tchernykh, A., et al.: Scalable data storage design for nonstationary IoT environment with adaptive security and reliability. IEEE Internet Things J. **7**(10), 10171–10188 (2020). https://doi.org/10.1109/jiot.2020.2981276
2. Conti, M., Gangwal, A., Hassan, M., Lal, C., Losiouk, E.: The road ahead for networking: a survey on ICN-IP coexistence solutions. IEEE Commun. Surveys Tutor. **22**(3), 2104–2129 (2020). https://doi.org/10.1109/comst.2020.2994526
3. Estrin, D., Zhang, L., Burke, J.: Named Data Networking (NDN) Project. Technical report, October 2010
4. Mejri, S., Touati, H., Kamoun F.: Hop-by-hop interest rate notification and adjustment in named data networks. In: 2018 IEEE Wireless Communications and Networking Conference (WCNC), pp. 1–6(2018)
5. Aboud, A., Touati, H.: Geographic interest forwarding in NDN-based wireless sensor networks. In: 2016 IEEE/ACS 13th International Conference on Computer Systems and Applications (AICCSA), pp. 1–8(2016). https://doi.org/10.1109/AICCSA.2016.7945683
6. Kardi, A., Touati, H.: NDVN: named data for vehicular networking. Int. J. Eng. Res. Technol. (IJERT) **4**(4), 1–6 (2015)
7. Touati, H., Aboud, A., Hnich, B.: Named data networking-based communication model for Internet of Things using energy aware forwarding strategy and smart sleep mode. Concurr. Comput. Pract. Exper. **34**(3) (2022). https://doi.org/10.1002/cpe.6584
8. Mejri, S., Touati, H., Kamoun, F.: Preventing unnecessary interests retransmission in named data networking. In: 2016 International Symposium on Networks, Computers and Communications (ISNCC) (2016). https://doi.org/10.1109/isncc.2016.7746058
9. NVD - CVE-2020-25681. https://nvd.nist.gov/vuln/detail/CVE-2020-25681. Accessed 17 Mar 2022
10. Deng, L., Gao, Y., Chen, Y., Kuzmanovic, A.: Pollution attacks and defenses for Internet caching systems. Comput. Netw. **52**(5), 935–956 (2008). https://doi.org/10.1016/j.comnet.2007.11.019
11. Kumar, N., Singh, A.K., Aleem, A., Srivastava, S.: Security attacks in named data networking: a review and research directions. J. Comput. Sci. Technol. **34**(6), 1319–1350 (2019). https://doi.org/10.1007/s11390-019-1978-9

12. Hidouri, A., Hadded, M., Hajlaoui, N., Touati, H., Muhlethaler, P.: Cache pollution attacks in the NDN architecture: impact and analysis. In: 2021 International Conference on Software, Telecommunications and Computer Networks (SoftCOM), 23 September 2021. http://dx.doi.org/10.23919/softcom52868.2021.9559049
13. Lauinger, T., Laoutaris, N., Rodriguez, P., Strufe, T., Biersack, E., Kirda, E.: Privacy implications of ubiquitous caching in named data networking architectures. Technical report, Northeastern University, 2012, June 2019. https://tobias.lauinger.name/papers/ccn-cache-attackstr-iseclab-0812-001.pdf
14. Buragohain, M., Nandi, S.: Demystifying security on NDN: a survey of existing attacks and open research challenges. In: Chakraborty, M., Singh, M., Balas, V.E., Mukhopadhyay, I. (eds.) The "Essence" of Network Security: An End-to-End Panorama. LNNS, vol. 163, pp. 241–261. Springer, Singapore (2021). https://doi.org/10.1007/978-981-15-9317-8_10
15. Xie, M., Widjaja, I., Wang, H.: Enhancing cache robustness for content-centric networking. In: 2012 Proceedings IEEE INFOCOM, March 2012. https://doi.org/10.1109/infcom.2012.6195632
16. Guo, H., Wang, X., Chang, K., Tian, Y.: Exploiting path diversity for thwarting pollution attacks in named data networking. IEEE Trans. Inf. Forensics Secur. 11(9), 2077–2090 (2016). https://doi.org/10.1109/tifs.2016.2574307
17. Kamimoto, T., Mori, K., Umeda, S., Ohata, Y., Shigeno, H.: Cache protection method based on prefix hierarchy for content-oriented network. In: 2016 13th IEEE Annual Consumer Communications & Networking Conference (CCNC), January 2016. https://doi.org/10.1109/ccnc.2016.7444816
18. Zhang, G., Liu, J., Chnag, X., Chen, Z.: Combining popularity and locality to enhance in-network caching performance and mitigate pollution attacks in content-centric networking. IEEE Access 5, 19012–19022 (2017). https://doi.org/10.1109/access.2017.2754058
19. Yao, L., Fan, Z., Deng, J., Fan, X., Wu, G.: Detection and defense of cache pollution attacks using clustering in named data networks. IEEE Trans. Dependable Secure Comput. 17(6), 1310–1321 (2020). https://doi.org/10.1109/tdsc.2018.2876257
20. Hidouri, A., Touati, H., Hadded, M., Hajlaoui, N., Muhlethaler, P.: A detection mechanism for cache pollution attack in named data network architecture. In: Barolli, L., Hussain, F., Enokido, T. (eds.) Advanced Information Networking and Applications, pp. 435–446. Springer, Cham (2022). https://doi.org/10.1007/978-3-030-99584-3_38
21. Park, H., Widjaja, I., Lee, H.: Detection of cache pollution attacks using randomness checks. In: 2012 IEEE International Conference on Communications (ICC), June 2012. https://doi.org/10.1109/icc.2012.6363885
22. Karami, A., Guerrero-Zapata, M.: An ANFIS-based cache replacement method for mitigating cache pollution attacks in Named Data Networking. Comput. Netw. 80, 51–65 (2015). https://doi.org/10.1016/j.comnet.2015.01.020
23. Kumar, N., Srivast, S.: IBPC: an approach for mitigation of cache pollution attack in NDN using interface-based popularity. Research Square Platform LLC (2021). http://dx.doi.org/10.21203/rs.3.rs-682924/v1
24. Lei, K., et al.: Blockchain-based cache poisoning security protection and privacy-aware access control in NDN vehicular edge computing networks. J. Grid Comput. 18(4), 593–613 (2020). https://doi.org/10.1007/s10723-020-09531-1
25. Lauinger, T., Laoutaris, N., Rodriguez, P., Strufe, T., Biersack, E., Kirda, E.: Privacy risks in named data networking: what is the cost of performance? ACM SIGCOMM Comput. Commun. Rev. 42(5), 54–57 (2012)

26. Ntuli, N., Han, S.: Detecting router cache snooping in Named Data Networking. In: 2012 International Conference on ICT Convergence (ICTC), October 2012. https://doi.org/10.1109/ictc.2012.6387155
27. Gao, M., Zhu, X., Su, Y.: Protecting router cache privacy in named data networking. In: 2015 IEEE/CIC International Conference on Communications in China (ICCC), November 2015. https://doi.org/10.1109/iccchina.2015.7448754
28. Kumar, N., Singh, A.K., Srivastava, S.: A triggered delay-based approach against cache privacy attack in NDN. Int. J. Netw. Distrib. Comput. **6**(3), 174 (2018). https://doi.org/10.2991/ijndc.2018.6.3.5
29. Gasti, P., Tsudik, G., Uzun, E., Zhang, L.:. DoS and DDoS in named data networking. In: 2013 22nd International Conference on Computer Communication and Networks (ICCCN), July 2013 . https://doi.org/10.1109/icccn.2013.6614127
30. Kim, D., Nam, S., Bi, J., Yeom, I.: Efficient content verification in named data networking. In: Proceedings of the 2nd ACM Conference on Information-Centric Networking, 30 September 2015. https://doi.org/10.1145/2810156.2810165
31. Ghali, C., Tsudik, G., Uzun, E.: Needle in a Haystack: Mitigating content poisoning in named-data networking. In: Proceedings 2014 Workshop on Security of Emerging Networking Technologies (2014). http://dx.doi.org/10.14722/sent.2014.23014
32. Dai, H., Wang, Y., Fan, J., Liu, B.: Mitigate DDoS attacks in NDN by interest traceback. In: 2013 IEEE Conference on Computer Communications Workshops (INFOCOM WKSHPS), April 2013. https://doi.org/10.1109/infcomw.2013.6970722
33. Compagno, A., Conti, M., Gasti, P., Tsudik, G.: Poseidon: mitigating interest flooding DDoS attacks in Named Data Networking. In: 38th Annual IEEE Conference on Local Computer Networks, October 2013. https://doi.org/10.1109/lcn.2013.6761300
34. Karami, A., Guerrero-Zapata, M.: A hybrid multiobjective RBF-PSO method for mitigating DoS attacks in Named Data Networking. Neurocomputing **151**, 1262–1282 (2015). https://doi.org/10.1016/j.neucom.2014.11.003

# IPAM: An Improved Penalty Aware VM Migration Technique

Garima Singh[1]($\boxtimes$), Ruchi Tailwal[2], Meenakshi Kathayat[2],
and Anil Kumar Singh[1]

[1] Motilal Nehru National Institute of Technology Allahabad, Prayagraj, UP, India
singhgarima4688@gmail.com, ak@mnnit.ac.in
[2] Govind Ballabh Pant Institute of Engineering and Technology, Pauri, UK, India

**Abstract.** In today's era, more and more businesses are moving on the cloud. The customer needs to be assured of the quality-of-service they desire from the cloud service provider. Service level agreement (SLA) is a significant medium for building this confidence. The services are often running on virtual machines (VMs) provided by service provider. Various cloud management activities require transferring of VMs among the servers. They make use of live migration to achieve these objectives. With multiple VMs being migrated, it is essential to assign the available bandwidth among the VMs to minimize the penalty incurred due to SLA violation during migration. However, depending upon the assigned transfer rates, some VMs in the group might complete the migration process earlier than the others. In this paper, we propose an algorithm and a controller to assign freed bandwidth to the remaining VMs in the group. With extensive simulations, it is found that the penalty, migration time, and downtime for VMs is significantly reduced compared to the state-of-the-art approaches.

**Keywords:** VM migration · Service Level Agreement (SLA) · SLA violation · Cloud service provider

## 1 Introduction

Cloud computing has surfaced as a major paradigm in the field of IT. It is not just because of the web services and high-power data centers. The onus of this shift goes to virtualization, which is the key enabling technology behind the cloud. One of the salient feature offered by virtualization is VM migration, allowing transfer of virtual machine (VM) between physical servers without any change to the physical infrastructure.

VM migration is the core technology for key management activities in the cloud, such as load balancing, fault tolerance, maintenance, etc. It can be accomplished in a live or non-live manner. In non-live/cold migration, the VM is first stopped, and then the VM memory is transferred to the destination host. Once the transfer is complete, the VM is resumed at the destination. With live/hot

O. Gervasi et al. (Eds.): ICCSA 2022, LNCS 13375, pp. 324–336, 2022.
https://doi.org/10.1007/978-3-031-10522-7_23

migration, the VM is running while the migration takes place. It has a short downtime during which the services running on the VM remains unavailable and is hardly noticed by the user.

If service level agreement (SLA) [8] regulates the availability of services on the VM, the overheads due to VM migration can not be disregarded [13]. Whenever VM is migrated, downtime is inevitable. During the downtime, the services hosted on the VM will remain inaccessible. Depending on the price paid for the SLA satisfaction, for the same downtime, different penalties would be charged for different VMs [11].

This work is an extension of the penalty aware VM migration (PAM) technique [11], which tries to minimize the penalty incurred while migrating multiple VMs. The initial transfer rates are assigned to VMs using PAM for the proposed algorithm. However, depending upon the assigned transfer rate, it is possible that some of the VM might complete the migration earlier than the other VMs in the same group, and the bandwidth that was allocated to VMs which completed the migration will be freed. If there are no new tasks that require bandwidth, this freed bandwidth can be allocated to the remaining VMs in the group which has not completed the migration yet. The main contributions of this work are:

- An algorithm to assign additional bandwidths to VMs that are still in the pre-copy phase while some of the VMs have completed the migration process.
- By allocating additional bandwidth to the remaining VMs, the bandwidth utilization is improved, and the total penalty charged is reduced.
- Simulations are conducted to analyze the effect of various parameters on performance matrices for the proposed approach.

The remaining paper is arranged as follows. Section 2 discusses VM migration techniques and related work. A brief description of a model for SLA aware migration is discussed in Subsect. 2.3. Section 3 discusses the proposed algorithm to improve the performance of penalty aware migration. The experimental results for various performance matrices is discussed in Sect. 4. Finally, Sect. 5 presents the conclusion.

## 2 Background

### 2.1 VM Migration Techniques

VM migration leverages process migration and tries to solve the problem of residual dependencies faced by the latter. It can be carried out in a live/non-live manner. As the downtime and consequently service un-availability duration is more with non-live migration, the research community focuses more on live VM migration. So, in this work, we will be discussing live migration techniques only.

Live VM migration can be further carried out in pre-copy, post-copy, or hybrid manner. Any live VM migration technique consists of a *push* and/or *pull* phase with a *stop-and-copy* phase. With *pre-copy* [2], there is a *push* phase followed by a small *stop-and-copy* phase. During the *push* phase, the VM memory data is transferred from the source host to the destination host in iterations. Each subsequent iteration transfers the memory that has been dirtied in the previous round. When some terminating condition is reached, the VM is stopped, and the remaining dirty pages are transferred, after which the VM is resumed on the destination host.

*Post-copy* [5] migration first executes the *stop-and-copy* phase followed by the *pull* phase. During *stop-and-copy* phase, a small amount of data containing the necessary information to start the VM is copied from the source to the destination host, while the VM is paused at the source host. Once the data is copied, the VM is resumed at the destination host. The remaining pages are copied from the source host during the *pull* phase. *Hybrid* migration is a blend of *pre-copy* and *post-copy* migration technique. There are a limited number of iterative rounds as *pre-copy* migration followed by a *stop-and-copy* phase, after which VM is resumed at the destination host. The remaining pages are transferred during the *pull* phase as in *post-copy* migration.

## 2.2  Related Work

Pre-copy migration is more robust in comparison to post-copy and hybrid migration. That is the reason why majority of the hypervisors like XEN and VMware uses pre-copy to migrate the VMs. A great amount of research focused on improving the performance of pre-copy migration, and this subsection aims at discussing some of them.

Compression is one technique that can be used to reduce the network traffic during live migration. Data compression exploits data regularities to enhance the capability of pre-copy migration. Jin et al. proposed *MECOM* [6] that adaptively compresses the pages of the VM using different compression techniques depending upon the similarity ratio of the page. The work in [10] proposes to optimize the total downtime of multiple migrating VMs by allocating transfer rates and compression rates to VMs depending upon the available bandwidth. To shorten the VM migration duration and total data transfer on the network, many techniques try to avoid sending duplicate pages while migrating VMs by checking for inter and intra VM similarity [3,9].

Migrating multiple VMs is a strenuous task compared to single VM migration and requires careful planning. The migration resources need to be allocated among the migrating VMs in an intelligent manner, and a proper migration schedule needs to be determined to reduce the impact of migration. Cerroni and Esposito [1] proposed a transfer rate assigning scheme for multiple VMs to optimize the total migration time and total downtime. Similarly, Liu and He proposed *VMBuddies* [1] for migrating multi-tier applications over WAN. They proposed an arbitrator for assigning bandwidth to VMs so as to limit the service interruption time. It ensures that all VMs finishes migration nearly at the same time.

Whenever VMs are migrated, there might be a possibility of SLA violation. Many works have considered the placement and consolidation of VMs to minimize the chances of SLA violation. An economically enhanced resource manager

(EERM) is proposed by Macias et al. [7] to escalate the returns of the service provider. Tsakalozos et al. [12] proposed a time-constrained live migration technique to minimize the possibility of SLA violation and service degradation experienced by the customer.

## 2.3   A Model for SLA Aware VM Migration

Before discussing IPAM - an improved penalty aware migration technique, it is essential to discuss modeling live migration in the light of SLA. Although it is already mentioned in the previous works [11], this section discusses penalty aware migration in a nutshell for a better comprehension of the proposed strategy.

Assume $VM_j$ has memory size, dirty rate, and transfer rate as $M_j$, $d_j$, and $r_j$ respectively. The size of dirty memory generated during the $i^{th}$ pre-copy round ($V_{i,j}$) and the time span of the $i^{th}$ pre-copy round ($t_{i,j}$) can be computed for $VM_j$ using Eq. 1.

$$V_{i,j} = \begin{cases} M_j, & \text{if } i = 0; \\ d_j t_{i-1,j}, & \text{else} \end{cases} \quad t_{i,j} = \begin{cases} \frac{M_j}{r_j}, & \text{if } i = 0; \\ \frac{d_j t_{i-1,j}}{r_j}, & \text{else} \end{cases} \tag{1}$$

Assume for $VM_j$, $\rho_j$ is the ratio of memory dirty rate ($d_j$) and transfer rate ($r_j$), i.e., $\rho_j = d_j/r_j$. With pre-copy migration, the dirty memory transferred during the different pre-copy iterations and the duration of each iteration can be enumerated as follows:

*Iteration 0*: $V_{0,j} = M_j$ and $t_{0,j} = \frac{M_j}{r_j}$

*Iteration 1*: $V_{1,j} = d_j t_{0,j} = M_j \rho_j$ and $t_{1,j} = \frac{V_{1,j}}{r_j} = \frac{M_j \rho_j}{r_j}$

*Iteration 2*: $V_{2,j} = d_j t_{1,j} = M_j \rho_j^2$ and $t_{2,j} = \frac{V_{2,j}}{r_j} = \frac{M_j \rho_j^2}{r_j}$

$$Finally : V_{i,j} = d_j t_{i-1,j} = M_j \rho_j^i \text{ and } t_{i,j} = \frac{V_{i,j}}{r_j} = \frac{M_j \rho_j^i}{r_j} \tag{2}$$

The migration time ($TM_j$) and downtime ($TD_j$) for $VM_j$ with $n$ number of pre-copy iterations, can be calculated using the following equation.

$$TM_j = \sum_{i=0}^{n} t_{i,j} = \frac{M_j}{r_j} \sum_{i=0}^{n} \rho_j^i \quad \text{and} \quad TD_j = \frac{M_j \rho_j^n}{r_j} \tag{3}$$

To remove the complexities in modeling the problem, it is presumed that the VMs start migrating concurrently. So the total migration time is the largest of the migration time of $m$ VMs, i.e., $TMT = max \{ TM_j \mid 1 \leq j \leq m \}$

Total downtime($TDT$) determines the service inaccessibility duration for $m$ VMs during migration and can be calculated as

$$TDT = \sum_{j=1}^{m} DT_j \tag{4}$$

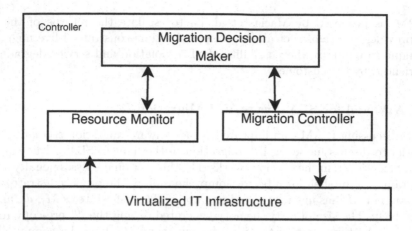

**Fig. 1.** Controller modules

The penalty incurred for migrating $VM_j$ with $Price_j$ paid by the customer for it's SLA satisfaction is assumed to be $Pen_j$. $Pen_j$ follows the properties of a Gompertz curve [14]. For this work, if the downtime is less than a threshold $TD_{min}$, no penalty is incurred. The value of $Pen_j$ is computed as follows.

$$Pen_j = \begin{cases} 0, & \text{if } TD_j \leq TD_{min}; \\ \dfrac{75}{100} e^{-e^{-100\frac{M_j \rho_j^n}{r_j} + \frac{e}{2}}} Price_j, & \text{otherwise.} \end{cases} \tag{5}$$

Further, the total penalty $(TP)$ for migrating $m$ VMs is:

$$TP(r_1, r_2, ..., r_m) = \{Pen_1 + Pen_2 + .... + Pen_m\} \tag{6}$$

Finally, the optimization problem that need to be solved is as given below:

$$\min_{r_1, r_2, ..., r_m} TP(r_1, r_2, ..., r_m) \tag{7}$$

such that

$$r_1 + r_2 + ................................ + r_m \leq B \tag{8a}$$

$$0 < r_j \leq B \tag{8b}$$

$$0 < d_j < MinRate \leq r_j \tag{8c}$$

Penalty aware migration uses Lagrange multiplier [4] for allocating transfer rates to VMs such that the objective function given in Eq. 7 is minimized, and the constrains described using Eqs. 8a–8c are satisfied. Here, $MinRate$ is the minimum guaranteed transfer rate for migrating each VM and is set to 30 Mbps in this works.

---

**Algorithm 1: Re-computeTxRate**

---

**Input:** $m$, $i$, $Rate$, $Finish$, $\alpha$

1   $Finish[i] \leftarrow 1$          ▷ $VM_i$ has completed the migration

2   $Num\_Remaining\_VMs \leftarrow m - \sum_{k=1}^{M} Finish[k]$

3   $Free\_BW \leftarrow Rate[i]$          ▷ Bandwidth freed by $VM_i$

4   $Temp\_BW \leftarrow \alpha * \frac{Free\_BW}{Num\_Remaining\_VMs}$     ▷ Extra Bandwidth to be allocated to
     remaining migrating VMs

5   **foreach** $VM_j$ **do**

6      **if** $Finish[j] \neq 1$ **then**

7          *Find min k s.t.* $\sum_{i=0}^{k} t_{i,j} >= TM_i + \tau$

8          $r_j = r_j + Temp\_BW$

9          Migrate VM$_j$ with the new transfer rate $r_j$ for round k onwards

---

## 3   Improved Penalty Aware VM Migration

Here, we put forward an algorithm to enhance the functioning of penalty aware migration, as discussed in the previous subsection. We propose a controller, as shown in Fig. 1 to regulate the allocation of transfer rates to migrating VMs depending upon the network bandwidth availability.

When a request comes to migrate multiple VMs in parallel, the migration decision maker module uses PAM to assign the initial transfer rates to VMs. The resource monitor module periodically monitors the VM performance and bandwidth availability. As some of the VMs complete migration, the resource monitor module informs the migration decision-maker about the freed bandwidth. The migration decision-maker then determines if additional bandwidth can be allocated to the remaining VMs or not.

When $VM_i$ is migrated successfully, the migration controller evokes the procedure $Re - computeTxRate$ as shown in Algorithm 1. Here, $Finish[i]$ denotes if the $VM_i$ has successfully migrated or not. Initially, $Finish[i]$ is set to 0 $\forall i \in \{1, 2, ..m\}$. When $VM_i$ successfully completes the migration, the algorithm sets the value of $Finish[i]$ to 1 (step 1). Next, we estimate the bandwidth allocated to $VM_i$ and the number of VMs which have not completed the migration, as shown in step 2 and 3. Assume $\alpha$ be the fraction of the bandwidth that the migration controller decided to assign to the remaining VMs. The additional bandwidth that can be assigned to the remaining migrating VMs are migrated is computed in step 4. Finally, step-5 to 8 assign the additional bandwidth as computed in step 4 to VMs. For simplicity, we assume that in case more bandwidth is available during the middle of pre-copy transfer round, the VM does not immediately switch to the new transfer rate. Rather, the transfer rate is updated in the subsequent rounds. Moreover, we assume that some constant time $\tau$ is required to switch to this new bandwidth. For experimental purposes, the value of $\tau$ is set to 1 sec in this work.

**Table 1.** Experimental parameters

| Parameter | Value |
|---|---|
| Max bandwidth for migration ($B$) | 1 Gbps |
| No. of pre-copy iterations ($n$) | 10 |
| Memory size of $VM_1$, $VM_2$ and $VM_3$ | [1, 1, 1] GB |
| Average memory dirtying rate for 3 VM's | [3000, 3000, 3000] pps |
| Price for $VM_1$, $VM_2$, and $VM_3$ | [1000, 500, 100] |
| Min. transfer rate ($MinRate$) | 30 MBps |

Allocating a portion of freed bandwidth to the VMs which are still migrating decreases the penalty, downtime, and migration time. However, it is possible that the migration controller decides not to assign the freed bandwidth to the remaining VMs, in such a case, the value of $\alpha$ will be 0 and the performance of IPAM will be the same as of PAM.

## 4    Experimental Results

Here we analyze the functioning of the following three approaches:

- Downtime Aware Migration (DTAM): This migration scheme tries to reduce the total downtime by efficient allocation of transfer rate as discussed in [1].
- Penalty Aware Migration (PAM): This approach tries to minimize the total penalty charged while migrating VMs as discussed in [11].
- Improved Penalty Aware Migration (IPAM): The suggested migration scheme to improve the performance of PAM.

The working of DTAM, PAM, and IPAM is analyzed in terms of penalty, migration time, and downtime experienced by the VMs during migration. The simulation parameters used in this paper are as in Table 1 until stated explicitly. Three VMs of 1 GB size each with price as 1000, 500, and 100 units are migrated under different environments. The value of $TD_{min}$ is 1 nanosecond. So, no penalty would be charged for migrating the VM if the downtime is less than or equal to 1 nanosecond. The value of $\alpha$ is 1/3 for Algorithm 1. Hence once a VM completes the migration, only one-third of the bandwidth assigned to that VM can be allocated to the remaining VMs. All the simulations are conducted in Matlab. To find the initial transfer rate for the optimization problem, *fmincon* and *globalsearch* functions provided in Matlab are used.

### 4.1    Effect of Pre-copy Rounds

This subsection studies the effect of pre-copy iterations on various parameters. Here all the 3 VMs have memory size and dirty rate fixed to 1 GB and

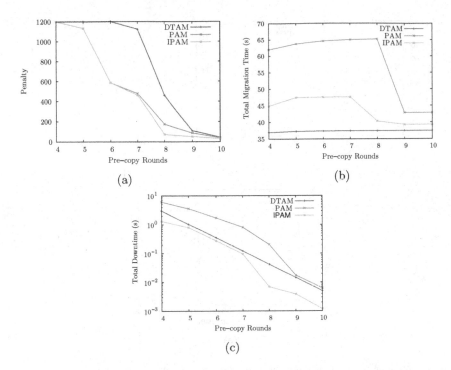

**Fig. 2.** Effect of pre-copy transfer rounds on different parameters for migrating 3 VMs with memory size and dirty rate as 1 GB and 3000 pages per second respectively. The maximum bandwidth for migration is set to 1 GB while the pre-copy rounds are varied from 4 to 10.

3000 pps[1], respectively. The maximum bandwidth available for migration is 1 Gbps, and the pre-copy iterations are varied from 4 to 10.

Figure 2a shows the penalty charged by the three approaches. With a small number of pre-copy iterations (4–6), the penalty charged by PAM and IPAM is almost the same. This is because, with a smaller number of rounds, IPAM can not reduce the downtime time of remaining VMs sufficiently. Further, as the number of rounds is increased from 6 to 9, the penalty charged by IPAM is found to be less compared to PAM. With IPAM, once a VM completes migration, the bandwidth allocated to that VM is assigned to the remaining migrating VMs, which reduces the penalty for the remaining VMs. Moreover, when the pre-copy round is 10, DTAM, PAM, and IPAM approximately impose the same penalty. All the approaches transfer the VMs with sufficiently small downtime resulting in a small penalty.

Figure 2b shows the total migration time for the different numbers of pre-copy rounds. The total migration time for IPAM is less compared to PAM but higher than DTAM. With IPAM, the VM with less price (VM$_2$ and VM$_3$) are migrated

---

[1] PPS is page dirtied per second. The size of each page is assumed to be 4 KB.

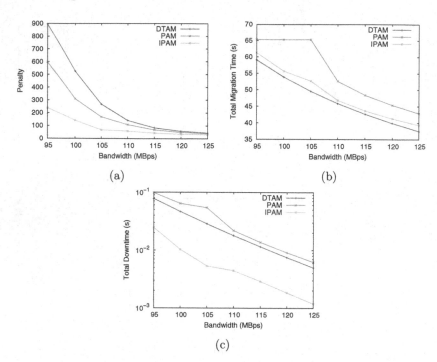

**Fig. 3.** Effect of available bandwidth for migration on different parameters for migrating 3 VMs with memory size and dirty rate as 1 GB and 3000 pages per second respectively. The number of pre-copy iterations is fixed to 10 while the maximum bandwidth available for migration is varied from 95 MBps to 125 MBps.

with less bandwidth during the initial pre-copy rounds. This results in a longer migration duration for the initial rounds. However, as $VM_1$ complete migration, the bandwidth assigned to it is available for the remaining VMs. IPAM assigns this freed bandwidth to $VM_2$ and $VM_3$ for the remaining pre-copy rounds. This results in a reduction in the migration time for $VM_2$ and $VM_3$ for the remaining pre-copy rounds.

Figure 2c shows that the total downtime for different number of pre-copy rounds. It can be seen that the total downtime for IPAM is less compared to DTAM and PAM because assigning more bandwidth to VM in the last round can significantly reduce its downtime and, consequently the total downtime will be reduced. In case multiple VMs are to be migrated and the controller decides to assign additional bandwidth to the remaining VMs, IPAM can migrate VMs with less total penalty, total migration time, and total downtime in comparison to PAM.

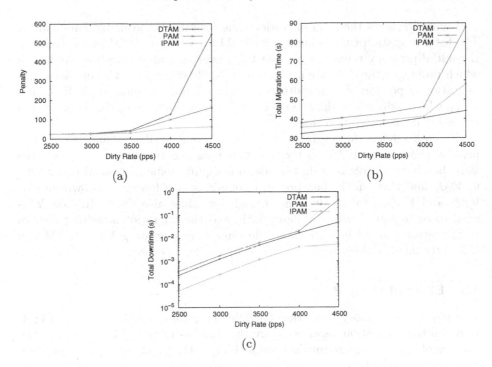

**Fig. 4.** Effect of dirty rate on different parameters for migrating 3 VMs with memory size as 1 GB. The number of pre-copy iterations and maximum bandwidth available for migration is fixed to 10 and 1 Gbps respectively. The average dirty rate is varied from 2500 pps to 4500 pps.

## 4.2 Effect of Available Bandwidth

Here, the simulation environment is the same as in Sect. 4.1 except for the number of pre-copy rounds, which is fixed to 10, while the bandwidth available for migration is varied from 95 MBps to 125 MBps.

Figure 3a presents the penalty imposed for transferring 3 VMs with different available bandwidths. It can be observed that for the same migration bandwidth, the penalty imposed by IPAM is less followed by PAM and DTAM. It is self-evident that with an increase in the bandwidth, the penalty is reduced. When more bandwidth is available for migration (125 MBps), the penalty imposed by all the approaches is approximately the same. This is because adequate bandwidth was allocated to VMs to transfer them with a small penalty. However, when the bandwidth available is reduced, the penalty imposed by IPAM was found to be less compared to PAM and DTAM. With less bandwidth, PAM allocated more bandwidth to VM with a higher price. The VMs with less price were migrated with low bandwidth, resulting in a surge in the penalty for such VMs. With IPAM, once few VMs finish the migration, a fraction of bandwidth allocated to them can be assigned to the remaining VMs for the further left pre-copy rounds.

Figure 3b shows the total migration time for different available bandwidths. The total migration time is highest for PAM followed by IPAM and DTAM. In the initial pre-copy rounds, $VM_2$ and $VM_3$ were migrated with less bandwidth which prolonged the duration of those rounds. However, as $VM_1$ completed the migration, a portion of bandwidth allocated to it was assigned to the $VM_2$ and $VM_3$, which reduced the duration of later pre-copy rounds resulting in an overall reduction in the migration time.

Figure 3c shows the total downtime for different available bandwidths. The penalty charged by IPAM is the lowest among the three approaches for the same bandwidth. This is again because of assigning some additional bandwidth to $VM_2$ and $VM_3$ in the last pre-copy rounds, which lowers the downtime for $VM_2$ and $VM_3$. Due to this, the overall downtime also drops. In case VMs need to be migrated with less bandwidth, and the migration scheduler decides to allocate the freed bandwidth to the remaining migrating VMs, IPAM can efficiently migrate them with a significantly reduced penalty.

### 4.3  Effect of Dirty Rate

The impact of memory dirty rate on different parameters is shown in Fig 4. Here, all the simulation parameters are the same as in Sect. 4.1 except that the number of the pre-copy rounds is fixed to 10, and the average rate is varied from 2500 pps to 4500 pps.

With a low dirty rate of 2500–3500 pps, the penalty imposed by PAM, IPAM, and DTAM is almost the same as shown in Fig. 4a. This is because all three approaches were able to migrate the VMs with sufficiently small downtime. This resulted in a significant reduction in the total penalty for all three. But as the dirty rate is increased beyond 3500 pps, the penalty imposed by IPAM was found to be less in contrast to PAM and DTAM. This was again because of assigning additional bandwidth to $VM_2$ and $VM_3$ during the last iteration, which reduced the downtime and consequently the penalty incurred for $VM_2$ and $VM_3$.

Figures 4b and 4c present the total migration time and total downtime for various dirty rates. The total migration time for IPAM is less compared to PAM and higher than DTAM. This is again due to less assignment of bandwidth during the initial rounds to $VM_2$ and $VM_3$ as explained in Sect. 4.2.

## 5  Conclusion and Future Work

The key technology behind cloud management activities is VM migration, providing features like resource optimization, fault tolerance, and load balancing. However, VM migration confronts various challenges. Service level agreement (SLA) is a significant factor while moving the business to the cloud and determines the degree of trust the customer puts on the service provider.

Whenever service level agreement (SLA) regulates the availability of services on the VM, the overheads due to VM migration can not be disregarded. The penalty aware migration (PAM) assigns transfer rate to the VMs to safeguard

SLA during migration. This work improves the performance of penalty aware migration by proposing an algorithm that efficiently utilizes the freed bandwidth. As few VMs in the group complete the migration process, the bandwidth allocated to them is free. This bandwidth is assigned to the remaining VMs in the group which are still in the pre-copy phase. It was found that the total migration time, total downtime, and the penalty incurred are sufficiently reduced with the proposed approach.

Although this work mathematically models live migration in the light of SLA to efficiently utilize the available bandwidth, real-time implementation is left for the future. Further, the work can be extended to consider multiple SLAs for a service and agreed-upon penalty clauses in case of their violation.

**Acknowledgment.** This work was supported by the Ministry of Electronics and Information Technology (MEITY), Government of India under Visvesvaraya PhD Scheme for Electronics and IT (Grant no. PhD-MLA-4(20)/2015–16).

# References

1. Cerroni, W., Esposito, F.: Optimizing live migration of multiple virtual machines. IEEE Trans. Cloud Comput. **6**(4), 1096–1109 (2016)
2. Clark, C., et. al.: Live migration of virtual machines. In: Proceedings of the 2nd Conference on Symposium on Networked Systems Design & Implementation, vol. 2, pp. 273–286 (2005)
3. Deshpande, U., Wang, X., Gopalan, K.: Live gang migration of virtual machines. In: Proceedings of the 20th International Symposium on High Performance Distributed Computing, pp. 135–146 (2011)
4. Gavin, H.P., Scruggs, J.T.: Constrained optimization using Lagrange multipliers. CEE 201L. Duke University (2012)
5. Hines, M.R., Deshpande, U., Gopalan, K.: Post-copy live migration of virtual machines. ACM SIGOPS Operating Syst. Rev. **43**(3), 14–26 (2009)
6. Jin, H., Deng, L., Wu, S., Shi, X., Chen, H., Pan, X.: MECOM: live migration of virtual machines by adaptively compressing memory pages. Future Gener. Comput. Syst. **38**, 23–35 (2014)
7. Macías, M., Rana, O., Smith, G., Guitart, J., Torres, J.: Maximizing revenue in grid markets using an economically enhanced resource manager. Concurrency Comput. Pract. Experience **22**(14), 1990–2011 (2010)
8. Parkin, M., Badia, R.M., Martrat, J.: A comparison of SLA use in six of the european commissions FP6 projects. Institute on Resource Management and Scheduling, CoreGRID-Network of Excellence, Tech. Rep. TR-0129 (2008)
9. Riteau, P., Morin, C., Priol, T.: Shrinker: improving live migration of virtual clusters over wans with distributed data deduplication and content-based addressing. In: Jeannot, E., Namyst, R., Roman, J. (eds.) Euro-Par 2011. LNCS, vol. 6852, pp. 431–442. Springer, Heidelberg (2011). https://doi.org/10.1007/978-3-642-23400-2_40
10. Singh, G., Singh, A.K.: Optimizing multi-VM migration by allocating transfer and compression rate using geometric programming. Simul. Model. Pract. Theory **106**, 102201 (2021)

11. Singh, G., Singh, A.K.: Optimization of SLA aware live migration of multiple virtual machines using lagrange multiplier. Future Gener. Comput. Syst. (2022)
12. Tsakalozos, K., Verroios, V., Roussopoulos, M., Delis, A.: Live VM migration under time-constraints in share-nothing IaaS-clouds. IEEE Trans. Parallel Distrib. Syst. **28**(8), 2285–2298 (2017)
13. Voorsluys, W., Broberg, J., Venugopal, S., Buyya, R.: Cost of virtual machine live migration in clouds: a performance evaluation. In: Jaatun, M.G., Zhao, G., Rong, C. (eds.) CloudCom 2009. LNCS, vol. 5931, pp. 254–265. Springer, Heidelberg (2009). https://doi.org/10.1007/978-3-642-10665-1_23
14. Winsor, C.P.: The Gompertz curve as a growth curve. Proc. Nat. Acad. Sci. U.S. Am. **18**(1), 1 (1932)

# Reducing Cache Miss Rate Using Thread Oversubscription to Accelerate an MPI-OpenMP-Based 2-D Hopmoc Method

F. L. Cabral[1]([✉]), C. Osthoff[1], and S. L. Gonzaga de Oliveira[2]

[1] Laboratório Nacional de Computação Científica (LNCC), CENAPAD,
Petrópolis, Brazil
{fcabral,osthoff}@lncc.br
[2] Universidade Federal de São Paulo, São José dos Campos, SP, Brazil
sanderson.oliveira@unifesp.br

**Abstract.** This paper applies the MPI-OpenMP-based two-dimensional Hopmoc method using the explicit work-sharing technique with a recently proposed mechanism to reduce implicit barriers in OpenMP. Specifically, this paper applies the numerical algorithm to yield approximate solutions to the advection-diffusion equation. Additionally, this article splits the mesh used by the numerical method and distributes them to over-allocated threads. The mesh partitions became so small that the approach reduced the cache miss rate. Consequently, the strategy accelerated the numerical method in multicore systems. This paper then evaluates the results of implementing the strategy under different metrics. As a result, the set of techniques improved the performance of the parallel numerical method.

**Keywords:** Parallel computing · OpenMP · MPI · High performance computing · Thread oversubscription

## 1 Introduction

Researchers use partial differential equations to describe relevant problems in different areas. Examples include scientific and engineering applications in aerospace, petroleum, environmental, chemical and biomedical engineering, geoscience, and elsewhere. In more specific problems, practitioners use partial differential equations to describe flow problems inherent in geology, oceanography, and the propagation of pollutants in different media such as water and air. Specifically, we consider the advection-diffusion equation $u_t + vu_x = du_{xx}$, where $v$ and $d$ are positive constants of velocity and diffusion, respectively.

A recent publication [1] used the two-dimensional Hopmoc method to approximate the solution of advection-diffusion equations with dominant convection [2]. The Hopmoc method calculates the convection process for each time semi-step,

© The Author(s), under exclusive license to Springer Nature Switzerland AG 2022
O. Gervasi et al. (Eds.): ICCSA 2022, LNCS 13375, pp. 337–353, 2022.
https://doi.org/10.1007/978-3-031-10522-7_24

eliminating the second term on the left side of the original equation, reducing the equation to the problem $u_t = du_{xx}$. Afterward, the method calculates the diffusion process by dividing the computational mesh into two subsets calculated alternately in each time semi-step, one with an explicit approach and the other with an implicit approach. Although it is an implicit method, this approach does not apply a linear equation systems solver.

Algorithms of this nature enable parallelism and other strategies. Furthermore, the two-dimensional Hopmoc method increases the application performance and low-cost approximate solutions using highly refined meshes [1]. These characteristics contribute to studying the results more accurately and closer to reality.

This paper studies the effect that thread oversubscription (i.e., a quantity of threads higher than the number of available threads) has on the performance of an MPI-OpenMP-based numerical method while also considering the influence of synchronization. Specifically, this paper analyzes the performance of a parallel resource thread oversubscription strategy applied in an MPI-OpenMP-based numerical algorithm in multicore computing environments. The study focuses on the potential benefits of oversubscription for reducing cache misses and increasing application speedup. Thus, the paper uses the 2-D Hopmoc method to approximate the solution to the advection-diffusion equation. Furthermore, the study provides two implementations of the approach for comparison. A naive version uses regular parallel work-sharing loops with barriers at the end of each semi-step. A second implementation, called MPI-OMP-EWS, uses fine-grain synchronization between consecutive regions, allowing a point-to-point synchronization between threads working on adjacent data.

This paper organizes the remainder of the text as follows. We present the related work in Sect. 2. Afterward, we describe the two-dimensional Hopmoc method implemented with OpenMP and MPI [3] in Sect. 3. In Sect. 4, we explain two variants of the Hopmoc algorithm. In Sect. 5, we describe how we performed the tests. In Sect. 6, we show the results. Finally, in Sect. 7, we address the conclusions.

## 2   Related Work

Practitioners have developed different techniques to reduce cache miss in applications executed in multicore systems (e.g., [4–6]). Cabral et al. [7] showed the performance of the Hopmoc method in a shared memory computing environment Intel® MIC Xeon® Phi using the OpenMP programming model. The publication compared a naive version of the Hopmoc algorithm with a strategy that used the explicit task chunk technique. The study concluded that this second alternative reduced overhead and spin times. Cabral et al. [7–11] employed a total variation diminishing scheme to increase the accuracy of the Hopmoc method.

Cabral et al. [9] implemented the Hopmoc method using the explicit work-sharing technique and more efficient OpenMP directives. The authors referred to this approach as the OMP-EWS strategy.

Cabral et al. [11] employed an explicit work-sharing approach alongside a specific synchronization mechanism. The strategies achieved reasonable speedups in both multi-core and manycore architectures.

A recent publication [1] proposed a mechanism to accelerate the hybrid MPI-OpenMP-based two-dimensional Hopmoc method in a multicore system. Furthermore, the study used a hybrid version of the two-dimensional Hopmoc algorithm based on MPI and OMP-EWS. The article referred to the strategy as MPI-OMP-EWS. The paper compared three two-dimensional numerical methods on different Intel® processors.

In general, publications avoid thread oversubscriptions because the technique introduces prohibitive overheads due to excessive thread preemptive scheduling, context switch costs, loss of locality, and contention on shared resources. On the other hand, previous studies have successfully explored the thread oversubscription technique [12–15].

Iancu et al. [12] evaluated the impact of task oversubscription on the performance of MPI, OpenMP, and UPC implementations of the NAS Parallel Benchmarks on UMA and NUMA multi-socket architectures. The authors evaluated explicit thread affinity management against the default Linux load balancing and considered sharing and partitioning system management strategies. The authors observed that sharing the available cores between applications provided better throughput than explicit partitioning. Modest levels of oversubscription improved system throughput by 27% and provided better performance isolation of applications. Their results indicated that the determining behavioral factor when applications share a system is the granularity of the synchronization tasks.

Navarro et al. [13] addressed the problem of the underutilization of the CPU core where a host thread operates. The authors evaluated a host thread blocking strategy combined with oversubscription that delegated to the operating system the duty of scheduling threads to available CPU cores to guarantee that all cores executed practical work. The authors observed that allowing oversubscription controlled by the operating system could be favorable under specified scenarios.

Jiang et al. [14] examined a shared memory multi-threaded approach to streamline tracing that targets data-intensive architectures. Their study pointed out that thread oversubscription of streamlined tasks is an effective technique for hiding I/O latency.

Huang et al. [15] conducted a comprehensive study of the overhead of thread oversubscription. The authors found that the direct cost of context switching does not cause a noticeable performance slowdown in most applications. Furthermore, the authors observed that oversubscription could be both constructive and destructive to the performance of CPU caches.

# 3    Hybrid Version of the Hopmoc Method Based on MPI and OpenMP

Hopmoc is a numerical strategy that provides approximate solutions to convection-dominated advection-diffusion equations. The method integrates features from the Hopscotch algorithm [16] and the modified method of characteristics (MMOC) [17]. Thus, the approach allows the separation of variables through characteristic curves.

The Hopmoc algorithm divides the computational mesh into two distinct sets. Then, the algorithm explicitly updates the first set of unknowns in the first time semi-step. Subsequently, the method implicitly updates the second set of unknowns in the second time semi-step. The algorithm alternates the two groups of unknowns at each time step. Thus, the method does not apply a linear system. Each iteration of the main while loop represents a time step. This main loop executes a set of loops responsible for alternately performing explicit and implicit calculations of the two time semi-steps of each time step. Algorithm 1 depicts the pseudocode of the Hopmoc method.

```
1  begin
2  |    Each MPI process computes its partition mesh
3  |    Each OMP thread computes its local
4  |    mesh inside the partition mesh allocated to a process
5  |    while time < FinalTime do
6  |    |    ...
7  |    |    lock
8  |    |    for columns in the thread local mesh do
9  |    |    |    for all lines in the input mesh do
10 |    |    |    |    MMOC or an explicit or implicit time semi-step
11 |    |    unlock
12 |    |    Each OMP thread waits for its neighbours
13 |    |    ...
```

**Algorithm 1:** Overview of the Hopmoc method.

The hybrid version of the Hopmoc method is a strategy that uses both OpenMP threads and MPI processes to split the workload and allow for efficient parallelization [1]. The implementation divides the input mesh into smaller partitions. The approach permanently assigns each of these partitions to a process. The strategy guarantees the first level of parallelism, using MPI processes exclusively. Next, each MPI process divides its workload among the available threads. Specifically, the approach parallelizes all inner for loops in the main outer while loop. This process guarantees the second level of parallelism, therefore, using threads exclusively.

## 4    Two Implementations of the Hopmoc Method

In this section, we present two implementations of the Hopmoc method. The two variations differ in the way thread parallelism is applied. Thus, we divided this section into two parts. The first, presented in Sect. 4.1, is intended to explain the naive implementation of the Hopmoc method. In Sect. 4.2, we describe the hybrid version of the MPI-OpenMP-based two-dimensional Hopmoc algorithm.

### 4.1  Naive Implementation

The thread-level parallelism of this implementation uses standard OpenMP directives. Furthermore, inner the outer loop, each for loop immediately precedes an OpenMP directive **#pragma omp parallel for**. Algorithm 2 shows an overview of the parallelization used in the naive implementation.

```
 1  begin
 2  │   while time < FinalTime do
 3  │   │   #pragma omp parallel for
 4  │   │   for all columns in the input mesh do
 5  │   │   │   for all lines in the input mesh do
 6  │   │   │   │   Modified method of characteristics

 7  │   │   #pragma omp parallel for
 8  │   │   for all columns in the input mesh do
 9  │   │   │   for all lines in the input mesh do
10  │   │   │   │   First explicit time semi-step

11  │   │   #pragma omp parallel for
12  │   │   for all columns in the input mesh do
13  │   │   │   for all lines in the input mesh do
14  │   │   │   │   First implicit time semi-step

15  │   │   #pragma omp parallel for
16  │   │   for all columns in the input mesh do
17  │   │   │   for all lines in the input mesh do
18  │   │   │   │   Second explicit time semi-step

19  │   │   #pragma omp parallel for
20  │   │   for all columns in the input mesh do
21  │   │   │   for all lines in the input mesh do
22  │   │   │   │   Second implicit time semi-step
```

**Algorithm 2:** Overview of the parallel naive implementation.

### 4.2  MPI-OMP-EWS Strategy

The MPI-OMP-EWS-based two-dimensional Hopmoc method relies on a parallelization mechanism consisting of two main techniques: explicit work-sharing (EWS) and synchronization between adjacent threads (AdjSync) [1]. The EWS technique explicitly divides the mesh partitions allocated to the MPI process among the available threads. The approach assigns permanently to each thread a mesh partition. Furthermore, the MPI-OMP-EWS strategy performs a 1-D partitioning of the mesh. For example, consider a mesh composed of $10^4 \times 10^4$ stencil points. In this example, each thread receives $10^4$ mesh lines. Moreover, each thread holds $10^4$ mesh lines divided by the number of threads set for the execution. For example, when the run uses 1,000 threads, each thread receives a partition composed of $10^4 \times 10$ stencil points.

The AdjSync mechanism is responsible for synchronizing the threads available in the process. With this approach, synchronization does not wait for all threads to reach the same synchronization point as performed in the naive implementation. Instead, the strategy only synchronizes adjacent threads. Furthermore, the approach only synchronizes each thread with its two adjacent threads, i.e., a previous thread and a succeeding thread.

Algorithm 3 shows an overview of the parallelization used in the implementation based on the MPI-OMP-EWS strategy. Before each inner for loop, the thread informs its neighbors of an execution block (see line 3 in Algorithm 3). Afterward, the thread removes this lock and waits until its neighbors perform the same operation (see line 7 in Algorithm 3).

```
1 begin
2 │   ...
3 │   lock
4 │   for columns in the partition mesh do
5 │   │   for all lines in the input mesh do
6 │   │   │   MMOC or an explicit or implicit time semi-step
7 │   unlock
8 │   ...
```

**Algorithm 3:** Pseudocode excerpt of parallel Hopmoc method using MPI-OMP-EWS.

The implementation allocates one MPI process to each machine's CPU in executions without thread oversubscription. Additionally, we executed the hybrid MPI-OMP-EWS strategy using from one thread to the maximum number of OpenMP threads per MPI process.

# 5   Description of the Tests

The first machine used in the tests featured a computer with two Intel® Xeon® processors E5-2698 v3, each composed of 32 physical cores, hyperthreading disabled, and total memory of 112 GB. The operating system was the CentOS Linux version 7.3.1611 (Core). We refer to this computer as the M1 machine. We extracted results from the Intel® VTune™ Amplifier performance profiler in executions performed on this machine.

The second machine used in the experiments a computer with four Intel®
Xeon® Gold 6230R, each composed of 26 physical cores, with hyperthreading
enabled (two threads per core) and total memory of 384 GB. We refer to this
computer as the M2 machine. We used the mpiicpc (Intel® C++ compiler) with
the optimization flags -O3 and -xHost to generate the executable codes in the
two computers.

We conducted an exploratory investigation to determine the number of iterations. With more than 1,000 iterations, there was no change in speedup in the
two versions of the two-dimensional Hopmoc method used in this study. With
less than 1,000 iterations, the speedup was worse than with 1,000 iterations. This
feature occurred because of a lack of workload. Thus, the simulations performed
1,000 iterations in each execution of the two-dimensional Hopmoc method.

At the beginning of an experiment, the experiment allocated an MPI process
to each CPU. This allocation meant that the execution used two (four) MPI
processes in the experiment performed on the M1 (M2) machine. Afterward, the
test increased the number of threads from 1 to 32 (52) in the simulation conducted on the M1 (M2) computer system. When the run used 32 (52) threads
per CPU, each physical core had one (two) thread(s) in the experiment performed on the M1 (M2) machine, recalling that we enabled the hyperthreading
on the M2 high-performance unit. Subsequently, the test over-allocated threads,
maintaining 32 (52) threads per process in the experiment performed on the M1
(M2) machine. Afterward, the simulation increased the number of MPI processes
from 2 to 200 (74), totaling 3,200 (3744) threads in the experiment performed
on the M1 (M2) machine. Above these quantities, the standard MPI aborted the
execution, indicating a system resource limit. The test incremented the number
of MPI processes by two (four) in the experiment executed on the M1 (M2)
machine so that each CPU had the same number of threads.

The runs had exclusive access to the hardware, i.e., no other tasks were running simultaneously. We calculated the speedup as the ratio between serial version and parallel implementation times. The experiments ensured convergence as
the 2-D Hopmoc method is convergent [18] and because the odd-even Hopscotch
method shows unconditional numerical stability [19].

# 6   Results and Analysis

This section shows speedup metrics for two high-performance systems and L1,
L2, and L3 cache miss for one of the systems. Additionally, we measured syn-
chronization overhead concerning the overall execution and spin times regarding
CPU time. Sections 6.1 and 6.2 show the experiment performed on the M1 and
M2 machines, respectively.

## 6.1   Experiment Performed on the M1 Machine

We executed the MPI-OMP-EWS-based implementation with a mesh composed
of $10^3 \times 10^3$ stencil points. In this test, the thread oversubscription technique

did not benefit the performance of the MPI-OMP-EWS-based implementation. Despite the small mesh partitions in each thread, the high overhead costs required to handle the high number of threads outweighed the cache miss rate reduction.

Additionally, we executed the MPI-OMP-EWS-based implementation using a mesh composed of $10^5 \times 10^5$ stencil points. Again in this test, the thread oversubscription technique did not benefit the performance of the MPI-OMP-EWS-based implementation. Thread oversubscription would require many threads to improve the MPI-OMP-EWS-based implementation executed with a large-scale mesh. With a high number of threads, the mesh partition of each thread would probably be small enough to reduce cache miss rates. However, the Intel® VTune™ Amplifier performance profiler indicated high cache miss rates even when the system reached the limits of MPI processes and OpenMP threads.

Figure 1 shows the speedup of executions of the two implementations evaluated in this study. The simulation used a two-dimensional mesh composed of $10^4 \times 10^4$ points, employing $10^{-4}$ as a variation of the mesh spacing. We performed executions with up to 3,200 threads. However, the figure shows the results of runs with 1,100 threads in the plot. Specifically, the behavior of the results does not differ when the runs used more than 1,100 threads. The serial versions of the naive and MPI/OMP-EWS implementations took 1423 s and 1420 s, respectively. Up to approximately 500, the speedup of the two approaches was very close ($\approx$6x) with slight superiority of the implementation with the MPI-OMP-EWS strategy. The speedup of the MPI-OMP-EWS approach increased to more than 25x when executed with more than 500 threads until approximately 1,000 threads. However, the speedup of the naive implementation remained at approximately 6x.

The naive version does not have the mesh partitioned as performed in the implementation using the MPI-OMP-EWS strategy. We implemented the former with the directive **#pragma omp parallel for** as reported in Sect. 4.1 and the latter as described in Sect. 4.2. Thus, the naive version distributes loop iterations among existing threads. Therefore, there is no data partitioning, and each thread does not know in advance its data partition, as performed in the implementation that uses the MPI-OMP-EWS strategy. Thus, the speedup of the naive version yielded a maximum of 6.5x with 32 threads.

Figures 2 and 3 show the L1 and L2 cache miss counts from executions of naive and MPI-OMP-EWS-based implementations of the two-dimensional Hopmoc method. This test varied the number of threads from 1 to 3,200. Figure 4 shows the results of the last level cache (LLC) miss rate for executions of the two implementations evaluated in this study. The results yielded by the two approaches in runs with up to 500 threads are very similar $\left( \approx 3 \cdot 10^9 \right)$. With executions using more than 500 threads, the cache miss rate in LLC memory with the naive implementation increases. With runs with threads ranging from 500 to 700, the cache miss rate in LLC memory of the code based on the MPI-OMP-EWS strategy decreases significantly, reaching less than $10^9$ in executions using more than 700 threads. With runs with the implementation based on the

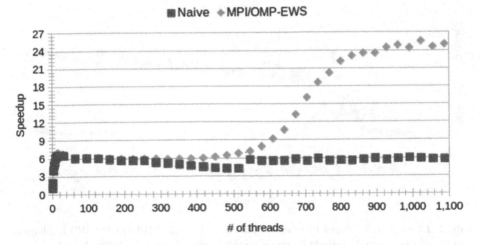

**Fig. 1.** Speedups from executions of naive and MPI-OMP-EWS implementations of the two-dimensional Hopmoc method using from 1 to 1,100 threads.

MPI-OMP-EWS approach using more than 500 threads, possibly, the mesh partitions are too small. Thus, we suppose the mesh partitions remain at the same cache memory level. We consider that the use of tread oversubscription creates mesh partitions very small. Consequently, we assume that the process efficiently allocates the small mesh partitions in the same cache memory level. This process possibly requires a short time to create and schedule these threads.

As previously mentioned, Fig. 4 shows that the cache miss rate in LLC memory becomes low when using more than 700 threads in the implementation based on the MPI-OMP-EWS strategy. Even with this number of threads, the implementation speedup was ≈16x (see Fig. 1). The speedup of the implementation was more than 25x when using more than 1,000 threads. Therefore, the cache hit rate in LLC memory does not explain this speedup gain. Thus, when the implementation employed 700 to 1,000 threads, the cache hit rate becomes higher in L2 cache-memory and subsequently in L1 cache memory (see Figs. 2 and 3).

Figure 5 shows the results of the ratio of Spin time to CPU time. Spin time is the time in synchronization barriers (i.e., the time the code waits for all threads to be synchronized and ready to work) in routines that process threads, such as the creation and scheduling. CPU time is the metric that represents the amount of time that a CPU uses for processing instructions of a process. Thus, CPU time is neither Spin time nor Overhead time, but the processing time in calculations and procedures specific to the method. Figure 5 shows that the ratio between Spin time and CPU time in the naive execution was always higher than in the MPI-OMP-EWS-based version.

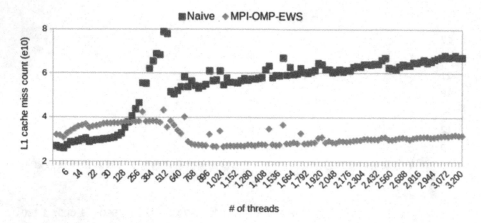

**Fig. 2.** L1 cache miss count from executions of naive and MPI-OMP-EWS implementations of the two-dimensional Hopmoc method using from 1 to 3,200 threads.

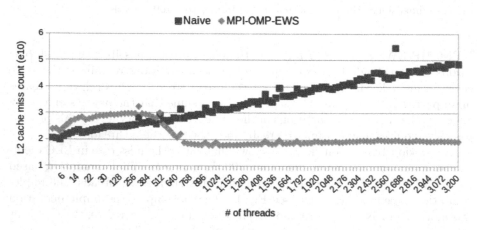

**Fig. 3.** L2 cache miss count from executions of naive and MPI-OMP-EWS implementations of the two-dimensional Hopmoc method using from 1 to 3,200 threads.

Figure 6 exhibits the results of the ratio of overhead time to CPU time. Overhead time is the time in the routines of the operating system. The figure also shows that the performance profiles change in executions using more than 500 threads. The proportion between overhead time and CPU time always grew. This proportion increased significantly when the runs used more than 500.

Figure 6 shows that the computational cost of creating, allocating, and scheduling several threads did not significantly increase the total running time. Specifically, for approximately 500 to 2,000 threads, the overhead time

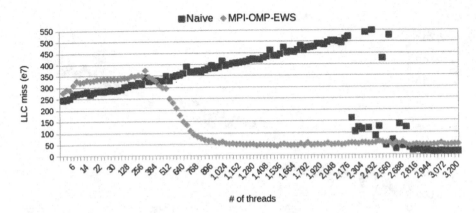

**Fig. 4.** LLC miss count from executions of naive and MPI-OMP-EWS implementations of the two-dimensional Hopmoc method using from 1 to 3,200 threads.

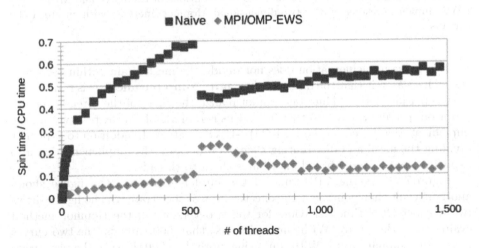

**Fig. 5.** Spin time by CPU time ratio of executions of the naive and MPI-OMP-EWS-based implementations of the two-dimensional Hopmoc method with up to 1,500 threads.

represented less than 2% of the productive processing time of the method. This result points out the effectiveness of the thread oversubscription technique in the MPI-OMP-EWS strategy: reducing mesh segments to their adequacy to the cache memory size compensated for the time to over-allocate threads (preemptive scheduling and context switching between threads).

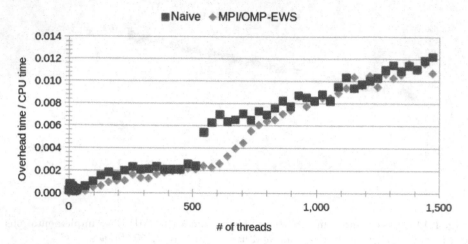

**Fig. 6.** Overhead time by CPU time ratio of executions of the naive and MPI-OMP-EWS implementations of the two-dimensional Hopmoc method with up to 1,500 threads.

The naive implementation does not divide the mesh again within each process. The reason is that the directive **#pragma omp parallel for** is responsible for the parallelization. Thus, one cannot realize the effect of the thread oversubscription technique. On the other hand, this is remarkable in the tests within the implementation based on the MPI-OMP-EWS strategy. In addition to explicitly dividing the mesh and distributing them to processes, this implementation also explicitly splits the mesh and distributes them to threads.

Figure 7 shows the CPU time of the implementations. The figure shows another result that points out the effectiveness of the strategy. The figure shows two distinct CPU time behaviors for the two versions of the Hopmoc method evaluated in this study. With runs using less than 500 threads, the two curves have a very similar profile. With runs using more than 500 threads, the two curves differ. There is a drop with discontinuity, and then the curve rises again with less slope in the curve representing the CPU time of the naive implementation. The CPU time is reduced continuously in the variant with the MPI-OMP-EWS strategy. Then, the results stabilize with executions with more than 700 threads.

These results reaffirm and agree with those presented in the plots that show the speedup, L1, L2, and last level cache rate miss (see Figs. 1, 2, 3, and 4). While there is a reduction in the cache miss in LLC, there is a significant decrease in CPU time for the Hopmoc method based on the MPI-OMP-EWS strategy, which directly leads to a higher speedup (see Fig. 1).

We previously mentioned that the naive implementation does not have an explicit second division inside each process as is performed in the MPI-OMP-EWS

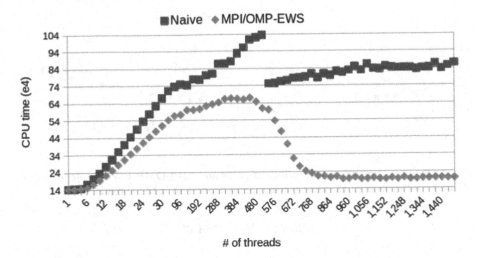

**Fig. 7.** CPU time of naive and MPI-OMP-EWS-based implementations of the two-dimensional Hopmoc method with up to 1,500 threads.

strategy. Thus, the naive implementation is less sensitive to cache miss reduction and, consequently, to its benefits.

Figure 8 shows the running times of other simulations performed with the two implementations evaluated in this study. The simulation used a two-dimensional mesh composed of $2 \times 10^4 \times 2 \times 10^4$ points, employing $2 \times 10^{-4}$ as a variation of the mesh spacing. The serial versions of the naive and MPI/OMP-EWS implementations took 5654 s and 5848 s, respectively. The two versions took similar running times when using up to 600 threads. When using more than 600 threads, the MPI-OMP-EWS-based implementation was remarkably faster than the naive implementation.

## 6.2   Experiment Performed on the M2 Machine

Figure 9 shows the speedup for the two implementations evaluated in this study. The simulations used a two-dimensional mesh composed of $10^4 \times 10^4$ points, employing $10^{-4}$ as a variation of the mesh spacing. The serial versions of the naive and MPI/OMP-EWS implementations took 1382 s and 1174 s, respectively.

The MPI-OMP-EWS-based implementation increased the speedup from 1 to 68 threads. We recall that 104 physical cores and 208 threads comprise the machine. Up to 416 threads, the speedup was approximately 33x. Then, the speedup increased to 165x with 3,744 threads. The serial version of the MPI-OMP-EWS-based version probably had a high cache miss rate. We used the

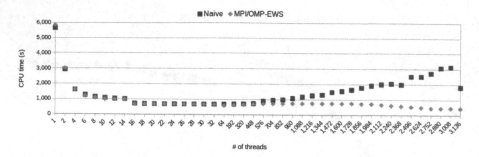

**Fig. 8.** Running times from executions of naive and MPI-OMP-EWS implementations of the two-dimensional Hopmoc method using from 1 to 3,136 threads.

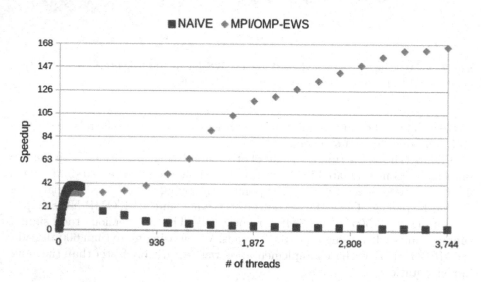

**Fig. 9.** Speedups from executions of naive and MPI-OMP-EWS-based implementations of the two-dimensional Hopmoc method using from 1 to 3,744 threads.

thread oversubscription technique to reduce this problem. Consequently, the use of the approach improved the performance of the implementation.

The naive implementation yielded a speedup of 40x using 106 to 248 threads. Then, the speedup of the implementation decreased, returning a speedup of 2x with 3,744 threads.

# 7    Conclusions

We performed an experiment using the MPI-OMP-EWS strategy in the two-dimensional Hopmoc algorithm in executions performed on a computer with two Intel® Xeon® processors E5-2698 v3, composed of 32 physical cores. The MPI-OMP-EWS-based implementation yielded a speedup of 7x running with 32 threads. When using the thread oversubscription technique, the speedup of the implementation increased to 25x, almost reaching a speedup equal to the number of physical cores of the machine.

We also experimented with the MPI-OMP-EWS-based implementation of the two-dimensional Hopmoc algorithm executions on a computer with four Intel® Xeon® Gold 6230R, composed of 104 physical cores and 208 threads. The MPI-OMP-EWS-based implementation yielded a speedup of 35x running with 208 threads. When using the thread oversubscription technique, the speedup of the implementation increased to 165x.

The focus of this study was to reduce the sizes of the numerical method mesh partitions so that they can fit in the same level of cache memory. As a result, communication between the segments would be less costly. The implementation achieved this objective using the thread oversubscription technique in the experiments.

Although the overhead time of allocation and scheduling (preemptive scheduling and context switching between threads) of threads, the experiment achieved a satisfactory result with the MPI-OMP-EWS strategy applied to implement a parallel version of the two-dimensional Hopmoc method in tandem with the thread oversubscription technique. Thus, this paper showed that the MPI-OMP-EWS process enables an efficient performance of the 2-D Hopmoc method using thread oversubscription. The approach allowed it by eliminating the implicit barriers of the OpenMP standard and reducing the spin time. The conclusion is that for fine-grain synchronization, oversubscription of threads through MPI is beneficial.

We intend to continue this study to confirm the possibility of extracting a high performance in parallelism and efficiently using the physical resources of a multicore system. We plan to conduct new experiments with the parallel techniques used in this study. We also plan to continue this study by employing the strategy in other numerical methods executed in different microarchitectures, such as the third-generation Intel® Xeon® Scalable processors.

**Acknowledgments.** CAPES - Coordenação de Aperfeioamento de Pessoal de Nvel Superior (Coordination for Enhancement of Higher Education Personnel, Brazil) supported this study.

# References

1. Cabral, F.L., Gonzaga de Oliveira, S.L., Osthoff, C., Costa, G.P., Brandão, D.N., Kischinhevsky, M.: An evaluation of MPI and OpenMP paradigms in finite-difference explicit methods for PDEs on shared-memory multi- and manycore systems. Concurrency Comput. Pract. Exp. **32**(20), e5642 (2020). e5642 cpe.5642
2. Oliveira, S., Kischinhevsky, M., Gonzaga de Oliveira, S.L.: Convergence analysis of the Hopmoc method. Int. J. Comput. Math. **86**, 1375–1393 (2009)
3. MPI Forum. MPI forum (2022). https://www.mpi-forum.org/. Accessed 20 Mar 2022
4. Prisaganec, M., Mitrevski, P.J.: Reducing competitive cache misses in modern processor architectures. Int. J. Comput. Sci. Inf. Technol. (IJCSIT) **8**(6), 49–57 (2016)
5. Cassales, G., Gomes, H., Bifet, A., Pfahringer, B., Senger, H.: Improving parallel performance of ensemble learners for streaming data through data locality with mini-batching. In: IEEE 22nd International Conference on High Performance Computing and Communications; IEEE 18th International Conference on Smart City; IEEE 6th International Conference on Data Science and Systems (HPCC/SmartCity/DSS), Yanuca Island, Cuvu, Fiji. IEEE (2020)
6. Alperen, A., Afibuzzaman, M., Rabbi, F., Ozkaya, M.Y., Catalyurek, U., Aktulga, H.M.: An evaluation of task-parallel frameworks for sparse solvers on multicore and manycore CPU architectures. In: ICPP 2021: 50th International Conference on Parallel Processing, pp. 1–11 (2021)
7. Cabral, F.L., Osthoff, C., Costa, G.P., Brandão, D., Kischinhevsky, M., Gonzaga de Oliveira, S.L.: Tuning up the TVD-HOPMOC method on Intel MIC Xeon Phi architectures with Intel Parallel Studio tools. In: 2017 International Symposium on Computer Architecture and High Performance Computing Workshops (SBAC-PADW), pp. 19–24. IEEE (2017)
8. Brandão, D.N., Gonzaga de Oliveira, S.L., Kischinhevsky, M., Osthoff, C., Cabral, F.: A total variation diminishing Hopmoc scheme for numerical time integration of evolutionary differential equations. In: Gervasi, O., et al. (eds.) ICCSA 2018. LNCS, vol. 10960, pp. 53–66. Springer, Cham (2018). https://doi.org/10.1007/978-3-319-95162-1_4
9. Cabral, F.L., Osthoff, C., Costa, G.P., Gonzaga de Oliveira, S.L., Brandão, D., Kischinhevsky, M.: An OpenMP implementation of the TVD–Hopmoc method based on a synchronization mechanism using locks between adjacent threads on Xeon Phi (TM) accelerators. In: Shi, Y., et al. (eds.) ICCS 2018. LNCS, vol. 10862, pp. 701–707. Springer, Cham (2018). https://doi.org/10.1007/978-3-319-93713-7_67
10. Cabral, F., et al.: An improved OpenMP implementation of the TVD–Hopmoc method based on a cluster of points. In: Senger, H., et al. (eds.) VECPAR 2018. LNCS, vol. 11333, pp. 132–145. Springer, Cham (2019). https://doi.org/10.1007/978-3-030-15996-2_10
11. Cabral, F.L., et al.: Fine-tuning an OpenMP-based TVD–Hopmoc method using Intel® parallel studio XE tools on Intel® Xeon® architectures. In: Meneses, E., Castro, H., Barrios Hernández, C.J., Ramos-Pollan, R. (eds.) CARLA 2018. CCIS, vol. 979, pp. 194–209. Springer, Cham (2019). https://doi.org/10.1007/978-3-030-16205-4_15
12. Iancu, C., Hofmeyr, S., Blagojevic, F., Zheng, Y.: Oversubscription on multicore processors. In: IEEE International Symposium on Parallel Distributed Processing (IPDPS), Atlanta, GA, pp. 1–11. IEEE (2010)

13. Navarro, A., Vilches, A., Corbera, F., Asenjo, R.: Strategies for maximizing utilization on multi-CPU and multi-GPU heterogeneous architectures. J. Supercomput. **70**, 756–771 (2014)
14. Jiang, M., Essen, B.V., Harrison, C., Gokhale, M.B.: Multi-threaded streamline tracing for data-intensive architectures. In: Childs, H., Pajarola, R., Vishwanath, V. (eds.) 4th IEEE Symposium on Large Data Analysis and Visualization, LDAV, Paris, France, pp. 11–18. IEEE Computer Society (2014)
15. Huang, H., et al.: Towards exploiting CPU elasticity via efficient thread oversubscription. In: HPDC 2021: Proceedings of the 30th International Symposium on High-Performance Parallel and Distributed Computing, pp. 215–226 (2021)
16. Gordon, P.: Nonsymmetric difference equations. SIAM J. Appl. Math. **13**, 667–673 (1965)
17. Douglas, J., Jr., Russell, T.F.: Numerical methods for convection-dominated diffusion problems based on combining the method of characteristics with finite element method or finite difference procedures. SIAM J. Numer. Anal. **19**, 871–885 (1982)
18. Robaina, D.: BDF-Hopmoc: an implicit multi-step method for the solution of partial differential equations based on alternating spatial updates along the characteristic lines. Ph.D. thesis, Instituto de Computação, Universidade Federal Fluminense, July 2018. (in Portuguese)
19. Gourlay, A.R.: Hopscotch: a fast second-order partial differential equation solver. IMA J. Appl. Math. **6**(4), 375–390 (1970)

# The Adoption of Microservices Architecture as a Natural Consequence of Legacy System Migration at Police Intelligence Department

Murilo Góes de Almeida[✉] and Edna Dias Canedo[✉]

Department of Computer Science, University of Brasília (UnB),
P.O. Box 4466, Brasília–DF, Brazil
murilow@gmail.com, ednacanedo@unb.br
http://ppca.unb.br/

**Abstract.** During the end of 2017, the systems developed by policemen in the Intelligence Department of São Paulo State Military Police were outdated in technology and did not follow any kind of pattern, neither had integration with services, databases and other systems, being very difficult to maintain. However, this kind of system could not be abandoned, because they were important in the organization. Thus, the managers of the Intelligence Department understood the need for modernization of architecture and system technologies. There are some approaches that can be chosen in this evolution process. A difficult question to be answered is related to which path is better to be followed in this process of system migration, mainly about the choosing of monolithic or microservices architecture. Although the microservice architecture is modern, it is not so easy to be implemented directly in a legacy system evolution process, because it depends on a strong domain of businesses areas and technology, which makes it difficult to involve of beginners developers. In this paper, we reported an experience about migrating a legacy system used in Intelligence Department of Sao Paulo State Military Police to a microservice-based architecture by re-engineering the legacy system as a monolith first and then decomposing it to microservices. We realized that microservices did not necessarily had to be adopted in the first place, but it could be a natural consequence of evolution, using a monolithic approach in the beginning. This process may also help the development team to improve their knowledge about the adopting of new technologies, architectures and better understanding of business.

**Keywords:** Monolithic · Microservice · Legacy system · Architecture migration · Software design tradeoffs

## 1 Introduction

Public security in Brazil is a state duty, guaranteed by Federal Constitution, that means, the public power is responsible to preserve the public order, security of people and property. There are law enforcement institutions created by Federal Constitution [7], each one having a specific duty in the public security context. Brazil is a Federal Republic, divided by 26 states plus a Federal District. The states have their own public security system, responsible for prevention and repression of crimes.

The organization responsible for preventing crimes is named Military Police. It has an intelligence department, that works for security public intelligence activities in São Paulo State and part of the brazilian public security intelligence subsystem [8]. This department develops its own systems, as also manages technology infrastructure which provides the systems sustentation. These activities are all developed by military police people, because of data sensitivity which is processed and stored, most of them classified. Thus, the intelligence department does not have an outsourced technical staff hired to work with technology, using policemen able to work in intelligence activity. Furthermore, it is very tricky to find a policeman with technology skills, because it is not required in the police admission process. Therefore, the policeman staff working with technology in intelligence is very reduced compared to other institutions, moreover, they do not have advanced knowledge in system development, although they have a great desire to learn it.

Because of the small number of police officers, added with limited knowledge in technology, at the end of 2017, systems developed by policemen in the Intelligence Department did not follow any kind of pattern, neither had integration with services or databases, thus, there were a lot of legacy monolithic systems that did not "talk" with each other. Each system had its own authentication system, frontend, backend and database.

The software development process used at that moment involved the use of a "scaffold" tool, that generates automatically all system code using a model first approach, that means, having a previously database modeled using some visual tool. Scaffold may be a good solution for programming learning, it is encouraged for novice programmers who have limited knowledge and experience [29]. The using of this process was justified because there was a reduced staff added with the client expectation of receiving a finished system in a short deadline.

In fact, the process mentioned above accelerated the process of development and delivery of systems, however, it did not accomplish the user's expectations. The system maintenance was very complicated, because the code generated by the scaffold tool was very difficult to read and edit. The most worrying was the fact of the systems, even of different business areas inside the police intelligence, did not communicate between them, neither with other corporate systems of Military Police, consequently, behaving as "black-boxes", and, in the majority of cases, storing exactly the same kind of data in different places, causing several redundancies of data. Last but not least, some intelligence business areas which did not have a developed application, used to store important data in files like spreadsheets, without any kind of integration with other areas. Figure 1 shows how the systems and database were organized in the scenario above.

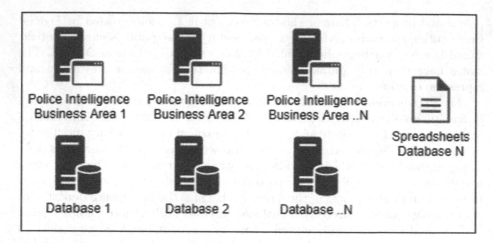

**Fig. 1.** Isolated and monolithic systems and databases developed in Intelligence Department

According to the presented scenario, the managers of the Intelligence Department understood the need for modernization of architecture and system technologies, assuming that the main goal had to be the data integration and systems interoperability. In this paper, we demonstrated how this process was developed, since the mapping of data by business fields, the choosing of system architecture and technologies. After that, it is discussed why we did not use microservices at first, but this adoption became a consequence of this system evolution process.

Accordingly, this paper presents the following contributions:

1. In a process of legacy systems migration, the microservices architecture is not necessarily the best option to be implemented immediately;
2. The use of a monolithic architecture combined with modern technologies helps the development team to understand the business areas that can later be transformed into microservices;
3. The need to use a microservices architecture may arise naturally when the monolithic architecture becomes unsustainable, but easy to be split into microservices;
4. The details about the migration process in a context of public service in which the development team is small and with little experience about this subject;

## 2   Background

### 2.1   Legacy Systems

Legacy systems, in the words of Bennett [3], can be defined informally as "large software systems that we don't know how to cope with but that are vital to our organization". Generally, the legacy systems become very difficult to maintain and evolve over time, however, the majority of them perform crucial work for their organization. Consequently, at a given time, legacy systems cost a lot of efforts, causing a paradox, although they are vital for the organization, at the same time are causing several problems for them. Therefore, there are several studies about legacy systems migration.

Bisbal et al. [4] suggested migration methodologies, no matter what will be the new technology or architecture. There is a methodology more aggressive where the entire legacy system is abandoned and redeveloped from the scratch, nevertheless, it is also possible to migrate taking advantage of what already exists. There are also studies about migration to specifics architectures, such as migrating legacy systems towards object-oriented platform [14] or even migration to more modern architectures such as microservices [23]. Indeed, migration of legacy systems is a challenge that can be faced by almost every organization in the world, what is demonstrated in this specific case of our study.

### 2.2 Services Oriented Architecture

The term SOA, abbreviation to Service Oriented Architecture, was first mentioned in the industry by Gartner Group in 1996 [1]. There are several definitions about Service Oriented Architecture, nevertheless, all of them agree that it is a paradigm which improves flexibility in systems [22]. An adequate SOA definition is a software architecture based on services, which are loosely coupled software components that can be orchestrated to increase business agility [17]. This concept helps us to understand that Services Oriented Architecture brings some advantages, such as reliability, scalability, reusability, loosely coupled, easy maintenance, among others. The understanding about SOA helps our comprehension about microservices architecture, which has a relationship with SOA concepts.

### 2.3 Monolithic Architecture

Monolithic Architecture is a traditional strategy to software development. In this architecture, the functions are encapsulated in the same application [13]. If the monolith application is simple, it is advantageous, because it is easy to develop, test and deploy [13]. Otherwise, it may be more complicated to manage in some scenarios, because a monolithic architecture shares the physical resources of the same machine, such as memory, databases or files. A very noted problem in this architecture is related to scalability and the aspects related to change and evolution of application [9].

In other words, if a monolithic application has a lot of functions, it is not possible to manage individually the amount of physical resources that each function has to consume. The entire resources will be provided to the monolith, not exclusively to functions. Finally, if some functionality has to be repaired or evolved, all application will have to be affected, because it is about the entire application, no matter what is the function.

## 2.4 Microservices Architecture

Microservices are small scalable applications that represent bounded business capabilities and is frequently deployed independently [9] and are mentioned in the bibliography as architecture and paradigm. Using this approach, each microservice works like an independent application representing a single business functionality. It helps in terms of scalability. Independent scalability is very different comparing to monolith, because in this case, when a microservice consumes more resources, it is easy to provide more physical resources especially for that application. There is also a pecuniary advantage in this case, because it is possible to scale the applications only when it is demanded [25].

It is important to mention that microservices also provide independent development. A single unit can be developed by a specific group, that can use a specific programming language [25]. The independent development also brings others benefits, in the words of Bucchiarone et al. [9], "Since each microservice represents a single business capability, which is delivered and updated independently, discovering bugs or adding minor improvements does not have any impact on other services and on their releases". It is a great advantage compared to monolith, which a simple maintenance or evolution could affect the entire application. The same author also points that the use of microservices can be developed and managed by a single team. In other words, it is possible to have an entire ecosystem of microservices and different groups working with each application, isolated.

The adoption of microservices architecture may brings some drawbacks and challenges, such as a more complex deployment, performance (generally microservices communicate over the network), physical resources consumption and others [27], thus, the adoption of microservices architecture will never necessarily be better than the monolithic one, because it depends on a specific case.

# 3  Business Field Data Mapping

In this section, we demonstrate an investigation about where the data of different business areas of Military Police of São Paulo are stored and how they can be consumed by intelligence applications.

The Military Police of São Paulo State has a specific Information Technology Department separated to Intelligence Department, also managed by police officers, having their own software factory and infrastructure, nevertheless, they can work with outsource professionals, being responsible by operational and administrative systems in the majority of business areas of police (except intelligence), such as operational, human resources, logistics, health and financial.

There was a general agreement that systems developed by the intelligence field had to store only data related to their own business areas, that means, only what is produced by the intelligence service. Data out of intelligence business domain, such as human resources, should be accessed through that system which stores this original data, using some kind of systemic integration.

The data sources from different business areas have been mapped, after that, we realized that the majority of them were under responsibility of the Information Technology Department from Military Police. There was possibility to access some data sources using web services. In this way, external data that in the past were replicated in a database of Intelligence Department, started to be accessed directly through web services. Because of that, Intelligence Department stopped storing redundant data, that used to consume unnecessary storage volume and sometimes did not have integrity.

During the mapping activity in the Information Technology Department of Military Police it was possible to figure out that there was available an authentication service that could be integrated in the intelligence applications. In this case, the majority of systems developed by that department uses an authentication service provided by Active Directory (AD). AD is a common repository for information about objects that reside on the network, such as users, among others [15]. The using of AD as authentication service would help to solve frequent complains from intelligence users and developers, because they used to forgot the password, and the intelligence systems did not have a password recovering functionality, thus, every time that some user forgot the password, they had to call or send an email to intelligence developers, that would be able to reset or change password.

We concluded that the authentication process had to be provided by AD, because the users and passwords stored in that service were used in the majority of police systems, therefore, the user would have less probability to forget it, and, even if that happened, they would have to deal directly with the Information Technology Department from Military Police, which has more staff to handle with it. Thus, the systems of intelligence stopped checking user authentication, it would be provided by AD service, however, the intelligence system had to check if a user had authorization to login and what functionalities he was able to access.

The correct understanding about what kind of data is related to intelligence business core provides a possibility to develop a system more flexible, integrated and without data redundancy, in addition to opening more discoveries of services for integration, such as the case of authentication service adoption. The result of this mapping provided a new system design integration as it is represented in Fig. 2. After this process, both development team and decision makers reinforced the understanding that system integration through a service oriented architecture helps to reduce data redundancy and keeps the data with a integrity assurance.

## 4   Legacy System Migration

In this section, we explained what happened during the legacy system migration process. It is pointed new routines that started to be followed, as a consequence of modernization. At the end, it is explained when the monolithic architecture started to be difficult to maintain, but easy to migrate into microservice architecture.

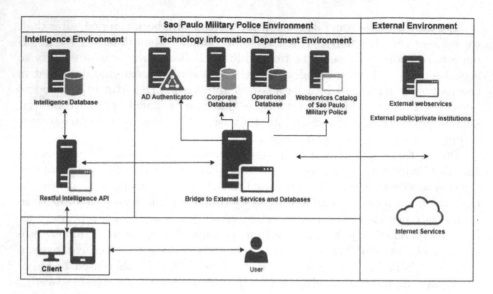

**Fig. 2.** New integration API proposed after a Business Field Data Mapping

After the process of business data understanding and mapping, it was proposed the building of a platform using only a frontend that concentrates all system functionalities, according to user system permissions. Different from legacy system, the new one has a total separation of frontend to backend, being this last one a RESTFUL API, able to communicate with externals web-services of different business areas. In RESTful applications, the method information goes into HTTP method [28], and implements REST (Representational State Transfer) [18], which has as key abstraction of information the resource, a conceptual mapping to a set of entities. For using the REST architecture, The use of a RESTFUL API approach seems easy to understand and implement, facilitating the integration with different clients, such as a mobile application, beyond only a frontend web application.

The using of a "scaffold" tool was abandoned, and the development team started to produce their own code, taking advantage of this moment to adopt a GIT repository, which did not existed in the system development process since now. GIT is a version control system (VCS), it allows you to track the iterative changes you make to your code [5]. The development team did not know how GIT worked, therefore, it was necessary a training, not only related to technical details, but also giving a better understanding about the importance of working with code versioning in a repository. It seems complicated at first, however, is a powerful tool that can improve code development and documentation [5].

In this first moment, we did not use a microservice architecture, because the crew had little knowledge about this subject, and also a difficult to know how to model each microservice according to application context, thus, we preferred to adopt a monolithic architecture. Although we used this approach, the source code organization was carefully organized, especially the classes, packages and their respective names, separated by their business areas or even the functionality performed by the class. This separation contributed to the development team having a greater understanding of what could actually be broken in microservice, if the need arose, throughout the evolution of the application.

Over the months, new features were added to the system, both from new business areas that were not integrated in the platform, as well as evolution of the existing ones. This made the project, even well organized, starting to have a higher number of classes and lines of codes, in addition to taking more time to build the application in the production environment, thus, a simple change in a specific module, it affected all users, without distinction. The high number of features was also making it difficult to monitor which ones were most accessed by users or even which consumed more hardware resources. If for some reason the application was slow, it ended up being scaled in its entirety, without the possibility of identifying the real reason for the slowness.

There was no continuous integration process in the sense of building automation, that is, the building of a new functionality in the production environment was generated and replaced by the old one manually, which made the system unavailable for a certain moment. This unavailability, even if temporally, caused certain annoyances, such as users contacting the technical team and informing them that the application was not working. The manual process of updating builds also made it risky. If the responsible did it incorrectly, making the roll-back process extremely difficult.

As the project started to increase the complexity in its source code, although well organized, it caused insecurity for the development team in carrying out maintenance or evolutions, especially regarding newer developers. The same insecurity was also on the part of the more experienced staff, fearing that the handing over of the project responsibilities to the beginning staff could somehow cause problems that would affect all application, and, because of that, the workload ended staying with the more experienced developers, preferring to perform actions that, in theory, the beginning staff would be able to work.

For theses reasons, the use of the microservices approach started to be considered. The expectation of the development team and decision makers was that breaking this monolith into microservices would solve the majority of these problems and maybe would not be risky, because at this point, the project was very well organized and modularized and the knowledge about the functionalities and business areas were very clear to all involved people in this project.

## 5   Microservices Adoption

In this section, we present which technologies were chosen to adopt microservices and the reasons, the advantages and the challenges faced during this process.

The monolithic application was being developed with the Java Spring Boot framework. According to official documentation, Spring makes it easier to create Java enterprise applications. It provides everything you need to embrace the Java language in an enterprise environment [21], and luckily, the same framework ecosystem has its own libraries for using applications as microservices, in this case, the monolithic to microservices migration process, it was used the library called "Spring Cloud". Spring Cloud is an umbrella project composed of several projects related to building cloud-based applications and microservices [12]. It provides basically, among other possibilities, a dependency named "Discovery Server" that behaves like a server where the other application subscribes to it, whenever they start up. Spring Cloud also provides another dependency that works as a "Gateway", which also subscribes to Eureka Server and checks which applications are subscribed there, and finally organizes all routes starting from a single address.

There was considerable ease in adopting the technologies mentioned above, because the development team was already acquainted with the Java programming language and the Spring framework. The separation of the project into microservices was not an obstacle either, after a certain time working with the monolithic approach, taking care to organize the code into specific packages, it helped to have a greater understanding of which of those features should present itself as an independent microservice, thereby, the monolithic application was broken into 13 (thirteen) independent microservices. Figure 3 shows a new environment using microservices in the intelligence infrastructure.

## 5.1  Advantages

The migration process to microservices also "forced" the development team to verify which tools would be best suited to support the applications. All microservices were hosted into Docker containers and The Windows Server operating system was replaced by a Linux distribution. The applications that are built in the docker are packaged with all the supporting dependencies into a standard form called container and brings some advantages such as speed, portability, scalability, rapid delivery, and density [6].

It also took the opportunity to resolve the issue of continuous integration. Due to the migration to microservices, there was a specific project for each microservice, therefore, using the GitFlow workflow in integration with the Jenkins Continuous Integration server, it was possible to create an automatic deploy flow in each microservice within a specific environment (development, approval and production) depending on the branch where the code was committed, such as deploy in the development environment for the branch marked as "feature", or in production for "master". Jenkins is a continuous integration tool, it can simplify and accelerate delivery by helping you automate the deployment process [30]. The implementation of it allowed us to automate the construction, testing and deployment of each microservice, greatly facilitating the continuous delivery process and GitFlow adoption, an important abstraction for flow state management which allows us to achieve higher levels of safety, provenance, ease

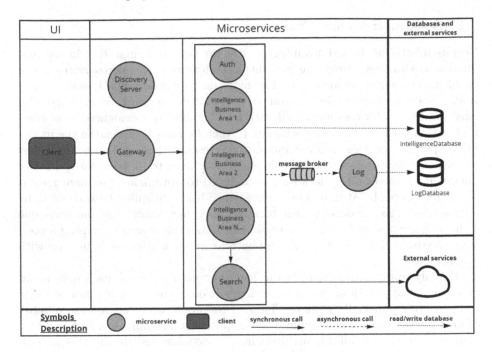

**Fig. 3.** Environment using microservices in intelligence side

of programmability, and support for multiple applications [16]. In addition to collaborating in this process, it enriched the development team's vision of good code versioning practices.

Breaking the monolithic application into smaller parts helped the more skilled developers to have greater confidence in making the source code available for the less skilled ones to explore it, because some of them isolated were very simple to understand and manipulate. There was a consensus that, if any incorrect code changes were made in some microservices, the impact would be minimal, as only that specific one would be affected, which actually happened, being easy to revert to the previous state. As a result, each developer became responsible for a specific application, according to their technical knowledge, increasing productivity and making the entire development team feel more involved with the project and more resolute in making their microservice best factored and evolved.

The use of microservices in containers facilitated scalability management, enabling a more rational distribution of hardware resources among them. At that time, it was evident that certain features of the monolithic application were less used compared to others, and after the separation, there was a better distribution of resources such as processing and memory in specific applications, unlike others that did not require as much computational resources.

## 5.2 Disadvantages and Challenges

Despite all the mentioned advantages, after the complete migration in the production environment from the monolithic architecture to microservices, some problems started to be identified. The first one happened when it was realized that a specific microservice consumed an expensive amount of memory, also affecting those who communicated with it. This difficulty evidenced slow communication with the database, which until then had not been seen in the monolithic approach, as this used a computational resource higher than what is used in each container individually. The moment was taken to improve the quality of queries performed on the database, in addition to optimizing the management of connection pools. At that time, what seemed like a difficulty, turned out to be advantageous, as the development team acquired new knowledge and overcame a challenge that would hardly be seen in the monolithic scenario, causing a positive refactoring in the source code and better communication configuration with the database.

Equally important to note is the fact that each microservice works as an independent application, therefore, it depends on a minimum amount of physical resources, especially memory. Thus, if the application has a large number of microservices, the available physical computational resources must be greater compared to the monolithic architecture. It was observed during this process because the virtual machine which hosts the monolithic application has 16GB of RAM memory comparing to 20GB in the virtual machine that runs the microservices ecosystem.

## 6 Related Work

Luz et al. [25] studied adoption of Microservices in Brazilian Government Institutions. They argue that there are many benefits in microservices adoption, including better scalability, productivity and maintainability. Nevertheless, it can be a challenging task in Government Institutions, mainly because it not only demands the understanding of new techniques and tools, but it also increases the need to automate tasks related to software deployment and software monitoring. They also conclude that it is difficult to break a monolithic system into microservices, mainly because there is a lack of guidelines with more precise descriptions about the expected granularity of a microservice. In fact, both advantages and disadvantages were faced in our migration process, the main difficulty was related to our development team skills and how to model the microservices, that were achieved during the modernization process.

Agilar et al. [31] studied a Service Oriented Approach to the Modernization of Legacy Systems in a Government University Institution. The use of Service Oriented Architecture (SOA) is mentioned as a way to solve the system modernization, using the Representational State Transfer (REST) architecture. In broad strokes, the using of REST is justified because of this simplicity and ease of understand, in addiction to the fact that the systems in study is able to work with HTTP requests. The use of a Service Oriented Architecture with REST in the Intelligence Department are justified in general with the same arguments.

Carvalho et al. [10] conducted a study about extraction of configurable and reusable microservices from legacy systems, interviewing specialists who worked in migration process from monolithic to microservices architecture. The majority of interviewed specialists answered that variability as useful or very useful to extract of microservices. Variability is the ability to create system variants for different market segments or contexts of use [11]. They also observed that microservices extraction can increase software customization. In our system migration, at the ending, we realized that the majority of microservices built were related to a specific business segment of the police intelligence activity.

Agilar et al. [2] has written a systematic mapping study on legacy system modernization. According to the paper, the main contribution of the study is to characterize software modernization according to the existing literature, discussing the related terms, classifying the related research contributions, and presenting the main reasons that motivate an effort of software modernization (also according to the literature). Although the literature presents a huge quantity of publication about software modernization, they generally were proposed without any practical evaluation, in other words, there are just a few studies reporting success experiences in modernizing legacy systems.

The migration process conducted in the Intelligence Department of São Paulo Military Police was not based in a specific method or technique published, but was made in an empiric way according to the real need of modernization. The experience during the migration process helped the team realize that a legacy system can be modernized at first using a monolithic approach and after some time, it will be necessary the use of microservices, that will be performed easily because of a better domain of business learned during the modernization process.

Laigner et al. [24] conducted a study about Big Data legacy System to Microservices Event-Driven Architecture, applying action research, investigating the reasons that motivate the adoption of a microservice-based event-driven architecture, intervening to define the new architecture, and documenting the challenges and lessons learned. Among the conclusions mentioned in the paper, it is worth mentioning that, in their words, defining microservices too early in the development process may yield into a wrong definition. Although microservices have a lot of benefits, if the requirements is not sufficiently mature, it can bring more problems than advantages.

Mazzara et al. [26] performed a case study based on the FX Core system, a mission critical system of Dankse Bank, the largest bank in Denmark. The migration process went through steps similar to those identified in the São Paulo police intelligence department. They also preferred to start the functionalities in a single application unit, which in their words, "allows the team and the organization to uniform the vision, but also the understanding of the specific approach and of the coding standard". After this step, the split into new services will be natural, such as was experimented in this study. Other important observation is the is the "attraction" of microservices architecture with DevOps. Mazzara et al. [26] related that "devops and microservices appear to be an indivisible pair for organizations aiming at delivering application and services at high velocity". When we started to migrate the monolithic system to the microservices architecture, we were not thinking about DevOps, however, we realized that it would be necessary to implement some tools to optimize the maintenance and deployment process.

Fritzsch et al. [20] investigated the migration process of 14 systems across different domains and sizes. They concluded that the intention of migrate legacy system is to overcome the difficulties of maintainability, which comes with some symptoms such as costs, changes are too costly or are prone to cause side effects and bad analyzability. There are also problems with traceability, long startup times and downtime during updates or difficulties to apply updates in general. This problems is quite similar to what was related about the situation of legacy systems in Intelligence Department. They also analysed why these companies chosen microservices. The main arguments used were scalability of the architecture, development teams, aiming for smaller and better manageable and maintainable units. These arguments also converge with what was reported previously, that is, dividing the system into small application units would facilitate the distribution of responsibility to the development team, in addition to improving the maintainability of each service.

Finally, it is very important to mention the "MonolithFirst" approach of Fowler [19], who alerts that going directly to a microservices architecture is risky. He explains that a monolith allows you to explore both the complexity of a system and its components boundaries. He provides some ways to execute a monolith-first strategy, such as designing a monolith carefully, paying attention to modularity within the software, both at the API boundaries and how the data is stored. It was the way that the monolithic architecture was developed during the legacy system migration and it helped to break our application in microservices, because paying attention in this process made our team have more knowledge about the system functionalities and business areas, consequently, our migration process became easy to perform.

## 7    Final Remarks

Based on what we have been exposed in this paper, we have figured out that in some time, legacy systems must be evolved, because it becomes very difficult to maintain, understand and is not user friendly. During the migration to modern technologies and architectures, the adoption of microservices architecture is not necessarily the only way of evolution, even though this approach brings a lot of benefits that are mentioned in this study.

The monolithic architecture does not mean that is outdated, in that case, it was a good start point to implement new technologies and service oriented architecture such as REST. It helped us also understand better the business areas of intelligence police department and the others of the Military Police. Thereby, microservices are not adopted as a starting point, but it became an inevitable consequence in the entire migration process, making it became a natural need at the time when certain difficulties emerged in the monolithic architecture, which began to make the development process costly, whether in the use of human or technological resources.

The initial adoption of the monolithic architecture, taking the necessary care in organizing the source code in the project, allowed for greater ease in the construction of microservices, enabling a clearer understanding of what a microservice actually has to be. It is important to point that all of these observations were confirmed by the development team, independently of experience level.

The final adoption of this architecture allowed the advantages of scalability, flexibility, control, monitoring, build automation, greater involvement of the development team and increased productivity, causing considerable evolution in the systems developed and maintained by the Military Police Intelligence Department of the State of São Paulo.

**Acknowledgments.** We want to thank the Ministry of Justice and Public Security of Brazil and the Military Police of São Paulo State for supporting this research.

# References

1. Abrams, C., Schulte, W.R.: Service-oriented architecture overview and guide to soa research. Technical Report G00154463, Gartner (2008). https://www.gartner.com/doc/575608/serviceoriented-architecture-overview-guide-soa
2. Agilar, E., Almeida, R., Canedo, E.D.: A systematic mapping study on legacy system modernization. In: The 28th International Conference on Software Engineering & Knowledge Engineering, SEKE, USA, pp. 345–350 (2016)
3. Bennett, K.: Legacy systems: coping with success. IEEE Softw. **12**(1), 19–23 (1995)
4. Bisbal, J., et al.: An overview of legacy information system migration. In: Proceedings of Joint 4th International Computer Science Conference and 4th Asia Pacific Software Engineering Conference, pp. 529–530. IEEE (1997). https://doi.org/10.1109/APSEC.1997.640219
5. Blischak, J.D., Davenport, E.R., Wilson, G.: A quick introduction to version control with git and github. PLoS Comput. Biol. **12**(1), e1004668 (2016)
6. Boettiger, C.: An introduction to docker for reproducible research. ACM SIGOPS Oper. Syst. Rev. **49**(1), 71–79 (2015)
7. Brazil: Constitution of the federative republic of brazil (1988). http://www.planalto.gov.br/ccivil_03/constituicao/constituicao.htm
8. Brazil: Decree n 3.695 of December 21 2020. Brazilian public security intelligence subsystem creation (2020). http://www.planalto.gov.br/ccivil_03/decreto/d3695.htm
9. Bucchiarone, A., Dragoni, N., Dustdar, S., Larsen, S.T., Mazzara, M.: From monolithic to microservices: an experience report from the banking domain. IEEE Softw. **35**(3), 50–55 (2018)
10. Carvalho, L., Garcia, A., Assunção, W.K.G., Bonifácio, R., Tizzei, L.P., Colanzi, T.E.: Extraction of configurable and reusable microservices from legacy systems: An exploratory study. In: Proceedings of the 23rd International Systems and Software Product Line Conference, SPLC 2019, vol. A, pp. 26–31. Association for Computing Machinery, New York (2019). https://doi.org/10.1145/3336294.3336319

11. Czarnecki, K.: Variability in software: state of the art and future directions. In: Cortellessa, V., Varró, D. (eds.) FASE 2013. LNCS, vol. 7793, pp. 1–5. Springer, Heidelberg (2013). https://doi.org/10.1007/978-3-642-37057-1_1

12. Davis, A.L.: Spring cloud. In: Spring Quick Reference Guide, pp. 231–246. Apress, Berkeley, CA (2020). https://doi.org/10.1007/978-1-4842-6144-6_18

13. De Lauretis, L.: From monolithic architecture to microservices architecture. In: 2019 IEEE International Symposium on Software Reliability Engineering Workshops (ISSREW), pp. 93–96. IEEE (2019) https://doi.org/10.1109/ICSM.1997.624238

14. De Lucia, A., Di Lucca, G., Fasolino, A., Guerra, P., Petruzzelli, S.: Migrating legacy systems towards object-oriented platforms. In: 1997 Proceedings International Conference on Software Maintenance, pp. 122–129. IEEE (1997). https://doi.org/10.1109/ICSM.1997.624238

15. Desmond, B., Richards, J., Allen, R., Lowe-Norris, A.G.: Active Directory: Designing, Deploying, and Running Active Directory. O'Reilly Media Inc., Newton (2008)

16. Dwaraki, A., Seetharaman, S., Natarajan, S., Wolf, T.: Gitflow: flow revision management for software-defined networks. In: Proceedings of the 1st ACM SIGCOMM Symposium on Software Defined Networking Research, pp. 1–6. ACM (2015) https://doi.org/10.1145/2774993.2775064

17. Erl, T.: Service-Oriented Architecture: Concepts, Technology, and Design. Prentice Hall PTR, Hoboken (2005)

18. Fielding, R.T.: Architectural styles and the design of network-based software architectures. University of California, Irvine, USA (2000)

19. Fowler, M.: Monolithfirst (2015). https://martinfowler.com/bliki/MonolithFirst.html

20. Fritzsch, J., Bogner, J., Wagner, S., Zimmermann, A.: Microservices migration in industry: intentions, strategies, and challenges. In: 2019 IEEE International Conference on Software Maintenance and Evolution (ICSME), pp. 481–490 (2019). https://doi.org/10.1109/ICSME.2019.00081

21. Johnson, R., et al.: The spring framework-reference documentation. Interface **21**, 27 (2004)

22. Josuttis, N.: SOA in Practice: The Art of Distributed System Design. O'Reilly Media, Newton (2007)

23. Knoche, H., Hasselbring, W.: Using microservices for legacy software modernization. IEEE Softw. **35**(3), 44–49 (2018)

24. Laigner, R., et al.: From a monolithic big data system to a microservices event-driven architecture. In: 2020 46th Euromicro Conference on Software Engineering and Advanced Applications (SEAA), pp. 213–220. IEEE (2020). https://doi.org/10.1109/SEAA51224.2020.00045

25. Luz, W., Agilar, E., de Oliveira, M.C., de Melo, C.E.R., Pinto, G., Bonifácio, R.: An experience report on the adoption of microservices in three Brazilian government institutions. In: Proceedings of the XXXII Brazilian Symposium on Software Engineering, SBES 2018, pp. 32–41. Association for Computing Machinery, New York (2018). https://doi.org/10.1145/3266237.3266262

26. Mazzara, M., Dragoni, N., Bucchiarone, A., Giaretta, A., Larsen, S.T., Dustdar, S.: Microservices: migration of a mission critical system. IEEE Trans. Serv. Comput. **14**(5), 1464–1477 (2021). https://doi.org/10.1109/TSC.2018.2889087

27. Merson, P.: Microservices beyond the hype: what you gain and what you lose (2015). https://insights.sei.cmu.edu/blog/microservices-beyond-the-hype-what-you-gain-and-what-you-lose

28. Richardson, L., Ruby, S.: RESTful Web Services. O'Reilly Media, Newton (2008)
29. Salleh, S.M., Shukur, Z., Judi, H.M.: Scaffolding model for efficient programming learning based on cognitive load theory. Int. J. Pure Appl. Math **118**(7), 77–83 (2018)
30. Smart, J.: Jenkins: The Definitive Guide. Oreilly and Associate Series, O'Reilly Media, Newton (2011)
31. de Vargas Agilar, E.: A Service Oriented Approach to the Modernization of UnB's Legacy Systems. Master's thesis, University of Brasília, Brasília, Brazil (2016)

...

# Geometric Modeling, Graphics and Visualization

# Eye Centre Localisation with Convolutional Neural Networks in High- and Low-Resolution Images

Wenhao Zhang(✉) and Melvyn L. Smith

Centre for Machine Vision, Bristol Robotics Laboratory, University of the West of England, Bristol BS16 1QY, UK
wenhao.zhang@uwe.ac.uk

**Abstract.** Eye centre localisation is critical to eye tracking systems of various forms and with applications in variety of disciplines. An active eye tracking approach can achieve a high accuracy by leveraging active illumination to gain an enhanced contrast of the pupil to its neighbourhood area. While this approach is commonly adopted by commercial eye trackers, a dependency on IR lights can drastically increase system complexity and cost, and can limit its range of tracking, while reducing system usability. This paper investigates into a passive eye centre localisation approach, based on a single camera, utilising convolutional neural networks. A number of model architectures were experimented with, including the Inception-v3, NASNet, MobileNetV2, and EfficientNetV2. An accuracy of 99.34% with a 0.05 normalised error was achieved on the BioID dataset, which outperformed four other state-of-the-art methods in comparison. A means to further improve this performance on high-resolution data was proposed; and it was validated on a high-resolution dataset containing 12,381 one-megapixel images. When assessed in a typical eye tracking scenario, an average eye tracking error of 0.87% was reported, comparable to that of a much more expensive commercial eye tracker.

**Keywords:** Eye centre localisation · Eye tracking · Deep learning

## 1  Introduction

Eye tracking has seen a long history of extensive use in differing application domains since its early-stage development in psychological studies tracking eye movements in reading [1, 2]. The increasing variety and quantity of commercial eye trackers [3, 4] and related research works [5] have provided strong evidence that this technology bears high potentials in contributing to multi-disciplinary research and to assistance with day-to-day human activities. For example, eye tracking was employed by marketers and designers to measure the effectiveness of advertisements in magazines [6]; and more recently to understand how users would view websites [7]. When applied to a distinctive discipline, eye tracking could assist with diagnosis of neurodegenerative diseases by providing eye movement biomarkers able to assess cognitive performance [8]. Another trending area of

O. Gervasi et al. (Eds.): ICCSA 2022, LNCS 13375, pp. 373–384, 2022.
https://doi.org/10.1007/978-3-031-10522-7_26

application concerns human-computer interaction, in the form of gaming-based learning [9] or control of a computer [10], for example.

Eye centre localisation is fundamental to development of eye tracking technologies, and it has a significant impact on eye tracking accuracy and precision. Choice of approach to eye centre localisation also directly affects complexity, cost, and usability of an eye tracking system. Generally, systems which work at a close proximity to eyes such as head-mounted eye trackers, and which have complex designs such as those utilising active illumination, can offer greater precision and accuracy but have lower affordability and usability. For example, a typical head-mounted system employed by psychological or medical research [11] can cost tens of thousands of pounds or more, resulting in limited adoption of such technologies. More importantly, uncomfortable intrusiveness of a head-mounted device is likely to undermine exhibition of natural user behaviours which are often critical to such studies. Although remote eye trackers exist, they usually have a limited range of working distance (e.g. 40 cm) as well as a lower accuracy than their head-mounted counterparts [12]. While offering a less expensive option, they are still far from being widely affordable.

Motivated by these challenges, this paper presents a deep learning based approach for eye centre localisation with a single camera, which aims to accelerate development of a cost-effective solution for remote and passive eye tracking with a high precision and accuracy. This research makes a contribution by investigating the effectiveness of different convolutional neural network (CNN) architectures for eye centre localisation, and by assessing the impact of image resolution on localisation accuracy. Based on research findings, a possible means to further improve the performance of the proposed approach is discussed and future works are recommended.

## 2   Related Works

Depending on whether active illumination is required, an eye centre localisation approach can be categorised as either active or passive, with the former being the predominant category due to the number of benefits active illumination can offer. Commonly, active illumination takes the form of infrared (IR) or near infrared light oriented towards the eyes. When an IR source is positioned close to the optical axis of a camera, active illumination causes the pupil to be lit, creating a brighter elliptical shape in high contrast to its neighbourhood. This is known as the bright pupil method. Different to this setup, the dark pupil method requires off-axis positioning of IR light(s), leading to a darker pupil but also an enhanced contrast [13]. In both methods, active illumination also causes cornea reflections, which provide additional features to allow conversion from eye centre locations to gaze positions taking into consideration head movements. For example, the Tobii Pro Nano device [12] employs an approach that switches between the bright pupil mode and the dark pupil mode according to environmental conditions. However, active eye centre localisation methods are often faced with real-world challenges. For example, as sunlight has a broad IR spectra, its interference to active illumination could lead to inaccurate eye centre localisation results in an outdoor application [14].

Different to these active methods, passive eye centre localisation approaches do not rely on active illumination, but they employ inherent eye appearance and/or geometry features under ambient lighting. While this can lead to a reduced system cost and complexity, there is a higher demand for and emphasis on overcoming interfering features, such as eyelids and makeup, which will often appear to be more prominent in unstructured image data due to a lack of active illumination. This has motivated various studies to exploit geometric features of the eyes by modelling circular (but realistically elliptical) contours of the pupil and iris. For example, one of the approaches [15] designed an objective function of gradient based features, drawing on the fact that gradients residing on the edge of a disk would be oriented towards its centre. This approach achieved reasonable eye centre localisation results by solving this optimisation problem, although its performance would be largely compromised by presence of strong gradients from shadows, other facial features such as eyebrows, and occluded pupil or iris. To deal with these interfering features, a study [16] based on image topography explicitly detected eyebrows such that false candidates from these regions could be removed during a multi-resolution analysis of iris features. Another method [17] tried to tackle this challenge by employing a two-stage approach to perform a coarse-to-fine estimation. In this approach, a convolution operator would be used to obtain an initial estimation of the eye centres based on geometric features; boundary tracing and ellipse fitting were then used to refine previous estimations. Similarly, the method proposed by [18] designed a two-stage approach combining gradient features and isophote features filtered by a bespoke selective oriented gradient filter to progressively reduce interfering features at a global scale before carrying out a local-level analysis in order to achieve improved accuracy. However, specularities and shadows mimicking geometric characteristics of pupil and iris still pose a fundamental challenge.

As machine learning approaches generally excel in dealing with complex patterns that cannot be easily and explicitly characterised, their capabilities have been leveraged to improve the accuracy of eye centre localisation. A method proposed in [19] employed a number of deep neural networks for face detection, eye detection, and openness assessment in succession; all as preliminary stages to eye centre localisation. However, instead of taking advantage of machine learning throughout all stages, they designed heuristic-based features for analysis of the iris. Similarly, the method presented in [20] only employed machine learning in a preliminary stage that served to identify a smaller region of interest. To achieve this, the Dlib toolkit [21] was utilised to detect facial landmarks including those of eye corners and eyelids. Both approaches reported incremental improvements, but occluded pupil and iris, as well as presence of glasses, still caused a large localisation error. A different approach [22] embracing a higher utilisation of machine learning designed an end-to-end CNN for predicting eye centre locations within face regions. Building on established network architectures, such as Inception-v3 [23] and ResNet [24], this approach achieved a significantly higher eye centre localisation accuracy.

## 3 Methodology

### 3.1 Datasets and Data Capture Experiments

Most state-of-the-art methods have reported results on a publicly available dataset, namely the BioID dataset [25, 26]. Therefore, we incorporated this dataset for developing and validating the proposed method to facilitate quantitative and comparative performance evaluation. This dataset consists of 1521 grayscale images of 23 different subjects, and it contains realistic challenges such as a variable ambient illumination, presence of glasses, and other types of inter-subject and intra-subject eye appearance variability. The images are of a low resolution, i.e., 384 × 288 pixels. Inclusion of a large background area means that the effective region of a face or an eye in these images has even fewer pixels. While deep learning is known to be able to handle small images effectively in a wide range of challenges such as object detection and classification, low-resolution data will inevitably limit eye tracking performance. In view of this, we constructed a new dataset that has a higher image resolution, and we assessed its impact on CNN models for eye centre localisation. To capture these data, we recruited ten participants at the University of the West of England (UWE), Bristol, including seven males and three females, aged between 18 and 55 years and of different ethnic backgrounds. The research experiments had been approved by UWE Faculty Research Ethics Committee (reference No: HAS.19.08.017). All data were recorded in a laboratory environment where overhead lighting was consistent but could lead to self-shadowing on faces. Each participant watched a five-minute video on a 27-inch screen positioned at approximately 60 cm away showing a moving visual target used to trigger eye movements. A chin rest was used to restrict large head movements such that eye movements would become more prominent. A machine vision camera (FLIR Grasshopper3) beneath the screen, angled towards the face regions, was set to capture images at 160 frames per second at a size of 1024 by 1024 pixels. A workstation with an Intel Xeon E5-2630 processor and 128 GB RAM hosted the control programme and interfaced with the camera. The experiment was repeated four times for each participant (i.e., four trials). The system setup and experiment procedure we employed are representative of those in eye tracking based psychological and medical studies, such as [27] and [28]. This would help place our research in context and would facilitate a more meaningful performance validation.

We manually annotated a random subset of data (12,381 images) from the first trials only, with pixel coordinates of eyes centres. The resolution of our data is 10 times as high as the BioID dataset (considering pixel count of an image). The camera field-of-view is primarily covered by face regions, leaving little background. Therefore, the pixel count of a face region is effectively over 20 times higher than the BioID dataset. The 60 cm screen-to-participant distance, the 27-in. screen size, and the moving visual target also caused eyes to move to extreme positions, horizontally, vertically, and diagonally. This introduced various levels of iris occlusions (by eyelids) contributing to data variability.

### 3.2  CNNs for Eye Centre Localisation

Building on the success of our prior investigation [22], in this study, we further employed different CNN architectures to solve eye centre localisation as a regression problem. We utilised an established CNN backbone to learn various levels of features. A global averaging pooling layer then condenses these features before passing them through fully connected layers, finally outputting the left and right eye centre coordinates. The Mean Squared Error (MSE) was used as the loss function. For the BioID dataset, we employed the Dlib library for face detection which successfully removed the background in each image. The face regions then became the input to our CNN models. For the new dataset we constructed, as the area of background is negligible, we directly input raw images to the CNN models. A number of backbones were experimented with, including Inception-v3 [23], the NASNet [29], MobileNetV2 [30] and the EfficientNetV2 (V2-L and V2-B3) [31]. Without unfolding the backbones and exhaustively listing all their layers, the general CNN architecture can be illustrated in Fig. 1.

| Backbone | | Inception-v3 |
|---|---|---|
| Concatenate | Input: | (8, 8, 320) |
| | | (8, 8, 768) |
| | | (8, 8, 768) |
| | | (8, 8, 192) |
| | Output: | (8, 8, 2048) |
| + | | |
| Global average pooling | Input: | (8, 8, 2048) |
| | Output: | 2048 |
| + | | |
| Fully connected | Input: | 2048 |
| | Output: | 4 |

**Fig. 1.** An illustration of the CNN architecture, using Inception-v3 as an example

All these different backbone architectures achieved outstanding top-1 and top-5 accuracy on the ImageNet [32] validation dataset, which evidenced their exceptional capabilities of feature extraction in general image classification tasks. Despite this, one of the problems these models may encounter is loss of spatial precision in a landmark localisation task. This is caused by spatial pooling of features typically occurring in a CNN, which is intended to progressively enlarge the overall receptive field while reducing the number of parameters. While it can serve this dual purpose, it effectively downsamples feature maps passed through the network; and therefore, this reduces localisation capability of the network. In view of this, without modifying the network architecture, we investigated into the impact of image resolution on CNN performance. In addition, from the perspective of eye tracking, acquisition of high-resolution images can also contribute to a higher accuracy.

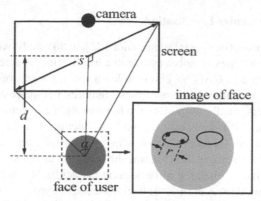

**Fig. 2.** Illustration of a screen-based eye tracking scenario where the two dots within image of face represent the extreme pupil centre positions, giving a maximum displacement value of $r$ pixels.

Taking a typical eye tracking scenario for example (depicted in Fig. 2) and assuming that a user gazes at information on a screen with a diagonal size of $s$ cm, while a remote eye tracker performs image-based eye centre localisation at a distance of $d$ cm; an eye centre localisation error of one pixel, namely the smallest value in the discrete image domain, corresponds to an error of $e_{deg}$ degrees that can be calculated by Eq. (1).

$$e_{deg} = \frac{2arctan\left(\frac{s}{2d}\right)}{r} \cdot \frac{180}{\pi} \tag{1}$$

This means that, when user distance $d$ and screen size $s$ are fixed, an increase in image resolution will proportionally increase displacement of pupil centre $r$, leading to a reduced error. Although high-resolution images can potentially reduce eye tracking error, an increased number of input neurons will drastically increase computation, consequently demanding a much larger GPU memory. Therefore, we employed the Dlib toolkit to detect eye corners in each face image, which informed extraction of two square eye regions from each face image, such that these smaller regions of interest could then become model input. This allowed utilisation of a reasonable batch size for training without having to downsample input size. Consequently, the model was changed to output coordinates of a single eye centre at a time.

## 4  Results and Discussions

The CNN models were implemented with Python 3.8, Tensorflow and Keras 2.8.0, and were evaluated on a workstation with an Intel i9-9940X CPU, 64 GB memory, and a Nvidia Titan RTX GPU.

As the number of samples in the BioID dataset is not particularly large in the context of deep learning, we employed the five-fold cross validation method with a 8:2 split for training and validation in each fold. We followed the commonly used relative error metric proposed by [23] to evaluate eye centre localisation accuracy. This metric calculates an error as the Euclidean distance between eye centre estimates and their ground truth before normalising this distance relatively to the pupillary distance. This is formulated by Eq. (2).

$$e_{max} = \frac{\max(d_l, d_r)}{\omega} \qquad (2)$$

where $d_l$ and $d_r$ are the absolute errors for the eye pair, and $\omega$ is the pupillary distance in pixels. The maximum value of $d_l$ and $d_r$ after normalisation is defined as the maximum normalised error $e_{max}$. A normalised error of 0.05 would be equivalent of the average pupil diameter. To train the model, cropped face regions from images were used, as mentioned previously. They were resized to 299 × 299 pixels, meaning that they had to be significantly upscaled. We used the Adam optimiser, a batch size of 32, a learning rate of 0.001. We observed that the model would generally converge within 300 epochs without showing severe overfitting; therefore, we do not emphasise the importance of hyperparameter tuning here. We first show in Fig. 3 that this CNN approach, when employing different backbones, could achieve highly accurate eye centre localisation results.

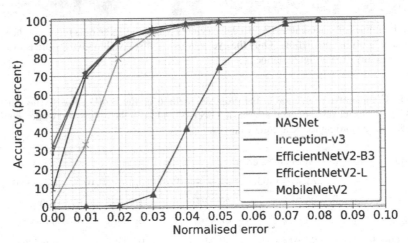

**Fig. 3.** Accuracy curves of the CNN model on the BioID dataset when utilising different architectures

These accuracy curves can demonstrate that accuracies with a tolerance of 0.05 normalised error approached 100%. The highest accuracy overall was obtained by EfficientNetV2-B3 that was one of the most compact models experimented with, able to perform inference at 46ms per step. The EfficientNetV2-L model achieved a similar overall accuracy, but its parameter count is over seven times higher. The Inception-v3 model produced a slightly worse accuracy but it could perform inference faster at 36ms per step. The lowest accuracy was from NASNet despite its large model size and topological depth, which overfitted when having not received further hyperparameter tuning. A few examples of inaccurate localisation results (where $e_{max} > 0.05$) by the

EfficientNetV2-B3 model are shown in Fig. 4. It can be seen that, in a few instances, the CNN predictions appear to be more accurate than the ground truth. Admittedly, manual annotation of data is prone to error, but this could be overcome by a CNN given a sufficient amount of correctly labelled data. We then compared the CNN performance with that of four other state-of-the-art methods on the BioID dataset. The results are shown comparatively in Table 1.

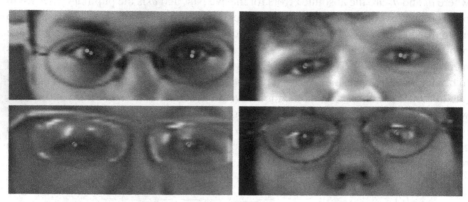

**Fig. 4.** Examples of inaccurately localised eye centres where the green dots represent the ground truth and red dots the predictions. Only the eye regions are displayed to give the areas of interest a better visibility. (Color figure online)

**Table 1.** Comparative evaluation of the proposed method on the BioID dataset. The * notation means that the exact value of accuracy has not been provided by the referenced works, but it was approximated according to the accuracy curves.

| Method | Normalised error | | | |
|---|---|---|---|---|
| | $e_{max} \leq 0.03$ | $e_{max} \leq 0.05$ | $e_{max} \leq 0.10$ | $e_{max} \leq 0.25$ |
| EfficientNetV2-L | 93.71% | 99.34% | 100% | 100% |
| EfficientNetV2-B3 | 94.65% | 98.52% | 99.92% | 99.92% |
| Inception-v3 | 95.80% | 99.34% | 99.92% | 99.92% |
| MobileNetV2 | 92.76% | 98.27% | 99.92% | 99.92% |
| NASNet | 6.25% | 74.34% | 100% | 100% |
| [20] | 52%* | 94.50% | 100% | 100% |
| [19] | / | 94.25% | 98.40% | 99.45% |
| [17] | 50%* | 85.08% | 94.30% | 98.13% |
| [16] | 62%* | 85%* | 94%* | 99.5%* |

As this demonstrates superior performance of the proposed method, we followed a similar process to evaluate it further on the high-resolution dataset we constructed, utilising the Inception-v3 model. As this dataset has approximately ten times as many images as the BioID dataset, it was partitioned into training, validation, and testing with a split of 8:1:1. With an input image size of $512 \times 512$ pixels, the model arrived at the minimum validation loss at epoch 62 within five hours of training. When further trained beyond this point, the model did not severely overfit. More details can be seen in Fig. 5.

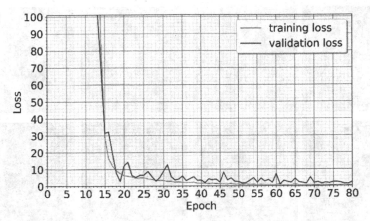

**Fig. 5.** Training and validation loss curves on the high-resolution dataset and the Inception-v3 model

Model performance was then evaluated on input images downsampled to different sizes, respectively. As mentioned in the preceding section, eye regions cropped by Dlib were also used to train the model. We compared these results and report them in Fig. 6.

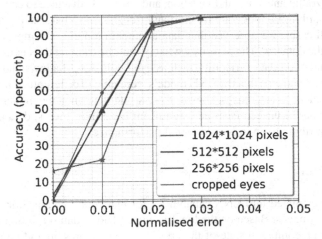

**Fig. 6.** Accuracy curves on the high-resolution dataset

When model input received uncropped images, high-resolution images contributed to improved model performances. When cropped eye regions were used to train the model, a further improvement on overall accuracy was achieved, as shown in Fig. 6.

This is one of the ways to increase the pixel count of the regions of interest (i.e., the eyes) without dramatically increasing the size of model input. Examples of inaccurate eye centre localisation were shown in Fig. 7. A normalised error $e_{max} > 0.02$ was used, as all instances had an error smaller than 0.05.

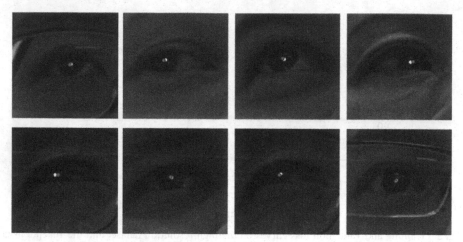

**Fig. 7.** Examples of inaccurate eye centre localization on the high-resolution dataset

Following Eq. (1), the average eye localisation error was calculated to be 0.87° and was similar for different resolutions of input. We also experimented with data augmentation to simulate data variability caused by head movements, such as roll, yaw and pitch of the head, horizontal and vertical translation, and a variable distance to camera. This was achieved by applying a moderate rotation and translation to batches of images during training. In all cases, we observed that data augmentation did not improve model performance on the datasets. The reasons are likely that the training data employed already sufficiently modelled data variability such as eye occlusion, shadows and specularities in the testing set; and also that the CNN models were able to differentiate between useful features from these interferences. However, we argue that when the models are exposed to a large number of unseen faces and significant head movements, data augmentation will likely contribute to an improved model performance.

## 5  Conclusions

This study investigated into CNN capabilities for eye centre localisation on high- and low-resolution images. Based on the low-resolution BioID dataset, it first validated the performance of a number of state-of-the-art CNN architectures, including Inception-v3, NASNet, MobileNetV2, and EfficientNetV2; and demonstrated superior localisation accuracies in comparison to other similar approaches. Both the Inception-v3 model and the EfficientNetV2 model achieved an eye localisation accuracy close to 100% with a normalised error of 0.05. Following this, the CNN model was evaluated on a high-resolution dataset; and it showed that a higher resolution could improve eye centre localisation performance, given the same model architecture. Additionally, we used Dlib to detect and crop eye regions as a preliminary step to CNN based eye centre localisation. By removing a large amount of background, this effectively increased resolution of the regions of interest only, such that the size of input to model remained relatively small. The proposed eye centre localisation approach, when placed in a typical eye tracking scenario, could achieve an error of 0.87°, comparable to a much more expensive commercial eye tracker. We also experimented with data augmentation for improving data variability, which did not lead to a higher model performance. However, we argue that the proposed data augmentation technique is likely to be able to make a contribute when large head movements are present.

In our future works, we will investigate into model architectures optimised for receiving high-resolution images as a means to further reduce eye centre localisation error. We also intend to combine localisation with tracking to overcome inaccuracies caused by eye blinks as well as to improve efficiency. We will also employ this cost-effective eye tracking approach to facilitate healthcare studies such as early diagnosis of eye diseases and neurodegeneration.

## References

1. Rayner, K.: Eye guidance in reading: fixation locations within words. Perception **8**(1), 21–30 (1979)
2. McConkie, G.W., Rayner, K.: The span of the effective stimulus during a fixation in reading. Percept. Psychophys. **17**(6), 578–586 (1975)
3. Tobii pro Homepage. https://www.tobiipro.com/. Accessed 02 Apr 2022
4. Gazepoint Homepage. https://www.gazept.com/. Accessed 08 Mar 2022
5. Duchowski, A.T.: A breadth-first survey of eye-tracking applications. Behav. Res. Methods Instrum. Comput. **34**(4), 455–470 (2002)
6. Krugman, D.M., Fox, R.J., Fletcher, J.E., Rojas, T.H.: Do adolescents attend to warnings in cigarette advertising? An eye-tracking approach. J. Advert. Res. **34**(6), 39–53 (1994)
7. Hervet, G., Guérard, K., Tremblay, S., Chtourou, M.S.: Is banner blindness genuine? Eye tracking internet text advertising. Appl. Cogn. Psychol. **25**(5), 708–716 (2011)
8. Crawford, T.J., Devereaux, A., Higham, S., Kelly, C.: The disengagement of visual attention in Alzheimer's disease: a longitudinal eye-tracking study. Front. Aging Neurosci. **7**, 118 (2015)
9. Kiili, K., Ketamo, H., Kickmeier-Rust, M.D.: Evaluating the usefulness of eye tracking in game-based learning. Int. J. Ser Games **1**(2), 51–65 (2014)
10. Zhang, X., Liu, X., Yuan, S.M., Lin, S.F.: Eye tracking based control system for natural human-computer interaction. Comput. Intell. Neurosci. **2017**, 1–9 (2017)
11. Mele, M.L., Federici, S.: Gaze and eye-tracking solutions for psychological research. Cogn. Process. **13**(1), 261–265 (2012)
12. Tobii pro nano. https://www.tobiipro.com/product-listing/nano/. Accessed 08 Mar 2022
13. Gneo, M., Schmid, M., Conforto, S., D'Alessio, T.: A free geometry model-independent neural eye-gaze tracking system. J. Neuroeng. Rehabil. **9**(1), 1–15 (2012)
14. Binaee, K., Sinnott, C., Capurro, K.J., MacNeilage, P., Lescroart, M.D.: Pupil Tracking under direct sunlight. In: ACM Symposium on Eye Tracking Research and Applications, pp. 1–4. Association for Computing Machinery, New York (2021)
15. Timm, F., Barth, E.: Accurate eye centre localisation by means of gradients. Visapp **11**, 125–130 (2011)

16. Villanueva, A., Ponz, V., Sesma-Sanchez, L., Ariz, M., Porta, S., Cabeza, R.: Hybrid method based on topography for robust detection of iris center and eye corners. ACM Trans. Multimed. Comput. Commun. Appl. (TOMM) **9**(4), 1–20 (2013)
17. George, A., Routray, A.: Fast and accurate algorithm for eye localisation for gaze tracking in low-resolution images. IET Comput. Vision **10**(7), 660–669 (2016)
18. Zhang, W., Smith, M.L., Smith, L.N., Farooq, A.: Gender and gaze gesture recognition for human-computer interaction. Comput. Vis. Image Underst. **149**, 32–50 (2016)
19. Ahmad, N., Yadav, K.S., Ahmed, M., Laskar, R.H., Hossain, A.: An integrated approach for eye centre localization using deep networks and rectangular-intensity-gradient technique. J. King Saud Univ.-Comput. Inf. Sci. (2022)
20. Khan, W., Hussain, A., Kuru, K., Al-Askar, H.: Pupil localisation and eye centre estimation using machine learning and computer vision. Sensors **20**(13), 3785 (2020)
21. King, D.E.: Dlib-ml: a machine learning toolkit. J. Mach. Learn. Res. **10**, 1755–1758 (2009)
22. Zhang, W., Smith, M.: Eye centre localisation with convolutional neural network based regression. In 2019 IEEE 4th International Conference on Image, Vision and Computing, pp. 88–94. IEEE (2019)
23. Szegedy, C., Vanhoucke, V., Ioffe, S., Shlens, J., Wojna, Z.: Rethinking the inception architecture for computer vision. In Proceedings of the IEEE Conference on Computer Vision and Pattern Recognition, pp. 2818–2826. IEEE (2016)
24. He, K., Zhang, X., Ren, S., Sun, J.: Deep residual learning for image recognition. In Proceedings of the IEEE Conference on Computer Vision and Pattern Recognition, pp. 770–778. IEEE (2016)
25. The BioID. Face database (2014). https://www.bioid.com/About/BioID-Face-Database. Accessed 05 Feb 2019
26. Jesorsky, O., Kirchberg, K.J., Frischholz, R.W.: Robust face detection using the Hausdorff distance. In: Bigun, J., Smeraldi, F. (eds.) Audio- and Video-Based Biometric Person Authentication. AVBPA 2001. Lecture Notes in Computer Science, vol. 2091. Springer, Heidelberg (2001). https://doi.org/10.1007/3-540-45344-X_14
27. Crutcher, M.D., Calhoun-Haney, R., Manzanares, C.M., Lah, J.J., Levey, A.I., Zola, S.M.: Eye tracking during a visual paired comparison task as a predictor of early dementia. Am. J. Alzheimer's Dis. Other Dement.® **24**(3), 258–266 (2009)
28. Oyama, A., et al.: Novel method for rapid assessment of cognitive impairment using high-performance eye-tracking technology. Sci. Rep. **9**(1), 1–9 (2019)
29. Zoph, B., Vasudevan, V., Shlens, J., Le, Q.V.: Learning transferable architectures for scalable image recognition. In: Proceedings of the IEEE Conference on Computer Vision and Pattern Recognition, pp. 8697–8710. IEEE (2018)
30. Sandler, M., Howard, A., Zhu, M., Zhmoginov, A., Chen, L.C.: Mobilenetv2: inverted residuals and linear bottlenecks. In: Proceedings of the IEEE Conference on Computer Vision and Pattern Recognition, pp. 4510–4520. IEEE (2018)
31. Tan, M., Le, Q.: Efficientnetv2: smaller models and faster training. In: International Conference on Machine Learning, pp. 10096–10106. PMLR (2021)
32. Russakovsky, O., et al.: Imagenet large scale visual recognition challenge. Int. J. Comput. Vision **115**(3), 211–252 (2015)

# Torus of Revolution Generated by Curves of Eight

Felícita M. Velásquez-Fernández[1]([⊠]) (iD), Sindy Pole Vega-Ordinola[1,2]([⊠]),
Carlos Enrique Silupu-Suarez[1,2]([⊠]), Robert Ipanaqué-Chero[2]([⊠]) (iD),
and Ricardo Velezmoro-León[2]([⊠]) (iD)

[1] Universidad Tecnológica del Perú, Av. Vice. Cdra 1, 20002 Piura, Peru
`C22852@utp.edu.pe`
[2] Universidad Nacional de Piura, Urb. Miraflores s/n Castilla, Piura, Peru
`sindypoleuct2019@gmail.com`, `ee_enrique1415@outlook.com`,
`{ripanaquec,rvelezmorol}@unp.edu.pe`

**Abstract.** Among the geometric bodies of revolution we find the torus
of revolution generated from a circumference that rotates around an axis.
Given the classic definition used in Mathematics, interest arises in finding
other curves that generate the torus of revolution when rotating around
an axis. There is already work done, about the construction of toruses of
revolution, using a lemniscatic curve. In this article, making the respective analysis and the necessary programming using the Mathematica 11.1
software, allowed us to carry out the necessary calculations and geometric visualizations of the mathematical object: So a torus of revolution
was built from the curve of eight in its parametric form and even the
equation of the torus in its Cartesian form. The study was extended
and the torus of revolution was generated from rational and irrational
curves that rotate around an axis. Curves were determined that were on
the torus generated by a curve of eight, which when properly projected
to planes, curves that have symmetries were obtained. When points on
these curves are properly taken, special irregular polygons are obtained.
By obtaining these results, a satisfactory answer to the research question
was obtained, as well as a way to define it. In addition, it has shown us
a wide path of research on the different curves that can generate a torus
of revolution.

**Keywords:** Torus · Turn of eight · Mathematica

## 1 Introduction

In the geometry of space we speak of geometric bodies of revolution, when they are
generated by turning a curve around an axis. Among this group is the bull of revolution. If we look for real examples where toroids are used, we can mention a wide
range of electronic circuits: inductors and toroidal transformers. Since its use has
increased enormously due to its symmetry, it has superior electrical performance
and low leakage of magnetic flux escaping from the core. Another example is the

particle accelerator, a machine that uses electromagnetic fields to propel charged particles at very high speeds and energies that travel in a toroidal-shaped tube contained in well-defined beams.

In Mathematics, according to [1] if we consider the circumference of radius "b" in the plane $y = 0$ whose center is at the point (a,0,0) with $a > b$. If "a" is on the circumference we rotate it around the z axis, then we generate a surface called Torus of Revolution.

Given the definition of a torus of revolution, the research question arises: Can a torus of revolution be generated from the figure eight curve as it is rotated around a straight line [2]. Once the research question has been formulated, the respective analysis is carried out to start the programming. The objectives set for this research are:

1. Generate a torus of revolution from the figure eight curve.
2. Define curves in the torus of eight.
3. Polygons whose vertices belong to a given parametric curve.

## 2    Torus of Revolution Generated by Curves of Eight Programmed in Mathematica

Once the research question has been formulated, the respective analysis is carried out to start the programming.

### 2.1    The Figure Eight Curve

To generate the parametric equation of the torus of revolution with figure eight curves, we consider the flat curve:

$$Ocho[t, (A, B)] = (A, Bsin(t), Bsin(t)cos(t)) \tag{1}$$

which is resting on the plane whose formulation $x = A$. With Mathematica we define it as follows:

$$Ocho[t_-, \{A_-, B_-\}] := \{A, BSin(t), BSin(t)Cos(t)\}$$

And we graph with Mathematica, according to Eq. (1) we have that (Fig. 1):

$$g1 = ParametricPlot3D\,[Ocho[t, \{1, 1\}], \{t, 0, 2\pi\}, PlotStyle \rightarrow Hue[0.75]]$$

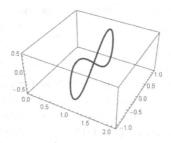

**Fig. 1.** Curve eight

## 2.2   Plane Where the Figure Eight Curve Rests

For the case that we are giving without a doubt is the equation $x = 1$. We corroborate this by graphing the equation of the plane by (Fig. 2).

$g2 = ParametricPlot3D[\{1, u, v\}, \{u, -1, 1\}, \{v, -1, 1\}, Mesh \rightarrow False,$
$PlotStyle \rightarrow Yellow]$

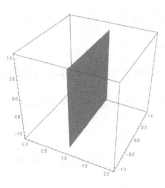

**Fig. 2.** Plane $x = 1$, where the figure eight curve is

Using the Show command we paste the figures g1 and g2: $Show[g1, g2]$

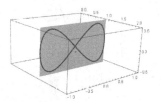

**Fig. 3.** The plane with the curve of eight

Now we calculate the maximum distance from the origin of coordinates to the points of the figure eight curve, for this we define the function squared distance (Fig. 3).

$$d[t\_] := (Ocho[t, \{A, B\}] - \{A, 0, 0\}).(Ocho[t, \{A, B\}] - \{A, 0, 0\})$$

We calculate the critical point:

$$Solve[d'[t] == 0, t]$$

We take the critical point $t_0 = \frac{\pi}{2}$ and evaluate the second and third drifts at that point.

$$(d''[t]/.t \rightarrow \frac{\pi}{2}) == (d'''[t]/.t \rightarrow \frac{\pi}{2}) == 0$$

But in the fourth derivative and evaluated at that point, we get:

$$d''''[t]/.t \to \frac{\pi}{2}$$
$$24B^2$$

Thus, the distance function has a maximum at $t_0 = \frac{\pi}{2}$. It is simply calculated

$$\sqrt{d[t]}/.t \to \frac{\pi}{2}//PowerExpand$$
$$B$$

Then we define the circle circumscribed to the figure eight curve (Fig. 4).

$$Cccocho[t\_], \{A\_, B\_\} := \{A, BCos[t], BSin[t]\}$$

With this we have:

$$g3 = \text{ParametricPlot3D}[Cccocho[t, \{1, 1\}], \{t, 0, 2\pi\}, \text{PlotStyle} \to \text{Red}]$$

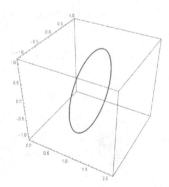

**Fig. 4.** Circumference

All this is reflected in the following (Fig. 5):

$$\text{Show}[g1, g2, g3, \text{PlotRange} \to \text{All}]$$

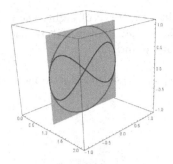

**Fig. 5.** Circle where the figure eight curve is inscribed

### 2.3   Generation of the Bull with the Curve of the Eight

If we have the Eq. (1), we will rotate it around the "Z" axis and we will obtain the torus of the curve of eight. We obtain the equation using the Mathematica software.

$ToroOcho[\{u\_, v\_\}, \{A\_, B\_\}] := \{\{Cos[v], -Sin[v], 0\}, \{Sin[v], Cos[v], 0\}, \{0, 0, 1\}\}.$
$Ocho[u, \{A, B\}]$

We run generically

$ToroOcho[\{u, v\}, \{A, B\}]$|When executing the command we get:
$\{ACos[v] - BSin[u]Sin[v], BCos[v]Sin[u] + Asin[v], BCos[u]Sin[u]\}$

To obtain the graph with Mathematica [3] we type

tor = ParametricPlot3D[ToroOcho[{u, v}, {1, 4}], {u, 0, π}, {v, 0, 2π},
PlotStyle → Directive[Opacity[0.7], Yellow, Specularity[White, 50]],
PlotPoints → 60]

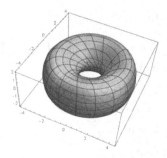

**Fig. 6.** Graph of the ToroOcho[{u, v}, {1, 4}]

Next, the torus of eight, the curve of eight, the circle circumscribed to the curve of eight and the plane that contains it to the curve that generates the torus of eight is shown (Figs. 6 and 7).

$$Show[g1, g2, g3, tor, PlotRange \rightarrow All]$$

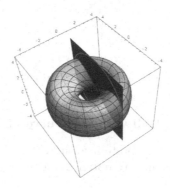

**Fig. 7.** Graph of the ToroOcho[$\{u, v\}, \{1, 4\}$], plane x=1, circumference and curve of the eight.

## 2.4  The Cartesian Equation of the Torus with the Curve of the Eight

It is natural to take into account the parametric equations of the torus of the curve of eight to obtain its Cartesian equation. We choose the abscissa component:

$$x = ToroOcho[\{u, v\}, \{A, B\}][[1]]$$
$$ACos[v] - BSin[u]Sin[v]$$

Then the ordered:

$$y = ToroOcho[\{u, v\}, \{A, B\}][[2]]$$
$$BCos[v]Sin[u] + ASin[v]$$

Finally, regarding the variable z:

$$z = ToroOcho[\{u, v\}, \{A, B\}][[3]]$$
$$BCos[u]Sin[u]$$

Later:

$$(x^2 + y^2 - A^2)(B^2 + A^2 - x^2 - y^2)//Simplify$$
$$B^4Cos[u]^2Sin[u]^2$$

With all this it is obtained that:

$$(x^2 + y^2 - A^2)(B^2 + A^2 - x^2 - y^2) = z^2B^2//Simplify$$

Consequently, the Cartesian equation of the torus of eight is:

$$(x^2 + y^2 - A^2)(B^2 + A^2 - x^2 - y^2) = z^2 B^2$$

Now it is graphed with Mathematica Software. Assuming the values: A=1; B=4 and considering (Fig. 8):

$tor0 = ContourPlot3D[(x^2 + y^2 - A^2)(B^2 + A^2 - x^2 - y^2) == B^2 z^2,$
$\{x, -4.2, 4.2\}, \{y, -4.2, 4.5\}, \{z, -4, 4\}, Mesh \rightarrow False,$
$PlotPoints \rightarrow 75, ContourStyle \rightarrow Directive[Yellow, Opacity[0.8]]]$

We will graph the torus of revolution together with the figure eight curve

$$Show[g1, tor0, PlotRange \rightarrow All]$$

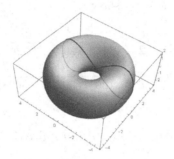

**Fig. 8.** Graph of the EightTorus[u,v,1,4] and curve of the eight that generates it.

## 2.5  Curves in the Torus with the Curve of the Eight

To define curves in the torus of eight, the parametric equation [4] of the torus of eight is used

$$\alpha[t_-, \alpha_1 : \{_-, _-\}, \{A_-, B_-\}] := ToroOcho[\{u, v\}, \{A, B\}] / . \{u \rightarrow \alpha[[1]], v \rightarrow \alpha[[2]]\}$$

For example:

$$\alpha[u, \{ArcCos[u], ArcSin[u]\}, \{1, 4\}] // TrigExpand$$

Which is an irrational curve and also generates the Bull of eight. which is graphically obtained by (Fig. 9).

$cur1 = ParametricPlot3D[\{\sqrt{1 - u^2} - 4u\sqrt{1 - u^2}, -4u^2 + u + 4, 4u\sqrt{1 - u^2}\},$
$\{u, -1, 1\}, PlotStyle \rightarrow Hue[0.]]$

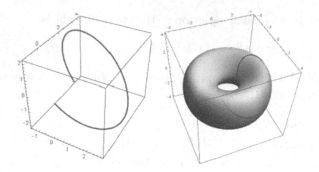

**Fig. 9.** Graph of the irrational curve that is in the torus of eight.

Considering the expansion of the function Cosine and Sine in Taylor series with a good approximation, as we show

$$cos[u\_] := 1 - \frac{u^2}{2} + \frac{u^4}{24} - \frac{u^6}{720} + \frac{u^8}{40320} - \frac{u^{10}}{3628800}$$
$$sin[u\_] := u - \frac{u^3}{6} + \frac{u^5}{120} - \frac{u^7}{5040} + \frac{u^9}{362880}$$

And we define the following matrix:

$$A1[u\_] := \{\{cos[u], -sin[u], 0\}, \{sin[u], cos[u], 0\}, \{0, 0, 1\}\}$$

Thus we have that the figure eight curve would be as follows

$$NewOcho[u\_, \{A\_, B\_\}] := \{A, Bsin[u], Bsin[u]cos[u]\}//Expand$$

In general, the figure eight curve would be:

$$NewOcho[u, \{A, B\}]$$
$$\{A, Bu - \frac{Bu^3}{6} + \frac{Bu^5}{120} - \frac{Bu^7}{5040} + \frac{Bu^9}{362880}, Bu - \frac{2Bu^3}{3} + \frac{2Bu^5}{15} - \frac{4Bu^7}{315} + \frac{2Bu^9}{2835}$$
$$- \frac{31Bu^{11}}{1209600} + \frac{Bu^{13}}{1555200} - \frac{101Bu^{15}}{9144576000} + \frac{Bu^{17}}{8128512000} + \frac{Bu^{19}}{1316818944000}\}$$

We define a rational algebraic version of the torus with the figure eight curve:

$$TorOchoR[\{u\_, v\_\}\{A\_, B\_\}] := A1[u].NewOcho[v, \{A, B\}]//Expand$$

Executing in general form by means of the command: $TorOchoR[\{u, v\}, \{1, 4\}]$ We will assume that A=1 and B=4 in the above equation. To graph it, use the command (Fig. 10):

$$TorochoR = ParametricPlot3D[TorOchoR[\{u, v\}, \{1, 4\}]//Evaluate$$
$$\{u, -\pi, \pi\}, \{v, 0, \pi\}]$$

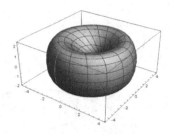

**Fig. 10.** Graph of the rational algebraic version of the torus with the curve of eight.

A version of this torus involving irrational functions

$$TorOchoI[\{u_-, v_-\}, \{A_-, B_-\}] := A1[u].\{\sqrt{1-v^2} - 4v\sqrt{1-v^2},$$
$$4 + v - 4v^2, 4v\sqrt{1-v^2}\}$$

When we evaluate in the command above for A=1 and B=4, $TorOchoI[\{u, v\},$ $\{1, 4\}]$, we get the torus version of eight in irrational equations. To plot we will use the command

$$ParametricPlot3D[TorOchoI[\{u, v\}, \{1, 4\}]//Evaluate, \{u, -\pi, \pi\},$$
$$\{v, -1, 1\}, PlotPoints \rightarrow 75]$$

## 2.6   Special Polygon with 12 Sides

To present the dodecangle, we consider the following plane curve (Fig. 11):

$$\beta[t_-]:=Delete[\alpha[t, \{3t, t\}, \{1, 4\}], 3]$$

When executing the command we get:

$$\beta[t]$$

$$\{Cos[t] - 4Sin[t]Sin[3t], Sin[t] + 4Cos[t]Sin[3t]\}$$

Its graph is achieved with

$$ParametricPlot[\beta[t], \{t, 0, 2\pi\}, PlotStyle \rightarrow Hue[0.65]]$$

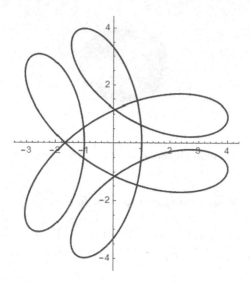

**Fig. 11.** Curve B(t)

Now, we construct with Mathematica a list in the domain of the curve that is $[0, 2\pi]$ with increments of $\frac{\pi}{24}$ eliminating the last term .

$$lis = Delete[Table[t, \{t, 0, 2\pi, \frac{\pi}{24}\}], -1]$$

With that list of dividing the interval, we evaluate the curve on all those elements.

$$pun = \beta/@lis$$

Then we consider a sublist

$$lis = \{pun[[36]], pun[[38]], pun[[12]], pun[[14]], pun[[4]], pun[[6]], pun[[28]],$$
$$pun[[30]], pun[[20]], pun[[22]], pun[[44]], pun[[46]]\}$$

Considering the mini program:

$$Angulo[\{P\_, Q\_, R\_\}] := ArcCos[\frac{(Q - P).(Q - R)}{Norm[Q - P]Norm[Q - R]}]$$

We calculate the interior angles of the dodecangle by:

$$Angulo/@Partition[Append[Append[lis1, pun[[36]]], pun[[38]], 3, 1]//N$$

It is obtained that the first two angle measures are equal and their approximate value is 2.87732. The third and fourth value are equal, Y its approximate value is of 2.35866. These two measures are repeated two by two alternately.

To get the length of the sides of the dodecangle we use:

$$Long[\{P\_, Q\_\}] := Norm[P - Q]$$
$$Long/@Partition[Append[lis1, pun[[36]]]], 2, 1]//N$$

So we have six sides that measure 0.99942, and two triplets of sides that measure 1.01817 and 4.64618. The polygon that is generated is an irregular dodecangle. Whose graph we obtain with the command (Fig. 12):

$$G2 = Graphics[\{Hue[0.75], Line/@Partition[Apepend[lis1, pun[[36]]], 2, 1]\}]$$

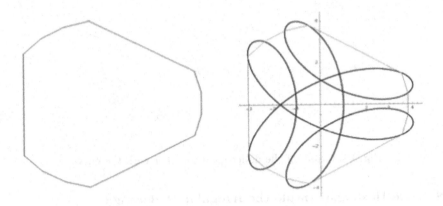

**Fig. 12.** Graph of the dodecangle and this together with the curve

## 2.7   Two Hexangles Inside the Irregular Dodecangle

From lis1 we extract the following sublist

$$lis11 = \{lis1[[1]], lis1[[3]], lis[[5]], lis1[[7]], lis1[[9]], lis[[11]]\};$$

And we calculate the measure of the interior angles.

$$Ang/@Partition[Append[Append[lis11, lis1[[1]], lis1[[3]], 3, 1]//FullSimplify$$

Obtaining 2pi 3 . We obtain the measure of the sides by:

$$Long/@Partition[Append[lis11, lis[[1]], 2, 1]//N$$

The approximate measure of the first sides is 2.0, 5.40083, which you alternate successively. Consequence of these two results, we conclude that it is a Hexangle. Análogamente de la sub lista

$$lis12 = \{lis1[[2]], lis1[[4]], lis[[6]], lis1[[8]], lis1[[10]], lis1[[12]]\};$$

It is also obtained that it is a hexaangle, and these two hexaangles are congruent and symmetric with respect to the X axis. The graphs show what is explained (Fig. 13):

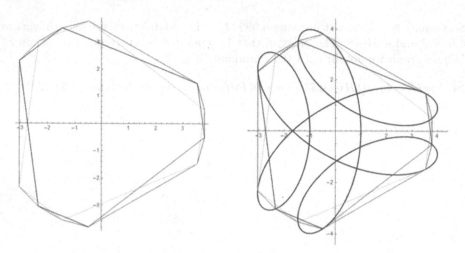

**Fig. 13.** Graph of the dodecangle together with the curve

## 2.8   Two Hexangles Inside the Irregular Dodecangle

To obtain the points of the triangles we create the following list

$$listris = Table[\{lis[[i]], lis1[[i+4]], lis1[[i+8]]\}, \{i, 1, 4\}]$$

Then we choose the first element of listris that ultimately gives us the vertices of the first triangle.

$$listris[[1]]$$

$$\{\{4Cos[\tfrac{\pi}{24}]Cos[\tfrac{\pi}{8}] - Sin[\tfrac{\pi}{24}], -Cos[\tfrac{\pi}{24}] - 4Cos[\tfrac{\pi}{8}]Sin[\tfrac{\pi}{24}]\},$$
$$\{Cos[\tfrac{\pi}{8}] - 4Cos[\tfrac{\pi}{8}]Sin[\tfrac{\pi}{8}], 4Cos[\tfrac{\pi}{28}]^2 + Sin[\tfrac{\pi}{8}]\},$$
$$\{-Cos[\tfrac{5\pi}{24}] - 4Cos[\tfrac{\pi}{8}]Sin[\tfrac{5\pi}{24}], -4Cos[\tfrac{\pi}{28}]Cos[\tfrac{5\pi}{24}] + Sin[\tfrac{5\pi}{24}]\}\}$$

Calculate the measures of the interior angles

$$Ang/@Partition[Append[Append[listris[[1]], listris[[1]][[1]]], listriz[[1]][[2]]], 3, 1]//Simplify$$
$$\{\tfrac{\pi}{3}, \tfrac{\pi}{3}, \tfrac{\pi}{3}\}$$

The length of the sides

$$Longitd/@Partition[Append[listris[[1]], listris[[1]][[1]]], 2, 1]//Simplify$$
$$\{\sqrt{3(9 + 4\sqrt{2})}, \sqrt{3(9 + 4\sqrt{2})}, \sqrt{3(9 + 4\sqrt{2})}\}$$

So we have that the points of listris[[1]] determine an equilateral triangle. To graph the four triangles involved, the following is used:

$$Triangulo[P : \{\_, \_\}, Q : \{\_, \_\}, R : \{\_, \_\}] :=$$
$$Graphics[\{Hue[Random[]], Line/@Partition[\{P, Q, R, P\}, 2, 1]\}]$$

And then we type (Fig. 14):

$$Show[Triangulo/@Table[\{list1[[i]], lis1[i+4]], lis1[[i+8]]\}, \{i, 1, 4\}]]$$

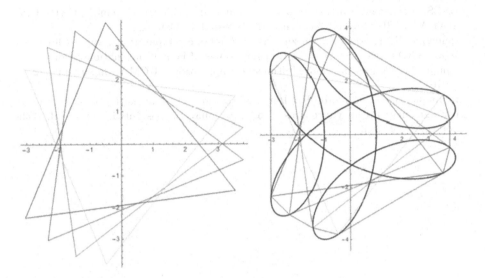

**Fig. 14.** Graph of the dodecangle along with the four equilateral triangles and curve

## 3   Conclusions

According to the results found, it is concluded that a torus of revolution can be constructed in its generic form from the curve of eight defined:

$$\{ACo[v] - BSin[u]Sin[v], BCos[v]Sin[u] + ASin[v], BCos[u]Sin[u]\}$$

The Cartesian equation of the torus generated by the figure eight curve was determined:

$$(x^2 + y^2 - A^2)(B^2 + A^2 - x^2 - y^2) = B^2z^2$$

The generated torus can be defined from rational and irrational curves.

The existing spatial curves on the torus generated by the figure eight curve were analyzed, taking into account the projections to the XY plane, observing existing symmetries. Points were taken from the curves that would be the vertices of special polygons such as irregular dodecangles, irregular hexagons, and equilateral triangles.

It is recommended to deepen the study of the polygons that are generated with the projection of special curves that are on the torus generated by a figure eight curve.

## References

1. Hasser, N., Lasalle, J., Sullivan, J.: Análisis Matemático Vol2 curso intermedio. Trillas, Mexico (1971)
2. LNCS Homepage. https://repositorio.unp.edu.pe/bitstream/handle/UNP/1648/MAT-VEG-SIL-2018.pdf?sequence=1. Accessed 15 Oct 2022
3. Ipanaque, R., Iglesias, A., Velezmoro, R.: Symbolic computational approach to construct a 3D torus via curvature. In: Proceedings of Fourth International Conference Ubiquitous Computing and Multimedia Applications, UCMA, Japan, pp. 22–24 (2010)
4. Ipanaque, R., Velezmoro, R.: Parameterization of some surfaces of revolution through curvature-varying curves: a computational analysis. Int. J. Hybrid Inf. Technol. **6**, 71–82 (2013)

# A Novel, Fast and Robust Triangular Mesh Reconstruction from a Wire-Frame 3D Model with Holes for CAD/CAM Systems

Vaclav Skala$^{(\boxtimes)}$ (iD)

Faculty of Applied Sciences, Department of Computer Science and Engineering,
University of West Bohemia, 301 00 Pilsen, Czech Republic
skala@kiv.zcu.cz
http://www.VaclavSkala.eu

**Abstract.** Polygonal meshes are used in CAD/CAM systems and in solutions of many of engineering problems. Many of those rely on polygonal representation using facets, edges and vertices. Today, due to numerical robustness as only three points can lie on a plane, limited numerical precision of the floating point representation, etc. the triangular facets are used nearly exclusively. This is a significant factor witch is not fully considered in triangular mesh representations and their processing.

This contribution presents a new approach to the 3D geometric model representation based on vertices and edges only, i.e. by the wire-frame data model, where no facet representation is needed, if the surface is formed by a triangular mesh.

The wire-frame representation use leads to significant reduction of data as there is no need to represent facets explicitly. It can be used for significant data compression, etc. Examples demonstrating the worst cases solutions are presented with a 3D print of those.

**Keywords:** Polygonal model · Edge model · Wire-frame model · Polygonal meshes · Triangular mesh · Surface model consistency · 3D geometric modeling · Surface representation · Data compression · Mesh surface reconstruction · CAD/CAM systems · Manufacturing · 3D print · Geometry hash function

## 1 Introduction

Geometric modeling of 3D surfaces is based on polygonal meshes, parametric surfaces or implicitly defined objects in the vast majority of cases. In the case of polygonal meshes a surface is represented by a polygonal mesh Botsch [6], Wenger [28], Apostol [2], Brentzen [7], Levy [21] which is usually represented by data structures as half-edge, winged-edge, etc.

Research supported by the University of West Bohemia - Institutional research support.

A significant effort is devoted to:

- polygon mesh repair Attene [4],
- mesh reconstruction from a set of triangles Glassner-1994 [12], Skala [25],
- memory optimization and mesh registration Le Clerc [19],
- hole filling in manifold meshes Gou [14],
- Boolean operations on polyhedral meshes Landier [18], Fu [11], Attene [3] and intersection problems Held [15],
- surface reconstruction from sketched drawings Company [9], Yu [32], or projections Lee [20], Alexei [1], Shin [24], Yan [31] and Fang [10].

A wire-frame representation is not considered as it does not represent a surface unambiguously in the case of polygonal faces Varley [26], Botsch [6]. Polygonal mesh reconstruction of objects without holes for

However, several attempts for reconstructions of 3D solid objects were made by Mirandi [23], Markowsky1980 [22] and Zabran [33], Inouse [17] and Bandla [5]. Necessity of facets in the surface representations is presented in nearly all books on computer graphics and geometric modeling.

However nowadays, the polygonal meshes are nearly exclusively represented by triangular meshes, as the only three points can lie on a plane due to limited numerical precision due to use of the IEEE-754 [29] floating point representation. This significant property has important consequences in many aspects, e.g. can lead to decrease of memory requirements, simpler data structures for data transmission, higher data compression ratio and to higher robustness.

In the following, a new robust method for triangular 3D surface mesh reconstruction from the wire-frame data model, i.e. object is only represented by vertices and edges, as a consequence of the triangular representation. This breaks the "axiom" on the ambiguity of 3D wire-frame models representation in the case of triangular meshes used for a surface representation of geometrical objects.

The proposed approach can also lead to new algorithms for geometric model consistency check, data compression for data transmission etc. Also, it can be extended for general polygonal meshes and for manifold objects using "virtual edges".

## 2    Data Structures

Mesh based data structures have several variants used in applications. They have to be evaluated especially from requirements and their properties point of view, e.g. algorithmic, topological, etc., see WiKi [30] The mesh data structures can be classified to:

- Face-based structures, which is a set of "unconnected" triangles. It is a simple data structure, where no information on neighbor triangles is directly available. Typical example is the STL format used in CAD/CAM systems for 3D printing. Non-trivial algorithms for a mesh reconstruction are to be used Glassner [13], Hradek [16] and Skala [25]

- Edge-based structures, where an edge is the edge shared by two polygons. The typical example is the winged-edge structure [Baumg72]
- Half-edge structure, which is based on splitting an edge to two oriented half-edges. More efficient modification was introduced in Campagna-1998 [8]

All data structures have several variants reflecting specific requirements from targeted application, the algorithmic point of view, memory requirements, consistency and robustness aspects etc. However, in some cases memory requirements are critical, e.g. in data compression and transmission, surface reconstruction from acquired data etc.

The CAD/CAM systems use different surface representations of geometrical objects and non-trivial operations with them, q.e. union, difference, etc. There are still problems with robustness and correctness of those operations, see Wassermann [27] as those issues are critical for the CAD/CAM systems.

The wire-frame data model, which contains only information on vertices coordinates and edges, is not defining the surface unambiguously, if the polygonal model is used, i.e. faces are not triangulated. The Fig. 1 presents the wire-frame model and three different interpretations of the wire-frame model, if polygonal mesh is used (triangulation of the faces is not considered).

It can be seen, that the holes can be front-back, left-right or top-bottom oriented in the case that the faces are un-triangulated polygons. This a typical example of an ambiguity of the wire frame model, in the case of the polygonal representation.

However, in the case of the objects with a triangular mesh, the triangular property of the given surface is so significant, that should have substantial influence to the algorithms and data structures, which represent a surface of the given object.

There is a question, whether a surface based on a triangular mesh can be represented unambiguously by vertices and edges only, i.e. by a wire-frame data model.

## 3    Wire-Frame Data Model

Data structures and algorithms used in polygonal meshing are widely described with many specific modifications. The wire-frame data structure, which contains only vertices coordinates and edges, is considered as ambiguous. In the case of polygonal meshes the ambiguity is clearly visible on the "4D-Cube" data model, see Fig. 1.

In the case of simple polygonal meshes which:

- do not have a hole, i.e. Genus zero
- are not self-intersecting, not touching on a vertex, edge and face
- surface is "water proof"

the simple algorithm based on "pairing" is quite simple and applicable for the most cases. It is based on finding cycles in a graph of the given edges of the

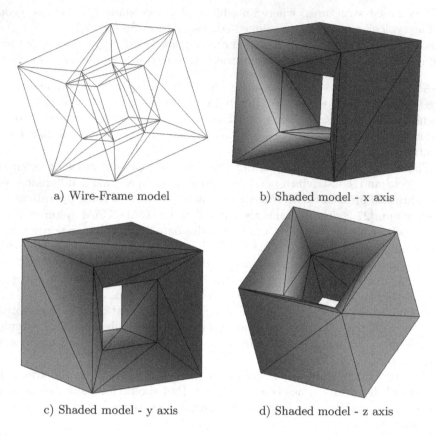

a) Wire-Frame model

b) Shaded model - x axis

c) Shaded model - y axis

d) Shaded model - z axis

**Fig. 1.** Different possible interpretations of the 4D-Cube wire-frame and shaded models

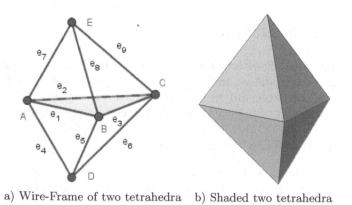

a) Wire-Frame of two tetrahedra    b) Shaded two tetrahedra

**Fig. 2.** Join of two tetrahedra

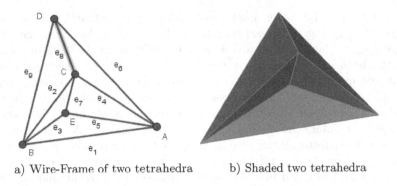

a) Wire-Frame of two tetrahedra          b) Shaded two tetrahedra

**Fig. 3.** Difference of two tetrahedra

length 3. However, such algorithm fails on very simple and similar cases, see Fig. 2, Fig. 3 and Fig. 4.

The situation gets more complicated in the case of objects with holes, which is a quite common case of models originated from CAD/CAM systems.

# 4  Wire-Frame for Triangle Meshes

The surfaces of geometric models are represented by triangular meshes nearly exclusively. It leads to better numerical precision of computation, etc.

As the knowledge, that the mesh is a triangular mesh, is so significant, that it should lead to significant data structure simplification or to a new data structure itself.

In the case of the triangular mesh it is expected that:

- a 3D surface is closed (but not necessarily)
- a surface of 3D object represented by a triangular mesh
- 3D surface is "water proof"
- each triangle is a triangle of the final surface
- any edge is shared by two triangles only (if the 3D surface is closed)
- 3D surface is non-manifold

When the object at Fig. 1 is represented by a triangular mesh, the correct surface can be generated. However, in some even simple cases, the algorithm of surface generation can be more complicated.

## 4.1  Non-trivial Cases Without Holes

The surface generation of 4D cube model at Fig. 1 proofs that restriction to triangular mesh representation is beneficial. However, such knowledge does not guarantee correctness of the surface generated.

Let us consider Computer Solid Geometry (CSG) representation and tetrahedrons $T_{ABCD}$, $T_{ABCE}$ and $T_{ABCF}$. Then, the object at Fig. 2 is given as

$T_{ABCD} \cup T_{ABCE}$, i.e. union operation, while the object at Fig. 3 is given as $T_{ABCD} - T_{ABCE}$, i.e. difference operation. The "pairing algorithm" generates a triangle $T_{ABC}$, which is an invalid as it is a residue from the CSG operation.

In the both cases, the simple algorithm fails, as it would generate a non-existent common face of those two tetrahedrons. In the first case, such incorrect face would be inside, in the second case, the invalid case would "close" the hole of the object at Fig. 3. On the other hand, some objects might have a hole similarly as in the "4D-Cube" case at Fig. 1. In this case, such simple algorithm would delivered correct result, if the wire frame model represents the triangular mesh. Actually it is due to a non-triangular cross section of the object. The simple algorithm would also fail in the case of a prism with a triangular profile, see Fig. 4. In this case also non-existent triangles in side of the object would be generated. It can be seen, that these simple examples demonstrate, that such simple algorithm would not work properly.

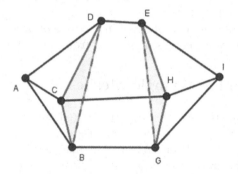

**Fig. 4.** Prism

However, in the case Fig. 5, the simple algorithm generates a correct triangular mesh. It can be seen that the triangular non-existent triangles or triangular holes causing problems in the correct triangular mesh generation.

## 4.2   Non-trivial Cases with Holes

The "triangular-ring" model at Fig. 6 represents the case, when "virtual triangles" at the corners can be generated from the wire-frame model, but they are not part of the surface of those objects, which are actually non-manifold unions of three prisms with triangular, Fig. 6a, and non-triangular, Fig. 6b, cross sections of the objects.

There are two main problems in unambiguity of the surface reconstruction given by the wire-frame model, if general polygonal faces:

- Ambiguous surface as in the case of the "4D-Cube" model, see Fig. 7
- Non-existent (fictive) faces generation as in the case of the "Triangular-ring" model, where 3 non-existent (inner) triangles would be generated on the intersection of two triangular prisms, see Fig. 6.

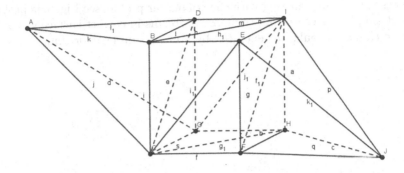

**Fig. 5.** Prism-rectangular-profile

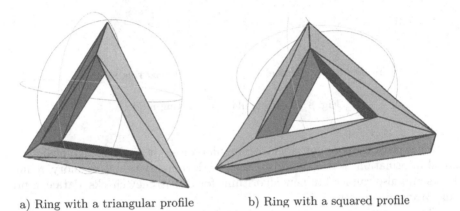

a) Ring with a triangular profile      b) Ring with a squared profile

**Fig. 6.** Triangular ring

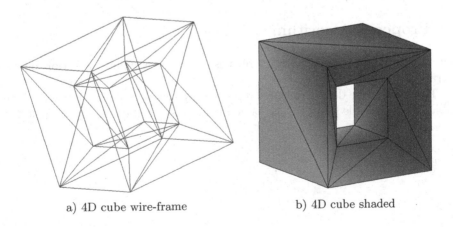

a) 4D cube wire-frame      b) 4D cube shaded

**Fig. 7.** 4D Cube testing model

In the case of a triangular ring with the triangular profile, see Fig. 8, is probably the most simple object causing the most problems in correct surface generation as 4 false triangles would be generated by a naive simple algorithm.

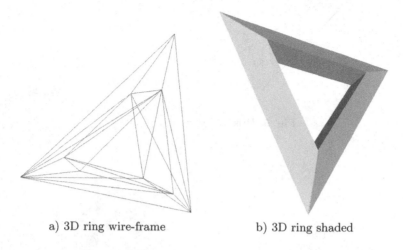

a) 3D ring wire-frame                    b) 3D ring shaded

**Fig. 8.** 3D triangular ring testing model

If a surface is represented as a triangular mesh, it gives us significant additional information, which should be used to decrease data, i.e. memory, requirements and also can lead to new algorithms for consistency checks, data compression, transmission, etc.

The unambiguous surface generation of the "triangular-ring" wire-frame model is possible, if triangular mesh is used, see Fig. 8b.

In the following the principle of the proposed algorithm will be described.

## 5    Proposed Algorithm

Let us consider a simple object which is result of a union operation on two tetrahedra Fig. 9.

The wire-frame data structures representing this polyhedron is given by the table of edges Table 1 and by the table of vertices coordinates $x, y, z$ Table 2.

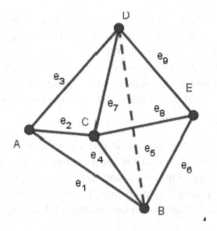

**Fig. 9.** Example - two joint tetrahedra

**Table 1.** Wire-frame data structure - edges

| $ID_E$ | 1 | 2 | 3 | 4 | 5 | 6 | 7 | 8 | 9 |
|---|---|---|---|---|---|---|---|---|---|
| $V_1$ | 1 | 1 | 1 | 2 | 2 | 2 | 3 | 3 | 4 |
| $V_2$ | 2 | 3 | 4 | 3 | 4 | 5 | 4 | 5 | 5 |

**Table 2.** Wire-frame data structure - vertices

|  | A | B | C | D | E |
|---|---|---|---|---|---|
| $ID_V$ | 1 | 2 | 3 | 4 | 5 |
| $x$ | 0 | 3 | 1 | 2 | 4 |
| $y$ | 0 | -2 | 1 | 2 | -2 |
| $z$ | 0 | 2 | 1 | -1 | 3 |

For the surface reconstruction from the wire-frame data model, actually only a table of edges is required, as vertex coordinates are not used in manifold single triangular surface model cases.

It should be noted that $ID_E$, resp. $ID_V$ are identifiers of edges, resp. vertices and are not actually part of data structures necessarily.

The proposed algorithm is actually very simple in principle for the closed surfaces.

1. Find all triangles sharing common edge twice only, generate those triangles and sign edges of those triangles as used   update data structures reflecting those changes
2. Find all triangles having the only one common edge shared three times, generate those triangles and sign edges of those triangles as used   update data structures reflecting those changes

3. Find all triangles having the only two common edges shared three times, generate those triangles and sign edges of those triangles as used  update data structures reflecting those changes
4. Find all triangles having all three common edges shared three times, generate those triangles and sign edges of those triangles as used  remove such a triangles from the set of given reminding triangles as those triangles are not part of the surface.

In the case, that the that the surface is not closed, i.e. it has the border, additional check is to be used to verify that the borders forms closed boundary curve.

The result of the algorithm is a non-ordered set of triangles, i.e. there is no information on the triangle neighbours. However, the basic algorithm can be modified and the triangular mesh can be generated, i.e. information of neighbours is generated as well.

It should be noted, that the reconstruction of a triangular mesh from a set of triangles is a nontrivial task. Triangular mesh reconstruction from a set of triangles is described in Glassner [13], Hradek [16] and Skala [25].

# 6    Experimental Results

The proposed algorithm was tested for several data sets, some of those were specifically constructed to "attack" the proposed algorithm, e.g.

- A "ring" shape polyhedron which has a triangular profile, see Fig. 7
- A "4D-Cube" model with triangular faces, see Fig. 6, Fig. 8
- Polyhedron with 6 faces formed as a union of two tetrahedrons with a "common" face, see Fig. 2, Fig. 3, Fig. 9, etc.

The resulting triangular meshes were stored in the PLY format and 3D printed. The Fig. 10 presents 3D print of the reconstructed "4D-Cube" and "triangular ring" data.

The experiments proved functionality of the proposed algorithm and correctness of its implementation in Pascal using Lazarus IDE.

The proposed algorithm can be easily modified for the case when some triangles on the surface of a model are missing. In this case the input data must contain information on those triangles in explicit form and they will be handled as non-existent virtual triangles.

**Fig. 10.** 3D print of "4D-Cube" and "triangular ring" reconstruction from the wire-frame model

## 7  Conclusion

Triangular meshes are used for surface models nearly exclusively due to many reasons. However, the triangular mesh properties have not been fully explored yet as far as the unambiguity mesh representation, storing, compression and transmission, etc. This paper presents a new algorithm, which enables to reconstruct faces of a triangular mesh surface from wire-frame data structure, which was considered as ambiguous representation in computer graphics, CAD/CAM systems.

The proposed algorithm breaks the "axiom" on the ambiguity of wire-frame 3D models representation in the case of triangular meshes. The proposed approach can also lead to new algorithms for mesh consistency checks, data compression applicable especially in CAD/CAM systems and transmission, etc. The proposed algorithm can reconstruct a surface of non-manifold objects is they share a common face, similarly as in the "triangular-ring" model.

**Acknowledgment.**
The author would like to thank to recent students at the VSB-Technical University and Ostrava University, University of West Bohemia as the method was designed during the Fall term in 2013 and verified by experimental implementations in Pascal.

Thanks also belong to colleagues at the University of West Bohemia and Shandong University (China) for their valuable comments, hints provided and for printing 3D model and to anonymous reviewers for their critical views and hints leading to significant paper improvement.

# References

1. Alexei, Z., Arkady, Z.: Three-dimensional reconstruction from projections based on incidence matrices of patterns. AASRI Procedia **9**, 72–77 (2014). https://doi.org/10.1016/j.aasri.2014.09.013. https://www.sciencedirect.com/science/article/pii/S2212671614001139. 2014 AASRI Conference on Circuit and Signal Processing (CSP 2014)
2. Apostol, K.: Polygonal Modeling. SaluPress (2012). https://doi.org/10.5555/2463089
3. Attene, M.: Indirect predicates for geometric constructions. CAD Comput. Aided Des. **126** (2020). https://doi.org/10.1016/j.cad.2020.102856
4. Attene, M., Campen, M., Kobbelt, L.: Polygon mesh repairing: an application perspective. ACM Comput. Surv. **45**(2) (2013). https://doi.org/10.1145/2431211.2431214
5. Bandla, S., Gurumoorthy, B.: Constructing a wire-frame from views on arbitrary view planes for objects with conic sections inclined to all view planes. CAD Comput. Aided Des. **43**(12), 1639–1653 (2011). https://doi.org/10.1016/j.cad.2011.08.010
6. Botsch, M., Kobbelt, L., Pauly, M., Alliez, P., Levy, B.: Polygon Mesh Processing. 1st edn. A K Peters/CRC Press (2010). https://doi.org/10.1201/b10688
7. Brentzen, J.A., Gravesen, J., Anton, F., Aans, H.: Guide to Computational Geometry Processing: Foundations, Algorithms, and Methods. Springer, London (2012). https://doi.org/10.5555/2349037
8. Campagna, S., Kobbelt, L., Seidel, H.P.: Directed edges-a scalable representation for triangle meshes. J. Graph. Tools **3**(4), 1–11 (1998). https://doi.org/10.1080/10867651.1998.10487494
9. Company, P., Varley, P.A.C., Plumed, R., Camba, J.D.: Detection of vertices in sketched drawings of polyhedral shapes. In: Vera-Rodriguez, R., Fierrez, J., Morales, A. (eds.) CIARP 2018. LNCS, vol. 11401, pp. 376–383. Springer, Cham (2019). https://doi.org/10.1007/978-3-030-13469-3_44
10. Fang, F., Lee, Y.: 3D reconstruction of polyhedral objects from single perspective projections using cubic corner. 3D Res. **3**(2), 1–8 (2012). https://doi.org/10.1007/3DRes.02(2012)1
11. Fu, Z.G., Zou, B.J., Chen, Y.M., Wu, L., Shen, Y.: Reconstruction of intersecting curved solids from 2D orthographic views. CAD Comput. Aided Des. **42**(9), 841–846 (2010). https://doi.org/10.1016/j.cad.2010.03.005
12. Glassner, A.: Building Vertex Normals from an Unstructured Polygon List, pp. 60–73. Academic Press Professional Inc, USA (1994)
13. Glassner, A.: Building vertex normals from an unstructured polygon list. In: Graphics Gems IV, pp. 60–73 (1994)
14. Gou, G., Sui, H., Li, D., Peng, Z., Guo, B., Yang, W., Huang, D.: Limofilling: Local information guide hole-filling and sharp feature recovery for manifold meshes. Remote Sens. **14**(2) (2022). https://doi.org/10.3390/rs14020289. https://www.mdpi.com/2072-4292/14/2/289
15. Held, M.: ERIT-a collection of efficient and reliable intersection tests. J. Graph. Tools **2**(4), 25–44 (1997). https://doi.org/10.1080/10867651.1997.10487482
16. Hrádek, J., Kuchar, M., Skala, V.: Hash functions and triangular mesh reconstruction. Comput. Geosci. **29**(6), 741–751 (2003). https://doi.org/10.1016/S0098-3004(03)00037-2

17. Inoue, K., Shimada, K., Chilaka, K.: Solid model reconstruction of wireframe cad models based on topological embeddings of planar graphs. J. Mech. Des. Trans. ASME **125**(3), 434–442 (2003). https://doi.org/10.1115/1.1586309
18. Landier, S.: Boolean operations on arbitrary polygonal and polyhedral meshes. CAD Comput. Aided Des. **85**, 138–153 (2017). https://doi.org/10.1016/j.cad.2016.07.013
19. Le Clerc, F., Sun, H.: Memory-friendly deep mesh registration. CSRN-Comput. Sci. Res. Notes **3001**(1), 1–10 (2020). https://doi.org/10.24132/CSRN.2020.3001.1
20. Lee, Y., Fang, F.: A new hybrid method for 3D object recovery from 2D drawings and its validation against the cubic corner method and the optimisation-based method. CAD Comput. Aided Des. **44**(11), 1090–1102 (2012). https://doi.org/10.1016/j.cad.2012.06.001
21. Levy, B., Zhang, H.R.: Elements of geometry processing. In: SIGGRAPH Asia 2011 Courses, SA 2011, pp. 1–48. ACM, New York (2011). https://doi.org/10.1145/2077434.2077439
22. Markowsky, G., Wesley, M.A.: Fleshing out wire frames. IBM J. Res. Dev. **24**(5), 582–597 (1980)
23. Minardi, P.: Reconstruction of 3-dimensional solid objects represented by wireframe descriptions. In: Earnshaw, R.A., Wyvill, B. (eds.) New Advances in Computer Graphics, pp. 489–503. Springer, Tokyo (1989). https://doi.org/10.1007/978-4-431-68093-2_31
24. Shin, B.S., Shin, Y.: Fast 3D solid model reconstruction from orthographic views. CAD Comput. Aided Des. **30**(1), 63–76 (1998). https://doi.org/10.1016/S0010-4485(97)00054-7
25. Skala, V., Kuchar, M.: The hash function and the principle of duality. In: Proceedings Computer Graphics International CGI 2001, pp. 167–174 (2001)
26. Varley, P.A., Company, P.P.: A new algorithm for finding faces in wireframes. Comput. Aided Des. **42**(4), 279–309 (2010). https://doi.org/10.1016/j.cad.2009.11.008
27. Wassermann, B., Kollmannsberger, S., Yin, S., Kudela, L., Rank, E.: Integrating CAD and numerical analysis: 'dirty geometry' handling using the finite cell method. Comput. Methods Appl. Mech. Eng. **351**, 808–835 (2019). https://doi.org/10.1016/j.cma.2019.04.017
28. Wenger, R.: Isosurfaces: Geometry, Topology, and Algorithms. A.K.Peters/CRC Press, New York (2013). https://doi.org/10.1201/b15025
29. Wikipedia: IEEE 754 - Wikipedia, the free encyclopedia (2021). https://en.wikipedia.org/wiki/IEEE_754. Accessed 11 July 2021
30. Wikipedia contributors: Polygon mesh - Wikipedia, the free encyclopedia (2021). https://en.wikipedia.org/wiki/Polygon_mesh. Accessed 19 Oct 2021
31. Yan, Q.W., Philip Chen, C., Tang, Z.: Efficient algorithm for the reconstruction of 3D objects from orthographic projections. Comput. Aided Des. **26**(9), 699–717 (1994). https://doi.org/10.1016/0010-4485(94)90020-5
32. Yu, H., He, Y., Zhang, W.: A new approach to analyzing interactions of two objects in space based on a specially- tailored local coordinate system. IEEE Access **9**, 60258–60264 (2021). https://doi.org/10.1109/ACCESS.2021.3074509
33. Zabran, M.: An algorithm recreating 3D triangle mesh faces from its edges. In: CESCG 2018, pp. 1–8 (2018). https://cescg.org/wp-content/uploads/2018/04/Zabran-An-Algorithm-Recreating-3D-Triangle-Mesh-Faces-from-Its-Edges.pdf

# A Free Web Service for Fast COVID-19 Classification of Chest X-Ray Images with Artificial Intelligence

Jose David Bermudez Castro[1]([✉])[iD], Jose E. Ruiz[1][iD],
Pedro Achanccaray Diaz[1][iD], Smith Arauco Canchumuni[1][iD],
Cristian Muñoz Villalobos[1][iD], Felipe Borges Coelho[1][iD],
Leonardo Forero Mendoza[2][iD], and Marco Aurelio C. Pacheco[1][iD]

[1] Pontifical Catholic University of Rio de Janeiro, Rua Marquês de São Vicente, 225, Gávea, Rio de Janeiro, RJ 22451-900, Brazil
prof.bermudez@ica.ele.puc-rio.br
[2] Rio de Janeiro State University, Block C - Floor 9, R. São Francisco Xavier, 524, Maracanã, Rio de Janeiro, RJ 20550-900, Brasil
https://www.puc-rio.br

**Abstract.** The coronavirus outbreak became a major concern for society worldwide. Technological innovation and ingenuity are essential to fight COVID-19 pandemic and bring us one step closer to overcome it. Researchers over the world are working actively to find available alternatives in different fields, such as the Healthcare System, pharmaceutic, health prevention, among others. With the rise of artificial intelligence (AI) in the last 10 years, IA-based applications have become the prevalent solution in different areas because of its higher capability, being now adopted to help combat against COVID-19. This work provides a fast detection system of COVID-19 characteristics in X-Ray images based on deep learning (DL) techniques. This system is available as a free web deployed service for fast patient classification, alleviating the high demand for standards method for COVID-19 diagnosis. It is constituted of two deep learning models, one to differentiate between X-Ray and non-X-Ray images based on Mobile-Net architecture, and another one to identify chest X-Ray images with characteristics of COVID-19 based on the DenseNet architecture. For real-time inference, it is provided a pair of dedicated GPUs, which reduce the computational time. The whole system can filter out non-chest X-Ray images, and detect whether the X-Ray presents characteristics of COVID-19, highlighting the most sensitive regions.

**Keywords:** COVID-19 · Deployed system · Free web service · Deep learning

O. Gervasi et al. (Eds.): ICCSA 2022, LNCS 13375, pp. 412–427, 2022.
https://doi.org/10.1007/978-3-031-10522-7_29

# 1    Introduction

The coronavirus disease 2019 (COVID-19) was declared a public health emergency of international concern by the World Health Organization (WHO) on January 30 [1]. COVID-19 has become a pandemic with more than 120 million confirmed cases and almost 3 million deaths around 223 countries [2] at the time of writing this work. There have been many efforts to fight COVID-19 around the world such as research a vaccine against COVID-19, massive creation of ventilators as well as personal protective equipment (PPE), development of fast diagnosis systems from chest X-Ray and/or thoracic computer tomography (CT), among others in many different fields.

Artificial Intelligence (AI) can be applied in many different ways to fight COVID-19. As stated in [3], between the most important applications of AI in COVID-19 pandemic are: early detection of the infection from medical imaging, monitoring and prediction of the spread of the virus and mortality rates, tracing the virus by identifying hot spots, and development of drugs and vaccines by helping in clinical trials. Landing AI [4] developed a monitoring tool that issues an alert when anyone is less than the desired distance from another person, promoting social distancing in the streets due to its effectiveness to slow down the COVID-19 spread. On the other hand, machine learning methods have been applied to predict the number of active cases around the world [5], for fast COVID-19 detection from CT [6] and X-Ray [7], and to develop systems for detection of those who are not wearing facial masks [8].

Using the viral nucleic acid detection using real-time polymerase chain reaction (RT-PCR) methods for testing in thousands of suspenseful patients is very delayed. To address this drawback, efforts have been made using AI to detect patients with COVID-19 in a very fast time through medical imaging technologies like CT and X-Ray images. It is because, COVID-19 causes acute, highly lethal pneumonia with clinical symptoms similar to those reported for SARS-CoV and MERS-CoV [9]. The most common and widely available method using this type of technologies is by chest X-Ray images because it is available in ambulatory care facilities, handy with portable X-Ray systems, and enabling rapid classification (speeding up the disease screening). In contrast, CT scanners may not be available in many underdeveloped regions, disabling its use for quick diagnoses. Despite the advantages to detect COVID-19 by X-Ray, one of the main bottlenecks is the need of specialists (radiologists) to interpret the images. Taking this "specialists" expertise as *a prior* knowledge to build an AI system can help them for quick triage, especially as a tool to triage patients for radiologists with case overloads.

## 1.1    Related Works

Several AI-based approaches have been proposed to detect patients with COVID-19 using X-Ray images. Most of them use pre-trained models and data augmentation, mainly due to the lack of data. [7] create a free repository of X-Ray image data collections to train machine learning approaches for COVID-19 classification. In addition, [10] published a survey on public medical imaging data resources (CT, X-Ray, MRT and others), which can be used to increase the number of X-Ray samples. Reviews of known deep learning models used to create an automatic detection of COVID-19 from X-Ray images are presented by [11] and [12], which used VGG-19, MobileNetV2, Inception, Xception and ResNetV2 as pre-trained models. They used a small number of X-Ray samples with confirmed COVID-19 (224, 50 and 25 respectively). [13] collected more X-Ray samples to increase the training dataset and use pre-trained models followed by highlighting class-discriminating regions using gradient-guided class activation maps(Grad-CAM) [14] for better visualization.

Abbas [15] introduced a model called Decompose, Transfer and Compose (DeTracC) to classify between healthy, severe acute respiratory syndrome (SARS) and COVID-19 in X-Ray images. This network was built in tree stages: (i) features extraction, (ii) class decomposition, and (iii) classification. The authors used AlexNet and ResNet18, as pre-trained models, and Principal Component Analysis (PCA), as a decomposition class. The training was performed with 80 samples of normal X-Ray, 105 samples of COVID-19, and 11 samples of SARS, and data augmentation to increase the dataset to 1764 was employed. Afshar [16] presented a new model based on capsule networks called COVIDS-CAPS to classify between non-COVID-19 (normal, Bacterial and Viral) and COVID-19 using less number of trainable parameters compared with pre-trained models. Their results show that COVIDS-CAPS is able to predict X-Ray with COVID-19. Despite the fact that the network was trained with few X-Ray samples, which poses uncertainties regarding the network suitability for new samples.

Not only AI-based research was developed (several papers using deep learning to predict COVID-19 in X-Ray images), also software and services have been created. The startup "DarwinIA" developed the COVID-Net [17], which can help to identify COVID-19 patients using chest X-Ray radiography. Also, they made a free Kubernetes Bundle for inferencing COVID-19 X-Rays images. In addition, Seoul-based medical AI software company Lunit[1] released its AI-powered software for chest X-Ray analysis with a limitation of 20 uses/day/user.

## 1.2  Contributions

In this context, this work presents a free and open source system available as a web service for fast detection of COVID-19 characteristics in chest X-Ray images using deep learning. This system employs deep learning models to detect COVID-19 effects on lungs from chest X-Ray, which can be used for classification, triage, and monitor COVID-19 cases.

The main contributions of this work can be summarized as follows: First, two deep learning models are presented, one to differentiate between X-Ray and non-X-Ray images based on Mobile-Net architecture, and another one to detect chest X-Ray images with characteristics of COVID-19 using a network bases on dense blocks and initialized from a pre-trained ImageNet. Second, we provide a

---

[1] Lunit: https://www.lunit.io/en/covid19/.

free and open-source service with dedicated GPUs to make inferences in real-time. The source code is available at https://github.com/ICA-PUC/ServiceIA-COVID-19.

The remainder of the paper is organized as.follows: Sect. 2 describes the proposed methodology for the Web Service's implementation, and Sect. 3 presents the datasets employed in our experiments. Then, Sect. 4 shows the results achieved by the X-Ray images filter and COVID-19 classifier. Finally, Sect. 5 summarizes the conclusions obtained from our experiments.

## 2   Methodology

This section presents the methodologies adopted for each of three parts of the project, the X-Ray image filter, the COVID-19 classifier and the Web page description. Figure 1 summarizes the workflow of the system.

The first box in Fig. 1, from left to right, illustrates the beginning of the detection process. It starts with a simple extension verification to check whether the uploaded file is an image (web interface). Next, the Backend (second box) sends and stores the input image to the GPU cluster (Server), which performs the network's inferences after the Backend verifies the correct uploading of the images to it. Finally, the last box shows how the web interface stores and displays the result of the inference.

### 2.1   X-Ray Images Filter

Due to the input of our system to predict COVID-19 are X-Ray images from frontal AP and PA views, we first guarantee that the inputs present these characteristics to have a correct assessment. Therefore, we implement a neural network based on Mobile-Net architecture to identify whether it is a valid image (pulmonary frontal X-Ray image) or a non-valid image (rotated pulmonary X-Ray images, colored or natural images, for instance).

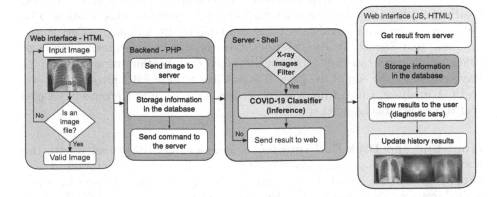

**Fig. 1.** Inference workflow for X-ray images. Each step refers to a single abstraction layer.

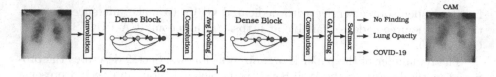

**Fig. 2.** Description of the neural architecture used in this work to classify X-Ray images for detection COVID-19. It is made of three DenseNet blocks, followed by a linear classifier.

## 2.2 COVID-19 Classifier

Figure 2 illustrates the processing scheme followed in this work to classify COVID-19 X-Ray images. The core of this system is a classifier built on the DenseNet [18] network with weights initialized from a pre-trained ImageNet [19] model. We selected a DenseNet-based architecture due to it has demonstrated high capability for classifying X-Ray images [20,21].

For optimizing the network parameters, we split this process into two stages due to the scarcity of COVID-19 samples. At the first stage, we train the DenseNet to discern between No Finding and Lung Opacity images, and at the second one, the model was finetuned incorporating the COVID-19 class information. During the first stage, COVID-19 samples were considered as Lung Opacity because of existing correlation between COVID-19 and Pneumonia, and processed independently in the second stage. By adopting this stratified training, we take advantage of the number of samples per class in the first stage to guarantee the learning of representative features for identifying opacities in the Lungs. Then, in the second stage, these features are finetuned to classify whether the opacity was originated by COVID-19 or not.

## 2.3 Web Page Description

The web page was created to display all the content of this research. Besides, health specialists may use the platform to support patients' classification. The web page is accessible worldwide, being available in two languages: Portuguese (original) and English. It also describes also, there is an area on the web page where public users can experience the predicted classification using personal X-Ray images. At the end of the page, it is possible to view a 3D projection based on PCA analyses, which from a set of images samples, forms groups of images that most resemble each other.

**Front-End and Back-End Interface - Service Architecture:** due to the web page was developed as a free service for providing a simple solution to perform image analysis, and that can be utilized by any user. The web page interface (called front-end) was developed in HyperText Markup Language (HTML), Cascading Style Sheets (CSS) and JavaScript (JS). The implemented service that maintains the operation of the website, known as backend, was developed in

Hypertext Preprocessor (PHP), Python, and Shell Command Language (Sh). The Deep Learning neural network models were implemented in Keras engine, using Tensorflow as backend. The server run over a Unix operating system, which controls the running process via Bourne-again shell (Bash).

# 3   X-Ray Dataset

Public data, collected from different places, was used for our implementations.

## 3.1   X-Ray Images Filter

For filtering frontal X-Ray images, we selected three public groups of images:

- Frontal pulmonary X-Ray [22].
- Frontal non-pulmonary X-Ray collected using Web Scraping.
- Other kind of images that are not X-Ray images: PASCAL VOC and Computational Vision at CALTECH dataset.

Taking into account that the performance of the classification system would be reduced if it process images inverted or rotated (90° clockwise and counterclockwise), we created a group of images with these characteristics to be identified as non-valid by the X-Ray filter. Particularly, we randomly selected a set of images from the X-Ray dataset and applied rotations of 90°, 180°, and 270° to each image. Table 1 summarizes the distribution of the dataset used for the filter network.

## 3.2   COVID-19 Classifier

For detecting COVID-19 using X-Ray imagery, we selected four publicly available datasets, two associated with COVID-19 and the others with opacities in Lungs caused by different pathologies, like pneumonia, infiltration, consolidation, among others. Both COVID-19 datasets, Cohen [7] and *Figure 1-COVID*[2] datasets, are community repositories updated regularly with X-Ray imagery from patients from different countries, already diagnosed or suspected of having COVID-19, and others pneumonia infections. At the date this paper was written, the Cohen dataset

**Table 1.** Dataset distribution for the X-ray images filter.

| Class | Data type | # of samples | | | |
|---|---|---|---|---|---|
| | | Train | Validation | Test | Total |
| Valid | Frontal pulmonary X-ray | 4,400 | 300 | 300 | 5,000 |
| | Rotated frontal pulmonary X-ray | 4,800 | 100 | 100 | 5,000 |
| Non-valid | Frontal non-pulmonary X-ray | 530 | 100 | 100 | 730 |
| | Not X-ray | 9,800 | 100 | 100 | 10,000 |

---

[2] https://github.com/agchung/Figure1-COVID-chestxray-dataset.

**Table 2.** Distribution of samples of Chest X-Ray, RSNA, and COVID-19 datasets.

| Pathology | Datasets | | |
|---|---|---|---|
| | Chest X-ray | RSNA | COVID-19 |
| No finding | 1,340 | 8,851 | – |
| Lung opacity | 1,346 | 6,012 | – |
| COVID-19 | – | – | 3616 |

contained 438 X-Ray images from AP and PA views, 359 associated with COVID-19, and 79 with the others pathologies. The *Figure 1-COVID* dataset is a smaller one comprising 40 images, where 35 are from patients confirmed with COVID-19, three with pneumonia caused by others infections, and two with no finding pathology. There is also a set of images from patients with symptoms not confirmed as positive of COVID-19 that were filtered out. We merged the Cohen and the *Figure 1-COVID* dataset forming the COVID-19 dataset.

The non-COVID-19 datasets are the Chest X-Ray Pneumonia [23] and the RSNA Pneumonia detection challenge [24]. The Chest X-Ray Pneumonia dataset contains a total of 5,863 PA view X-Ray images, collected from pediatric patients from one to five years old. The dataset is distributed into two categories: Normal or Pneumonia, and it is already organized into training, validation, and testing sets. Additionally, it also reported whether the pneumonia was caused by a virus or bacterial. From the RSNA dataset, we selected the images corresponding to the "No Finding" and "Lung Opacity" classes, filtering out the images rotated at $(90°\text{--}270°)$ approx using the X-Ray filter. Table 2 summarizes the final distribution of samples after performed this process. In this work, we rename the images labeled as Normal and Pneumonia to the non-Finding and Lung opacity class to have the same nomenclature of RSNA dataset. Examples of the "No Finding" and "Lung Opacity" classes are shown in Fig. 3.

## 4   Results

This section presents the experimental protocol used to develop the networks. Afterward, it is shown and analyzed the results obtained. All experiments were carried out in an NVIDIA GPU Tesla P100 of 16 GB of RAM and 3584 Cuda cores.

### 4.1   X-Ray Images Filter

**Experimental Protocol.** The images were resized to $224 \times 224 \times 1$ and normalized between zero to one. Besides, the training samples were augmented by performing random rotations of 5° and zooming up to 10%. Table 3 summarizes the hyper-parameters setup used for training.

**Result.** The training time was 30 min approximately, running a total of 69 epochs, when the early-stopping was activated. The network achieved the best

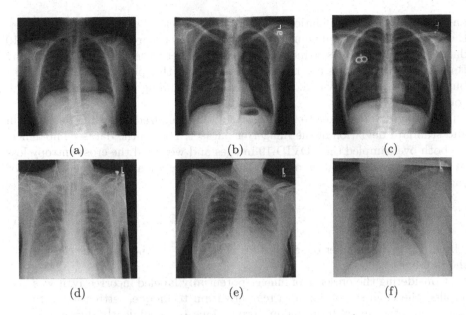

**Fig. 3.** Examples of images from patients labeled as no finding (a, b, c) and Lung Opacity (d, e, f).

**Table 3.** Training configuration used in the filter network.

| Configurations | Value |
| --- | --- |
| Batch | 128 |
| Steps by epoch | 5 |
| Number of epochs | 100 (maximum) |
| Optimizer | Adam |
| Learning rate | 0.001 (decay a 0.5 factor each 5 epochs) |
| Stop criteria | Follow up the loss function (15) |
| Metrics | Accuracy |

performance at epoch 54, with a loss function value of 0.0075, and 99.83% of accuracy in the validation set. Similar classification rates were obtained by evaluating the trained network in the testing set, reaching an accuracy of 99.3%.

## 4.2    COVID-19 Classifier

**Experimental Protocol.** We first split each dataset into three groups: training, validation, and testing sets, adopting different criteria for each dataset. In the COVID-19 datasets, we selected the samples according to the patient to avoid having samples from the same patient in training and validation/testing sets, respectively. Specifically, we selected a proportion of 80%, 10%, and 10% of patients for training, validation, and testing, respectively. In the RSNA dataset, the samples were split randomly following the same proportion of the COVID-19 datasets because there is no more than one image per patient. In the Chest X-Ray Pneumonia dataset was not necessary to perform this procedure as this distribution was already provided. Finally, the corresponding groups were merged to constitute the final sets.

All images were resized to $224 \times 224 \times 3$ and normalized according to the mean and standard deviation of the ImageNet dataset. Due to the dataset imbalance, we both oversampled the COVID-19 images and weighted the cross-entropy loss to enhance the classification of COVID-19 imagery. We assigned the weights for each class using Eq. 1,

$$\omega_{c_i} = \frac{N_{c_i}}{N_{c_{max}}}, 0 < i < C \tag{1}$$

where $N_{c_i}$ is the number of samples for class $i$, $N_{c_{max}}$ the majority class and $C$ the number of classes.

Considering the presence of images potentially labeled incorrectly, it was also applied the label smoothing as a regularization technique, setting alpha to 0.1. It prevents the model from making predictions too confidently during training that can be reflected in poor generalization. Then, cross-entropy loss takes the form described in Eq. 2,

$$L = y_{soft} * \log(\hat{y}) * \omega_{c_i} + (1 - y_{soft}) * \log(1 - \hat{y}) \tag{2}$$

where $y_{soft} = (1 - \alpha) * y + \alpha/C$, and $y$ and $\hat{y}$ the true and predicted labels, respectively.

Besides, we also augmented the training and validation samples by performing random horizontal flipping, rotation, brightness, scaling, occlusions at top of the images, cropping, and resize transformations. This procedure was carried out to avoid the network learns to maximize the inter-class differences based on the distribution of the noise that characterizes each dataset. During training, we monitored the validation loss function applying early stopping when no improvements were observed throughout five consecutive epochs. Also, the learning rate was reduced by a factor of 0.5 after a plateau on the validation loss. We initiated the learning rate of Adam optimizer to $1e{-}5$, fixing the other parameters to default values.

We assessed the performance of the model quantitatively and qualitatively. The foremost was performed in terms of Confusion Matrix, sensitivity and specificity metrics, which quantifies the classifier's ability to avoid false negatives and false positives, respectively. In particular, we report the sensitivity as diagonal of the confusion matrix. Also, the qualitative assessment was performed by analyzing the generated Class Activation Maps (CAM), which indicates the regions that were more relevant in the classification of the evaluated image.

Finally, a Visual Transformer (VIT) [25] model and four traditional machine learning techniques, Support Vector Machine (SVM), Random Forest (RF), XGBoost [26], and Multilayer Perceptron (MLP), respectively, were also evaluated and used as a baseline for our proposed methodology.

**Table 4.** Median and standard deviation normalized confusion matrix obtained by evaluating all classifier in the corresponding testing set after running the experiments 50 times.

| | | Predicted | | |
|---|---|---|---|---|
| | | No finding | Lung opacity | COVID-19 |
| Ours | No finding | **95.80 ± 1.40%** | 2.50 ± 0.80% | 1.50 ± 1.20% |
| | Lung opacity | 8.80 ± 1.70% | **90.00 ± 1.80%** | 0.80 ± 0.50% |
| | COVID-19 | 1.40 ± 0.90% | 0.60 ± 0.60% | **97.80 ± 1.10%** |
| SVM | No finding | 88.22 ± 0.15% | 7.53 ± 0.10% | 4.25 ± 0.10% |
| | Lung opacity | 11.73 ± 0.05% | 82.80 ± 0.08% | 5.47 ± 0.07% |
| | COVID-19 | 10.17 ± 0.11% | 9.12 ± 0.00% | 80.72 ± 0.11% |
| RF | No finding | 89.80 ± 0.20% | 11.20 ± 0.20% | 6.00 ± 0.40% |
| | Lung opacity | 14.00 ± 0.30% | 78.50 ± 0.40% | 4.10 ± 0.40% |
| | COVID-19 | 4.10 ± 0.20% | 2.30 ± 0.20% | 83.80 ± 0.50% |
| VIT | No finding | 90.60 ± 1.30% | 6.20 ± 1.10% | 3.10 ± 0.60% |
| | Lung opacity | 15.40 ± 1.40% | 80.00 ± 1.60% | 4.80 ± 0.90% |
| | COVID-19 | 4.70 ± 1.00% | 6.60 ± 1.20% | 88.70 ± 1.50% |
| XGBoost | No finding | 91.99 ± 0.83% | 2.21 ± 0.24% | 5.80 ± 0.63% |
| | Lung opacity | 1.63 ± 0.12% | 82.77 ± 0.18% | 15.60 ± 0.18% |
| | COVID-19 | 1.54 ± 0.05% | 5.98 ± 0.22% | 92.48 ± 0.27% |
| MLP | No finding | 85.39 ± 0.59% | 5.58 ± 0.35% | 9.02 ± 0.59% |
| | Lung opacity | 17.82 ± 0.84% | 76.46 ± 1.02% | 5.71 ± 0.55% |
| | COVID-19 | 9.66 ± 1.23% | 14.91 ± 0.95% | 75.41 ± 1.38% |

**Table 5.** Results obtained by the classifier in terms of Specificity metric. It is reported the mean and standard deviations statistics as percentage (NF: No Finding, LO: Lung Opacity, C-19: COVID-19).

| | SVM | RF | VIT | XGBoost | MLP | Ours |
|---|---|---|---|---|---|---|
| NF | 88.8 ± 0.0 | 83.1 ± 0.3 | 88.1 ± 1.1 | 98.4 ± 0.1 | 92.4 ± 0.5 | **93.7 ± 1.2** |
| LO | 92.1 ± 0.1 | 92.8 ± 0.2 | 93.6 ± 1.0 | 95.2 ± 0.2 | 91.9 ± 0.4 | **97.9 ± 0.6** |
| C-19 | 95.2 ± 0.1 | 97.9 ± 0.1 | 96.1 ± 0.6 | 87.8 ± 0.3 | 84.9 ± 0.8 | **98.8 ± 0.9** |

**Results.** Tables 4 and 5 summarize the performance of all assessed models in terms of the confusion matrix and specificity metrics, respectively, after executing the experiments 50 times. Specifically, we report the result in terms of the median and the standard deviation statistics for all evaluated metrics.

Results demonstrate the high capability of our method to discern between the assessed classes. In particular, it is observed that the classifier exhibits a lower rate of misclassification regarding the COVID-19 class, although the lower amount of samples. Notice the most confusion occurs between Lung Opacity and

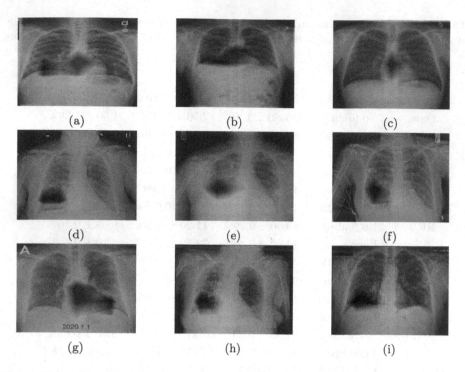

**Fig. 4.** Examples of images from patients labeled as non-finding (a, b, c), Lung Opacity (d, e, f), and COVID-19 (g, h, i), respectively.

No Finding samples. These results are expected considering that some of the Lung Opacity samples are very similar to the No Finding, indicating a possible early stage of the disease. These results are reflected in the specificity metric, where the classification rates are above 90.0% in median for all classes. However, it is necessary the collection of more COVID-19 images to improve the capability of the models for this task. For a real scenario, it is important to have a classifier with a lower rate of false positives to reduce the propagation of the virus, as well as with lower false positives to avoid classifying healthy persons. Additionally, it is required to have samples from different sensors to make the model more robust against particular artifacts and landmarks. Regarding the performance of other evaluated techniques, it notorious the superiority of our method in all metrics. We obtained rates above 90 for all metrics, whereas most of the others are below 90%. Interestingly, the VIT performed similarly to traditional techniques, although it has demonstrated high performance in other domains. We hypothesize that its performance was affected by the low quantity of available samples for the X-Ray domain. Among the traditional techniques, XGBoost got the higher metrics values, obtaining rates in some cases above 90%, and among all methods, it got the lowest standard deviation.

| Actual | COVID-19 | Lung Opacity | No Finding |
|--------|----------|--------------|------------|
| CAM | | | |
| Predicted | Lung Opacity | COVID-19 | Lung Opacity |

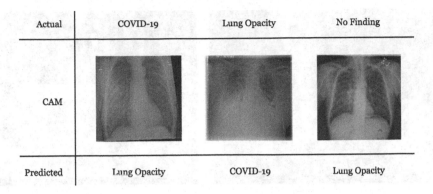

**Fig. 5.** Examples of images missclassified.

Figure 4 shows three examples per class of CAMs corresponding to images from the testing set. Specifically, it is shown a composition of the images and the associated CAM as heatmaps. By performing this analysis, it can be determined the most relevant regions considered by the network to make the final classification. In fact, it can be noticed the higher intensities on heatmaps are localized around the lungs as expected, and artifacts as rows or letters present on the images are ignored by the network to make the final prediction. These results suggest that the network is not making the final decision based on the noise characteristics of each dataset. In the dataset there are artifacts that can easily be identified by the network to discern between images from the assessed classes. Regarding images belonging to Lung Opacity, it is remarked that the network was able to identify the regions where these opacities occur. Similar behavior can be observed in the COVID-19 images where the network also highlights the most whited regions. These results are expected considering the high correlation between COVID-19 image and Pneumonia, as COVID-19 causes Pneumonia. For the Non Finding class, the heatmaps are concentrated in the central part of the chest, between the Lungs.

Finally, Fig. 5 shows examples of images missclassified. It can be observed that images classified as COVID-19 being of Lung Opacity, presents similar characteristics and vice-versa. This situation is expected to be common in patients with advanced degrees of pneumonia. This situation is expected to be common for patients with advanced stages of pneumonia independently the cause of it.

## 4.3 Web Page Interface

The site is structured in three sections, being the first one, where the user can interact with the website to test owned X-Ray images or examples available on the website. The second one describes the motivation and objectives of the project, and the third one presents the proposed solution as well as the technical explanation of its implementation.

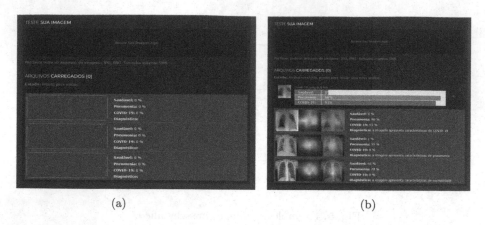

(a)                                                    (b)

**Fig. 6.** (a) Initial state of the site, where the user can send an X-Ray image to obtain a prediction of COVID-19. (b) Section of results: history and classification of X-Ray images tested.

Figure 6a displays a snip of the first section of the web site at its initial state, while Fig. 6b shows examples of testing performed on it. In particular, it is illustrated in diagrams of bars the result obtained for the actual test, and a history of the last experiment carried out. Besides, for each test, it is shown a brief description of the results, indicating if the image evaluated is from a healthy person, with opacity in the Lungs, or with characteristics of COVID-19.

Finally, the web page also shows an Embedding projector [27] to visualize and interpret the features extracted from 294 X-Ray images from the dataset. For instance, this projection are visualizing a basic clustering (No Finding and COVID-19 images) using the PCA algorithm.

## 5    Conclusion

In this work, a free web service for fast corona virus 2019 (COVID-19) classification using chest X-ray images is presented. The web service is handy and accessible, being possible to use it from desktop computer or mobile devices. It has dedicated GPUs for real-time inference and relies on two deep learning models: a model to differentiate between X-Ray and non-X-Ray images, and a model to detect COVID-19 characteristics in chest X-ray images.

The web service is composed of three main parts: a friendly web interface, an X-Ray image filter, and a COVID-19 classifier. The web interface allows the user to upload a chest X-Ray image for consultation and receive a classification, which can be Healthy, Characteristics of Pneumonia, or COVID-19. Moreover, a heatmap with the Class Activation Maps (CAM) is generated, which indicates the regions that were more relevant in the classification of the evaluated image.

An X-Ray image filter have been implemented to differentiate between valid images (pulmonary frontal X-Ray images), and non-valid images (rotated pulmonary X-Ray images, natural images, other kind of images). A pre-trained

MobileNet architecture have been employed for this purpose, achieving an accuracy of 99.3%.

The COVID-19 Classifier was implemented by optimizing a pre-trained ImageNet DenseNet. Results demonstrated the capability of the model to discern between the assessed classes, recording values above 90% in terms of sensitivity and specificity metrics. Additionally, a qualitative evaluation, based on the analysis of the generated CAM, indicates that the trained network makes its decisions focuses on the regions of the image where the Lungs are located. This analysis shows that the strategy of augmenting the data and replicating the COVID-19 samples helped to mitigate the problem of overfitting considering the scarcity of COVID-19 samples. Additionally, we evaluated the VIT, a new DL approach for image classification, and four traditional machine learning techniques. Results demonstrated that out method the highest capability for classification among all assessed methods

Future works consider the assessment of the system in hospitals to have feedback from specialists. We will provide a platform to annotate samples to increase the dataset, and retrain the network to have a more accurate model.

Besides, we will extend our methodology to make classification in Computerized Tomography images where more COVID-19 images are available.

## Impact Statement

This work generates a technological impact by providing a user-friendly web service deployed using free frameworks and public datasets. It is easy to access from any device connected to the internet such as desktop computers or mobile phones. Besides, the service core is developed using Artificial Intelligence techniques to classify the X-Ray images. Moreover, this work contributes socially by helping the health sector in this time of crisis, providing a tool for decision support about COVID-19 diagnosis using X-Ray images. Furthermore, the code is open source to allow the scientific community to modify it and collaborate to improve it.

## Disclaimer of Liability

It is noteworthy that there is no way to guarantee 100 % effectiveness in any predictive process. For this reason, it is extremely important that any medical diagnosis is made by specialized healthcare professionals. The objective of this project is only to assist decision-making by specialists.

**Acknowledgement.** This work could not have been done without the collaboration of the entire team of the Applied Computational Intelligence Laboratory (ICA) and Cenpes/Petrobras, partners for 21 years in the research and development of artificial intelligence projects for oil and gas sector.

# References

1. World Health Organization Homepage. WHO Timeline - COVID-19 (2020). www. who.int/news-room/detail/27-04-2020-who-timeline--covid-19. Accessed 5th June 2020
2. World Health Organization Homepage. Coronavirus disease (COVID-19) pandemic (2020). https://www.who.int/emergencies/diseases/novel-coronavirus-2019. Accessed 22nd June 2020
3. Vaishya, R., Javaid, M., Khan, I.H., Haleem, A.: Artificial intelligence (AI) applications for COVID-19 pandemic. Diabetes Metab. Syndr. Clin. Res. Rev. **14**(4), 337–339 (2020)
4. Landing AI. Tool to help customers monitor social distancing in the workplace (2020). https://landing.ai/. Accessed 26th May 2020
5. Institute for New Economic Thinking Homepage - University of Cambridge Faculty of Economics. (INET) (2020). http://covid.econ.cam.ac.uk/linton-uk-covid-cases-predicted-peak. Accessed 27th May 2020
6. Gozes, O., et al.: Rapid AI development cycle for the coronavirus (COVID-19) pandemic: initial results for automated detection & patient monitoring using deep learning CT image analysis (2020)
7. Cohen, J.P., Morrison, P., Dao, L.: COVID-19 Image Data Collection (2020)
8. LeewayHertz. Face mask detection system (2020). https://www.leewayhertz.com/face-mask-detection-system/. Accessed 26th May 2020
9. Li, Y.-C., Bai, W.-Z., Hashikawa, T.: The neuroinvasive potential of SARS-CoV2 may play a role in the respiratory failure of COVID-19 patients. J. Med. Virol. **92**(6), 552–555 (2020)
10. Kalkreuth, R., Kaufmann, P.: COVID-19: a survey on public medical imaging data resources (2020)
11. Apostolopoulos, I.D., Mpesiana, T.A.: Covid-19: automatic detection from X-ray images utilizing transfer learning with convolutional neural networks. Phys. Eng. Sci. Med. **43**(2), 635–640 (2020). https://doi.org/10.1007/s13246-020-00865-4
12. Hemdan, E.E.-D., Shouman, M.A., Karar, M.E.: COVIDX-Net: a framework of deep learning classifiers to diagnose COVID-19 in X-ray images (2020)
13. Karim, Md.R., Döhmen, T., Rebholz-Schuhmann, D., Decker, S., Cochez, M., Beyan, O.: DeepCOVIDExplainer: explainable COVID-19 predictions based on chest X-ray images (2020)
14. Selvaraju, R.R., Cogswell, M., Das, A., Vedantam, R., Parikh, D., Batra, D.: Grad-CAM: visual explanations from deep networks via gradient-based localization. In: 2017 IEEE International Conference on Computer Vision (ICCV), pp. 618–626 (2017)
15. Abbas, A., Abdelsamea, M., Gaber, M.: Classification of COVID-19 in chest X-ray images using DeTraC deep convolutional neural network. medRxiv (2020)
16. Afshar, P., Heidarian, S., Naderkhani, F., Oikonomou, A., Plataniotis, K.N., Mohammadi, A.: COVID-CAPS: a capsule network-based framework for identification of COVID-19 cases from X-ray images. Pattern Recogn. Lett. **138**, 638–643 (2020)
17. Wang, L., Lin, Z.Q., Wong, A.: COVID-NET: a tailored deep convolutional neural network design for detection of COVID-19 cases from chest X-ray images. Sci. Rep. **10**(1), 1–12 (2020)
18. Huang, G., Liu, Z., Van Der Maaten, L., Weinberger, K.Q.: Densely connected convolutional networks. In: 2017 IEEE Conference on Computer Vision and Pattern Recognition (CVPR), pp. 2261–2269 (2017)

19. Deng, J., Dong, W., Socher, R., Li, L.-J., Li, K., Fei-Fei, L.: ImageNet: a large-scale hierarchical image database. In: 2009 IEEE Conference on Computer Vision and Pattern Recognition, pp. 248–255. IEEE (2009)
20. Gündel, S., Grbic, S., Georgescu, B., Liu, S., Maier, A., Comaniciu, D.: Learning to recognize abnormalities in chest X-rays with location-aware dense networks. In: Vera-Rodriguez, R., Fierrez, J., Morales, A. (eds.) CIARP 2018. LNCS, vol. 11401, pp. 757–765. Springer, Cham (2019). https://doi.org/10.1007/978-3-030-13469-3_88
21. Baltruschat, I.M., Nickisch, H., Grass, M., Knopp, T., Saalbach, A.: Comparison of deep learning approaches for multi-label chest X-ray classification. Sci. Rep. 9(1), 1–10 (2019)
22. Kermany, D.S., et al.: Identifying medical diagnoses and treatable diseases by image-based deep learning. Cell 172(5), 1122–1131 (2018)
23. Kermany, D., Zhang, K., Goldbaum, M.: Labeled Optical Coherence Tomography (OCT) and Chest X-Ray Images for Classification (2018). Mendeley Data, v2, https://doi.org/10.17632/rscbjbr9sj, https://nihcc.app.box.com/v/ChestXray-NIHCC
24. Wang, X., Peng, Y., Lu, L., Lu, Z., Bagheri, M., Summers, R.M.: ChestX-ray8: hospital-scale chest X-ray database and benchmarks on weakly-supervised classification and localization of common thorax diseases. In: Proceedings of the IEEE conference on Computer Vision and Pattern Recognition, pp. 2097–2106 (2017)
25. Dosovitskiy, A., et al.: An image is worth 16x16 words: transformers for image recognition at scale. ICLR (2021)
26. Chen, T., Guestrin, C.: XGBoost: a scalable tree boosting system. CoRR, abs/1603.02754 (2016)
27. Smilkov, D., Thorat, N., Nicholson, C., Reif, E., Viégas, F.B., Wattenberg, M.: Embedding projector: interactive visualization and interpretation of embeddings. arXiv preprint arXiv:1611.05469 (2016)

# Interference Level Estimation for a Blind Source Separation in Document Restoration

Antonio Boccuto[1] ⓘ, Ivan Gerace[1(✉)] ⓘ, and Valentina Giorgetti[2] ⓘ

[1] Dipartimento di Matematica e Informatica, via Vanvitelli, 1, 06123 Perugia, Italy
{antonio.boccuto,ivan.gerace}@unipg.it
[2] Dipartimento di Matematica e Informatica,
viale G. B. Morgagni 67/A, 50134 Firenze, Italy
valentina.giorgetti@unifi.it

**Abstract.** We deal with the problem of blind separation of the components, in particular for documents corrupted by bleed-through and show-through. So, we analyze a regularization technique, which estimates the original sources, the interference levels and the blur operators. We treat the estimate of the interference levels, given the original sources and the blur operators. In particular, we investigate several GNC-type algorithms for minimizing the energy function. In the experimental results, we find which algorithm gives more precise estimates of the interference levels.

**Keywords:** Blind source separation · Image restoration · Document restoration · Bleed-through · Show-through · GNC technique

## 1 Introduction

In this paper we deal with a *Blind Source Separation* (BSS) problem for the analysis of digital documents. Digital imaging for documents is very important, because it allows to have digital achieves, to make always possible the accessibility and the readability. The *Digital Document Restoration* consists of a set of processes finalized to the visual and aesthetic improvement of a virtual reconstruction of a corrupted document, without risk of deterioration.

We deal with *show-through* and *bleed-through* effects. The show-through is a front-to-back interference, caused by the transparency of the paper and the scanning process, and by means of which the text in the one side of the document can appear also in the other side. The bleed-through is an intrinsic front-to-back physical deterioration caused by ink seeping, and its effect is similar to that of show-through. The physical model for the show-through effect has to take into account the spreading of light in the paper, the features of the paper, the reflectance of the verso and the transmittance parameters, and so, in general, it turns to be rather complicated. In [20], G. Sharma gave a nonlinear mathematical model which was first analyzed and then further approximated so to become

O. Gervasi et al. (Eds.): ICCSA 2022, LNCS 13375, pp. 428–444, 2022.
https://doi.org/10.1007/978-3-031-10522-7_30

easier to handle. A nonlinear modified Sharma model is proposed in [12,17,19]. In particular, in [12] it is proved that the results given there by the nonlinear model improve those obtained by means of data decorrelation or independent component analysis. In [17] a cost function is introduced, which includes the non-linear model together with a regularization term related to Total Variation. In [19] the interference levels are estimated a priori and then an iterative procedure is used for the estimates of the recto and verso of documents. Some nonlinear models which assume that the interference levels depend on the location are presented in [9,11,22]. So, the model turns to be non-stationary, that is not translation invariant. The algorithms in [9,22] for the resolution of the related inverse problem are fast heuristics. In [4], a non-stationary model is proposed. However, in order to obtain more precise results, a computationally more expensive regularized problem has been sketched in [8] and [21]. Now we analyze in detail the iterative technique to solve such a model, in which the sources, the blur operators and the interference level are computed separately at every step, until a fixed point is found. In this paper, in particular, we deal with determining the interference levels, by fixing the blur operators and the ideal sources. To this aim, we use a GNC-type technique (see, e.g., [1–3,5,6,10,13–16,18]). Note that a correct estimate of the interference levels is crucial in our approach for a right recognition of the letters in documents.

In this paper we analyze four different GNC-type algorithms to determine the interference level. Such algorithms are experimentally compared, and we have chosen the algorithm which has given estimates of the interference levels closest to ideal levels, improving the results presented in [8] and [21].

In a forthcoming paper, the steps about finding the blur operators and the ideal sources will be treated.

The paper is structured as follows. In Sect. 2 we deal with the regularization of the modified Sharma model. In Sect. 3 we describe the alternating iterative algorithm, used to find the minimum of the energy function. In Sect. 4 we analyze the technique to determine the interference levels, given the blur operator and the ideal sources. In Sect. 5 we propose different types of convex approximations. In Sect. 6 we present GNC-type alternative minimization techniques. In Sect. 7 we compare the proposed technique by means of the experimental results.

## 2   Regularization of the Problem

In this paper we consider a modified Sharma-type model related to the show-through phenomenon in paper documents, as follows (see, e.g., [8,21]):

$$r^d(i,j) = r(i,j)e^{q_v(i,j)\left(\frac{z_v(i,j)}{N}-1\right)}, \quad v^d(i,j) = v(i,j)e^{q_r(i,j)\left(\frac{z_r(i,j)}{N}-1\right)}, \qquad (1)$$

where $N$ is the maximum value of the light intensity, which is assumed to correspond with the background of the analyzed document; $r = [r(i,j)]$, $v = [v(i,j)] \in \mathbb{R}^{nm}$ are the vectors which represent the ideal images of the recto and the verso of the document (expressed in the lexicographic form); $q_r(i,j)$ is the interference level which affects the light intensity of interferences from the recto to the verso; $q_v(i,j)$ is the interference level which affects the light intensity of interferences from the verso to the recto; $r^d = [r^d(i,j)], v^d = [v^d(i,j)] \in \mathbb{R}^{nm}$ are the vectors which represent the observed data mixtures (expressed in the lexicographic form); $z_r = [z_r(i,j)] = Af, z_v = [z_v(i,j)] = Ar$ are the blurred images of the recto and the verso, where $A \in \mathbb{R}^{(nm)\times(nm)}$ is the blur operator, which in general has the form of a matrix with Toeplitz blocks. The problem of the blind separations of components consists of finding an estimate of the recto/verso pair of the source document, which is denoted by $s = (r,v)$, of the interference level $q = (q_r, q_v)$ and of the blur operator $A$, given as input the observed images of the recto and the verso. This is an ill-posed problem in the Hadamard sense. To estimate the solution of the problem, some regularization techniques are used. Thus, the solution of the regularized problem is $(s^*, q^*, A^*) = \arg\min_{(s,q,A)} E(s,q,A)$, where

$$E(s,q,A) = T(s,q,A) + \widehat{S}(s) + S(q_r) + S(q_v) + S_c(q_r,q_v) \tag{2}$$

is the *energy function*, and

$$T(s,q,A) = T_r(q_v) + T_v(q_r) = \sum_{i=1}^{n}\sum_{j=1}^{m}\left(r^d(i,j) - r(i,j)e^{-q_v(i,j)\left(1-\frac{z_v(i,j)}{N}\right)}\right)^2$$

$$+ \sum_{i=1}^{n}\sum_{j=1}^{m}\left(v^d(i,j) - v(i,j)e^{-q_r(i,j)\left(1-\frac{z_r(i,j)}{N}\right)}\right)^2 \tag{3}$$

is the *consistency term*, which measures the faithfulness of the solution to the data, and $\widehat{S}(s)$ is the *regularization term*, which is chosen according to the properties which the estimated source has to satisfy. Moreover, the last terms of (2) are given by

$$S(q_w) = \lambda_w^2 \sum_{i=1}^{n}\sum_{j=1}^{m}\left[\left(q_w(i,j) - q_w(i-1,j)\right)^2 + \left(q_w(i,j) - q_w(i,j-1)\right)^2\right],$$

where $w \in \{r,v\}$, $\lambda_w$ is the regularization parameter related to the interference level of the recto (resp. verso), if $w = r$ (resp., $w = v$), and

$$S_c(q_r, q_v) = \sum_{i=1}^{n}\sum_{j=1}^{m}\lambda_c^2(q_r(i,j) - q_v(i,j))^2$$

is the joint smoothness term. The parameter $\lambda_c$ is the regularization parameter between the interference of the recto and the verso with respect to the same pixel.

## 3   Alternating Techniques

To minimize the function in (2), we use a strategy of *alternating minimization*, which consists of the estimation of the minimum of the function with respect to each single variable, fixing the other ones. We proceed as follows:

initialize $k = 0$, $s_0, q_0, A_0$
while a stationary point of $E$ is not found
   $k = k + 1$
   $s_k = \arg\min_s E(s, q_{k-1}, A_{k-1})$
   $q_k = \arg\min_q E(s_{k-1}, q, A_{k-1})$
   $A_k = \arg\min_A E(s_{k-1}, q_{k-1}, A)$

To solve the problem of minimization of the dual energy, which in general is not convex, a technique introduced by Blake and Zisserman can be used (see, e.g., [1–3,5,6,10,13–16,18]). With such a technique, called GNC (*Graduate Non-Convexity*), the energy function $E$, is approximated by means of a finite family $\{F^{(p)}\}$ of functions, in such a way that the first one is convex and the last one coincides with the given function. Moreover, we call $\mathbf{x}$ the variable with respect to which we will compute the minimum of $E$. The algorithm is structured as follows: every energy function is minimized by starting with the minimum achieved by optimizating the approximation of the energy function obtained at the previous step. By choosing different approximating functions, it is possible to obtain various formulations of the GNC algorithm. The minimization of each of the approximating functions $E^{(p)}$ can be done by means of an algorithm called NL-SOR (*Non Linear Successive Over-Relaxation*) (see, e.g., [7]).

## 4   Determining the Interference Levels

In this paper, we deal with finding only the interference levels, fixed the recto, the verso and the blur mask. The other steps of the alternating algorithm will be treated in a forthcoming paper. The energy function with respect to the interference level is given by

$$E(s_{k-1}, q, A_{k-1}) = k + \sum_{i=1}^{n}\sum_{j=1}^{m}\left(r^d(i,j) - r(i,j)e^{-q_v(i,j)\left(1-\frac{z_v(i,j)}{N}\right)}\right)^2 \quad (4)$$

$$+ \sum_{i=1}^{n}\sum_{j=1}^{m}\left(v^d(i,j) - v(i,j)e^{-q_r(i,j)\left(1-\frac{z_r(i,j)}{N}\right)}\right)^2 + S(q_r) + S(q_v) + S_c(q_r, q_v),$$

where $k = \widehat{S}(s_{k-1})$ is a constant. It is possible to prove that the smoothness terms are convex. Now, define $\psi : \{v, r\} \rightarrow \{v, r\}$ by

$$\psi(r) = v, \quad \psi(w) = r. \quad (5)$$

It is not difficult to see that the Hessian matrix of the data consistency term is positive-definite if and only if

$$q_w(k,t) < -\frac{\ln\left(\frac{(\psi(w))^d(k,t)}{2\,\psi(w)(k,t)}\right)}{1 - \frac{z_w(k,t)}{N}} \quad \text{for all } w \in \{r, v\},\ k \in \{1, \ldots, n\},\ t \in \{1, \ldots, m\}.$$

Thus, the energy function related to the interference level is given by the sum of the terms of data consistency, which are not necessarily convex, and the smoothness terms, which are convex. Hence, in general the uniqueness of the global minimum is not guaranteed.

# 5   Convex Approximation of the Data Consistency Term

To approximate the term of faithfulness to the data, it is possible to approximate $T_v$ and $T_r$ separately. Moreover, we can approximate each term of the sum in (3) separately too. Fixed $i \in \{1, \dots, n\}$, $j \in \{1, \dots, m\}$ and $v \in \{f, r\}$, let $\psi$ be as in (5), and denoting by $\alpha = \dfrac{\psi(w)(i,j)}{\psi(w^d)(i,j)}$, $\gamma = \dfrac{z_w(i,j)}{N} - 1$, $q = q_w(i,j)$, the term related to the faithfulness to the data can be expressed as

$$T(s,q,A) = T_r(q_v) + T_v(q_r) = \sum_{i=1}^{n} \sum_{j=1}^{m} \left( r^d(i,j) - r(i,j) e^{-q_v(i,j)\left(1 - \frac{z_v(i,j)}{N}\right)} \right)^2$$

$$+ \sum_{i=1}^{n} \sum_{j=1}^{m} \left( v^d(i,j) - v(i,j) e^{-q_r(i,j)\left(1 - \frac{z_r(i,j)}{N}\right)} \right)^2 \tag{6}$$

$$= \sum_{i=1}^{n} \sum_{j=1}^{m} \sum_{w \in \{r,v\}} \psi(w)^d(i,j) \, \varphi_{i,j,w}(q),$$

where

$$\varphi_{i,j,w}(q) = \left( 1 - \alpha \, e^{q\gamma} \right)^2 = 1 - 2\alpha \, e^{q\gamma} + \alpha^2 \, e^{2q\gamma}. \tag{7}$$

Therefore, to make the function $\varphi_{i,j,w}$ in (7) convex, we will proceed in several ways. In particular, in this paper we approximate the quantity $g_{i,j,w}(q) = e^{q\gamma}$ by a line of the type $\tilde{g}(q) = \tilde{A}q + \tilde{B}$. So, the approximation of $\varphi_{i,j,w}(q)$ is given by $\tilde{\varphi}(q) = (1 - \alpha\tilde{A}q - \tilde{B})^2$, which is a convex function.

## 5.1   Interpolating Approximation

Now we approximate $g_{i,j,w}(q)$ with the line $p_{i,j,w}^{(1)}(q)$ interpolating at the points $(3, e^{3\gamma})$ and $(0, 1)$. It is not difficult to see that

$$p_{i,j,w}^{(1)}(q) = q\left( \frac{e^{3\gamma}}{3} - \frac{1}{3} \right) + 1.$$

Thus, the convex approximation of $\varphi_{i,j,w}(q)$ is given by

$$\varphi_{i,j,w}^{(1)}(q) = \left( 1 - \alpha q \frac{e^{3\gamma} - 1}{3} - \alpha \right)^2. \tag{8}$$

## 5.2   The Best Line Approximation

Now we approximate $g_{i,j,w}(q)$ by the line $p_{i,j,w}^{(2)}(q)$ of best approximation with respect to the 2-norm in $P_1([0,3]) = \{p : [0,3] \to \mathbb{R} | \; p$ is a polynomial of degree at most 1$\}$. It is not difficult to see that (Figs. 1, 2)

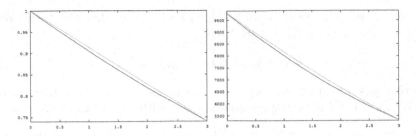

**Fig. 1.** On the left side: Graph of $g_{i,j,w}(q)$ in blue and $p^{(1)}(q)$ in red. On the right side: Graph of $\varphi_{i,j,w}(q)$ in blue and $\varphi^{(1)}(q)$ in red ($\alpha = 100$, $\gamma = 0.1$). (Color figure online)

$$p_{i,j,w}^{(2)}(q) = A^{(2)} q + B^{(2)}, \text{ where}$$

$$A^{(2)} = \frac{2}{3\,\gamma}\left(2e^{3\gamma} - \frac{2(e^{3\gamma} - 1)}{3\,\gamma} - e^{3\gamma} + 1\right),$$

$$B^{(2)} = -\frac{5\,e^{3\gamma}}{3\,\gamma} - \frac{4}{3\,\gamma} + \frac{2\,e^{3\gamma}}{3\,\gamma^2} - \frac{2}{3\,\gamma^2} + \frac{e^{3\gamma}}{\gamma}.$$

The convex approximation of $\varphi_{i,j,w}(q)$ is

$$\varphi_{i,j,w}^{(2)}(q) = \left(1 - \alpha\,A^{(2)}\,q - B^{(2)}\right)^2. \tag{9}$$

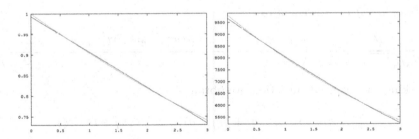

**Fig. 2.** On the left side: Graph of $g_{i,j,w}(q)$ in blue and $p^{(2)}(q)$ in red. On the right side: Graph of $\varphi_{i,j,w}(q)$ in blue and $\varphi^{(2)}(q)$ in red ($\alpha = 100$, $\gamma = 0.1$). (Color figure online)

Note that this is the first convex approximation chosen in the GNC-type algorithm proposed in [8] and [21].

### 5.3 Hybrid Best Approximation and Interpolation

Now we approximate $g_{i,j,w}(q)$ by means of the line $p_{i,j,w}^{(5)}(q)$ of best approximation related to the 2-norm in $P_1([0,3]) = \{p : [0,3] \to \mathbb{R}|\ p \text{ is a polynomial of degree at most 1}\}$, which interpolates $g_{i,j,w}(q)$ at a chosen point $\bar{q}$. (Figs. 3, 4)

Now we make a change of coordinates, in such a way that the "new" origin coincides with $(\bar{q}, g_{i,j,w}(\bar{q}))$. Let us define

$$\tilde{g}(q) = g_{i,j,w}(q + \bar{q}) - g_{i,j,w}(\bar{q}). \tag{10}$$

Note that $\tilde{g}$ is a translation of $g_{i,j,w}$ in the Cartesian plane. Now we determine the polynomial $\tilde{p}^{(5)}$ of best approximation of $\tilde{g}$ with respect to the 2-norm in

$$P_1([-\bar{q}, 3 - \bar{q}]) = \{p : [-\bar{q}, 3 - \bar{q}] \to \mathbb{R} \mid p \text{ is a polynomial of degree at most 1}\}$$

which interpolates $\tilde{g}$ at 0. We use the Gram-Schmidt method to find an orthonormal basis $\{e_1\}$ of the space $\{p \in P_1([-\bar{q}, 3 - \bar{q}]) \mid p(0) = 0\}$. A basis for this space is given by $x_1 = q$. By normalizing, we get

$$\|x_1\| = \sqrt{\int_{-\bar{q}}^{3-\bar{q}} q^2 \, dq} = \sqrt{3} \left( \sqrt{\bar{q}^2 - 3\bar{q} + 3} \right),$$

So, the normalized basis is given by

$$e_1 = \frac{x_1}{\|x_1\|} = \frac{q\sqrt{3}}{3(\sqrt{\bar{q}^2 - 3\bar{q} + 3})}.$$

The polynomial $\tilde{p}^{(5)}(q)$ of best approximation of $\tilde{g}_{i,j,w}(q)$ is

$$\tilde{p}^{(5)}(q) = c_1 e_1(q),$$

where $c_1 = \langle \tilde{g}, e_1 \rangle$ is equal to

$$-\frac{\sqrt{3}}{3(\sqrt{\bar{q}^2 - 3\bar{q} + 3})} e^{\bar{q}\gamma} \left( \frac{(\bar{q} - 3)e^{(3-\bar{q})\gamma} - \bar{q}\, e^{-\bar{q}\gamma}}{\gamma} + \frac{e^{(3-\bar{q})\gamma} - e^{-\bar{q}\gamma}}{\gamma^2} + \frac{9 - 6\bar{q}}{2} \right).$$

By taking the inverse translation, we obtain

$$p_{i,j,w}^{(5)}(q) = \tilde{p}^{(5)}(q - \bar{q}) + g_{i,j,w}(\bar{q}) = A^{(5)}(\bar{q})\, q + B^{(5)}(\bar{q}),$$

where

$$A^{(5)}(\bar{q}) = -\frac{e^{\bar{q}\gamma}}{6(\bar{q}^2 - 3\bar{q} + 3)} \left( \frac{(2\bar{q} - 6)e^{(3-\bar{q})\gamma} - 2\bar{q}\, e^{-\bar{q}\gamma}}{\gamma} \right.$$
$$\left. + 2\frac{e^{(3-\bar{q})\gamma} - e^{-\bar{q}\gamma}}{\gamma^2} + 9 - 6\bar{q} \right),$$

$$B^{(5)}(\bar{q}) = \frac{\bar{q}\, e^{\bar{q}\gamma}}{6(\bar{q}^2 - 3\bar{q} + 3)} \left( \frac{(2\bar{q} - 6)e^{(3-\bar{q})\gamma} - 2\bar{q}\, e^{-\bar{q}\gamma}}{\gamma} \right.$$
$$\left. + 2\frac{e^{(3-\bar{q})\gamma} - e^{-\bar{q}\gamma}}{\gamma^2} + 9 - 6\bar{q} \right) + e^{\bar{q}\gamma}.$$

In particular, for $\bar{q} = 0$ we get

$$A^{(3)} = A^{(5)}(0) = \frac{1}{18}\left(\frac{6e^{3\gamma}}{\gamma} - 2\frac{e^{3\gamma} - 1}{\gamma^2} - 9\right),$$

$$B^{(3)} = B^{(5)}(0) = \frac{1}{18}e^{3\gamma}\left(\frac{6e^{-3\gamma}}{\gamma} + 2\frac{e^{-3\gamma} - 1}{\gamma^2} + 9\right),$$

while for $\bar{q}=3$ we have

$$A^{(4)} = A^{(5)}(3) = \frac{1}{18}e^{3\gamma}\left(\frac{6e^{-3\gamma}}{\gamma} + 2\frac{e^{-3\gamma} - 1}{\gamma^2} + 9\right),$$

$$B^{(4)} = B^{(5)}(3) = \frac{1}{6}e^{3\gamma}\left(\frac{6e^{-3\gamma}}{\gamma} + 2\frac{e^{-3\gamma} - 1}{\gamma^2} + 9\right) + e^{3\gamma}.$$

From this it follows that two possible convex approximation of $\varphi_{i,j,w}(q)$ are

$$\varphi^{(\kappa)}_{i,j,w}(q) = \left(1 - \alpha A^{(\kappa)}q - \alpha B^{(\kappa)}\right)^2, \quad \kappa = 3,4. \tag{11}$$

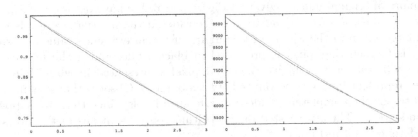

**Fig. 3.** On the left side: Graph of $g_{i,j,w}(q)$ in blue and $p^{(3)}(q)$ in red. On the right side: Graph of $\varphi_{i,j,w}(q)$ in blue and $\varphi^{(3)}(q)$ in red ($\alpha = 100$, $\gamma = 0.1$). (Color figure online)

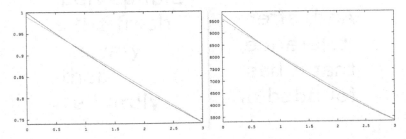

**Fig. 4.** On the left side: Graph of $g_{i,j,w}(q)$ in blue and $p^{(4)}(q)$ in red. On the right side: Graph of $\varphi_{i,j,w}(q)$ in blue and $\varphi^{(4)}(q)$ in red ($\alpha = 100$, $\gamma = 0.1$). (Color figure online)

# 6  The GNC Approximation Families

The first convex approximation of the consistency term of the energy function related to the interference level of the verso is expressed by

$$T^{(\kappa)}(s,q,A) = \sum_{i=1}^{n}\sum_{j=1}^{m}\sum_{w\in\{r,v\}} \psi(w)^d(i,j)\,\varphi_{i,j,w}^{(\kappa)}(q), \quad \kappa = 1,2,3,4. \tag{12}$$

We define the following families of functions of convex approximations. Let $T_p^{(\kappa)} = pT^{(\kappa)} + (1-p)T$. For $p = 1$, we get the first convex approximation associated with $\kappa$, while for $p = 0$ we have the original function $T$. Note that for $\kappa = 2$ we get the family of approximations used in the GNC-type algorithm proposed in [8] and [21].

# 7  Experimental Results

In this section we compare the experimental results, by using the four different GNC algorithms proposed in the previous sections. We have assumed two different pairs of original images, given in Figs. 5 and 6. We have used a uniform blur mask of dimension $5 \times 5$, and we have considered the interference levels to be estimated given in the Fig. 7. In this figure, if the interference value of a single pixel is 0, then that pixel is presented in black while, and if the interference value is 3 (that is very high), then that pixel is presented in white. The gray pixels represent interference values between 0 and 3. Observe that it is not possible to assume completely random interference levels, since they are supposed to be smooth. Thus, we tested our algorithms only by means of the proposed interference level in Fig. 7.

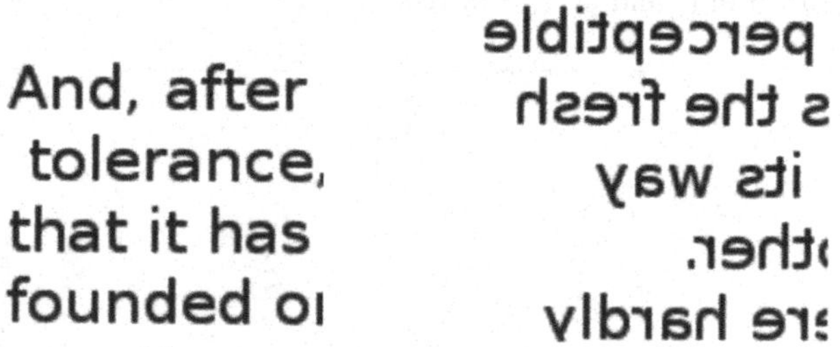

(a)                    (b)

**Fig. 5.** First pair of ideal sources

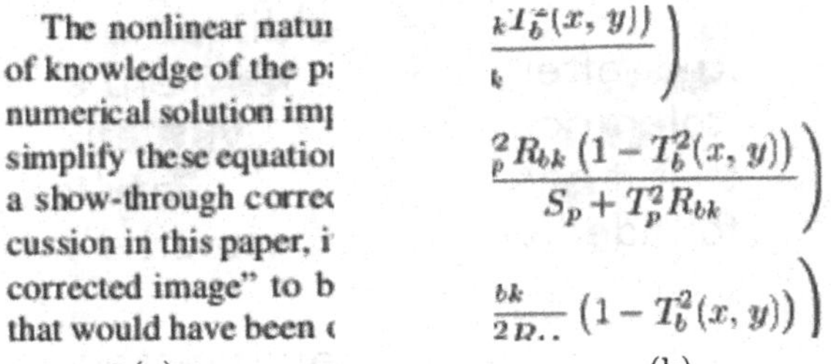

The nonlinear natur
of knowledge of the p:
numerical solution im[
simplify these equatio1
a show-through correc
cussion in this paper, i
corrected image" to b
that would have been (

(a)

$$k I_b^+(x, y)) \Bigg)$$

$$\frac{_p^2 R_{bk} \left( 1 - T_b^2(x, y) \right)}{S_p + T_p^2 R_{bk}} \Bigg)$$

$$\frac{bk}{2R..} \left( 1 - T_b^2(x, y) \right) \Bigg)$$

(b)

**Fig. 6.** Second pair of ideal sources

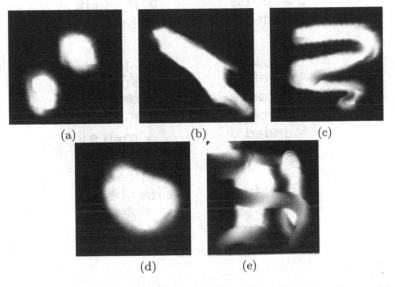

(a)        (b)        (c)

(d)        (e)

**Fig. 7.** Interference levels: (a) $q_f^{(1)} = q_r^{(1)}$; (b) $q_f^{(2)} = q_r^{(2)}$; (c) $q_f^{(3)} = q_r^{(3)}$; (d) $q_f^{(4)} = q_r^{(4)}$; (e) $q_f^{(5)} = q_r^{(5)}$.

Note that we have assumed that the ideal interference levels of the recto and of the verso coincide. Considering the first pair of original sources given in Fig. 5 and the interference levels given in Fig. 7, we obtain the data mixtures given in Fig. 8. We have tested the four GNC algorithms, assuming the following regularization parameters:

$$\lambda_f = \lambda_r = 50, \quad \lambda_c = 100.$$

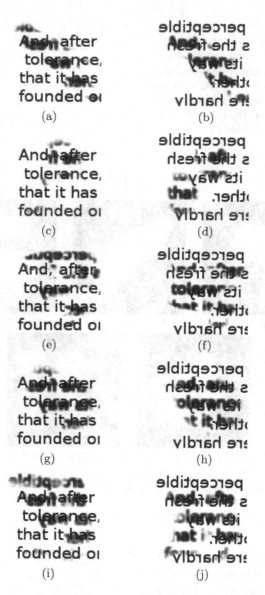

**Fig. 8.** (a–b) Document in Fig. 5 degraded by the interference level $q_r^{(1)} = q_v^{(1)}$; (c–d) document in Fig. 5 degraded by the interference level $q_r^{(2)} = q_v^{(2)}$; (e–f) document in Fig. 5 degraded by the interference level $q_r^{(3)} = q_v^{(3)}$; (g–h) document in Fig. 5 degraded by the interference level $q_r^{(4)} = q_v^{(4)}$; (i–j) document in Fig. 5 degraded by the interference level $q_r^{(5)} = q_v^{(5)}$.

We have compared the four proposed algorithms in terms of mean square error (MSE) between the estimate of the obtained interference level and the ideal interference level given in Fig. 7. In Table 1 there are the errors in terms of MSE obtained by the proposed algorithms, by considering the pair of original sources presented in Fig. 5 and the interference levels $q_f^{(i)} = q_r^{(i)}$, $i = 1, \ldots, 5$, given in Fig. 7. The effectiveness of the algorithm has been tested by using some images, created to highlight the capacity of the algorithm to eliminate the degradations due to the effect of show-through.

**Table 1.** MSE of the proposed algorithms, using the original sources in Fig. 5.

| | $q_f^{(1)}$ | $q_r^{(1)}$ | $q_f^{(2)}$ | $q_r^{(2)}$ | $q_f^{(3)}$ | $q_r^{(3)}$ | $q_f^{(4)}$ | $q_r^{(4)}$ | $q_f^{(5)}$ | $q_r^{(5)}$ |
|---|---|---|---|---|---|---|---|---|---|---|
| $\kappa = 1$ | 0.0571 | 0.0533 | 0.0719 | 0.0831 | 0.0798 | 0.0784 | 0.0821 | 0.0792 | 0.1021 | 0.0987 |
| $\kappa = 2$ | 0.0358 | 0.0374 | 0.0338 | 0.0412 | 0.0440 | 0.0398 | 0.0314 | 0.0267 | 0.0373 | 0.0417 |
| $\kappa = 3$ | 0.0318 | 0.0400 | 0.0372 | 0.0394 | 0.04183 | 0.0427 | 0.0273 | 0.0264 | 0.0413 | 0.0398 |
| $\kappa = 4$ | 0.0214 | 0.0235 | 0.0232 | 0.0224 | 0.0314 | 0.0303 | 0.0098 | 0.0113 | 0.0352 | 0.0388 |

The best results obtained in Table 1 are indicated in red. As it is possible to observe, the best algorithm for the first pair of images is associated to the family of approximations obtained with $\kappa = 4$. In Fig. 9 we present the interference levels estimated by the algorithm related to $\kappa = 4$.

Regarding the second pair of original sources in Fig. 6 and the interference levels in Fig. 7, and taking a uniform mask of type $5 \times 5$, we have the data mixtures in Fig. 10. We have tested the four GNC algorithms, using the previous regularization parameters. In Table 2 the errors in terms of MSE obtained by the proposed algorithms, by considering the pair of original sources presented in Fig. 6 and the interference levels $q_f^{(i)} = q_r^{(i)}$, $i = 1, \ldots, 5$, given in Fig. 7. In Table 2 the best results which we obtained are indicated in red. So it is possible to notice that in the 100% of the examined cases the algorithm which gives the best results is that corresponding with $\kappa = 4$.

As we see in Table 2, the best algorithm for the first pair of images is again that related to the family of approximations with $\kappa = 4$. In Fig. 11 there are the interference levels estimated by the algorithm corresponding with $\kappa = 4$.

**Table 2.** MSE of the proposed algorithms, using the original sources in Fig. 6.

| | $q_f^{(1)}$ | $q_r^{(1)}$ | $q_f^{(2)}$ | $q_r^{(2)}$ | $q_f^{(3)}$ | $q_r^{(3)}$ | $q_f^{(4)}$ | $q_r^{(4)}$ | $q_f^{(5)}$ | $q_r^{(5)}$ |
|---|---|---|---|---|---|---|---|---|---|---|
| $\kappa = 1$ | 0.0523 | 0.0497 | 0.0613 | 0.0671 | 0.0942 | 0.0817 | 0.1218 | 0.1375 | 0.1129 | 0.1567 |
| $\kappa = 2$ | 0.0337 | 0.0302 | 0.0363 | 0.0337 | 0.0479 | 0.0328 | 0.0371 | 0.0442 | 0.0385 | 0.0406 |
| $\kappa = 3$ | 0.0315 | 0.0313 | 0.0332 | 0.0353 | 0.0318 | 0.0338 | 0.0418 | 0.0573 | 0.0397 | 0.0393 |
| $\kappa = 4$ | 0.0238 | 0.0252 | 0.0243 | 0.0254 | 0.0102 | 0.0175 | 0.0258 | 0.0323 | 0.0332 | 0.0358 |

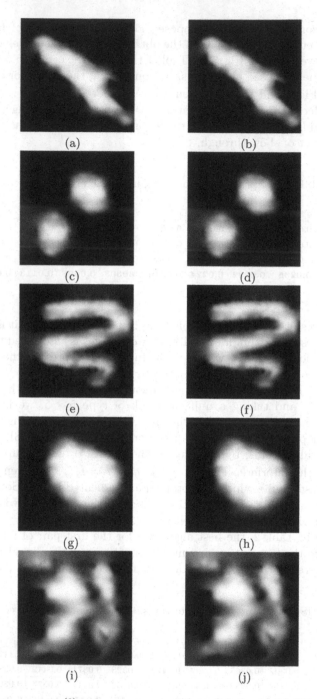

**Fig. 9.** (a) estimation of $q_f^{(1)}$; (b) estimation of $q_r^{(1)}$; (c) estimation of $q_f^{(2)}$; (d) estimation of $q_r^{(2)}$; (e) estimation of $q_f^{(3)}$; (f) estimation of $q_r^{(3)}$; (g) estimation of $q_f^{(4)}$; (h) estimation of $q_r^{(4)}$; (i) estimation of $q_f^{(5)}$; (j) estimation of $q_r^{(5)}$.

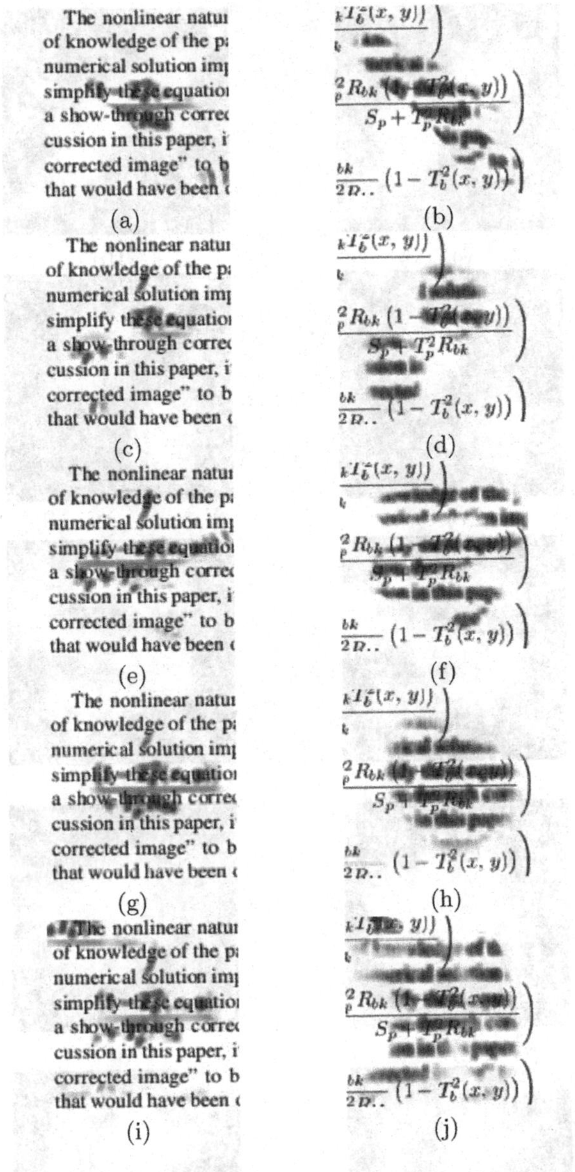

The nonlinear natur
of knowledge of the pa
numerical solution imp
simplify these equation
a show-through correc
cussion in this paper, i
corrected image" to b
that would have been

$kI_b^-(x,y)\}$

$\dfrac{{}^2_\rho R_{bk}\left(1 - T_p^2(x,y)\right)}{S_p + T_p^2 R_{bk}}$

$\dfrac{bk}{2R..}\left(1 - T_b^2(x,y)\right)$

(a)　　　　　　　　(b)

The nonlinear natur
of knowledge of the pa
numerical solution imp
simplify these equation
a show-through correc
cussion in this paper, i
corrected image" to b
that would have been

$kI_b^-(x,y)\}$

$\dfrac{{}^2_\rho R_{bk}\left(1 - T_b^2(x,y)\right)}{S_p + T_p^2 R_{bk}}$

$\dfrac{bk}{2R..}\left(1 - T_b^2(x,y)\right)$

(c)　　　　　　　　(d)

The nonlinear natur
of knowledge of the pa
numerical solution imp
simplify these equation
a show-through correc
cussion in this paper, i
corrected image" to b
that would have been

$kI_b^-(x,y)\}$

$\dfrac{{}^2_\rho R_{bk}\left(1 - T_b^2(x,y)\right)}{S_p + T_p^2 R_{bk}}$

$\dfrac{bk}{2R..}\left(1 - T_b^2(x,y)\right)$

(e)　　　　　　　　(f)

The nonlinear natur
of knowledge of the pa
numerical solution imp
simplify these equation
a show-through correc
cussion in this paper, i
corrected image" to b
that would have been

$kI_b^-(x,y)\}$

$\dfrac{{}^2_\rho R_{bk}\left(1 - T_b^2(x,y)\right)}{S_p + T_p^2 R_{bk}}$

$\dfrac{bk}{2R..}\left(1 - T_b^2(x,y)\right)$

(g)　　　　　　　　(h)

The nonlinear natur
of knowledge of the pa
numerical solution imp
simplify these equation
a show-through correc
cussion in this paper, i
corrected image" to b
that would have been

$kI_b^-(x,y)\}$

$\dfrac{{}^2_\rho R_{bk}\left(1 - T_b^2(x,y)\right)}{S_p + T_p^2 R_{bk}}$

$\dfrac{bk}{2R..}\left(1 - T_b^2(x,y)\right)$

(i)　　　　　　　　(j)

**Fig. 10.** (a–b) Document in Fig. 6 degraded by the interference level $q_r^{(1)} = q_v^{(1)}$; (c–d) document in Fig. 6 degraded by the interference level $q_r^{(2)} = q_v^{(2)}$; (e–f) document in Fig. 6 degraded by the interference level $q_r^{(3)} = q_v^{(3)}$; (g–h) document in Fig. 6 degraded by the interference level $q_r^{(4)} = q_v^{(4)}$; (i–j) document in Fig. 6 degraded by the interference level $q_r^{(5)} = q_v^{(5)}$.

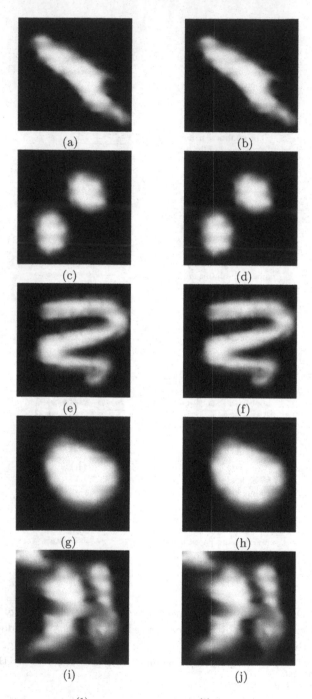

**Fig. 11.** (a) estimation of $q_f^{(1)}$; (b) estimation of $q_r^{(1)}$; (c) estimation of $q_f^{(2)}$; (d) estimation of $q_r^{(2)}$; (e) estimation of $q_f^{(3)}$; (f) estimation of $q_r^{(3)}$; (g) estimation of $q_f^{(4)}$; (h) estimation of $q_r^{(4)}$; (i) estimation of $q_f^{(5)}$; (j) estimation of $q_r^{(5)}$.

Thus, we propose to use the family of approximations given for $\kappa = 4$, improving the results obtained in [8] and [21], where the family of approximation with $\kappa = 2$ is used.

## Conclusions

We studied the problem of blind separation of the components, in particular concerning ancient documents corrupted by bleed-through and show-through. We dealt with the problem of studying a regularization technique, which estimates the original sources, the interference levels and the blur operators. We investigated the estimate of the interference levels, given the original sources and the blur operators. In particular, we analyzed various GNC algorithms for minimizing the involved energy function. Such algorithms are different because of the choice of the first convex approximation. By means of the experimental results, we determined which algorithm gives more accurated estimates of the interference levels, improving the results given in [8] and [21]. In a forthcoming paper we will analyze the other steps of the technique here proposed, for the joint estimate of the original sources, the blur operator and the interference level.

**Acknowledgment.** This work was partially supported by University of Perugia, G.N.A.M.P.A. (Italian National Group of Mathematical Analysis, Probability and Applications) and I.N.d.A.M. (Italian National Institute of Higher Mathematics).

## References

1. Bedini, L., Gerace, I., Tonazzini, A.: A deterministic algorithm for reconstruction images with interacting discontinuities. Comput. Vis. Graph. Image Process.: Graph. Models Images Process. **56**, 109–123 (1994)
2. Blake, A., Zisserman, A.: Visual Reconstruction. MIT Press, Cambridge, MA (1987)
3. Boccuto, A., Gerace, I.: Image reconstruction with a non-parallelism constraint. In: Proceedings of the International Workshop on Computational Intelligence for Multimedia Understanding, Reggio Calabria, Italy, 27–28 October 2016, IEEE Conference Publications, pp. 1–5 (2016)
4. Boccuto, A., Gerace, I., Giorgetti, V.: A blind source separation technique for document restoration. SIAM J. Imaging Sci. **12**(2), 1135–1162 (2019)
5. Boccuto, A., Gerace, I., Martinelli, F.: Half-quadratic image restoration with a non-parallelism constraint. J. Math. Imaging Vis. **59**(2), 270–295 (2017)
6. Boccuto, A., Gerace, I., Pucci, P.: Convex approximation technique for interacting line elements deblurring: a new approach. J. Math. Imaging Vis. **44**(2), 168–184 (2012)
7. Brewster, M.E., Kannan, R.: Nonlinear successive over-relaxation. Numerische Math. **44**(2), 309–315 (1984)
8. Gerace, I., Martinelli, F., Tonazzini, A.: Restoration of recto-verso archival documents through a regularized nonlinear model. In: Proceedings of 20th European Signal Processing Conference EUSIPCO, pp. 1588–1592 (2012)

9.  Gerace, I., Palomba, C., Tonazzini, A.: An inpainting technique based on regularization to remove bleed-through from ancient documents. In: 2016 International Workshop on Computational Intelligence for Multimedia Understanding (IWCIM), pp. 1–5 (2016)
10. Hazan, E., Levy, K.Y., Shalev-Shwartz, S.: On graduated optimization for stochastic non-convex problems. In: Proceedings of the 33rd International Conference on Machine Learning, New York, NY, USA, 2016. JMLR: W& CP 48, pp. 1–9 (2016)
11. Khan, M.R., Imtiaz, H., Hasan, M.K.: Show-through correction in scanned images using joint histogram. SIViP **4**(3), 337–351 (2010)
12. Martinelli, F., Salerno, E., Gerace, I., Tonazzini, A.: Nonlinear model and constrained ML for removing back-to-front interferences from recto-verso documents. Patt. Recogn. **45**, 596–605 (2012)
13. Mobahi, H., Fisher, J.W.: A theoretical analysis of optimization by Gaussian continuation. In: Wong, W.-K., Lowd, D. (eds.) Proceedings of the Twenty-Ninth Conference on Artificial Intelligence of the Association for the Advancement of Artificial Intelligence (AAAI), Austin, Texas, USA, 25–30 January 2015, pp. 1205–1211 (2015)
14. Nikolova, M.: Markovian reconstruction using a GNC approach. IEEE Trans. Image Process. **8**(9), 1204–1220 (1999)
15. Nikolova, M., Ng, M.K., Tam, C.-P.: On $\ell_1$ data fitting and concave regularization for image recovery. SIAM J. Sci. Comput. **35**(1), A397–A430 (2013)
16. Nikolova, M., Ng, M.K., Zhang, S., Ching, W.-K.: Efficient reconstruction of piecewise constant images using nonsmooth nonconvex minimization. SIAM J. Imaging Sci. **1**(1), 2–25 (2008)
17. Ophir, B., Malah, D.: Show-through cancellation in scanned images using blind source separation techniques. In: Proceedings of IEEE International Conference on Image Processing (3), pp. 233–236 (2007)
18. Robini, M.C., Magnin, I.E.: Optimization by stochastic continuation. SIAM J. Imaging Sci. **3**(4), 1096–1121 (2010)
19. Salerno, E., Martinelli, F., Tonazzini, A.: Nonlinear model identification and see-through cancelation from Recto/Verso data. Int. J. Document Anal. Recogn. (IJDAR) **16**(2), 177–187 (2013)
20. Sharma, G.: Show-through cancellation in scans of duplex printed documents. IEEE Trans. Image Process. **10**, 736–754 (2001)
21. Tonazzini, A., Gerace, I., Martinelli, F.: Document image restoration and analysis as separation of mixtures of patterns: from linear to nonlinear models. In: Gunturk, B.K., Li, X. (eds.) Image Restoration - Fundamentals and Advances, pp. 285–310. CRC Press, Taylor & Francis, Boca Raton (2013)
22. Tonazzini, A., Savino, P., Salerno, E.: A non-stationary density model to separate overlapped texts in degraded documents. SIViP **9**(1), S155–S164 (2014). https://doi.org/10.1007/s11760-014-0735-3

# A Blind Source Separation Technique for Document Restoration Based on Image Discrete Derivative

Antonio Boccuto[1] , Ivan Gerace[1(✉)] , Valentina Giorgetti[2] ,
and Gabriele Valenti[1]

[1] Dipartimento di Matematica e Informatica, Via Vanvitelli, 1, 06123 Perugia, Italy
{antonio.boccuto,ivan.gerace}@unipg.it
[2] Dipartimento di Matematica e Informatica, viale G. B. Morgagni, 67/A,
50134 Firenze, Italy
valentina.giorgetti@unifi.it

**Abstract.** In this paper we study a *Blind Source Separation* (BSS) problem, and in particular we deal with document restoration. We consider the classical linear model. To this aim, we analyze the derivatives of the images instead of the intensity levels. Thus, we establish non-overlapping constraints on document sources. Moreover, we impose that the rows of the mixture matrices of the sources have sum equal to 1, in order to keep equal the lightnesses of the estimated sources and those of the data. Here we give a technique which uses the symmetric factorization, whose goodness is tested by the experimental results.

**Keywords:** Blind source separation · Image restoration · Document restoration · Image derivative · Symmetric factorization

## 1 Introduction

In this paper we deal with a *Blind Source Separation* (BSS) problem, which is widely studied in signal processing and presents various developments in several areas. We consider both *show-through* and *bleed-through* deteriorations. The show-through is due mostly to the scanning operation. The bleed-through is a physic phenomenon, due to the ink infiltration between the sides of the document.

We analyse a usual linear and stationary recto-verso model (see, e.g., [8–10,16]), and deal with the problem of finding an estimate of the ideal source images of both sides of the document and of the mixture matrix which describes the bleed-through and show-through effects. The BSS problem is ill-posed in the sense of Hadamard (see, e.g., [7]). Indeed, given any mixture matrix, there exists a corresponding pair of ideal images, which are solutions of the problem.

Among the *Independent Component Analysis* (ICA) techniques, many methods are proposed, in which it is supposed to have a mutual independence of

O. Gervasi et al. (Eds.): ICCSA 2022, LNCS 13375, pp. 445–461, 2022.
https://doi.org/10.1007/978-3-031-10522-7_31

the related sources (see, e.g., [5]). The most used ICA technique is the Fas-tICA method (see, e.g., [8–12]), by means of which it is possible to determine an orthogonal rotation of the data which maximizes non-Gaussianity, using a fixed-point iteration.

Other techniques impose that the estimated sources are mutually uncorrelated. In this case, they are found by a linear transformation of the data, determined by assuming an orthogonality condition, as in *Principal Component Analysis* (PCA), or an orthonormality property, like in *Whitening* (W) and *Symmetric Whitening* (SW) methods (see, e.g., [15,16]).

In [1] a change of variables concerning the data is made, so that the presence and absence of text in the analysed document are associated respectively with high and low intensities of the light, and a nonnegativity constraint concerning the estimated sources is posed (see, e.g., [3,4,6,13]). Moreover, as the lightness of the background of the source is expected to coincide with the lightness of the data, we suppose that all rows of the mixing matrix have sum equal to one.

In [1] the *overlapping matrix* of both the observed data is defined, from which it is possible to deduce the *overlapping level*, which measures the intersections between the letters of the recto and the verso. The technique given in [1] is called *minimum amount of text overlapping in document separation* (MATODS).

In this paper the technique proposed in [1] is modified, and it is dealt with the derivatives of the images of the original sources. In general, the derivatives are related to the edges of the letters contained in the analyzed documents. In particular, we distinguish between horizontal and vertical derivatives. While it is probable that some letters of the recto overlap with some letters of the verso, there is a very low probability that the vertical (horizontal) derivatives of the recto overlap with the vertical (horizontal) derivatives of the verso. Thus, in our proposed technique, we assume that the overlapping level is equal to zero. The knowledge of the overlapping level allows to the proposed technique to eliminate the iterative phase necessary to MATODS to determinate such a level. Thus, it is possible to effectively reduce the computational costs. By means of our experimental results, we show that the proposed technique improves the results obtained in [1] when the source images are noisy. We refer to this method as the *Zero Edge Overlapping in Document Separation* (ZEODS) algorithm.

In Sect. 2 we present the linear model. In Sect. 3 we develop the ZEODS algorithm to deal with the linear problem. In Sect. 4 we compare experimentally the ZEODS algorithm with other fast and unsupervised methods existing in the literature.

## 2    The Linear Model

The classical linear model is the following (see, e.g., [8–10,14,16]):

$$\widehat{x}^T = A\,\widehat{s}^T, \tag{1}$$

where $\cdot^T$ is the transpose operator, $\widehat{x} \in [0, 255]^{nm}$ is the $n \times m$ *data document*, $\widehat{s} \in [0, 255]^{nm}$ is the $n \times m$ *source document*, $A \in \mathbb{R}^{2\times 2}$ denotes the *mixture matrix*. Here we deal with the problem of evaluating the mixture matrix and the ideal sources from the data assuming (1).

However, analogously as in [1], as the paper has the same color for every side of the document, we suppose that the value of the source background is the same as the background of the data. To impose this condition, we require that $A$ is a *one row-sum matrix*, namely

$$a_{11} + a_{12} = a_{21} + a_{22} = 1. \tag{2}$$

Now we introduce a structural modification to the model proposed in [1]. Indeed we will show how, dealing with the first derivatives of the images, the algorithm in [1] will be considerably simplified, reducing computational costs and obtaining significantly better reconstructions in several experimental results. We begin with introducing the concept of *clique* as the set of pixels on which the finite difference of first order is well-defined. The vertical cliques are of the type

$$c = \{(i,j), (i+1,j)\}, \tag{3}$$

while the horizontal cliques have the form

$$c = \{(i,j), (i,j+1)\}. \tag{4}$$

We denote by $C$ the set of all cliques. Note that $|C| = 2nm - m - n$, where $C$ denotes the cardinality of $C$.

Given a vertical clique $c = \{(i,j), (i+1,j)\}$, the finite difference operator on it is $\Delta_c \widehat{\mathbf{x}} = \widehat{x}_{i,j} - \widehat{x}_{i+1,j}$. Moreover, given a horizontal clique $c = \{(i,j), (i,j+1)\}$, the associated finite difference operator is $\Delta_c \widehat{\mathbf{x}} = \widehat{x}_{i,j} - \widehat{x}_{i,j+1}$. We consider the linear operator $D \in \mathbb{R}^{|C| \times nm}$. Note that, in this matrix, every row index corresponds to a clique, while every column index corresponds to a pixel. To every row it is possible to associate a vertical or horizontal clique. Then, if we consider a vertical clique $c = \{(i,j), (i+1,j)\}$, we get

$$D_{c,(l,k)} = \begin{cases} 1, & \text{if } (l,k) = (i,j), \\ -1, & \text{if } (l,k) = (i+1,j), \\ 0, & \text{otherwise;} \end{cases}$$

and, if $c = \{(i,j), (i,j+1)\}$ is a horizontal clique, we have

$$D_{c,(l,k)} = \begin{cases} 1, & \text{if } (l,k) = (i,j), \\ -1, & \text{if } (l,k) = (i,j+1), \\ 0, & \text{otherwise.} \end{cases}$$

Let $\dot{x} \in \mathbb{R}^{|C| \times 2}$ be the *data derivative document matrix* defined by

$$\dot{x} = D\widehat{x}. \tag{5}$$

Analogously, the *source derivative matrix* $\dot{s} \in \mathbb{R}^{|C| \times 2}$ is defined by

$$\dot{s} = D\widehat{s}. \tag{6}$$

Notice that the involved images contain letters. If we assume that the colours of the letters and of the background are uniform, then the finite differences are null, while they are different from zero in correspondence with the edges of the letters.

From (1), (5) and (6) we deduce

$$\dot{x}^T = \widehat{x}^T D^T = A\widehat{s}^T D^T = A\dot{s}^T. \tag{7}$$

Note that the linear model obtained by considering the data document derivative matrix and the source derivative matrix is equal to that obtained by treating the data document and the source document in (1).

Analogously as in [1], here we define the following $2 \times 2$ *data derivative overlapping matrix* of the observed data:

$$\dot{C} = \begin{bmatrix} \dot{c}_{11} & \dot{c}_{12} \\ \dot{c}_{21} & \dot{c}_{22} \end{bmatrix} = \dot{x}^T \dot{x} = \begin{bmatrix} \dot{x}_r^T \cdot \dot{x}_r & \dot{x}_r^T \cdot \dot{x}_v \\ \dot{x}_v^T \cdot \dot{x}_r & \dot{x}_v^T \cdot \dot{x}_v \end{bmatrix}. \tag{8}$$

The matrix $\dot{C}$ indicates how much the edges of the letters in the front overlap with those of the back. The *source derivative overlapping matrix* can be defined similarly as

$$\dot{P} = \begin{bmatrix} \dot{p}_{11} & \dot{p}_{12} \\ \dot{p}_{21} & \dot{p}_{22} \end{bmatrix} = \dot{s}^T \dot{s} = \begin{bmatrix} \dot{s}_r^T \cdot \dot{s}_r & \dot{s}_r^T \cdot \dot{s}_v \\ \dot{s}_v^T \cdot \dot{s}_r & \dot{s}_v^T \cdot \dot{s}_v \end{bmatrix}.$$

It is not difficult to see that the matrices $\dot{C}$ and $\dot{P}$ are symmetric and positive semidefinite. We refer to the value

$$\dot{k} = \dot{p}_{12} = \dot{p}_{21} = \dot{s}_r^T \cdot \dot{s}_v \tag{9}$$

as the *source derivative overlapping level*. We assume that $\dot{k} = 0$, that is the edges of the recto of the document do not overlap with those of the verso. Note that in [1] the value of the source overlapping level $k$ could not be assumed equal to 0, but could be estimated by searching a fixed point of such a value by means of an iterative method. Such iterative phases caused the algorithm in [1] more computationally expensive than that we are presenting here.

## 3   A Technique for Solving the Linear Problem

The set of all orthogonal $2 \times 2$ matrices is given by the union of all rotations and reflections in $\mathbb{R}^2$, which are expressed as

$$Q^1(\theta) = \begin{bmatrix} \sin\theta & -\cos\theta \\ \cos\theta & \sin\theta \end{bmatrix} \quad \text{and} \quad Q^{-1}(\theta) = \begin{bmatrix} \sin\theta & \cos\theta \\ \cos\theta & -\sin\theta \end{bmatrix}, \tag{10}$$

respectively, as $\theta$ varies in $]0, 2\pi]$. As $\dot{C} = \dot{C}^{1/2}(\dot{C}^{1/2})^T = \dot{C}^{1/2}\dot{C}^{1/2}$ is a symmetric factorization of $\dot{C}$, then it is possible to check that all factorizations of $\dot{C}$ have the form

$$Z^{(\iota)}(\theta) = \dot{C}^{1/2}Q^{(\iota)}(\theta) = \begin{bmatrix} \rho_{11} & \rho_{12} \\ \rho_{21} & \rho_{22} \end{bmatrix} Q^{(\iota)}(\theta) = \begin{bmatrix} z_{11}^{(\iota)}(\theta) & z_{12}^{(\iota)}(\theta) \\ z_{21}^{(\iota)}(\theta) & z_{22}^{(\iota)}(\theta) \end{bmatrix}, \quad (11)$$

where $\theta \in ]0, 2\pi]$ and $\iota \in \{-1, 1\}$. Moreover, we get

$$z_{11}^{(1)}(\theta) = z_{11}^{(-1)}(\theta), \; z_{12}^{(1)}(\theta) = -z_{12}^{(-1)}(\theta), \; z_{21}^{(1)}(\theta) = z_{21}^{(-1)}(\theta), \; z_{22}^{(1)}(\theta) = -z_{22}^{(-1)}(\theta). \quad (12)$$

We assume that

$$\dot{C} = \dot{x}^T \dot{x} = A \dot{s}^T \dot{s} A^T = A \widetilde{P} A^T, \quad (13)$$

where $\widetilde{P}$ denotes a symmetric positive-definite estimate of the source derivative overlapping matrix $\dot{P}$. We put

$$\widetilde{p}_{12} = \widetilde{p}_{21} = 0. \quad (14)$$

Observe that we do not assign a value to $\widetilde{p}_{11}$ and $\widetilde{p}_{22}$, since they will be found later by posing that the estimated mixture matrix is one row-sum. Let us consider

$$\widetilde{P} = YY^T \quad (15)$$

as a symmetric factorization, where $Y$ is a nonsingular matrix fulfilling

$$y_{11}\,y_{21} + y_{12}\,y_{22} = 0, \quad (16)$$

thanks to (14). From (13) and (15) we get

$$\dot{C} = AYY^T A^T = AY(AY)^T,$$

namely $AY$ is a factorization of $\dot{C}$. For each $\theta \in ]0, 2\pi]$ and $\iota \in \{-1, 1\}$, we consider an estimate $\widetilde{A}^{(\iota)}(\theta)$ of the mixture matrix $A$ as a matrix with the property that $\widetilde{A}^{(\iota)}(\theta) = Z^{(\iota)}(\theta)Y^{-1}$, with $Z^{(\iota)}(\theta)$ as in (11). We have

$$a_{11}^{(\iota)}(\theta) = \frac{z_{11}^{(\iota)}(\theta)y_{22} - z_{12}^{(\iota)}(\theta)y_{21}}{y_{11}\,y_{22} - y_{21}\,y_{12}}, \qquad a_{12}^{(\iota)}(\theta) = \frac{z_{12}^{(\iota)}(\theta)y_{11} - z_{11}^{(\iota)}(\theta)y_{12}}{y_{11}\,y_{22} - y_{21}\,y_{12}}, \quad (17)$$

$$a_{21}^{(\iota)}(\theta) = \frac{z_{21}^{(\iota)}(\theta)y_{22} - z_{22}^{(\iota)}(\theta)y_{21}}{y_{11}\,y_{22} - y_{21}\,y_{12}}, \qquad a_{22}^{(\iota)}(\theta) = \frac{z_{22}^{(\iota)}(\theta)y_{11} - z_{21}^{(\iota)}(\theta)y_{12}}{y_{11}\,y_{22} - y_{21}\,y_{12}}.$$

By requiring that $\widetilde{A}^{(\iota)}(\theta)$ fulfils (2), we get

$$z_{11}^{(\iota)}(\theta)y_{22} - z_{12}^{(\iota)}(\theta)y_{21} + z_{12}^{(\iota)}(\theta)y_{11} - z_{11}^{(\iota)}(\theta)y_{12} = y_{11}\,y_{22} - y_{21}\,y_{12}, \quad (18)$$

$$z_{21}^{(\iota)}(\theta)y_{22} - z_{22}^{(\iota)}(\theta)y_{21} + z_{22}^{(\iota)}(\theta)y_{11} - z_{21}^{(\iota)}(\theta)y_{12} = y_{11}\,y_{22} - y_{21}\,y_{12}.$$

Therefore the matrix $Y$ fulfils properties (16) and (18). The nonlinear system in (16) and (18) admits infinitely many solutions. Among the possible solutions, we take

$$y_{11} = \frac{\det \dot{C}}{(z_{22}^{(\iota)}(\theta) - z_{12}^{(\iota)}(\theta)) \det Z^{(\iota)}(\theta)}, \quad y_{12} = 0, \tag{19}$$

$$y_{21} = 0, \quad\quad\quad y_{22} = \frac{\det Z^{(\iota)}(\theta)}{z_{11}^{(\iota)}(\theta) - z_{21}^{(\iota)}(\theta)}.$$

Note that, by (12) and (17), we obtain that $\widetilde{A}^{(1)}(\theta) = \widetilde{A}^{(-1)}(\theta)$ for every $\theta \in ]0, 2\pi]$. Furthermore, by (10) and (11) we get that $Z(\theta) = -Z(\theta + \pi)$ for any $\theta \in ]0, \pi]$, and hence from (17) and (19) we deduce that

$$\widetilde{A}(\theta) = \widetilde{A}(\theta + \pi), \tag{20}$$

for each $\theta \in ]0, \pi]$.

So, in the following we deal with the case $\iota = 1$, we put $\widetilde{A}(\theta) = \widetilde{A}^{(1)}(\theta)$ and $Z(\theta) = Z^{(1)}(\theta)$ for each $\theta \in ]0, \pi]$.

Note that $Y$ has to be non-singular, since $Y$ is a symmetric factorization of $\dot{P}$.

When the equations in (19) are not defined, that is if $z_{11}(\theta) = z_{21}(\theta)$ or $z_{12}(\theta) = z_{22}(\theta)$, we get that $\theta = \varphi + t\frac{\pi}{2}$, where

$$\varphi = \begin{cases} \arctan\left(\dfrac{\dot{\rho}_{22} - \dot{\rho}_{12}}{\dot{\rho}_{11} - \dot{\rho}_{21}}\right), & \text{if } \dot{\rho}_{11} \neq \dot{\rho}_{21}, \\[2mm] \dfrac{\pi}{2}, & \text{if } \dot{\rho}_{11} = \dot{\rho}_{21}, \end{cases} \tag{21}$$

and $\dot{\rho}_{i,j}$, $i, j = 1, 2$, are the entries of the matrix $\dot{C}^{1/2}$.

For every $\theta \in ]\varphi, \varphi + \frac{\pi}{2}[\cup]\varphi + \frac{\pi}{2}, \varphi + \pi[$, we get that an estimate of the source derivative matrix $\dot{s}$ is expressed by

$$\widetilde{s}(\theta)^T = [\widetilde{s}_r(\theta) \; \widetilde{s}_v(\theta)]^T = \widetilde{A}^{-1}(\theta)\dot{x}^T, \tag{22}$$

which, since $\widetilde{A}^{-1}(\theta) = \widetilde{A}^1(\theta) = Z^{(1)}(\theta)Y^{-1}$ and thanks to (18), yields

$$\widetilde{s}_r(\theta) = -\frac{z_{22}(\theta)}{z_{12}(\theta) - z_{22}(\theta)}\dot{x}_r + \frac{z_{12}(\theta)}{z_{12}(\theta) - z_{22}(\theta)}\dot{x}_v; \tag{23}$$

$$\widetilde{s}_v(\theta) = -\frac{z_{21}(\theta)}{z_{11}(\theta) - z_{21}(\theta)}\dot{x}_r + \frac{z_{11}(\theta)}{z_{11}(\theta) - z_{21}(\theta)}\dot{x}_v.$$

Note that the obtained formulas are simpler than the corresponding ones given in [1], because here we consider derivatives of images instead of images. As we supposed that the derivatives of our estimated sources take values between 0 and $2\,\mathrm{m}$, where $m$ is the maximum value of the observed image, we compute the orthogonal projection of $\widetilde{s}(\theta)$ on $[0, 2m]^{nm \times 2}$ related to the Frobenius norm.

We consider the non-negative projections $\tau(\widetilde{s}_{r,\iota}(\theta))$ and $\tau(\widetilde{s}_{v,\iota}(\theta))$ as the new estimates of the derivatives of the sources. Thus we find a value $\widetilde{\theta}$ minimizing the *objective function*

$$g(\theta, \dot{C}) = \tau(\widetilde{s}_r(\theta))^T \cdot \tau(\widetilde{s}_v(\theta)), \ \theta \in ]\varphi, \varphi + \frac{\pi}{2}[\cup]\varphi + \frac{\pi}{2}, \varphi + \pi[. \qquad (24)$$

Observe that, thanks to (20) and (22), the function $g$ has period $\pi$ with respect to $\theta$. The function $g$ is minimized by means of the algorithm given in [1].

The proposed algorithm can be written in the following way.

**function ZEODS($\widehat{x}$)**
$\dot{x} = D\widehat{x}$;
$\dot{C} = \dot{x}^T \dot{x}$;
$\widetilde{\theta} = argmin(\textbf{function } g(\cdot, \dot{C}))$;
$Z(\widetilde{\theta}) = \dot{C}^{1/2} Q_1(\widetilde{\theta})$;
compute $\widetilde{s}_r(\widetilde{\theta})$ and $\widetilde{s}_v(\widetilde{\theta})$ as in (23);
**return** $D^{-1}\tau(\widetilde{s}(\widetilde{\theta}))$

The function $g(\cdot, \cdot)$ is determined as follows:

**function $g(\theta, \dot{C})$**
$Z(\theta) = \dot{C}^{1/2} Q^1(\theta)$;
compute $\widetilde{s}_r(\theta)$ and $\widetilde{s}_v(\theta)$ as in (23);
**return** $(\tau(\widetilde{s}_r(\theta)))^T \cdot \tau(\widetilde{s}_v(\theta))$

We refer to this method as the *Zero Edge Overlapping in Document Separation* (ZEODS) algorithm. Note that ZEODS is an unsupervised technique.

## 4   Experimental Results

In our experimental results we use quite noisy ideal sources, from which the observed documents are synthetically constructed from suitable mixture matrices. We examine RGB color images. The channels $R$, $G$ and $B$ are treated separately.

The first case we investigate is a symmetric mixture matrix. For each channel $R$, $G$ and $B$, the related matrices are

$$A_R = \begin{pmatrix} 0.6 & 0.4 \\ 0.4 & 0.6 \end{pmatrix}, A_G = \begin{pmatrix} 0.6 & 0.4 \\ 0.4 & 0.6 \end{pmatrix}, A_B = \begin{pmatrix} 0.6 & 0.4 \\ 0.4 & 0.6 \end{pmatrix}. \qquad (25)$$

Now we see the behavior of the presented algorithms. We consider the ideal images in Fig. 1, and using the above indicated mixture matrices, we synthetically obtain the degraded images in Fig. 2.

By applying the algorithms we get, as estimates, the results in Figs. 3, 4, 5, 6, 7 and 8.

(a) original recto          (b) original verso

**Fig. 1.** Ideal images

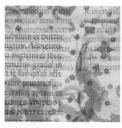

(a) degraded recto          (b) degraded verso

**Fig. 2.** Degraded images

(a)  recto  estimated          (b)  verso  estimated
by ZEODS                        by ZEODS

**Fig. 3.** Estimates by ZEODS

(a)  recto  estimated          (b)  verso  estimated
by MATODS                       by MATODS

**Fig. 4.** Estimates by MATODS

(a)  recto  estimated
by FastIca

(b)  verso  estimated
by FastIca

**Fig. 5.** Estimates by FastIca

(a) recto estimated
by  Symmetric
Whitening

(b) verso  estimated
by  Symmetric
Whitening

**Fig. 6.** Estimates by Symmetric Whitening

(a)  recto  estimated
by Whitening

(b)  verso  estimated
by Whitening

**Fig. 7.** Estimates by Whitening

454    A. Boccuto et al.

(a) recto estimated by PCA    (b) verso estimated by PCA

**Fig. 8.** Estimates by PCA

**Table 1.** Errors of the estimations of the document in Fig. 1 degraded by the mixture matrix in (25).

| Used technique | MSE Recto | MSE Verso | MSE of A |
|---|---|---|---|
| ZEODS | 5.0766 | 0.6228 | $1.020 \cdot 10^{-4}$ |
| MATODS | 12.5173 | 49.0506 | 0.0011 |
| FASTICA | 58.2382 | 212.8663 | 0.0546 |
| Symmetric whitening | 428.0422 | 373.6753 | 0.00183 |
| Whitening | $7.7086 \cdot 10^3$ | $6.2362 \cdot 10^3$ | 0.3561 |
| PCA | $1.4943 \cdot 10^4$ | $5.2861 \cdot 10^3$ | 0.3770 |

In Table 1 we present the mean square errors with respect to the original documents obtained by means of the aforementioned algorithms for estimating the recto and the verso of Fig. 1.

We now present the next case. For every channel $R$, $G$ and $B$, we consider the following mixture matrices.

$$A_R = \begin{pmatrix} 0.7 & 0.3 \\ 0.2 & 0.8 \end{pmatrix}, A_G = \begin{pmatrix} 0.45 & 0.55 \\ 0.4 & 0.6 \end{pmatrix}, A_B = \begin{pmatrix} 0.7 & 0.3 \\ 0.51 & 0.49 \end{pmatrix}. \tag{26}$$

Now we see the behavior of the presented algorithms, regarding both errors and the visual point of view. We consider the ideal images in Fig. 9. Using the above indicated mixture matrices, we synthetically obtain the degraded images in Fig. 10. By applying the algorithms we obtain, as estimates, the results in Figs. 11, 12, 13, 14, 15 and 16. In Table 2 we present the mean square errors with respect to the original documents obtained by means of the above algorithms for the estimate of the recto and the verso of Fig. 9.

Finally, we present the results related to the following images in Fig. 17. For the channels $R$, $G$ and $B$, we deal again with the mixture matrices in (26).

Using the abovementioned mixture matrices, we synthetically get the degraded images in Fig. 18.

By means of the algorithms we get, as estimates, the results in Figs. 19, 20, 21, 22, 23 and 24.

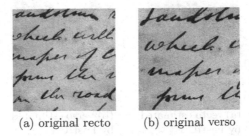

(a) original recto          (b) original verso

**Fig. 9.** Ideal images

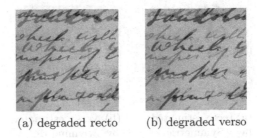

(a) degraded recto          (b) degraded verso

**Fig. 10.** Degraded images

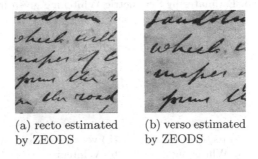

(a) recto estimated         (b) verso estimated
by ZEODS                    by ZEODS

**Fig. 11.** Estimates by ZEODS

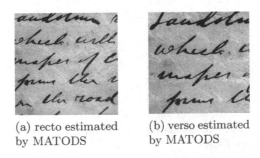

(a) recto estimated         (b) verso estimated
by MATODS                   by MATODS

**Fig. 12.** Estimates by the algorithm MATODS given in [1]

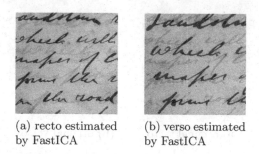

(a) recto estimated
by FastICA

(b) verso estimated
by FastICA

**Fig. 13.** Estimates by the algorithm FastICA given in [10]

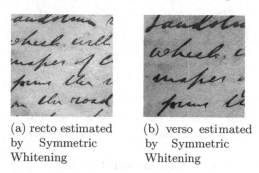

(a) recto estimated
by    Symmetric
Whitening

(b)  verso  estimated
by    Symmetric
Whitening

**Fig. 14.** Estimates by Symmetric Whitening given in [16]

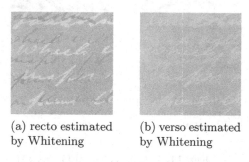

(a) recto estimated
by Whitening

(b) verso estimated
by Whitening

**Fig. 15.** Estimates by Whitening given in [16]

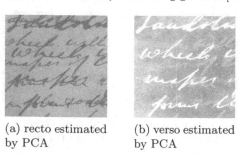

(a) recto estimated
by PCA

(b) verso estimated
by PCA

**Fig. 16.** Estimates by PCA given in [16]

**Table 2.** Errors of the estimations of the document in Fig. 9 degraded by the mixture matrix in (26).

| Used technique | MSE Recto | MSE Verso | MSE of A |
|---|---|---|---|
| ZEODS | 1.2642 | 2.6337 | $2.2806 \cdot 10^{-5}$ |
| MATODS | 62.2418 | 85.4395 | 0.0026 |
| FastICA | 353.226 | 182.7357 | 0.0303 |
| Symmetric Whitening | 409.8490 | 495.5137 | 0.1435 |
| Whitening | $7.7216 \cdot 10^3$ | $3.5975 \cdot 10^3$ | 0.4449 |
| PCA | $1.2810 \cdot 10^4$ | $2.5195 \cdot 10^3$ | 0.4473 |

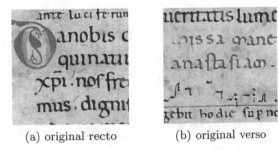

(a) original recto          (b) original verso

**Fig. 17.** Ideal images

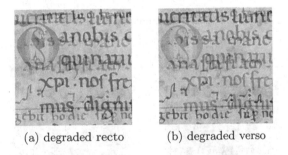

(a) degraded recto          (b) degraded verso

**Fig. 18.** Degraded images

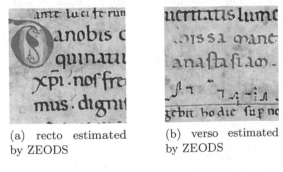

(a) recto estimated by ZEODS          (b) verso estimated by ZEODS

**Fig. 19.** Estimates by ZEODS

(a) recto estimated by MATODS

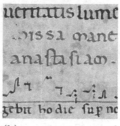

(b) verso estimated by MATODS

**Fig. 20.** Estimates by MATODS

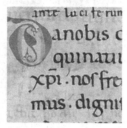

(a) recto estimated by FastIca

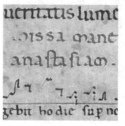

(b) verso estimated by FastIca

**Fig. 21.** Estimates by FastIca

(a) recto estimated by Symmetric Whitening

(b) verso estimated by Symmetric Whitening

**Fig. 22.** Estimates by Symmetric Whitening

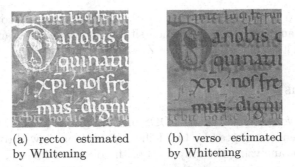

(a)  recto  estimated
by Whitening

(b)  verso  estimated
by Whitening

**Fig. 23.** Estimates by Whitening

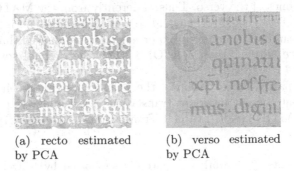

(a)  recto  estimated
by PCA

(b)  verso  estimated
by PCA

**Fig. 24.** Estimates by PCA

In Table 3 there are the mean square errors with respect to the original documents obtained using the above algorithms for the estimate of the recto and the verso of Fig. 17.

**Table 3.** Errors of the estimations of the document in Fig. 17 degraded by the mixture matrix in (26).

| Used technique | MSE Recto | MSE Verso | MSE of A |
|---|---|---|---|
| ZEODS | 3.2977 | 3.6252 | $1.090 \cdot 10^{-4}$ |
| MATODS | 35.0124 | 42.8569 | $1.5041 \cdot 10^{-4}$ |
| FASTICA | 232.7229 | 147.4355 | 0.0304 |
| Symmetric Whitening | 235.6894 | 607.9245 | 0.1441 |
| Whitening | $1.4669 \cdot 10^{4}$ | $6.6340 \cdot 10^{3}$ | 0.5272 |
| PCA | $1.9414 \cdot 10^{4}$ | $3.9348 \cdot 10^{3}$ | 0.4795 |

It is possible to note how the here proposed ZEODS algorithm obtains always results which are qualitatively and quantitatively better than algorithms which assume the same linear model.

In [2] we examined various other cases, in which the ideal sources are quite noisy images, and in almost all studied situations we get the same results, and the better results are obtained by the ZEODS method.

## Conclusions

In this article we extended the MATODS method proposed in [1] for the restoration of documents corrupted by bleed-through and/or show-through. In particular, instead of analyzing the gray level of the observed images, we studied the derivatives of the gray level in those images. In this case, there is a very low probability that the horizontal (or vertical) derivatives of the recto overlap with the respective ones of the verso. Thus, differently from the MATODS, the overlapping level is established to be equal to zero. Therefore, no iterative phase is necessary to estimate such a level. Experimentally, we showed that the proposed method is more efficient than MATODS when the original sources are noisy images.

We are preparing an extension of the ZEODS method, to include the case in order to treat the not invariant translation case, similarly to that proposed by the NIT-MATODS (Not Invariant Translation MATODS) ([1]), to deal with real documents.

**Acknowledgments.** This work was partially supported by University of Perugia, G.N.A.M.P.A. (Italian National Group of Mathematical Analysis, Probability and Applications) and I.N.d.A.M. (Italian National Institute of Higher Mathematics).

## References

1. Boccuto, A., Gerace, I., Giorgetti, V.: A blind source separation technique for document restoration. SIAM J. Imaging Sci. **12**(2), 1135–1162 (2019)
2. Boccuto, A., Gerace, I., Giorgetti, V., Valenti, G.: A Blind Source Separation Technique for Document Restoration Based on Edge Estimation. http://viXra.org/abs/2201.0141 (2022)
3. Chan, T.-H., Ma, W.-K., Chi, C.-Y., Wang, Y.: A convex analysis framework for blind separation of non-negative sources. IEEE Trans. Signal Process. **56**(10), 5120–5134 (2008)
4. Cichocki, A., Zdunek, R., Amari, S.-I.: New algorithms for non-negative matrix factorization in applications to blind source separation. In: Proceedings of the 2006 IEEE International Conference Acoustics, Speech and Signal Processing, Toulouse, France, pp. 1–4 (2006)
5. Comon, P.: Independent component analysis, a new concept? Signal Process. **36**, 287–314 (1994)
6. Gillis, N.: Successive nonnegative projection algorithm for robust nonnegative blind source separation. SIAM J. Imaging Sci. **7**(2), 1420–1450 (2014)
7. Gillis, N.: Sparse and unique nonnegative matrix factorization through data preprocessing. J. Mach. Learn. Res. **13**, 3349–3386 (2012)
8. Hyvärinen, A.: Fast and robust fixed-point algorithms for independent component analysis. IEEE Trans. Neural Netw. **10**(3), 626–634 (1999)

9. Hyvärinen, A.: The fixed-point algorithm and maximum likelihood estimation for independent component analysis. Neural Process. Lett. **10**(1), 1–5 (1999)

10. Hyvärinen, A., Oja, E.: A fast fixed-point algorithm for independent component analysis. Neural Comput. **9**(7), 1483–1492 (1997)

11. Khaparde, A., Madhavilatha, M., Manasa, M.B.L., Pradeep Kumar, S.: FastICA algorithm for the separation of mixed images. WSEAS Trans. Signal Process. **4**(5), 271–278 (2008)

12. Malik, R. K., Solanki, K.: FastICA based blind source separation for CT imaging under noise conditions. Int. J. Adv. Eng. Technol. **5**(1), 47–55 (2012)

13. Ouedraogo, W.S.B., Souloumiac, A., Jaidane, M., Jutten, C.: Non-negative blind source separation algorithm based on minimum aperture simplicial cone. IEEE Trans. Signal Process. **62**(2), 376–389 (2014)

14. Tonazzini, A., Gerace, I., Martinelli, F.: Multichannel blind separation and deconvolution of images for document analysis. IEEE Trans. Image Process. **19**(4), 912–925 (2010)

15. Tonazzini, A., Gerace, I., Martinelli, F.: Document image restoration and analysis as separation of mixtures of patterns: from linear to nonlinear models. In: Gunturk, B.K., Li, X. (eds.) Image Restoration - Fundamentals and Advances, pp. 285–310. CRC Press, Taylor and Francis, Boca Raton (2013)

16. Tonazzini, A., Salerno, E., Bedini, L.: Fast correction of bleed-through distortion in greyscale documents by a blind source separation technique. Int. J. Doc. Anal. **10**(1), 17–25 (2007)

17. Vavasis, S.: On the complexity of nonnegative matrix factorization. SIAM J. Optim. **20**(3), 1364–1377 (2009)

# Information Systems and Technologies

# Scalable Solution for the Anonymization of Big Data Spatio-Temporal Trajectories

Hajlaoui Jalel Eddine(✉)

Lambda Lab, Paris, France
hajlaouijalel_ig@yahoo.fr

**Abstract.** Regardless of the collection location, mobile traffic data contains information about many aspects of subscribers' lives, including their activities, interests, schedules, travel and preferences. It is precisely the ability to access such information on unprecedented scales that is of critical importance for studies in a wide variety of fields. However, access to such a rich source also raises concerns about potential infringements on the rights of mobile customers regarding their personal data: among other things, individuals can be identified, their movements can be modified, their movements can be tracked and their mobile stage fright can be monitored. As a result, regulators have been working on legislation to protect the privacy of mobile users. In this optic, we provide a scalable solution to anonymize Big Data Spatio-temporal Trajectories of mobile users.

**Keywords:** Big Data · Anonymization · Privacy

## 1 Introduction

Mobile traffic transmits information about people's movements, interactions and mobile service consumption on unprecedented scales. Traditional techniques data collection, e.g., census, population surveys or phone interviews, cannot provide a perspective, even from a comparable distance, on human activities. As a result, as soon as the rise of the mobile communications became obvious - about a decade ago - sociologists, epidemiologists, transport and telecommunication experts have seen in the collected data set by mobile network operators a clear opportunity to perform their analyses while maintaining a high level of detail for each individual [1–4]. The first landmark studies using large mobile traffic datasets were conducted in the United States towards 2006. Since then, the growth of mobile traffic analysis has been spectacular and has grown at an annual rate of 90%. The main reason for this phenomenon is the nature of mobile traffic databases, allowing large-scale research relevant to different disciplines [5]. However, other factors contributed to the success of telephony mobile traffic analyses. The increase in the volume of workload is primarily based on the growing availability of datasets. As mentioned above, mobile operators have always monitored mobile traffic in their networks, for maintenance, efficiency and billing purposes. Yet they have traditionally been very careful about sharing the collected data. This attitude has changed in recent years, as more and more operators are inclined to open their data to analytical processing in the broad sense. On the one hand, operators driven by the value that mobile traffic data can have, are still deploying more advanced probes in their networks allowing more detailed measurement of subscriber activities. On the other hand, mobile services have been developed from simple calling and texting to permanent applications based on Cloud applications [6,11]: this leads to much more frequent interactions between users (or their devices) and the network, which leads to a significantly higher granularity of activity samples recorded at the operator's side. A third key element, resulting from the first two preceding ones, is the emergence of a very active company and an interdisciplinary community which brings together researchers and industrial players. The cohesion of university-industry partnerships have important consequences: for example, mobile operators encourage fundamental and applied research on mobile traffic in response to targeted challenges. As examples, we can cite challenges of Telecom Italia[1].

In this paper we implement our scalable solution of spatio-temporal trajectories merging based on our Cartesian Product k-merge (FCP-k-merge) algorithm which extends the k-merge algorithm. In Sect. 2, we discuss the taxonomy of mobile traffic analysis approaches. In Sect. 3, we illustrate the architectural aspect of our application while focusing on the optimization of the algorithm for calculating the aggregation cost of the movements of mobile users by generalizing their spatio-temporal trajectories. In Sect. 4, we conclude the paper and highlight perspectives of our work.

## 2    Taxonomy of Mobile Traffic Analysis Solutions

The adopted classification [12] of traffic analysis works revolves around the study topics, each of which includes multidisciplinary contributions. The roadmap of the proposed hierarchy is illustrated in Fig. 1. In the upper layer, authors explicit three macro-research topics across multiple domains: they cite the social analysis, mobility analysis and network analysis, respectively. Then, a topic tree is detailed within each macro-topic. Below, we show a taxonomy of the topics included in the classification:

- *Social analysis* explore the relationships between mobile traffic and a broad set of social features. The research focuses on characterizing the social structure of mobile user interactions, and on studying the impact of demographic, economic or environmental factors on the way of mobile services consumption. This topic includes works which exploit social characteristics, inferred from mobile traffic, for the characterization and mitigation of epidemics.
- *Mobility analysis* deal with the extraction of mobility information from mobile traffic. Mobility is considered here in its largest sense, and focus on generic human movements, both individual and collective, as well as specialized patterns followed by specific users, for example trips on transport systems.

---

[1] http://www.telecomitalia.com/bigdatachallenge/.

This branch also defines the reliability of mobile traffic data as a source of mobility information.

– *Network analysis* have a more technical perspective, as they focus on understanding the dynamics of mobile traffic demand and how to evolve the mobile network infrastructure to better accommodate it. The work in this category therefore relates either to the characterization of the uses of mobile services, or to the operation of this knowledge to implement different sophisticated technological solutions. The wide majority of the categories described above are interdisciplinary in nature. In the lower part of Fig. 1, authors provide a representation of the importance of five main areas for the different topics of mobile traffic analysis. The relationships are not probably clear cut, but it can be seen that mobility studies are the ones that capture the tremendous attempts to contribute. Most of the categories have sense for two or three disciplines. The only non-multidisciplinary subjects is devoted to develop solutions for mobile networks: being fairly specific and very technical subjects, it is evident that they entice contributions only from the networking community.

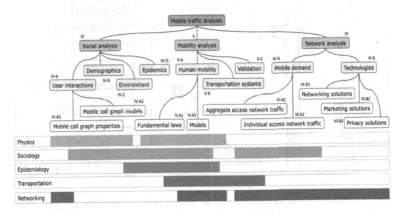

**Fig. 1.** Functional architecture of the mobile data clustering application.

## 3   Spatio-Temporal Big Data Clustering Solution

In this section, we present our contribution to the anonymization of user mobility data within $\lambda\_Company^2$, this massively collected data makes it possible to trace the movement of people. The anonymization of these Big Data consists of aggregating them using clustering techniques so as not to be able to re-identify people from call logs or probe data and anonymize their movements. Thus, we apply our technique of aggregation/fusion of spatiotemporal trajectories in a Big Data ecosystem with the Spark platform and the Scala language.

---

[2] For the sake of anonimity of the company owning the data set.

## 3.1 Reference Architecture

Data storage focuses on how to efficiently store a huge volume of data, allowing faster read/write speeds during processing. The storage layer must take care to store all types of data and continue to evolve with the exponential growth of data. In our case, the source data is csv files stored in HDFS and transformed into Spark for batch processing for offline analysis. We have added a streaming module for real-time processing in order to extend the scope of the reference architecture. A real-time processing system connects directly to the data ingestion layer and is applicable for online analysis; it should provide low latency processing results. The cluster manager is trained by resource managers to accommodate resource provisioning and scheduling throughout the distributed system. Communication between Spark applications and transactional nodes, masters and workers, and intercommunication between drivers and Spark executors can be secure (i.e., encrypted). Encryption must be configured individually on each node of the cluster (Fig. 2).

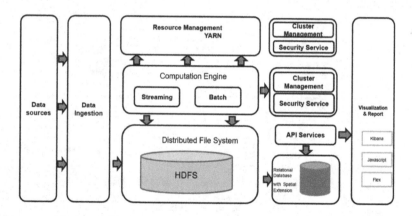

**Fig. 2.** Reference architecture of the mobile data clustering application.

The data visualization layer is the presentation layer. Dashboards can be created to help the user perform visual analysis directly from the ingested source or processed data. In Big Data environments - Hadoop [13] and Spark [14] echosystem - there are no integrated components for data visualization. Flex, JavaScript or Kibana can be used as a visualization tool to present the dashboards in real time.

Apache Hadoop, introduced by Yahoo in 2005, is the open source implementation of the MapReduce programming paradigm. The main characteristic of Hadoop is to use hardware base mainly distributed for the parallel processing of batch jobs. The heart of Hadoop is its fault-tolerant Hadoop Distributed File Systems (HDFS) file system which can be explicitly set to span many machines. In HDFS, the data block is much larger than a traditional file system (4 KB vs. 128 MB). Therefore, it reduces the memory required to store the metadata on the locations of the data blocks. In addition, it reduces the search operation in large files. In addition, it dramatically improves network usage because only fewer network connections are required for random read operations. In the architecture of HDFS, there are mainly two types of nodes: Name Node and Data Node. The Name Node contains the metadata of HDFS blocks and the Data Node is the location where the actual data is stored. By default, three copies of the same block are stored on data nodes to make the system fault tolerant. Hadoop's resource manager is called Yarn. It is composed a central resource manager that resides in the master node and many node managers that live on the slave nodes. When an application is submitted to the cluster, the application master negotiates resources with the resource manager and starts the container (where the actual processing takes place) on the slave nodes. The main disadvantage of Hadoop was that it stored intermediate results on disk. Therefore, for intensive shuffle operations (the rearrangement of data between machines, by keys, so that entire operations can be handled) like iterative machine learning, a huge amount of data is stored on disk and transferred. On the network, which represents a significant overload on the entire system.

Apache Spark is one of the world's premier big data processing platforms. It is a large scale, open source data processing framework. It primarily focuses on high-speed server cluster computing and provides scalable and interactive analysis through high-level APIs. Spark supports batch or streaming data analysis, machine learning, and graph processing. It can also access various data sources such as HDFS, HBase, Cassandra, etc. and use Resilient Distributed Dataset (RDD), Data Frame (DF), or Data Set (DS) structures for data abstraction. Compared to Hadoop system tasks, Apache Spark can perform most in-memory calculations and offers better performance for some applications such as iterative algorithms. When the results do not fit in memory, the intermediate results are written to disk. Spark can run locally on a single machine, in a local cluster, and in the cloud. It runs on Hadoop Yarn, Apache Mesos, and the standalone cluster manager by default. Applications or jobs are divided into several sets of tasks called stages that are interrelated. All of these steps form a directed acyclic graph (DAG), where each step is executed one after the other.

## 3.2   Functional Dimension

The data pre-processing step includes flexible procedures that are applied before storing and analyzing the trajectory data, such as data format transformation and associating the stamped movement sequences to each user. After being properly treated, all trajectories are kept in memory to support efficient analysis and rapid restitution of results. A (raw) sample of a space-time trajectory represents the position of a subscriber at a given time, and we model it with a real vector of length $3_s = (t(s),\ x(s),\ y(s))$. Since a data set is characterized by a finite granularity in time and space, the sample is actually a niche covering a minimum of time and spatial intervals. A spatiotemporal (sub)trajectory describes the movements of a single subscriber during the duration of the occurrence of the movements in the data set. Formally, each trajectory is an ordered vector

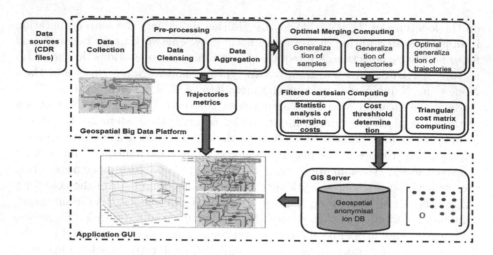

**Fig. 3.** Functional architecture of the mobile data clustering application.

of samples $S = (s_1, ..., s_N)$, where the order is induced by the time coordinate, i.e., $t(si) < t(si')$ si et seulement si $i \leq i'$.

A generalized trajectory, obtained by merging different trajectories, is defined as an ordered vector of generalized samples $G = (G_1, ..., G_Z)$. Here, the order is more subtle, and based on the fact that the time intervals extended by the generalized samples do not overlap, a property that will be called temporal consistency. Once able to optimally merge the (sub) trajectories, the calculation of the cost of merging trajectories is a combinatorial treatment that involves all combinations of the trajectories one by one. The computation result is a matrix $n \times n$ where $n$ is the number of trajectories. We perform a statistical computation in order to determine a threshold (i.e., a mean cost value). The resulting matrix is a triangular matrix where the cost values are not duplicated. The results of the merged trajectories are stored in a geospatial anonymization database (Fig. 3).

## 3.3 Algorithm for Merging Trajectories

To calculate the cost between trajectories to merge, we implemented $k - merge$ [15–17] an algorithm to efficiently search the set of raw samples $S$, extract the subset of elementary partitions, $K^\times$, and identify the optimal partition $G^\times$. The k-merge algorithm, detailed in Algorithm 1, starts by filling a set of raw samples $S$, whose items $s_{i,j}$ are sorted according to their time value $t(s_{i,j})$ (lines 1 to 3). Then, it processes all the samples according to their time order (line 6). More precisely, the algorithm tests, for each sample $s_\theta$ in position $\theta$, all the sets $\{s_{\theta'}, ..., s_\theta\}$, with $\theta' \leq \theta$, as follows. The first loop ignores incomplete sets that do not contain at least one sample of each input path (line 8). The second loop runs until the first non-elemental set is encountered (line 10). Here, the algorithm generates the current set (complete and elementary) $\{s_{\theta'}, ..., s_\theta\}$ to $G$, and checks if $G$ reduces the total cost of merging down to $s_\theta$. If so, the cost is updated by adding $c(G)$ to the cumulative cost up to $s_{\theta'-1}$, and the resulting $S$ (partial) score that includes $G$ is stored (lines 11 through 14). Once out of the loops, the cost associated with the last sample is the optimal cost, and just navigate to arrive in the structure of the partition to retrieve the associated $G^\times$ (lines 16–17). Note that, in order to update the inclusion cost of the current sample $s_\theta$ (line 13), the algorithm checks only the previous samples in time. Therefore, the optimal decision up to $s_\theta$ should not depend on any of the samples in the initial trajectories that come later than $s$.

---

**Algorithm 1: k-merge algorithm pseudocode.**

---

**input** : Trajectories $\mathbf{S}_1, \ldots, \mathbf{S}_k$, where $\mathbf{S}_i = (s_{i,1}, \ldots, s_{i,N_i})$
**output**: Generalized sample set $\mathbf{G}^*$, Cost $C(\mathbf{G}^*)$
1 **foreach** $i \in [1, k]$ **do**
2  $\quad S_i = \bigcup_{j=1}^{N_i} \{s_{i,j}\}$;
3 $S \leftarrow$ timesort $(S_1 \cup \cdots \cup S_k)$;
4 Cost $\leftarrow (0, \infty, \ldots, \infty)$;
5 Partition $\leftarrow$ (NULL, $\ldots$, NULL);
6 **foreach** $s_\theta \in S$ **do**
7  $\quad \theta' = \theta - 1$;
8  $\quad$ **while** incomplete $(s_{\theta'}, \ldots, s_\theta)$ **do**
9  $\quad\quad \theta' = \theta' - 1$;
10 $\quad$ **while** elementary $(s_{\theta'}, \ldots, s_\theta)$ **do**
11 $\quad\quad \mathcal{G} \leftarrow$ generalize $(s_{\theta'}, \ldots, s_\theta)$;
12 $\quad\quad$ **if** Cost$[\theta] > c(\mathcal{G}) +$ Cost$[\theta' - 1]$ **then**
13 $\quad\quad\quad$ Cost$[\theta] \leftarrow c(\mathcal{G}) +$ Cost$[\theta' - 1]$;
14 $\quad\quad\quad$ Partition $\leftarrow (\theta' - 1, \mathcal{G})$;
15 $\quad\quad \theta' = \theta' - 1$;
16 $\mathbf{G}^* \leftarrow$ visit (Partition);
17 $C(\mathbf{G}^*) \leftarrow$ Cost$[|S|]$;

---

## 3.4    Filtered Cartesian Product k-merge (FCP-k-merge) Algorithm

The Filtered Cartesian Product k-merge (FCP-k-merge) algorithm allows optimizing the execution of the k-merge algorithm which, once executed with a consequent set of users, runs in exponential time. For every 1000 users, k-merge completes its execution in about 6 h in $\lambda$_Company's private cluster. The idea is to limit the cost calculation only for pairs of trajectories whose merging cost does not exceed a certain threshold $\lambda$. As a result, we avoid an exhaustive cartesian product and thus reduce the processing space in the triangular cost matrix. The FCP-k-merge algorithm allows us to determine an average threshold by performing the steps shown in Algorithm 2.

First, this algorithm accumulates the number of costs using a spark *accumulator* that retrieves the costs of each worker node of the cluster. Then, the final number of costs is assigned to each bin or segment of the vector. Finally, the threshold value $\lambda$ is calculated and in the ideal case it corresponds to the histogram's median. In the case where the last bin contains an important value, i.e. the distribution of bins values is unbalanced, we repeat the execution with a higher bin width and a higher number of bins (lines 8–10) (Fig. 4).

---

**Algorithm 2:** Filtered cartesian computing

---

1  Cost matrix: $Cn * n$,
2  $n\_bins$: bins number
3  $w\_bin$: bin width
4  Threshold $\lambda$
   /* initialisation                                                    */
5  $\lambda = 0$ // threshold
6  Max_bin_value = n_bins * w_bin // Maximum value
7  bin_accunt[ ] = Array(Int) of size $nbin + 1$
8  //step 1:
9  **for**  *(i := 0 to n )* **do**
10 |   For $(j = 0$ to n)
11 |   **if** *(Sij $\geq$ max_bin_value)* **then**
12 |   |   do: bin_accum[nbin+1]+=1
13 |   **else**
14 |   |   do: index=(int) ((Sij)/wbin)
15 |   |   bin_acc[index]+=1
16 |   **if** $bin\_acc[n + 1] \gg medium\_value$ **then**
17 |   |   repeat step 1 with w_binNew $\succ$ w_bin and n_binsNew $\succ$ n_$bins$
18 |   **else**
19 |   |   return $\lambda = Median(bin\_acc)$

---

## 3.5   Used Mobility Data

Mobile traffic is most often in the form of CRA (Call Detail Record), or CDR (Call Detail Record). It can include several fields but for mobility studies only 3 are essential:

- User ID (cell phone number or SIM card number).
- Time stamp of connection to the mobile network.
- Mobile network identifier (CELL_ID).

   This third element is composed of 2 sub-identifiers (Figs. 5 and 6):

- LAC = Location Area Code
- CI (Cell Identification) or SAC (Service Area Code) or ECI (E-UTRAN Cell Identifier) depending on the technology (2G, 3G or 4G)

On 2G and 3G networks both elements (LAC and CI/SAC) are needed to identify an antenna (CI and SAC codes are guaranteed to be unique within a LAC). On the 4G network the ECI code is unique for each antenna and is therefore sufficient to identify it. An example of CRA data is shown as depicted in the Fig. 7:

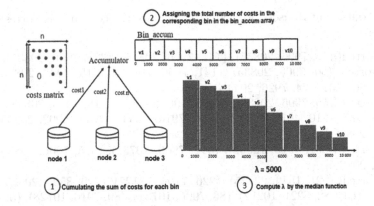

**Fig. 4.** Steps to calculate the $\lambda$ cost threshold.

```
User_id;datetime;LAC;CELL
935b0906b5cdb56a4407c4098ae754ac846911e7;2015-09-15 12:32:35;1054;19851
15637b4580e2a5e8f6a0cc2c62d50f74b67d6b3c;2015-09-15 12:32:05;1054;6775
e384f05b9f7b6a240e6161b203b80d02cfe36b15;2015-09-15 12:32:36;1054;49616
15637b4580e2a5e8f6a0cc2c62d50f74b67d6b3c;2015-09-15 12:32:25;1054;6771
c8444c5e849ef6a03e948f3e1a863c139790b4fd;2015-09-15 12:32:37;1054;56057
4355c1a7e14a1eb898dc71937ed92e2653e13747;2015-09-15 12:32:21;1054;37453
4355c1a7e14a1eb898dc71937ed92e2653e13747;2015-09-15 12:32:41;1054;37453
```

**Fig. 5.** CRA mobile data.

The datetime field can be given in clear as in the example but also in unix epoch (number of seconds since 1/1/1970). The data are in no particular order. To build a trajectory, it is therefore necessary to extract the data from a user and sort them according to the datetime field. An example of reference data for the datetime is shown in the Fig. 8: The X/Y positions are given in Lambert 2 extended projection. It is an Euclidean projection so to calculate the distances between the points, we can use the Pythagorean theorem.

```
CELL ;LAC ;SITE ;X ;Y
19851;1054;00000493H3;0;3G;795782;2081272
6775;1054;00000119H3;150;3G;792940;2082960
```

**Fig. 6.** Network antenna data.

## 3.6   Experimentations

The experiments are performed on a local Dell computer with 32 GB RAM and an Intel(R) Core(TM) i7-8700, 3.2 GHZ, 6-core processor. Let the following test set containing 10 users, we want to calculate the cost matrix corresponding to them:

- $U_1$: sorted([(58, 7906, 20835), (141, 7906, 20835), (321, 7906, 20835)])
- $U_2$: sorted([(50, 7906, 20835), (141, 7906, 20835), (315, 7906, 20835), (870, 6972, 20868), (874, 7926, 2044)])
- $U_3$: sorted([(55, 7906, 20835), (147, 7906, 20835), (318, 7906, 20835)])
- $U_4$: sorted([(210, 4916, 12532), (366, 7916, 12330), (371, 5902, 20835), (380, 7906, 20868)])
- $U_5$: sorted([(331, 4916, 12532), (512, 7906, 10731), (515, 7906, 20835), (524, 7906, 20868)])
- $U_6$: sorted([(221, 1549, 22125), (226, 7104, 73122), (229, 8506, 20835)])
- $U_7$: sorted([(82, 5221, 10212), (86, 7906, 10731), (89, 7916, 10728), (524, 7916, 10788)])
- $U_8$: sorted([(918, 7906, 20835), (944, 1045, 30442), (946, 1054, 71754), (952, 1054, 178)])
- $U_9$: sorted([(775, 1080, 12532), (760, 1080, 7980), (764, 1080, 2563), (766, 1080, 219)])
- $U_{10}$: sorted([(1220, 32519, 12362), (1221, 76, 10731), (1224, 1706, 235), (1228, 1902, 868)])

| | $U_1$ | $U_2$ | $U_3$ | $U_4$ | $U_5$ | $U_6$ | $U_7$ | $U_8$ | $U_9$ | $U_{10}$ |
|---|---|---|---|---|---|---|---|---|---|---|
| $U_1$ | 0 | 19089 | 15 | 2361162 | 6130776 | 6408512 | 2951165 | 70202010 | 19704074 | 62114524 |
| $U_2$ | 0 | 0 | 11017084 | 12208579 | 10364685 | 23532079 | 9708766 | 70847574 | 17045958 | 62577783 |
| $U_3$ | 0 | 0 | 0 | 2426703 | 6170160 | 6270386 | 3081974 | 70437324 | 19786403 | 62273656 |
| $U_4$ | 0 | 0 | 0 | 0 | 1932290 | 2818218 | 2609514 | 58286864 | 15557076 | 54085463 |
| $U_5$ | 0 | 0 | 0 | 0 | 0 | 21082096 | 1462174 | 48788436 | 12226820 | 47663146 |
| $U_6$ | 0 | 0 | 0 | 0 | 0 | 0 | 13194158 | 58857192 | 44583150 | 1.06173648e+08 |
| $U_7$ | 0 | 0 | 0 | 0 | 0 | 0 | 0 | 68328208 | 13290100 | 051122937 |
| $U_8$ | 0 | 0 | 0 | 0 | 0 | 0 | 0 | 0 | 15138534 | 32350220 |
| $U_9$ | 0 | 0 | 0 | 0 | 0 | 0 | 0 | 0 | 0 | 20991033 |
| $U_{10}$ | 0 | 0 | 0 | 0 | 0 | 0 | 0 | 0 | 0 | 0 |

$C =$

**Fig. 7.** Cost matrix for 10 mobile users.

From the cost matrix $C$ depicted in Fig. 7, we notice that users $U_1$ and $U_3$ have trajectories whose merging cost is equal to 15 because they look very similar. Users $U_6$ and $U_{10}$ have trajectories whose merging cost is very huge and is equal to 1.06173648e+08 because the trajectories are quite far in time and geographical coordinates. Figure 8 shows the execution time of the k-merge algorithm for 100 users combined with a number of users ranging from 100 to 1500 users. The maximum execution time is 9888 ms or less than one second. With the FCP-k-merge, this time is likely to be half optimized.

Currently, we are conducting deep experiments on the private $\lambda\_Company$ cluster to see the behavior of the FCP-k-merge algorithm in terms of the execution time considering that with the k-merge algorithm, we can reach about 6 h for a combination of 1000 users.

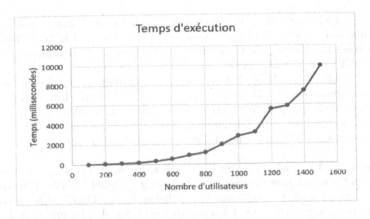

**Fig. 8.** Execution time of the FCP-k-merge algorithm.

## 4   Conclusion

This work, focused mainly on privacy, ultimately allowed the development of a proof of concept application, in order to help organizations concerned with the privacy of mobile users by anonymizing their trajectories. The main objective has therefore been the implementation of the k-merge algorithm under Spark with the Scala language. There are still a number many points to improve, especially at the level of partitioning, but the solution is functional and fulfills the objectives that we have set, to perform the clustering of spatiotemporal trajectories. The secondary objective is the optimization of k-merge by the Filtered Cartesian Product k-merge (FCP-k-merge) algorithm which help to optimize execution time by offloading memory with additional processing. In the future we plan to deploy our solution in an elastic Kubernetes infrastructure for the sake of the orchestration of our containerized infrastructure and its high scalability.

## References

1. Zhang, C., Fiore, M., Ziemlicki, C., Patras, P.: Microscope: mobile service traffic decomposition for network slicing as a service. In: Proceedings of the 26th Annual International Conference on Mobile Computing and Networking, pp. 1–14, September 2020
2. Pullano, G., Valdano, E., Scarpa, N., Rubrichi, S., Colizza, V.: Evaluating the effect of demographic factors, socioeconomic factors, and risk aversion on mobility during the COVID-19 epidemic in France under lockdown: a population-based study. Lancet Digit. Health **2**(12), e638–e649 (2020)
3. Zhao, Y., Luo, Y., Yu, Q., Hu, Z.: A privacy-preserving trajectory publication method based on secure start-points and end-points. Mob. Inf. Syst. (2020)
4. Bennati, S., Kovacevic, A.: Privacy metrics for trajectory data based on k-anonymity, l-diversity and t-closeness. arXiv preprint arXiv:2011.09218 (2020)
5. Tan, R., Tao, Y., Si, W., Zhang, Y.-Y.: Privacy preserving semantic trajectory data publishing for mobile location-based services. Wirel. Netw. **26**(8), 5551–5560 (2019). https://doi.org/10.1007/s11276-019-02058-8

6. Hajlaoui, J.E., Omri, M.N., Benslimane, D.: Multi-tenancy aware configurable service discovery approach in cloud computing. In: 2017 IEEE 26th International Conference on Enabling Technologies: Infrastructure for Collaborative Enterprises (WETICE), pp. 232–237. IEEE, June 2017

7. Hajlaoui, J.E., Omri, M.N., Benslimane, D., Barhamgi, M.: QoS based framework for configurable IaaS cloud services discovery. In: 2017 IEEE International Conference on Web Services (ICWS), pp. 460–467. IEEE, June 2017

8. Azouzi, S., Hajlaoui, J.E., Ghannouchi, S.A., Brahmi, Z.: E-Learning BPaaS discovery in cloud based on a structural matching. In: SoMeT, pp. 176–189, September 2019

9. Khemili, W., Hajlaoui, J.E., Omri, M.N.: Energy aware fuzzy approach for placement and consolidation in cloud data centers. J. Parallel Distrib. Comput. (2021)

10. Mokni, M., Yassa, S., Hajlaoui, J.E., Chelouah, R., Omri, M.N.: Cooperative agents-based approach for workflow scheduling on fog-cloud computing. J. Ambient Intell. Human. Comput. 1–20 (2021)

11. Mokni, M., Hajlaoui, J.E., Brahmi, Z.: MAS-based approach for scheduling intensive workflows in cloud computing. In: 2018 IEEE 27th International Conference on Enabling Technologies: Infrastructure for Collaborative Enterprises (WETICE), pp. 15–20. IEEE, June 2018

12. Naboulsi, D., Fiore, M., Ribot, S., Stanica, R.: Large-scale mobile traffic analysis: a survey. IEEE Commun. Surv. Tutor. **18**(1), 124–161 (2015)

13. Zeebaree, S.R., Shukur, H.M., Haji, L.M., Zebari, R.R., Jacksi, K., Abas, S.M.: Characteristics and analysis of hadoop distributed systems. Technol. Rep. Kansai Univ. **62**(4), 1555–1564 (2020)

14. Zaharia, M., et al.: Apache spark: a unified engine for big data processing. Commun. ACM **59**(11), 56–65 (2016)

15. Gramaglia, M., Fiore, M., Tarable, A., Banchs, A.: $k^{\tau,\epsilon}$-anonymity: Towards privacy-preserving publishing of spatiotemporal trajectory data. arXiv preprint arXiv:1701.02243 (2017)

16. Gramaglia, M., Fiore, M., Tarable, A., Banchs, A.: Preserving mobile subscriber privacy in open datasets of spatiotemporal trajectories. In: IEEE INFOCOM 2017-IEEE Conference on Computer Communications,pp. 1–9. IEEE, May 2017

17. Fiore, M., et al.: Privacy in trajectory micro-data publishing: a survey. arXiv preprint arXiv:1903.12211 (2019)

# Big Data Software Architectures: An Updated Review

Tiago Vinícius Remígio da Costa, Everton Cavalcante(⊠) ⓘ,
and Thais Batista ⓘ

Federal University of Rio Grande do Norte, Natal, Brazil
everton.cavalcante@ufrn.br

**Abstract.** Big Data usually refers to the unprecedented growth of data and associated processes to gather, store, process, and analyze them to provide organizations and users with useful insights and information. The intrinsic complexity and characteristics of systems handling Big Data require software architectures as founded drivers for these systems to meet functional and quality requirements. In light of the relevant role of software architectures for Big Data systems, we investigate the current state of the art of Big Data software architectures. This paper presents the results of a systematic mapping study that updates existing literature reviews on this topic. We selected and analyzed 23 primary studies published in the last five years. We identified 11 architecture-related quality requirements and six architectural modules relevant to the design of software architectures for Big Data systems, besides analyzing whether existing proposals of reference architectures comply with these requirements and modules. We expect the results presented in this paper can provide a continuous update of the state of the art while highlighting essential concerns in the design of software architectures for Big Data systems.

**Keywords:** Software architecture · Big Data · Systematic mapping study

## 1 Introduction

The adoption of recent computing paradigms such as Cloud Computing, the Internet of Things (IoT), and 5G networks has been a major force to *Big Data*. This is an umbrella term usually referring to data sets whose size grows to an extent beyond the ability of traditional methods and tools to gather, store, process, and analyze the available data at a tolerable time [1,20]. Big Data is often defined by its characteristics, the so-called 5V's [2,12]: *Volume* (amount of data), *Velocity* (how quickly data are generated and transmitted), *Variety* (diversity of data types and sources), *Veracity* (quality and accuracy of data), and *Value* (what it is possible to do with data). The relevance of Big Data nowadays is noticeable: 96% of 85 interviewed companies from different domains

© The Author(s), under exclusive license to Springer Nature Switzerland AG 2022
O. Gervasi et al. (Eds.): ICCSA 2022, LNCS 13375, pp. 477–493, 2022.
https://doi.org/10.1007/978-3-031-10522-7_33

manifested strongly investing in Big Data and Artificial Intelligence in 2021 [16]. Big Data systems (BDS) can indeed be found in many fields, providing valuable insights and information to organizations and users [1].

Software architectures are widely recognized as the backbone of any successful software-intensive system, thereby fundamentally contributing to achieving both business goals and quality requirements. This challenging scenario draws attention to designing Big Data software architectures. A software architecture for a BDS can aggregate different constituent elements related to functionalities such as data extraction, processing, integration, analysis, and visualization. More than this, decisions made at the software architecture level directly affect how these systems can meet quality attributes intrinsic to this context, such as scalability, availability, high performance, etc.

The relevance of BDS nowadays and the significant role of software architectures in meeting functional and quality requirements in these systems makes it worth investigating the literature to obtain a panorama of Big Data software architectures. This panorama can allow reflecting on the current state of the art and understanding the essential elements and quality requirements to consider when designing software architectures for BDS. The literature already provides secondary studies with this goal [1,20,21]. However, these existing works consider only primary studies published until 2017 and miss a time window of almost five years with recent work, despite adopting a systematic methodology.

To achieve the goal of investigating the current state of the art of the literature on Big Data software architectures while avoiding wasting time and effort with an unnecessary literature review, we grounded on a decision framework that helped us assess the need for updating existing secondary work on this topic [5,13]. After obtaining confidence that such an update would be worth it, we carried out a *systematic mapping study* (*systematic mapping*, in short) focusing on collecting, selecting, and analyzing primary studies on Big Data software architectures published since 2017. A systematic mapping is a form of secondary study that uses a systematic, rigorous procedure to obtain a comprehensive panorama of a research topic and identify research and development gaps from primary studies available in the literature [17]. This paper reports the main results of the performed systematic mapping with architecture-related requirements and modules relevant to software architectures for these systems and whether existing proposals of reference architectures to BDS encompass these elements. Our main intention with this work is that the presented results can contribute to both researchers and practitioners to design better software architectures for BDS.

The remainder of this paper is organized as follows. Section 2 discusses secondary studies related to this work. Section 3 describes the methodology to carry out the systematic mapping. Section 4 presents and discusses the results from the analysis of the relevant primary studies. Section 5 brings some conclusions.

## 2   Related Work

Kumar and Alencar [11] carried out a wide-scope secondary study on the interplay of Software Engineering activities in the development of BDS. After retrieving results by combining manual and automated search using three electronic databases, these authors selected 170 primary studies covering the different phases of the software development life cycle. Architectural design was found in 40% of the selected studies, being acknowledged as an essential concern in building BDS. Nonetheless, this study is quite generic and did not specifically focus on Big Data software architectures.

To the best of our knowledge, Sena et al. [20] were pioneers in presenting the state of the art specifically related to Big Data software architectures. Their systematic mapping selected and analyzed 19 primary studies available in seven electronic databases, identifying eight architecture-related quality requirements and five modules regarded as essential to coping with the characteristics of BDS at the architectural level. Further work of these authors [21] specifically focused on investigating the use of well-known architectural patterns to design software architectures for BDS. From the set of studies selected in their previous work, they analyzed 11 studies that reported the use of architectural patterns for BDS. They concluded that the architectural patterns commonly used for BDS do not differ from those used in other contexts, and a layered model stood out as the most used pattern. The body of work analyzed by these two studies is now almost five years old since they considered primary studies published until mid-2017.

Avci et al. [1] carried out a systematic literature review aiming to investigate software architectures for BDS. They selected and analyzed 43 primary studies available in five electronic databases, identifying the domains in which Big Data software architectures have been applied, the application domains where they have been observed, and relevant quality attributes and architectural patterns considered. Despite having been published in 2020, these authors considered only primary studies published between 2010 and 2017, i.e., the study results are not up-to-date with the recent literature.

Rahman and Reza [19] and Montero et al. [14] recently carried out systematic mappings focusing on quality requirements relevant to BDS. The former study selected and analyzed 14 primary studies published between 2012 and 2019, retrieved from four electronic sources. The authors identified quality requirements and mapped them to the quality attributes defined in the ISO/IEC 25010:2011 International Standard [7], concluding that six of them (namely *performance efficiency, functional stability, reliability, security, usability,* and *scalability*) would be crucial to be considered in BDS design. The latter study selected and analyzed 67 primary studies published in the last decade (2010–2020), retrieved from two electronic sources and snowballing. The authors aimed to identify models proposed in the context of BDS to assess the quality of these systems. The set of analyzed studies reported 12 different quality models, and almost half of them focused on measuring the quality of data. The focus of both studies was on quality requirements, not explicitly relating them to the architectural level.

Our analysis of these systematic literature reviews and mapping studies served as driving motivations for this paper. The studies investigating the literature on Big Data software architectures covered only primary studies published until 2017, and recent work with new perspectives has been available since then.

Furthermore, recent concepts associated with BDS, such as *data lake* and *data platform*, were not considered even though they can impact architecture decisions and the overall quality of BDS. A data lake is a Big Data repository that stores raw data in their original, heterogeneous format with on-demand integration and enables users to query and explore these data [6]. A data platform is a cohesive infrastructure that provides organizations and users with several tools and utilities to develop, integrate, deploy, and manage Big Data applications and their data. Performing another literature review from scratch with no framed time window would not be efficient and worth of time and effort because the existing secondary studies adopted a rigorous, systematic methodology. Therefore, we opted to update one of these secondary studies considering the most recent literature published from 2017 to 2021.

## 3  Methodology

Before undertaking a systematic mapping, researchers need to ensure that the study is both needed and feasible. Kitchenham et al. [10] highlight that it is essential to consider whether the study (i) can produce outcomes that are likely to contribute to the knowledge about the addressed research topic and (ii) is distinct enough from already existing secondary studies in the same research topic, e.g., not comprehensively covering the research topic or being out of date.

This section describes the methodology adopted to carry out the systematic mapping. Section 3.1 grounds on a decision framework to assess the need for updating existing secondary work on Big Data software architectures. Section 3.2 presents the systematic mapping protocol in terms of research questions, search strategy, and selection criteria. Section 3.3 describes the process for selecting relevant primary studies.

### 3.1  The Need for an Updated Review

Updating a systematic mapping provides a continuous update of state of the art on a research topic and can identify how it evolves regarding the stability of existing research findings. Mendes et al. [13] point out that there have been no systematic proposals on whether and when to update systematic literature reviews and mapping studies in Software Engineering despite their increasing use in the last 15 years. These authors suggested using the Garner et al.'s decision framework [5] to guide the update (or not) of systematic literature reviews in the Software Engineering field. Figure 1 depicts the decision framework.

We followed Mendes et al. [13] on using the decision framework to check whether the existing secondary studies on Big Data software architectures would be worth updating. Table 1 summarizes the questions and answers to the framework for this work, which are provided in the following.

**Currency of the Research Topic.** Big Data software architectures have been evolving through the years, mainly due to the growth of data to handle (volume) and how fast they should be available (velocity) for analysis and predictions. Therefore, software architectures for these systems should have components able to address and balance the 5V's characteristics. Existing secondary

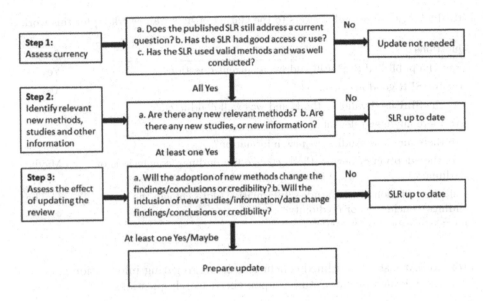

**Fig. 1.** The decision framework to assess the need for updating secondary studies [13].

studies on Big Data software architectures (see Sect. 2) have been all carried out by following valid systematic methods.

**Relevant New Methods, Studies, and Other Information.** BDS have evolved to comply with technological advances and data governance regulations. Early Big Data concerned distributed processing in enterprise data centers (e.g., using Hadoop/MapReduce), whereas there has been a recent technology shift to cloud-based solutions. Furthermore, the enforcement of regulations worldwide (e.g., GDPR in Europe, CCPA in the USA, and LGPD in Brazil) implies considering constraints posed by these legal bases in designing, developing, and deploying secure BDS. Therefore, BDS are no longer just about data ingestion, processing, storage, and visualization.

**Effect of Updating the Review.** The inclusion of new methods and requirements changes how software architectures or reference architectures are designed to settle new aspects. New modules and new quality requirements can impact how a Big Data software architecture is designed.

### 3.2   Review Protocol

Once the need for updating the existing secondary work on Big Data software architecture has been identified, we followed consolidated guidelines available in the literature [18] to carry out our systematic mapping. We first devised a protocol with research questions to answer, the adopted search strategy, the criteria to select studies, and the data extraction and synthesis methods. Next, we searched for, selected, and analyzed the primary studies according to the

**Table 1.** Questions and answers to the Garner et al.'s framework [5] for this work.

| Questions | Answers |
|---|---|
| Does the published SLR still address a current question? | Yes |
| Has the SLR good access or use? | Yes |
| Has the SLR used valid methods and was well conducted? | Yes |
| Are there any new relevant methods? | No |
| Are there any new studies, or new information? | Yes |
| Will the adoption of new methods change the findings/conclusions or credibility? | Maybe |
| Will the inclusion of new studies/information/data change the findings/conclusions or credibility? | Maybe |

SLR = systematic literature review

protocol. At last, we outlined conclusions by aggregating information extracted from the relevant primary studies upon the research questions.

**Research Questions.** This study aimed to investigate the recent state of the art of the literature on the design of software architectures for BDS. We grounded on the Sena et al.'s work [20] since it was the pioneering secondary study on Big Data software architectures. We considered the following research questions (RQs):

RQ1: What are the main requirements for building software architectures for BDS?

RQ2: What are the main modules/components in software architectures of BDS?

RQ3: What requirements and modules are found in existing proposals of reference architectures for BDS?

**Search Strategy.** We used an automated search process to retrieve primary studies with the potential to answer the posed RQs. We considered six well-known electronic publication databases with good coverage of the literature, namely IEEEXplore, ACM Digital Library, ScienceDirect, Scopus, Web of Science, and Enginering Village. Two primary keywords were initially identified from the defined RQs: *Big Data* and *software architecture*. To increase coverage of the literature search, we have built the following search string:

```
(big data OR data lake OR data platform) AND
(software architecture OR reference architecture OR reference model)
```

**Selection Criteria.** We used selection criteria to include studies potentially relevant to answering the posed RQs and exclude those that would not contribute to answering them. We have preserved the two inclusion criteria (ICs) and the

five exclusion criteria (ECs) from Sena et al. [20]. However, we added EC6 to exclude studies published before 2017 since our work is an updated review:
Inclusion criteria:

IC1: The primary study addresses software architectures in the context of BDS.
IC1: The primary study proposes a reference architecture or a reference model for BDS.

Exclusion criteria:

EC1: The primary study is a table of contents, tutorial description, or a summary of a conference/workshop.
EC2: The primary study is written in a language other than English.
EC3: The study is a previous version of a more complete one on the same research or of the same authors.
EC4: The full text of the primary study is not available.
EC5: The primary study is out of scope of the systematic mapping.
EC6: The primary study was published before 2017.

### 3.3  Selection Process

We carried out the systematic mapping in the last quarter of 2021, thus considering studies published so far. We used the Parsifal[1] Web tool to support all activities of searching, filtering, selecting, and extracting data from the retrieved studies. The automated search process considered adaptations to the base search string (see Sect. 3.2) according to the specificities of each publication electronic database and the title, abstract, and keyword fields.

Figure 2 depicts the process for selecting the relevant primary studies. The automated search procedure retrieved 1,378 results, of which 730 were removed as duplicates, i.e., studies retrieved by more than one publication database. The remaining 648 unique studies underwent a selection process in two stages. The first stage aimed to apply the selection criteria (ICs and ECs) established in the systematic mapping protocol to the title, abstract, and keywords of the retrieved results, resulting in 32 studies. Next, we fully read the study and applied the selection criteria to check if it could answer any RQ. This resulted in a final set of 23 studies relevant to this work. The selected primary studies are listed in the Appendix, identified as S1 to S23.

## 4  Results and Discussion

This section summarizes and discusses the results of the systematic mapping considering the RQs described in Sect. 3.2 and the data extracted and synthesized from the analyzed primary studies. Section 4.1 gives an overview of the selected primary studies. Sections 4.2 to 4.4 present the answers to each RQ.

---

[1] https://parsif.al/.

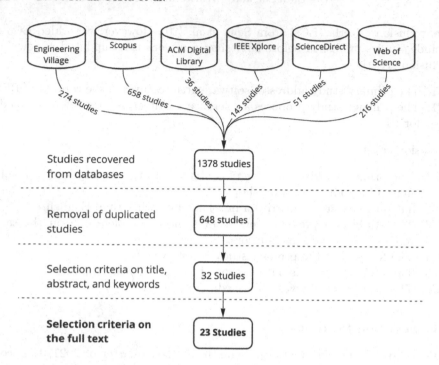

**Fig. 2.** Process for selecting the relevant primary studies.

## 4.1   Overview of the Selected Studies

**Distribution of the Studies over the Years.** Figure 3a shows the distribution of the publication of studies on software architectures for BDS. We observed an average of 4.6 studies (median = 4) published per year.

**Publication Venues.** Figure 3b illustrates the types of venues in which the selected primary studies were published. Most of the studies were published in international conference proceedings, possibly indicating a minor degree of maturity for the proposals. Only one study (S20) was published in a venue directly related to the Software Architecture field. In contrast, most studies were published in conferences and journals focusing on Big Data and its applications. The studies spread over different venues, with no one standing out among them.

**Application Domains.** Figure 4 shows the application domains addressed by the selected primary studies. We noticed that most of the selected studies are related to Big Data infrastructure, i.e., with no specific application domain.

## 4.2   Quality Requirements

RQ1 aimed to identify the main quality requirements to be considered in designing software architectures for BDS. Sena et al. [20] elicited eight requirements and associated them to the *Systems and software Quality Requirements and*

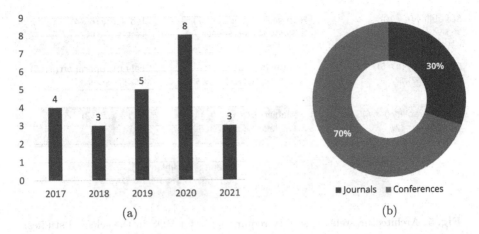

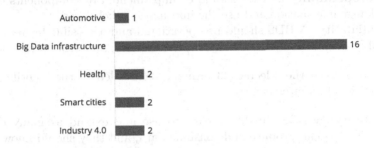

**Fig. 3.** Distribution of the selected primary studies per publication year (a) and type of publication venue (b).

**Fig. 4.** Application domains addressed by the selected primary studies.

*Evaluation* (SQuaRE) model defined in the ISO/IEC 25010:2011 International Standard [7]. Our findings confirm the relevance of these quality requirements in the selected primary studies. These eight requirements are:

1) **Scalability:** A BDS should be able to scale storage and computational resources to deal with growing data.
2) **High performance:** A BDS should deal with different needs to process and serve data, supporting batch and streaming processing.
3) **Modularity:** A BDS software architecture should be composed of several independent, loosely coupled components.
4) **Consistency:** Data must be retrieved in the same format and compatible with previous data [22].
5) **Security:** A BDS should protect information and data so that people or other products or systems have the degree of data access appropriate to their types and levels of authorization.
6) **Real-time operation:** A BDS should be able to process data in real-time, using streaming processing to provide data when time-serving constraint is required.

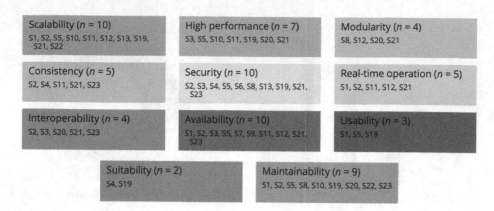

**Fig. 5.** Architecture-related quality requirements for BDS in the selected studies.

7) **Interoperability:** A BDS should be implemented by components that can exchange information and use the information exchanged.
8) **Avaliability:** A BDS should be operational and accessible for use, usually applying fault-tolerant mechanisms, redundancy, and other strategies.

Our analysis of the selected 23 primary studies led to the identification of three additional requirements:

9) **Usability:** A BDS should be easy to use and extend as many different stakeholders can produce and consume data, and they should know how to operate the system.
10) **Suitability:** BDS should be functional according to requirements stated in architecture design, and data should comply with the predefined constraints.
11) **Maintainability:** A BDS should be easily changed to evolve, correct, and be adaptable according to data characteristics.

Figure 5 shows the 11 architecture-related quality requirements for BDS in the selected primary studies. We observed that the most frequent requirements are *scalability, security, availability,* and *maintainability,* appearing in more than 40% of the studies. Scalability is an essential requirement since volume is the most basic characteristic of Big Data. Consequently, BDS are inherently expected to scale ingestion, processing, and storage to accommodate the large volumes of data. The availability of a BDS concerns making the system operational and its data ready to use. It can be achieved through replication, horizontal scaling, distributed cluster nodes, and disaster response (e.g., studies S3 and S9). Security is also widely mentioned in terms of related characteristics such as authenticity, confidentiality, and integrity, which are required to govern data accordingly as legal regulations apply to personal data. Finally, the separation of concerns through modules and storage layers increases maintainability, which is important for managing modifications and preserving the BDS stability.

### 4.3  Architectural Modules

RQ2 aimed to identify modules/components common to software architectures for BDS. We mapped six architectural modules, being *Data Governance* found in addition to the five other architectural modules identified by Sena et al. [20]:

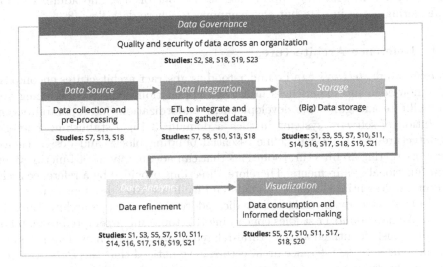

**Fig. 6.** Architectural modules in software architectures for BDS.

1) **Data Source:** Processes where data are captured, collected, or actively sent to a BDS. In practice, this can be done by capturing (relational) databases, streaming data to the BDS storage, or even retrieving data through API calls.
2) **Data Integration:** After ingesting sources, data must be transformed from a raw, brute format through ETL (Extract, Transform, and Load) processes to a refined state that helps data analysts.
3) **Storage:** Storage technologies can be adopted in a Big Data software architecture for different purposes.
4) **Data Analytics:** Refinement of processed data.
5) **Visualization:** Data consumption and decision-making aligned with business-related roles.
6) **Data Governance:** Processes and responsibilities to ensure the quality and security of the data used across an organization.

Identifying these architectural modules is relevant to design better software architectures for BDS, including the conception of a reference architecture for these systems. Figure 6 depicts the relationships among these modules, which can be organized into a pipeline structure encompassing the generation, processing, analysis, and consumption of data. It is also worth observing that *Data*

*Governance* represents a crosscutting concern that impacts the other modules, clearly defining roles and data ownership levels and policies.

Study S2 argues that storage and governance modules precede the creation of any further resources in a data-centric architecture like the ones driving BDS, where data assets play a prominent role. Moreover, data governance defines metadata and policies enabling appropriate access control, use, and administration, considering not only data but also components where data flow [8,9].

## 4.4   Reference Architectures

*Reference architectures* can be understood as abstract architectures encompassing knowledge and experiences in a given application domain, thus being able to facilitate and guide the development, standardization, interoperability, and evolution of software systems in such a domain [3,15]. Establishing reference architectures for BDS can define essential building blocks and design choices for constructing architectural solutions that can adequately meet functional and non-functional requirements. Therefore, directions provided by a reference architecture are essential elements to guide and facilitate BDS development.

RQ3 specifically investigated studies addressing reference architectures for BDS. We have found 17 studies concerning this topic and attempted to map how the previously identified architectural-related quality requirements and modules are present in those reference architectures. We noticed that the *Data Analytics* ($n = 9$), *Storage* ($n = 5$), and *Data Governance* ($n = 5$) modules were presented as the main building blocks in reference architectures for BDS. Seven studies have detailed scalability as an essential quality requirement to be encompassed by reference architectures since software architectures for BDS must be scalable to support the high volume and velocity of data. Security is also considered an essential quality requirement for reference architectures in seven studies, suggesting a relationship with the *Data Governance* module.

Our results partially confirm the ones of Sena et al. [20] regarding the essential architectural modules in reference architectures for BDS, except for the newly *Data Governance* module. However, the security requirement seems to have gained more attention in recent years when observing the previously existing results. In the previous systematic mapping, 21.03% (4/19) of the studies were found addressing this requirement in 2017, against 30.43% (7/23) now. This increase may be a consequence of the enforcement of major regulations on data, which became effective only in the last two to four years (GDPR in Europe in 2018, CCPA in the USA and LGPD in Brazil in 2020). Furthermore, data privacy and security have been a genuine concern because of recent data breaches, misuses, and other threats to companies and people.

We also noticed few studies with at least four architectural modules in the proposed reference architectures, thus meaning that these proposals do not fully meet the common relevant modules for software architectures tailoring BDS. Moreover, there are studies (e.g., S7) in which the *Data Integration* and *Storage* modules are bound as a single module, probably as a consequence of technology choice. These discrepancies regarding the architectural modules in the existing proposals of reference architectures for BDS and how these elements are organized may point to a lack of maturity and failure in following a systematic design process, as recently observed by Garcés et al. [4].

## 5   Conclusion

This paper presented the results of a systematic mapping to investigate the current state of the art on how Big Data has been addressed at the architectural level. This systematic mapping updates a previous secondary study from mid-2017 [20] on software architectures for BDS, covering primary studies published in the last five years. We have systematically analyzed 23 studies available in the literature to (i) identify essential quality requirements for the design of BDS software architectures, (ii) define the main modules composing these architectures, and (iii) investigate how existing reference architectures comply with those requirements and modules.

Our analysis resulted in some findings that update the state of the art on software architecture and reference architectures for BDS. This work confirms previous findings on essential eight architecture-related quality requirements, with particular attention to scalability and availability due to the intrinsic nature of Big Data and security as a consequence of recent regulations on the use of data. Three new quality requirements were identified (usability, suitability, and maintainability) as also relevant to the design of software architectures for BDS.

We also identified six architectural modules relevant to design better software architectures for BDS. Five of these modules were identified in previous work [20], and we included *Data Governance* as a new one as referring to processes and responsibilities to ensure the quality and security of the data used across an organization. These architectural modules can also be a foundation for the conception of reference architectures for BDS, a topic we investigated in this work. Most of the primary studies concerned reference architectures for BDS, but we noticed that these proposals do not encompass all the elicited quality requirements and architectural modules in Big Data software architectures. We also had an insight into the lack of a systematic process guiding the design of existing reference architectures, an issue to be addressed in future research.

## Appendix

[S1] Sfaxi, L., Ben Aissa, M.M.: Babel: A generic benchmarking platform for Big Data architectures. Big Data Research **24** (2021). http://doi.org/10.1016/j.bdr.2021.100186

[S2] López Martínez, P., Dintén, R., Drake, J.M., Zorrilla, M.: A Big Data-centric architecture metamodel for Industry 4.0. Future Generation Computer Systems **125**, 263–284 (2021). http://doi.org/10.1016/j.future.2021.06.020

[S3] Shah, S.A., Seker, D.Z., Rathore, M.M., Hameed, S., Yahia, S.B., Draheim, D.: Towards disaster resilient smart cities: Can Internet of Things and Big Data analytics be the game changers? IEEE Access **7**, 91885–91903 (2019). http://doi.org/10.1109/access.2019.2928233

[S4] Wahyudi, A., Kuk, G., Janssen, M.: A process pattern model for tackling and improving Big Data quality. Information Systems Frontiers **20**, 457–469 (2018). http://doi.org/10.1007/s10796-017-9822-7

[S5] Quinde, C., Guillermo, D., Siguenza-Guzman, L., Orellana, D., Pesántez-Cabrera, P.: A software architecture proposal for a data platform on active mobility and urban environment. In: Morales, G.R., C., E.R.F., Salgado, J.P., Pérez-Gosende, P., Cordero, M.O., Berrezueta, S. (eds.) Information and Communication Technologies, Communications in Computer and Information Science, vol. 1307, pp. 501–515. Springer Nature Switzerland AG (2020). http://doi.org/10.1007/978-3-030-62833-8_37

[S6] Moreno, J., Serrano, M.A., Fernández-Medina, E., Fernández, E.B.: Towards a security reference architecture for Big Data. In: Proceedings of the 20th International Workshop on Design, Optimization, Languages and Analytical Processing of Big Data co-located with 10th EDBT/ICDT Joint Conference, CEUR Workshop Proceedings, vol. 2062. CEUR-WS, Germany (2018)

[S7] Sang, G.M., Xu, L., de Vrieze, P.: Simplifying Big Data analytics systems with a reference architecture. In: Camarinha-Matos, L.M., Afsarmanesh, H., Fornasiero, R. (eds.) Collaboration in a Data-Rich World, IFIP Advances in Information and Communication Technology, vol. 506, pp. 242–249. IFIP, Switzerland (2017). http://doi.org/10.1007/978-3-319-65151-4_23

[S8] Awaysheh, F.M., Aladwan, M.N., Alazab, M., Alawadi, S., Cabaleiro, J.C., Pena, T.F.: Security by design for Big Data frameworks over Cloud Computing. IEEE Transactions on Engineering Management (2020). http://doi.org/10.1109/tem.2020.3045661

[S9] Garises, V., Quenum, J.: The road towards Big Data infrastructure in the health care sector: The case of Namibia. In: Proceedings of the 19th IEEE Mediterranean Electrotechnical Conference. pp. 98–103. IEEE, USA (2018). http://doi.org/10.1109/melcon.2018.8379075

[S10] Henning, S., Hasselbring, W., Möbius, A.: A scalable architecture for power consumption monitoring in industrial production environments. In: Proceedings of the 2019 IEEE International Conference on Fog Computing. pp. 124–133. IEEE, USA (2019). http://doi.org/10.1109/icfc.2019.00024

[S11] Aissa, M.M.B., Sfaxi, L., Robbana, R.: Decisional architectures from Business Intelligence to Big Data: Challenges and opportunities. In: Proceedings of the 2nd International Conference on Digital Tools & Uses Congress. ACM, USA (2020). http://doi.org/10.1145/3423603.3424049

[S12] Haroun, A., Mostefaoui, A., Dessables, F.: A Big Data architecture for automotive applications: PSA Group deployment experience. In: Proceedings of the 17th IEEE/ACM International Symposium on Cluster,

Cloud and Grid Computing. pp. 921–928. IEEE, USA (2017). http://doi.org/10.1109/ccgrid.2017.107

[S13] Joaquim, J.L.M., dos Santos Mello, R.: An analysis of confidentiality issues in data lakes. In: Proceedings of the 22nd International Conference on Information Integration and Web-based Applications & Services. pp. 168–177. ACM, USA (2020). http://doi.org/10.1145/3428757.3429109

[S14] Cuzzocrea, A., Loia, V., Tommasetti, A.: Big-Data-driven innovation for enterprises: Innovative Big Value Paradigms for next-generation digital ecosystems. In: Proceedings of the 7th International Conference on Web Intelligence, Mining and Semantics. ACM, USA (2017). http://doi.org/10.1145/3102254.3102271

[S15] Zhu, Y., Liu, H.: Research on data-driven models of teaching quality evaluation. In: Proceedings of the 2020 International Conference on Computer Communication and Information Systems. pp. 10–14. ACM, USA (2020). http://doi.org/10.1145/3418994.3419001

[S16] Kaufmann, M.: Big Data Management Canvas: A reference model for value creation from data. Big Data and Cognitive Computing 3(1) (2019). http://doi.org/10.3390/bdcc3010019

[S17] Iglesias, C.A., Favenza, A., Álvaro Carrera: A Big Data reference architecture for emergency management. Information 11(12) (2020). http://doi.org/10.3390/info11120569

[S18] Arass, M.E., Ouazzani-Touhami, K., Souissi, N.: Data life cycle: Towards a reference architecture. International Journal of Advanced Trends in Computer Science and Engineering 9(4), 5645–5653 (2020). http://doi.org/10.30534/ijatcse/2020/215942020

[S19] Xiaofeng, L., Jing, L.: Research on Big Data reference architecture model. In: Proceedings of International Conference on Artificial Intelligence and Big Data. pp. 205–209. IEEE, USA (2020) http://doi.org/10.1109/icaibd49809.2020.9137451

[S20] Cerezo, F., Cuesta, C.E., Moreno-Herranz, J.C., Vela, B.: Deconstructing the Lambda Architecture: An experience report. In: 2019 IEEE International Conference on Software Architecture Companion. pp. 196–201. IEEE, USA (2019). http://doi.org/10.1109/icsa-c.2019.00042

[S21] Garises, V., Quenum, J.: An evaluation of Big Data architectures. In: Proceedings of the 8th International Conference on Data Science, Technology and Applications. pp. 152–159. SciTePress, Portugal (2019). http://doi.org/10.5220/0007840801520159

[S22] Salavati, H., Gandomani, T.J., Sadeghi, R.: A robust software architecture based on distributed systems in Big Data health care. In: Proceedings of the 2017 International Conference on Advances in Computing, Communications and Informatics. pp. 1701–1705. IEEE, USA (2017). http://doi.org/10.1109/icacci.2017.8126088

[S23] Giebler, C., Gröger, C., Hoos, E., Schwarz, H., Mitschang, B.: A zone reference model for enterprise-grade data lake management. In: Proceedings of the IEEE 24th International Enterprise Distributed Object Computing Conference. pp. 57–66. IEEE, USA (2020). http://doi.org/10.1109/edoc49727.2020.00017

# References

1. Avci, C., Tekinerdogan, B., Athanasiadis, I.N.: Software architectures for Big Data: a systematic literature review. Big Data Anal. **5** (2020). https://doi.org/10.1186/s41044-020-00045-1
2. Beyer, M., Laney, D.: The importance of 'Big Data': A definition. Technical report, Gartner, USA, June 2012
3. Cloutier, R., Muller, G., Verma, D., Nilchiani, R., Hole, E., Bone, M.: The concept of reference architectures. Syst. Eng. **13**(1), 14–27 (2010). https://doi.org/10.1002/sys.20129
4. Garcés, L., et al.: Three decades of software reference architectures: a systematic mapping study. J. Syst. Softw. **179** (2021). https://doi.org/10.1016/j.jss.2021.111004
5. Garner, P., et al.: When and how to update systematic reviews: Consensus and checklist. BMJ **354** (2016). https://doi.org/10.1136/bmj.i3507
6. Hai, R., Geisler, S., Quix, C.: Constance: an intelligent data lake system. In: Proceedings of the 2016 International Conference on Management of Data, pp. 2097–2100. ACM, USA (2016). https://doi.org/10.1145/2882903.2899389
7. ISO/IEC 25010: Systems and software engineering - Systems and software Quality Requirements and Evaluation (SQuaRE) - System and software quality models. ISO, Switzerland (2011)
8. Janssen, M., Brous, P., Estevez, E., Barbosa, L.S., Janowski, T.: Data governance: Organizing data for trustworthy Artificial Intelligence. Govern. Inf. Q. **37**(3) (2020). https://doi.org/10.1016/j.giq.2020.101493
9. Kim, H.Y., Cho, J.S.: Data Governance Framework for Big Data implementation with a case of Korea. In: Proceedings of the 2017 IEEE International Congress on Big Data (2017). https://doi.org/10.1109/bigdatacongress.2017.56
10. Kitchenham, B.A., Budgen, D., Brereton, P.: Evidence-Based Software Engineering and systematic reviews. Chapman and Hall/CRC Press, USA (2016)
11. Kumar, V.D., Alencar, P.: Software Engineering for Big Data projects: domains, methodologies and gaps. In: Proceedings of the 2016 IEEE International Conference on Big Data, pp. 2886–2895. IEEE, USA (2016). https://doi.org/10.1109/bigdata.2016.7840938
12. Laney, D.: 3D data management: Controlling Data Volume, Velocity, and Variety. Technical report, META Group, USA, February 2001
13. Mendes, E., Wohlin, C., Felizardo, K., Kalinowski, M.: When to update systematic literature reviews in Software Engineering. J. Syst. Softw. **167** (2020). https://doi.org/10.1016/j.jss.2020.110607
14. Montero, O., Crespo, Y., Piatini, M.: Big data quality models: a systematic mapping study. In: Paiva, A.C.R., Cavalli, A.R., Ventura Martins, P., Pérez-Castillo, R. (eds.) QUATIC 2021. CCIS, vol. 1439, pp. 416–430. Springer, Cham (2021). https://doi.org/10.1007/978-3-030-85347-1_30
15. Nakagawa, E.Y., Oquendo, F., Maldonado, J.C.: Reference architectures. In: Oussalah, M.C. (ed.) Software Architecture 1, pp. 55–82. ISTE/John Wiley & Sons Inc., United Kingdom (2014). https://doi.org/10.1002/9781118930960.ch2

16. NewVantage: Big Datra and AI Executive Survey 2021: Executive summary of findings. techreport, NewVantage Partners LLC, USA, January 2021
17. Petersen, K., Feldt, R., Mujtaba, S., Mattsson, M.: Systematic mapping studies in Software Engineering. In: Proceedings of the 12th International Conference on Evaluation and Assessment in Software Engineering, pp. 68–77. British Computer Society, United Kingdom (2008). https://doi.org/10.14236/ewic/ease2008.8
18. Petersen, K., Vakkalanka, S., Kuzniarz, L.: Guidelines for conducting systematic mapping studies in Software Engineering: an update. Inf. Softw. Technol. **64**, 1–18 (2015). https://doi.org/10.1016/j.infsof.2015.03.007
19. Rahman, M.S., Reza, H.: Systematic mapping study of non-functional requirements in Big Data system. In: Proceedings of the 2020 IEEE International Conference on Electro Information Technology, pp. 025–031. IEEE, USA (2020). https://doi.org/10.1109/eit48999.2020.9208288
20. Sena, B., Allian, A.P., Nakagawa, E.Y.: Characterizing Big Data software architectures: a systematic mapping study. In: Proceedings of the 11th Brazilian Symposium on Software Components, Architectures, and Reuse. ACM, USA (2017). https://doi.org/10.1145/3132498.3132510
21. Sena, B., Garcés, L., Allian, A.P., Nakagawa, E.Y.: Investigating the applicability of architectural patterns in Big Data systems. In: Proceedings of the 25th Conference on Pattern Languages of Programs. ACM, USA (2018)
22. Wahyudi, A., Kuk, G., Janssen, M.: A process pattern model for tackling and improving big data quality. Inf. Syst. Front. **20**(3), 457–469 (2018). https://doi.org/10.1007/s10796-017-9822-7

# Acoustic Nudging-Based Model for Vocabulary Reformulation in Continuous Yorùbá Speech Recognition

Lydia Kehinde Ajayi[1]([✉]) [iD], Ambrose Azeta[2] [iD], Isaac Odun-Ayo[3] [iD],
and Enem Theophilus Aniemeka[4] [iD]

[1] ENSI Department, National Identity Management Commission, Lagos, Nigeria
lydia4reel@gmail.com
[2] Department of Computer Science, Namibia University of Science and Technology, Windhoek, Namibia
aazeta@nust.na
[3] Department of Computer Science, Chrisland University, Abeokuta, Nigeria
isaac.odun-ayo@chrislanduniversity.edu.ng
[4] Department of Cybersecurity, Faculty of Computing, Air Force Base, Kaduna, Nigeria
ta.enem@afit.edu.ng

**Abstract.** Speech recognition is a technology that aid processing of speech signals through communicating with computer applications. Previous studies exhibits speech recognition errors arising from users' acoustic irrational behavior. This research paper provides acoustic nudging-based model for reformulating the persistence of automatic speech recognition errors that involve the user's acoustic irrational behavior and distortion of speech recognition accuracy. Gaussian mixture model (GMM) helped in addressing the low-resourced attribute of Yorùbá language to achieve better accuracy and system performance. From the implemented results, it was observed that the proposed acoustic nudging-based model improves accuracy and system performance based on Word Error Rate (WER), validation, testing and training accuracy. The evaluation results for the mean WER was 4.723% when compared to existing models. This approach thereby reduces error rate when compared with previous models by GMM (1.1%), GMM-HMM (0.5%), CNN (0.8%), and DNN (1.4%). Therefore, this work was able to discover a foundation for advancing the current understanding of under-resourced languages and development of an accurate and precise model for speech recognition.

**Keywords:** Acoustic nudging model · Gaussian mixture model · Automatic speech recognition · Communication and nudging

## 1 Introduction

Speech is one of the most convenient means of communication between people and humans [1–4]. Human-computer interaction is based on the syntactic arrangement of lexical names drawn from huge vocabularies [3]. Yorùbá language is an indigenous

O. Gervasi et al. (Eds.): ICCSA 2022, LNCS 13375, pp. 494–508, 2022.
https://doi.org/10.1007/978-3-031-10522-7_34

language exiting in the second largest ethnic group in Nigeria spoken by more than 50 million people with 30 million speaking Standard Yorùbá [5] [6].

There are three different spoken languages in Nigeria which are Yorùbá, Igbo, and Hausa with their accents, however, the focus of this study is on Standard Yorùbá. The Yoruba is one of the 12 languages of the Edekiri branch from the family of West Benue-Congo. Yorùbá is a native language spoken by Nigeria, Togo, Ghana, Sudan, Cote D'Ivoire, Sierra-Leone, and Benin. Standard Yorùbá is also spoken beyond Africa in countries like Cuba, Brazil, Trinidad and Tobago where a large number of these languages are be located [7, 8].

Yorùbá also borrow different words from Arabic, Hausa, Igbo and English [9]. Yorùbá language is a language that falls under the low-resourced languages as it doesn't have a massive amount of speech and text information for speech recognition. Speech processing for under-resourced language such as Yoruba is a current field of research that has experienced significant progress. Under-resourced language is defined as a language that lacks unique writing system and has limited presence on the Web. They are also called low-density, low-data, low-resourced, or resource-poor languages [10].

Several efforts have been made over the years to develop vocally interactive system to realize voice to speech synthesis [2]. There are different classifications of automatic speech recognition which are based on utterances that are broken down into isolated, continuous, spontaneous and connected. This paper is organized as follows: Sect. 2 highlights related works, Sect. 3 described the acoustic nudging-based models. The results and discussions are contained in Sect. 4, while Sect. 5 provides conclusion and further works of the study.

## 2 Related Work

ASR also known as speech-to-text converts a speech signal into textual information i.e., a sequence of spoken words using an algorithm that is implemented by a hardware or software module into text data [10, 11]. [12] designed HMM-based Tamil Speech Recognition based on limited Tamil words exhibiting low recognition accuracy. [13] developed a GMM based isolated speech recognition using MATLAB, where he designed a speaker-dependent speech recognition system based only on isolated digits of 0–9 and gives an accuracy ratio greater than 70%. [14] developed a speech-to-text converter using GMM where the paper focused on the extraction of features of the speech signal by MFCC for multiple isolated words to train audio files to get spoken words recognized and gave an accuracy of 98%, but the limitation is that it uses isolated words. Automatic speech recognition for Tunisian dialect, which is also an under-resourced language was developed in [17]. The HMM-GMM model using MFCC and HMM-GMM with LDA were compared in the study. These approaches gave a WER of 48.8% and 48.7%. [17] proposed an enhanced ASR system for Arabic using Kaldi Toolkit to build the system around, after which the acoustic models were trained using the HMM-GMM model, and the data collected was based on Standard Arabic news broadcasts. The language model was trained with two Corpora, including GigaWord3 Arabic corpus (1000 words) and the acoustic training data transcription (315000 words). The result gave a WER of 14.42%.

[3] provided a Mobile Tourist Assistance for Yorùbá Language developed for tourists and implemented on Android application. The researchers developed a speech-to-text system for easy communication between locals and tourists. The text data were gathered from on-site interaction with the native speakers in four different domains: Market, Media, Hospital, Motor-Park and Restaurant. The recording of the Yorùbá phone-set was done using Praat software through a male voice. The recording of the Yorùbá phone-set was done using Praat software and a male voice. The accuracy of the system was established to be 85% for clarity and 88% for naturalness. The limitation of this system is that it is a one-way interactive system, based on isolated words. [18] also developed a Home Automation speech-to-text system that lets a user control computer function and dictates text by voice using HMM as acoustic modeling, MFCC for feature extraction and for feature training of the dataset. [19] developed a standard Yorùbá Isolated speech-to-text system using HTK, which can recognize isolated words spoken by users using previous data. The system adopted a syllable-based approach using six '6' native speakers speaking 25 bi-syllabic and 25 tri-syllabic words under an acoustically-controlled room based on HMM and MFCC. The overall accuracy recognition ratio gave 76% and 84% for bi-syllabic and tri-syllabic words.[21] proposed a continuous Fongbe ASR system, an African language spoken in Benin, Togo, and a minimal part of Nigeria, but the system exhibited low accuracy of 71.07%, and no inclusion of tone diacritization.

All the existing studies have no consideration for automatic correction of ASR errors involving user's acoustic irrational behavior. Moreso, existing studies didn't consider tone diacritization as it is needed especially in Yoruba language to avoid ambiguity. To improve speech recognition accuracy and system performance, acoustic nudging-based model is proposed in this paper. The research process reduces word error rate and sentence error rate at a very significant level when compared to other existing models.

## 3 The Acoustic Nudging-Based Model

Acoustic nudging is a concept adapted from behavioural science for aligning speech interactions that appears distorted. This study focused on large vocabulary, speaker independent, and tone-diacritized continuous standard Yorùbá speech recognition, which is the recognition of continuously spoken words with a comparatively high number of different words. The continuous word recognition system for standard Yorùbá based on the AN model is developed in three stages as follows: (i) System training with standard Yorùbá speech samples, (ii) System validation with standard Yorùbá speech samples, and (iii) System testing with standard Yorùbá test samples. The training phase of the CSYSTT system consists of building and learning the acoustic model, which is regarded as the major component of any automatic speech recognition "ASR" or speech-to-text "STT" engines [6]. The training and recognition of parameters are based on an AN speaker-independent tone-diacritized continuous standard Yorùbá speech recognition system capable of handling large vocabularies. The approach for modeling standard Yorùbá sounds consists of generated/trained acoustic models and language models for standard Yorùbá speech data (see Fig. 1).

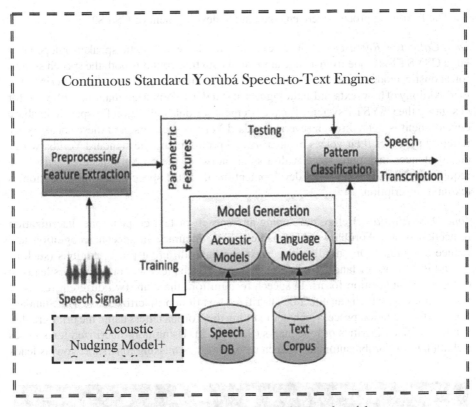

**Fig. 1.** The proposed acoustic nudging-based model

**Acoustic Nudging Model:** The entire process that makes up the acoustic nudging model is adapted from this study [20]. The acoustic nudging model is needed for automatic reformulation of the user's acoustic irrational behavior which involves tracking/monitoring, detecting, and reformulation of user's acoustic behavior in real-time.

*Gaussian Mixture Model:* The Gaussian Mixture Models (GMM) was used to address the low-resourced attribute of Yoruba Language [21]. Research has recorded GMM to be a tremendous success in the speech domain due to their high word detection accuracy ratio for language with low training data. GMM has been applied in many domains like artificial intelligence, image recognition and phoneme classification. one of the powerful attributes of GMM is its ability to form smooth approximations to arbitrarily shaped densities [24]. The Gaussian mixture density model for speech assumes that an M component mixture model with component weights $P(w_m)$ and its parameters $\theta_m$ represents the shape of each spectral. A univariate mixture model is represented in [21]. The developed ANGM modeling technique trained more than a trial to optimize the final training parameters. The accuracy of the model and loss is checked when tuning the parameters for optimization purposes. The ANGM model is a universal approach that can deal with both discrete and continuous data.

The following process were engaged in the development of CSYSTT:

*Data Collection Requirement.* The development of the automatic speaker-independent large CSYSTT is made from a large amount of data that contains both the speech signals for acoustic modeling and text data for language modeling. This stage describes the methodology of how texts and audio signals of standard Yorùbá language are collected for designing the CSYSTT system. The requirement for data collection for speech database development is done through several standard Yorùbá speakers, and these speakers are required to record their voices by uttering and pronouncing the standard Yorùbá words and sentences in a pure voice with a small noise in the background area. Also, the requirement for the text corpus development involves the speech data file collection as textual transcription.

*Tone Diacritization.* Before developing any speech or text corpus, tone diacritization is needed in any Yorùbá words to achieve high accuracy in speech recognition and reduce ambiguity. One un-diacritized text can have different pronunciations (such as ile and ile - house or land). Therefore, having a Yorùbá text without diacritics leads to different pronunciation forms. In speech recognition, there are two different forms of textual training, which can either be diacritized text or non-diacrtized text. The Standard Yorùbá diacritization process includes marking the Yorùbá letters using the orthographic symbols called diacritics or tone marks (See Fig. 2). Using non-diacritized texts poses a challenge to Yorùbá automatic speech recognition as missing tone/short vowels leads

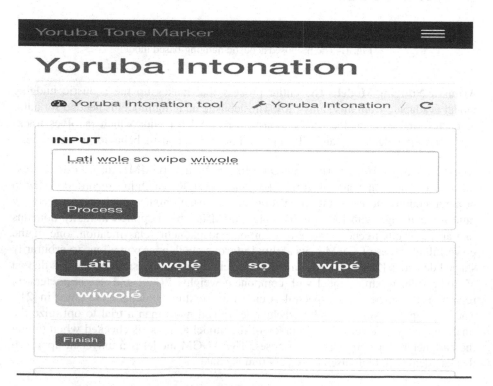

**Fig. 2.** A Semi-Supervised Standard Yorùbá Tone Diacritization Process

to some confusion in the learning and training process. Identification of syllables with the appropriate tone helps to determine the stress and intonation of that particular word.

In *Yorùbá* language, for diacritization process, having deep knowledge of syllables is essential and the allowed syllables in *Yorùbá* language are V, CV, and N", where V represents vowel sound, CV represents Consonant-Vowel sound and N represents Syllabic Nasal. Furthermore, *Yorùbá* language contains twenty-six '26' letters (consonants and vowels), seven '7' oral vowel sounds, and eighteen '18' consonant sounds. One of the consonant sounds is a digraph denoted as "D" and the rest as "C" with three '3' upper tonal signs (high, mid and low: á, a, and à) and under vowel sign (o, ọ) to distinguish words with the same spellings but different meaning and pronunciation. They are known as the consonants – sounds and vowel-sounds given below;

*Consonant-sounds*
b,  d,  f,  g,  gb,  j,  k,  l,  m,  n,  p,  r,  s,  ṣ,  t,  u,  w,  y
*Vowel-sounds*
Oral-vowel:      a,        e,        ẹ,        i,        o        ọ        u
Nasal vowel:     an        ẹn        in        ọn        u

**Recorded Speech Signal (Speech Database Development).** The speech corpus was created through data collection by training and validating and testing Yorùbá speech samples. The collection of data to develop the speech corpus is based on very large vocabulary for continuous speech recognition. A very large vocabulary generally implies that the system will have a vocabulary of roughly 20,000 to 60,000 words. The dataset was collected using 47 different Yorùbá speakers making a total of 22,312 data points and sums up to 2880.8 hours as each speaker utters different standard Yorùbá words and sentences (such as single word utterances, multiple word utterances, long sentences, etc) one after the other in different record notes. The data was further divided into training, validation and testing dataset (See Table 1). Moreso, for the acoustic nudging model process, 16 speech data were collected based on a normal, angry, panicked, sore throat, and stressed acoustic behavior from different age brackets for males and females. The speakers are from different states in Nigeria, consisting of female and male speakers of a large variety of ages, i.e., both children and adults. The dataset was gathered from different social apps such as Facebook, WhatsApp, Messenger, Twitter, as the speakers recorded their voices in short mp3 files.

**Table 1.** Speech corpus statistics

|            | No of speakers | No of files | No of sentences | No of words |
|------------|----------------|-------------|-----------------|-------------|
| Train      | 22             | 17,850      | 6392            | 11458       |
| Validation | 10             | 2,162       | 851             | 1311        |
| Test       | 15             | 2,300       | 918             | 1382        |
| Total      | 47             | 22312       | 8161            | 14151       |

The data gathered from different locations; each location consisted of varying noises. Some voice samples embedded low/noise room recordings, while some were affected by outdoor noises (such as by air-conditioner, children playing, car horning, dog barking, siren, street music, low music playing, people talking, etc.). Therefore, to create a high-end accurate and robust voice system, noise and silence removal was required as there are varying voice samples based on these outdoor noises. Therefore, it was important to perform pre-processing/feature extraction on each signal separately. The noise-free voice samples were given as a batch of different voice notes by each speaker. (See Table 2).

**Table 2.** System parameters

| Speaking mode | Continuous words |
|---|---|
| Sampling Rate | 44 kHz |
| Training/Enrolment | Speaker-Independent |
| Vocabulary Size | Large |
| Equipment | Smart Voice Recorder Application (QuickRec), Woefzela, Social Media Application |
| Number of Channels | 1, Mono |
| Audio Data File Format | .wav |
| Speech Acquisition | 2-Level (Word Level and Sentence Level) |
| Speech Corpus | 22,312 words and sentences |
| Number of Speakers | 47 |
| Language | Standard Yorùbá |

**Text Corpus Development.** In addition to the speech database, there is the resultant text corpus, which involves developing the text corpus. The collection of proper and suitable text is significant for the development of a text corpus. For the standard Yorùbá text corpus, the text collection was mainly done through the utilization of newspaper articles, Yorùbá online books, newspapers, texts embedded on the m-commerce platform, and online Yorùbá text dictionary. The next process was diacritizing each text using the Yorùbá tonal marks with the aid of a semi-supervised diacritizer. The full vocalization of the Yorùbá script was provided by the insertion of diacritics in the text. The approach employed in this process is a semi-automatic diacritization approach using Online Yorùbá Tone Marker (OYTM). The steps include the following: (i) Entering Standard Yorùbá text, one paragraph at a time, (ii) Tone mark each paragraph one syllable at a time by choosing syllable option using the correct tone mark either do, re, or mi with the tone under-marking for short vowel. Table 3 contains standard Yoruba continuous speech sample Dataset and its English version.

**Table 3.** A Standard Yorùbá Continuous Speech Sample Dataset and its English Version.

| S/N | English version | Standard Yorùbá version |
|---|---|---|
| 1 | Welcome, please put in your email and password | Káàb`ọ j`ọw´ọ fí ímeèlì àti `ọr`ọ ìgbaniwólé rẹ |
| 2 | I want to buy men's watches | Mo fẹ rà aago àwọn okúnrin |
| 3 | I want to buy women's shoes | Mo fẹ rà bàtà àwọn obìnrin |
| 4 | Diving Watch | Ìluw`ẹ´ẹ aago |
| 5 | Pay now by saying pay now | Sánwó ní báyìí nípa sísọ sánwó ní báyìí |
| 6 | men's bag | baagì àwọn okúnrin |
| 7 | women watch | aago àwọn obìnrin |

**Data Labeling.** All the data collected must be in proper order. After all the speech samples were processed, it was necessary for the speech samples to be divided and labeled, which is done by labeling and exporting multiple speech samples from one sample using the corresponding text transcription. Thereafter, the speaker's name was added to each speech sample and each speech sample was then divided to put each word is in one separate file.

**Pre-processing/Feature Extraction.** As the data were gathered from different locations, it followed with varying noises. Some voice samples embedded low/minimal noise (room recordings), while some were affected by outdoor noises (by air-conditioner, children playing, car horning, dog barking, siren, street music, low music playing, people talking, etc.). This is referred to as environmental variations, and to minimize this problem, it is essential to create a high-end, accurate, and robust voice system where noise and silence removal is required. Therefore, it was important to perform pre-processing/feature extraction on each signal separately. The voice samples were given as a batch of different voice notes by each speaker, which is ultimately necessary for each sample to be noise-free. It involves compressing all the speech signal samples to a vector that makes meaningful information. Before developing and training the model, feature extraction of audio files is required to eliminate unwanted signals such as noise and silence. This stage includes noise removal and silence removal. The silence removal is to eliminate the unvoiced and silent art of the speech signal. This stage explains how the file format of all the separated words/sentences with 22,312 speech files were converted into a wav format to execute the feature extraction algorithm. This study makes use of the Mel-frequency cepstral coefficient (MFCC). MFCC in speech research has been known as one feature extraction algorithm that works well with continuous speech recognition tasks for finding features compared to other feature extraction algorithms [19]. It reduces vulnerability to noise disturbance. They are created by taking the spectrum of a spectrogram ('a cepstrum') and discarding some of the higher frequencies that are less significant to the human ear [11].

**Acoustic Reformulation and Modeling.** In this study, the statistical representation adopted is Acoustic Nudging (AN) model and the Gaussian Mixture Model (GMM). The ANGM (GMM + AN) Model was used in statistically representing the relationships between the speech signals and the language phonemes. These models were combined to develop the acoustic representation model of this study. This proposed model (ANGM) helps in automatically reformulating user's acoustic irrational behavior, by correcting ASR error, to minimize the error rate embedded in speech data and at the same time, address the issue of low-resourced attributes of Yoruba Language.

**Pronunciation Dictionary.** The Pronunciation dictionary (PD) is also known as the lexicon. It contains all the 37,536 words with the sentences when broken down into a single word followed by their pronunciation called the phonetic transcription based on Standard Yorùbá language. The pronunciation dictionary was created after a deep study of Standard Yorùbá phonetics and also, different rules were used in pronouncing the words. Multiple entries are entered for words that are diacritized due to their homonym's characteristics e.g., words with the same spelling but different pronunciation. Table 4 presents the phonetic dictionary list of some words used in training the system. This pronunciation dictionary acts as an intermediary between the acoustic model and the language model to achieve a good recognition result.

**Table 4.** The phonetic dictionary used in the training

| Aago | a a go | Ìgbaniwólé | e gba ni wo le |
|---|---|---|---|
| Àbájáde | a ba ja de | | |
| àdírésì | a di re sii | | |
| àkóólè | a koo lee | look for the same spellings and different | |
| àmì | a mi | meanings | |
| àwo | a woo | | |
| àwon | a wo n | | |
| àsàyàn | a sa yan | . | |
| baagì | ba gi | . | |
| báyìí | ba yi | . | |
| béè béè | bee be | . | |
| bèèrè | beee re | | |
| èka | e ka | Yan – ya a un | |

## 4   Result and Discussion

To facilitate comparison with previous results, the ANGM model for the CSYSTT system was evaluated based on Word Error Rate (WER). The WER was calculated using Eq. 1:

$$WER = 100 \times \frac{Sw + Ds + ls}{N}$$

(1)

$$\text{Where } N = D + S + C$$

Also, the Word Recognition Rate (WRR) metric is a complement of the Word Error Rate (WER) given by Eqs. 1 and 2:

$$WRR = WER^1 \tag{2}$$

$$Accuracy(WRR) = (1 - WER) * 100\% \tag{3}$$

The ANGM model achieved a word error rate (WER) average score of 4.723% and mean accuracy (WRR) of 95.277. The best performance in terms of WER using 15 speakers was achieved using 128 MFCCs with 2.453% from speaker 10 (female adult) (see Table 5).

**Table 5.** WER Results for 15 different Test Speakers using ANGM Model

| S/N | Speakers | No of speech files | Mean accuracy (WRR)% | WER % |
|---|---|---|---|---|
| 1 | Speaker 1 (Male Adult) | 170 | 94.576 | 5.424 |
| 2 | Speaker 2 (Female Adult) | 190 | 95.692 | 4.308 |
| 3 | Speaker 3 (Female Adult) | 160 | 96.785 | 3.215 |
| 4 | Speaker 4 (Female Child) | 80 | 92.452 | 7.548 |
| 5 | Speaker 5 (Male Adult) | 148 | 96.683 | 3.317 |
| 6 | Speaker 6 (Male Child) | 90 | 92.643 | 7.357 |
| 7 | Speaker 7 (Female Adult) | 185 | 95.856 | 4.144 |
| 8 | Speaker 8 (Male Adult) | 160 | 96.932 | 3.068 |
| 9 | Speaker 9 (Male Child) | 85 | 93.593 | 6.407 |
| 10 | Speaker 10 (Female Adult) | 190 | 97.547 | 2.453 |
| 11 | Speaker 11 (Male Adult) | 160 | 95.327 | 4.673 |
| 12 | Speaker 12 (Male Child) | 82 | 94.735 | 5.265 |

(*continued*)

Table 5.  (*continued*)

| S/N | Speakers | No of speech files | Mean accuracy (WRR)% | WER % |
|-----|----------|-------------------|---------------------|-------|
| 13 | Speaker 13 (Female Adult) | 280 | 96.855 | 3.145 |
| 14 | Speaker 14 (Male Adult) | 170 | 94.954 | 5.046 |
| 15 | Speaker 15 (Male Adult) | 150 | 94.532 | 5.468 |
| | | Total = 2300 | Average = 95.277 | Average = 4.723 |

**Comparison with other Existing Models.** To evaluate the efficacy of the ANGM model for the CSYSTT system, this study compares the performance of the ANGM model with existing models that have been popularly used in literature with the application as either single models or hybrid models such as GMM, GMM-HMM, CNN, GMM-CNN and DNN. These models have been widely studied in different application scenarios where the training dataset was large and small with a dataset of 500 and above. The main purpose of this comparative study is to show how the ANGM model performs compared with popular speech recognition models. In the results presented in Table 6 and Fig. 4, the WER of each model was obtained by taking the average of each continuous Yorùbá speech sentence from the 2300 test dataset using different speakers with different age brackets conducted under a natural environment where there is noise interference.

Table 6.  WER Results for 5 Existing Speech Recognition Models with ANGM Model

| S/N | Sentences used | ANGM | GMM | GMM-HMM | CNN | GMM-CNN | DNN |
|-----|----------------|------|-----|---------|-----|---------|-----|
| 1 | Mo fẹ rà bàtà àwọn okúnrin | 4.248 | 5.324 | 4.957 | 5.823 | 4.667 | 5.483 |
| 2 | Fi si k`ẹk´ẹ ìgb´ẹru | 4.108 | 5.478 | 4.802 | 5.392 | 4.598 | 5.356 |
| 3 | Àjọsọpọ ti nmí kekere bàtà tàwọn obìnrin | 4.203 | 5.362 | 4.723 | 5.237 | 4.747 | 5.823 |
| 4 | Sánwó ní báyìí | 3.315 | 5.056 | 4.623 | 4.965 | 4.492 | 5.623 |
| 5 | Mo fẹ rà ọmọ wẹwẹ kanfasi | 3.623 | 5.256 | 4.701 | 4.813 | 4.276 | 5.600 |
| 6 | Mo fẹ rà baagì àwọn obìnrin | 6.757 | 7.789 | 6.334 | 6.934 | 6.534 | 7.893 |
| 7 | Mo fẹ rà bàtà awọ ilẹ | 4.255 | 4.911 | 4.612 | 4.833 | 4.335 | 5.064 |

(*continued*)

**Table 6.** (*continued*)

| S/N | Sentences used | ANGM | GMM | GMM-HMM | CNN | GMM-CNN | DNN |
|---|---|---|---|---|---|---|---|
| 8 | mo fẹ rà bàtà àwọn obìnrin | 3.967 | 4.567 | 3.845 | 3.867 | 3.267 | 4.834 |
| 9 | Mo fẹ rà bàtà àwọn okúnrin | 3.921 | 4.578 | 3.822 | 3.805 | 3.235 | 4.745 |
| 10 | Àwọn bata alawọ goolu | 3.145 | 4.283 | 3.941 | 4.002 | 4.122 | 4.782 |
| 11 | Mo fẹ rà aago àwọn okúnrin | 145 | 4.803 | 4.197 | 4.397 | 4.523 | 5.324 |
| Average WER | | **4.091** | **5.219** | **4.596** | **4.915** | **4.436** | **5.503** |

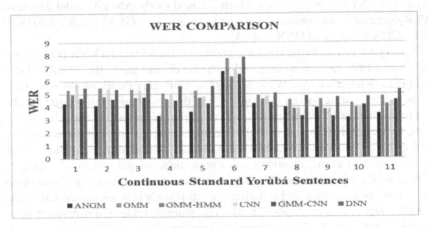

**Fig. 3.** WER comparison chart

The WER for ANGM, GMM, GMM-HMM, CNN, GMM-CNN and DNN models were estimated to be 4.091%, 5.219%, 4.596%, 4.915%, 4.436% and 5.503% respectively. The WER decrease was obtained between two systems and analyzed using Eq. 4.

$$\%\text{Decrease} = \left| \frac{\text{WER}_{p2} - \text{WER}_{p1}}{\text{WER}_{p1}} \right| \times 100 \qquad (4)$$

The average CSYSTT performance which is based on the ANGM model demonstrates a WER decrease of GMM (1.1%), GMM-HMM (0.5%), CNN (0.8%), and DNN (1.4%). when compared with previous models. The results of the experiment obtained in Tables 4 and 5 are compared with a column chart in Fig. 4. In this study, WER comparison was also made based on existing literature studies for under-resourced languages [22–24] with this present study having different WER ranges of 11.27%, 10.07%, 5.48%, 5.45%, 4.92%, etc. The existing African language speech recognition system [8,20] also achieved a WER range of 9.48%, 14.83%, 18%, and when compared with this current study, the ANGM model has a significantly lower average WER of 4.091% using 2300 test sentences.

## 5  Conclusion and Future Works

After the development of the indigenous vocabulary Continuous Standard Yorùbá Speech-to-Text reformulation engine for seamless communication, the system was evaluated using WER. The mean Word Error Rate (WER) is 4.723%. To evaluate the efficacy of the ANGM model, this study compared the performance of the ANGM model with existing models that have been popularly used in literature with an application as either single models or hybrid models using 11 CSY test datasets. The ANGM model achieved the least mean WER % of 4.091 compared to the afore-mentioned existing speech recognition models with mean WER% of 5.219, 4.596, 4.915, 4.436, and 5.503. The average CSYSTT performance which is based on the ANGM model demonstrates a WER decrease when compared with previous models- GMM (1.1%), GMM-HMM (0.5%), CNN (0.8%), and DNN (1.4%).

Existing African language speech recognition also achieved a WER range of 9.48%, 14.83%, and 18%, and when compared with this current study, the ANGM model has a significantly lower average WER of 4.091%. Our study caters for the observed limitations of the existing speech domain through the development of a large vocabulary Continuous Standard Yorùbá Speech-to-Text Engine as opposed to the existing Isolated Yorùbá Speech-to-Text Engine with consideration of tone diacritization and an Acoustic Nudging-based Gaussian Mixture (ANGM) Model. The essence is to allow automatic correction of ASR errors, involving user's acoustic irrational behavior in speech with low-resourced attributes for any language to achieve better accuracy and system performance. The Yoruba speech engine derived from this study may also be used as a platform to host the applications in Media, [25–27]. This study provides future research direction including the design of a Voice Engine System for other Yorùbá Accents, design of a Voice Engine System for other African Languages, and application of the ANGM model in other languages for enhanced accuracy and system performance.

## Abbreviations

| | |
|---|---|
| ANGM | Acoustic Nudging-based Gaussian Mixture Model |
| WRR | Word Recognition Rate |
| WER | Word Error Rate |
| ASR | Automatic Speech Recognition |
| STT | Speech-to-Text |
| TTS | Text-to-Speech |
| CSYSTT | Continuous Standard Yoruba Speech-to-Text |
| VQ | Vector Quantization |
| HMM | Hidden Markov Model |
| CNN | Convolution Neural Network |
| DNN | Deep Neural Network |
| CSY | Continuous Standard Yorùbá |

# References

1. Gaikwad, S.K., Gawali, B.W., Yannawar, P.: A review on speech recognition technique. Int. J. Comput. Appl. **10**(3), 16–24 (2010). https://doi.org/10.5120/1462-1976
2. Nwakanma, P.C., Ibe, R.C.: Globalization and economic growth. An econometric dimension drawing evidence from Nigeria. Int. Rev. Manage. Bus. Res. **3**(2), 771 (2014)
3. Deborah, N.O., Rhoda, I.A., Williams, O.A.: Development of a Mobile Tourist Assistance for a Local Language. **6**(1), 5–9 (2017). https://doi.org/10.5923/j.tourism.20170601.02
4. Prachi, U., Bhope, G.: Voice Based Collaborative Banking (2015)
5. Akintola, A., Ibiyemi, T.: Machine to Man Communication in Yorùbá Language. Annal. Comput. Sci. Ser. **15**(2) (2017)
6. Sebastian, B.W., Sebastian, B., Pinar, T., Leon, D.: Software Development: Advanced Computing. IT University of Copenhagen, October 2018
7. Levis, J., Suvorov, R.: Automatic speech recognition. The encyclopedia of applied linguistics (2012). https://doi.org/10.1002/9781405198431.wbeal0066
8. Wahab, A., Atanda, F., Azmi, S., Yusof, M., Hariharan, M.: Yorùbá Automatic Speech Recognition: A Review Yorùbá Automatic Speech Recognition : A Review, June 2013
9. Oluseye, A.: Yorùbá: A Grammar Sketch: Version 1.0; Journal of National Technical Support (2014)
10. Le, V.B., Besacier, L.: Automatic speech recognition for under-resourced languages: application to Vietnamese language. IEEE Trans. Audio Speech Lang. Process. **17**(8), 1471–1482 (2009). https://doi.org/10.1109/TASL.2009.2021723
11. Saksamudre, K.S., Shrishrimal, P.P., Deshmukh, R.R.: A review on different approaches for speech recognition system. Int. J. Comput. Appl. **115**(22), 23–28 (2015). https://doi.org/10.5120/20284-2839
12. Thangarajan, R.: Speech Recognition for Agglutinative Languages. Modern Speech Recognition Approaches with Case Studies (2012). https://doi.org/10.5772/50140
13. Vu, N.T., Kraus, F., Schultz, T.: Rapid building of an ASR system for under-resourced languages based on multilingual unsupervised training. In: Proceedings of the Annual Conference of the International Speech Communication Association, INTERSPEECH, pp. 3145–3148, August 2017
14. Vyas, J.V.: Study of Speech Recognition Technology and its Significance in Human-Machine Interface. **3**(10), 416–422 (2017)
15. Mohanty, S., Swain, B.K.: Markov Model Based Oriya Isolated Speech Recognizer-An Emerging Solution for Visually Impaired Students in School and Public Examination. Special Issue IJCCT **2**(2,3,4), 107–111 (2010). https://www.researchgate.net/publication/266268918
16. Ltaief, A., Ben, E.Y., Graja, M., Belguith, L.H.: Automatic speech recognition for Tunisian dialect, pp. 1–8 (2016)
17. Das, P., Acharjee, K., Das, P., Prasad, V.: Voice Recognition System : Speech-To-Text, July 2016
18. Adetunmbi, O.A., Obe, O.O., Iyanda, J.N.: Development of Standard Yorùbá speech-to-text system using HTK. Int. J. Speech Technol. **19**(4), 929–944 (2016). https://doi.org/10.1007/s10772-016-9380-2
19. Laleye, F.A., Besacier, L., Ezin, E.C., Motamed, C.: First automatic fongbe continuous speech recognition system: Development of acoustic models and language models. In: 2017 Federated Conference on Computer Science and Information Systems (FedCSIS), pp. 477–482. IEEE, September 2017
20. Galvan, R.F., Barranco, V., Galvan, J.C., Batlle, S., Fajardo, F., García, S.: We are IntechOpen , the world's leading publisher of Open Access books Built by scientists, for scientists TOP 1%. Intech, i(tourism) **13** (2016). http://dx.doi.org/https://doi.org/10.5772/57353

21. Ajayi L.K., Azeta, A.A., Odun-Ayo I., Chidozie, F, Ajayi, PT. Automatic Re-Formulation of user's Irrational Behavior in Speech Recognition using Acoustic Nudging Model. J. Comput. Sci. **16**. 17ss31–1741. https://doi.org/10.3844/jcssp.2020.1731.1741
22. Beserra, A.A.V., Silva, W.L.S., Serra, G.L.D.O.: A GMM/CPSO speech recognition system. In: IEEE International Symposium on Industrial Electronics, 2015-September (December 2018), 26–31. https://doi.org/10.1109/ISIE.2015.7281438
23. Stuttle, M.N.: A Gaussian Mixture Model Spectral Representation for Speech Recognition, p. 163, July 2003
24. Huggins-daines, D., Kumar, M, Chan, A, Black, AW, Ravishankar, M, Rudnicky, AI, Avenue, F, Pocketsphinx : A Free , Real-Time Continuous Speech Recognition System For Hand-Held Devices Language Technologies Institute (dhuggins , mohitkum , archan , awb , rkm , air)@ cs . cmu . edu., pp. 185–188 (2016)
25. Azeta, A., Da-Omiete, A.I., Azeta, I.V., Emmanuel, O.I.,. Fatinikun, D.O., Ekpunobi, E.: Implementing a medical record system with biometrics authentication in E-Health. In: IEEE AFRICON: Science, Technology and Innovation for Africa, AFRICON2017, pp. 18–20. September 2017; The Avenue V&A Waterfront Cape Town South Africa
26. Ajayi, L.K., et al.: Enhancing the low adoption rate of M-commerce in Nigeria through Yorùbá voice technology. In: Abraham, A., Hanne, T., Castillo, O., Gandhi, N., Nogueira Rios, T., Hong, T.-P. (eds.) HIS 2020. AISC, vol. 1375, pp. 516–524. Springer, Cham (2021). https://doi.org/10.1007/978-3-030-73050-5_52
27. Azeta, A.A., Ayo, C.K., Atayero, A.A., Ikhu-Omoregbe, N.A.: Application of VoiceXML in e-Learning Systems", Cases on Successful E-Learning Practices in the Developed and Developing World: Methods for the Global Information Economy. Chapter 7, Published in the United States of America by Information Science Reference (an imprint of IGIGlobal). Edited by Bolanle A. Olaniran., pp. 92–108 (2009)

# Ontology Quality Evaluation Methodology

R. Shyama I. Wilson[1,2](✉) (iD), Jeevani S. Goonetillake[2] (iD), Athula Ginige[3] (iD),
and Walisadeera Anusha Indika[4] (iD)

[1] Uva Wellassa University, Badulla, Sri Lanka
shyama@uwu.ac.lk
[2] University of Colombo School of Computing, Colombo 07, Sri Lanka
jsg@ucsc.cmb.ac.lk
[3] Western Sydney University, Penrith, NSW, Australia
a.Ginige@westernsydney.edu.au
[4] University of Ruhuna, Matara, Sri Lanka
waindika@dcs.ruh.ac.lk

**Abstract.** Lack of methodologies for ontology quality evaluation causes a challenge in producing good quality ontologies. Thus, we developed an iterative quality methodology to address this gap by analyzing the existing quality theories defined in ontology engineering, as well as, the theories in software engineering. Accordingly, this paper presents the developed methodology including how the other ontology quality theories get associated with it. Moreover, a use case in the agriculture domain has been demonstrated in order to provide an understanding of how the methodology can be applied in a real context. In the future, many experiments are expected to be carried out to fine-tune the methodology and to illustrate its usefulness.

**Keywords:** Ontology quality · Quality evaluation · Ontology · Agriculture

## 1 Introduction

Ontology engineering is a field that concerns the ontology development process (i.e., planning, designing, building, and maintaining) and studies methodologies, methods, tools and languages to produce a well-engineered ontology [1, 2]. However, it is debatable whether a well-engineered ontology is fit for the intended purpose, in other terms, it can be questioned whether a well-engineered ontology meets the requirements of the considered use case. This can be ensured only through a rigorous quality evaluation across the ontology development. However, the existing well-known ontology methodologies such as Uschold and King's method [3] TOVE [4], METHONTLOGY and On-to-Knowledge, have identified ontology evaluation as a phase of a methodology rather than considering it as an ongoing task which begins in the early stages of the developmental process. Moreover, these methodologies have not provided a detailed description of the quality evaluation. As a result, the attention to be provided for quality evaluation of ontologies got limited. Consequently, quality problems could not be detected until the ontology is used in an operational environment. Thus, in turn, it can adversely affect the overall quality of

O. Gervasi et al. (Eds.): ICCSA 2022, LNCS 13375, pp. 509–528, 2022.
https://doi.org/10.1007/978-3-031-10522-7_35

a system in which the ontology is integrated. Moreover, solving those quality problems requires an extra effort and not only that, it can be expensive and time-consuming. Thus, quality evaluation of ontologies cannot be underestimated.

As explained in [5, 6], quality evaluation requires a proper understanding of the intended purpose of the ontology and the domain to be modeled. Moreover, it is an iterative process that should be initiated at the requirements analysis phase and should be carried out in parallel with the development of the ontology. In analyzing the existing works, it has been identified that these notions have not been considered. Instead, the studies have discussed several other aspects such as quality scopes, evaluation levels, quality characteristics, tools, stages, approaches and techniques (see Fig. 1). To this end, we proposed an iterative methodology for ontology quality evaluation by analyzing quality theories in software engineering and also based upon the experience gained through ontology development and evaluation. Moreover, we made an effort to map the existing quality theories with the relevant steps of the proposed methodology (see Sect. 3). This, in turn, provides a better understanding of how the quality theories are getting associated with the quality evaluation process. Accordingly, the paper has been structured as follows.

Section 2 discusses the quality aspects: *levels, characteristics, scopes, techniques, stages, tools* and *approaches* considered in the previous works. Section 3 presents the proposed methodology for ontology quality evaluation. This has been further exemplified in Sect. 4. Finally, Sect. 5 concludes the discussed methodology by highlighting the future work.

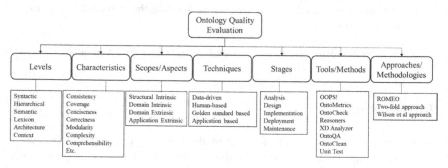

**Fig. 1.** Overview of ontology quality evaluation.

# 2   Overview of the Ontology Quality

Ontology quality has been discussed under several aspects such as (see Fig. 1):

- Levels of ontologies: syntactic, semantic, hierarchy/taxonomy, architecture/structure, lexicon and context [7, 8]
- Characteristics (i.e., criteria, principles): consistency, conciseness, completeness, accuracy, adaptability, clarity, etc. [8–10]

- Scopes: conceptualization/structure, domain and technical/application [11, 12]
- Evaluation aspects: structural intrinsic, domain intrinsic, domain extrinsic and application extrinsic [5, 6]
- Techniques: data-driven, golden standard-based, human-based and application-based [7, 8, 11]
- Stages in the ontology life cycle: analysis, design (i.e., conceptualization, formalization), implementation, deployment and maintenance [5]
- Tools/methods [6, 13, 14]
- Approaches/methodologies [10, 15, 16]

The following sub-sections discuss the aforementioned aspects in detail.

## 2.1 Ontology Quality Evaluation Levels

In evaluating an ontology, different levels namely syntactic, hierarchical, semantic, lexicon, architecture and context have been taken into account rather than evaluating ontology as a whole component [7]. For instance, under the syntactic level, ontology is evaluated to confirm whether it complies with the specification and syntax defined in the representation language. Under the hierarchy level, the properties related to the taxonomic structure (i.e., subsumption relationship) of an ontology are evaluated. Thus, it is also known as the taxonomy level evaluation. OntoClean [17] is one of the well-known methodologies that supports assessing the taxonomic properties such as *essence*, *identity*, and *unity* of an ontology. Under the semantic level, it is checked whether the ontology content is coherent with the domain knowledge that has been used to model the ontology. Typically, precision and recall measures have been used to assess the characteristics (i.e., semantic consistency, domain coverage and conciseness) related to the domain coherency [10, 15, 18]. In addition to that, the ontology taxonomic measures such as maximum depth, maximum breadth and structural variance have been adopted to assess the semantic level of an ontology [19, 20]. Under the lexicon level of an ontology, the vocabulary used to identify the ontology components (i.e., concepts, relationships, attributes, and individuals) is evaluated. The pre-defined representation principles are evaluated under the architecture level and the practical usefulness in the operational environment is evaluated under the context level [7, 8].

## 2.2 Ontology Dimensions, Characteristics and Measures

Various characteristics/attributes and measures have been proposed for ontology evaluation. Initially, the author in [3, 9] proposed five characteristics such as clarity, coherence, expandability, minimum encoding bias and minimal ontological commitment for ontology evaluation. Thereafter, the author in [8] has proposed another set of characteristics by associating them with the ontology evaluation levels (see Table 1). For instance, the characteristic: correctness has been defined to evaluate the lexicon and syntactic levels of ontologies. Later, the researchers in [21] have proposed a set of quantitative attributes to assess the quality of an ontology. This set of attributes can also be utilized to select a suitable ontology from the ontology repositories for the intended purpose. Based on that, the tools: OntoQA [21] and OntoMetrics [22] have been developed which support ontology developers to easily assess ontologies by avoiding the cost of manual evaluation.

Meanwhile, the semiotic metric suit has been proposed that consists of ten attributes grouped into four dimensions, namely: syntactic, semantic, pragmatic and social. Moreover, a set of measures to evaluate each attribute has been provided through that metric suit. Another comprehensive set of measures has also been introduced for ontology quality assessment in [23]. To this end, the attributes have been classified into three dimensions, namely: *structural, functional* and *usability-related*. Similarly, many researchers have proposed different characteristics, attributes and measures by grouping them into different dimensions (see Table 1). Therefore, we had to perform a comprehensive literature analysis to identify a set of characteristics that can be used for ontology quality evaluation [15, 24, 25]. Consequently, we proposed a quality model which consists of nineteen characteristics associated with different evaluation scopes [25]. Moreover, when analyzing the existing works, several discrepancies associated with the definitions provided for the characteristics, attributes and measures were observed. To this end, we made an effort to provide definitions for each characteristic identified through the literature that has been further discussed in [24, 25].

**Table 1.** Ontology quality characteristics.

| Citation | Dimension | Characteristics/Attributes |
|---|---|---|
| [9] | | Clarity, coherence, expandability, minimum encoding bias and minimal ontological commitment |
| [8] | Architecture | Soundness |
| | Syntax and lexicon | Correctness |
| | Content | Consistency, completeness, conciseness, expandability and sensitiveness |
| [21] | Schema | Relationship richness, attribute richness, inheritance richness |
| | Data | Class richness, average population, cohesion, importance, fulness, relationship richness, inheritance richness, connectivity and readability |
| [26] | Syntactic | Lawfulness, richness |
| | Semantic | Interpretability, consistency, clarity |
| | Pragmatic | Comprehensiveness, accuracy, relevance |
| | Social | Authority, history |
| [23] | Structural | Topological, logical, meta-logical |
| | Functional | Accuracy, precision, recall |
| | Usability-related | Recognition annotation, efficiency annotation, and interfacing annotation |

*(continued)*

**Table 1.** (*continued*)

| Citation | Dimension | Characteristics/Attributes |
|----------|-----------|----------------------------|
| [27] | – | Structural, functional adequacy, reliability, operability, maintainability, compatibility, transferability, etc.[a] |
| [18] | – | Language conformance<br>Completeness<br>Conciseness<br>Correctness (syntactic correctness, semantic correctness, representation) correctness, usefulness |
| [28] | Content | Correctness (internal consistency, external consistency, compatibility), completeness (syntactic completeness, semantic completeness) |
| | Presentation | Well-formedness, conciseness (non-redundancy), structural complexity (size, relation), modularity (cohesion, coupling) |
| | Usage | Applicability (definability, description complexity), adaptability (tailorability, composability, extendibility, transformability), efficiency (search efficiency, composition efficiency, invocation efficiency), comprehensibility |

[a] http://miuras.inf.um.es/evaluation/oquare/Contenido.html.

## 2.3 Ontology Evaluation Scopes and Aspects

The researchers have discussed different scopes/aspects to be considered in quality evaluation. The authors in [11, 12] have presented the three main scopes, namely: conceptual scope, domain scope and technical scope. Conceptual scope evaluates whether the concepts associated with the taxonomy of ontologies are well represented. When comparing with the ontology levels, it can be understood that the quality of the taxonomic level is considered in this scope. The domain scope evaluates whether the ontology represents the domain knowledge required to accomplish the specified tasks in the considered use case. To this end, the authors in [12] have shown that the domain scope considers the evaluation of the lexicon and architectural levels. Moreover, the technical scope evaluates whether the ontology meets the specified application requirements which are required for ontology integration and application in practice [5, 7].

Similar to the evaluation scopes described just above, the ontology summit has also proposed a set of scopes (i.e., evaluation aspects) to be considered in evaluating the quality of ontologies [6]. However, they have defined four main scopes, namely: *structural intrinsic, domain intrinsic, domain extrinsic and application extrinsic.*

The domain extrinsic and application extrinsic consider the evaluation of domain requirements and application requirements of an ontology which are specifically needed for a particular application respectively. These evaluations are very much similar to the "black-box" or "task-based" testing in software engineering [29]. Thus, the quality assessment is performed without peering at the ontology structure and the content. This has also been defined as ontology validation in [5, 8]. In general, the quality under the extrinsic aspect is determined by analyzing the correctness of the answers provided to competency questions with the involvement of users and domain experts [4].

The structural intrinsic and domain intrinsic scopes focus on the ontology structural and content quality evaluation respectively. In the structural intrinsic scope, the focus is given to the syntactic and structural requirements (i.e., syntactic, structural, architectural levels) which involve the specified conceptualization such as language compliance, conceptual complexity, and logical consistency. In the domain intrinsic aspect, quality is evaluated with reference to the domain knowledge which is used for the knowledge representation. At this stage (i.e., in the intrinsic aspect), mainly, the evaluation is performed by ontology engineers by considering the ontology as an isolated component separated from the system [5]. Somehow, ontology engineers need to obtain the assistance of domain experts when evaluating the domain intrinsic aspect as it requires some domain understanding. As we understood through the literature review, the semantic, vocabulary and architectural levels of ontologies are evaluated under the domain intrinsic aspect. Furthermore, the quality evaluation performed under the structural and domain intrinsic aspects are similar to the paradigm of "white-box" testing in software engineering [29]. Thus, the verification is being done under the intrinsic scope to ensure whether the ontology is built in the right way [8, 29].

### 2.4 Ontology Quality Evaluation Techniques

There are various techniques for carrying out a quality evaluation. The most commonly discussed techniques are human-based evaluation, data-driven evaluation, golden standard-based evaluation and application-based evaluation [7]. These techniques can be selected based upon the purpose, characteristics, scope, and/or levels to be evaluated of an ontology [24, 30]. For instance, the human-based technique is performing the quality assessment with the intervention of domain experts and/or users, and all the ontology levels can be assessed using this technique. In contrast to that, the data-driven evaluation assesses the ontology using a valid corpus and it is more suitable for ontology evaluation when it is difficult to acquire domain experts. However, this technique typically is used to evaluate the vocabulary and semantic levels of an ontology. When considering the golden-standard-based technique, it uses a standard ontology for the quality assessment and also it can be used in evaluating the levels: vocabulary, structure and semantics. However, the main difficulty of this technique is to find a standard ontology that has the quality at an acceptable level for the specified use case. The application-based technique is used to evaluate an ontology in an operational environment after it is integrated into the application. Thus, this technique can be adopted to evaluate the practical usefulness of an ontology and therefore, is suitable for assessing the context level of an ontology.

### 2.5 Ontology Evaluation Across the Ontology Life Cycle

Ontology quality could also depend on the success of activities that are followed to develop an ontology. For instance, if the requirement specification of an ontology is poorly performed at the requirement development phase, then, the resulting ontology will not succeed in providing knowledge to the specified tasks. To this end, the authors in

[5] have introduced a comprehensive set of criteria that can be used to evaluate the activities performed under each stage (i.e., *requirement development, ontological analysis, ontology design, system design, ontology development & reuse, system development & integration, deployment* and *maintenance*) of the ontology development.

In addition to that, the author in [31] has performed a comprehensive survey and analyzed quality criteria that can be used to evaluate ontologies at the design and implementation stages of the development. Consequently, it has been identified that a set of possible criteria such as *accuracy, adaptability, cognitive adequacy, completeness, conciseness, consistency, expressiveness* and *grounding* can be used for evaluating the design of an ontology. Moreover, the criteria: *computational efficiency, congruency, practical usefulness, precision* and *recall*, can be used to evaluate ontologies at the implementation stage. Nonetheless, as shown by the author in [31], the previous works have used only a few characteristics from these to evaluate the ontologies at each stage. Mainly, there is a piece of evidence in using the characteristic: *functional completeness (i.e., expressiveness)* and *practical usefulness* frequently in the previous works. To this end, the authors in [15, 31] have pointed out the necessity of introducing a complete methodology or approach for ontology evaluation in order to avoid the quality evaluation getting limited to a certain set of characteristics.

## 2.6 Ontology Quality Evaluation Tools

Appropriate tools can be utilized to make the ontology quality evaluation process easy, efficient and cost-effective. In the previous studies, many tools have been introduced and a few of them are summarized in Table 2. In analyzing the tools, it can be realized that a number of tools are available for evaluating the syntactic and structural properties. The tools: S-OntoEval, RepOSE, DoORS and OntoKeeper support to assess the characteristics in structural and domain intrinsic aspects. Nevertheless, it can be observed that only a few tools are available to use online such as RDF validator, OWL validator, OOPS!, OntoMetrincs, DoORS and RepOSE.

**Table 2.** Ontology tools and methods.

| Tool/Method | Characteristics/Attributes | Aspects |
|---|---|---|
| RDF Validation Service [32] | Language compliance | Structural intrinsic |
| OWL Validator [33] | Language compliance | Structural intrinsic |
| OntoAnalyser [34] | Language compliance and internal consistency | Structural intrinsic |
| OntoKick [34] | Accuracy and functional completeness | Domain extrinsic |

*(continued)*

**Table 2.** (*continued*)

| Tool/Method | Characteristics/Attributes | Aspects |
|---|---|---|
| OntoQA [21] | Complexity: relationship richness, attribute richness, inheritance richness, class richness, Average population, fullness<br>Modularity: cohesion, importance, connectivity, instance relationship richness, etc | Structural intrinsic |
| S-OntoEval tool [35] | Complexity, modularity, internal consistency, external consistency, comprehensibility | Structural intrinsic and domain intrinsic |
| OntologyTest [36] | Accuracy and functional completeness | Domain extrinsic |
| OntoCheck [37] | Comprehensibility | Structural intrinsic attributes that are complementary to the domain intrinsic aspect have been automated |
| XD analyzer [38] | Coverage: isolated entities, missing types, missing domain or range in properties, missing inverse,<br>Comprehensibility: instance missing labels and comments, unused imported ontologies | Structural intrinsic attributes that are complementary to the domain intrinsic aspect have been automated |
| RepOSE[a] [39] | Compliance and external consistency | Structural intrinsic and domain intrinsic |
| OOPS![b] [40] | Detect common pitfalls<br>Compliance: e.g., P34, P35 and P38<br>Consistency: e.g., P05, P06, P07, P19 and P24<br>Coverage: e.g., P04, P10, P11, P12 and P13<br>Conciseness: e.g., P02, P03, P21 and P32<br>Comprehensibility: e.g., P08, P20 and P22<br>Availability: e.g., P36 and P37 | Structural intrinsic, domain intrinsic/extrinsic and application extrinsic (i.e., only automated structural intrinsic metrics) |

(*continued*)

**Table 2.** (*continued*)

| Tool/Method | Characteristics/Attributes | Aspects |
|---|---|---|
| OntoMetric[c] [41] | Complexity: basic metric, knowledge base metric Modularity: graph metrics, class metrics Comprehensibility: annotation metrics | Structural intrinsic and domain intrinsic (i.e., only automated structural intrinsic metrics) |
| OntoDebug [42] | Internal Consistency | Structural intrinsic |
| DoORS[d] [43] | Compliance, external consistency, conciseness, comprehensibility, accuracy, relevancy, and credibility | Structural intrinsic, domain intrinsic and domain extrinsic |
| OntoKeeper [44] | Compliance: lawfulness, richness, conciseness, comprehensibility, accuracy, relevancy, and credibility | Structural intrinsic, domain intrinsic, and domain extrinsic |
| Delta [45] | Complexity, modularity | Structural intrinsic |

[a] RepOSE: https://www.ida.liu.se/~patla00/research/RepOSE/
[b] OOPS!: http://oops.linkeddata.es/
[c] OntoMetric: https://ontometrics.informatik.uni-rostock.de/ontologymetrics/
[d] DoORS: https://owlparser.herokuapp.com/

## 2.7 Ontology Quality Approaches and Methodologies

It is vital to have approaches and methodologies that systematically describe theories to be used, processes to be followed and the steps to be carried out in doing some work. With respect to the ontology quality evaluation, a few contributions can be found, such as the ROMEO methodology [10], the Two-Fold quality assurance Approach [16] and the Wilson et al. approach [15]. ROMEO methodology provides a set of guidelines to identify the intrinsic ontology quality characteristics from the defined ontology quality requirements of a system. Mainly, it has been constructed by employing the Goal-Question-Metrics (GQM) paradigm in information systems [46]. The Two-Fold quality approach has been introduced to monitor and assess the quality of an evolving knowledge base. It consists of two main phases, namely: coarse grain analysis and fine-grain analysis. During the coarse grain analysis, a quantitative analysis is performed to detect the high-level changes and common quality issues in a knowledge base. On the other hand, fine-grain analysis is performed to detect the detailed changes in a knowledge base and to detect all possible quality issues. The Wilson et al. approach mainly presents the steps to be carried out in determining quality characteristics from the intended needs of an ontology and presents how the identified characteristics are evaluated. Similar to the ROMEO methodology, this approach is also based on the GQM paradigm. However, the Wilson et al. approach supports to separately identify both intrinsic and extrinsic quality characteristics considering the ontology evaluation aspects (i.e., scopes).

# 3   Ontology Quality Evaluation Methodology

Although quality evaluation has been considered as a phase in most of the ontology methodologies, it is an iterative process that consists of several activities such as; *identification of intended needs, elicitation of quality requirements from the identified needs, prioritizing the quality requirements, specifying quality characteristics* (i.e., intrinsic and extrinsic aspect) and *performing quality assessment* across the ontology development [5, 47]. Moreover, these activities should be carried out in parallel with the development of the ontology starting from the stage of requirements analysis. However, there is no proper methodology that provides a set of steps that need to be followed under the quality evaluation of ontologies. To this end, we propose a methodology for the ontology quality evaluation by examining software quality theories described in SQuaRE (Systems and software Quality Requirements and Evaluation) [48] and also based on the experience gained through our previous studies [15, 24]. Accordingly, the proposed methodology consists of four main steps, namely: *quality requirement specification, plan & design, execution* and *user acceptance test* (see Fig. 2). These steps should be followed in parallel with the steps in the ontology development as illustrated in Fig. 3. The outer circle of Fig. 3 presents the steps in the ontology development life cycle as defined in [5]. The inner-circle presents the steps to be followed through our methodology which are further described in the below subsections.

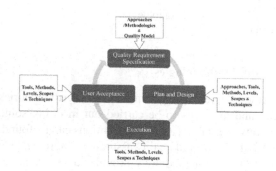

**Fig. 2.** Ontology quality evaluation methodology.

**Fig. 3.** The quality evaluation stages associated with the ontology life cycle.

## 3.1   Quality Requirement Specification

Under this stage, mainly, the quality requirements to be achieved through an ontology should be identified. It is noteworthy that quality requirements have been also defined as *quality characteristics* [49]. Thus, hereinafter, we use the term *quality characteristics* to refer to the term *quality requirements*. To identify the quality characteristics, initially, it is required to recognize,

- Who are the intended users?
- What is the intended purpose of using an ontology/ontology-driven system?

- What is the context of use?
- What are the intended needs[1] in the considered context (i.e., use case)? What are the competency questions?
- What is the scope of the ontology? What set of Competency Questions (CQs)/user needs will be covered through the ontology?
- What are the resources available for the ontology quality evaluation (i.e., text corpora, documents, domain experts, other related ontologies, users, tools, budget, time)?

Generally, ontology engineers identify the aforementioned factors at the requirement analysis phase in ontology development [5]. Thus, they can be considered when specifying the quality characteristics during this step. To this end, an appropriate approach/methodology can be followed. For instance, the Wilson et al. approach [15] can be used which explains how the characteristics for evaluating each aspect (i.e., intrinsic and extrinsic) are derived from the intended needs. In addition to this approach [15], the ROMEO methodology can also be used. However, it only supports deriving the characteristics associated with the intrinsic aspect of an ontology [10]. Moreover, quality models are required for the mentioned approaches that support determining the characteristics. This is due to the fact that quality models[2] present a possible set of characteristics that are applicable for an artifact evaluation. In software engineering, ISO/IEC 25010 defines a quality model that supports specifying the characteristics required for the considered software product [48]. Moreover, it describes a set of measures that can be used to assess quality characteristics. However, for ontology engineering, there are no such agreed quality models that can be used for the quality requirement specification. Instead, a number of characteristics/metrics proposed in the previous works can be seen such as characteristics/metrics proposed in [3, 8, 23, 26, 43]. Nevertheless, it is difficult for researchers and developers to analyze all these existing works and to identify a proper set of quality characteristics. To this end, we constructed an ontology quality model after performing a comprehensive literature analysis that presents nineteen main characteristics [15, 25]. Meantime, it describes a set of measures that can be used to assess characteristics. Therefore, this model can be utilized when following any of the aforementioned approaches to specify quality characteristics.

The followings should be the outputs of this stage.

- Specification of ontology quality requirements (i.e., quality characteristics)
- Specification of quality measures

### 3.2 Plan and Design

After specifying the quality characteristics, evaluators (i.e., ontology engineers, and curators) can identify the related ontology levels or scopes (see Fig. 1) in which the characteristics are associated. Moreover, they can further identify the measures to be

---

[1] Intended needs: business requirements that the intended users (i.e., persons, parties or organizations) expect from the ontology/ ontology driven information system.

[2] Quality model consists of a set of characteristics and the relationships between them that provide the basis for specifying quality requirements and evaluating quality [49].

used to assess each characteristic under each level with the support of a quality model. Also, they can define the decision criteria[3] for the selected measures. Furthermore, the evaluators can select the tools to be utilized, methods and techniques to be applied in order to assess the measures derived for the characteristics. For instance, assume that *functional accuracy* has been identified as a quality characteristic for an ontology in a particular context. Then, it can be derived through the approaches [10, 15, 18] and the quality model [15, 25], that *external consistency, internal consistency* and *syntactic accuracy* are a set of quality characteristics that are to be achieved through the ontology for *functional accuracy*. Meantime, the levels and scopes in which the characteristics are associated can be identified with the support of approaches. Table 3 represents the levels and scopes related to the characteristics that we have identified. Moreover, it includes the related measures, tools/methods, and techniques that can be used to assess the characteristics. When selecting techniques and tools/methods, it is required to analyze the resources that are available for the evaluation. For instance, *external consistency* is "the degree to which an ontology (i.e., ontology definitions) is coherent with the specified domain knowledge" [15, 25]. To this end, a frame of reference is required to check the domain coherency. A frame of reference could be a text corpus, domain experts and a standard ontology. If we have a valid text corpus to check the domain coherency, then the data-driven evaluation techniques can be utilized to assess the *external consistency*. On the other hand, if the domain expert intervention is readily available to the evaluators, then the human-based techniques can be easily carried out to evaluate the characteristic. Similarly, for all the relevant quality characteristics, the factors: *scope, tool, method* and *techniques* should be identified and shall be documented under this stage.

**Table 3.** The quality aspects related to the selected user requirement: functional accuracy.

| Characteristic | Scope | Level | Measures | Tool/Methods | Techniques |
|---|---|---|---|---|---|
| External consistency | Domain intrinsic | Semantic | Precision | Manually | Data driven, Human based |
| Internal consistency | Structural intrinsic | Semantic and structural | Logical contradictions | Reasoners | An evaluator can use the tools to observe the logical contradictions |
| Syntactic accuracy | Structural intrinsic | Syntactic | Lawfulness | OOPS!, protégé | An evaluator can use the tools to observe the syntactic violence |

---

[3] Decision criteria may be *"numerical threshold that used to determine the level of confidence in a given results. These will often be set with respect to quality requirements and corresponding evaluation criteria"* [48].

The following should be the outputs of this stage.

- Specification of the selected quality measures, tools, methods, and techniques to be used in the quality evaluation.
- Specification of decision criteria for ontology quality measures.
- Specification of resources available for the evaluation.
- Specification of detailed quality evaluation plans including time and budget [48].

### 3.3 Execution

During the execution stage, the selected quality measures of the characteristics shall be applied to the developed ontology or ontology being developed to check the required quality characteristics are achieved. In other terms, both *white-box testing* (i.e., domain intrinsic and structural intrinsic) and *black-box testing* (i.e., domain extrinsic and application extrinsic) shall be performed under this stage. Then, the results of the measures shall be reported and reviewed using the decision criteria. Consequently, any specific deficiencies can be identified with regard to the quality requirements. Thereafter, those deficiencies can be informed to the ontology developers to take the required actions to address them. Moreover, any limitations, constraints and exclusions in an evaluation can be reported including their impact on the use [48].

The following should be the outputs of this stage.

- Results of the ontology quality measures associated with the characteristics.
- Report of the limitations, constraints and exclusions in an evaluation.

### 3.4 User Acceptance

Under this stage, an ontology shall be evaluated in order to ensure whether the ontology meets the intended needs. In the case of an ontology-driven system, the ontology shall be assessed with the intervention of end-users of the system. To this end, the criteria and techniques defined for the acceptance testing in system and software engineering [48] can also be adopted due to the ontology will not appear as an individual component to the end-users at this level. In the case where the ontology is deployed as a standalone reference ontology, the appropriate application-based techniques can be used to observe whether the intended needs in an operational environment are achieved through the ontology [5, 7, 18].

Through this stage, the intended needs that are not covered through the ontology can be detected. These needs may be (i.) a set of new requirements for the ontology or (ii.) the requirements that have been identified during the requirement analysis, but, have not been addressed through the development. In these cases, the missing requirements shall be reported to the development team for further action. Consequently, the quality requirement specification can be refined and the methodology can be repeated.

The following should be the outputs of this stage.

- Results of the user acceptance test, i.e., new user needs, user feedback, comments and suggestions.

# 4 Application

**Quality Rquirement Specification:** to exemplify the methodology that we have proposed, we consider a use case in the agriculture domain explained in [15, 50]. In Sri Lanka, agriculture is one of the main industries, of which, the farmer is the main stakeholder who struggles to access the right information at the right time to make the right decisions. To address this issue, the requirement of producing an agricultural ontology and the intended needs to be achieved through that ontology have been identified in [50]. With respect to our methodology, we initially identified the answers to the questions which are highlighted in Sect. 3.1 and have been summarized in Table 4. A few of the identified intended needs were selected for the explanation as given below.

a) Users need the necessary and sufficient contextual information.
b) Users need trustworthy information.
c) Users need information in an understandable way.
d) Users need up-to-date information.

These needs are a set of inputs for the quality requirement specification in the proposed quality methodology. We illustrate how the quality requirement (i.e., characteristics) can be specified considering only the first requirement (i.e., *a*) in order to maintain the simplicity of the explanation. However, Table 4 summarized the quality characteristics which are associated with the other needs specified from **b** to **d**.

To identify the quality characteristics which are expressed in the user need: *"a"*, we employed the Wilson et al. approach [15]. Accordingly, we formulated the questions by considering the need mentioned below.

Q1: Does the ontology provide contextual information in a specified context of use?

Q2: Does the ontology provide necessary and sufficient information in a specified context of use?

With the support of the ontology quality model in [15, 25], we identified that the mentioned questions describe the characteristics: *relevancy* and *completeness* of ontology information respectively. By further subdividing these questions, the ontology characteristics to be achieved at the domain intrinsic and structural intrinsic levels were identified. For example, the characteristics: *conciseness* and *compliance* have been identified as characteristics to be satisfied at the intrinsic level (i.e., domain, structural) to achieve *relevancy* (Q1). To achieve *completeness* (Q2), the required internal ontology characteristics have been identified as *coverage* and *compliance*. Similarly, the ontology characteristics associated with the other user needs can also be identified. Due to the page limitation, we have not described in this paper the steps in detail which are to be followed in deriving the quality characteristics and further detail is available in [15]. Accordingly, Table 4 presents all the related quality characteristics derived from the mentioned needs.

**Table 4.** Summarization of the quality requirements.

| Main users | Farmers, Agriculture Instructors, Experts |
|---|---|
| Purpose | To support the decision-making process of farmers |
| Context of use | Pest and disease management in Brinjal |
| Resources | Agronomist, domain experts, terminology documents, list of packages of practices, tools: Protégé, OOPS! (online), OntoMetrics (online), etc |
| User needs | Quality requirement (see Q1–Q6 in [15]) |
| a | Q1. Relevancy: conciseness and compliance<br>Q2. Completeness: coverage and compliance |
| b | Q3. Accuracy: external consistency and internal consistency<br>Q4. Credibility |
| c | Q5. Understandability: comprehensibility and compliance |
| d | Q6. Timeliness |
| Scope and CQs | Scope and CQs are defined in [15, 50] |

**Plan and Design:** During this stage, it is required to plan and design how the specified quality characteristics shall be evaluated. Accordingly, we identified the measures that can be used to assess the specified quality characteristics (i.e., relevancy, completeness, conciseness, coverage and compliance), the tools, methods, and techniques based upon the available resources (see Table 5). In selecting the measures for the characteristic evaluation, we utilized the quality model that we have constructed in [15, 25]. To evaluate the structural intrinsic characteristics, the available tools were explored and selected such as OOPS! [40], OntoMetrics [22], Protégé [51] (see Table 5). Moreover, we defined the data-driven techniques to measure the characteristics: *external consistency, conciseness, comprehensibility* and *coverage* as we have the documents provided by the domain experts. To assess the domain extrinsic scope, the human-based techniques were defined as the domain expert and user assistance can be obtained for the considered context. To this end, the unit test discussed in [52, 53] can also be performed by maintaining test cases. Thus, in that case, all the required test cases should be documented and then, they can be used during the test execution. Similarly, the appropriate evaluation measures, tools, methods, techniques and scope are required to decide during this stage in order to use in the quality execution phase.

**Table 5.** Quality characteristics and the related evaluation aspects. *Note: *E* denotes extrinsic characteristics, *I* denotes intrinsic characteristics, *O* denotes a modeled ontology, and *F* denotes a frame of reference.

| Characteristics | Measures | Techniques | Methods/Tools |
|---|---|---|---|
| Relevancy (E) | The number of competency questions received relevant answers | Human-based | Protégé, |

(continued)

**Table 5.** (*continued*)

| Characteristics | Measures | Techniques | Methods/Tools |
|---|---|---|---|
| Completeness (E) | The number of competency questions received sufficient answers | Human-based | Protégé, |
| Accuracy (E) | Number of competency questions received correct answers | Human-based | Protégé, |
| Credibility (E) | | Human-based | Manual |
| Understandability (E) | | Human-based | Manual |
| Timeliness (E) | Average update rate | | Manual |
| Conciseness (I) | Precision (O; F) | Data-driven | Manual |
| Coverage (I) | Recall (O; F) | Data-driven | Manual |
| External consistency (I) | Precision (O; F) | Data-driven Human-based | Manual |
| Internal consistency (I) | Number of logical contradictions | Human-based | Reasoners |
| Compliance (I) | Measures of lawfulness, richness, class richness, naming conventions, etc. [15] | Human-based | Protégé, OOPS! and OntoMetrics |

**Execution:** As planned and designed in the previous stage, the quality evaluation can be performed in this stage. According to the example, during the intrinsic level, the structural intrinsic characteristics were evaluated using the selected tools such as OOPS! [40], OntoMetrics [22], Protégé [51] and reasoners [54]. The characteristics in the domain intrinsic scope were assessed manually using data-driven techniques. Finally, the characteristics in the domain extrinsic scope were evaluated using Protégé by running the SPARQL queries defined for the CQs. In this case, the answers produced to the CQs were validated using the documents provided by the domain experts and obtaining their support. After assessing the identified measures using the selected methods and techniques, the results of this evaluation were reported. The evaluation results related to this example, i.e., the use case in agriculture, can be found in [15].

**User Acceptance Test:** In the considered use case, an ontology is used as a component of a decision support system. Therefore, the user acceptance test can be performed by giving the ontology-driven system to the end-users, i.e., farmers and agriculture inspectors. To this end, the quality in use criteria defined in ISO/IEC 25010 can be used to assess the effectiveness, efficiency and user satisfaction of the ontology-driven system [49]. Due to the main system being under development, the acceptance test in a real environment has not yet been performed for the use case. In the future, we expect to present a thorough result analysis including this step.

## 5    Conclusion

The usefulness of a methodology for ontology quality evaluation has been identified through theoretical and empirical reviews. As an initial step, we constructed a methodology by analyzing the theories in software engineering, i.e., SQuaRE [48, 49] and experience gained through the development and evaluation of ontologies. Consequently, the developed methodology consists of four main steps, namely: *quality requirement specification, plan & design, execution* and *user acceptance test* (see Fig. 2). These steps can be performed iteratively and parallelly with the ontology development life cycle. The applicability of this methodology for real applications has been exemplified by discussing a use case in agriculture. Moreover, the methodology has been introduced for undergraduate students who are currently doing research in ontology engineering. Most of the students provided positive feedback by highlighting that the methodology is useful for them to understand the proper set of characteristics to be assessed and how the quality concepts discussed in the literature are associated with it. To this end, we further expect to observe the results of the experiments using the proposed methodology in many use cases and to enhance it with a more comprehensive set of guidelines.

**Acknowledgement.** The author acknowledges the support received from the LK Domain Registry (https://www.domains.lk/index.php/outreach/research-grants) in publishing this paper.

## References

1. Gal, A.: Ontology engineering. In: Liu, L., Özsu, M.T. (eds.) Encyclopedia of Database Systems, pp. 1972–1973. Springer, Boston (2009). https://doi.org/10.1007/978-1-4614-8265-9
2. Gómez-Pérez, A., Fernández-López, M., Corcho, O.: Theoretical foundations of ontologies. In: Gómez-Pérez, A., Fernández-López, M., Corcho, O. (eds.) Ontological Engineering: With Examples from the Areas of Knowledge Management, e-Commerce and the Semantic Web, pp. 1–45. Springer, London (2004). https://doi.org/10.1007/1-85233-840-7_1
3. Uschold, M., Gruninger, M.: Ontologies: principles, methods and applications. Knowl. Eng. Rev. **11**, 93–136 (1996)
4. Gruninger, M., Fox, M.S.: Methodology for design and evaluation of ontologies. In: Workshop on Basic Ontological Issues in Knowlege Sharing (1995)
5. Neuhaus, F., et al.: Towards ontology evaluation across the life cycle: the ontology summit 2013. Appl. Ontol. **8**, 179–194 (2013)
6. Ontology Summit 2013. http://ontolog.cim3.net/OntologySummit/2013/. Accessed 26 June 2021
7. Brank, J., Grobelnik, M., Mladeni, D.: A survey of ontology evaluation techniques. In: Proceedings of the Conference on Data Mining and Data Warehouses, pp. 166–170 (2005)
8. Gómez-Pérez, A.: Towards a framework to verify knowledge sharing technology. Expert Syst. Appl. **11**, 519–529 (1996)

9. Gruber, T.R.: Toward principles for the design of ontologies used for knowledge sharing. Int. J. Hum. Comput. Stud. **43**, 907–928 (1993)
10. Yu, J., Thom, J.A., Tam, A.: Requirements-oriented methodology for evaluating ontologies. Inf. Syst. **34**(8), 766–791 (2009). https://doi.org/10.1016/j.is.2009.04.002. ISSN 0306-4379
11. Pak, J., Zhou, L.: A framework for ontology evaluation. In: Sharman, R., Rao, H.R., Raghu, T.S. (eds.) WEB 2009. LNBIP, vol. 52, pp. 10–18. Springer, Heidelberg (2010). https://doi.org/10.1007/978-3-642-17449-0_2
12. Lantow, B.: OntoMetrics: putting metrics into use for ontology evaluation. In: KEOD, pp. 186–191 (2016)
13. Corcho, O., Fernández-López, M., Gómez-Pérez, A.: Methodologies, tools and languages for building ontologies. Where is their meeting point? Data Knowl. Eng. **46**, 41–64 (2003)
14. Aruna, T., Saranya, K., Bhandari, C.: A survey on ontology evaluation Tools. In: 2011 International Conference on Process Automation, Control and Computing, pp. 1–5 (2011)
15. Wilson, S.I., Goonetillake, J.S., Ginige, A., Walisadeera, A.I.: Towards a usable ontology: the identification of quality characteristics for an ontology-driven decision support system. IEEE Access **10**, 12889–12912 (2022)
16. Rashid, M., Torchiano, M., Rizzo, G., Mihindukulasooriya, N., Corcho, O.: A quality assessment approach for evolving knowledge bases. Semant. Web **10**, 349–383 (2019)
17. Guarino, N., Welty, C.A.: An overview of OntoClean. In: Staab, S., Studer, R. (eds.) Handbook on Ontologies, pp. 151–171. Springer, Heidelberg (2004). https://doi.org/10.1007/978-3-540-24750-0_8
18. Rico, M., Caliusco, M.L., Chiotti, O., Galli, M.R.: OntoQualitas: a framework for ontology quality assessment in information interchanges between heterogeneous systems. Comput. Ind. **65**, 1291–1300 (2014)
19. Sánchez, D., Batet, M., Martínez, S., Domingo-Ferrer, J.: Semantic variance: an intuitive measure for ontology accuracy evaluation. Eng. Appl. Artif. Intell. **39**, 89–99 (2015)
20. Fernández, M., Overbeeke, C., Sabou, M., Motta, E.: What makes a good ontology? A case-study in fine-grained knowledge reuse. In: Gómez-Pérez, A., Yu, Y., Ding, Y. (eds.) ASWC 2009. LNCS, vol. 5926, pp. 61–75. Springer, Heidelberg (2009). https://doi.org/10.1007/978-3-642-10871-6_5
21. Tartir, S., Arpinar, I.B., Moore, M., Sheth, A.P., Aleman-Meza, B.: OntoQA: metric-based ontology quality analysis. In: The IEEE Workshop on Knowledge Acquisition from Distributed, Autonomous, Semantically Heterogeneous Data and Knowledge Sources (2005)
22. Lantow, B.: OntoMetrics: application of on-line ontology metric calculation. In: BIR Workshops, pp. 1–12 (2016)
23. Gangemi, A., Catenacci, C., Ciaramita, M., Lehmann, J.: Modelling ontology evaluation and validation. In: Sure, Y., Domingue, J. (eds.) ESWC 2006. LNCS, vol. 4011, pp. 140–154. Springer, Heidelberg (2006). https://doi.org/10.1007/11762256_13
24. Wilson, R.S.I., Goonetillake, J.S., Indika, W.A., Ginige, A.: Analysis of ontology quality dimensions, criteria and metrics. In: Gervasi, O., et al. (eds.) ICCSA 2021. LNCS, vol. 12951, pp. 320–337. Springer, Cham (2021). https://doi.org/10.1007/978-3-030-86970-0_23
25. Wilson, R.S.I.: A Conceptual Model for Ontology Quality Assessment. http://semantic-web-journal.net/system/files/swj3003.pdf. Accessed 04 Apr 2022
26. Burton-Jones, A., Storey, V.C., Sugumaran, V., Ahluwalia, P.: A semiotic metrics suite for assessing the quality of ontologies. Data Knowl. Eng. **55**, 84–102 (2005)
27. Duque-Ramos, A., Fernández-Breis, J.T., Stevens, R., Aussenac-Gilles, N.: OQuaRE: a SQuaRE-based approach for evaluating the quality of ontologies. J. Res. Pract. Inf. Technol. **43**, 159–176 (2011)
28. Zhu, H., Liu, D., Bayley, I., Aldea, A., Yang, Y., Chen, Y.: Quality model and metrics of ontology for semantic descriptions of web services. Tsinghua Sci. Technol. **22**, 254–272 (2017)

29. McDaniel, M., Storey, V.C.: Evaluating domain ontologies: clarification, classification, and challenges. ACM Comput. Surv. **52**, 1–44 (2019)
30. Raad, J., Cruz, C.: A survey on ontology evaluation methods. In: Proceedings of the 7th International Joint Conference on Knowledge Discovery, Knowledge Engineering and Knowledge Management, pp. 179–186. SCITEPRESS - Science and and Technology Publications, Lisbon (2015)
31. Degbelo, A.: A snapshot of ontology evaluation criteria and strategies. In: Proceedings of the 13th International Conference on Semantic Systems, pp. 1–8. Association for Computing Machinery, New York (2017)
32. W3C RDF Validation Service. https://www.w3.org/RDF/Validator/. Accessed 29 Dec 2021
33. Horridge, M.: OWL 2 Validator. http://mowl-power.cs.man.ac.uk:8080/validator/. Accessed 29 Dec 2021
34. Sure, Y., Erdmann, M., Angele, J., Staab, S., Studer, R., Wenke, D.: OntoEdit: collaborative ontology development for the semantic web. In: Horrocks, I., Hendler, J. (eds.) ISWC 2002. LNCS, vol. 2342, pp. 221–235. Springer, Heidelberg (2002). https://doi.org/10.1007/3-540-48005-6_18
35. Dividino, R., Romanelli, M., Sonntag, D.: Semiotic-based ontology evaluation tool S-OntoEval. In: Proceedings of the Sixth International Conference on Language Resources and Evaluation (LREC 2008) (2008)
36. García-Ramos, S., Otero, A., Fernández-López, M.: OntologyTest: a tool to evaluate ontologies through tests defined by the user. In: Omatu, S., et al. (eds.) IWANN 2009. LNCS, vol. 5518, pp. 91–98. Springer, Heidelberg (2009). https://doi.org/10.1007/978-3-642-02481-8_13
37. Schober, D., Tudose, I., Svatek, V., et al.: OntoCheck: verifying ontology naming conventions and metadata completeness in Protégé 4. J. Biomed. Semant. **3**, S4 (2012). https://doi.org/10.1186/2041-1480-3-S2-S4
38. Daga, E.: XDTools - NeOn Wiki. http://neon-toolkit.org/wiki/XDTools.html. Accessed 29 Dec 2021
39. Lambrix, P., Liu, Q.: Debugging the missing is-a structure within taxonomies networked by partial reference alignments. Data Knowl. Eng. **86**, 179–205 (2013)
40. Poveda-Villalón, M., Gómez-Pérez, A., Suárez-Figueroa, M.C.: Oops! (ontology pitfall scanner!): an on-line tool for ontology evaluation. Int. J. Semant. Web. Inf. Syst. IJSWIS. **10**, 7–34 (2014)
41. Lozano-Tello, A., Gomez-Perez, A.: ONTOMETRIC: a method to choose the appropriate ontology. J. Database Manag. JDM **15**, 1–18 (2004)
42. Schekotihin, K., Rodler, P., Schmid, W.: OntoDebug: interactive ontology debugging plug-in for Protégé. In: Ferrarotti, F., Woltran, S. (eds.) FoIKS 2018. LNCS, vol. 10833, pp. 340–359. Springer, Cham (2018). https://doi.org/10.1007/978-3-319-90050-6_19
43. McDaniel, M., Storey, V.C., Sugumaran, V.: Assessing the quality of domain ontologies: metrics and an automated ranking system. Data Knowl. Eng. **115**, 32–47 (2018)
44. Amith, M., et al.: OntoKeeper: semiotic-driven ontology evaluation tool for biomedical ontologists. In: 2018 IEEE International Conference on Bioinformatics and Biomedicine (BIBM), pp. 1614–1617 (2018)
45. Kondylakis, H., et al.: Delta: a modular ontology evaluation system. Information **12**, 301 (2021)
46. van Solingen, R., Basili, V., Caldiera, G., Rombach, H.D.: Goal question metric (GQM) approach. In: Encyclopedia of Software Engineering. American Cancer Society (2002)
47. Carriero, V.A., Gangemi, A., Mancinelli, M.L., Nuzzolese, A.G., Presutti, V., Veninata, C.: Pattern-based design applied to cultural heritage knowledge graphs. Semantic Web. **12**, 313–357 (2021)

48. ISO/IEC 25040:2011(en), Systems and software engineering — Systems and software Quality Requirements and Evaluation (SQuaRE) — Evaluation process. https://www.iso.org/obp/ui/# iso:std:iso-iec:25040:ed-1:v1:en. Accessed 03 Jan 2022

49. ISO/IEC 25010:2011(en), Systems and software engineering — Systems and software Quality Requirements and Evaluation (SQuaRE) — System and software quality models. https://www. iso.org/obp/ui/#iso:std:iso-iec:25010:ed-1:v1:en. Accessed 26 June 2021

50. Walisadeera, A.I., Ginige, A., Wikramanayake, G.N.: User centered ontology for Sri Lankan farmers. Ecol. Inform. **26**, 140–150 (2015). https://doi.org/10.1016/j.ecoinf.2014.07.008

51. Protégé. https://protege.stanford.edu/. Accessed 14 Nov 2021

52. Vrandečić, D., Gangemi, A.: Unit tests for ontologies. In: Meersman, R., Tari, Z., Herrero, P. (eds.) OTM 2006. LNCS, vol. 4278, pp. 1012–1020. Springer, Heidelberg (2006). https:// doi.org/10.1007/11915072_2

53. Fernández-Izquierdo, A., García-Castro, R.: How to validate ontologies with themis. In: Hitzler, P., et al. (eds.) ESWC 2019. LNCS, vol. 11762, pp. 52–57. Springer, Cham (2019). https://doi.org/10.1007/978-3-030-32327-1_11

54. List of Reasoners | OWL research at the University of Manchester. http://owl.cs.manchester. ac.uk/tools/list-of-reasoners/. Accessed 14 Nov 2021

# Impact of Radio Map Size on Indoor Localization Accuracy

Madikana S. Sediela[1](✉), Moses L. Gadebe[2], and Okuthe P. Kogeda[3]

[1] Department of Computer Science, Faculty of ICT, Tshwane University of Technology, Private Bag X680, Pretoria 0001, South Africa
sedielams@tut.ac.za

[2] Department of Advanced Internet of Things, Council for Scientific and Industrial Research (CSIR), P.O. Box 395, Pretoria 0001, South Africa
MGadebe@csir.co.za

[3] Department of Computer Science and Informatics, Faculty of natural and agricultural sciences, University of the Free State, P.O. Box 339, Bloemfontein 9300, South Africa
KogedaPO@ufs.ac.za

**Abstract.** Nowadays Indoor Positioning Systems (IPS) are attracting attention in literature because of Global Positioning System (GPS) challenge to track and navigate indoors. These IPSs intend to provide information about a wireless object's current position indoor. GPS-based localization is the most successful Location-Based Service (LBS) application deployed in an outdoor environment. However, GPS faces a challenge of the line of sight indoor. GPS is affected extensively by the multipath-effects. IPS technologies such as Wi-Fi are deployed for indoor localization, in an attempt to alleviate the GPS indoor challenges. Most IPS employs the Fingerprinting algorithm, whereby a radio-map is generated during the offline phase by collecting measurements of Received Signal Strength Indicator (RSSI) at known locations and, positioning of devices at an unknown location is performed during the online phase by utilizing Machine Learning (ML) Algorithms. The radio-map dataset plays a major role in the accuracy performance of the classifiers deployed during the online phase. RSSI fluctuates indoors because of fading, interferences, and shadowing, therefore, the correction of the radio-map RSSI measurements is mandatory to improve the classifiers performance. In this paper, we looked into the impact of the size of the calibration radio-map on the accuracy of the predictive model. We applied the Mean and Standard Deviation filter on three datasets of different sizes to reduce the RSSI instability at each required point and conducted comparative performance on how ML classification models perform on the three radio-map different in size. The radio-map was generated using our EMPsys application. The results of the simulations show that the accuracy of the Kernel Naïve Bayes significantly improved with filter as the radio-map size increased, from 64.4% with 453 observations in the first scenario to 95.4% with 1054 observations in the third scenario. We, therefore, conclude that the performance of the classifier to be used during the online phase of the fingerprinting algorithm relies on both the size of the radio-

© The Author(s), under exclusive license to Springer Nature Switzerland AG 2022
O. Gervasi et al. (Eds.): ICCSA 2022, LNCS 13375, pp. 529–543, 2022.
https://doi.org/10.1007/978-3-031-10522-7_36

map and the filtering methods used to correct the RSSI measurements of the radio-map.

**Keywords:** Fingerprinting · Mean · Standard deviation · RSSI · GPS · Wi-Fi · IPS · LBS

# 1 Introduction

With a rapid development of a diverse wireless sensor networks, Location-Based Services (LBS) applications have attracted more attention in the research community. LBS provides useful information about a person's or object's current position [1]. LBS positioning technologies can be categorized into an outdoor and indoor system. The GPS technology is the most successful outdoor, however, its applicability is constrained in a closed indoor environment because of non-line-of-sight propagation and multipath effects [2–4]. With GPS challenge indoor, Indoor Positioning Systems (IPS) are explored to close the GPS gap Indoor. The main goal of the IPS is to provide a cost effective, high accuracy and real time solution [5]. IPS utilizes short-ranged technologies such as Wi-Fi [3,6] and Bluetooth [7,8].

These short-ranged technologies are usually deplored with the Fingerprinting Algorithm due to its low deployment cost and convenient signal acquisition [2]. The Fingerprinting Algorithm is divided into two phases, the offline phase for radio-map generation and the online phase for location estimation using the Machine Learning (ML) algorithms. The measurements of the Received signal strength indicator (RSSI) are collected together with the transmitter device's MAC Address and SSID to form a radio-map at known locations during the offline phase. In the online phase, the RSSI scanned at unknown location by the receiver device is matched with the data of the radio-map by utilizing a prediction algorithm.

The success of the model that utilizes the Fingerprinting algorithm is eminently dependent on the radio-map or the dataset collected during the offline phase. Nevertheless, the RSSI measurements are sensitive to environmental settings and without RSSI correction of the radio-map, the localization error of the prediction algorithms in an online phase is too high to achieve the needs of IPS. Continuous attention to correct the RSSI measurements in an effort to improve the performance of the ML model has been explored in literature, without considering the effect of the size of the radio-map on the performance of the ML algorithm. Radio-map generation is a very time consuming process [2], and its size may impact the outcome of models and thus also affect the classification performance [9,10].

In this study, we investigate the impact of the size of radio-map, and correct the RSSI measurements to simulate the effect of the outcomes of the performance of the prediction model. Our RSSI filtering approach presented in [1] uses the mean and standard deviation to identify and correct the RSSI measurements. We discuss our three incremental dataset scenarios resulting in one dataset.

We, therefore, provide comparative performance metrics of Machine learning classification algorithms and analyse the performance of the models as the size in radio-map increases. Our results show that the accuracy of the Kernel Naïve Bayes significantly improved with filter as the radio-map size increases, from 64.4% with 453 observation in the first scenario to 95.4% with 1054 observations in the third scenario. We therefore conclude that the performance of the classifier to be used during the online phase of the fingerprinting algorithm relies on both the size of the radio-map and the filtering method used to correct the RSSI measurements of the radio-map.

The remainder of this paper is structured as follows: In Sect. 2, we present related work. In Sect. 3, we present the methodology followed to improve indoor location estimation. In Sect. 4, we present testing and results. Finally, we provide conclusion and future work in Sect. 5.

## 2   Related Work

Several studies in literature have continuously attempted to address the issue of unstable RSSI measurements of the radio-map during the offline phase of the fingerprinting algorithm, to improve the performance of the ML algorithms deployed during the online phase. A little work was done to evaluate both the effect of the size of the radio map and corrected RSSI measurements on indoor localization model accuracy.

The authors in [11], examined the ability of the predictive model to induce based on different untrained dataset. The study utilized MATLAB to evaluate if the dataset size has an effect on the accuracy of the predictive model. The study discovered that the training dataset size should be good enough to represent the entire dataset. The author utilized three Neural Networks and the simulation results showed that the learning model produced the most accurate and stable results with the largest dataset.

Similarly, the authors in [9], examined the effect of medical domain dataset size on the performance of supervised Machine Learning algorithms. The authors used three datasets of different sizes to analyze the models performance with respect to accuracy, precision, recall, f-score, specificity and under the ROC curve (AUC). The study concluded that the success of a classifier depends on the dataset representation of the original observations rather than dataset size. Both studies in [9,11] evaluated the impact of the dataset size, however, the studies were not focusing on the hash indoor localization radio-map RSSI values. Our studies evaluate the impact of both radio-map size and the RSSI filtering mechanism.

In recent years, the Bluetooth and Wi-Fi localisation technologies gained a boost because of the evolution of smartphone devices with in-built sensors [12]. The authors in [13], developed a system for locating wireless nodes in a home environment requiring a single access point based on Wi-Fi. Wi-Fi requires that the area in which the devices are used have Access point. Received signal strength indicator was used as a sensor reading (RSSI). Bayesian filtering was used to compute location estimates based on sample sets derived by Monte Carlo sampling. The model proposed in [13] has similarities to the model proposed in [14]. The author in [14] exploited sensor fusion approach by combining the landmarks, Wi-Fi and Pedestrian Dead Reckoning (PDR). Their system runs fully on the smartphone in an effort to cut costs, then used the Kalman Filter to denoise the RSSI measurements. The landmark approach was introduced to overcome the error of initial positioning, which in turn improves the accuracy when predicting the walking directions. Nevertheless, the RSSI training dataset of the Fingerprinting algorithm remains vulnerable because of changes in the environmental conditions.

More research are rather focusing on dealing with the RSSI challenges because of the environmental conditions. Up to a certain extent, acceptable results have been achieved. The authors in [15] proposed a Wi-Fi integrated Device-free localisation (Dfl) system for intrusion detection of the human body. The system uses RSSI patterns generated when a person in motion passes through the system. All the generated RSSI measurements are therefore filtered using the Alpha Trim Mean Filter, which considers extreme high and extreme low RSSI as noise or outliers. The study in [16], has a different view because according to the authors, extremely high RSSI values represent almost the real value of RSSI.

The above mentioned studies have one thing in common, they are all attempting to close the gap that comes with the GPS-based localisation indoor. In attempting to close the gap, more attention was given to correction of measurements by filtering the RSSI errors. In this study, we focus on both the impact of the size of radio-map and corrected the RSSI measurements of the radio-map.

## 3    Methodology

In this section, we investigate the impact of the size of radio-map generated during the offline phase of the fingerprinting algorithm on the classification performance. In order to achieve this goal, we developed a system called EMPsys that was implemented following the fingerprinting algorithm. The EMPsys was developed using Java programming language on Android platform using Android Studio Integrated Development Environment (IDE) and XML for interface design. The EMPsys was used during experimentation to generate the radio-map during the offline phase. Three radio-maps of different sizes were used to examine the impact of increasing the size of radio-map on the performance of Machine learning algorithms used for location determination. Each radio map was filtered using the mean and standard deviation to evaluate both the radio-map size and filter impact. The performance of the classifiers is evaluated with respect to accuracy, precision and recall. In the following sub-sections, we discuss the system architecture and classification models.

### 3.1    System Architecture

The design of EMPsys is based on the fingerprinting algorithm. It is divided into two phases, the offline phase and the online phase. During offline phase the radio-map is generated by collection RSSI measurements together with the transmitter device's SSID and MAC Address at known locations and store the data in a real-time Firebase database. The radio-map is then filtered for outliers at each required point, by using the mean and standard deviation filtering approach.

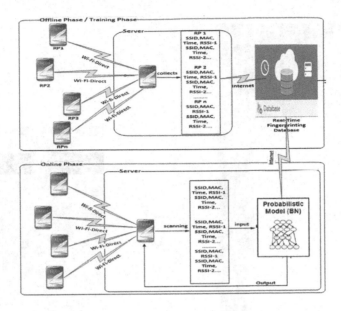

**Fig. 1.** System architecture [1]

All RSSI values found to be outliers are replaced with the mean value. These radio-map plays a major role during the online phase, because it is used for matching purposes by the prediction model. Machine learning algorithms such as the KNN, Naïve Bayes and decision trees are used during the online phase to localize transmitter devices at unknown locations. The system architecture is presented in Fig. 1.

### 3.2    Radio Map Generation

We therefore focus on the offline phase collection of the radio-map and correction of the RSSI measurements, and then evaluate the effect of its size on the classification algorithm to be utilized during the online phase as the radio-map size increases. In Fig. 2, Fig. 3, Fig. 4 and Fig. 5, we present the screenshots of the EMPsys application that is used to generate the radio-maps used in this study. We used the offline phase of the EMPsys as represented in the navigation bar of the application in Fig. 2. When the user clicks on the offline tap, the calibration interface is activated as presented in Fig. 3.

The user would therefore be required to click on Off button to start the calibration phase. During this process, the application checks if the receiver device Wi-Fi is enabled or not, if not, the application uses the WiFiManager library to switch the device Wi-Fi on. Then the calibration phase begins with the user prompted to specify the location of the transmitter device at known location to start gathering the radio-map dataset as illustrated in Fig. 4. The application therefore starts scanning for the RSSI, SSID and MAC Address of

**Fig. 2.** Offline phase

**Fig. 3.** Calibration interface

**Fig. 4.** Start radio-map generation

**Fig. 5.** Gathering radio-map dataset

the device that is broadcasting its signal at known location as presented in Fig. 4. The application keeps on scanning if it senses change in signal strength, otherwise, the user also has control to re-scan using the floating button.

### 3.3  Classification Algorithms

The radio-map is used by the location estimation algorithms such as the KNN [29], Decision Tree [30] and Naïve Bayes [31–33]. We looked into how these models localise and made comparisons.

   The **K-Nearest Neighbourhood (KNN)** is used to perform the classification by determining the distance between nodes [17]. When using the KNN algorithm, the coordinates of a location from a measured transmitters are acquired by averaging the values of the Euclidean distance of K required points [18]. A given weight determined by the difference between the true measurements and positioning points. When the average value of the Euclidean distance is calculated, the fingerprinting K data are weighted.

The KNN classifier follows the following steps:

1. Initialise the value of K,
2. Compute the distance the measured location and the true location,
3. Sort the distances,
4. Choose the top K nearest neighbors,
5. Apply simple majority and,
6. Estimate location with more neighbors from measured location.
7. The location estimate is returned by Eq. (1):

$$L(x,y) = \frac{\sum_{m=1}^{k} d_m}{\sum_{n=1}^{k} d_n}(x_m, y_m) \tag{1}$$

where:

- $L(x,y)$ is the coordinates of the measured location,
- $(x_m, y_m)$ is the coordinates of the m-th required point and,
- $d_m$ is the Euclidean distance between the RSSI readings at location $(x, y)$ and $(x_m, y_m)$.

The Euclidean distance $d_m$ is given by Eq. (2):

$$d_m = \sum_{m=1}^{k} \sqrt{(RSSI_{(x,y)} - RSSI_{(x_m, y_m)})^2} \tag{2}$$

   **A decision tree** is a non-parametric supervised learning method for classification and regression algorithms expressed as a recursive partition of the instance space [19]. It splits dataset into smaller subsets, while at the same time an associated decision tree is incrementally developed, and the results is a tree with decision notes [20]. For instance, in localisation, The RSSI and orientation are used in the internal node conditions, and the locations or required points are used in the leaf nodes [21]. Classification of data collected is performed by navigating the tree from the root down to the leaf, based on the outcome of the conditions [22]. The main goal of the decision trees is to deduce the suitable decision tree by reducing the error.

The **Bayesian Network** uses a probabilistic approach to localisation. It utilises the conditional probability and Bayesian inference to estimate the location of a device at unknown location. The Bayesian algorithms such as the Naïve Bayes classifier models the statistical distribution of signal strengths collected at each required point during the offline or training phase of the fingerprinting algorithm as a histogram. Then use it as a prior in a Bayesian framework, and use it to determine the probability of having a specific histogram of signal strengths at a new location using a Naïve Bayes algorithm [23]. For location estimation, the Naïve Bayes is given by Eq. (3):

$$p(L_i|RSSI_i) = \frac{p(L_i).p(RSSI_i|L_i)}{\sum_{i=1}^{n} p(L_n).p(RSSI_i|L_n)} \tag{3}$$

where:

- $L_i$ is the location to be estimated,
- $RSSI_i$ is the recent received RSSI at an unknown location i,
- $p(L_i)$ is the prior probability of location $i$,
- $p(RSSI_i \mid L_i)$ is the likelihood function and,
- $p(L_i \mid RSSI_i)$ is the posterior function or conditional probability.

Using Eq. (3), the conditional probability at $L_i$ computed for fingerprints and the location corresponding to the maximum likelihood is chosen as the best matching location of the device at unknown location.

In Table 1, we provide a comparison of these location estimation models.

Table 1. Comparison of machine learning algorithms

| Algorithm | Advantages | Limitations |
| --- | --- | --- |
| KNN | No Training Period (It does nor learn anything in the training period). | Does not work well with large dataset and sensitive to noisy data, sing values and outliers [24] |
| Decision Tree | Requires less effort for data preparation and produce accurate result [25]. Missing values do not affect the process of building a decision tree [26] | A small change in the data can cause large change in the structure of the decision tree causing instability. Can be computationally expensive. |
| Naïve Bayes | It requires short computational time for training. It improves the classification time by removing the irrelevant features [27] | Requires very large number of records to obtain good results. |

## 4    Experimentation and Results

The datasets or radio-maps used in this study are of different sizes. The datasets increase in each EMPsys data collection experimentation and, simulations are performed in MATLAB. The classification models are constructed based on the size of the radio-maps generated in each scenario generated during the offline phase of the Fingerprinting algorithm, with known target outputs. The data collection experiments were performed in an indoor environment with a dimension of 9 m × 10 m. The building has five rooms named Room 1, Room 2, Room 3, Room 4 and Room 5, which are our points of data collection during the offline phase and the target outputs during the online phase. The experimental environment is presented in Fig. 6.

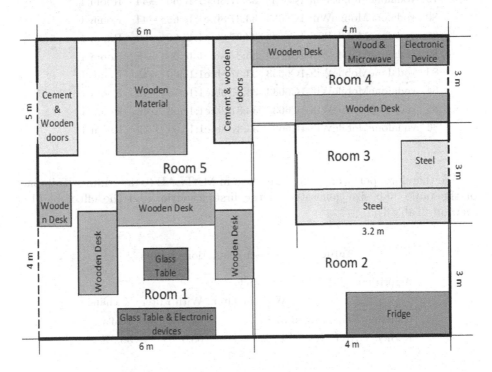

**Fig. 6.** The experimental environment

**Scenario 1:** In the first data collection experiment, 15 points were selected at each room and six measurements from each point were collected from the transmitter device used for data collection. A total of 90 measurements were taken from each room. The radio-map size for the first experiment was 453 observations. A sample of the measurements collected from room 1 is shown in Table 2.

**Table 2.** Comparison of machine learning algorithms

| ID | SSID | MacAddress | RSSI | RequirePoint |
|----|------|------------|------|--------------|
| 71 | vodafoneMobileWifi-1C6633 | 33:37:8b:c1:1c:66 | −56 | Room 1 |
| 72 | vodafoneMobileWifi-1C6633 | 33:37:8b:c1:1c:66 | −46 | Room 1 |
| 73 | vodafoneMobileWifi-1C6633 | 33:37:8b:c1:1c:66 | −45 | Room 1 |
| 74 | vodafoneMobileWifi-1C6633 | 33:37:8b:c1:1c:66 | −44 | Room 1 |
| 75 | vodafoneMobileWifi-1C6633 | 33:37:8b:c1:1c:66 | −44 | Room 1 |
| 76 | vodafoneMobileWifi-1C6633 | 33:37:8b:c1:1c:66 | −46 | Room 1 |
| 77 | vodafoneMobileWifi-1C6633 | 33:37:8b:c1:1c:66 | −46 | Room 1 |
| 78 | vodafoneMobileWifi-1C6633 | 33:37:8b:c1:1c:66 | −45 | Room 1 |
| 79 | vodafoneMobileWifi-1C6633 | 33:37:8b:c1:1c:66 | −44 | Room 1 |
| 80 | vodafoneMobileWifi-1C6633 | 33:37:8b:c1:1c:66 | −44 | Room 1 |
| 81 | vodafoneMobileWifi-1C6633 | 33:37:8b:c1:1c:66 | −50 | Room 1 |
| 82 | vodafoneMobileWifi-1C6633 | 33:37:8b:c1:1c:66 | −48 | Room 1 |
| 83 | vodafoneMobileWifi-1C6633 | 33:37:8b:c1:1c:66 | −48 | Room 1 |
| 84 | vodafoneMobileWifi-1C6633 | 33:37:8b:c1:1c:66 | −48 | Room 1 |
| 85 | vodafoneMobileWifi-1C6633 | 33:37:8b:c1:1c:66 | −48 | Room 1 |
| 86 | vodafoneMobileWifi-1C6633 | 33:37:8b:c1:1c:66 | −35 | Room 1 |

We therefore, performed the simulation in MATLAB to determine the impact of the radio-map size generated in the first scenario, and the effect of filter method (Table 3).

**Table 3.** Scenario 1 simulations results

| Algorithm | Accuracy | | |
|-----------|----------|--|--|
| | Without filter | With Filter | % change |
| Gaussian Naïve Bayes | 37.8 % | 64.4 % | 70.4% |
| Kernel Naïve Bayes | 44 % | 68.9 % | 56.6% |

The simulation result of the first scenario with dataset of size 453 observations shows that the accuracy result of the Gaussian and Kernel have both improved with filter feature. The Kernel Naïve Bayes classifier out-performed the Gaussian Naïve Bayes classifier with 68.9%. However, at this stage we observed that the percentage change was high for the Gaussian Naïve Bayes with 70.4%, which shows that the filter was more effective for the Gaussian Nave Bayes classifier.

**Scenario 2:** In the second data collection experiment, the number of points remained at 15 at each room, however, the measurements taken at each point has increased by 66.67% from 6 measurements at a point in the first scenario to additional 4 measurement to make 10 measurements per point. A total of 150 measurements were taken from each room. Therefore, the size of the radio-map was 753 observations (Table 4).

**Table 4.** Scenario 2 simulations results

| Algorithm | Accuracy | | |
|---|---|---|---|
| | Without filter | With Filter | % change |
| Gaussian Naïve Bayes | 50.7 % | 70.7 % | 39.4% |
| Kernel Naïve Bayes | 53.3 % | 76.0 % | 42.6% |

At the second scenario results with a radio-map of size 753 observations, we observed that both percentage change and the model accuracy favoured the Kernel Naïve Bayes Classifier with 42.6% percentage increase and 76.0% accuracy with filter. The model accuracy also improved in accuracy from 68.9% to 76.0% with the Kernel Naïve Bayes Classifier from the radio-map size 453 to 753 observations. At this stage, we observed that both the radio-map size and the filter have an impact on the predictive model accuracy.

**Scenario 3:** In the third data collection experiment, the number of points remained unchanged. The number of measurements collected from each point increased from 10 measurements in the second scenario to 14 measurements with a percentage increase of 40%. At this point of the experimentation, 211 measurements were taken from each room, to give a radio-map with 1054 observations size (Table 5).

**Table 5.** Scenario 3 simulations results

| Algorithm | Accuracy | | |
|---|---|---|---|
| | Without filter | With Filter | % change |
| Gaussian Naïve Bayse | 45.7 % | 79.0 % | 72.9% |
| Kernel Naïve Bayse | 49.5 % | 95.2 % | 92.3% |

During the third and final simulation results with a radio-map of size 1054 observations, we observed that the Kernel Naïve Bayes outperforms the Gaussian Naïve Bayes with an accuracy of 95.2% to 72.9%. The accuracy of the Kernel Naïve Bayes with filter also increased from scenario 1, 2 and 3 from 68.9%, 76.0% and 95.2%, which shows that the predictive model depends on both the radio-map size and the filtering mechanism, because the results without a filter are too low in all three scenarios with different radio-maps to achieve the goal of IPS that its model should be accurate.

We further applied the radio-map generated in scenario 3 on different filtering methods and different classifiers in Fig. 7.

The classifiers used in Fig. 7, exhibited different reaction on radio-map of size 1054 observation based on different filters used. The result shows that the accuracy of a localisation model is affected by both the radio-map size and the filtering mechanism. Our proposed filter and the Median (+-3) filter mechanisms performed well with the radio-map of size 1054 observations. It is notable that our proposed method with the kernel Naïve Bayes and the Fine Decision Tree are most effective. Lastly, the moving average filter and exponential smoothing results were not effective in correction of RSSI measurements and thus resulted in poor performance on the predictive models with the radio-map of size 1054 observations.

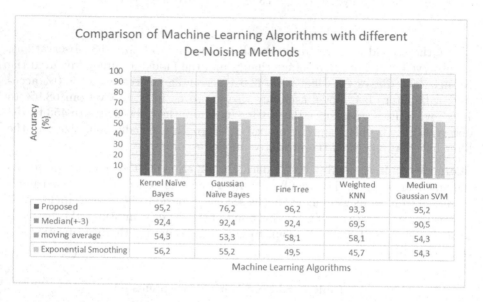

**Fig. 7.** Effect of different filters using radio-map size 1054 on ML accuracy

Finally, we made comparison with Dataset generated by another study in Table 6.

**Table 6.** Comparison with dataset generated by another study.

|  | Our study dataset | Dataset used in [28] |
|---|---|---|
| Radio-Map size | 1054 | 56099 |
| Kernel Naïve Bayes Accuracy with Filter | 95.4% | 94.5% |
| McConville et.al [28] | N/A | 92% |

Interestingly, we made a comparison between our study with a radio-map of 1054 observations and the radio-map generated by a study in [28], and we observed a percentage decrease 0.9% in the Kernel Naïve Bayes Accuracy with Filter, which indicates that there is a very low difference in the model's accuracy between the two datasets. We also observe the Kernel Naïve Bayes Accuracy with Filter outperformed the model used in [28], with 94.5% to 92% respectively. We, therefore, conclude that up to a certain extent that both the size of the radio map and the filter method have an effect on the accuracy of the classification.

# 5  Conclusion

In recent years, indoor positioning systems have attracted attention, with an effort to close the GPS gap indoor and localize objects or human beings holding devices. The Fingerprinting algorithm is being used because of its cost-effective mechanism. Nevertheless, the Fingerprinting algorithms utilized ML algorithms during its online phase to localize and these ML models performance eminently depend on the radio-map. In this study, we investigated both the impact of the size of the radio-map and the effect of the RSSI filtering method on the performance on classification models. We developed a system called the EMPsys that we utilized to generate the radio-maps used to evaluate the effect on classification algorithms. The data scenarios were divided into three radio-maps of different sizes. We observed that the accuracy of the Kernel Naïve Bayes significantly improved with filter as the radio-map size increases, from 64.4% with 453 observation in the first scenario to 95.4% with 1054 observations in the third scenario. We, therefore, conclude that the performance of the classifier to be used during the online phase of the fingerprinting algorithm relies on both the size of the radio-map and the filtering method used to correct the RSSI measurements of the radio-map.

In future, we seek to investigate what constitute radio-map to be too small or too large in order for a classifier to maximize its performance.

**Acknowledgements.** The authors would like to thank Tshwane University of Technology and University of the Free State for financial support. The authors declare that there is no conflict of interest regarding the publication of this paper.

# References

1. Sediela, M.S., Gadebe, M.L., Kogeda, O.P.: Indoor localization with filtered and corrected calibration RSSI. In: Zitouni, R., Phokeer, A., Chavula, J., Elmokashfi, A., Gueye, A., Benamar, N. (eds.) AFRICOMM 2020. LNICST, vol. 361, pp. 59–73. Springer, Cham (2021). https://doi.org/10.1007/978-3-030-70572-5_4
2. Qiao, W., Kang, X., Li, M.: An improved XGBoost indoor localization algorithm. DEStech Trans. Comput. Sci. Eng. cisnr (2020)
3. Owuor, D.L., Kogeda, O.P., Agbinya, J.I.: Three tier indoor localization system for digital forensics. Int. J. Electr. Comput. Energetic Electron. Commun. Eng. **11**(6), 602–610 (2017)

4. Khan, M., Kai, Y.D., Gul, H.U.: Indoor Wi-Fi positioning algorithm based on combination of Location Fingerprint and Unscented Kalman Filter. In: 2017 14th International Bhurban Conference on Applied Sciences and Technology (IBCAST), pp. 693–698. IEEE (2017)

5. Li, S., Rashidzadeh, R.: Hybrid indoor location positioning system. IET Wirel. Sensor Syst. **9**(5), 257–264 (2019)

6. Zhou, Z., Yang, Z., Wu, C., Sun, W., Liu, Y.: LiFi: Line-of-sight identification with WiFi. In: 2014 Proceedings IEEE INFOCOM, pp. 2688–2696. IEEE (2014)

7. Oksar, I.: A Bluetooth signal strength based indoor localization method. In: 2014 International Conference on Systems, Signals and Image Processing (IWSSIP), pp. 251–254. IEEE (2014)

8. Huh, J.-H., Seo, K.: An indoor location-based control system using bluetooth beacons for IoT systems. Sensors **17**(12), 2917 (2017)

9. Althnian, A., et al.: Impact of dataset size on classification performance: an empirical evaluation in the medical domain. Appl. Sci. **11**(2), 796 (2021)

10. Rácz, A., Bajusz, D., Héberger, K.: Effect of dataset size and train/test split ratios in QSAR/QSPR multiclass classification. Molecules **26**(4), 1111 (2021)

11. Ajiboye, A., Abdullah-Arshah, R., Hongwu, Q.: Evaluating the effect of dataset size on predictive model using supervised learning technique (2015)

12. Roy, P., Chowdhury, C.: A survey of machine learning techniques for indoor localization and navigation systems. J. Intell. Robot. Syst. **101**(3), 1–34 (2021). https://doi.org/10.1007/s10846-021-01327-z

13. Zàruba, G.V., Huber, M., Kamangar, F., Chlamtac, I.: Indoor location tracking using RSSI readings from a single Wi-Fi access point. Wireless Netw. **13**(2), 221–235 (2007)

14. Chen, Z., Zou, H., Jiang, H., Zhu, Q., Soh, Y.C., Xie, L.: Fusion of WiFi, smartphone sensors and landmarks using the Kalman filter for indoor localization. Sensors **15**(1), 715–732 (2015)

15. Pirzada, N., Nayan, M.Y., Hassan, M.F., Subhan, F.: Multipath fading in device-free indoor localization system: measurements and interpretation. Mehran Univ. Res. J. Eng. Technol. **34**, no. S1 (2015)

16. Xue, W., Qiu, W., Hua, X., Yu, K.: Improved Wi-Fi RSSI measurement for indoor localization. IEEE Sens. J. **17**(7), 2224–2230 (2017)

17. Bahl, P., Padmanabhan, V.N.: RADAR: an in-building RF-based user location and tracking system. In: Proceedings IEEE INFOCOM 2000. Conference on Computer Communications. Nineteenth Annual Joint Conference of the IEEE Computer and Communications Societies (Cat. No. 00CH37064), vol. 2, pp. 775–784. IEEE (2000)

18. Zhu, X.: Indoor localization based on optimized KNN. Network Commun. Technol. **5**(2), 1–34 (2021)

19. Cleophas, T.J., Zwinderman, A.H.: Decision Trees. In: Machine Learning in Medicine, pp. 137–150. Springer, Dordrecht (2013). https://doi.org/10.1007/978-94-007-7869-6_14

20. Seçkin, A.Ç., Coçkun, A.: Hierarchical fusion of machine learning algorithms in indoor positioning and localization. Appl. Sci. **9**(18), 3665 (2019)

21. Sánchez-Rodríguez, D., Hernández-Morera, P., Quinteiro, J.M., Alonso-González, I.: A low complexity system based on multiple weighted decision trees for indoor localization. Sensors **15**(6), 14809–14829 (2015)

22. Maimon, O., Rokach, L.: Data mining and knowledge discovery handbook (2005)

23. Mirowski, P., Milioris, D., Whiting, P., Ho, T.K.: Probabilistic radio-frequency fingerprinting and localization on the run. Bell Labs Tech. J. **18**(4), 111–133 (2014)

24. Mohamed, A.E.: Comparative study of four supervised machine learning techniques for classification. Inf. J. Appl. Sci. Technol. **7**(2) (2017)

25. Archana, S., Elangovan, K.: Survey of classification techniques in data mining. Int. J. Comput. Sci. Mob. Appl. **2**(2), 65–71 (2014)

26. Dhiraj, K.: Top 5 advantages and disadvantages of Decision Tree Algorithm. ed (2020)

27. Jadhav, S.D., Channe, H.: Comparative study of K-NN, naive Bayes and decision tree classification techniques. Int. J. Sci. Res. (IJSR) **5**(1), 1842–1845 (2016)

28. McConville, R., Byrne, D., Craddock, I., Piechocki, R., Pope, J., Santos-Rodriguez, R.: Understanding the quality of calibrations for indoor localisation. In: 2018 IEEE 4th World Forum on Internet of Things (WF-IoT), pp. 676–681. IEEE (2018)

29. Guo, G., Wang, H., Bell, D., Bi, Y., Greer, K.: KNN model-based approach in classification. In: Meersman, R., Tari, Z., Schmidt, D.C. (eds.) On The Move to Meaningful Internet Systems 2003: CoopIS, DOA, and ODBASE. OTM 2003. LNCS, vol. 2888. Springer, Heidelberg. https://doi.org/10.1007/978-3-540-39964-3-62

30. Brijain, R., Patel, R., Kushik, M.R., Rana. K.: A survey on decision tree algorithm for classification (2014)

31. Huang, Y., Li, L.: Naive Bayes classification algorithm based on small sample set. In: IEEE International Conference on Cloud Computing and Intelligence Systems 2011, pp. 34–39 (2011). https://doi.org/10.1109/CCIS.2011.6045027

32. Ssengonzi, C., Kogeda, O.P., Olwal, T.O.: A survey of deep reinforcement learning application in 5G and beyond network slicing and virtualization. Elsevier: Array **14**, 100142 (2022). https://doi.org/10.1016/j.array.2022.100142. https://www.sciencedirect.com/science/article/pii/S2590005622000133. ISSN 2590-0056

33. Gadebe, M.L., Kogeda, O.P., Ojo, S.: A Smartphone Naïve Bayes Human Activity Recognition using Personalized dataset. J. Adv. Comput. Intell. Intell. Inf. **24**(5), 685–702 (2020). https://doi.org/10.20965/jaciii.2020.p0685. https://www.fujipress.jp/jaciii/jc/jaciii002400050685/. ISBN: 1343-0130/1883-8014

# A Deep Learning Model for Mammography Mass Detection Using Mosaic and Reconstructed Multichannel Images

Nada M. Hassan[1]([⊠]) [iD], Safwat Hamad[2], and Khaled Mahar[3]

[1] College of Computing and Information Technology, Arab Academy for Science and Technology, Cairo, Egypt
nadamahmoud@aast.edu
[2] Faculty of Computer and Information Sciences, Ain Shams University, Cairo, Egypt
[3] College of Computing and Information Technology, Arab Academy for Science and Technology, Alexandria, Egypt

**Abstract.** Breast cancer is the most publicized cancer that hits women around the world. It's considered as the second cause of death among females. Early detection helps a lot in increasing the survival rate, and the probability of recovery from this disease. The mammogram is the main screening modality that is used regularly for breast cancer diagnosis. The accurate interpretation of the mammogram is very important for mass detection and diagnosis. The rapid evolution of deep learning is contributing to introduce more accurate systems that can act as a second opinion for the radiologists, and accordingly, this can help in providing an accurate diagnosis. In this paper, we propose a model for mass detection and classification based on You Look Only Once (YOLO)v4. We designed the experiment to investigate the performance of different augmentation techniques using YOLOv4 including mosaic that was introduced by YOLOv4. Furthermore, in the preprocessing phase, the images were reconstructed to be in a multichannel format which enhanced the detection accuracy by almost $\simeq 10\%$. The model was evaluated with the usage of different combinations of augmentation techniques (mosaic, mix-up, and conventional augmentation). The experiments were conducted on the INbreast and MIAS datasets, the results of INbreast showed that mosaic with YOLOv4 achieved the best results with mAP (mean average precision), precession, and recall of almost $\simeq 99.5\%$, 98%, and 94% respectively for detection. In addition, the proposed model achieved AP of 99.16% and 99.58% for classifying the detected masses as benign and malignant respectively. Furthermore, the best results on MIAS achieved mAP, precession, and recall of 95.28%, 93%, and 90% respectively. Finally, our methodology showed competitive performance compared to other similar studies.

**Keywords:** Mammogram · Mass detection · CAD system · INbreast · YOLOv4 · Mosaic

O. Gervasi et al. (Eds.): ICCSA 2022, LNCS 13375, pp. 544–559, 2022.
https://doi.org/10.1007/978-3-031-10522-7_37

# 1 Introduction

According to the Global Observatory Cancer (GLOBOCAN) estimates for 2020 [1], breast cancer is the most diagnosed cancer with 2.3 million new cases which represents 11.7% of the whole newly diagnosed cancer cases. It's considered as the first cancer type that causes death with 15.5% of the whole deaths from cancer among the females in the world. The clinical studies proved that the early detection of breast cancer can enhance the survival rate [2] and increase the chances of early recovery from this cancer type. Mammogram is one of the screening modalities that is mostly used as a regular screening tool and for early breast cancer diagnosis. It provides to some extent a good quality image that is produced through a low dose of x-rays.

The accurate diagnosis mainly needs a well-experienced radiologist, however, with a large number of cases that need examination this can lead to the wrong diagnosis. Recently, clinical trials proved that the Computer-Aided (Detection/Diagnosis) CAD systems can act as a second opinion for radiologists, and also it can be used to reduce the efforts of the manual annotation of the mammographic images. The importance of the existence of such systems that can perform accurately in detecting the masses, especially the small ones is increasing. The deep learning-based object detection models showed substantial success in achieving high accuracy with good computational power.

YOLO [3] is considered as the state of art model among the deep learning-based object detection models, as it surpassed other models such as the regional-based Convolutional Neural Network (RCNN) and Single Shot multi-box Detector (SSD) with competing performance at both accuracy and speed. There are four versions of YOLO which are YOLO v1 [3], YOLO v2 [4], YOLOv3 [5] and the recent one is YOLOv4 [6] which has many enhancements that affect positively in terms of accuracy. YOLOv4 enhanced the average precision by almost 10% more than YOLOv3 on the benchmark dataset Microsoft Common Objects in Context (MS COCO).

In this work, the model is designed for mass detection and classification based on YOLOv4. The paper aims to investigate the impact of the newly introduced augmentation techniques mosaic and mix-up on detecting the masses in the mammographic images and how these techniques will affect the performance of the model. Furthermore, the effect of converting the images into multichannel images on the performance of the model was investigated.

The main contribution of this paper can be summarized as the following:

1. Enhance the appearance of the breast masses and tissues by reconstructing the mammographic images into multi-channel-colored images.
2. Evaluate the impact of enhancing the appearance of the breast masses and tissues on the performance of the YOLOv4 on mammographic images.
3. Utilizing and evaluating the impact of using Mosaic and Mix-up with conventional augmentations and with different combinations.
4. Evaluate the generalization of the model with unseen images from other datasets that were obtained from different scanners.

The paper is organized as the following; Sect. 2 presents the related work, then Sect. 3 gives an overview of the used methods in this research including the used dataset in the experiments and the implementation details. Then Sect. 4 presents the experimental results and provides a discussion of these results. Finally, Sect. 5 contains the conclusion and directions for future work.

## 2  Related Work

In the last few years, efforts increased towards developing more accurate CAD systems that can be used clinically. The leap that occurred in the object detection and the computer vision fields due to the appearance of deep learning and transfer learning contributes hugely to introducing more reliable systems.

The main advantage of deep learning is the automated extraction of the features that the network learned through training. Furthermore, transfer learning helped a lot to overcome the problem of the need for large datasets for deep learning, in addition, it reduces the training time.

Researchers are still exploiting the benefits of deep learning and transfer learning with medical images to introduce reliable CAD systems. In [7], Al-antari et al. introduced a breast cancer CAD system based on YOLO to detect the masses in mammograms. Their proposed system was fully automated in the phases of mass detection, segmentation, and classification. YOLO was used to both detect and localize the masses; Full Resolution Convolutional Network (FRCN) was used to segment the detected masses and finally, these segmented masses were classified into benign and malignant through a pre-trained CNN with AlexNet architecture. Their experiment was conducted on the INbreast dataset and their model achieved an accuracy of 98.96% for detection, 92.97% for segmentation, and 95.64% for classification. Moreover, in [8], they modified the segmentation and classification phases in the same model they introduced in [7]. The model achieved an accuracy of 97.27%, and 92.97% for detection and segmentation respectively. For classification, they used InceptionResNet-V2 with an average overall accuracy of 95.32%.

Ribli et al. [9] introduced a model based on Regional Convolutional Network R-CNN for localizing the masses and classifying them. They investigated the impact of the different resolutions on the performance of the model, their experiments proved that the higher resolution images give better results. The model detected almost 90% of the malignant masses in the INbreast dataset and achieved an AUC of 95% for classification.

In [10], Agarwal et al. proposed a CAD system based on Faster R-CNN for mass detection and classification. They conducted their experiments on three datasets INbreast, OPTIMAM, and private dataset. Their model achieved sensitivity ranging from 95% to 71% and a specificity of 70% for detection. In their work, they used images that were obtained from different scanners.

Peng et al. [11] modified the backbone of the Faster R-CNN model; they used a multiscale feature pyramid network between the output layers of the backbone, this modification was mainly done to enhance the small mass detection in their experiments. Their model achieved a True Positive Rate (TPR) of 0.934 for CBIS-DDSM and o.955 for INbreast datasets.

These reviewed researches utilized various deep learning-based object detection models in their introduced models for mammographic mass detection and classification and these approaches achieved promising results. However, the majority of these researches didn't focus too much on enhancing the quality of the images themselves before the training. Furthermore, the detection of the small masses and the detection of the masses generally within the dense breast tissues are still considered as open challenges [12]. This paper mainly contributes to addressing these problems by firstly enhancing the visibility of the breast tissues in the mammographic image by reconstructing the images in a multichannel format. Accordingly, this can increase the discriminant features the model can learn. Secondly, utilizing a new augmentation technique named mosaic increased the complexity of the model at the training phase and improved the model's ability at detecting masses at smaller and different scales.

## 3 Methodology and Background

In this work, YOLOv4 has been used for mass detection and classification in mammogram images. Also, the mosaic and mix-up data augmentation techniques were used to investigate their effects on the detection of the existing masses in the breast.

### 3.1 Background

**You Look Only Once (YOLO).** YOLO works through a single neural network trained in an End-to-End fashion which takes an image as input in a single shot and predicts bounding boxes and class labels for each bounding box directly. The YOLO algorithm splits the input image into ($s \times s$) grid cells. The cell is considered to be responsible for detecting an object if the center of this object falls in this cell. Each cell predicts the location of a fixed number of bounding boxes as well as their Confidence Score. The coordinates of the bounding box are represented by 4 values (x, y, w, h) where x and y are representing the center point of the box. On the other hand, the confidence score is calculated as shown in Eq. (1), where the Intersection over Union IoU is representing the overlapped area between the predicted bounding box and the ground truth. If the box contains an object, it predicts a probability of this object belonging to every class Ci, where i = 1,..., K as K represents the number of the classes in the dataset which is 2 in our experiments. The output for each bounding box is represented by a vector composed of the bounding box coordinates and the probability of the class that the object belongs to.

$$Confidence\ score = prob(containing\ an\ object) \times IoU\ (predicted\ bb,\ ground\ truth) \tag{1}$$

The basic building block of the YOLO detector family is composed of three parts; backbone, neck, and head. The backbone extracts the feature maps from the input image and this part can be VGG16, ResNet-50, SpineNet, EffecientNet-B0/B7, CSPResNeXt50, or CSPDarknet53 which is recommended in the paper of YOLOv4 [6] based on many experiments. The neck is responsible for enhancing the feature discriminability and robustness via adding extra layers between the backbone and the head to enrich the information that feeds into the head. Finally, the head which is also named dense prediction is mainly responsible for locating the bounding boxes and classifying the objects inside these boxes.

YOLOv4 utilizes the Cross Stage Partial (CSP) connections with the Darknet-53 as a backbone for feature extraction. While in the neck they used a modified Path Aggregation Network (PAN) [13], a modified Spatial Attention Module (SAM) [14], and Spatial Pyramid Pooling (SPP) [15]. In addition, they introduced in YOLOv4 bag of freebies and a bag of specials that are used for the backbone and the detector to enhance the performance of the network. Figure 1 illustrates the architecture of YOLOv4.

In this work, the new data augmentation technique that was introduced in YOLOv4 which is called Mosaic was used, in addition to Mix-up data augmentation to investigate how these techniques can affect the performance of the model at detecting the masses in the mammograms and classifying them into benign and malignant. Also, the CSPDarknet53 was used as a backbone for extracting the discriminant features from the input mammogram images to detect two types of masses benign and malignant.

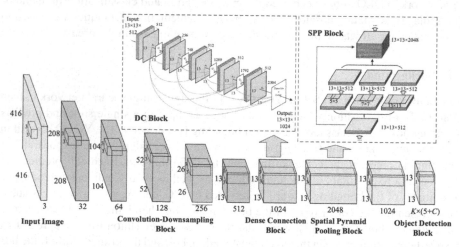

**Fig. 1.** YOLOv4 architecture [16]

**Mosaic Data Augmentation.** In this paper, mosaic augmentation was used to increase the size of the training set, in addition to gaining the benefit from this technique in identifying the small masses. Mosaic is one of the newest techniques for data augmentation which was introduced in [6]. The idea behind this algorithm is to combine four of the training images into one image with the original size of the single image, so the objects in each image of the four are appearing on a smaller scale. Accordingly, this augmentation technique can enhance the performance of the model in identifying the objects at small scales. Furthermore, with this technique, there's no need for a large mini-batch size through training. The algorithm mainly depends on locating the four corners of the image (the upper left, upper right, lower left, and lower right) to apply the processing of the data augmentation respectively on the four corners. This approach increases the learning ability of the model four times of learning the original image; and accordingly, that enhances the performance of the model.

**Mix-up Data Augmentation.** In addition to the Mosaic, we used the Mix-up augmentation technique which was introduced in 2018 [17]. Mix-up blends the features of two images in one image with their corresponding labels from the training set. The mix-up algorithm can be represented in the following formula:

$$\hat{x} = \lambda x_i + (1 - \lambda)x_j \tag{2}$$

$$\hat{y} = \lambda y_i + (1 - \lambda)y_j \tag{3}$$

In Eq. (2) $x_i$ and $x_j$ are the raw input vectors of the images while $y_i$ and $y_j$ in Eq. (3) represent the one hot-encoders for the labels of these images. These pairs $(x_i, y_i)$ and $(x_j, y_j)$ are randomly selected from the training set. Accordingly, from Eqs. (2) and (3), it can be said that Mix-up expands the training distribution by factoring in the prior knowledge that linear interpolations of feature vectors should result in linear interpolations of the targets.

### 3.2 Implementation

**Dataset.** The experiments were done using three different datasets INbreast, MIAS, and CBIS-DDSM.

*INbreast.* The dataset [18] contains 410 mammograms for 115 cases and 90 cases were diagnosed with cancer. The dataset images were acquired using Siemens MammoNovatio scanner which provided Full Field Digital Mammograms (FFDM) that have high quality than the Digital Mammogram (DM), the dataset includes different breast abnormalities. The dataset has 107 mammograms containing masses (benign and malignant) which were used in the experiments. In the experiments that were done in this work, the masses that have BI-RADS scores of 1, 2, and 3 were considered benign, while the ones that have a score of 4, 5, and 6 were considered malignant. The images are provided in DICOM format, also the dataset contains images in both views Medio Lateral Oblique (MLO) and Carnio Caudal (CC) view.

*MIAS.* MIAS [19] is a mammographic dataset that is composed of 322 mammography images in Portable Gray Map (PGM) format. The dataset contains only images with MLO view only; the images are at 50-micron resolution. The type of the images is Screening Film Mammography (SFM), and the ground truth data are associated with the dataset. Different abnormalities are included in the dataset in addition to normal images; 55 images with masses were used from this dataset in the experiments.

*CBIS_DDSM.* Some images were used in the experiments from the Curated Breast Images Subset of Digital Database for Screening Mammography (CBIS_DDSM) [20]. The dataset contains 10239 images for 1566 patients with images containing a total of 1696 tumors. However, the dataset is considered as the largest publicly available mammographic dataset, the quality of the images isn't good as these images are in DM format. The dataset includes both views MLO and CC, all the images are in the DICOM format. The ROIs are provided with the dataset in addition to CSV files that describes the pathological information for the patients. The images of this dataset were obtained from four different scanners DBA, LUMISYS, and HOWTEK (A/D).

**Data Preprocessing and Augmentation.** The images were converted from DICOM to JPEG in INbreast and from PMG to JPEG, then these images were scaled into 8 bits. The images were cropped to extract the breast region and accordingly minimize the area of the background; so, the Gaussian filter and Otsu's thresholding [21, 22]were used. After that, the images were normalized to normalize the pixels intensity distribution of the ROI of the breast region to be in the range of (0–255). The Contrast Limited Adaptive Histogram Equalization (CLAHE) [23]was applied at two different clip limits. CLAHE is an improved version of the Adaptive Histogram Equalization (AHE), and this technique aims to decrease the amplified noise by distributing equally the histogram part that surpass the clip limit.

The mammography images are considered as grayscale images that consist of black, white and shades of gray and this make these images challenging at learning their features, however, the edges and the texture features are affecting hugely the mass identification. Accordingly, to enhance the mass appearance in the mammogram and the contrast of the breast region, a new multi-channel image for the mammographic image was reconstructed by merging three single-channel images which are (normalized, and the other two images after CLAHE). This step enhanced the appearance of the masses and the breast tissues as shown in Fig. 2.

Due to the small size of the INbreast and MIAS datasets, traditional data augmentation techniques were applied on both training and testing sets to increase the size of the dataset by augmenting the original images with processed ones using operations of (blur, random brightness contrast, shift scale rotation, random rotate, transpose, multiplicative noise, and vertical flip) as shown in Fig. 3. The INbreast dataset increased to be 801 mammographic images and MIAS became 382 images after this step.

The mosaic and mix-up augmentation techniques were applied only on the training dataset through enabling them in the network settings to investigate their impact on the performance of the model in detecting the masses. Figure 4 shows samples for the mosaic augmentation on the INbreast mammographic images.

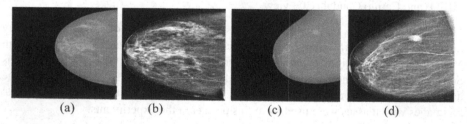

(a)              (b)                    (c)                    (d)

**Fig. 2.** Images from INbreast before preprocessing (a,c) and after preprocessing (b,d).

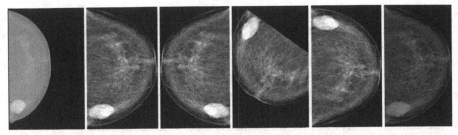

**Fig. 3.** A mammogram from INbreast before and after preprocessing in addition to samples of its corresponding images after applying conventional data augmentation techniques (flipping, brightness, and rotation).

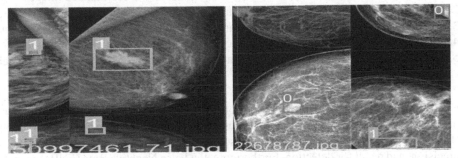

**Fig. 4.** Images from INbreast with mosaic data augmentation with annotations where 0 refers to benign and 1 to malignant.

**Implementation Environment.** The experiments were done on a workstation with an Intel® Core i7-11700k processor with 32 GB RAM, 3.200 GHz frequency, and NVIDIA GeForce RTX 3080Ti GPU with 12 vRAM. The proposed CAD system was implemented using C++ and Python 3.8 on the Windows 10 operating system.

**Implementation Design.** The images were split randomly into a training set and testing set with a ratio of 80%–20% respectively. The experiment was designed to evaluate the effectiveness of the multichannel images on the detection performance. In addition, it evaluated the performance of the mosaic and the mix-up augmentation techniques using the YOLOv4 network to investigate the impact of using such techniques on detecting the masses and classifying them into benign and malignant.

Some parameters have to be settled for the Yolov4 network, the value of these parameters is changed based on the domain and the used dataset in the experiment. For this work these parameters have been set as the following for both datasets INbreast and MIAS:

- The input image size for the network is 416 x 416.
- The number of classes is 2 which represents benign and malignant.
- Learning Rate (LR) is 0.001 based on different experiments that show that this value gives better results.

- The Scales that were used in the experiments to change the value of the LR are 0.1,0.1.
- The steps that represent the number of iterations and act as checkpoints for applying the scales on the learning rate, were set to 3200, and 3600 respectively. This means that the LR will be adjusted by multiplying its value by 0.1 after 3200 batches and multiplying it again by 0.1 after 3600 batches.
- Max_batches (number of iterations) was set to 4000 based on the equation mentioned in [3] (number of classes x 2000).
- The number of filters was set to 21 which is set to (number of classes + 5) × 3

The experiments were done over the following combinations:

1. YOLOv4 + Conventional Machine Learning + Mosaic + Normalized images
2. YOLOv4 + Conventional Machine Learning + Mosaic + Multichannel images
3. YOLOv4 + Conventional Machine Learning + Multichannel images
4. YOLOv4 + Conventional Machine Learning + Mixup + Multichannel images
5. YOLOv4 + Conventional Machine Learning + Mosaic + Mixup + Multichannel images

**Evaluation Metrics.** In this work, the performance of the model in the conducted experiments was evaluated through various metrics. These metrics are Intersection over Union (IoU), mean Average Precision (mAP), F1-score, True Positive (TP), False Positive (FP) precision, and recall for detection. Furthermore, the False Negative Rate (FNR) was calculated for mass detection according to Eq. (4) because of its importance in diagnosing diseases. For classification, the Average Precision (AP), TP, and FP were used.

$$FNR = \frac{False\ Negative}{True\ Positive + False\ Negative} \tag{4}$$

The mAP is calculated to evaluate the model accuracy for a set of object detections compared to its ground truth annotations. It's mainly calculated based on taking the average of the Average Precision (AP) for each class (benign and malignant).

$$mAp = \frac{1}{N} \sum_{i=1}^{N} (AP)_i, \text{ where } N \text{ is the number of classes.} \tag{5}$$

IoU is describing to what extent the ground truth is overlapping with the predicted bounding box, and it can be calculated as the following:

$$\frac{A \cap B}{A \cup B}, \text{ where } A \text{ is the predicted bounding box and } B \text{ is the ground truth box.} \tag{6}$$

For each prediction, the IoU is calculated and then thresholded to a value between (0.5 – 0.9). In our experiments, we used the value of 0.5 as a threshold where the detected masses are considered as a correct detection (TP) only if the IoU $>=$ 0.5. In addition, the precision, sensitivity, and F1-score are calculated according to the following Eqs. (7), (8), and (9) respectively.

The precision here is describing the percentage of the correct predictions, in other words, the percentage of the true positives regarding the total detected positive cases. While the recall determines the percentage of the ability of the model at detecting the positive cases regarding the total cancer cases.

Average precision was used to describe the area under the curve (AUC) for the precision and recall curve. The AP is calculated to evaluate the accuracy of the model predictions for each class.

$$Precision = \frac{True\ Positive}{True\ Positive + False\ Positive} \tag{7}$$

$$Recall\ (senstivity) = \frac{True\ Positive}{True\ Positive + False\ Negative} \tag{8}$$

$$F1 - score = 2 \times \frac{precision \times recall}{precision + recall} \tag{9}$$

## 4   Experimental Results and Discussion

This section illustrates and discusses the results of the conducted experiments. Two experiments are conducted to assess the performance of the model before and after the step of converting the images into multichannel images. In addition, another four experiments were performed to evaluate the impact of the different augmentation techniques on the model performance, these techniques were applied to the training set only. The first trial was applied with the mosaic, the second one with the mix-up, while in the third trial both mosaic and mix-up were applied, and finally, the last trial was done with just only the traditional augmentation techniques that were applied to the whole dataset as mentioned in Sect. 3.2.

Table 1 shows that the multichannel images enhanced significantly the mAP of the detection by almost $\simeq 10\%$ and the sensitivity by $\simeq 7\%$, moreover, it improved the classification accuracy for each class. It can be noticed from Table 1 that the number of TP increased while the number of FP and FN decreased which means that this step enhanced the detection of the truly existing masses. Based on these results, it can be demonstrated that preprocessing can overcome the problem of small datasets. Deep learning models need large datasets to provide higher accuracy, however, the experiments showed that enhancing the images can provide more discriminant features and this can ease the learning process of the model.

Considering the results from Table 2 and 3 mosaic augmentation achieved the best mAP among the other techniques; furthermore, the mosaic improved the number of TP and FN of mass detection, whether for INbreast or MIAS, as mosaic allowed the model to learn the masses at different scales and different contexts. The mix-up and mosaic together showed competitive performance; They achieved almost the same sensitivity (recall) score as mosaic however it showed lower mAP than mosaic only. Possibly this happens because of mix-up, as it changes the pixel values of the mammogram image when mixing up two images; This perhaps affects the appearance of the mass shape and the surrounding tissues and, accordingly, the detection task.

Figure 5, 6, Table 4, and 5 showed the results of testing unseen images from different datasets that were digitized with different scanners using the model that was trained on INbreast only; these images are from CBIS-DDSM which provides mammographic images in DM format and MIAS that composed of (SFM) images. In the experiments, 21 images with masses from MIAS were used as unseen images for testing the model that was trained on INbreast with mosaic.

FFDM has better accuracy in detecting breast cancer than SFM [24] and this obviously can be demonstrated from the results in Table 2 and 3. In addition, this can explain the results that showed in Table 4; The model which was trained with conventional + mosaic combination using INbreast dataset only succeeded in testing some unseen images from MIAS dataset for detecting masses in them. The testing results of this experiment showed mAP of 71.93%. It is important to note that MIAS dataset is composed of SFM images while INbreast is composed of FFDM images only and accordingly this can clarify this result as the model was trained on FFDM images and tested on SFM images which have lower quality. However, the model with conventional + mosaic combination when trained and tested on MIAS showed good results as shown in Table 3.

The training with the mosaic combination and the conventional augmentation allowed for better generalization rather than the other combinations, and also it increased the learning ability of the model. The main advantage of mosaic especially in these experiments over the other evaluated techniques is mainly in producing new images at different and smaller scales which allowed a variation of the different mass sizes that may exist in the mammogram and this increased the ability of the model at detecting the masses with variant sizes that range from very small to very large. The variation of the mass sizes and shapes in the medical images specifically 2D images makes the detection and localization task challenging.

The mix-up with conventional augmentation combination showed better results than the conventional augmentation only due to generating new images with linearly mixing up features of two mammographic images; this combination showed more stability and reduces the bad predictions rather than using the conventional augmentation only. Conventional augmentation techniques may resolve the problem of overfitting however, it doesn't improve the generalization too much compared to Mosaic and Mix-up. Furthermore, the Mosaic and Mix-up outperformed the conventional augmentation in terms of detection and distinction between benign and malignant masses as shown in Table 2 and 3.

It can be deduced from these results that the proposed model with combination of mosaic and multichannel images has a good level of generalization and robustness. Furthermore, the model was able to differentiate between the benign masses and malignant masses with AP of 99.16% and 99.58% respectively on INbreast; 91.87% and 98.69% for MIAS. The model showed competitive performance compared to other recent similar studies in terms of accuracy and inference time as shown in Table 6.

**Table 1.** INbreast detection results of the experimental trials for the model with the normalized images and mosaic vs. multichannel images with mosaic in terms of mAP, F1-score, number of TP, number of FP, Recall, Precision, and FNR. In addition, the results for distinguishing Benign (B) and Malignant (M) masses in terms of AP, TP, and FP.

| # | Technique | mAP(%)@IoU = 0.5 | F1-score (%) | TP | FP | FN | Recall (%) | Precision (%) | FNR | B-AP (%) | M-AP (%) | TP-FP (B) | TP-FP (M) |
|---|---|---|---|---|---|---|---|---|---|---|---|---|---|
| Trial 1 | Normalized images + mosaic | 88.89% | 90% | 74 | 5 | 11 | 87% | 94% | 0.129 | 81.85% | 95.94% | 21–0 | 53–5 |
| Trial 2 | Multichannel images + mosaic | 99.37% | 96% | 80 | 2 | 5 | 94% | 98% | 0.058 | 99.61% | 99.58% | 24–0 | 56–2 |

**Table 2.** INbreast detection results of the four experimental trials in terms of mAP, F1-score, TP, FP, Recall, Precision, and FNR. In addition, the results for distinguishing the Benign and Malignant masses in terms of AP, TP, and FP.

| # | Augmentation technique | mAP(%)@IoU = 0.5 | F1-score (%) | TP | FP | FN | Recall (%) | Precision (%) | FNR | B-AP (%) | M-AP (%) | TP-FP (B) | TP-FP (M) |
|---|---|---|---|---|---|---|---|---|---|---|---|---|---|
| Trial 1 | Conventional + Mosaic | 99.37% | 96% | 80 | 2 | 5 | 94% | 98% | 0.058 | 99.16% | 99.58% | 24–0 | 56–2 |
| Trial 2 | Conventional + Mix-up | 83.37% | 84% | 71 | 14 | 14 | 84% | 84% | 0.164 | 75.86% | 90.87% | 18–5 | 53–9 |
| Trial 3 | Conventional + Mosaic + Mix-up | 95.14% | 96% | 81 | 3 | 4 | 95% | 96% | 0.047 | 91.19% | 99.09% | 24–1 | 57–2 |
| Trial 4 | Conventional | 75.25% | 79% | 61 | 8 | 24 | 72% | 88% | 0.282 | 66.11% | 84.39% | 13–2 | 48–6 |

**Table 3.** MIAS detection results of the four experimental trials in terms of mAP, F1-score, TP, FP, Recall, Precision, and FNR. In addition, the results for distinguishing the Benign and Malignant masses in terms of AP, TP, and FP.

| # | Augmentation technique | mAP(%)@IoU = 0.5 | F1-score (%) | TP | FP | FN | Recall (%) | Precision (%) | FNR | B-AP (%) | M-AP (%) | TP-FP (B) | TP-FP (M) |
|---|---|---|---|---|---|---|---|---|---|---|---|---|---|
| Trial 1 | Conventional + Mosaic | 95.28% | 92% | 84 | 6 | 9 | 90% | 93% | 0.096 | 91.87% | 98.69% | 51–4 | 33–2 |
| Trial 2 | Conventional + Mix-up | 92.34% | 84% | 79 | 17 | 14 | 85% | 82% | 0.150 | 90.11% | 94.57% | 46–1 | 33–16 |
| Trial 3 | Conventional + Mosaic + Mix-up | 93.20.65% | 93% | 83 | 2 | 10 | 89% | 98% | 0.107 | 89.33% | 97.06% | 51–2 | 32–0 |
| Trial 4 | Conventional | 65.79% | 64% | 56 | 26 | 37 | 60% | 68% | 0.397 | 50.74% | 80.83% | 26–10 | 30–16 |

**Table 4.** Results of testing on 21 unseen images from MIAS (B and M refer to Benign and Malignant respectively) on the model that trained on INbreast with Mosaic.

| mAP(%)@IoU = 0.5 | F1-score (%) | TP | FP | FN | Recall (%) | Precision (%) | FNR | B-AP (%) | M-AP (%) | TP-FP (B) | TP-FP (M) |
|---|---|---|---|---|---|---|---|---|---|---|---|
| 71.93% | 70% | 15 | 7 | 6 | 71% | 68% | 0.285 | 68.75% | 75.11% | 6–1 | 9–6 |

**Table 5.** Results of testing unseen images from CBIS_DDSM and MIAS dataset on the model that trained on INbreast with Mosaic.

| # | Dataset | Image-id | Detection |
|---|---|---|---|
| a | CBIS-DDSM | P_00118_RIGHT_CC | 1 mass (Malignant with ≃ 97%) |
| b | | P_00332_LEFT_MLO | 2 masses (Benign with ≃ 37%and94%) |
| c | | P_00265_RIGHT_CC | 1 mass (Malignant with ≃ 99%) |
| d | | P_00273_LEFT_CC | 1 mass (Benign with ≃ 96%) |
| e | MIAS | Mdb023 | 1 mass (Malignant with ≃ 79%) |
| f | | Mdb142 | 1 mass (Benign with ≃ 92%) |
| g | | Mdb202 | 1 mass (Malignant ≃ 100%) |
| h | | Mdb010 | 1 mass (Benign ≃ 92%) |

**Table 6.** Comparison between some of the recent works based on YOLO and the proposed model

| Reference | Method | Dataset | Detection Accuracy | Inference time/image (sec) |
|---|---|---|---|---|
| Aly et al.[25] | YOLOv3 | INbreast, DDSM | 89.5% | 0.009 |
| Al-antari et al.[7] | YOLO | INbreast | 98.96% | 3 |
| Baccouche et al.[26] | YOLO based Fusion models | INbreast, CBIS-DDSM | 98.1% | 0.58, 0.55 |
| Platania et al.[27] | YOLO based ROI Classifier | CBIS-DDSM | 90% | – |
| Al-antari et al.[28] | YOLO | INbreast | 97.27% | 0.025 |
| Proposed Model | YOLOv4 + Mosaic + Multichannel images | INbreast | 99.37% | 0.0112 |
| | | MIAS | 95.28% | 0.0111 |

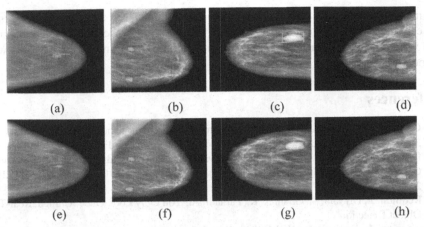

**Fig. 5.** Results of the model on unseen images (a), (b), (c), and (d) images from CBIS-DDSM and their corresponding ground-truth (e), (f), (g), and (h).

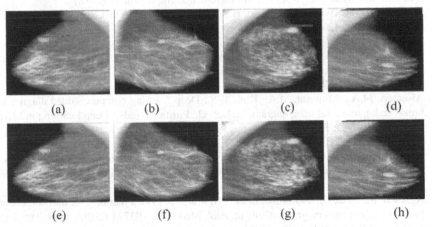

**Fig. 6.** Results of the model on unseen images (a), (b), (c), and (d) images from MIAS and their corresponding ground-truth (e), (f), (g), and (h)

## 5   Conclusion

In this paper, we proposed a CAD system for breast mass detection and classification, this model is based on YOLOv4. The model utilized the mosaic data augmentation which was applied only to the training set after applying conventional augmentation techniques to the whole dataset (training and testing). Furthermore, the images were converted to multichannel images which improved the visibility of the breast tissues and the masses; this accordingly enhanced the mAP by almost 10% however the model was working on 416 x 416 input size. The proposed model achieved mAP of 99.37% with a False Negative Rate (FNR) of 0.06; moreover, the model was able to detect masses with different sizes when tested on unseen images from other datasets which means that the model can be generalized. In addition, the model enhanced the classification results for each mass type (benign and malignant). In future work, we are intended to extend this work to detect other abnormalities in the mammograms and to evaluate this work on other datasets.

# References

1. Global Cancer Statistics: GLOBOCAN Estimates of Incidence and Mortality Worldwide for 36 Cancers in 185 Countries. Enhanced Reader (2020). Accessed 28 Feb 2022
2. Hadjiiski, L., Sahiner, B., Chan, H.P.: Advances in CAD for diagnosis of breast cancer. Curr. Opin. Obstet. Gynecol. **18**, 64 (2006). https://doi.org/10.1097/01.GCO.0000192965.29449.DA
3. Redmon, J., Divvala, S., Girshick, R., Farhadi, A.: You Only Look Once: Unified, Real-Time Object Detection
4. Redmon, J., Farhadi, A.: YOLO9000: Better, faster, stronger. In: Proceedings of the 30th IEEE Conference on Computer Vision and Pattern Recognition, CVPR 2017, pp. 6517–6525 (2016). https://doi.org/10.1109/CVPR.2017.690
5. Redmon, J., Farhadi, A.: YOLOv3: An Incremental Improvement (2018)
6. Bochkovskiy, A., Wang, C.-Y., Liao, H.-Y.M.: YOLOv4: Optimal Speed and Accuracy of Object Detection (2020)
7. Al-antari, M.A., Al-masni, M.A., Choi, M.T., Han, S.M., Kim, T.S.: A fully integrated computer-aided diagnosis system for digital X-ray mammograms via deep learning detection, segmentation, and classification. Int. J. Med. Inform. **117**, 44–54 (2018). https://doi.org/10.1016/J.IJMEDINF.2018.06.003
8. Al-antari, M.A., Al-masni, M.A., Kim, T.-S.: Deep learning computer-aided diagnosis for breast lesion in digital mammogram. In: Lee, G., Fujita, H. (eds.) Deep Learning in Medical Image Analysis. AEMB, vol. 1213, pp. 59–72. Springer, Cham (2020). https://doi.org/10.1007/978-3-030-33128-3_4
9. Ribli, D., Horváth, A., Unger, Z., Pollner, P., Csabai, I.: Detecting and classifying lesions in mammograms with deep learning. Sci. Rep. **8**(1), 1–7 (2018). https://doi.org/10.1038/s41598-018-22437-z
10. Agarwal, R., Díaz, O., Yap, M.H., Lladó, X., Martí, R.: Deep learning for mass detection in full field digital mammograms. Comput. Biol. Med. **121**, 103774 (2020). https://doi.org/10.1016/J.COMPBIOMED.2020.103774
11. Peng, J., Bao, C., Hu, C., Wang, X., Jian, W., Liu, W.: Automated mammographic mass detection using deformable convolution and multiscale features. Med. Biol. Eng. Comput. **58**, 1405–1417 (2020). https://doi.org/10.1007/S11517-020-02170-4/FIGURES/7
12. Hassan, N.M., Hamad, S., Mahar, K., Tools, M.: Mammogram breast cancer CAD systems for mass detection and classification: A review. Multimedia Tools Appl. **81**, 1–33 (2022). https://doi.org/10.1007/S11042-022-12332-1
13. Liu, S., Qi, L., Qin, H., Shi, J., Jia, J.: Path aggregation network for instance segmentation. In: Proceedings of the IEEE Computer Society Conference on Computer Vision and Pattern Recognition, pp. 8759–8768 (2018). https://doi.org/10.1109/CVPR.2018.00913
14. Woo, S., Park, J., Lee, J.-Y., Kweon, I.S.: CBAM: Convolutional block attention module. In: Ferrari, V., Hebert, M., Sminchisescu, C., Weiss, Y. (eds.) ECCV 2018. LNCS, vol. 11211, pp. 3–19. Springer, Cham (2018). https://doi.org/10.1007/978-3-030-01234-2_1
15. He, K., Zhang, X., Ren, S., Sun, J.: Spatial pyramid pooling in deep convolutional networks for visual recognition. In: Fleet, D., Pajdla, T., Schiele, B., Tuytelaars, T. (eds.) ECCV 2014. LNCS, vol. 8691, pp. 346–361. Springer, Cham (2014). https://doi.org/10.1007/978-3-319-10578-9_23

16. Huang, Z., Wang, J.: DC-SPP-YOLO: Dense Connection and Spatial Pyramid Pooling Based YOLO for Object Detection
17. Zhang, H., Cisse, M., Dauphin, Y.N., Lopez-Paz, D.: Mixup: Beyond Empirical Risk Minimization
18. Moreira, I.C., Amaral, I., Domingues, I., Cardoso, A., Cardoso, M.J., Cardoso, J.S.: INbreast: Toward a full-field digital mammographic database. Acad. Radiol. **19**, 236–248 (2012). https://doi.org/10.1016/J.ACRA.2011.09.014
19. Mammographic Image Analysis Society (MIAS) database v1.21. https://www.repository.cam.ac.uk/handle/1810/250394. Accessed 26 Mar 2022
20. Lee, R.S., Gimenez, F., Hoogi, A., Miyake, K.K., Gorovoy, M., Rubin, D.L.: A curated mammography data set for use in computer-aided detection and diagnosis research. Sci. Data **4**(1), 1–9 (2017). https://doi.org/10.1038/sdata.2017.177
21. D'Haeyer, J.P.F.: Gaussian filtering of images: A regularization approach. Signal Process. **18**, 169–181 (1989). https://doi.org/10.1016/0165-1684(89)90048-0
22. Otsu, N.: Threshold selection method from gray-level histograms. IEEE Trans. Syst. Man Cybern. SMC **9**, 62–66 (1979). https://doi.org/10.1109/TSMC.1979.4310076
23. Pizer, S.M., et al.: Adaptive histogram equalization and its variations. Comput. Vis. Graph. Image Process. **39**, 355–368 (1987). https://doi.org/10.1016/S0734-189X(87)80186-X
24. Song, S.Y., Park, B., Hong, S., Kim, M.J., Lee, E.H., Jun, J.K.: Comparison of digital and screen-film mammography for breast-cancer screening: A systematic review and meta analysis. J. Breast Cancer **22**, 311–325 (2019). https://doi.org/10.4048/jbc.2019.22.e24
25. Aly, G.H., Marey, M., El-Sayed, S.A., Tolba, M.F.: YOLO based breast masses detection and classification in full-field digital mammograms. Comput. Methods Programs Biomed. **200**, 105823 (2021). https://doi.org/10.1016/J.CMPB.2020.105823
26. Baccouche, A., Garcia-Zapirain, B., Olea, C.C., Elmaghraby, A.S.: Breast lesions detection and classification via YOLO-based fusion models. Comput. Mater. Continua **69**, 1407–1425 (2021). https://doi.org/10.32604/CMC.2021.018461
27. Platania, R., Shams, S., Yang, S., Zhang, J., Lee, K., Park, S.-J.: Automated breast cancer diagnosis using deep learning and region of interest detection (BC-DROID). In: Proceedings of the 8th ACM International Conference on Bioinformatics, Computational Biology, and Health Informatics (2017). https://doi.org/10.1145/3107411
28. Al-antari, M.A., Han, S.M., Kim, T.S.: Evaluation of deep learning detection and classification towards computer-aided diagnosis of breast lesions in digital X-ray mammograms. Comput. Methods Programs Biomed. **196**, 105584 (2020). https://doi.org/10.1016/J.CMPB.2020.105584

# A Stacking Recommender System Based on Contextual Information for Fashion Retails

Heitor Werneck[1], Nicollas Silva[2], Carlos Mito[1], Adriano Pereira[2], Elisa Tuler[1], Diego Dias[1(✉)], and Leonardo Rocha[1]

[1] Universidade Federal de São João del-Rei, São João del Rei, Brazil
{werneck,mito}@aluno.ufsj.edu.br, {etuler,diegodias,lcrocha}@ufsj.edu.br
[2] Universidade Federal de Minas Gerais, Belo Horizonte, Brazil
{ncsilvaa,adrianoc}@dcc.ufmg.br

**Abstract.** The recent success of distinct e-commerce systems has driven many fashion companies into the online marketplace, allowing consumers to quickly and easily access a worldwide network of brands. However, to succeed in this scenario, it is necessary to provide a tailored, personalized, and reliable fashion shopping experience. Moreover, unfortunately, current solutions on marketing have provided a general approach to push and suggest the most popular or purchased items in most cases. Thus, this paper proposes a new **ensemble recommendation system** based on the stacking of classical approaches associated with contextual information about customers and products. Our idea is to incorporate user preferences and item characteristics to ensure a desirable level of personalization to commonly applied methods. Our method is a Neural Collaborative Filtering algorithm that can combine any recommendation system with contextual domain information. The results are promising, showing significant gains of up to 80% MRR, 70% NDCG, and 108% Hits when compared to popular baselines for this same scenario.

**Keywords:** Recommendation systems · Stacking · Word embeddings

## 1 Introduction

E-commerce applications are related to the use of digital communication applied to business. E-commerce is now present in the daily lives of businesses and consumers, affecting and changing how the parties involved in the transactions interact. In all these applications, there is a disproportion between the availability and the ability of people to evaluate the information [20]. This volume of data has led researchers to strive to analyze the information generated by users, modeling a personalized profile according to their preferences. These profiles are used to feed predictive models that aim to match users with available items

Supported by CAPES, CNPq, Finep, Fapesp and Fapemig.

O. Gervasi et al. (Eds.): ICCSA 2022, LNCS 13375, pp. 560–574, 2022.
https://doi.org/10.1007/978-3-031-10522-7_38

in the domain. Such models are known as Recommendation Systems (RS) [16], whose goal is to identify relevant items according to user preferences, defined throughout interactions. To illustrate the importance of RS, we can mention the profit gains observed in several businesses, for example, 35% increase in sales at a DVD retailer [22] and at eBay, a 6% increase in profit was observed in the implementation of a new recommendation method [6].

More recently, we have observed a scenario in which online marketing has been growing at a swift pace in recent years – the luxury fashion [9]. This growth is associated with the behavioral change of consumers in the traditional fashion industry who now have quick and easy access to a worldwide network to retailers of major luxury fashion brands. It is necessary to provide a tailored, personalized, and reliable fashion shopping experience to succeed in this scenario, which makes the role of RS even more important in the user journey, allowing customers to discover products that suit their style, complement their choices, or challenge them with bold new ideas. Coupled with these issues, the sparsity of data in these applications is even greater. In addition to many existing products common to traditional recommendation scenarios, other characteristics significantly increased the number of possible options, making the scenario even more challenging.

The RS literature on the fashion domain was scarce for a long time compared to the literature in other traditional domains. However, recently we have observed a growing interest in this domain. Some of the existing proposals are adaptations of traditional collaborative filtering strategies that use implicit information from user/item interaction (i.e., clicks and navigation links) [23], or explicit (i.e., rate, purchase) information [10, 12, 15, 17, 27, 31]. There are proposals that present solutions from other perspectives, such as integrating fashion and human perception themes about custom body shapes and knowledge of professional designers [28] and using 3D body shape information [8]. While these usually present exciting results, they require a set of information that the user is not always comfortable to provide. While all of these proposals present interesting results in particular domains (i.e., datasets), we have not found a method in the literature that can be generalized to different domains. Neither did we find a robust quantitative evaluation, comparing with state-of-the-art methods, to prove the good results.

In this paper, we propose a solution that aims to generalize to different fashion RS by combining different context information: (i) customer-product interaction (i.e., day, week); (ii) items characteristics (e.g., material, color, size, price); (iii) customer behavior (i.e., number of interactions, number of items consumed), with different traditional state-of-the-art RS. Our approach is a *stacking* that combines RS predictions with contextual meta-data. It enables the exploitation of pre-existing user-item interaction modeling using existing methods (e.g., LightGCN) with a context that can recognize new user-item interaction patterns. This work sets out to accomplish:

1. An evaluation of multiple competitive RS in the fashion recommendation domain;

2. A best-fit approach for the fashion domain, exploiting context information along with a state-of-the-art method in RS;
3. To demonstrate the importance of context in the fashion recommendation task;
4. To improve recommendations for different types of users through contextual information.

Our proposal is general enough to allow different RSs to be combined. Specifically, in the present work, we present a first instantiation that combines a collaborative filtering neural network method, a classical non-personalized method, and the domain context information. In our experimental evaluation, considering two Amazon data collections, the results showed significant gains of up to 80% MRR, 70% NDCG, and 108% Hits when compared to methods considered state-of-the-art for the fashion recommendation scenario.

The remainder of the paper is organized as follows. Section 2 describes some basic concepts related to RSs, the main works in the fashion domain, and the main associated challenges. In Sect. 3, we detail our proposal. In Sect. 4, we discuss the instantiation of the proposal and the achieved results compared to several existing proposals in the literature. Finally, Sect. 5 presents our conclusions and directions for future work.

## 2  Related Works

### 2.1  Recommendation Systems

Recommendation Systems (RSs) can be broadly divided into two classes, namely, personalized and non-personalized [3]. Non-customized techniques are a bit simpler, as they recommend items not based on the user's taste but rather on user preferences in general (i.e., most popular, highest rated, among others). On the other hand, personalized techniques can be considered more complex than non-personalized ones, as they need to extract from the users' information possible tastes and use them to recommend items that are more similar to the user's profile. Such information can be obtained through user feedback, a click on a website or a review of an item bought/watched on the internet. As we will discuss, our proposal allows combining approaches from both classes.

Regarding personalized RSs, the most traditional approaches are content-based filtering [25] and collaborative filtering [1]. In content-based strategies, the user will receive recommendations of items similar to those he has consumed in the past, i.e., the system will recommend the items whose attributes most closely resemble the items consumed by the user. On the other hand, in strategies based on collaborative filtering, users with similar preferences in the past tend to have similar preferences in the future. The system not only uses the items consumed by a user in the past but also acts by matching his preferences with the preferences of similar users. This approach ignores the notion of actions having a context [2] and that users interact with the system in a particular context, and preferences related to items may be dependent on the context the user is in, a prevalent aspect in the fashion domain.

Another set of personalized RSs is the context-based ones that use various types of contextual information to make recommendations. Contextual information can be [11]: spatial (those contexts that define the geographic state or environment of users, or items), static (those contexts that do not change over time and affect the recommendation, such as age and gender), and temporal (those contexts that change temporally and are dynamic, such as social relationships). These RSs are very pertinent to the fashion recommendation domain since, for example, clothing can have seasons and can be recommended depending on the season and the country of the user. Contextual information can improve the effectiveness of the recommendation process and, in this domain, is often essential. These RSs proposals are the most suitable to be combined in our proposal.

## 2.2  General Challenges of Recommendation Systems

In the recommendation task, systems can suffer from several problems in domains, such as [18] cold start problem, which happens when a new user or item enters the system, or also in a lighter definition, these same elements have little history of interactions; explainability, which is commonly found to lack this same concept in neural network-based recommender systems; grey sheep, where one user does not agree with any other group (collaborative filtering methods usually suffer from this problem); sparsity, where users usually interact in a system with an extensive catalog of items and the distinction between interactions over user items makes the interaction matrix sparse, which can lead to less accurate recommendations. The fashion recommendation scenario also deals with all these problems. In this paper, we will focus on the problem of data sparsity.

## 2.3  Fashion Recommendation Systems

Finally, this section presents some of the main works related specifically to fashion RSs. In [4] the authors propose a method of stacking, used in more traditional domains, combining a few attributes (created from interaction data). The proposal is limited to simple models with little ability to combine attributes at a high level. [23] proposes a simple recommendation approach for the fashion domain in which it uses item price, popularity, and how recent the item is to aid in recommendations, being a simple strategy with very little diversification in exploiting attributes of the domain. In [17] the authors propose the insertion of visual attributes into RSs from adaptations to improve the recommendation of fashion items. [30] proposes a fashion compatibility knowledge learning method that incorporates visual compatibility relationships as well as style information. In [7] the authors propose a framework to jointly train feed-forward neural networks with embeddings and a linear model with attribute transformations. While the proposal is interesting, there is no discussion of using other recommendation models as input to the model. Other work explores the recommendation task generically but without the use of additional information beyond the [13,14,29] interactions. With this, these models suffer from problems in domains where context is essential; however, they still describe an important part of modeling user-item interaction, and new ways of reusing pre-existing methods can be investigated.

Most approaches in the literature are concerned with specific challenges in recommending fashion items and do not address an evaluation with current state-of-the-art methods of traditional recommender systems. Furthermore, generic approaches that integrate context information are complex for hyper-parameter tuning and do not discuss the use of pre-existing systems for information aggregation. Our work goes in another direction and presents itself as an approach with the potential to be applied in practical recommender scenarios.

## 3   Stacking for Fashion Recommendation Systems

All contextual information is equally important for the fashion recommendation domain and must be considered when proposing solutions. A complete system should consider at least three types of information: (1) those related to the user-item interaction (i.e., day and week of interaction); (2) those related to the items (e.g., material, color, size, and price); and those related to the users (i.e., number of interactions and number of items consumed). In this sense, the main approaches related to fashion recommendation already use this information to model the users' interest in the available items and thus make their recommendations. Some of these approaches rely on non-personalized information, such as the popularity of their products, to achieve more sales. On the other hand, other approaches try to understand users' preferences better and recommend the products they are most interested in. The main hypothesis of this work is that both approaches are equally important for a scenario where the system has to please its users and constantly sell its products. For this reason, our proposal is an RSs stacking that aims to combine the predictions of distinct approaches with existing contextual information about users and items. We propose adopting models based on neural networks since these models can match attributes at multiple levels.

### 3.1   Our Neural Network

Our proposal consists of a simple and effective approach to combine multiple data instances known as Multilayer Perceptron (MLP). MLP is a class of feed-forward artificial neural networks that consist of at least three layers of nodes: (1) an input layer, (2) a hidden layer, and (3) an output layer. Except for the input nodes, each node is a neuron that uses a nonlinear activation function. Its architecture is highly dependent on the problem to be studied, and its results can change sharply according to its variation. In this case, it is essential to perform a hyperparameter search method. Moreover, MLP uses a supervised learning technique called backpropagation. Its multiple layers and nonlinear activation

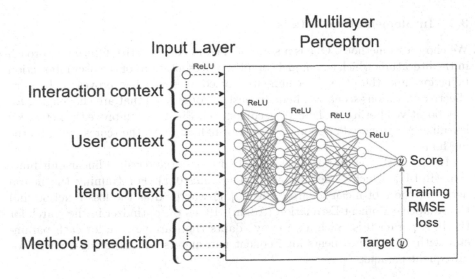

**Fig. 1.** Stacking created over distinct models and contextual information for fashion.

distinguish MLP from a linear perceptron [26]. Figure 1 depicts our proposal, combining different inputs to our neural network.

MLP has the following attributes as input: predictions from the recommendation models (e.g., SVD and SVD++); data about the user; data about the interaction; and data about the item. To use the contexts more appropriately with MLP, we proposed an initial pre-processing step on the data. This pre-processing transforms categorical attributes into vectors of Boolean attributes (one-hot encoding). For the attributes with many available categories, we propose to use only the 100 most popular ones to avoid the problem of high dimensionality in the recommendations. In terms of recommendation models, our initial proposal consists of combining only two proposals: (i) non-customized model named Popular that ranks the items according to their popularity, defined in this work as the number of different users who have clicked on the item; and (ii) LightGCN [13], a method that learns user and item embeddings by propagating them linearly in the user's interaction graph with the item, using the weighted sum of the learned embeddings across all layers as the final embedding. Thus, the combined information is:

1. Context: consists of the contextual information of users, items, and user-item interaction;
2. LightGCN item: consists of the information obtained from the user-item modeling generated by the LightGCN method (score assigned to each item for each user);
3. Popular item: score assigned by the non-personalized Popular method to each item (independent of the user).

## 3.2   Implementation Details

. We chose two methods. One is a state-of-the-art collaborative filtering approach in the literature, which can model complex representations of the user interaction behavior; and the other is a non-customized method that proves to be very effective in various scenarios, being robust in some cases that are challenging for collaborative filtering methods (i.e., cold-start). Finally, to improve the network's learning, we proposed applying z-score normalization to the scores given by the methods.

In our work, the proposed neural network uses the rectified linear unit function (ReLU), which is defined as $f(x) = max(0, x)$. For training the neural network, the root-mean-square error (Eq. 1) was used as the loss function and the Adaptive Moment Estimation (Adam) [19] as the optimizer in the search for the best parameters. Such a strategy adapts the learning rate for each parameter with small adjustments for frequent parameters and large adjustments for infrequent parameters.

$$L_{RMSE} = \sqrt{\Sigma_{i=1}^{n} \frac{(\hat{y} - y)^2}{n}} \tag{1}$$

# 4   Experimental Evaluation

This section presents the set of experiments performed to evaluate our proposal. First, we present our experimental setup, describing the datasets and their pre-processing steps performed, the evaluation methodology and metrics used, and the baselines considered in our comparison. Next, we discuss the experimental results. Finally, we present an experiment with different combinations of information and algorithms to evaluate each component's impact on the final result of the proposed stacking method.

## 4.1   Setup

### 4.1.1   Datasets
First, we select two classic datasets in the literature with user ratings on Amazon products. These two datasets contain data about the user's interaction with a product (i.e., rating and timestamp) and the item (i.e., color and size).

- **Amazon Fashion.** It is a dataset of user ratings on items in the fashion section of Amazon; and
- **Amazon Clothing.** It is a dataset of user reviews of items in the clothing section (e.g., clothing, shoes, and jewelry). We prepared an initial random sampling of 100,000 users to use the Amazon Clothing dataset due to the large number of interactions.

Without any special processing, these two datasets have a large portion of users with few interactions. This characteristic is not effective for an assertive quantitative evaluation of RSs. Thus, for a more diverse evaluation, we perform a filtering process in the two datasets, where we removed users with less than **n** interactions from the datasets. For evaluating two important recommendation scenarios, we used $n = 5$ to evaluate the dataset with users with little and much knowledge and $n = 10$ to evaluate users that contain a reasonable number of interactions (i.e., knowledge for the system). Furthermore, to simplify the application of the methods and evaluation, the user's ratings, which are integer values from 1 to 5, were transformed to 1 if the rating was $\geq 4$ and 0, otherwise. Table 1 presents the main statistical measures about the created datasets. It is important to highlight the high sparsity index, a remarkable characteristic of the fashion domain.

**Table 1.** Dataset statistics.

| Dataset | #User | #Item | #Interactions | Sparsity |
|---|---|---|---|---|
| Amazon Fashion (n = 5) | 2,056 | 7,433 | 13,452 | 99.91% |
| Amazon Fashion (n = 10) | 128 | 1,382 | 1,654 | 99.06% |
| Amazon Clothing (n = 5) | 7,528 | 51,029 | 70,172 | 99.98% |
| Amazon Clothing (n = 10) | 2,152 | 28,338 | 36,011 | 99.94% |

### 4.1.2   Evaluation Methodology

To measure the quality of the methods in the recommendation task, we used a leave-one-out split, which is commonly applied by the literature of RSs [14,24]. In this data splitting technique, we insert the last interaction of each user (in temporal order) into the test set and use the remaining data as training. In addition, due to the high time cost of classifying all items in a base, we adopt the strategy [21] of generating a random sample of 99 items that are not interacted by the user for each existing interaction.

The performance of each item on the recommended list is evaluated in this paper by three distinct metrics [5]:

- Hit Ratio (HR): represents the number of items recommended correctly, based on the set of items consumed by the target user (test).
- Mean Reciprocal Rank (MRR): is a statistical measure to evaluate the user's "effort" to find an item relevant to her/him. The closer to the top of a ranking the correct items are for a user, the closer the MMR is to 1, and consequently, the better the solution.
- Normalized Discounted Cumulative Gain (NDCG): is a statistical measure to evaluate the quality of a ranking. The NDCG value is high when the items of higher estimated relevance appear higher up the actual ranking when compared to the items of lower estimated relevance.

We compare our proposal with several algorithms commonly used in the fashion scenario. These algorithms consist of generic and specific strategies for the fashion recommendation scenario:

1. Random: simple model, to define the lower bound of the problem, recommends items randomly.
2. Popular: traditional baseline model of recommender systems, this method ranks the items according to the most popular. We defined Popularity in this work as the number of different users who clicked on the item.
3. SVD (Singular Value Decomposition): SVD is a matrix factorization method used in RSs for collaborative filtering.
4. SVD++: This method minimizes an objective function, which includes an overall bias and two others for users and items, using Stochastic Gradient Descent (SGD) and regularization with L2.
5. BilinearNet: it is a method of embeddings learning with neural networks, which does not use any layers and learns the representations of users and items.
6. NeuMF [14]: is a neural network-based method, which merges generalized matrix factorization using neural networks with multilayer perceptron layers.
7. LightGCN [13]: is a method that learns user and item embeddings by propagating them linearly in the graph of user interaction with the item and uses the weighted sum of the learned embeddings in all layers as the final embedding.

For the selection of the best hyper-parameters of the methods, a search for hyper-parameters' values was performed using an execution over the training from the *leave-one-out*. More specifically, we applied the same data splitting (i.e., *leave-one-out*) in training set to generate a new training and validation set. We executed the methods for a set of hand-picked hyper-parameters in the new training set and validation set. Then we selected the hyper-parameters' set with the highest MRR to the final evaluation in the test set for each method.

We have adopted a recent strategy to evaluate the generated lists [14], which selects the top 10 items to evaluate all metrics. Thus HR measures whether the test item is present in the top 10 list, and NCDG accounts for the hit position by assigning higher scores to hits in the first ranks, while MRR assigns higher scores to the first hits with a smoother (linear) score decrease. We computed the scores for the three metrics for each user, and the average was stored. The entire evaluation process was run five times, with the random sampling of items being different for each of the five runs. All this enables a later statistical evaluation of the methods' gains. This statistical evaluation was done using the Student's t-test with $p = 0.05$. The evaluation methodology is presented in Fig. 2.

## 4.2   Results

We divided the presentation of the results into two parts. First, we compared the results achieved by our proposal with the results obtained by the other strategies, following the methodology presented in the previous section. Then, we compared different combinations of the information and strategies considered in our proposal to evaluate each component's impact on the final result of the stacking proposal.

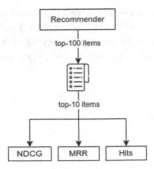

**Fig. 2.** Evaluation of the list of recommended items.

### 4.2.1 Comparison to Baselines

Table 2 presents the results of the methods on the databases according to the evaluation policy previously described. Evaluating the baselines previously selected for this work, we can notice that the non-personalized algorithms tend to behave better when we apply less aggressive filtering on the collections data ($n = 5$). Such approaches keep many users with little information (i.e., associated ratings). Thus, techniques that exploit global user interest may be favored in this scenario. However, in the other scenarios, we see the superiority of traditional methods and recently applied strategies in the fashion retail scenario.

In general, it is also possible to observe that our proposed method presents a significantly better result when compared to all baselines, considering all evaluated metrics and datasets. In some scenarios, such as the Amazon Fashion dataset ($n = 10$), our proposal achieves gains of 80% for MRR, 70% for NDCG, and 108% for Hits. These results validate our primary hypothesis that combining multiple pieces of information is effective for the fashion domain. Moreover, even in highly sparse scenarios (with less aggressive filtering), our strategy can also present the best results due to its ability to compose multiple information for user preference prediction.

### 4.2.2 Evaluating Stacking Components

This subsection presents an experiment in which we vary the combinations over inputs to the proposed stacking method. The main goal of this experiment is to identify the explanations for the results obtained through the method and what are the primary impact factors for the final result. There will always be one of the methods in the input sets, LightGCN or Popular. Table 3 shows the results obtained from this experiment, where we highlight the use of context through the symbol "*" in front of the word MLP (MLP*).

We can see the impact of including contextual information about users on the learning of our stacking model with this analysis. Although there are some cases where the combination of methods without context is competitive with the best combinations, overall, the best values for each metric are obtained using contextual information. This occurs because this information can guide our neural

**Table 2.** Performance of the different strategies on four datasets. The best results are highlighted in bold. The stacking method (MLP) achieves statistically significant improvements, outperforming all baselines. The symbol ▲ denotes significant gains and • denotes statistical ties by applying Student's t-test with a $p$ value $= 0.05$ over the best baseline.

|  | MRR | NDCG | Hits |
|---|---|---|---|
| **Amazon Fashion (n = 5)** | | | |
| Random | 0.03079 | 0.01036 | 0.10438 |
| Popular | 0.24759 | 0.04396 | 0.32160 |
| SVD | 0.23278 | 0.03781 | 0.27986 |
| SVD++ | 0.04975 | 0.01436 | 0.12996 |
| BilinearNet | 0.23848 | 0.03713 | 0.27160 |
| NeuMF | 0.24200 | 0.03942 | 0.30068 |
| LightGCN | 0.25016 | 0.03966 | 0.28385 |
| MLP* (LightGCN + Popular) | **0.30309▲** | **0.06172▲** | **0.52578▲** |
| **Amazon Fashion (n = 10)** | | | |
| Random | 0.02915 | 0.01025 | 0.09219 |
| Popular | 0.06004 | 0.01181 | 0.09531 |
| SVD | 0.07039 | 0.01319 | 0.11094 |
| SVD++ | 0.08332 | 0.02058 | 0.15625 |
| BilinearNet | 0.06967 | 0.01056 | 0.07969 |
| NeuMF | 0.08320 | 0.01513 | 0.12187 |
| LightGCN | 0.06568 | 0.01206 | 0.09688 |
| MLP* (LightGCN + Popular) | **0.15010▲** | **0.03511▲** | **0.32500▲** |
| **Amazon Clothing (n = 5)** | | | |
| Random | 0.02976 | 0.01016 | 0.10181 |
| Popular | 0.08635 | 0.02169 | 0.17545 |
| SVD | 0.05184 | 0.01231 | 0.10670 |
| SVD++ | 0.07245 | 0.01915 | 0.16400 |
| BilinearNet | 0.09200 | 0.01599 | 0.12375 |
| NeuMF | 0.09753 | 0.01838 | 0.14859 |
| LightGCN | 0.09131 | 0.01731 | 0.13116 |
| MLP* (LightGCN + Popular) | **0.13566▲** | **0.03294▲** | **0.26637▲** |
| **Amazon Clothing (n = 10)** | | | |
| Random | 0.03062 | 0.01033 | 0.10390 |
| Popular | 0.06673 | 0.01475 | 0.11803 |
| SVD | 0.05201 | 0.00990 | 0.08327 |
| SVD++ | 0.08378 | 0.02174 | **0.18374** • |
| BilinearNet | 0.07173 | 0.01186 | 0.09247 |
| NeuMF | 0.07917 | 0.01586 | 0.13429 |
| LightGCN | 0.07110 | 0.01282 | 0.09684 |
| MLP* (LightGCN + Popular) | **0.10998▲** | **0.02353▲** | **0.18494**• |

**Table 3.** Results of the proposed factorial experiment. The asterisk "*" indicates the use of context. The largest values are highlighted in **bold**.

|  | MRR | NDCG | Hits |
|---|---|---|---|
| **Amazon Fashion (n = 5)** | | | |
| MLP* (Popular + LightGCN) | 0.30309 | **0.06172** | **0.52578** |
| MLP* (Popular) | 0.09041 | 0.01810 | 0.17247 |
| MLP* (LightGCN) | 0.07032 | 0.01716 | 0.15691 |
| MLP (Popular) | 0.24572 | 0.04366 | 0.32179 |
| MLP (LightGCN) | 0.05444 | 0.01093 | 0.08317 |
| MLP (Popular + LightGCN) | **0.30633** | 0.05973 | 0.49368 |
| **Amazon Fashion (n = 10)** | | | |
| MLP* (Popular + LightGCN) | 0.15010 | 0.03511 | 0.32500 |
| MLP* (Popular) | **0.31656** | **0.09285** | 0.77656 |
| MLP* (LightGCN) | 0.06457 | 0.01280 | 0.10156 |
| MLP (Popular) | 0.25637 | 0.08096 | 0.72969 |
| MLP (LightGCN) | 0.02594 | 0.00547 | 0.05000 |
| MLP (Popular + LightGCN) | 0.24800 | 0.08222 | **0.80625** |
| **Amazon Cloth (n = 5)** | | | |
| MLP* (Popular + LightGCN) | 0.13566 | 0.03294 | 0.26637 |
| MLP* (Popular) | 0.07004 | 0.01872 | 0.14926 |
| MLP* (LightGCN) | **0.19476** | 0.03778 | 0.28536 |
| MLP (Popular) | 0.19086 | **0.04515** | **0.38982** |
| MLP (LightGCN) | 0.10115 | 0.02085 | 0.15444 |
| MLP (Popular + LightGCN) | 0.06994 | 0.01887 | 0.14880 |
| **Amazon Cloth (n = 10)** | | | |
| MLP* (Popular + LightGCN) | 0.10998 | 0.02353 | 0.18494 |
| MLP* (Popular) | **0.34585** | **0.08145** | **0.64870** |
| MLP* (LightGCN) | 0.17003 | 0.02881 | 0.22007 |
| MLP (Popular) | 0.33231 | 0.07267 | 0.54610 |
| MLP (LightGCN) | 0.04105 | 0.00744 | 0.05604 |
| MLP (Popular + LightGCN) | 0.09538 | 0.02007 | 0.15409 |

network to more assertive decisions about the preferences of these users. Something interesting to mention is also the applicability of popular strategies that can always be used with other recommendation algorithms. Furthermore, by combining non-personalized and personalized strategies with contextual information, our proposal stands out regardless of the application scenario. We intend in the future to evaluate how other strategies and information can be incorporated into our proposal and analyze their impact in the fashion domain.

# 5   Conclusion and Future Work

This paper presents a fashion recommendation proposal that combines different contextual information of users, items, and their interactions with other recommendation models through a stacking process. For dealing with distinct information (i.e., raw contextual information and information derived from modeling processes with distinct recommendations), we proposed using models based on neural networks since these models can combine attributes at multiple levels. From this generic proposal, we instantiated a first solution that uses an MLP with only two recommendation models: (i) non-customized model named Most Popular; and (ii) a personalized method based on LightGCN [13]. We evaluated our proposal on two Amazon data collections, comparing it with seven state-of-the-art proposals in fashion recommendation. Overall, our method showed significant gains of up to 80% MRR, 70% NDCG, and 108% Hits over the other models.

We intend to investigate and expand our analysis on future work by including other baselines and other stacking proposals. We also aim to apply other techniques for tabular data that are simple and efficient for aggregating information from RS scores with context.

# References

1. Adomavicius, G., Tuzhilin, A.: Toward the next generation of recommender systems: a survey of the state-of-the-art and possible extensions. IEEE Trans. Knowl. Data Eng. **17**(6), 734–749 (2005)
2. Adomavicius, G., Tuzhilin, A.: Context-aware recommender systems. In: Ricci, F., Rokach, L., Shapira, B., Kantor, P.B. (eds.) Recommender Systems Handbook, pp. 217–253. Springer, Boston, MA (2011). https://doi.org/10.1007/978-0-387-85820-3_7
3. Akshita, S., Smita, A.: Recommender system: review. Int. J. Comput. Appl. **71**(24), 38–42 (2013)
4. Bao, X., Bergman, L., Thompson, R.: Stacking recommendation engines with additional meta-features. In: Proceedings of the Third ACM Conference on Recommender Systems, pp. 109–116 (2009)
5. Bobadilla, J., Ortega, F., Hernando, A., Gutiérrez, A.: Recommender systems survey. Knowl.-Based Syst. **46**, 109–132 (2013)
6. Brovman, Y.M., et al.: Optimizing similar item recommendations in a semi-structured marketplace to maximize conversion. In: Proceedings of the 10th ACM Conference on Recommender Systems, pp. 199–202 (2016)
7. Cheng, H.-T., et al.: Wide & deep learning for recommender systems. In: Proceedings of the 1st Workshop on Deep Learning for Recommender Systems, pp. 7–10 (2016)
8. Dong, M., Zeng, X., Koehl, L., Zhang, J.: An interactive knowledge-based recommender system for fashion product design in the big data environment. Inf. Sci. **540**, 469–488 (2020)
9. Farfetch (2021)

10. Frejlichowski, D., Czapiewski, P., Hofman, R.: Finding similar clothes based on semantic description for the purpose of fashion recommender system. In: Nguyen, N.T., Trawiński, B., Fujita, H., Hong, T.-P. (eds.) ACIIDS 2016. LNCS (LNAI), vol. 9621, pp. 13–22. Springer, Heidelberg (2016). https://doi.org/10.1007/978-3-662-49381-6_2

11. Haruna, K., et al.: Context-aware recommender system: a review of recent developmental process and future research direction. Appl. Sci. **7**(12), 1211 (2017)

12. He, R., McAuley, J.: Ups and downs: modeling the visual evolution of fashion trends with one-class collaborative filtering. In: proceedings of the 25th International Conference on World Wide Web, pp. 507–517 (2016)

13. He, X., Deng, K., Wang, X., Li, Y., Zhang, Y., Wang, M.: LightGCN: simplifying and powering graph convolution network for recommendation (2020)

14. He, X., Liao, L., Zhang, H., Nie, L., Hu, X., Chua, T.-S.: Neural collaborative filtering. In: Proceedings of the 26th International Conference on World Wide Web, pp. 173–182 (2017)

15. Hu, Y., Yi, X., Davis, L.S.: Collaborative fashion recommendation: a functional tensor factorization approach. In: Proceedings of the 23rd ACM International Conference on Multimedia, pp. 129–138 (2015)

16. Jannach, D., Jugovac, M.: Measuring the business value of recommender systems. ACM Trans. Manag. Inf. Syst. (TMIS) **10**(4), 1–23 (2019)

17. Kang, W.-C., Fang, C., Wang, Z., McAuley, J.: Visually-aware fashion recommendation and design with generative image models. In: 2017 IEEE International Conference on Data Mining (ICDM), pp. 207–216. IEEE (2017)

18. Khusro, S., Ali, Z., Ullah, I.: Recommender systems: issues, challenges, and research opportunities. In: Kim, K., Joukov, N. (eds.) Information Science and Applications (ICISA) 2016. LNEE, vol. 376, pp. 1179–1189. Springer, Singapore (2016). https://doi.org/10.1007/978-981-10-0557-2_112

19. Kingma, D.P., Ba, J.: Adam: a method for stochastic optimization. arXiv preprint arXiv:1412.6980 (2014)

20. Konstan, J.A., Riedl, J.: Recommender systems: from algorithms to user experience. User Model. User-Adap. Inter. **22**(1), 101–123 (2012)

21. Koren, Y.: Factorization meets the neighborhood: a multifaceted collaborative filtering model. In: Proceedings of the 14th ACM SIGKDD International Conference on Knowledge Discovery and Data Mining, pp. 426–434 (2008)

22. Lee, D., Hosanagar, K.: Impact of recommender systems on sales volume and diversity (2014)

23. Nguyen, H.T., et al.: Learning to rank for personalised fashion recommender systems via implicit feedback. In: Prasath, R., O'Reilly, P., Kathirvalavakumar, T. (eds.) MIKE 2014. LNCS (LNAI), vol. 8891, pp. 51–61. Springer, Cham (2014). https://doi.org/10.1007/978-3-319-13817-6_6

24. Rendle, S., Freudenthaler, C., Gantner, Z., Schmidt-Thieme, L.: BPR: Bayesian personalized ranking from implicit feedback. arXiv preprint arXiv:1205.2618 (2012)

25. Ricci, F., Rokach, L., Shapira, B.: Introduction to recommender systems handbook. In: Ricci, F., Rokach, L., Shapira, B., Kantor, P.B. (eds.) Recommender Systems Handbook, pp. 1–35. Springer, Boston, MA (2011). https://doi.org/10.1007/978-0-387-85820-3_1

26. Taud, H., Mas, J.F.: Multilayer perceptron (MLP). In: Camacho Olmedo, M.T., Paegelow, M., Mas, J.-F., Escobar, F. (eds.) Geomatic Approaches for Modeling Land Change Scenarios. LNGC, pp. 451–455. Springer, Cham (2018). https://doi.org/10.1007/978-3-319-60801-3_27

27. Wakita, Y., Oku, K., Huang, H.-H., Kawagoe, K.: A fashion-brand recommender system using brand association rules and features. In: 2015 IIAI 4th International Congress on Advanced Applied Informatics, pp. 719–720. IEEE (2015)
28. Wang, L., Zeng, X., Koehl, L., Chen, Y.: Intelligent fashion recommender system: fuzzy logic in personalized garment design. IEEE Trans. Hum.-Mach. Syst. 45(1), 95–109 (2014)
29. Wu, J., et al.: Self-supervised graph learning for recommendation. In: Proceedings of the 44th International ACM SIGIR Conference on Research and Development in Information Retrieval, pp. 726–735 (2021)
30. Yin, R., Li, K., Lu, J., Zhang, G.: Enhancing fashion recommendation with visual compatibility relationship. In: The World Wide Web Conference, pp. 3434–3440 (2019)
31. Zeng, X., Koehl, L., Wang, L., Chen, Y.: An intelligent recommender system for personalized fashion design. In: 2013 Joint IFSA World Congress and NAFIPS Annual Meeting (IFSA/NAFIPS), pp. 760–765. IEEE (2013)

# Monitoring the Cathedral of Milan: An Archive with More Than 50 Years of Measurements

Luigi Barazzetti[1]([✉]), Francesco Canali[2], Stefano Della Torre[1], Carmelo Gentile[1], Mattia Previtali[1], and Fabio Roncoroni[3]

[1] Politecnico di Milano, Department of Architecture, Built Environment and Construction Engineering, Piazza Leonardo da Vinci 32, Milan, Italy
{luigi.barazzetti,stefano.dellatorre,carmelo.gentile, mattia.previtali}@polimi.it
[2] Veneranda Fabbrica del Duomo di Milano, Via Carlo Maria Martini 1, Milan, Italy
dl.cantieri@duomomilano.it
[3] Polo territoriale di Lecco, via Previati 1/c, Lecco, Italy
fabio.roncoroni@polimi.it

**Abstract.** The paper describes the origin and evolution of the monitoring system of the Duomo di Milano, which was installed during the 1960s. In that period, differential movements induced by the extraction of groundwater (among other factors) caused significant instability and risk of collapse of the monument. Today, the monitoring system is still operative. Instruments, techniques, and calculation procedures were continuously updated considering the continuity of the time series, resulting in a precious archive for structural health monitoring and conservation. The actual configuration of the monitoring system includes a large variety of both automatic and manual sensors, digital and mechanical, in real-time or with an established periodicity. Moreover, the monitoring system inside the cathedral still preserves continuity with the original measurements thanks to continuous maintenance carried out over time. The manuscript illustrates and discusses the original system as well as the updates related to activities that began more than half a century ago.

**Keywords:** Conservation · Digital archive · Dynamic/Static monitoring · Sensor · Subsidence

## 1 Introduction

The Cathedral of Milan (Duomo di Milano, Fig. 1) is an imposing gothic masterpiece located in the heart of Milan. The construction began in 1386 over the ancient basilicas of Santa Maria Maggiore and Santa Tecla, whose remains are still visible in the archeological area. Veneranda Fabbrica del Duomo di Milano (VFD) is the institution founded in 1387 in charge of the completion and conservation of the Duomo. In the same year, the marble of Candoglia quarries

© The Author(s), under exclusive license to Springer Nature Switzerland AG 2022
O. Gervasi et al. (Eds.): ICCSA 2022, LNCS 13375, pp. 575–590, 2022.
https://doi.org/10.1007/978-3-031-10522-7_39

was made available for construction. Today, the marble is used for continuous restoration activities, which are essential for preserving the monument.

The aim of this paper is not an extensive description of the Duomo and its rich and complex history, and the reader is referred to specific textbooks, such as [1,2]. The authors intend to illustrate and discuss the origin and evolution of the monitoring system of the Cathedral, whose initial version was installed during the 1960s, and it has been continuously updated and integrated during the following decades.

Starting from the second half of the 1900s, differential movements caused by sudden variations of the water table in the city center (coupled with other factors) caused significant instability and risk of collapse of the monument.

Ferrari da Passano [3] describes the causes of instability considering both historical and constructive aspects (e.g., size and constructive methods of foundations and columns, construction of the round arches, main spire, and the three smaller spires) as well as movements induced by "modern" factors: vibrations due to vehicular traffic on three sides around the Duomo (North, East, South), the metro underground line (North), and subsidence for the rapid change in the water table.

**Fig. 1.** The Duomo di Milano.

The initial monitoring system allowed specialists to measure the differential vertical movements and rotations of 12 columns, mainly along a line through the transept, as well as the four columns of the tiburium [3] (Fig. 2).

Continuous upgrades were carried out to extend the system to the entire church and the surrounding area, including the square and other buildings. The evolution of the monitoring system followed the numerous restoration activities, especially during the interventions on the columns, the facade, and the main spire.

The paper describes the history of a 50-year time series of monitoring data, the integrations, and the actual multi-sensor configuration. A link between main restoration activities and the upgrade of the monitoring systems is also illustrated and discussed, along with the maintenance required to guarantee the posterity of the system.

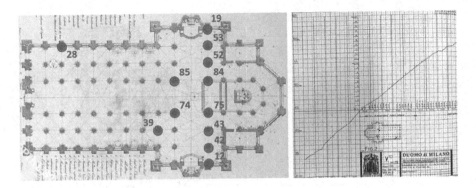

**Fig. 2.** The first system installed to capture vertical movements of some piers.

## 2    Actual Configuration of High Precision Levelling Networks for Subsidence Monitoring

### 2.1    The Archive of Differential Movements for Subsidence Monitoring

The actual configuration of the leveling network is the result of continuous updates in network configuration, number of points and their distribution, instruments, and processing methods.

The installation of a leveling network started in 1961 when the rapid change of the water table in the city caused differential movements of the structures of the Duomo [4]. As mentioned in the introduction, the first measurements were in the transept area. Nowadays, the internal leveling network (Fig. 3) is made up of 59 benchmarks installed on the columns. It provides a time series of vertical differential movements since 1969 that goes back to 1965 for a subset of points. The configuration and installation of the monitoring system were defined by Veneranda Fabbrica del Duomo di Milano and the Institute of Surveying, Photogrammetry, and Geophysics of Politecnico di Milano, i.e. the Polytechnic University of Milan.

Measurements are still acquired twice a year (always in May and November), notwithstanding initial data in 1965–1978 were also acquired with a higher frequency (4 seasons). The network features several closed loops, and measurements are adjusted via least squares, obtaining elevations with a precision of $\pm 0.1$ mm. As no stable benchmark is available in the area, point 39 has always been assumed as a reference since the first measurements.

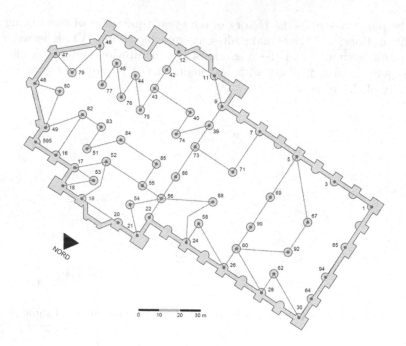

**Fig. 3.** The internal leveling network

Figure 4 shows a contour line representation obtained by interpolating vertical movements in the period 1970–2020 using rational basis splines, obtaining a DEM representation from which contours can be generated. As mentioned, differential movements are calculated with respect to column 39. For these reasons, columns show both positive and negative variations. The settlement of the transept is rather evident, with a maximum value reached from the middle towards the south.

An external leveling network is installed on buildings around the Duomo (Fig. 5). Points are distributed on the Cathedral, the square, and the main buildings and streets in the area (Palazzo Ducale, Galleria Vittorio Emanuele, etc.). Measurements are acquired once a year (always in May), obtaining adjusted elevations with a precision of ±0.1 mm for 92 points.

The first measurements were taken in 1966. Such measurements confirm that the maximum negative displacement is in the transept (Fig. 6). The software today used for least squares adjustment was implemented in MATLAB and allows a combined adjustment of internal and external leveling networks. It replaced a previous software implementation, which could not run the simultaneous adjustment of the two networks. Different tests carried out on smaller networks of other projects confirmed the consistency of the numerical outputs of the two software.

Recently, additional leveling benchmarks were added to the church's bell tower of S. Gottardo (2014). The aim was to include the belltower, using a

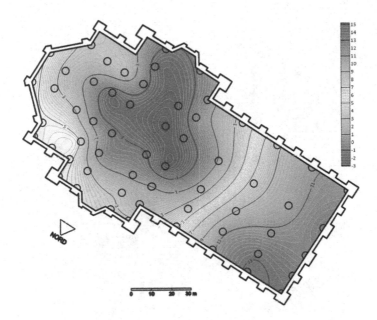

**Fig. 4.** Relative vertical displacements in the period 1970–2020 represented as contour lines.

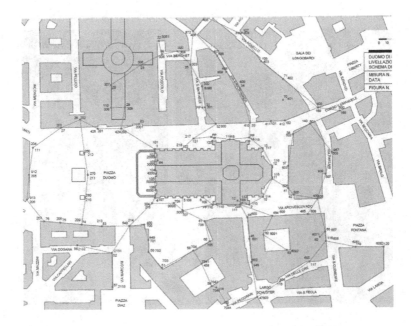

**Fig. 5.** Scheme of the external leveling network.

**Fig. 6.** Vertical movements in the square represented as contour lines (in mm/100) between 1966 and 2018.

**Fig. 7.** The supporting structure placed around the columns during restoration.

system to detect vertical movements and rotations. As benchmarks are installed on opposite sides, the relative vertical movements also provide information about the structure's rotation.

Internal and external leveling networks allowed one to quantify the differential movements after and before major restoration works of the 4 large columns of the tiburium, which was carried out in 1981–1984 [3]. The measured vertical movements measured in that period for the 4 main columns were 1.40 mm (column n. 74), 2.12 mm (n. 75), 2.16 mm (n. 84), and 2.89 mm (n. 85). The operation entailed the replacement of damaged material equivalent to approximately thirty percent of their volume, restoring stability to the Duomo's core (Fig. 7).

A graph of the differential movements of a subset of selected piers is shown in (Fig. 8). As can be seen, variations were much more rapid in 1970–80/85.

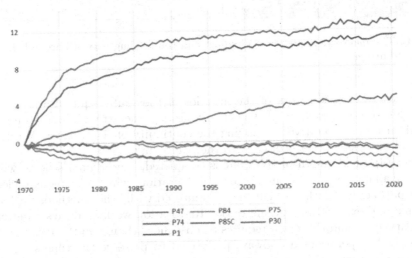

**Fig. 8.** Graph of differential vertical settlements (in mm) in the period 1970–2020 for a subset of columns.

## 2.2    Differential Vertical Movements of the Main Spire

An additional leveling network was also installed in 2008 at the bottom of the main spire called "guglia maggiore". The aim was to monitor vertical movements during the restoration work of the main spire, which required the installation of a scaffolding placed around the spire and reaching the top (Fig. 9).

Reference benchmarks are installed on two external spires (1000 and 2000), whereas point 3000 is a reference point connected to the top of the spire with an invar wire. The remaining points are installed at the base level of the tiburium. More details about the systems installed on the main spire of the Duomo (including both manual and automatic sensors and tools) are described in [5].

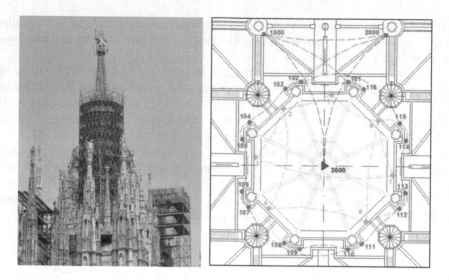

**Fig. 9.** The main spire and the scaffolding, and the leveling network around the base of the tiburium.

Recent restoration work of the intrados of the vault required a scaffolding that changed the geometry of the network. Today, the external loop around the tiburium is still operative, preserving the continuity of the archive. Additional points were instead added directly to the scaffolding.

Once the restoration of the vault is completed, the original scheme will be again available. This is an important consideration, which can be extended to other parts of the Cathedral currently monitored with other methods, including internal and external leveling networks. Restoration work is always required in the Cathedral, and this often requires a consequent change in the measurement strategy. All operations are always performed to preserve the time series, i.e., without removing points and protecting them if restoration activities are carried out in the area.

## 3   Tilt Monitoring

A tilt monitoring system was installed on several columns of the Cathedral in May 1972. Additional measurement points were added in the following years, obtaining the actual configuration shown in Fig. 10. Measurements are carried out with the manual reading of a vertical wire using the plumb bob principle. The instrument allows one to measure the variation of inclination between a point on top (where the wire is fixed) and the base of the column, where the instrument can be placed through a special plate. Variation of inclination is calculated from two readings providing the position of the wire with a precision of ±0.1 mm. The system can be removed, leaving only the wire and connection plate. It can therefore be used for the other columns.

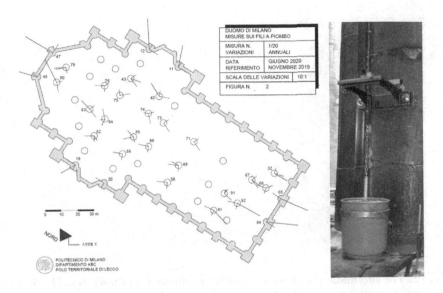

**Fig. 10.** Scheme of verticality variations measured with the plumbline using a 2-axis coordinatometer (precision ±0.1 mm).

**Fig. 11.** Measurements of tilt variations using an optical plumb installed on the façade and apse of the Duomo. The configuration on the left allows the connection of a vertical surface. The figure on the right shows the installation on a permanent reference on the floor.

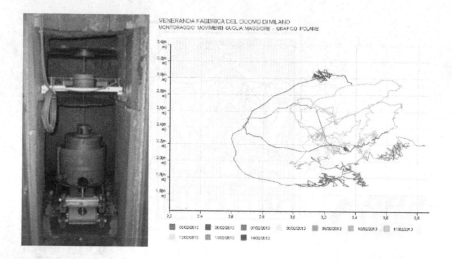

**Fig. 12.** The automatic plumb for verticality measurements of the spire. The figure on the right shows the movements of the spire using a polar graph representation.

Today, 32 columns are monitored. Moreover, the 4 columns of the tiburium and two columns of the façade have a double plumb system, i.e., wires connected at two different levels to check movements on top and at an intermediate level.

Measurements are carried out every 6 months, always in May and November, i.e., following the periodicity of leveling measurements. Data are reported on maps using a vector-based representation showing annual, partial, and total variations with respect to the first measurement epoch.

A different system is instead used to monitor the variation of inclination outside the Cathedral. 5 monitoring points are installed on the façade, and 2 on the columns of the apse. As the wire cannot be used outside, an optical plummet (Fig. 11) placed on a micrometric sled is used to collimate reference points and measure inclination variations.

The inclination of the spire is also monitored with an automatic plumb able to provide continuous measurements. The original system (Fig. 12) was recently renovated with a more modern sensor.

### 3.1   Other Monitoring Tools in the Duomo: A Short Overview

The monitoring system of the Duomo includes several other sensors and tools. Restoration activities and maintenance are a continuous process in the Cathedral and the installation of temporary solutions able to provide monitoring information has an active role in the operations. An example is the monitoring system able to capture the relative movement between the spire and the scaffolding around it with the use of GNSS technology. Figure 13 shows the configuration of the system, which has a master (reference) GNSS antenna installed on the roof, a GNSS on top of the spire (close to the Madonnina), and a third GNSS receiver on the scaffolding.

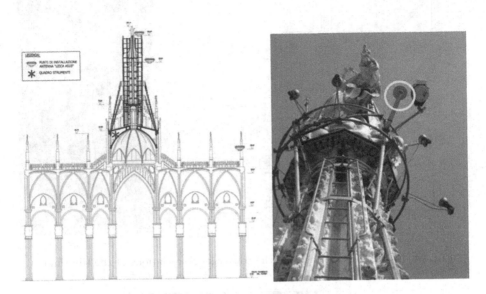

**Fig. 13.** Measuring in real-time the relative position between spire and scaffolding using GNSS techniques.

The system was developed to track 3D relative movements between scaffolding and spire in real-time during the restoration work of the spire, including cleaning of surfaces and replacing damaged tie rods and marble ashlars caused by iron oxidation.

In some cases, the installed sensors have become permanent and are now integrated into the archive. In other cases, continuous automatic measurements are coupled with manual measurements to verify the system itself periodically. An example is the convergence measurement of the tiburium carried out with LVDTs with an additional manual comparator with a precision of $\pm 0.01$ mm (Fig. 14). More recently, the restoration of the vault of the tiburium (currently in progress) has required the installation of temporary scaffoldings. The wires were removed so that it is possible to reposition all of them after completing restoration works.

It is worth mentioning that the monitoring system of the Cathedral includes several other sensors and tools installed in different periods to integrate the original configuration with new measurements. It is impossible to describe all the systems used and those still available in just a paper. In addition, different instruments and sensors have been tested during about 60 years of measurements, ranging from mechanical tools to digital sensors and techniques Fig. 15 shows just a selection of the previously mentioned systems. The authors intend to demonstrate that several other sensors and tools provide distance variations, 1D

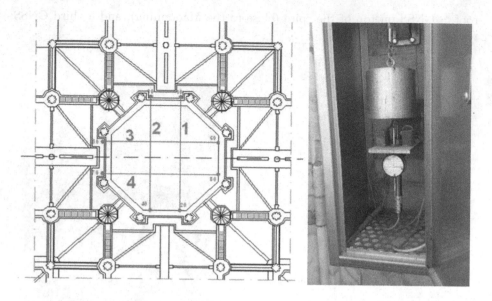

**Fig. 14.** LVDTs used to measure the convergence variations of the tiburium.

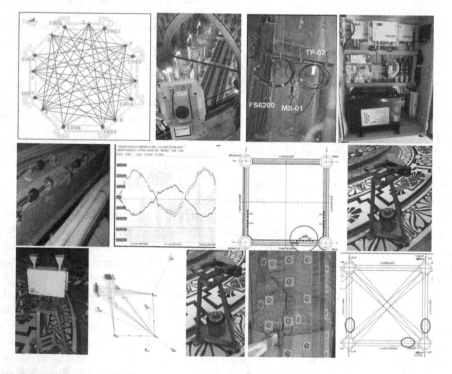

**Fig. 15.** Some of the monitoring sensors installed in the Cathedral of Milan. Different systems are still operative, whereas others were replaced with more modern versions.

/2D/3D displacements, crack convergence, and inclination variations, verticality deviations, among the others.

## 4  Continuous Monitoring

In recent years, a new continuous monitoring system was installed on the Cathedral and the spire. The system is entirely computer-based and provides an automatic transmission of the collected data, measuring 4 main types of physical quantities [6,7]:

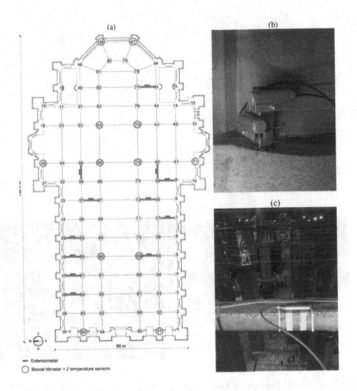

**Fig. 16.** (a) General layout of the static monitoring system installed in the Cathedral; (b) bi-axial tiltmeters mounted on a capital; (c) extensometer installed on a tie-rod.

- quasi-static measurements of inclination at the top of selected columns and 3 levels of the main spire;
- quasi-static strain measurements (using wireless vibrating wire extensometers) on selected tie-rods;
- measurements of internal and external environmental parameters (temperature and humidity);

- velocity measurements using electro-dynamic sensors on top of selected columns and 3 levels of the main spire.

The automatic monitoring sub-system installed on the main spire is conceptually similar to the one already used during the restoration work of the main spire [8]. Unfortunately, the system was significantly damaged by lightning strike in 2016, so that substitution was carried out with sensors featuring technical characteristics compatible with the new monitoring system.

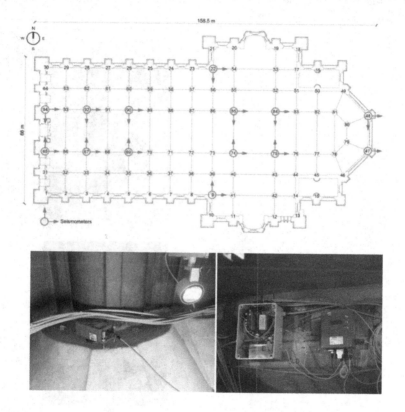

**Fig. 17.** General layout of the seismometers installed in the Cathedral.

The static monitoring system includes the following sensors:

- 12 bi-axial tiltmeters inside the church (Fig. 16) a and b), with ±0.5° range and ±0.5 mm/m resolution;
- 3 bi-axial tiltmeters with integrated temperature sensors installed at different levels (+65.87 m, +74.99 m, +91.67 m) of the main spire;
- 12 vibrating wire extensometers installed on 10 tie-rods;
- 12 hygrometers close to the extensometers;
- a weather station installed on the highest accessible level of the main spire (+91.67 m).

The dynamic monitoring system consists of:

- 13 biaxial seismometers and 1 mono-axial seismometer, installed at the top of selected columns inside the Cathedral (Fig. 17). They can measure the velocity in two orthogonal directions: N-S (transversal) and E-W (longitudinal);
- $3 times 3$ mono-axial seismometers, installed at the same levels of the main spire together with the biaxial tiltmeters of the static monitoring system.

## 5    Conclusions

The monitoring system of the Duomo di Milano includes a variety of methods and has a long history. The first measurements taken in the '60 have been continuously integrated following technological advancements. Special attention has always been paid to the continuity of the time series.

The archive of leveling measurements includes more than 50 years of data. The historical archive of measurements has been restructured, offering advanced functions and tools for data visualization and processing in GIS and statistical software. The system is also integrated with a Web-GIS application able to provide rapid access to measurements.

A report with numerical data, graphs, schemes, and a description of the system and the observed movements is constantly produced and delivered every six months [9]. New sensors were installed in different years of technological advances, and local solutions are continuously developed to support minor and major interventions that are an essential part of the daily activity of Veneranda Fabbrica del Duomo.

The importance of considering past observations and guaranteeing the continuity of the archive and the integration with new sensors will continue in the collaboration between Veneranda Fabbrica del Duomo di Milano and Politecnico di Milano.

**Acknowledgment.** The work was carried out within the framework of the agreement between Veneranda Fabbrica del Duomo di Milano and Politecnico di Milano.

## References

1. Ferrari da Passano, C: Storia della Veneranda Fabbrica, Milano, pp. 37–46 (1998)
2. Romussi, R.: Il Duomo di Milano tra arte e storia. Meravigli edizioni, Milano (2014)
3. Ferrari da Passano, C.: Il Duomo rinato: Storia e tecnica del restauro statico dei piloni del tiburio del Duomo di Milano. Veneranda Fabbrica del Duomo (Diakronia), Milan (1988). (in Italian)
4. Croce, A.: Questioni geotecniche sulle fondazioni del Duomo di Milano. In: Il Duomo rinato: Storia e tecnica del restauro statico dei piloni del tiburio del Duomo di Milano, vol. 2 (1970)
5. Alba, M., Roncoroni, F., Barazzetti, L., Giussani, A., Scaioni, M.: Monitoring of the main spire of the Duomo di Milano. In: Joint International Symposium on Deformation Monitoring, 2–4 November, Hong Kong, China, 6 p. (2011)

6. Gentile, C., Canali, F.: Continuous monitoring the cathedral of Milan: design, installation and preliminary results. In: The Eighteenth International Conference of Experimental Mechanics, vol. 2, p. 5354 (2018). https://doi.org/10.3390/ICEM18-05354
7. Gentile, C., Ruccolo, A., Canali, F.: Continuous monitoring of the Milan Cathedral: dynamic characteristics and vibration-based SHM. J. Civ. Struct. Heal. Monit. 9(5), 671–688 (2019). https://doi.org/10.1007/s13349-019-00361-8
8. Cigada, A., Dell'Acqua, L., Castiglione, B., Scaccabarozzi, M., Vanali, M., Zappa, E.: Structural health monitoring of an historical building: the main spire of the Duomo Di Milano. Int. J. Arch. Heritage 11 (2016)
9. Barazzetti, L., Roncoroni, F.: Relazione sulle misure eseguite per il controllo delle deformazioni del Duomo di Milano. Semestral report for the Veneranda Fabbrica del Duomo di Milano. 39 p. (2020)

# Computerized Adaptive Testing: A Unified Approach Under Markov Decision Process

Patricia Gilavert[ID] and Valdinei Freire[(✉)][ID]

School of Arts, Sciences and Humanities, University of São Paulo, São Paulo, Brazil
{patifernan,valdinei.freire}@usp.br

**Abstract.** Markov Decision Process (MDP) is the most common planning framework in the literature for sequential decisions under probabilistic outcomes; MDPs also underlies the Reinforcement Learning (RL) theory. Computerized Adaptive Testing (CAT) is an assessment approach that selects questions one after another while conditioning each selection on the previous questions and answers. While MDP defines a well-posed optimization planning-problem, shortsighted score functions have solved the planning problem in CATs. Here, we show how MDP can model different formalisms for CAT, and, therefore, why the CAT community may benefit from MDP algorithms and theory. We also apply an MDP algorithm to solve a CAT, and we compare it against traditional score functions from CAT literature.

**Keywords:** Computerized adaptive testing · Markov Decision Process

## 1 Introduction

Computerized Adaptive Testing (CAT) is an approach to assessment that tailors the administration of test items to the trait level of the examinee. Instead of applying the same question to every examinee, as in a traditional paper and pencil test, CATs apply questions one after another and each question selection is conditioned on the previous questions and answers [17]. The number of applied questions to each examinee can also vary to reach a better trade-off between precision, a correct trait estimation, and efficiency, a small number of questions. CATs reduce the burden of examinees in two ways; first, examinees do not need to complete a lengthy test; second, examinees answer questions tailored to their trait level avoiding too difficult or too easy questions [18].

Because examinees do not solve the same set of questions; an appropriate estimation of the latent trait level of the examinee must be considered. In the case of dichotomic questions, the item response theory (IRT) can be used to find the probability of an examinee to score one item as a function of his/her trait and therefore provide a coherent estimator. CAT in combination with IRT makes it possible to calculate comparable proficiencies between examinees who

O. Gervasi et al. (Eds.): ICCSA 2022, LNCS 13375, pp. 591–602, 2022.
https://doi.org/10.1007/978-3-031-10522-7_40

responded to different sets of items and at different times [6,8]. This probability is influenced by item parameters, as difficulty and discrimination.

In every CAT we identify at least six components [22,23]: (*i*) an item bank, (*ii*) an entry rule, (*iii*) a response model, (*iv*) an estimation mechanism, (*v*) an item selection criterion, and (*vi*) a stop criterion. The item bank determines questions that are available for the test; usually, items are selected without replacement. The entry rule specifies *a priori* knowledge from the examinee; in a Bayesian framework, it represents an *a priori* distribution over latent traits, and, in a Likelihood framework, it represents an initial estimation. The response model describes the chance of scoring for each examinee on each question in the item bank; the response model supports the estimation mechanism to estimate the latent trait of the current examinee. The item selection criterion chooses the question to be applied to the current examinee, while the stop criterion chooses when to stop the test; usually, both criteria may be supported by the current estimation, the item bank, and the response model.

Markov Decision Process (MDP) models problems where an agent makes sequential decisions and the results of these actions are probabilistic [12]. The agent's objective is to choose a sequence of actions so that the system acts optimally according to previously defined criteria. Such a sequence of actions follows a policy, which maps each observed state into an action. While MDP algorithms consider the model of the optimization problem to be known; Reinforcement Learning (RL) considers the same optimization problem when the model is unknown and must be learnt through trial-and-error interaction with the process [20].

Although CAT may be seen as a planning problem, where a long horizon must be taken into account to act optimally, mostly CAT methods consider shortsighted score-functions which select questions through an immediate analysis. Just a few works in literature has applied MDP framework to CAT, mostly by framing the sequential decision problem as Reinforcement Learning. [5] has applied RL to Sequential Mastery Testing, when a CAT is designed to classify each examinee as master or non-master; in this work, only two examinee is considered and questions follow the same response model; therefore, state can be simply defined as the difference between wrong and right answer and the only decision is when to stop the test. [15] make use of Recurrent Neural Networks to model the state space, mainly to account for an embedded representation of questions already applied; overexposure of items are avoided by penalizing overexposed items.

Although a few previous works frame the CAT problem as an MDP, they do so under a specific scenario. In this paper we show how MDP can model different formalisms for CAT, in particular, we frame CAT problems under the POMDP formalism, when agents does not observe the state fully [7]. We also gives an empirical example of how MDPs can be used for solving CAT problems, and we compare it against traditional shortsighted solutions from CAT literature.

# 2  Computerized Adaptive Testing

CATs are applied in an adaptive way to each examinee by computer. Based on predefined rules of the algorithm, the items are selected sequentially during the test after each answer to an item [18]. A classic CAT can be described by the following steps [9]:

1. The first item is selected;
2. The latent trait is estimated based on the first item answer;
3. The next item to be answered is selected;
4. The latent trait is recalculated based on previous answers; and
5. Repeat steps 3 and 4 until an answer is no longer necessary according to a pre-established criterion, called stop criterion.

## 2.1  Response Model and Latent Trait Estimator

Usually, a CAT is used to estimate some latent trait of an examinee. A university may use CAT to rank student by estimating a grade for each candidate. A doctor may diagnose some patient condition under a multidimensional spectrum. The Government may give a driver license to a teenager.

Generically, we can consider a latent trait $\theta_j \in \Theta$ for an examinee $j$, where $\Theta$ is the support set for latent trait. This trait can be unidimensional or multidimensional. When a question $i$ is submitted to the examinee $\theta_j$, an answer is given and a result $x_{ij}$ is observed.

Results may be dichotomic, polithomic, or continuum. A response model considers parameterized questions, i.e., a question $i$ is represent by a parameter vector $\gamma_i$ and a support set $\mathcal{X}_i$ for possible results. After a question $i$ is submitted to an examinee $j$, a random variable $X_{ij} \in \mathcal{X}_i$ representing the observed result is generated and the response model defines a probability distribution for the possible results[1], i.e., for all $x \in \mathcal{X}_i$:

$$\Pr(X_{ij} = x | \gamma_i, \theta_j).$$

Given an examinee $\theta$ and a sequence of $n$ answers $\mathbf{x}_n = (x_{i_1}, x_{i_2}, \ldots, x_{i_n})$, the latent trait $\theta$ can be estimated by Bayesian procedure or Maximum Likelihood (ML) [1].

We consider here a Bayesian estimator based on expected *a posteriori* (EAP), i.e.,

$$\hat{\theta} = \mathrm{E}\left[\theta | \mathbf{x}_n\right] = \int \theta \frac{f(\theta) \prod_{k=1}^{n} \Pr(X_{i_k} = x_{i_k} | \theta)}{\Pr(\mathbf{X}_n = \mathbf{x}_n)} d(\theta), \tag{1}$$

where $f(\theta)$ is the *a priori* distribution on the latent trait $\theta$, usually considered the standard normal distribution.

---

[1] We consider the case when $\mathcal{X}_i$ is enumerate for a briefer exposition.

The ML estimator estimates the latent trait by $\hat{\theta} = \max_\theta L(\theta|\mathbf{x}_n)$ where the likelihood is given by:

$$L(\theta|\mathbf{x}_n) = \prod_{k=1}^{n} \Pr(X_{i_k} = x_{i_k}|\theta). \tag{2}$$

If the objective of the CAT is to classify an examinee among options category $\mathcal{C}$, a classification function $C : \Theta \to \mathcal{C}$ may be defined after latent trait estimation $\hat{\theta}$ or a category estimator $\hat{C}$ may be directly defined.

## 2.2  Efficiency, Precision and Constraints

A CAT may be evaluated under two main criteria: precision and efficiency. Precision is related to how good is the estimation $\hat{\theta}$, while efficiency is related to the effort made by the examinee or examiner.

If the objective of the CAT is to ranking examinees, a common evaluation for precision is the mean square error (MSE):

$$MSE = \mathrm{E}\left[(\theta - \hat{\theta})^2\right] = \int (\theta - \hat{\theta})^2 f(\theta) d(\theta).$$

If the objective of the CAT is to classify an examinee, a common evaluation for precision may be accuracy (ACC):

$$ACC = \mathrm{E}[\mathbb{1}_{C_\theta = \hat{C}}],$$

where $\mathbb{1}_A$ is the indicator function for the condition $A$, and $C_\theta$ is the correct category.

Efficiency is usually evaluated by the length of the CAT, i.e., how many questions the examinee answered. Efficiency may also be evaluated by the time spent by the examinee because some questions may require more time than others, or some other effort measure.

Finally, CAT may pursue precision and efficiency under some restriction. The commonest restriction is regarding question repetition; in a test a question can only be applied once. A examiner may also be concerned with test content balancing and item exposure control. Content balancing considers that the item bank is clustered into groups of question and the test should choose question from all of the groups with a minimum rate. Item exposure control considers that a question should not be submitted to many examinee; if a question is overexposed, examinees will know it beforehand and the CAT will lost precision.

A particular restriction is considered in the multistage CAT [11]. In the multistage CAT, the test is subdivide into stages, and, in any stage, a set of question must be revealed at once to the examinee. After the examinee answers all the questions in a stage, he/she is routed individually to a new stage.

## 2.3   CAT as an Optimization Problem

All the elements described in the previous section allow us to define an optimization problem. Given a bank of items $Q$, we first model the CAT problem as a process:

1. A examinee $\theta$ is drawn from a distribution $f(\theta)$. Although the distribution $f(\theta)$ may be known to the examiner, the process does not reveals the examinee $\theta$.
2. While examiner does not decide to stop the test, at any stage $t = 1, 2, \ldots$
   (a) the examiner chooses a question $q_t \in Q$ and submits to the examinee[2].
   (b) By answering the question, the examinee generates a result $x_t$.
3. The examiner estimates the latent trait $\theta$ through an estimation $\hat{\theta}$[3].

The result of the CAT process is a random history $h = (\theta, q_1, x_1, q_2, x_2, \ldots, q_N, x_N, \hat{\theta})$. An optimal examiner is obtained from the following optimization problem:

$$\min \quad E_\theta[U(h)]$$
$$\text{s.t.} \quad Z(f(\theta), h) \cdot$$

$U$ is an objective function. For example, if the examiner wants to minimize MSE, then, $U(h) = (\theta - \hat{\theta})^2$. If the examiner wants to minimize the test length, then, $U(h) = N$. The objective function can also combine both objectives.

$Z$ is a constraint function. If the examiner wants to constraint item to maximum $\alpha$ exposition, then, $Z(\cdot) = \{h | E[\sum_{t=1}^{N} \mathbb{1}_{q_t = q}] \leq \alpha \ \forall q \in Q\}$. If the examiner wants to avoid question repetition, then, $Z(\cdot) = \{h | \sum_{t=1}^{N} \sum_{t'-t+1}^{N} \mathbb{1}_{q_t = q_{t'}} = 0 \ \forall q \in Q\}$. Note that in the first example, constraints are on the expectation over the random variable $h$, while in the second example constraints are on the samples of the random variable.

# 3   Markov Decision Process

We consider a special case of Markov Decision Process, the Stochastic Shortest Path (SSP) problem [2]. A SSP is defined by a tuple $\langle S, A, P, C, s_0, G \rangle$ where: $s \in S$ are the possible states; $a \in A$ are possible actions; $P : S \times A \times S \to [0, 1]$ is the transition function; $C : S \times A \to R^+$ is the cost function; $s_0 \in S$ is the initial state; and $G$ is the set of goal states.

A SSP defines a process of an agent interacting with an environment and at all time step $t$: $(i)$ the agent observes a state $s_t$, $(ii)$ the agent chooses an action $a_t$, $(iii)$ the agent pays a cost $c_t$; and $(iv)$ the process moves to a new state $s_{t+1}$. The process ends when a goal state $s \in G$ are reached. Transitions and costs present Markov's property, i.e., they both depend only on the current state $s_t$ and chosen action $a_t$.

---

[2] In the multistage CAT, the examiner must choose a set of questions.
[3] In a classification CAT, the examiner can estimate directly a category instead of a the latent trait $\theta$.

The solution for a SSP consists of policies that describe which actions should be taken in each situation. Here we consider probabilistic stationary policies $\pi : \mathcal{S} \rightarrow (\mathcal{A} \rightarrow [0,1])$ that maps each state for a probability distribution over actions.

The objective of a SSP is to find an optimal policy $\pi^*$ that minimizes the expected cumulative cost, i.e., we define a value function of a policy $\pi$ by $V^\pi = \mathbb{E}[\sum_{t=0}^{\infty} c_t | \pi]$ and defines the optimal policy as $\pi^* = \arg\max_\pi V^\pi$. There are many algorithms in the literature to find optimal policies for MDPs [12]. Here, we focus on Linear Programming algorithms, in particular the dual criterion formulation [21].

### 3.1  Linear Programming Solution

The Linear Programming Dual Formulation considers variables $x_{s,a}$ for all $s \in \mathcal{S}, a \in \mathcal{A}$ that indicates an expected accumulated occurrence frequency for every pair state-action. The SSP dynamics restricts the solutions by specifying an $in(s)$ and $out(s)$ flow model for every state $s$. Every state but initial state and goal state must equalize $in(s)$ and $out(s)$. Initial state $s_0$ presents a unity in-out difference, while goal states in $\mathcal{G}$ has no output. For every state $s \in \mathcal{S}$, we have:

$$in(s) = \sum_{s' \in \mathcal{S}, a \in \mathcal{A}} x_{s',a} P(s|s',a) \quad \text{and} \quad out(s) = \sum_{a \in \mathcal{A}_{(s)}} x_{s,a}. \tag{3}$$

Define the linear programming LP1 as follows:

$$
\begin{aligned}
\text{LP1} \quad &\min_{x_{s,a}} \quad \sum_{s \in \mathcal{S}, a \in \mathcal{A}} x_{s,a} \mathcal{C}(s,a) \\
&\text{s.t. } x_{s,a} \geq 0 &&\forall s \in \mathcal{S}, a \in \mathcal{A}(s) \\
&\quad out(s) - in(s) \leq 0 &&\forall s \in \mathcal{S} \setminus (\mathcal{G} \cup s_0). \\
&\quad out(s_0) - in(s_0) \leq 1 \\
&\quad \sum_{s_g \in \mathcal{G}} in(s_g) = 1
\end{aligned}
\tag{4}
$$

The optimal policy $\pi^*$ to the SSP can be obtained from expected accumulated occurrence frequency $x_{s,a}$ in LP1 by:

$$\pi^*(a|s) = \frac{x_{s,a}}{\sum_{a' \in \mathcal{A}} x_{s,a'}} \quad \forall s \in \mathcal{S},$$

and $\pi^*$ incurs in expected cost $c_{min} = \sum_{s \in \mathcal{S}, a \in \mathcal{A}} x_{s,a} \mathcal{C}(s,a)$.

### 3.2  Partial-Observable MDP

A formulation to sequential decision problem more generic than MDPs or SSPs is the Partial-Observable MDP (POMDP) [7]. In an MDP, the agent is considered to observe immediately the state of the process, this guarantee that an optimal policy can be find in the state space, i.e., the optimal decision is based only on the current state observation.

In a POMDP, the agent observes the process state mediate by a probabilistic observation function $O : S \rightarrow (\mathcal{O} \rightarrow [0,1])$. A POMDP defines a process of an agent interacting with an environment and at all time step $t$: $(i)$ the agent makes an observation $o_t \sim O(s_t)$, $(ii)$ the agent chooses an action $a_t$, $(iii)$ the agent pays a cost $c_t$; and $(iv)$ the process moves to a new state $s_{t+1}$.

In a POMDP, the optimal policy must consider the history for the current time step t, i.e., $h_t = (o_0, a_0, c_0, \ldots, o_t)$ or a belief state $b_t$ which is a probability distribution over state space given the history of observations. Note that the history grows exponentially with the time step $t$ and finding an optimal policy to a POMDP is only computational practical when the state space is finite and small. Usually, algorithms try to find a quasi-optimal policy [7].

### 3.3   Augmented States

MDPs and SSPs are very strict regards Markov property. First, the agent must observes the full state of the process. Second, the cost function must depend only on the current state. Third, the objective function considers a random variable that is simply the sum of immediate costs. If any of this properties is not presented, most of time, the optimal policy is not restricted to the MDP state space.

The POMDP solution is an example. In this case, the policy must be defined in an augmented state space, the history space. In general, Markov property can be recovered under an appropriated augmented state space. For example, if the process ends after some fixed times step $T$, the state space must be augmented with the current time $t$, i.e., $(s, t)$.

Although augmented state space can be a general technique to find out optimal policies, we have already seem with POMDP, that the augmented state space may grows exponentially.

## 4   CAT as a POMDP

Remember that in the process of a CAT, initially an examinee is drawn from a probability distribution $f(\theta)$. Then, given any question, the examiner observes the answer for that question, which depends on the question itself and the latent trait $\theta$ of the examinee. However, the examiner never observes directly the latent trait $\theta$. A CAT can be seen as a POMDP by:

1. Considering the state space as the tuple $(\theta, q_t)$, i.e., the latent trait and the last question.
2. Considering the action space as the set of question in the item bank, plus a termination action.
3. Considering deterministic transitions. First, $\theta$ never changes and the question $q_t$ changes following the examiner choices.
4. Considering the observation of the process as the result of the examinee answering the last question, i.e., the CAT response model.

Figure 1 shows a scheme connecting CAT and POMDP. There, the belief state is obtained from the *a posteriori* distribution based on Bayesian method. Next, we show how POMDPs can represent different formulations of CAT. $I$ is the belief state, while $\tau$ is the model to generate the *a posteriori* belief state.

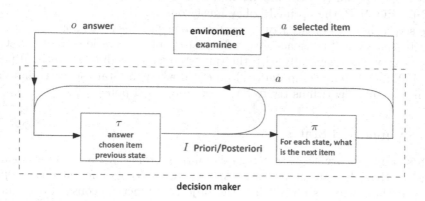

**Fig. 1.** CAT framed in a POMDP with belief state.

**Minimize MSE with Fixed-Length $N$ Without Repeated Questions.** Note that we do not formulate yet the cost function. Essentially it depends on the trade-off between precision and efficiency. In this scenario, it is desired to obtain the smallest MSE (utility function $U$) with at maximum $N$ questions (restriction function $Z$).

To do so, we must augment the observation space with all the question submitted to the examinee and respective results. Then, a terminal cost is payed based on the variance of the *a posteriori* distribution. The action space depends on the observation, i.e., $a_t \in \mathcal{A}(o_t)$ and if a question was already submitted, such a question is not included in $\mathcal{A}(o_t)$. After $N$ questions, the only question available in $\mathcal{A}(o_t)$ is the termination action.

**Item Exposure Control: Every Action is Exposed Equally.** Consider the LP1 formulation in Sect. 3.1, if every question must be exposed equally, the following constraint must be considered for every pair $a, a' \in \mathcal{A}$:

$$\sum_{s \in \mathcal{S}} x_{s,a} = \sum_{s \in \mathcal{S}} x_{s,a'}.$$

Remember that $x_{s,a}$ indicates the expected amount of occurrence of the pair $(s, a)$. The sum $\sum_{s \in \mathcal{S}} x_{s,a}$ is the expected total occurrence for action $a$, therefore, a question $a$.

**Multi-stage CAT: $K$ Questions Per Stage.** In this case, an action is a subset of the item bank $Q$ with $K$ questions, i.e., $\mathcal{A} = \{A \in 2^Q \text{ and } |A| = K\}$, where $2^Q$ is the power set of $Q$.

Note that although the formulations here presented may be not practical to be solved optimally, they are described under the same framework, MDPs and POMDPs. In the next section we give a practical result of our theoretical formulation.

# 5    Approximating a CAT by an MDP

In this section we show that the theoretical result showed in the previous section can elucidate results in the CAT literature. We consider a traditional CAT problem: fixed-length with a dichotomous item bank. We approximate this CAT by an MDP, which can be solved optimally, and we show that traditional selection criterion such as Fisher Information may be close to optimal solution.

## 5.1    Response Model: Item Response Theory

It is possible to build a CAT based on the item response theory (IRT), a mathematical model that describes the probability of an individual to score an item as a function of the latent trait level $\Pr(X_i = 1 \mid \theta)$. We consider the logistic model with three parameters [3]. A bank of 45 items calibrated from a national mathematics exam was used in our experiment [19].

## 5.2    Normalized and Discretized Bayesian Method

As said before, one way of recovering Markov property in a process is to consider augmented state or belief state. The *a posteriori* distribution by following Bayes method is exactly the belief state of our CAT POMDP. However, the state space of such distribution is the continuum $\aleph_1$. We construct a finite MDP from such belief states.

First, we normalized every *a posteriori* distribution by a Gaussian distribution with equivalent mean and variance. Second, we discretized such pair of values; we consider 100 mean values (between −4 and 4) and 1,000 variance values (between 0.001 and 1). Finally transitions are defined among normalized discretized belief states.

Usually, a CAT does not repeat an item in the same exam. Therefore, the state space must be augmented with the applied questions. In this case, the number of state is exponential in the number of questions. To reduce the number of states, we allow the CAT to repeat questions; in this case the state space does not need to be augmented. Remember that answers to questions are probabilistic; therefore, the user may answer differently for the same question.

We consider the CAT optimization problem of minimize MSE with fixed-length $N$ with repeated questions. In this case, an optimal policy can easily be founded. In the next section we compare it to traditional approach from CAT literature.

## 5.3    Experimental Result

We consider two score functions from CAT literature: Fisher Information (FI) [10,16] and Minimizing the Expected Posterior Variance (MEPV) [14]. The first one, FI, is well-known in the literature and is also the cheapest method. The second one, MEPV, is a costly score function, which consider the next potential belief states given every possible question in the item bank; it is optimal in our normalized discretized MDP when only one question is allowed. We define policies based on each score function and evaluated them under the MDP framework; because of the MDP framework the value function $V^\pi$ for each score function can be calculated exactly.

Score functions are shortsighted, in fact, they do not even take into account the fixed-length horizon $N$. They are clearly suboptimal, however, it is far from clear how far from the optimal policy they are. We make use of an MDP algorithm to obtained an optimal policy for every length between 1 and 45 questions. Every other policies, we compare against this gold standard.

Figure 2 shows our results. We plot the difference between the root MSE (RMSE) for every policy and the gold standard. Besides FI and MEPV policies, we also plot optimal policies behaviour for fixed-length 15, 30, and 45. Note that optimal policies may be far from gold standard during the first questions, but in the end (15, 30, or 45 questions) the gold standard is reached. Because policies based on score functions choose questions that gives return immediately, they are always close to the gold standard, but never is optimal. Despite score function not being optimal, we can see that the largest difference is not more than 0.01.

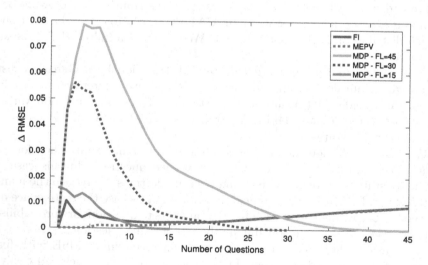

**Fig. 2.** Comparison of policies based on shortsighted score-functions and MDP optimal policies.

# 6   Conclusion

We formulated CAT formalisms as MDPs and showed in an experiment that despite being optimal, the gain with MDPs may not compensate since suboptimal solution must be considered in real scenarios. However, the formulation as MDPs allows to formulate CAT as optimization problem and describe many CAT formulations under the same framework.

We believe that such a framework and experiments as the one here showed, may elucidate the limits of a myriad of methods in the CAT literature, mainly regarding CAT under constraints. Recently we showed that Fixed-length stop criterion has great advantages against other stop criteria, with this framework we can investigate how it compares against optimality under different evaluations [4]. For example, the MDP framework allows to define risk-sensitive optimality [13]; Risk-sensitive MDPs would allow a CAT to weight worst scenarios regarding the length of the test or the MSE so that CAT is fair for every examinee.

# References

1. de Andrade, D.F., Tavares, H.R., da Cunha Valle, R.: Teoria da resposta ao item: conceitos e aplicações. ABE, São Paulo (2000)
2. Bertsekas, D.P., Tsitsiklis, J.N.: An analysis of stochastic shortest path problems. Math. Oper. Res. **16**(3), 580–595 (1991)
3. Birnbaum, A.L.: Some latent trait models and their use in inferring an examinee's ability. Statistical theories of mental test scores (1968)
4. Blind: Comprehensive empirical analysis of stop criteria in computerized adaptive testing. In: Submitted to International Conference on Computer Supported Education (CSEDU) (2021)
5. El-Alfy, E.S.M.: A reinforcement learning approach for sequential mastery testing, pp. 295–301 (2011)
6. Hambleton, R.K., Swaminathan, H.: Item Response Theory: Principles and Applications. Springer, Dordrecht (2013). https://doi.org/10.1007/978-94-017-1988-9
7. Hoerger, M., Kurniawati, H.: An on-line POMDP solver for continuous observation spaces (2020)
8. Kreitzberg, C.B., Stocking, M.L., Swanson, L.: Computerized adaptive testing: principles and directions. Comput. Educ. **2**(4), 319–329 (1978)
9. van der Linden, W.J., Glas, C.A.: Computerized Adaptive Testing: Theory and Practice. Springer, Boston (2000). https://doi.org/10.1007/0-306-47531-6
10. Lord, F.M.: Applications of Item Response Theory to Practical Testing Problems. Routledge, Abingdon (1980)
11. Magis, D., Yan, D., von Davier, A.A.: Computerized Adaptive and Multistage Testing with R: Using Packages CatR and MstR, 1st edn. Springer, Cham (2017). https://doi.org/10.1007/978-3-319-69218-0
12. Mausam, K.A.: Planning with Markov decision processes: an AI perspective. Synth. Lect. Artif. Intell. Mach. Learn. **6**(1) (2012)
13. Minami, R., da Silva, V.F.: Shortest stochastic path with risk sensitive evaluation. In: Batyrshin, I., González Mendoza, M. (eds.) MICAI 2012. LNCS (LNAI), vol. 7629, pp. 371–382. Springer, Heidelberg (2013). https://doi.org/10.1007/978-3-642-37807-2_32

14. Morris, S.B., Bass, M., Howard, E., Neapolitan, R.E.: Stopping rules for computer adaptive testing when item banks have nonuniform information. Int. J. Test. **20**(2), 146–168 (2020)
15. Nurakhmetov, D.: Reinforcement learning applied to adaptive classification testing. In: Veldkamp, B.P., Sluijter, C. (eds.) Theoretical and Practical Advances in Computer-based Educational Measurement. MEMA, pp. 325–336. Springer, Cham (2019). https://doi.org/10.1007/978-3-030-18480-3_17
16. Sari, H.I., Raborn, A.: What information works best?: A comparison of routing methods. Appl. Psychol. Meas. **42**(6), 499–515 (2018)
17. Segall, D.O.: Computerized adaptive testing. Encyclopedia Soc. Meas. **1**, 429–438 (2005)
18. Spenassato, D., Bornia, A., Tezza, R.: Computerized adaptive testing: a review of research and technical characteristics. IEEE Lat. Am. Trans. **13**(12), 3890–3898 (2015)
19. Spenassato, D., Trierweiller, A.C., de Andrade, D.F., Bornia, A.C.: Testes adaptativos computadorizados aplicados em avaliaçoes educacionais. Revista Brasileira de Informática na Educação **24**(02), 1 (2016)
20. Sutton, R.S., Barto, A.G.: Reinforcement Learning: An Introduction. MIT Press, Cambridge (1998)
21. Trevizan, F., Teichteil-Königsbuch, F., Thiébaux, S.: Efficient solutions for stochastic shortest path problems with dead ends. In: Proceedings of the Thirty-Third Conference on Uncertainty in Artificial Intelligence (UAI) (2017)
22. Wainer, H., Dorans, N.J., Flaugher, R., Green, B.F., Mislevy, R.J.: Computerized Adaptive Testing: A Primer. Routledge, Abington (2000)
23. Wang, C., Chang, H.H., Huebner, A.: Restrictive stochastic item selection methods in cognitive diagnostic computerized adaptive testing. J. Educ. Meas. **48**(3), 255–273 (2011)

# C-Libras: A Gesture Recognition App for the Brazilian Sign Language

Tiago Trotta[1], Leonardo Rocha[1], Telma Rosa de Andrade[1],
Marcelo de Paiva Guimarães[2], and Diego Roberto Colombo Dias[1]

[1] Universidade Federal de São João del-Rei, São João del-Rei, MG, Brazil
{trotta,lcrocha,telmadelac,diegodias}@ufsj.edu.br
[2] Universidade Federal de São Paulo, Osasco, SP, Brazil
marcelo.paiva@unifesp.br

**Abstract.** Sign languages are visual representations used by hearing or speech impaired people to communicate between themselves and with other people. There are over 140 sign languages globally, and they can be developed by deaf communities or derived from other existing sign languages. The signs made in this context are not considered gestures but words articulated primarily by the hands, while possibly involving facial expressions and trunk movements, making it far from trivial to understand them. Thus, automatic sign language recognition supported by machine learning has shown significant advancement in recent years. This paper presents a mobile application capable of recognizing gestures representing the letters of the Brazilian Sign Language's (Libras) alphabet. Our methodology has three steps: the construction of the gesture dataset containing all the letters of the Libras alphabet; the training of the machine learning model used in the gesture classification; and the development of the desktop/mobile application used to capture the gestures to be classified.

**Keywords:** Sign language recognition · Machine learning · Augmented reality

## 1 Introduction

Sign languages are visual representations based on hand gestures and facial and body expressions. They are distinct from conventional languages, such as English and Portuguese, because they are not auditory and do not require vocal expression. Because they develop within deaf communities, they are considered a natural language, provided with grammar, phonology, morphology, syntax, and semantics. Thus, sign languages are more complex than just a set of hand gestures. Therefore, due to their complexity, recognizing their gestures can be classified as a challenge to be beaten by machine learning techniques.

---

Supported by CNPq, FAPEMIG and Huawei.

O. Gervasi et al. (Eds.): ICCSA 2022, LNCS 13375, pp. 603–618, 2022.
https://doi.org/10.1007/978-3-031-10522-7_41

There is no universal sign language, and they can vary worldwide. In Brazil, there is the Brazilian Sign Language (Libras). According to research conducted by the Brazilian Institute of Geography and Statistics (IBGE) in 2019, in Brazil, 2.3 million people two years of age or older (1.1% of the population) suffer from hearing disabilities, out of which 22.4% of the people between 5 and 40 years of age know Libras [8].

In 2002 President Luís Inácio "Lula" da Silva sanctioned Law No. 10.436, which regulated Libras and recognized it as a legal and genuine means of communication. Through this law, Libras allows the deaf to use gestures instead of oral communication legitimately. In 2005, federal decree No. 5626 was published, establishing the mandatory teaching of Libras by universities in their undergraduate, pedagogical, and speech therapy courses. Thus, the use of sign language has gained space in Brazil, which has favored the development of deaf and hard-of-hearing children from an early age [9].

Among the many fields of study around sign languages, Sign Language Recognition (SLR) aims to develop computational approaches capable of automatically identifying a sequence of signs and correctly understand their meaning [5]. Many SLR approaches treat the problem simply as gesture recognition, but sign languages are far more complex and nuanced than just collections of specific gestures. A more manageable challenge within SLR would be to correctly classify the alphabet of a sign language, since these gestures are usually much simpler and less context-sensitive.

One of the techniques frequently used in SLR is Machine learning (ML), a subfield of artificial intelligence (AI) that automates the building of analytical models, allowing machines to adapt to various scenarios independently. ML has been applied to solve various problems of our daily lives related to image interpretation, voice command recognition, and even disease identification, such as COVID-19 [12]. In the area of SLR, it has not been different. Several works in the literature address the topic [3,4,7]. However, it is still an open area that demands research both in the preparation of datasets and the training of intelligent models.

Thus, in this paper, we proposed and developed a mobile and desktop application capable of capturing hand gestures and classifying them like letters of the Libras's alphabet using a Support Vector Machine (SVM). We tested the application with different SVM models, trained using different sets of letters and different numbers of example gestures per letter, and discovered that the number of examples per letter affects the model's accuracy. Our tests also show that the number and choice of letters recognized by the model affect accuracy as well.

In Sect. 2 we present and discuss the main sign language recognition (SLR) approaches, in Sect. 3 we explain the development of our application, Sect. 5 contains the results of our tests, and in Sect. 6 we present our conclusions and talk about future work.

# 2   Sign Language Recognition Approaches

Among the several approaches currently applied to SLR, we can highlight the use of inertial sensors and computer vision. In this section, we talk about the two technologies, technical development solutions, and some work that has set out to create tracking devices.

## 2.1   Sensor Based Approaches

Sensors have been widely employed in motion detection, so they are helpful in body tracking. In the specific case of sign languages, most gestures are concentrated on the upper limbs, specifically the hands.

The advance in virtual reality has enabled the proposal of several unconventional interaction devices. Among them, we can highlight the gloves (Data Gloves and Power Gloves), widely used in the context of SLR [1,11,15].

Despite gloves having been widely used to track hand gestures, other kinds of sensors have been employed, such as inertial sensors, made up of accelerometers, gyroscopes and compasses [19,20].

One of the great benefits of employing sensors in body tracking is the accuracy achieved. Since the sensors are attached to the user's body, they do not suffer from occlusion issues, something common in image capture-based solutions that employ computer vision.

## 2.2   Computer Vision-Based Approaches

Computer vision-based tracking techniques allow body tracking without any device or sensor attaching to the user's body, enabling mobility and naturality in movement execution.

Usually, vision-based tracking is performed by cameras, either RGB or infrared, such as the Kinect, which has both kinds of cameras. Among the solutions that only use infrared cameras, we can highlight the Leap Motion Controller [16]. On the side of the spectrum, some solutions only use RGB cameras, of which we can highlight MediaPipe, a framework used to build multimedia applications that require body tracking, allowing the detection of objects, faces, hands, hair segmentation among other features [10]. MediaPipe uses intelligent models developed by Google, using their machine learning framework - TensorFlow and TensorFlow Lite. In this work, we employ MediaPipe to capture gestures, both from webcam feed and from previously recorded video.

Although gloves are predominantly sensor-based, some approaches have explored the use of computer vision, such as colored gloves or colored markers positioned on the wrist or fingertips [6,18]. In 2017, Sadek et al. proposed and developed a low-cost smart glove capable of analyzing the anatomical shape of the hands [14]. However, despite the low cost, the use of the device required computer vision techniques since it used colored markers. The device proposed in 2015 by Rossol et al. also uses computer vision as tracking technology [13]. However, it employs the Leap Motion device as a tracking medium instead of

RGB cameras. The Leap Motion is a device specially designed to perform hand and finger tracking, allowing the identification of hands, fingers, orientation, and palm location.

# 3   Methodology

This work was developed in three steps, illustrated in Fig. 1. The first step was the construction of a gesture dataset containing examples of the Libras' alphabet gestures to be used as training data for an ML model. This step can be divided into three sub-steps: (1) The capturing of the gestures from videos downloaded from YouTube or recorded by RGB cameras; (2) The processing of the captured footage to extract the hands' joints, using the MediaPipe [10] framework; and (3) The storing of the gestures in the ReBase [2] database.

**Fig. 1.** Illustration of the methodology.

The second step was training an ML model, more specifically an SVM, to classify new gestures. Finally, the third and last step was the development of a desktop and mobile application, using the Unity game engine [17], to capture gestures from webcams and use the trained SVM to classify them.

## 3.1   Gesture Dataset Construction

The training dataset is a collection of several gesture examples for each of the letters in the Libras' alphabet, taken from video files recorded by regular RGB cameras. Some videos were recorded by members of the research team, and others were downloaded from various YouTube channels via a Python script using the *pytube* library.

Once downloaded, all the videos were processed by another Python script, using the *MediaPipe* and *OpenCV* libraries, in order to extract the hands' joints, as illustrated by Fig. 2. After extracting the joints' coordinates, the gestures received labels to be used as classes by the SVM. The labels were automatically chosen based on the original video's title, using various regular expressions - for example, a video named "Libras Alphabet - Letter A" would be labeled "libras_a". Finally, the gestures' coordinates and labels were written into JSON files, so they could be processed and inserted into the ReBase database.

ReBase is a database dedicated to storing body movements, specifically neuromotor rehabilitation movements. All the movements are stored in the form of

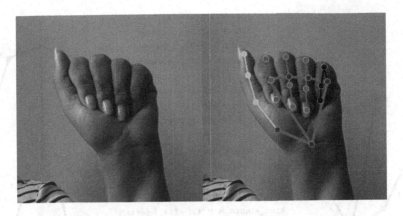

**Fig. 2.** MediaPipe processing to extract the hand's joints.

the rotations of the body's joints over time, which take up much less storage space than video files. In addition, working with joints and rotations means the movements can be recorded by any kind of body tracking device, such as the Kinect or even RGB cameras using MediaPipe, in addition to preserving the anonymity of the data, since no images of the subjects are stored. Even though ReBase was designed with a different context in mind - body movements instead of hand gestures - its data format is flexible enough to be adapted to other use cases.

MediaPipe's hand tracking module defines 21 joints for the hand, while ReBase defines 20 joints for key parts of the body. For this application, 20 of the hand joints defined by MediaPipe were mapped to the joints defined by ReBase, as shown in Fig. 3, thus making it possible to store hand gestures in the database. The joints 4, 8, 12, 16, and 20 were purposely ignored because they represent the tips of the fingers and cannot be rotated. The movements were then inserted into ReBase as JSON files, following ReBase's format, via the Unity ReBase API. For this purpose, we developed a Unity application to utilize the abstractions provided by the API. The application was also responsible for converting the joints' coordinates into rotations.

**Pre-processing.** Before being submitted to the ML model, the gestures were pre-processed. First, all the rotations were normalized between $0°$ and $306°$, as shown by Eq. 2, to avoid any negative rotations that could result from the conversion process. In addition, the gestures had their durations normalized to *30 frames*, the length of the shortest example. Every gesture over 30 frames had frames removed from different points along its duration, in regular intervals, until their length was equal to 30, as shown in Listing 1.1. The gestures were then converted into an array containing all the rotations in the $x$ axis, followed by all the rotations in the $y$ axis, followed by all the rotations in the $z$ axis, as defined by Expression 1, where n represents the gesture's number of frames.

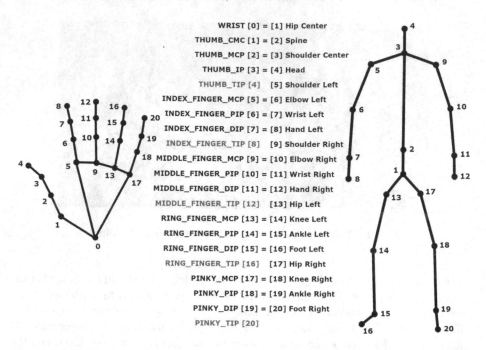

**Fig. 3.** MediaPipe's hand joints (left) mapped to ReBase's joints (right). The joints in red were ignored. (Color figure online)

```
def reduce_frames(gesture, n_frames):
    length = n_frames
    # While the gesture's length is larger than 30 frames
    while length > TARGET_LENGTH:
        count = 0
        # Remove frames in regular intervals
        step = math.ceil(length / TARGET_LENGTH)
        for i in range(0, length, step):
            gesture[i] = None
            count += 1
            length -= 1
            if length == TARGET_LENGTH:
                break
        gesture = [x for x in gesture if x != None]
    return gesture
```

**Listing 1.1.** Gesture length normalization

$$[x_1, x_2, ..., x_n, y_1, y_2, ..., y_n, z_1, z_2, ..., z_n] \tag{1}$$

$$NormalizeRotation(x) : \begin{cases} x - 360 & \text{if } x > 360 \\ 0 & \text{if } -0.1 < x < 0 \\ x & \text{otherwise} \end{cases} \qquad (2)$$

## 3.2   Gesture Classification

Once the training dataset had been constructed, processed, and stored in ReBase, we used it to train SVMs to classify new gestures. The SVMs were constructed in Python, using the *scikit-learn* library. The Radial Basis Function (RBF) was the chosen kernel function, and all of SVMs' parameters were set to scikit-learn's default values. For this application, each of the 27 letters of the Libras' alphabet represent a class.

There are no official Python APIs for ReBase, but it is possible to retrieve the data from the ReBase REST Server via HTTP requests. Thus, we created a Python script to download the training dataset, process it, and feed it to the SVMs, using the *requests* library. After training, the SVMs were dumped into files using the *Joblib* library so that they could be used later in the C-Libras application.

## 4   The C-Libras Application

The C-Libras application was developed for PC and Android smartphones and allows users to have their gestures classified in real-time by the trained SVMs. C-Libras follows the client-server architecture, as illustrated by Fig. 4. The clients are responsible for capturing the users' gestures, processing them and sending them to the server, which submits them to the SVM for classification and sends back the results. Each client communicates with the server via a WebSocket.

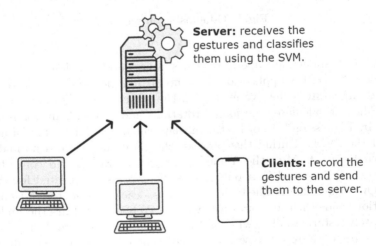

**Server:** receives the gestures and classifies them using the SVM.

**Clients:** record the gestures and send them to the server.

**Fig. 4.** C-Libras' client-server architecture.

**The C-Libras Client.** The C-Libras client was developed in Unity, using the *MediaPipe Unity Plugin* to process the gestures and extract the joints and the *WebSocketSharp* library to establish a WebSocket connection to the server.

Once the users start the application, they are presented with the C-Libras' main screen (Fig. 5), where they can perform the gestures to be classified. After each gesture is classified, the alphabet letter corresponding to the classification is displayed on the top section of the screen. The text display can be cleared by clicking the "Limpar" ("Clear") button. From this screen, the user can also access the camera configurations window (Fig. 6) by clicking the leftmost button. The configurations include selecting the video source from a list of cameras connected to the device, changing the camera's resolution, etc.

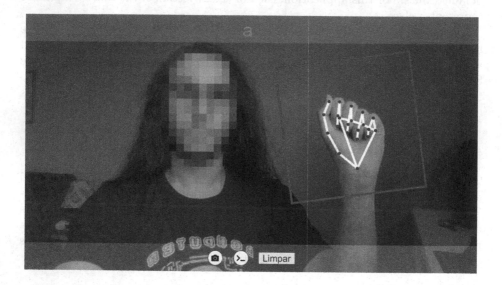

**Fig. 5.** C-Libras' main screen.

The client application operates in a simple workflow, described by Fig. 7. Once every frame, the application uses the MediaPipe Unity Plugin to process the latest frame from the live feed - i.e., the webcam - and extract the hands' joints. Then, it calculates the joints' rotations and stores them in an array, as defined by Expression 1, in order to translate the data to the same format used to train the SVMs. During this process, the rotations are also normalized as described by Eq. 2. After the frames' joints are extracted and converted, the resulting array is stored in a buffer, and the process is repeated for the next frame. Once the buffer is filled with 30 arrays - each representing a frame - the application sends them to the server via the WebSocket, clears the buffer, and immediately restarts to fill it while waiting for the classification. When the client receives a response from the server, the corresponding letter of the alphabet is displayed.

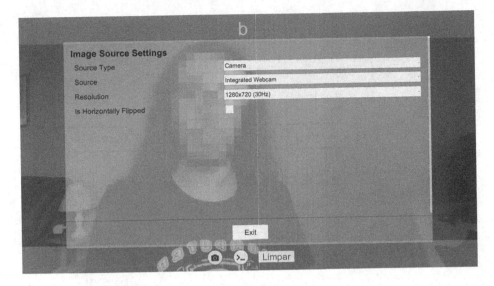

Fig. 6. C-Libras' camera configuration window.

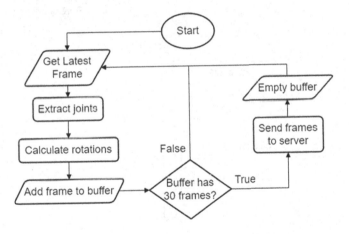

Fig. 7. C-Libras client workflow.

**The C-Libras Server.** The C-Libras server was developed in Python, using the *Django* web framework. Similar to the client, the server also has a simple workflow (Fig. 8). On startup, the server loads an SVM model from a file, using the Joblib library, and begins listening for connections. Once a WebSocket connection is established, the server waits for a message containing the 30 frames for classification. When the frames are received, the server only has to submit them to the SVM, since the client has already done all the pre-processing. Lastly, the results are sent back to the client via the WebSocket, and the server waits for the following message. A sequence diagram is presented in Fig. 9, exemplifying the interactions between the server and the client.

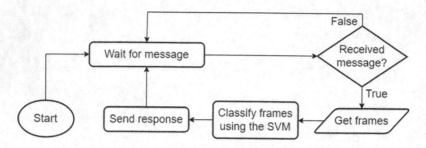

**Fig. 8.** C-Libras server workflow.

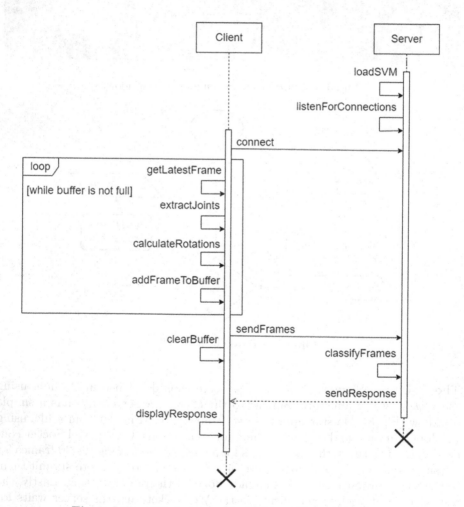

**Fig. 9.** Interaction between the C-Libras client and server.

# 5    Results

We performed three experiments to measure the accuracy of our application. In the first experiment, we trained multiple SVM models using seven examples per letter, varied the letters for each, and measured their accuracy. We chose to use 7 gestures for each letter for this example because this was the number of gestures available for the letters we had the least gestures.

In the second experiment, we trained multiple models using only the letters 'A', 'B', and 'C', varied the number of examples per letter, and measured their accuracy. We chose these letters for this experiment because they had the most examples available. The third experiment was the same as the second, but we used the letters 'A', 'E', and 'S'.

To measure the application's accuracy with a given SVM model, we calculated the accuracy for all letters and divided it by the number of letters, as represented by Eq. 3, where $L$ is the set of letters recognized by the model. The accuracy of each letter was calculated by executing the gesture ten times and dividing by ten the number of times the SVM model classified it correctly, as represented by Eq. 4, where $c$ is the number of correct classifications.

$$TotalAccuracy = \frac{\sum_{i \in L} Accuracy(i)}{|L|} \tag{3}$$

$$Accuracy(i) = \frac{c}{10} \tag{4}$$

When training an ML model, it is essential to use a large and diverse dataset. As this application is still in its initial stages, the training dataset is not as large as preferable, but already provides an excellent foundation to expand upon. In total, the training dataset contains 339 examples of gestures. There are 7 examples for each of the 27 letters of the Libras' alphabet, including the letter 'Ç' (c cedilla), out of which 3 were recorded by 3 different volunteers and 4 were taken from YouTube educational videos. There are also 50 additional examples for the letters 'A', 'B', and 'C', recorded by a member of the research team.

Table 1 presents the results for Experiment 1, ordered by the number of letters recognized by the model, which we will call the "size" of the model, and by accuracy. We can see that the SVM trained to recognize the full Libras' alphabet obtained an extremely low accuracy. There were too few examples for each gesture and too many classes, which resulted in an SVM model of poor quality. Usually, when working with ML classifications, especially when there are many classes, the number of examples for each class can easily reach the thousands.

We also noted that the size of the SVM affects the accuracy of the model, as evidenced by the overall tendency of smaller models to have a higher accuracy score - except for the model trained with the letters 'A', 'B', 'M', 'P', and 'W', which scored lower than the larger "A to F" model. Furthermore, the selection of the letters also influenced the accuracy score. That is because, with so few examples for each letter, there is a very high chance that the SVM will confuse

**Table 1.** Results for the first experiment, with varying letters and fixed number of gestures per letter.

| Letters | Accuracy |
| --- | --- |
| Full alphabet | 14.4% |
| A to M | 30.8% |
| A to F | 61.7% |
| A, B, M, P, W | 42% |
| A, C, T, X | 67.5% |
| A, C, N, T | 95% |

letters with similar signs, such as 'F' and 'T', 'A' and 'S', or even 'A' and 'X' (Figs. 10a, b and c). This concept is evidenced by the higher accuracy score of the last SVM compared to the penultimate one: both models had the same size, but the last one had a set of letters more distinct from each other.

Table 2 presents the results for Experiment 2, ordered by accuracy and by the number of examples for each letter. The total accuracy for the SVMs trained to recognize only the letters 'A', 'B', and 'C' is much higher than the accuracy of the more general models used in Experiment 1. That is because it is easier for the model to distinguish between fewer classes, as evidenced in Experiment 1. Moreover, the letters used in this experiment are distinct enough from each other (Fig. 10d) that it allowed the model to accurately distinguish between them with as few as seven examples per letter.

**Table 2.** Results for the second experiment, with fixed letters and varying number of gestures per letter.

| Size | Acc. for 'A' | Acc. for 'B' | Acc. for 'C' | Total Acc. |
| --- | --- | --- | --- | --- |
| 1 | 100% | 0% | 100% | 66.7% |
| 5 | 70% | 100% | 90% | 86.7% |
| 7 | 100% | 100% | 100% | 100% |
| 10 | 100% | 100% | 100% | 100% |

The results of Experiment 3, presented in Table 3, establish the importance of the letters set. This experiment used an SVM of the same size as the one used in Experiment 2, but the letters used are much more similar to each other (Fig. 10e). As a result, the total accuracies of the models in Experiment 3 were much lower than those of the ones used in experiment 2, even though they had the same size. It is also important to note that, in both Experiment 2 and 3, while an increase in the model's size translated to an increase in total accuracy,

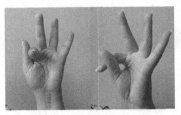

(a) 'F' and 'T'.

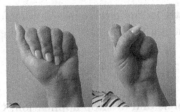

(b) 'A' and 'S'.

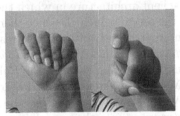

(c) 'A' and 'X'.

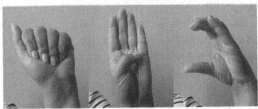

(d) 'A', 'B' and 'C'.

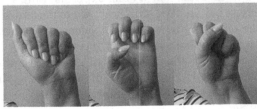

(e) 'A', 'E' and 'S'.

**Fig. 10.** Comparisons of similar letters of the Libras' alphabet.

**Table 3.** Results for the third experiment, with fixed letters and varying number of gestures per letter.

| Size | Acc. for 'A' | Acc. for 'E' | Acc. for 'S' | Total Acc. |
|------|-------------|-------------|-------------|-----------|
| 1    | 50%         | 0%          | 30%         | 26.7%     |
| 5    | 10%         | 20%         | 0%          | 40%       |
| 7    | 90%         | 100%        | 0%          | 63.3%     |

it did not translate directly to an increase in accuracy for all letters, because the size was not yet large enough to eliminate confusion between letters.

## 6   Conclusion

This work presents a mobile and desktop application, C-Libras, capable of capturing hand gestures and classifying them as letters of the Libras's alphabet. C-Libras follows a server-client architecture in which the client captures the gestures and sends them to the server, which classifies them by using an SVM. The training dataset was constructed by capturing the gestures with regular RGB cameras, processing them with Google's MediaPipe to extract the hands' joints, calculating their rotations, and storing them in the ReBase database.

We tested many SVMs with different sets of letters and different numbers of examples per letter. We concluded that, besides the number of examples per letter, the size of the letter set affects the model's accuracy. Our SVM trained with seven examples per letter to recognize the entire Libras' alphabet obtained an accuracy of 14.4%, while our models with fewer letters obtained much higher scores, such as the model for the letters 'A', 'B' and 'C', which obtained 100% accuracy with the same number of examples per letter. We also concluded that the letters included in the set affect accuracy as well: our model for the letters 'A', 'E' and 'S' obtained only 63.3% accuracy with the same number of letters and examples per letter as the 'A', 'B' and 'C' model.

In the future, we plan to expand our training dataset by recording more examples for each letter of the Libras' alphabet, executed by different voluntaries. We also plan to fine-tune our SVMs, experimenting with different kernel functions and different parameters. This way, we expect to be able to train an SVM to classify the entire Libras's alphabet accurately. Furthermore, to measure usability and reliability, we plan to test and validate our application in real scenarios with real users, including members of the deaf community. Finally, we plan on implementing a reverse approach, allowing the application to receive text input and display the corresponding alphabet signs.

# References

1. Assaleh, K., Shanableh, T., Zourob, M.: Low complexity classification system for glove-based Arabic sign language recognition. In: Huang, T., Zeng, Z., Li, C., Leung, C.S. (eds.) ICONIP 2012. LNCS, vol. 7665, pp. 262–268. Springer, Heidelberg (2012). https://doi.org/10.1007/978-3-642-34487-9_32
2. Barbosa, T., et al.: Rebase: data acquisition and management system for neuromotor rehabilitation supported by virtual and augmented reality. In: Anais do XXIII Simpósio de Realidade Virtual e Aumentada, pp. 181–185. SBC, Porto Alegre, RS, Brasil (2021). https://sol.sbc.org.br/index.php/svr/article/view/17535
3. Cheok, M.J., Omar, Z., Jaward, M.H.: A review of hand gesture and sign language recognition techniques. Int. J. Mach. Learn. Cybern. **10**(1), 131–153 (2017). https://doi.org/10.1007/s13042-017-0705-5
4. Chong, T.W., Lee, B.G.: American sign language recognition using leap motion controller with machine learning approach. Sensors **18**(10), 3554 (2018)
5. Cooper, H., Holt, B., Bowden, R.: Sign Language Recognition, pp. 539–562. Springer, London (2011). https://doi.org/10.1007/978-0-85729-997-0_27
6. El-Bendary, N., Zawbaa, H.M., Daoud, M.S., Hassanien, A.E., Nakamatsu, K.: ArSLAT: Arabic sign language alphabets translator. In: 2010 International Conference on Computer Information Systems and Industrial Management Applications (CISIM), pp. 590–595. IEEE (2010)
7. Elakkiya, R.: Machine learning based sign language recognition: a review and its research frontier. J. Ambient. Intell. Humaniz. Comput. **12**(7), 7205–7224 (2021)
8. de Geografia e Estatistica (IBGE), I.B.: PNS 2019: país tem 17,3 milhões de pessoas com algum tipo de deficiência. Agência de Notícias - IBGE. https://agenciadenoticias.ibge.gov.br/en/agencia-press-room/2185-news-agency/releases-en/31465-pns-2019-brazil-has-17-3-million-persons-with-some-type-of-disability. Accessed May 2022
9. Fitzpatrick, E.M., et al.: Sign language and spoken language for children with hearing loss: asystemantic review. Pediatrics **137**(1) (2016)
10. Google: MediaPipe. https://google.github.io/mediapipe/. Accessed Mar 2021
11. Mohandes, M., A-Buraiky, S., Halawani, T., Al-Baiyat, S.: Automation of the arabic sign language recognition. In: Proceedings. 2004 International Conference on Information and Communication Technologies: From Theory to Applications, pp. 479–480. IEEE (2004)
12. Roberts, M., et al.: Common pitfalls and recommendations for using machine learning to detect and prognosticate for Covid-19 using chest radiographs and CT scans. Nat. Mach. Intell. **3**(3), 199–217 (2021)
13. Rossol, N., Cheng, I., Basu, A.: A multisensor technique for gesture recognition through intelligent skeletal pose analysis. IEEE Trans. Hum.-Mach. Syst. **46**(3), 350–359 (2015)
14. Sadek, M.I., Mikhael, M.N., Mansour, H.A.: A new approach for designing a smart glove for Arabic sign language recognition system based on the statistical analysis of the sign language. In: 2017 34th National Radio Science Conference (NRSC), pp. 380–388. IEEE (2017)
15. Shukor, A.Z., et al.: A new data glove approach for Malaysian sign language detection. Procedia Comput. Sci. **76**, 60–67 (2015)
16. Ultraleap: Leap Motion Controller. https://www.ultraleap.com/product/leap-motion-controller/. Accessed Mar 2021
17. Unity: Unity - Game Engine. https://unity.com/pt. Accessed Mar 2021

18. Wang, R.Y., Popović, J.: Real-time hand-tracking with a color glove. ACM Trans. Graph. (TOG) **28**(3), 1–8 (2009)
19. Zhang, H., Wang, Y., Deng, C.: Application of gesture recognition based on simulated annealing BP neural network. In: Proceedings of 2011 International Conference on Electronic and Mechanical Engineering and Information Technology, vol. 1, pp. 178–181. IEEE (2011)
20. Zhang, X., Chen, X., Li, Y., Lantz, V., Wang, K., Yang, J.: A framework for hand gesture recognition based on accelerometer and EMG sensors. IEEE Trans. Syst. Man Cybern. Part A Syst. Hum. **41**(6), 1064–1076 (2011)

# A Deep Learning Approach for Automatic Counting of Bales and Product Boxes in Industrial Production Lines

Rafael J. Xavier[1], Charles F. O. Viegas[1], Bruno C. Costa[1], and Renato P. Ishii[2]

[1] See Working, Goias, 405, 79020-100 Campo Grande, MS, Brazil
{rafael,charles,bruno}@seeworking.com
[2] Federal University of Mato Grosso do Sul, Campo Grande, MS, Brazil
renato.ishii@ufms.br
https://seeworking.com, https://www.facom.ufms.br/

**Abstract.** Recent advances in machine learning and computer vision have led to widespread use of these technologies in the industrial sector. Quality control and production counting are the most important applications. This article describes a solution for counting products in an industrial production line. It consists of two main modules: i) hardware infrastructure and ii) software solution. In ii) there are modules for image capture and product recognition using the Yolov5 algorithm and modules for tracking and counting products. The results show that our solution achieves 99.91% accuracy in product counting and classification. Furthermore, these results were compared to the current manual counting system used in the industry considered in this study. This demonstrated the feasibility of our solution in a real production environment.

**Keywords:** Detection · Classification · Tracking · Counting · Machine learning · Deep learning · Industry 4.0

## 1 Introduction

Nowadays, the automation of the productive chain has been a major factor in the industry business. Increasingly more people are being replaced by machinery that is, in many cases, more efficient and productive, especially in repetitive tasks [4]. Indeed, all the cycles of production and supply networks are being integrated and automated through emerging technologies that provide real-time data gathering, allowing better analysis and information for the organization. This trend is being recognized as the fourth industrial revolution or Industry 4.0. This concept puts the industry business in a new level of technology, integrating several areas of knowledge like: the Internet of Things (IoT), Computer Vision and Big Data, with the goal to make industries more flexible and adaptable, providing a productive chain that can automatically change itself to make customized products in large scale [14].

O. Gervasi et al. (Eds.): ICCSA 2022, LNCS 13375, pp. 619–633, 2022.
https://doi.org/10.1007/978-3-031-10522-7_42

Recently, computer vision has been used to automate production lines and replace humans [12]. This technology is strongly supported by academics in counting and checking products. Neural networks are one of the most important of these technologies for classification and object recognition. The YOLO network in particular has recently gained a lot of insights [5,9–11] and is becoming the most important network for recognition. However, many of the solutions available on the market are expensive and no longer economically viable for small businesses. This paper discusses a solution that uses computer vision and artificial intelligence and aims to reduce the costs associated with current processing capacity in small and medium-sized enterprises.

Semalo Industry[1], a snack industry with plants in Campo Grande – MS and João Pessoa – PB in Brazil and Asunción in Paraguay, has advanced in automation and technology. Several recent investments have been made in automatic product packaging machines and production control software. Despite the progress, the factory has many difficulties in controlling its stocks, especially in reconciling the quantities of products entering and leaving the expedition area. Often the shop management system shows negative stocks, which is a serious anomaly. The production count is done visually by the employee responsible for taking products off a conveyor belt (finished and packaged products from the production area) and placing them on pallets. Problems occur when there is a difference between the production count and what actually arrives in the warehouse and when pallets are sent directly to delivery trucks due to contractual deadlines, making stock control difficult.

In this sense, the objective of this paper is to propose a solution that uses computer vision in the form of object recognition to automatically count bales and packages of storable products on pallets that provide satisfactory accuracy and performance for a real-time application. To perform this evaluation, we consider the following steps: Image capture, bounding box labelling, training the deep learning network, testing and collecting the results. The results show that our solution achieves 99.91% accuracy in product counting and classification. Furthermore, these results were compared with the current manual counting system used in the industry considered in this study. This demonstrated the feasibility of our solution in a real production environment.

The rest of this article is organized as follows: Sect. 2 describes related work on both tasks that uses similar methods to our approach. In Sect. 3, we describe the neural network architecture and its properties. In Sect. 4, we explain our solution approach in detail. The data set and the modeling problems are presented in Sect. 5. In Sect. 6, we present and discuss the experimental results. After discussing these results, we draw a conclusion and mention our thoughts on future work.

---

[1] https://semalo.com.br/.

## 2   Related Works

In this section, we review the recent detecting, tracking, and counting-based methods in the literature. Especially, we reveal the limitations in very few existing count classification-based methods to show the necessity of our research. We also discuss some works dealing with the imperfect targets to show the superiority of our method.

In the study [8], the authors present a method for detecting and counting pistachios transported on conveyor belts. These pistachios are then classified into two types (opened and closed). The study recorded a precision rate of over 92% using the RetinaNet network [7] with a pre-trained ResNet50 backbone. The study [6] uses smart cameras that run detection and counting algorithms. This technology allows for faster processing since no data needs to be transmitted, and is considered ideal for industrial inspections with large amounts of data. However, smart cameras are very expensive and not easily accessible. Using YOLO9000 [9], the authors [3] propose a method to integrate images from different cameras in a production line and process them as a single image. With this technique, the product can be tracked throughout the production line. However, according to the authors, this method requires a large data stream and high computational costs. Ulaszewski et al. [13] apply computer vision methods for real-time egg detection on a production line. They evaluate 3 neural network models: SSD-Mobilenetv2, FR-CNN, and Yolov3, and they identified that Yolov3 was the best performing with 93% effectiveness of detection, tracking ad counting process. Bahaghighat et al. [1] propose a new model for blister counting in drug production lines. The total accuracy of more than 88% was obtained based on our best model using Haar cascade, Radon transform, and KNN. These previous works do not provide information about your performance related to the manual real counting results in the conveyor belt.

## 3   Neural Network Architecture

To solve the above problems, this study proposes to use Yolov5 as the main tool to identify and classify products in industrial production lines. For this purpose, we need to re-train the network with the products we want to identify. Therefore, we had to create an extended data set with the object classes (boxes and bales) of the numerous products transported in Semalo's production lines.

### 3.1   YOLOv5

In this section, we discuss the implementation of Yolov5 [5]. Notice that this version is implemented using the Pytorch framework, different from previous versions. Its architecture is robust, with easy implementation and integration with any other python software. Moreover, Yolov5 brings 4 different architectures, each one with its own pre-trained models with different performances and assertiveness.

In this section we discuss the implementation of `Yolov5` [5]. Note that unlike previous versions, this version was implemented using the `Pytorch` framework. Its architecture is robust and easy to implement and integrate with any other Python software. Also, `Yolov5` provides 4 different architectures, each with its own pre-trained models with different performance and assertiveness.

Table 1 shows the differences between these networks and their mAP (mean Average Precision – the higher the better). `Yolov5x` has 2.2% higher accuracy than `Yolov5l`, although `Yolov5l` is 37.7% faster than `Yolov5x`.

**Table 1.** Comparative precision and speed table of different `Yolov5` versions.

| Model | Size (pixels) | mAP val 0.5:0.95 | mAP test 0.5:0.95 | mAP val 0.5 | Speed V100 (ms) |
|---|---|---|---|---|---|
| YOLOv5s | 640 | 36.7 | 36.7 | 55.4 | **2.0** |
| YOLOv5m | 640 | 44.5 | 44.5 | 63.1 | 2.7 |
| YOLOv5l | 640 | 48.2 | 48.2 | 66.9 | 3.8 |
| YOLOv5x | 640 | **50.4** | **50.4** | **68.8** | 6.1 |

Therefore, we chose the `Yolov5l` network for our proposal because it requires less processing capacity and allows running multiple instances of the model on less expensive and processing-limited hardware without compromising the accuracy of the solution.

## 3.2 Metrics

`Yolov5` uses many different metrics to calculate the quality of the network. The most important of these is the mean mAP, which uses Intersection over Union (IoU). Intersection over Union is a scoring metric used to measure the accuracy of an object detector in a given data set. In the numerator of the Eq. 1, we calculate the area of overlap between the predicted bounding box and the ground truth bounding box. The denominator is the area of union, or more simply, the area enclosed by both the predicted bounding box and the ground truth bounding box. If you divide the area of overlap by the area of union, you get our final value – the intersection over union.

The IoU, which tests the similarities between two records is expressed in the following Eq. 1.

$$J(A, B) = \frac{|A \cap B|}{|A \cup B|} = \frac{|A \cap B|}{|A| + |B| - |A \cap B|} \tag{1}$$

Here $A$ and $B$ are surfaces and $J(A, B)$ is the coefficient of 0 and 1. The higher the value, the greater the similarity between two sets. This coefficient is used in object recognition to test how close the model recognition is to a human recognition. Based on the tested coefficient, we can calculate whether the detections are positive, false-positive or false-negative.

**Algorithm 1:** Type of Detection Decision

---

**if** *Valid detection* **then**
    **if** *IoU* >= 50% **then**
        | Positive Detection;
    **else**
        | False-Positive Detection;
    **end**
**else**
    | False-Negative Detection;
**end**

---

Considering $IoU \geq 50\%$ the Algorithm 1 therefore defines the type of detection.

Furthermore, the metrics of performance, precision and recall are defined in Eq. 2 and 3, respectively.

$$Precision = \frac{TP}{TP + FP} \tag{2}$$

$$Recall(TPR) = \frac{TP}{TP + FN} \tag{3}$$

where, TP = *True-Positive*, FP = *False-Positive* and FN = *False-Negative*.

The metric *average precision* required to calculate the mAP is given by the area *under the curve* of each class, represented by the Eq. 4.

$$AP = \int_0^1 p(r)\,dx \tag{4}$$

The mAP 0.5 is the computation of the average accuracy, given by Eq. 5, of all classes computed by AP with the condition IoU > 0.5. The mAP 0.5 : 0.95 is the average of AP with IoU > 0.5 to Iou > 0.95, where the different instances of IoUs are added with 0.5. Thus, mAP 0.5 : 0.95 is the most important metric for measuring the quality of the model, because it measures not only the quality of the network classification in a test data set, but also the quality of the object localization in an image using different IoUs.

$$mAP = \frac{1}{N}\sum_{i=1}^{N} APi \tag{5}$$

## 4   The Solution Architecture

The developed solution enables the capture, decoding, recognition, tracking and counting of all products in the Semalo industry. In this section we describe in detail how we developed the physical and technological part of our solution.

## 4.1   Physical

In Semalo's production line, the camera is located on the side of the conveyor belt that transports products between the production and storage areas. When a product is detected by a camera, its image is captured and sent to a server. To perform the counting in real time and avoid data loss, we send the images over a high-speed wired network. Figure 1 illustrates this process.

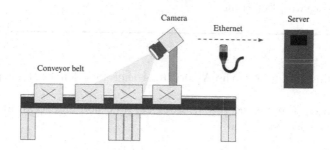

**Fig. 1.** The diagram shows the process of capturing and uploading images through a communication network.

By positioning the camera on the side of the conveyor belt and perpendicular to the products, we were able to capture more details of the bales and boxes, such as brand, color, logo, shape and texture. These features are important because many products are very similar and often differ only in color and size. Figure 2 shows some examples of products.

In addition, the production is divided into 5 different conveyor belts according to characteristics. On conveyor belts 1 and 2 the corn chips are transported, they go through the extrusion process, then they are roasted, flavored and packed in bales or boxes made of plastic. Conveyor belt 3 transports the conventional wheat or corn chips. They are roasted, shaped and also packed in bales and boxes.

Finally, conveyor belts 4 and 5 carry chips made mainly by potatoes, these are only packed in boxes. Table 2 overviews the output of products on the conveyor belts.

Finally, conveyors 4 and 5 carry French fries, which consist mainly of potatoes and are packed only in boxes. The Table  2 gives an overview of the product outputs on the conveyors.

**Table 2.** Table of the groups of conveyor belts by type of products.

| Group of conveyor belts | Types of products | Packing |
|---|---|---|
| Conveyor belts 1 and 2 | Extruded | Bales and boxes |
| Conveyor belt 3 | Conventional chips | Bales and boxes |
| Conveyor belts 4 and 5 | Potatoes | Boxes |

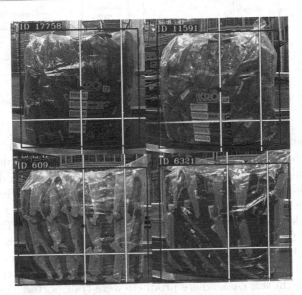

**Fig. 2.** Example of packed products **Kró** detected by our solution in the moment of count.

## 4.2 Technological

The software that does the acquisition, detection, and counting was created in Python. We divided this software into 5 modules (initialization, video, detection, tracking, and counting). The following diagram Fig. 3 shows the basic interactions between these modules.

The first module is the initialization. It contains a `Docker` configuration file that initializes the application without requiring you to manually check dependencies. It also installs the application in a container that is separate from the main computing environment. Also, this module initializes the cameras and prepares them for the next module. The second module is the video module. It receives the images captured by the cameras via the RTSP (Real Time Streaming Protocol) protocol and converts these images to a 640x640 resolution compatible with the `Yolov5` detector.

The third module takes care of recognition, fetches the converted frames, and, using Yolov5, returns all the bounding boxes with their respective product classifications. So, this information is sent to the next module.

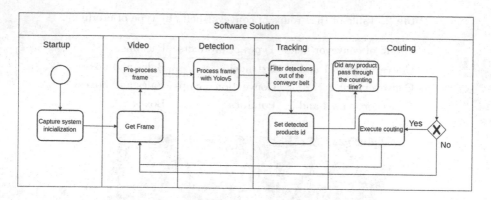

**Fig. 3.** Diagram with the basic interactions between our solution modules.

The fourth module is tracking, which first filters what is not on the conveyors. This module, which is one of the most complex parts of the solution, has gone through several iterations. The first was based on tracking products by their centroids. In this method, we tracked a product through 3 virtual lines, 2 vertical, the first of which is responsible for marking a product as ready to count and the second for marking a product as ready to count in our database. The third line is horizontal and filters products from the conveyor belt. Figure 4 shows these lines in Semalo's industry. These triggers were activated whenever the centroid of a product passed through the lines. This method works well for tracking people and objects, but in this case, where products were transported along a conveyor belt, it proved to be faulty at moments when products accumulated and got stuck in the belt. When this happened, IDs were swapped or duplicated, leading to errors in the count.

**Fig. 4.** Frame captured in the conveyor belt with the virtual lines for counting and filtering

Therefore, we reconstructed the tracking and counting software using an open-source technology called SORT [2]. This algorithm also uses centroids and Euclidean distances, but counts with the prediction of an object in the future. This helps with conjugation between a product in a previous frame and the same product in the current frame, making it a good solution for our tracking.

We made several modifications to help with the counting, loss of frames, detection failures and classification by the neural network. For this, we implemented one algorithm, to operate with SORT, that saves the history of classifications and its probabilities when a product passes through the conveyor belt. This way, when a product passed through the counting lines it was possible to verify the most common classification for such a product and define a normalized product, lowering the chances of a wrong count because of factors like illumination, temporary loss of connection and other external influences. Algorithm 2 is used to update a unique products position when they are being carried by a belt.

We made several changes to facilitate counting, frame loss, detection errors, and classification by the neural network. For this purpose, we implemented an algorithm that works with SORT and stores the history of classifications and their probabilities when a product passes through the conveyor belt. In this way, when a product passes through the counting lines, it was possible to check the most frequent classification for such a product and define a normalized product, reducing the probability of a wrong count due to factors such as lighting, temporary interruption, and other external influences. The Algorithm 2 is used to update the position of a single product when it is worn by a belt.

---

**Algorithm 2:** *SORT* update per frame

---
**foreach** *Registered product* **do**
  **if** *Correspondent detected in frame* **then**
    Returns updated product position;
    Returns updated normalized product;
  **else**
    Returns predicted product position;
  **end**
**end**

---

## 5 Data Set Construction and Modeling

To enable the training of the neural network, we first had to create the data set.

### 5.1 Data Set Construction Methodology

Due to the variability and availability of the 68 products produced by Semalo, we built the data set iteratively. In the beginning, only a few examples of each product were included. As the solution improved, we took new images to try to improve the low accuracy in classifying and identifying the products. One challenge we faced was the change in brightness over the course of a day in the industry. To solve this problem, we had to take images throughout the production cycle (morning, day, evening and night). In this way, we were able to improve the generalization of our model.

However, during the measurement tests in production, it became clear that it would not be possible to eliminate all the variations that could occur in a product and affect its classification. Therefore, to improve generalization, we took and annotated the product images in a laboratory environment, a neutral and completely different environment from the production environment. Figure 5 shows an example of image acquisition in the lab environment and others in production.

**Fig. 5.** Image captured in the laboratory and in production, respectively.

## 5.2 Data Set Features

In total, we annotated and merged 199,356 images, of which 79,083 were taken in production and 120,458 in the lab. There are 68 types of unique products manufactured by Semalo. We took these images in different environments that vary in terms of lighting, camera, assembly line, and background. The main camera we used was the `HikvisionDS-2CD3025G0-I` (B), with the RTSP recording protocol. We labeled the bounding boxes to identify the products in the images, which is essential for training the algorithm. This task was done using `LabelImg`. This tool exports the labels with their coordinates in a format compatible with `Yolov5`.

We had to perform many tests to properly define the basic parameterization of the network. We considered accuracy, training time and overfitting.

## 5.3 Network Training

As explained in Sect. 5.1, when training the model, we divided the products into the same groups used in Semalo's industry. This subdivision improved the accuracy and reduced the number of models. The performance of the model is shown later in Sect. 6.

## 5.4 Network Configuration Tests

In order to configure the parameterization of the network, two tests were performed. In the first, epochs were defined, i.e., the number of iterations a network performs through a data set. The number of epochs affects accuracy and had to be defined to reduce training time while maintaining the accuracy of the network. With 200 epochs and the amount of data collected, the training would take 8 days.

For the epoch test, we assumed that the data set consisted of images taken in different environments. Then we randomly ordered it and used 80% of them for training and 20% for testing.

We tested the following number of epochs: $10, 25, 50, 100$ and $200$. With a number of 924 products divided into 4 different types, we chose 50 epochs. This resulted in an accuracy of 99.7%, a good processing time without affecting the quality of the network, and solved the problem of overfitting that occurred with longer training times. Figure 6 shows the training hours required for each epoch and their accuracy in counting and classifying.

We then tested how the images are distributed between tests and training. We tested the following distributions: 1 – completely random distribution, 80% for training and 20% for tests; 2 – completely random distribution, 50% for training and 50% for tests; 3 – distribution with images from the lab and production, 10% of each data set was randomly transferred to each other. For illustration, using 4 and 5 conveyors as examples, we used $59, 423$ images from the lab and $55, 059$ from production for testing. After separating these 2 groups, we took 10% from each of these groups and mixed in the others.

The results showed that the best distributions were 1 and 3, both had a hit rate of 100% in counting and classifying, the 3 distribution had a small advantage over the 1 in the mAP@.5 test, reaching 91.2%, while the 1 distribution reached 90.4%, a difference of 0.8%.

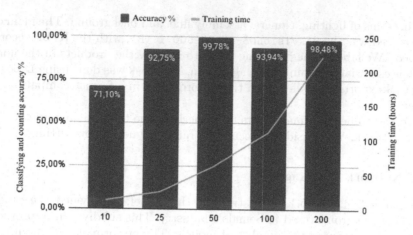

**Fig. 6.** Epoch tests with counting and classification accuracy and their training time.

In summary, the final baseline network configuration includes 50 epochs and a distribution with images from the lab and from production, with 10% of each data set randomly applied to each other.

## 5.5   Network's Hyper-parameters

The hyper-parameters are an important factor in the accuracy of a model. The parameters used in data augmentation are the most important because they directly affect how an image is used in training. We have changed the following elements:

- *hsv_h (hue), hsv_s (saturation) and hsv_v (value)* have values 0.005, 0.05, and 0.05, respectively. The parameterization of these elements was used to minimize drastic changes to the color of the product during training. These could change important properties of the products, making them more difficult for the network to recognize;
- *flipud*: Vertical flipping was used with a ratio of 1/10 because flipped products can be transported on the conveyors;
- *mosaic*: Mosaic was used for data augmentation, the ratio 5/10. It cuts many training images into one. Figure 7 shows an example of a mosaic.

The parameters not associated with *data augmentantion* are:

- *batch* size: 4;
- Initial learning rate: 0.01;
- Number of epochs: 50;
- Optimizer: *stochastic gradient descent* (SGD) with *momentum* 0.937 and *weighted descent*: 0.0005;
- Image size limit: 640 pixel height and 640 pixel width.

**Fig. 7.** Example of *data-augmentation* of type *mosaic*.

## 6   Results

The results of the trained models, grouped by conveyor belt, are shown in Table 3, and their metrics were explained in Sect. 3.

**Table 3.** Counting table

| Group of conveyor belts | Precision | Recall | mAP@.5 | mAP@.5:.95 |
|---|---|---|---|---|
| Conveyor belts 1 e 2 | 98.07% | 98.33% | 99.27% | 95.35% |
| Conveyor belt 3 | 97.27% | 98.82% | 99.02% | 95.69% |
| Conveyor belts 4 e 5 | 97.70% | 96.54% | 98.50% | 96.70% |

To validate our solution, we recorded videos of the neural network counting 10 products at different moments and did the manual counting as well, so we could compare the results. A total of 4.442 bales and 1384 boxes were counted, each type representing 5 different products. Figure 4 shows the results.

To validate our solution, we recorded videos in which the neural network counted 10 products at different time points, and we also performed the counting manually to compare the results. A total of 4, 442 bales and 1, 384 boxes were counted, and each type represented 5 different products. Figure 4 shows the results.

**Table 4.** Counting table

| Type | Manual counting | Solution counting | Accuracy rate |
|------|-----------------|-------------------|---------------|
| Bales | 4,442 | 4,437 | 99.88% |
| Boxes | 1,384 | 1,384 | 100% |

The results prove that our solution is suitable for counting products in industrial lines, with an overall accuracy rate of 99.91%. Even though the accuracy rate is very high, changes in the environment can drastically reduce the accuracy rate, resulting in fewer products being counted than should be.

## 7   Conclusion and Future Works

In this paper, we have presented an approach to recognition, classification and counting using the `Yolov5` Deep Learning technique. Our main goal is to maximize quality control and production counting in industrial environments. The results show that our solution achieves 99.91% accuracy in product counting and classification. Moreover, these results were compared to the current manual counting system used in the industry considered in this study. This proves the feasibility of our solution in a real production environment, i.e. Semalo's industry.

We foresee the solution evolution in order to make it possible to count products with a low-power embedded system containing both software and hardware artifacts, without the need for a dedicated server to process and count the products in an even cheaper way. As another future work, we envisage the use of the current solution in other industries with characteristics different from those exposed by this paper.

**Acknowledgments.** This paper was only possible thanks to the help of the Semalo Indústria e Comércio de Alimentos and its workers. We thank the support of the UFMS (Universidade Federal de Mato Grosso do Sul), PET (Programa de Educação Tutorial – FNDE), FUNDECT, Finep, and Ministério da Ciência, Tecnologia, Inovações e Comunicações, funded by FNDCT. We also thank the support of the INCT of the Future Internet for Smart Cities funded by CNPq, proc. 465446/2014-0, Coordenação de Aperfeiçoamento de Pessoal de Nível Superior - Brasil (CAPES) - Finance Code 001, and FAPESP, proc. 2014/50937-1 and 2015/24485-9.

Any opinions, findings, and conclusions or recommendations expressed in this material are those of the authors and do not necessarily reflect the views of FUNDECT, Finep, FAPESP, CAPES and CNPq.

## References

1. Bahaghighat, M., Akbari, L., Xin, Q.: A machine learning-based approach for counting blister cards within drug packages. IEEE Access **7**, 83785–83796 (2019). https://doi.org/10.1109/ACCESS.2019.2924445

2. Bewley, A., Ge, Z., Ott, L., Ramos, F., Upcroft, B.: Simple online and realtime tracking. In: 2016 IEEE International Conference on Image Processing (ICIP), pp. 3464–3468 (2016). https://doi.org/10.1109/ICIP.2016.7533003
3. Deac, C., Popa, C.L., Ghinea, M., Cotet, C.: Machine vision in manufacturing processes and the digital twin of manufacturing architectures, pp. 0733–0736 (2017). https://doi.org/10.2507/28th.daaam.proceedings.103
4. Frank, A.G., Dalenogare, L.S., Ayala, N.F.: Industry 4.0 technologies: implementation patterns in manufacturing companies. Int. J. Prod. Econ. **210**, 15–26 (2019). https://doi.org/10.1016/j.ijpe.2019.01.004, http://www.sciencedirect.com/science/article/pii/S0925527319300040
5. Jocher, G., et al.: ultralytics/yolov5: v5.0 - YOLOv5-P6 1280 models, AWS, Supervise.ly and YouTube integrations (2021). https://doi.org/10.5281/zenodo.4679653
6. Lee, S., Yang, C.: A real time object recognition and counting system for smart industrial camera sensor. IEEE Sens. J. **17**(8), 2516–2523 (2017)
7. Lin, T.Y., Goyal, P., Girshick, R., He, K., Dollar, P.: Focal loss for dense object detection. In: Proceedings of the IEEE International Conference on Computer Vision (ICCV) (2017)
8. Rahimzadeh, M., Attar, A.: Introduction of a new dataset and method for detecting and counting the pistachios based on deep learning (2020)
9. Redmon, J., Divvala, S., Girshick, R., Farhadi, A.: You only look once: unified, real-time object detection (2015)
10. Redmon, J., Farhadi, A.: Yolo9000: better, faster, stronger (2016)
11. Redmon, J., Farhadi, A.: Yolov3: an incremental improvement (2018)
12. Shrestha, A., Mahmood, A.: Review of deep learning algorithms and architectures. IEEE Access **7**, 53040–53065 (2019)
13. Ulaszewski, M., Janowski, R., Janowski, A.: Application of computer vision to egg detection on a production line in real time. Electron. Lett. Comput. Vision Image Anal. **20**, 113–143 (2021). https://doi.org/10.5565/rev/elcvia.1390
14. Wang, S., Wan, J., Zhang, D., Li, D., Zhang, C.: Towards smart factory for industry 4.0: a self-organized multi-agent system with big data based feedback and coordination. Comput. Netw. **101**, 158–168 (2016). https://doi.org/10.1016/j.comnet.2015.12.017, http://www.sciencedirect.com/science/article/pii/S1389128615005046

# Voice Gender Recognition Using Acoustic Features, MFCCs and SVM

Fadwa Abakarim[✉] and Abdenbi Abenaou

Research Team of Applied Mathematics and Intelligent Systems Engineering, National School
of Applied Sciences, Ibn Zohr University, 80000 Agadir, Morocco
fadwa.abakarim@gmail.com

**Abstract.** This paper presents a voice gender recognition system. Acoustic features and Mel-Frequency Cepstral Coefficients (MFCCs) are extracted to define the speaker's gender. The most used features in these kinds of studies are acoustic features, but in this work, we combined them with MFCCs to test if we will get more satisfactory results. To examine the performance of the proposed system we tried four different databases: the Ryerson Audio-Visual Database of Emotional Speech and Song (RAVDESS), the Saarbruecken Voice Database (SVD), the CMU_ARCTIC database and the Amazigh speech database (Self-Created). At the pre-processing stage, we removed the silence from the signals by using Zero-Crossing Rate (ZCR), but we kept the noises. Support Vector Machine (SVM) is used as the classification model. The combination of acoustic features and MFCCs achieves an average accuracy of 90.61% with the RAVDESS database, 92.73% with the SVD database, 99.87% with the CMU_ARCTIC database and 99.95% with the Amazigh speech database.

**Keywords:** Signal processing · Gender recognition · Acoustic features · Mel-Frequency Cepstral Coefficients · Zero-crossing rate · Support Vector Machine

## 1 Introduction

A voice gender recognition system is one of the most relevant and useful systems in applications such as sorting telephone calls by gender, security systems, human-machine interaction, targeted advertising, and voice recognition in crime scenarios [1–3].

It is easy for a human to differentiate the male voice from the female voice and vice versa. On the other hand, it is a difficult task for a machine. Therefore, several methods are developed to provide the machine with an optimal result. One of the most commonly used approaches is the extraction of the voice frequency features, because the female voice has higher frequency features than those of the male voice. Moreover, the most common of these features is the fundamental frequency (F0). The voice fundamental frequency of a male is from 85 Hz to 180 Hz while that of a female is from 165 Hz to 255 Hz [4, 5].

O. Gervasi et al. (Eds.): ICCSA 2022, LNCS 13375, pp. 634–648, 2022.
https://doi.org/10.1007/978-3-031-10522-7_43

Archana and Malleswari [3] presented gender identification and performance analysis of speech signals. They mentioned that pitch is the most used feature for voice gender identification, but it is not useful in cases when female and male pitch are similar. Therefore, they used other features such as Mel-Frequency Cepstral Coefficients (MFCCs), energy entropy and frame energy estimation. The classification methods used are the Artificial Neural Network (ANN) and the Support Vector Machine (SVM). The database used in this work is collected from 10 speakers, 5 female and 5 male, and 15 audio files are recorded by each speaker. The test phase is done by using 10 utterances. The experimental results show that SVM performs better than ANN. SVM reaches an accuracy of 80.00% and ANN reaches an accuracy of 40.00%.

Ahmad et al., [6] developed a gender identification system for telephone applications using Mel-Frequency Cepstral Coefficients (MFCCs). This work presented a comparative study between five classification methods: K-Nearest Neighbor (KNN), Naïve Bayes (NB), Multilayer Perceptron (MLP), Random Forest (RF) and Support Vector Machine (SVM). The voice features are extracted by MFCCs. The database used is collected from Korean speakers, and it contains two types of speech recordings: a short speech that lasts a few seconds and long telephone conversations that last between 5 and 8 min. The authors test the performance of their system by varying the size of the training dataset. When the training dataset is small, the classification performance becomes very low. As the size of the training dataset increases, the classification performance increases as well. The experimental results show that SVM performs better than other classification models for both short speech and long telephone speech.

Shareef, Abd and Mezaal [7] realized a gender voice classification with a high accuracy rate. The features are extracted by the well-known method, Mel-Frequency Cepstral Coefficients (MFCCs), and then the Vector Quantization (VQ) is applied for feature selection. In addition, other features are extracted from each voice: the mean, standard deviation (STD), zero-crossing (ZC) and amplitude (AMP). A set of 16 features is collected (12 MFCCs features and 4 features of mean, STD, ZC and AMP). Classification is performed using the machine learning algorithm (J 48). The database used in this work is collected from the CMU_ARCTIC database. The number of voice recordings used is 2770, including 1138 male and 1132 female. The proposed system reaches a high accuracy rate of 99.80%.

Buyukyilmaz and Cibikdiken [8] presented a voice gender recognition system using deep learning. A total of 21 acoustic features is used in this study. The classification step is performed by one of the best neural network models, the Multilayer Perceptron (MLP). The system is examined by 3168 utterances, including 1584 male and 1584 female. The authors succeeded in achieving a high accuracy of 96.74%.

Ramdinmawii and Mittal [9] realized a system of gender identification from speech signals. The features used in this work are Mel-Frequency Cepstral Coefficients (MFCCs), pitch and signal energy. The classification is done by linear Support Vector Machine (SVM). The performance of the proposed system is tested using the Texas Instruments Massachusetts Institute of Technology (TIMIT) database. 120 speech recordings are used, and 6 utterances are recorded by each of 10 male and 10 female speakers. The experimental results show that MFCC coefficients give a higher accuracy of 69.23% compared to the other features, which obtained an accuracy below 60.00%.

Uddin et al., [10] created a gender voice recognition system. The authors use a multilayer architecture with two layers. The first one contains the following features: fundamental frequency, spectral entropy, spectral flatness, mode frequency and mapping. The second one contains the MFCCs features. Two different classification models are used in this work: K-Nearest Neighbors (KNN) and Support Vector Machine (SVM). The performance of the proposed system is tested by three different databases: TIMIT (Texas Instruments Massachusetts Institute of Technology), RAVDESS (Ryerson Audio-Visual Database of Emotional Speech and Song) and a BGC database created by authors. The proposed system achieved a higher accuracy of 96.80% using the TIMIT database and KNN classifier.

These research studies showed that the commonly used methods for voice gender identification are acoustic features, Mel coefficients, and SVM classifier [3, 6–10]. In this paper, we combine acoustic features and MFCCs. In order to test the performance of the proposed system, we leave the speech signals unfiltered. Only the silence is removed but we keep the noises and other disturbances. Four different databases are used with different accents, languages, emotions, voice pitches, diseases and ages. Moreover, only half of each database is used for training and the other half for testing, in order to determine whether the system can reach satisfactory results. Indeed, the larger the training dataset, the better the performance [6, 11].

The rest of the article is organized as follows: the second section describes the set of approaches used for voice gender identification, then in the third section, the experimental results are presented with a discussion and finally the conclusion comes in the fourth section.

## 2 Applied Methods

In our study, we conducted a three-step process to identify the voice gender:

The first step is pre-processing, in which we removed silence from the input voice signals to compress their length using Zero-Crossing Rate (ZCR). However, we kept the noises and any disturbances found to evaluate the performance.

The second step is feature extraction, in which we used two different approaches. The first approach is to extract acoustic features from the input signals by calculating the mean frequency, standard deviation, median frequency, first quartile, third quartile, interquartile range, skewness, kurtosis, spectral entropy, spectral flatness and mean voice fundamental frequency. In addition, the second approach is to extract MFCCs features.

Finally, the last step is classification, in which two methods are used. The first method is to determine a threshold from the acoustic features of the training dataset. Then, we test whether the average of the acoustic features of the test signals is below or above the threshold. If it is below, then the voice gender is male, if it is the opposite, then the voice gender is female. This method is only valid for acoustic features because they are extracted from the voice fundamental frequencies and frequency spectrums. Moreover, the second method is one of the widely used classifiers in the field of speech recognition, the SVM model.

Figure 1 shows the three-step process used in our study.

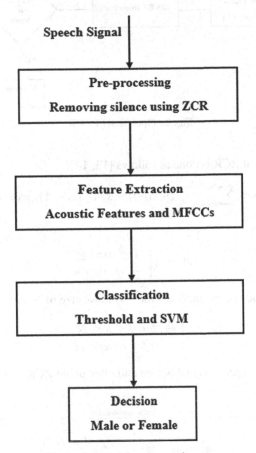

**Fig. 1.** Steps of the proposed system.

## 2.1  Pre-processing

Signal pre-processing is an important step in speech recognition. It allows us to compress the signals and to keep their qualities by removing the useless information. In our study, we used the Zero-Crossing Rate (ZCR) method to detect the unvoiced parts of the signal and remove them to obtain a 100% voiced signal.

The Zero-Crossing Rate is a measure of the number of times the amplitude of the speech signals crosses the value zero in a given frame. When ZCR is high, the speech signal is unvoiced and when it is low, the speech signal is voiced, as shown in Fig. 2 [12, 13].

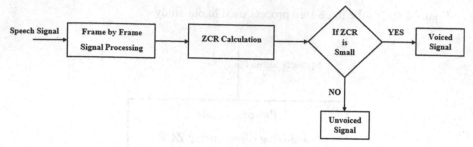

**Fig. 2.** Operation of ZCR.

The calculation of ZCR is done as follows [13, 14]:

$$Z(n) = \sum_{m=-\infty}^{\infty} |sgn[x(m)] - sgn[x(m-1)]| w(n-m) \tag{1}$$

where

$$sgn[x(n)]\begin{cases} 1 \; if \; x(n) \geq 0 \\ -1 \; if \; x(n) < 0 \end{cases} \tag{2}$$

with $w(n)$ is the windowing function with a window size of $N$ samples:

$$w(n)\begin{cases} \frac{1}{2N} \; for \; 0 \leq n \leq N-1 \\ 0 \; for \; otherwise \end{cases} \tag{3}$$

Figure 3 presents the speech signal before and after using ZCR.

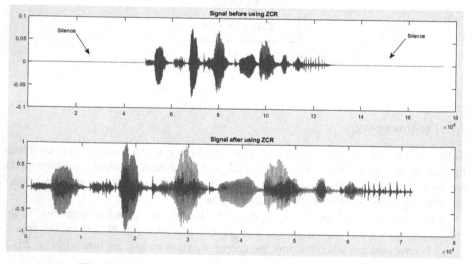

**Fig. 3.** Removing silence from the speech signal by using ZCR.

## 2.2   Feature Extraction

Feature extraction has a significant impact on the identification of processed signals. There are several methods for extracting important information from signals. Among them are acoustic features and Mel-Frequency Cepstral Coefficients.

**Acoustic Features.** Acoustic features are a set of properties that identify the voice, including the frequency features that are extracted after transforming the signal from the time domain to the frequency domain.

In our study, we extracted the following 11 features [4, 10]:

*Mean Frequency.* The mean frequency of a speech is the average value of the speech frequency in a specific interval of the frequency spectrum. It is calculated as the sum of the frequencies in the spectrum divided by the total number of frequency frames in a spectrum. Equation (4) presents the calculation:

$$f_{mean} = \frac{\sum_{i=0}^{n} f_i}{n} \tag{4}$$

where $f_i$ is the frequency of $i^{th}$ frame and $n$ is the number of frequency frames in the spectrum.

*Standard Deviation.* The standard deviation of a speech frequency is a measure of the frequencies in a spectrum that differ from the mean frequency. It is calculated as follows:

$$f_{sd} = \sqrt{\frac{\sum_{i=0}^{n}(f_i^2 - f_{mean}^2)}{n}} \tag{5}$$

where $f_i$ is the frequency of $i^{th}$ frame, $n$ is the number of frequency frames in the spectrum and $f_{mean}$ is the mean frequency mentioned at Eq. (4).

*Median Frequency.* The median frequency of a speech is the median value of the speech frequency in a specific interval of the frequency spectrum. It is calculated as follows:

$$f_{median} = \frac{\sum_{i=0}^{n} f_i}{2} \tag{6}$$

where $f_i$ is the frequency of $i^{th}$ frame and $n$ is the number of frequency frames in the spectrum.

*First Quartile.* To find the first quartile called Q1, we have to sort the frequency values obtained from the spectrum, and then it is the median of the lower half of the speech frequency set.

*Third Quartile.* To find the third quartile called Q3, we have to sort the frequency values obtained from the spectrum, and then it is the median of the upper half of the speech frequency set.

*Interquartile Range.* To find the interquartile range called IQR, we first have to find the first quartile (Q1) and the third quartile (Q3), and then calculate the difference between them.

*Skewness.* Skewness is a measure of the lack of symmetry. A distribution is symmetric if it looks the same to the left and right of the mean. It is calculated as follows:

$$f_{skewness} = \frac{\frac{1}{n}\sum_{i=0}^{n}(f_i - f_{mean})^3}{f_{sd}^3} \tag{7}$$

where $f_i$ is the frequency of $i^{th}$ frame, $n$ is the number of frequency frames in the spectrum, $f_{mean}$ is the mean frequency mentioned at Eq. (4) and $f_{sd}$ is the standard deviation value mentioned at Eq. (5).

*Kurtosis.* Kurtosis determines the heaviness of the distribution tails. It is calculated as follows:

$$f_{kurtosis} = \frac{\frac{1}{n}\sum_{i=0}^{n}(f_i - f_{mean})^4}{f_{sd}^4} \tag{8}$$

where $f_i$ is the frequency of $i^{th}$ frame, $n$ is the number of frequency frames in the spectrum, $f_{mean}$ is the mean frequency mentioned at Eq. (4) and $f_{sd}$ is the standard deviation value mentioned at Eq. (5).

*Spectral Entropy.* Spectral entropy is a measure of spectral power distribution of a speech signal. it is calculated as follows:

$$f_{spent} = \frac{-sum(\sum_{i=0}^{n} y_i * \log(\sum_{i=0}^{n} y_i))}{\log(n)} \tag{9}$$

where $y_i$ is the relative amplitude value of the frequency at the $i^{th}$ frame and $n$ is the number of frequency frames in the spectrum.

*Spectral Flatness.* Spectral flatness is the ratio of geometric mean to the arithmetic mean of a power spectrum.

*Mean Voice Fundamental Frequency.* The fundamental frequency is also known as the voice pitch. It is the frequency of the vocal folds and to calculate it we used autocorrelation.

Autocorrelation is a time domain method and a mathematical function that used to determine the similarity degree. Moreover, it is one of the most used methods for the extraction of the pitch, and the following equation shows the calculation:

$$A(\tau) = \frac{1}{T}\sum_{t=0}^{T-1} S(t)S(t + \tau) \tag{10}$$

with $\tau = [0, T - 1]$.

where $A(\tau)$ is the autocorrelation function at lag $\tau$, $T$ is the size of the frame of a speech signal, $S(t)$ is the speech signal and $\tau$ is the lag number or delay time. When lag, $\tau = 0$ the autocorrelation value always represents the maximum value.

After calculating the autocorrelation value, we used Eq. (11) to calculate the fundamental frequency $f_0$, then we calculated the mean value.

$$f_0 = \frac{1}{T} \tag{11}$$

**Mel-Frequency Cepstral Coefficients.** The Mel-Frequency Cepstral Coefficients is one of the most commonly used methods by researchers for speech recognition. Since speech is a non-stationary signal, short-term spectral analysis is the most common way to characterize the speech signal [3].

In our study, we obtained 14 Mel coefficients by following these steps [1, 4, 7, 10, 15]:

The first step to extract MFCCs features is to segment the speech into multiple frames, the size of each frame should be neither shorter nor longer. If it is shorter, it will not be enough to extract special information from the signal. On the other hand, if it is longer, the signal will be highly changed throughout the frame. The optimal solution is to segment the signal into a length of 20–40 ms for each frame. Then we used the Hamming Window to minimize the discontinuities of the speech signal before and after each frame of the window. Equation (12) shows the calculation of the Hamming Window:

$$W(n) = 0.54 - 0.46 \cos[\frac{2\pi n}{N - 1}] \tag{12}$$

with $0 \leq n \leq N - 1$.

where $W(n)$ is the window operation, $n$ is the number of each individual sample and $N$ is the total number of speech samples.

The next step is to transform each frame of the speech signal from the time domain to the frequency domain. Therefore, the Fast Fourier Transform (FFT) is applied to obtain the spectrum of each frame. The frequency range of the FFT spectrum is very wide and the speech signal does not follow the linear scale. Therefore, the bank of filters is processed according to the Mel scale. Equation (13) is used to convert a given frequency in Hz to Mel scale:

$$Mel(f) = 1125 * \ln(1 + \frac{f}{700}) \tag{13}$$

where $f$ is the given frequency in Hz and $Mel(f)$ is the perceived Mel frequency.

The final step is to convert the log Mel to the time domain by using the Discrete Cosine Transform (DCT). The result of this operation is called the Mel-Frequency Cepstrum Coefficient and the set of these coefficients is the acoustic vectors.

Figure 4 shows the steps of MFCCs extraction.

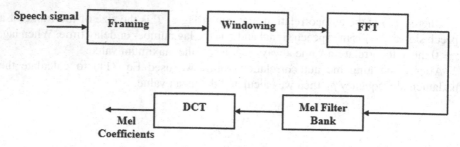

**Fig. 4.** Steps to get MFCC coefficients.

## 2.3  Classification

Classification is the next step that comes after feature extraction. The choice of a classification model is very important as it affects the final decision and the performance of the system. In this study, we used two methods of classification. The first one consists in classifying the test signals by using a threshold based on the average of the training dataset features, and the second one is the Support Vector Machine (SVM) model [16].

**Threshold.** The frequency features help the machine to differentiate the male voice from the female voice since the frequency data of the female voice is higher than of the male voice. Therefore, we calculated the mean value of the training dataset features for male and female. As a result, we obtain a threshold. If the mean value of the test signal features is above the threshold, it is a female voice and if it is below, it is a male voice [4, 5]. This classification approach is only valid with frequency features and not with MFCCs.

**Support Vector Machine.** Support Vector Machine (SVM) is one of the most powerful classifiers in the field of speech recognition. SVM supports binary classification. In this work, we have the female class and the male class. SVM goes through two steps, in the first step, it is very important to choose a kernel function. We chose the Radial Basic Function (RBF) kernel, which performs a low to high dimensional feature transformation. This transformation allows non-linearly separable data to be linearly separable at a higher dimension. Then, in the second step, a maximum margin hyperplane is constructed to draw the decision boundary between the classes [6, 17, 18].

## 3  Experimental Results and Discussion

In this section, we describe the four databases used in this study and we present and discuss the results obtained.

### 3.1  Data

To test the performance of our work we used four different databases: the Ryerson Audio-Visual Database of Emotional Speech and Song (RAVDESS) [19], the Saarbruecken Voice Database (SVD) [20], the CMU_ARCTIC database [21] and the Amazigh speech database (Self-Created).

**RAVDESS.** The Ryerson Audio-Visual Database of Emotional Speech and Song (RAVDESS) is a widely used database for speech emotion recognition. It contains 1440 audio files in .wav format with a frequency of 48 kHz, recorded by 24 authors, including 12 male and 12 female. The database is composed of 8 emotions: calm, happy, sad, angry, fearful, surprised, neutral and disgusted [22]. The language of the audio files is English. This database is chosen to test the performance of our system with speech signals having different tones. We divided the database in two, the first half for training and the second for testing as shown in Table 1.

**SVD.** The Saarbruecken Voice Database (SVD) is a widely used database for voice pathology detection. It is a German database, which contains a set of voice recordings from more than 2000 people, including males and females of different ages. The voice recordings contain the vowels /a/, /i/, and /u/ in a normal, high, low, and low-high-low pitch. Moreover, they contain the sentence "Guten Morgen, wie geht es Ihnen?" which means "Good morning, how are you?" in English. The length of each voice recording is between 1 and 4 s with a frequency of 50 kHz. The database contains 71 type of voice pathologies. In our study, we used the audio files of the recorded sentence "Guten Morgen, wie geht es Ihnen?". The SVD is chosen to test the performance of our system with pathology speech signals [23]. We divided the database in two, the first half for training and the second for testing as shown in Table 1.

**CMU_ARCTIC Database.** The CMU_ARCTIC database is widely used for voice gender recognition. It contains 1132 audio files in .wav format with a frequency of 32 kHz for female gender and 1138 audio files in .wav format with a frequency of 16 kHz for male gender. The language of the audio files is English. We chose to test the performance of our system with the CMU_ARCTIC database because it is commonly used by researchers for voice gender recognition [4, 24]. We divided the database in two, the first half for training and the second for testing as shown in Table 1.

**Amazigh Speech Database.** The Amazigh speech database is a self-created database that contains 300 audio files of numbers from one to five in the Amazigh language (yan, sin, krad, kuz, smmus) [12, 25, 26]. The duration of each audio file is between 1 and 3 s with a frequency of 16 kHz. A total of 60 people participated in the recording, including 30 male and 30 female. We created this database to test the performance of our system with a new type of language and accent. We divided the database in two, the first half for training and the second for testing as shown in Table 1.

**Table 1.** Information about databases used in this study.

| Database name | Number total of audio files | | Training dataset | | Test dataset | |
|---|---|---|---|---|---|---|
| | Male | Female | Male | Female | Male | Female |
| RAVDESS | 720 | 720 | 360 | 360 | 360 | 360 |
| SVD | 880 | 1108 | 440 | 554 | 440 | 554 |
| CMU_ARCTIC database | 1138 | 1132 | 569 | 566 | 569 | 566 |
| Amazigh database | 150 | 150 | 75 | 75 | 75 | 75 |

## 3.2 Results

The aim of this work was to detect the gender of the speech: whether it is male or female. This system can be used in several fields including security systems and human-machine interaction. In our study, we extracted a total of 25 features using two approaches, 11 acoustic features and 14 MFCCs features. The classification is done by two methods, the first method is to use a threshold as mentioned in Sect. 2 part 3, and the second method is to use the SVM classifier. To test the performance of the proposed system, we did not filter the input signals; we only removed the silence. The experiments were performed on a MATLAB 2019 platform using an Intel Core i7 processor with 8 GB of RAM and a 64-bit operating system.

Table 2 shows the accuracy rates of voice gender recognition using acoustic features. As mentioned in Sect. 2, part 3, a threshold was created to perform the classification. We obtained good results using this classifier, but they are not as good as those obtained using the SVM classifier. We also observe that the RAVDESS database has the lowest results compared to the other databases. With the threshold, RAVDESS achieved a rate of 78.06% for male recognition and 80.28% for female recognition. Furthermore, with the SVM classifier, it achieved a rate of 88.61% for male recognition and 90.22% for female recognition. On the other hand, the Amazigh speech database obtained the best results compared to the other databases. With the threshold, it reached a rate of 96.15% for male recognition and 95.01% for female recognition. Moreover, with the SVM classifier, it reached a rate of 99.80% for male recognition and 99.83% for female recognition.

**Table 2.** The accuracy rates of voice gender recognition using acoustic features.

| Classifier | Databases | | | | | | | |
|---|---|---|---|---|---|---|---|---|
| | RAVDESS (%) | | SVD (%) | | CMU_ARCTIC (%) | | Amazigh database (%) | |
| | Male | Female | Male | Female | Male | Female | Male | Female |
| Threshold | 78.06 | 80.28 | 83.86 | 89.35 | 82.60 | 86.11 | 96.15 | 95.01 |
| SVM | 88.61 | 90.22 | 90.27 | 94.43 | 99.47 | 99.65 | 99.80 | 99.83 |

Table 3 shows the accuracy rates of voice gender recognition using MFCCs features. The threshold mentioned in Table 2 is only valid for frequency features. Since females have higher frequency information than males, only the SVM classifier is used for the MFCCs features.

We can see in Table 3 that the results obtained are lower than the ones obtained in Table 2 using the acoustic features with the SVM classifier. However, it is not the same with the CMU_ARCTIC database. We can observe that it has higher results than those in Table 2, where it reached an accuracy rate of 99.47% for male recognition and 99.65% for female recognition. On the other hand, with MFCCs it achieved an accuracy rate of 99.73% for male recognition and 99.77% for female recognition. This is a difference of 0.26% for male recognition and a difference of 0.12% for female recognition.

**Table 3.** The accuracy rates of voice gender recognition using MFCCs features.

| Classifier | Databases | | | | | | | |
|---|---|---|---|---|---|---|---|---|
| | RAVDESS (%) | | SVD (%) | | CMU_ARCTIC (%) | | Amazigh database (%) | |
| | Male | Female | Male | Female | Male | Female | Male | Female |
| SVM | 87.22 | 88.39 | 90.15 | 93.50 | 99.73 | 99.77 | 99.23 | 95.22 |

After using the acoustic and MFCCs features individually, we combined them to see if this would provide better results than the ones obtained in Tables 2 and 3.

Table 4 shows that the results of the RAVDESS database are always the lowest, whether the acoustic and MFCCs features are used separately or in combination. Indeed, the signals in the database present 8 different emotions: calm, happy, sad, angry, fearful, surprised, neutral and disgusted. Therefore, they have different tones and each of them varies in a different way. In addition, for the four databases, we did not remove noises and other disturbances that also affect the results. However, in the end, we obtained higher results even though we did not filter the signals and used different databases with different standards.

The Amazigh speech database reaches an almost 100% accuracy for the recognition of male and female gender. The same goes for the CMU_ARCTIC database, while the SVD and RAVDESS databases achieve more than 90.00% accuracy.

**Table 4.** The accuracy rates of voice gender recognition by combining acoustic features and MFCC coefficients.

| Classifier | Databases | | | | | | | |
|---|---|---|---|---|---|---|---|---|
| | RAVDESS (%) | | SVD (%) | | CMU_ARCTIC (%) | | Amazigh database (%) | |
| | Male | Female | Male | Female | Male | Female | Male | Female |
| SVM | 90.44 | 90.78 | 90.68 | 94.77 | 99.85 | 99.89 | 99.91 | 99.98 |

Table 5 presents the results obtained in our study with the results of other existing studies.

**Table 5.** The highest results obtained in our study with other existing studies

| State of the art | Proposed method | Database | Accuracy (%) |
|---|---|---|---|
| [7] | MFCC, VQ and machine learning algorithm (J 48) | CMU_ARCTIC | 99.80 |
| [10] | Fundamental frequency, spectral entropy, spectral flatness, mode frequency, MFCCs features and KNN classifier | TIMIT | 96.80 |
| [27] | GMM-SV based SVM developed with PLP features | aGender | 90.40 |
| [28] | Pitch, energy and MFCC | TIMIT | 96.45 |
| [29] | Pitch, MFCC | OGI multilingual corpus | 96.53 |
| [30] | VAD, MFCC and PCA | RAVDESS | 98.88 |
| [31] | MFCC and BiLSTM | QDAT | 94.01 |
| Current study | Acoustic features, MFCC coefficients and SVM | Amazigh speech database (with highest results) | 99.91 (Male) 99.98 (Female) |

# 4 Conclusion

In this work, gender voice recognition goes through three steps: pre-processing, feature extraction and finally classification. First, ZCR is used to compress the input signals by removing silence. Then we extracted the acoustic and MFCCs features. Finally, we used threshold and SVM as classifiers. As mentioned in the introduction section, the researchers used a limited number of signals for training and testing, as it was stated that a small training dataset would lead to a low system performance. Therefore, we want to experiment the opposite and used 50% of the database for testing and the other 50% for training. As a result, although we used unfiltered signals and different databases with different ages, accents, languages, emotions and diseases, our system performed perfectly, especially when we combined the acoustic features with the MFCC coefficients. The accuracy rate was almost 100% for the Amazigh speech and CMU_ARCTIC databases, as well as over 90% for the RAVDESS and SVD databases. The execution time was fast in the second and third steps, but the pre-processing step takes more time. The system can for example be used for human-machine interaction, security systems, and digital advertisements by changing the graphical interface if the detected voice is male or female. In the future, we will improve our work by realizing a gender and emotion recognition system with an Amazigh speech database, which is rarely used in the field of speech recognition. In addition, we will use cross-training and cross-testing to perform the system.

**Acknowledgment.** A special thanks to Mr. T. Hobson from the Anglosphere English Center for reviewing for spelling and grammatical mistakes. In addition, to all participants who recorded their voices for this research.

# References

1. Alkhawaldeh, R.S.: DGR: Gender recognition of human speech using one-dimensional conventional neural network. Sci. Program. (2019). https://doi.org/10.1155/2019/7213717
2. Ng, C.B., Tay, Y.H., Goi, B.M.: Vision-based human gender recognition: A survey. In: Proceedings of the Computer Vision and Pattern Recognition (2012). https://doi.org/10.48550/arXiv.1204.1611
3. Archana, G.S., Malleswari, M.: Gender identification and performance analysis of speech signals. In: Proceedings of the 2015 Global Conference on Communication Technologies (GCCT), pp. 483–489. IEEE (2015). https://doi.org/10.1109/GCCT.2015.7342709
4. Hong, Z.: Speaker gender recognition system, Master's thesis, degree programme in wireless communications engineering. University of Oulu, Oulu, Finland, p. 54 (2017)
5. Titze, I.R.: Measurements for voice production: Research and clinical applications. J. Acoust. Soc. Am. (1998)
6. Ahmad, J., Fiaz, M., Kwon, S.I., Sodanil, M., Vo, B., Baik, S.W.: Gender identification using MFCC for telephone applications - a comparative study. Int. J. Comput. Sci. Electron. Eng. 3(5), 351–355 (2015). https://doi.org/10.48550/arXiv.1601.01577
7. Shareef, M.S., Abd, T., Mezaal, Y.S.: Gender voice classification with huge accuracy rate. Telkomnika 18(5), 2612–2617 (2020). https://doi.org/10.12928/TELKOMNIKA.v18i5.13717
8. Buyukyilmaz, M., Cibikdiken, A.O.: Voice gender recognition using deep learning. In: Proceedings of the 2016 International Conference on Modeling, Simulation and Optimization Technologies and Applications (MSOTA), vol. 58, pp. 409–411. Atlantis Press (2016)
9. Ramdinmawii, E., Mittal, V.K.: Gender identification from speech signal by examining the speech production characteristics. In: Proceedings of the 2016 International Conference on Signal processing and Communication (ICSC), pp. 244–249. IEEE (2016). https://doi.org/10.1109/ICSPCom.2016.7980584
10. Uddin, M.A., Hossain, M.S., Pathan, R.K., Biswas, M.: Gender recognition from human voice using multi-layer architecture. In: Proceedings of the 2020 International Conference on Innovations in Intelligent Systems and Applications (INISTA), pp. 1–7. IEEE (2020). https://doi.org/10.1109/INISTA49547.2020.9194654
11. Garg, D., Kaur, S., Arora, D.: Comparative analysis of speech processing techniques for gender recognition. Int. J. Adv. Electr. Electron. Eng., 278–283(2012)
12. Abakarim, F., Abenaou, A.: Amazigh isolated word speech recognition system using the adaptive orthogonal transform method. In: Proceedings of the 2020 International Conference on Intelligent Systems and Computer Vision (ISCV), pp. 1–6. IEEE (2020). https://doi.org/10.1109/ISCV49265.2020.9204291
13. Bachu, R.G., Kopparthi, S., Adapa, B., Barkana, B.D.: Separation of voiced and unvoiced using zero crossing rate and energy of the speech signal. In: Proceedings of the American Society for Engineering Education (ASEE) zone conference proceedings, pp. 1–7 (2008)
14. Shete, D.S., Patil, S.B., Patil, S.: Zero crossing rate and energy of the speech signal of devanagari script. IOSR J. VLSI and Signal Process. 4(1), 01–05 (2014). https://doi.org/10.9790/4200-04110105

15. Muda, L., Begam, M., Elamvazuthi, I.: Voice recognition algorithms using mel frequency cepstral coefficient (MFCC) and dynamic time warping (DTW) techniques. J. Comput. **2**(3), 138–143 (2010)

16. Noble, W.S.: What is a support vector machine? Nat. Biotechnol. **24**(12), 1565–1567 (2006). https://doi.org/10.1038/nbt1206-1565

17. Fokoue, E., Ma, Z.: Speaker gender recognition via MFCCs and SVMs. Rochester Institute of Technology RIT Scholar Works, pp. 1–9 (2013)

18. Jena, B., Mohanty, A., Mohanty, S.K.: Gender recognition and classification of speech signal. In: Proceedings of the 2021 International Conference on Smart Data Intelligence (ICSMDI), pp. 1–7. SSRN (2021)

19. Livingstone, S.R., Russo, F.A.: The ryerson audio-visual database of emotional speech and song (ravdess): A dynamic, multimodal set of facial and vocal expressions in north American english. PLoS ONE **13**(5), e0196391 (2018). https://doi.org/10.1371/journal.pone.0196391

20. Barry, W.J., Putzer, M.: Saarbruecken voice database. http://www.stimmdatenbank.coli.uni-saarland.de/. Accessed 01 Mar 2022

21. Kominek, J., Black, A.: The CMU Arctic speech databases for speech synthesis research. Language Technologies Institute, Carnegie Mellon University, Pittsburgh, PA, Tech. Rep. CMULTI-03-177 (2003). http://www.festvox.org/cmu_arctic/. Accessed 20 Feb 2022

22. Bhavan, A., Chauhan, P., Hitkul, Shah, R.R.: Bagged support vector machines for emotion recognition from speech. Knowl.-Based Syst. (2019)

23. Abakarim, F., Abenaou, A.: Voice pathology detection using the adaptive orthogonal transform method, SVM and MLP. Int. J. Online Biomed. Eng. **17**(14), 90–102 (2021)

24. Livieris, I.E., Pintelas, E., Pintelas, P.: Gender recognition by voice using an improved self-labeled algorithm. Mach. Learn. Knowl. Extr. **1**(1), 492–503 (2019). https://doi.org/10.3390/make1010030

25. Idhssaine, A., El Kirat, Y.: Amazigh language use, perceptions and revitalisation in Morocco: The case of rabat-sale region. J. North Afr. Stud. **26**(3), 465–479 (2021). https://doi.org/10.1080/13629387.2019.1690996

26. Zaid, H., El Allame, Y.E.K.: The place of culture in the Amazigh language textbooks in Morocco. L1-Educ. Stud. Lang. Lit. **18**, 1–20 (2018). https://doi.org/10.17239/L1ESLL-2018.18.01.01

27. Yücesoy, E., Nabiyev, V.V.: A new approach with score-level fusion for the classification of a speaker age and gender. Comput. Electr. Eng. **53**, 29–39 (2016). https://doi.org/10.1016/j.compeleceng.2016.06.002

28. Chaudhary, S., Sharma, D.K.: Gender identification based on voice signal characteristics. In: Proceedings of the 2018 International Conference on Advances in Computing, Communication Control and Networking (ICACCCN), pp. 869–874. IEEE (2018). https://doi.org/10.1109/ICACCCN.2018.8748676

29. Keyvanrad, M.A., Homayounpour, M.M.: Improvement on automatic speaker gender identification using classifier fusion. In: Proceedings of the 2010 18th Iranian Conference on Electrical Engineering, pp. 538–541. IEEE (2010). https://doi.org/10.1109/IRANIANCEE.2010.5507010

30. Nashipudimath, M.M., Pillai, P., Subramanian, A., Nair, V., Khalife, S.: Voice feature extraction for gender and emotion recognition. In: Proceedings of the ITM Web Conferences, vol. 40, p. 03008. EDP Sciences (2021). https://doi.org/10.1051/itmconf/20214003008

31. Mohammed, A.A., Al-Irhayim, Y.F.: Speaker age and gender estimation based on deep learning bidirectional long-short term memory (BiLSTM). Tikrit J. Pure Sci. **26**(4), 76–84 (2021)

# Exploring Neural Embeddings and Transformers for Isolation of Offensive and Hate Speech in South African Social Media Space

Oluwafemi Oriola[1,2]([✉]) [ID] and Eduan Kotzé[1] [ID]

[1] University of the Free State, Bloemfontein, South Africa
[2] Adekunle Ajasin University, Akungba, Nigeria
oluwafemi.oriola@aaua.edu.ng

**Abstract.** Our previous study on classification and detection of abusive language in South African social media space has shown the high prospect of surface level features and classical machine learning models in terms of accuracy. However, much improvement is still needed in the aspect of F1-score. Therefore, the state-of-the-arts such as neural embeddings (Word2Vec, Doc2Vec, GloVe) and neural network-based transformer models (BERT and mBERT) which have performed well in many hate speech isolation tasks are explored in this work. In the evaluation of classical machine learning algorithms, Word2Vec with Support Vector Machine outperformed the previous models, Doc2Vec and GloVe in terms of F1-score. In the evaluation of neural networks, all the neural embedding and transformer models performed worse than the previous models in terms of F1-score. In conclusion, the impressive performance of Word2Vec neural embedding with classical machine learning algorithms in terms of best F1-score of 0.62 and accuracy of 0.86 shows its good prospect in the isolation of abusive language and hate speech in South African social media space.

**Keywords:** Computational model · Neural models · South African abusive languages · Classification

## 1 Introduction

Toxic comments are not limited to verbal violence but include harassment, profanity, hate speech and cyberbullying [1], which unfortunately have pervaded the social media landscape. In response to the menace, many research efforts have gone into ridding out these ills from the social media using text mining. In South Africa particularly, they are treated with the acts of parliament using the instrument of laws [2]. However, the dispensation of justice has been impeded by lack of adequate provision of laws or skills, which automatic hate speech isolation tool can ameliorate [3].

According to South African Hate Crime Bill [2], hate speech is hinged on discrimination based on race, colour, ethnicity, gender, sexual orientation, nationality, or religion

O. Gervasi et al. (Eds.): ICCSA 2022, LNCS 13375, pp. 649–661, 2022.
https://doi.org/10.1007/978-3-031-10522-7_44

and targets citizens in manners that are potentially harmful to them. It is different from offensive speech, which is often less discriminatory compared to hate speech [4]. Thus, social media hate speech would be better distinguished from offensive speech and free speech using advanced technology such as Machine Learning and Deep Learning that could carry out in-depth data analysis.

The survey of existing works in the domain of offensive and hate speech isolation according to Fortuna and Nunes [5] showed that surface-level features such as N-Gram, term frequency inverse document frequency (TF-IDF), stylometry and user profile as well as neural embedding and transformer models have been employed during feature extraction and engineering step. Also, classical machine learning algorithms such as Logistic Regression (LogReg), Support Vector Machine (SVM), Random Forest (RF) and Gradient Boosting (GB), Convolutional Neural Networks (CNN) and Recurrent Neural Networks (RNN) have been employed in the classification step, with some impressive outcomes according to Parihar *et al.* [6]. Thus, our initial efforts in this domain went into exploring the surface level features and classical machine learning techniques to segregate offensive and hate speech from free speech in South African context [7]. However, the results obtained are below the expectation particularly in the aspect of F1-score. This paper therefore moves further by exploring neural embedding and transformer models for offensive and hate speech isolation on social media.

## 2 Background

Since the current work is building on our previous work [7], the subsections below illustrate the key aspects of the previous work.

The previous work focused on automatic detection of hate and offensive South African tweets in a multiclass classification problem space using both classical and ensemble machine learning models. N-gram, syntactic, negative sentiment-based surface level features and their combinations were investigated. Since no corpus existed, we first developed a golden standard Twitter corpus for the South African abusive language context using Twitter Archiver, a Google Sheets plugin which is based on Twitter Search API. We relied on South African laws in [2] to define and describe hate speech, offensive speech and free speech for annotation tasks. Hate speech (HT) in the South African context was defined as any unfairly discriminatory expression that demonstrates a clear intention to be harmful or to incite harm; promote or propagate hatred against a person or group of persons. Offensive speech (OFF) was defined as any fair or unfair expression that is not hate speech but discriminatory against a person or group of persons, while free speech (FS) was any expression that justifies the freedom of expressions' right. The FS was neither hate speech nor offensive speech.

About 21K tweets were initially collected but upon removal of duplicates, irrelevant and incorrectly annotated tweets, 14,896 resulted. During annotation, the tweets were divided according to the language of discourse into 7,100 for (English, English + Afrikaans), 4,102 for (English, English + Sesotho) and 4,500 for (English, English + IsiZulu) and two experienced human annotators, who were literate in each category of language labelled the tweets. By applying Cohen Kappa Agreement Test [8] for inter-annotator reliability, agreement scores of 0.837, 0.579 and 0.633, respectively were obtained. The resulting tweets were then pre-processed, as indicated in [7] since tweets can be very noisy and could distort the findings of the experiment.

The results showed that RF with word N-gram was the most effective in terms of accuracy of 0.893; SVM with character N-gram was the most effective in terms of true positive rate of 0.894 for HT detection; and GB with word N-gram was the most effective with true positive rate of 0.867 for OFF detection. By applying stacked ensemble generalization with multi-tier meta-features (multi-tier stacking ensemble), the true positive rates for HT and OFF were improved. However, the F1-scores remained poor with the best score of 0.56.

Therefore, this work explores ways of improving the performance, most especially F1-score by exploring neural embeddings and transformers.

## 3   Related Works

Literature has not reported the application of neural embeddings and transformer models for isolation of South African offensive and hate speech, but they have been employed in other contexts.

### 3.1   Neural Embeddings

Wang *et al.* [9] evaluated different embeddings models including skip-gram and continuous bag of words (CBOW) embeddings based on Word2Vec, GloVe, FastText, N-Gram2Vec and Dict2Vec for different applications using CNN and bidirectional LSTM. The intrinsic and extrinsic evaluators found skip-gram (Word2Vec) to be mostly efficient and outstanding in terms of accuracy for both neural networks.

Kumar *et al.* [10] employed GloVe pre-trained word embeddings, which included six billion tokens at 100 dimensions each to create a dense embedded matrix. They found that CNN + bidirectional LSTM ensemble classifier outperformed other deep learning neural networks such as CNN and bidirectional LSTM.

A classification experiment based on racist, sexist and neither classes was carried out using 16K annotated tweets in Badjatiya *et al.* [11]. The experiment made use of bag of word, TF-IDF weighted features, random embeddings as well as pre-trained GloVe and FastText character embeddings. From classification with several classifiers (LR, RF, SVM, GB, CNN and LSTM), the results showed that the random embedding with combination of LSTM and GB was the best with F-score of 0.93.

In Wang and Koopman [12], Word2Vec word embedding model outperformed pre-trained GloVe and Ariadne with an accuracy score of 0.627. An investigation into document embeddings also found Doc2Vec to be better than Ariadne, with least recall of 0.826 for both information classes.

### 3.2   Transformer-Based Deep Learning Models

In our model, BERT based neural transformer models are considered for their good performance [13]. Mozafari *et al.* [14] evaluated BERT on Waseem's racism and sexism dataset and Davidson's hate and offensive dataset. They employed CLS, non-linear layer,

CNN and LSTM classifiers. While all the classifiers recorded good performances, CNN was the most outstanding with F1-score of 0.92. Sohn and Lee [15] developed a multi-channel BERT for Classification of three popular hate speech datasets. The multichannel BERT consisted of mBERT, BERT and Chinese BERT, which have been pretrained and fine-tuned with pooling weight. The results of accuracy and F1-score were better than the individual models.

The reviewed works have shown that neural embeddings such as Word2Vec, Doc2Vec, GloVe and BERT transformer models performed well for different instances of hate and offensive speech isolation. In this work, however, both GloVe and BERT are not considered to avoid of the issue of out-of-vocabulary which might emanate due to the presence of many South African indigenous words in the evaluation dataset. This study, therefore, analyzes classical machine learning and neural network classifiers based on Word2Vec, Doc2Vec and mBERT.

# 4 Research Methods

## 4.1 Features Description

Firstly, two neural embeddings-based vector spaces were constructed from the vocabularies of the corpus using both Word2Vec and Doc2Vec models. Secondly, Multilingual Bidirectional Encoder Representations from Transformers (mBERT) was used to evaluate transformer-based model.

### 4.1.1 Word2Vec

Word2Vec [16] consists of a neural network architecture of an input layer, a projection layer and an output layer. It defines the probability of observing the target word $w_t$ in a document D given its local context $c_t$.

Mikolov et al. [16] introduced the Skip-gram model which is an efficient method for learning vector representations of words from unstructured text data. Unlike previous neural network embeddings before it, the training does not involve dense matrix multiplications. The training objective is to find word representations that are useful for predicting the surrounding words in a sentence or a document.

Given a sequence of training words $w_1$, $w_2$, $w_3$,..., $w_T$, skip-gram model objective is to maximize the average log probability which is:

$$\frac{1}{T}\sum_{t=1}^{T}\sum_{-c\leq j\leq c, j\neq 0} \log p(w_{t+j}|w_t) \tag{1}$$

where c is the size of the context.

The basic Skip-gram formulation defines $p(w_{t+j}|w_t)$ using the softmax function:

$$p(w_o|w_I) = \frac{\exp(v_{wO}^{\prime T}v_{w1})}{\sum_{w=1}^{W}\exp(v_{W}^{\prime T}v_{w1})} \tag{2}$$

where $v_w$ is the input and $v'_w$ is the output vector representations of w, and W is the number of words in the vocabulary. Because of the impracticality of softmax function, $p(w_0|w_I)$ is replaced by negative sampling as:

$$log\sigma\left(v_{wo}^I T_{Vw1}\right) + \sum\nolimits_{i=1}^{k} \mathbb{E}_{wi\sim P_n(w)}\left[log\sigma\left(-v_{wi}^I T_{Vw1}\right)\right] \tag{3}$$

### 4.1.2 Doc2Vec

Doc2Vec [17], an extension of Word2Vec forms document representation by averaging word embeddings of all the words in a document. Doc2Vec consists of an input layer, a projection layer, and an output layer. The embeddings include target word and neighbouring words, which form the local contexts and the entire documents serving as the global contexts. Doc2Vec makes use of two approaches to learn paragraph and document representations, namely the distributed memory (DM) model and the distributed bag-of-words (DBOW) model.

Doc2Vec defines the probability of observing a target word $w_t$ given its local context $c_t$ as well as the global context X as

$$P\left(w^t|c^t, X\right) = \frac{\exp(v_{w^t}^T\left(U_{c^t} + \frac{1}{T}UX\right))}{\sum_{w^l \in V} \exp(U_{c^t} + \frac{1}{T}UX)} \tag{4}$$

$U_{c^t}$ is the local context and $\frac{1}{T}UX$ is the global context and T is the length of the document. Thereafter, negative sampling is applied as presented in Word2Vec. The projection matrix from input space to hidden space U and projection matric from hidden space to output V are then learned to minimize the loss

$$l = -\sum\nolimits_{i=1}^{n} \sum\nolimits_{t=1}^{T_i} f\left(w_i^t, c_i^t, X_i^t\right) \tag{5}$$

Given the learned projection matrix U, each document is represented simply as an average of the embeddings of the words in the document.

$$d = \frac{1}{T}\sum\nolimits_{w\in D} U_w \tag{6}$$

The DBOW approach, which predicts target word based on contexts is used in this work.

### 4.1.3 Multilingual Bidirectional Encoder Representations from Transformers

Multilingual Bidirectional Encoder Representations from Transformers (mBERT) is the multilingual version of Bidirectional Encoder Representations from Transformers (BERT) [13], which is a bidirectional transformer encoder pretrained on English Wikipedia and Book Corpus. Unlike word embeddings, BERT models capture the contexts of texts, an improvement over existing contextual embeddings that learn either left-wise or right-wise. It makes use of masked language model to beat the challenge of bidirectional learning before and the next sentence prediction step. The pre-trained

BERT is fine-tuned by passing the word inputs through 12-layers of transformer encoder consisting of self-attention, add/normalise and feed-forward processes. The fine-tuned embeddings go through the neural prediction layer to produce the outputs. Figure 1 presents the architecture of the BERT.

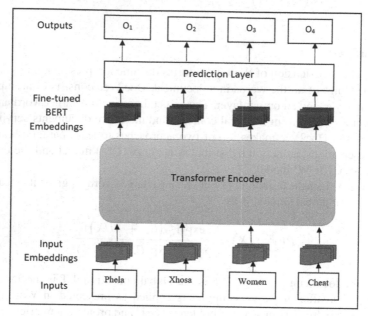

**Fig. 1.** The BERT architecture

The mBERT is used in this research because of its ability to accommodate different languages including Afrikaans, Sesotho and IsiZulu.

## 4.2   Classification Models

The classical machine learning algorithms such as *Logistic Regression* (LogReg), *Suport Vector Machine* (SVM), *Random Forest* (RF) and *Gradient Boosting* (GB) were evaluated and compared with the deep learning algorithms such as *Convolutional Neural Network* (CNN), *Long Short-term Memory* (LSTM), Bidirectional *Long Short-term Memory* (LSTM), *Gated Recurrent Unit* (GRU), Bidirectional *Gated Recurrent Unit* (GRU) and their various ensembles. We made use of Python's scikit-learn library by Pedregosa *et al.* [18] for the classical machine learning modelling and Keras by Chollet [19] for the deep learning modelling.

# 5   Experimental Setup

## 5.1   Dataset Description

Since the paper builds on the previous works, the models were evaluated using the abusive language dataset[1] used in [7]. The total and average distribution of words and characters in the dataset is presented in Table 1. The distribution shows that there were 28,912 unique words from which English words was about 28 times the size of South African words.

**Table 1.** Corpus statistics

| Parameters | Values |
|---|---|
| Total number of unique words | 28,912 |
| Number of unique English words | 27,466 |
| Number of unique non-English South African words | 1,446 |
| Average number of words per tweet | 23.76 |
| Average length of words per tweet | 142.75 |
| Total number of tweets | 14,896 |

## 5.2   Pre-processing

The tweets were cleaned and formatted by first tokenizing the tweets using Tweet-Tokenizer of Natural Language Processing Toolkit (NLTK) [20] before stemming the English words using WordNet Lemmatizer in NLTK [20]. Unwanted text such as user-name, punctuations, emoticons, emojis, special characters and hash symbols in hash tags were also removed. To avoid the omission of important terms as stop words, only English stopwords which are not present in other South African languages are extracted. We finally changed all text to lower case format.

## 5.3   Implementation

After implementing the pre-processing procedure using NLTK 3.5 [21], the dataset (n = 14,896) was divided into training (n = 11,172) and testing samples (n = 3,724) for the classification tasks. The parameter settings and their values for classical machine learning models are presented in Table 2. The selection of the best machine learning models was done using an exhaustive grid-search optimization over several hyperparameter configurations as highlighted in [7], while the Deep Leaning models were developed using 100 epochs, batch size of 64 and early stopping criteria (validation = loss, mode = min, verbose = 1, patience = 10, min_delta = 0.0001) without exhaustive grid-search due to extensive computing power requirements.

---

[1] https://github.com/oriolao/AbusiveLanguage.

Gensim [21] was used to implement the Word2Vec and Doc2Vec. For the Word2Vec, we used the skip-gram model [22] to create a 300-dimensional dense vector space. The model was implemented with minimum word count of 1, context window size of 10, workers of 8 and epoch of 30. For the Doc2Vec, we used DBOW (sg = 0) [12], which is built on a skip-gram model to create a 300-dimensional dense vector space. The parameters of Doc2Vec included negative, which set at 20 and learning rate, which is set at 0.002. The two embeddings were oversampled using synthetic minority oversampling technique (SMOTE) [23] to avoid imbalance in training.

In addition, *BERT-Base, Multilingual Cased Type* of transformer model with 104 languages, 12-layer, 768-hidden, 12-heads and 178,446,340 (170M) parameters was used to model mBERT. It was evaluated with batch size of 16bits, epoch of 5 and learning rate of 0.00001. The Python codes can be accessed here[2].

## 5.4 Performance Evaluation

The performance of the models was evaluated using accuracy and macro-averaging F1-score ($F1_m$). Also, macro-averaging precision ($precision_m$) and macro-averaging recall ($recall_m$) scores were evaluated for thorough comparison with the previous work [7]. Only the macro-averaging metrics were employed in the evaluation because the scores of the micro-averaging scores are always identical to the accuracy in multiclass classification. The equations for estimating accuracy, $F1_m$, $precision_m$ and $recall_m$ are presented in Eq. 7, 8, 9, 10.

$$Accuracy = \frac{TP + TN}{TP + FP + TN + FN} \tag{7}$$

$$F1_m = \frac{2X(Recall_m X Precision_m)}{(Recall_m + Precision_m)} \tag{8}$$

$$Precision_m = \frac{\sum_{i=1}^{l} \frac{TP}{TP+FP}}{l} \tag{9}$$

$$Recall_m = \frac{\sum_{i=1}^{l} \frac{TP}{TP+FN}}{l} \tag{10}$$

where TP is true positive; TN is true negative; FP is false positive; FN is false negative; and l is the number of classes.

## 6 Results

The test results for the $F1_m$ and accuracy performances of Word2Vec, Doc2Vec and mBERT based on classical and neural networks are presented in Table 2.

---

[2] https://github.com/oriolao/AbusiveLanguage.

**Table 2.** Test results for $F1_m$ and accuracy of the models

| Type of model | Semantic embedding | Machine learning model | $F1_m$ | Accuracy |
|---|---|---|---|---|
| Classical Machine Learning Model | Word2Vec | LogReg | 0.31 | 0.884 |
| | | SVM | 0.62 | 0.882 |
| | | RF | 0.59 | 0.885 |
| | | GB | 0.58 | 0.819 |
| | Doc2Vec | LogReg | 0.31 | 0.884 |
| | | SVM | 0.44 | 0.597 |
| | | RF | 0.58 | 0.884 |
| | | GB | 0.58 | 0.744 |
| Neural Networks | Word2Vec | MLP | 0.44 | 0.577 |
| | | CNN | 0.31 | 0.501 |
| | | LSTM | 0.35 | 0.815 |
| | | GRU | 0.37 | 0.653 |
| | | BiLSTM | 0.33 | 0.647 |
| | | BiGRU | 0.41 | 0.752 |
| | | Double CNN | 0.38 | 0.872 |
| | | Double LSTM | 0.43 | 0.748 |
| | | Double GRU | 0.36 | 0.840 |
| | | CNN + LSTM | 0.36 | 0.784 |
| | | CNN + GRU | 0.41 | 0.850 |
| | Doc2Vec | MLP | 0.31 | 0.884 |
| | | CNN | 0.36 | 0.800 |
| | | LSTM | 0.32 | 0.695 |
| | | GRU | 0.25 | 0.432 |
| | | BiLSTM | 0.28 | 0.482 |
| | | BiGRU | 0.09 | 0.145 |
| | | Double CNN | 0.24 | 0.350 |
| | | Double LSTM | 0.06 | 0.093 |
| | | Double GRU | 0.24 | 0.403 |
| | | CNN + LSTM | 0.27 | 0.440 |
| | | CNN + GRU | 0.29 | 0.468 |
| | Transformer model | BERT | 0.46 | 0.833 |

The results show that Word2Vec with SVM recorded the highest $F1_m$ of 0.62, followed by Word2Vec with RF of 0.59. Both Doc2Vec with RF and GB recorded $F1_m$ of 0.58 each. Word2Vec with GB also recorded accuracy of 0.58. The performances of Word2Vec and Doc2Vec for all the neural models were poor with the highest of 0.44 recorded by MLP. The neural network models including deep learning models performed less impressively in terms of $F1_m$

In terms of accuracy, Word2Vec and Doc2Vec, with RF were impressive with accuracy scores of 0.885 and 0.884, respectively. Also, Word2Vec with SVM performed well with accuracy of 0.882. Doc2Vec with GB recorded an accuracy of 0.744. Both SVM and RF also performed effectively with little bias for the majority class. The mBERT accuracy was however moderate at 0.833.

In comparing the performance of the current models with the previous models [7], accuracy and TPR performances are presented in Table 3 and F1m, precision$_m$ and recall$_m$ are presented in Table 4. From Table 3, the current models performed worse than the previous models in terms of accuracy but the TPR for the current machine learning models, most especially SVM were closer to the previous models. The best of each type of models are indicated in boldface.

**Table 3.** Comparison of Accuracy and TPR of the current and previous models

| Model | Feature | Type | Machine Leaning Model | TPR | | | Accuracy |
|-------|---------|------|----------------------|-----|-----|-----|----------|
| | | | | HT | OFF | FS | All |
| Previous Model[7] | N-gram surface level features | Classical | SVM | **0.894** | 0.069 | 0.864 | 0.646 |
| | | | RF | 0.094 | 0.631 | **0.966** | **0.893** |
| | | | GB | 0.529 | 0.867 | 0.804 | 0.803 |
| | | Baseline solution | Multitier stacking ensemble | 0.858 | **0.887** | 0.646 | 0.674 |
| Current Model | Neural Networks | Word2Vec | SVM | 0.376 | 0.738 | 0.910 | 0.882 |
| | | | RF | 0.224 | 0.646 | **0.928** | **0.885** |
| | | | GB | 0.576 | 0.804 | 0.827 | 0.819 |
| | | Doc2Vec | SVM | **0.718** | **0.827** | 0.570 | 0.597 |
| | | | RF | 0.235 | 0.637 | 0.927 | 0.884 |
| | | | GB | 0.682 | 0.778 | 0.742 | 0.744 |
| | | Transformer model | BERT | 0.000 | 0.31 2 | 0.687 | 0.833 |

The results in Table 4 show that the current models with the highest $F1_m$ of 0.62 outperformed the previous models that recorded the highest $F1_m$ of 0.56. The precision$_m$ and recall$_m$ of the current models were worse than the previous models. The results in

Table 3 and Table 4 also show that Word2Vec was slightly better than Doc2Vec. The best of each type of models are indicated in boldface.

The Cochrans-q test [24] was conducted on both the predictions of Word2Vec and the baseline solution. The results showed that at 0.05 significance, p-value of 0 (Q = 1854.77) was obtained meaning there was no significance difference. This shows that the current model is comparable to the previous model in terms of accuracy.

**Table 4.** Comparison of $Precision_m$, $Recall_m$ and $F1_m$ for the proposed statistical models and previous models

| Model | Feature | Type | Machine Leaning Model | $Precision_m$ | $Recall_m$ | $F1_m$ |
|---|---|---|---|---|---|---|
| Previous Model [7] | N-gram surface level features | Classical | SVM | **0.65** | 0.55 | 0.35 |
| | | | RF | 0.55 | 0.47 | 0.50 |
| | | | GB | 0.52 | 0.73 | **0.56** |
| | | Baseline | Multitier Stacking Ensemble | 0.50 | **0.80** | 0.50 |
| Current Model | Neural Networks | Word2Vec | SVM | **0.58** | 0.67 | **0.62** |
| | | | RF | 0.57 | 0.61 | 0.59 |
| | | | GB | 0.53 | **0.74** | 0.58 |
| | | Doc2Vec | SVM | 0.46 | 0.70 | 0.44 |
| | | | RF | 0.57 | 0.60 | 0.58 |
| | | | GB | 0.50 | 0.73 | 0.58 |
| | | Transformer model | BERT | 0.44 | 0.48 | 0.46 |

# 7   Conclusion

In this work, we have explored neural embedding and transformer models and compared their performances to our previous work [7]. The aim of the current work was to improve the F1-score in the classification of abusive languages for the purpose of effective isolation of offensive and hate speech. Based on the review of neural-based embedding and transformer models, we employed Word2Vec, Doc2vec and multilingual Bidirectional Encoder Representations from Transformers to classify abusive South African tweets into hate, offensive and free speech. Using the existing South African election dataset of 14K, the classical machine learning models such as Logistic Regression, Support Vector Machine, Random Forest and Gradient Boosting were first used to evaluate the neural features. Thereafter, different models of neural networks were explored.

With the exception of Logistic Regression, the results showed that the classical machine learning models based on Word2Vec was impressive with F1-score performance of 0.62 as against 0.56 of the previous model [7]. In terms of accuracy, a baseline performance of 0.885, which is less than the previous model by negligible value of 0.008 was recorded. On the other hand, the deep learning models performed worse than the classical machine learning models but the multilayer perceptron neural networks recorded high true positive rate for hate speech and offensive speech. The outcomes of the experiment showed that Word2Vec with Support Vector Machine performed best in terms of F1-score. In future work, Word2Vec will be enhanced through feature augmentation.

# References

1. Georgakopoulos, S.V., Tasoulis, S.K., Vrahatis, A.G., Plagianakos, V.P.: Convolutional neural networks for toxic comment classification. In: the 10th Hellenic Conference (2018). https://doi.org/10.48550/arxiv.1802.09957
2. Prevention and Combating of Hate Crimes and Hate Speech Bill. (2018). https://www.justice.gov.za/legislation/hcbill/B9-2018-HateCrimesBill.pdf
3. PeaceTech Lab: Monitoring and Analysis of Hateful Language in South Africa Report #6. *PeaceTech Lab* (2019). https://www.peacetechlab.org/south-africa-report-6. Accessed: 15 Nov 2019
4. Mehdad, Y., Tetreault, J.: Do characters abuse more than words? In: Proceedings of the 17th Annual Meeting of the Special Interest Group on Discourse and Dialogue 299–303 (Association for Computational Linguistics) (2016). https://doi.org/10.18653/v1/w16-3638
5. Fortuna, P., Nunes, S.: A survey on automatic detection of hate speech in text. ACM Comput. Surv. **51**(4), 51 (2018)
6. Parihar, A.S., Thapa, S., Mishra, S.: Hate speech detection using natural language processing : applications and hate speech detection using natural language processing: applications and challenges. In: Proceedings of the Fifth International Conference on Trends in Electronics and Informatics (ICOEI) 1302–1308. IEEE (2021). https://doi.org/10.1109/ICOEI51242.2021.9452882
7. Oriola, O., Kotzé, E.: Evaluating machine learning techniques for detecting offensive and hate speech in South African tweets. IEEE Access **8**, 21496–21509 (2020)
8. Cohen, J.: A coefficient of agreement for nominal scales. Educ. Psychol. Meas. **20**, 37–46 (1960)
9. Wang, B., Wang, A., Chen, F., Wang, Y., Kuo, C.: Evaluating word embedding models: methods and experimental results. APSIPA Trans. Signal and Inf. Process. **8**(E19), 1–13 (2019). https://doi.org/10.1017/ATSIP.2019.12
10. Kumar, S.: Fake news detection using deep learning models : a novel approach. Trans Emerg. Tel Tech. **31**(2), 1–23 (2019). https://doi.org/10.1002/ett.3767
11. Badjatiya, P., Gupta, S., Gupta, M., Varma, V.: Deep Learning for Hate Speech Detection in Tweets. In: International World Wide Web Conference Committee (IW3C2), pp. 759–760 (2017)
12. Wang, S., Koopman, R.: Semantic embedding for information retrieval. In: BIR 2017 Workshop on Bibliometric-enhanced Information Retrieval, pp. 122–132 (2017)
13. Devlin, J., Chang, M.W., Lee, K., Toutanova, K.: BERT: pre-training of deep bidirectional transformers for language understanding. In: 2019 Conference of the North American Chapter of the Association for Computational Linguistics: Human Language Technologies, pp. 4171–4186 (2019)

14. Mozafari, M., Reza Farahbakhsh, R., Crespi, N.: A BERT-based transfer learning approach for hate speech detection in online social media. In: 8th International Conference on Complex Networks and their Applications (2019). https://doi.org/10.48550/arXiv.1910.12574

15. Sohn, H., Lee, H.: MC-BERT4HATE: hate speech detection using multi-channel bert for different languages and translations. In: 2019 International Conference on Data Mining Workshops (ICDMW) 551–559. IEEE (2019). https://doi.org/10.1109/ICDMW.2019.00084

16. Mikolov, T., Chen, K., Corrado, G., Dean, J.: Efficient estimation of word representations in vector space. arXiv preprint arXiv:1301.3781 (2013)

17. Le, Q., Mikolov, T.: Distributed representations of sentences and documents. In: Proceedings of the 31 st International Conference on Machine Learning 32, pp. 1188–1196 (2014). https://proceedings.mlr.press/v32/le14.html

18. Pedregosa, F., et al.: Scikit-learn: machine learning in Python. J. Mach. Learn. Res. **12**, 2825–2830 (2011)

19. Chollet, F.: *Deep Learning with Python.* (Simon and Schuster, 2021)

20. Bird, S., Kliein, E., Loper, E.: Analyzing Texts with Natural Language Toolkit: Natural Language Processing with Python. (O'Reilly, 2009)

21. Radim, R., Valletta, P.S.: Software framework for topic modelling with large corpora. In: Proceedings of LREC 2010 workshop New Challenges for NLP Frameworks, Pp. 46–50 (2010)

22. Mikolov, T., Chen, K., Corrado, G., Dean, J.: Distributed Representations of Words and Phrases and their Compositionality, pp. 1–9 (2013). https://doi.org/10.48550/arXiv.1310.4546

23. Chawla, N.V, Bowyer, K.W., Hall, L.O.: SMOTE: synthetic minority over-sampling technique. J. Artificial Intelligence Res. **16**, 321–357 (2002)

24. Raschka, S.: MLxtend: providing machine learning and data science utilities and extensions to python' s scientific computing stack. J. Open Source Softw. **3**, 24–25 (2018)

# Commercialization of Open Software, Knowledge Flow, and Patents

Shixuan Yu[1](✉) 📵 and Ping Yu[2]

[1] Shanghai Institute of Technology, Shanghai 200030, China
yushixuan8@163.com
[2] Communication University of China, Beijing 100024, China

**Abstract.** Open source communities as large-scale paradigm innovations have attracted a lot of attention from scholars. In this paper, we analyze the possible effects that software companies' participation in open source communities can have on corporate patents through knowledge flow theory. Technological innovation resulting from the acquisition of technical knowledge by open source communities shortens the cycle of corporate technological innovation. However, since firms' technological innovation activities can only be imitations and follow-the-flow innovations, they may sometimes cause the failure of firms' technological innovation.

**Keywords:** Open software · Commercialization · Knowledge flow · Patents

## 1 Introduction

The early practices of the open source community originated from well-known open source software projects such as Linux and Apache. Following the great success of these open source projects, open source software (OSS) has attracted the attention of different academic fields. Some studies have focused on the motivations that drive users and developers to contribute to OSS projects [1], how the innovation process works [2], and the governance issues of the OSS community [3]. Open source software (OSS) is attracting commercial interest from a growing number of companies. The best known examples are IBM, Sun Microsystems, and Oracle, all of which have begun to invest in and legitimize Linux for enterprise applications [4]. As early as the first quarter of 2005, Novell had already realized $44 million in Linux-related product revenue, or 15% of its total sales for the same period. Other companies, such as Red Hat, have specialized as OSS distributors, aggregating, integrating and optimizing the latest software code offered by the OSS community. So why should for-profit companies get involved in the commercialization of OSS products?

Since becoming commercialized [5], another line of research on OSS has focused on for-profit companies that work with the OSS community [6, 7], which companies use to ensure the intellectual property protection mechanisms to ensure their return from the open business model [1, 8] and the competitive dynamics introduced by OSS [9].

O. Gervasi et al. (Eds.): ICCSA 2022, LNCS 13375, pp. 662–672, 2022.
https://doi.org/10.1007/978-3-031-10522-7_45

Although the potential benefits of widespread OSS adoption for participants have been largely established [8], there is still a lack of empirical evidence on the impact that OSS commercialization may have on patents of for-profit companies. According to Chesbrough [10], the real social impact of an innovation only arrives after it is commercialized. In an open innovation model, IP does not languish; it creates value, either directly or via licensing or other inside-out mechanisms. In a knowledge-based economy, knowledge capital is a more important source of value creation than are natural or capital resources. In such an economy, technology innovation is achieved through active knowledge flow between knowledge actors. Thus, it is important for firms to establish a strategy considering knowledge flow to improve innovation ability through the use of knowledge coming from open source [11, 12]. Many innovative firms have use a great variety of external sources to create new innovations and sustain existing ones [11]. One of the key challenges of open innovation is 'motivating outsiders to supply an ongoing stream of external innovations' [13]. In addition, Nelson and Winter [14] mentioned that one characteristic of innovation is commercialization of the invention.

Therefore, when firms commercialize, it will inevitably have an impact on innovation. Based on the knowledge-based theory of the firm, this paper first combines knowledge flow and open source communities, briefly discusses the impact of commercial participation in open source communities on patents, and argues that this impact is mainly reflected in technology innovation mode and cycle. Therefore, when firms try to profit from open source communities, it inevitably have an impact on internal innovation. Based on the knowledge-based theory of the firm, this paper combines knowledge flow and open innovation literature to briefly explore the impact of business participation in open source communities on patents, and argues that this impact is mainly reflected in technology innovation mode and cycle.

## 2 Knowledge Management and Open Innovation

### 2.1 Innovation and Open Source

According to Chesbrough [15], open innovation can utilize inbound and outbound knowledge flows to facilitate the growth of their innovation outputs. There are two stages: utilizing external innovations internally, and externally commercializing internal innovations [11]. The former is the basis for commercial companies to use open-source communities to develop commercial software. One of the important arguments is that companies can benefit from individual participants outside the company. Utilizing external innovations internally can be seen as a process includes three phases: obtaining, integrating, and commercializing external innovations [13].

The acquisition of external resources for open innovation includes customers, competitors, consumer public research institutions, universities and other types of organizations, while simultaneously using creative methods to exploit a firm's resulting IP [11]. Enterprises also enter professional fields beyond their boundaries through various mechanisms, including license agreement alliances, joint ventures, and informal social interactions. When the new technology reduces the transmission cost, promotes the rapid exchange and dissemination of information, and expands the scope of dissemination to potential participants, the diffusion characteristics of the innovation process are particularly obvious.

For new products,there are significant trade-offs between innovation speed, development costs, and competitive advantage for relying on external rather than internal learning [16]. Therefore, when the existence of external knowledge cannot be incorporated into innovation activities by the enterprise, the enterprise will lose huge profits. Only after the company's external knowledge is absorbed, can the company begin to adopt further measures to promote internal innovation results, such as licensing of IP, patent pooling and so on. Open innovation can reflect a shift in how companies manage and use their IP.

Open source software is an important output of the open source community in the software industry, and it is also a practice in open innovation. Compared with patent software, OSS users have the authority to modify enhance and extension software by a wide range of software licenses. In contrast, patented software strictly protects the source code. Using communication technology, participants in open-source projects can jointly create advanced software solutions and share new results in a collective manner within the community. Joining the open-source community may ensure that companies continue to produce new results.

## 2.2  Knowledge Flow and Open Innovation

From the perspective of knowledge capital, knowledge management influences the change of organizational management model with the development of the knowledge economy era, that is, the focus on product process management in the past has changed to the current focus on the management of enterprise knowledge capital and human capital. For the definition of knowledge management, most scholars focus on explaining knowledge management from the knowledge flow process. Alavi and Leidner [17] believes that knowledge management is the process of knowledge creation, knowledge storage, knowledge transfer and knowledge application for organizational knowledge capital. Knowledge management is an activity that enhances the competitiveness of enterprises through screening and acquiring and synergizing knowledge within a hierarchical organization.

Open innovation focuses on the acquisition and development of internal and external knowledge, and its essence is to comprehensively utilize the convenient knowledge flow across the internal and external organizations to accelerate the process of internal knowledge innovation. Therefore, the process of open innovation is the process of management and application of knowledge flow. In the knowledge network formed by enterprises, based on the embedded perspective, knowledge is always in a dynamic flow. This kind of knowledge flow usually has two directional vector interpretations. From the horizontal vector, the uneven distribution of knowledge among knowledge subjects and the higher requirements of specialized knowledge for carriers are the manifestations of knowledge heterogeneity. The internal demand and market demand it brings have led to the flow of knowledge among subjects. In terms of the vertical vector, the knowledge potential difference caused by the gap in the knowledge stock between subjects leads to the directional flow of knowledge due to the difference in social division of labor and resource endowments.

The value created by the flow of knowledge does not directly come from intellectual capital, but from the interaction between elements of intellectual capital. Interorganizational knowledge flows is an important factor for organizational innovation and new knowledge creation as it can increase company's innovation capabilities what in turn increases its competitive advantage. The commercialization of open source software involves two organizations of different nature: open source communities and enterprises. Therefore, it is particularly important to study the knowledge flow between them. According to previous research [18], knowledge flow can be summarized into 4 stages: knowledge acquisition, knowledge transfer, knowledge integration, knowledge creation and application.

## Knowledge Acquisition

Knowledge acquisition means that enterprises provide a knowledge base for open innovation through searching, absorbing and sharing internal and external knowledge, and lay the foundation of knowledge source for the next stage of knowledge transformation. The sources of knowledge flow in the open innovation framework can be diversified, such as upstream suppliers, university scientific research institutions and even competitors. These knowledge flows enter the knowledge inventory through absorption and sharing, and increase the knowledge stock of enterprises. Knowledge acquisition itself means that companies must establish a powerful search capability mechanism when searching for knowledge sources, so as to quickly find complementary knowledge or enhance knowledge. It is worth noting that in open innovation, most companies focus too much on searching "Opening up" knowledge and neglecting the development of the enterprise's own knowledge. The enterprise itself has a large amount of tacit knowledge, which is usually expressed as the intellectual capital of employees. After the acquisition of external knowledge, the enterprise and employees absorb and internalize their own knowledge storage, Knowledge sharing plays an intermediary role in this process.

Enterprises can benefit from personal creativity outside the enterprise, but the inflowing ideas and innovations from outside are not spontaneous, and new strategic working methods must be adopted to match the behavior of the enterprise with the resources and capabilities available from the external environment. In this context, free and open source software companies are an extreme example because innovations are provided by individuals who merge into the community, which means that traditional methods (such as contracts) to deal with other companies' external inputs are no longer suitable.

Focusing uncontrollably on innovations that benefit from external sources is difficult to be productive. For innovative activities, enterprises need to control many elements in the innovation network to a certain degree. Openness is beneficial, and this benefit decreases with the intervention of too many external sources of innovation. How to coordinate external knowledge to make the company open and get enough feedback to survive is a challenge.

If firms want to use external knowledge, companies need to know where the knowledge exists how to obtain it, and how to use it later. In order to deal with this, companies need to develop internal expertise to identify and absorb external results. Although absorptive capacity initially focused on identifying and evaluating possible external knowledge, in the future it will focus on how companies recognize and understand, absorb and apply external knowledge. Absorptive capacity shows that the external assimilation knowledge partly depends on the internal knowledge, because it simultaneously guides search behavior and the possibility of evaluating and using resources.

## Knowledge Transfer

Knowledge transfer is the process of transportation and transformation of knowledge resources. Al-Laham et al.[19] believes that knowledge has time value, and the value of knowledge gradually decreases with the passage of time, which will also bring about the shrinking of the organizational knowledge inventory." From a formal point of view, knowledge transfer is the process of tacit knowledge through coding and The process of the diffusion and externalization of the formal channels of the organization; from the perspective of knowledge flow, knowledge transfer is the transfer of the acquired knowledge source to the individual or department of knowledge demand: from the perspective of external performance, the transfer of knowledge at the individual level is generally through communication and other informal channels are used, and department-level knowledge transfer is usually achieved through formal channels such as meetings and teamwork.

## Knowledge Integration

Knowledge integration refers to the organization, reorganization and interpretation of existing knowledge in order to create new knowledge and maximize knowledge collaboration. This process is usually manifested as the storage, fusion and combination of coded knowledge. The knowledge integration process contains the transformation and fusion of individual knowledge to collective knowledge. Through multiple combinations of different unit knowledge, the stock and quality of enterprise knowledge are improved. Knowledge integration is a cyclical process. In the internal network composed of nodes and subnets within the enterprise, knowledge integration makes the node knowledge diffuse into subnet knowledge through the network, and the subnet knowledge is accepted by the nodes. This process makes the scattered individual knowledge integrated into Organize collective knowledge. However, it should be noted that knowledge integration is often through the organization's traditional knowledge fusion mechanism, that is, the manager's conventions and commands, which will lead to the blind obedience of knowledge subjects and the decline of innovation performance.

## Knowledge Creation and Application

Knowledge creation and application are the embodiment of "knowledge creation value", the result of the entire knowledge process and open innovation. From the perspective of knowledge stock, through the early knowledge acquisition, transfer and integration, the knowledge stock at this time is compared with the acquisition The time has dropped drastically and shows a high degree of coding and specialization. At the same time, the flow rate has been relatively accelerated, forming a process of knowledge appreciation. This knowledge appreciation is not linear and horizontal, but a spiral increase. In addition, the value of knowledge creation and application is reflected in the innovation of enterprises. Performance and innovative products are the commercialization and marketization of knowledge. Through the analysis of the knowledge flow process in open innovation, we can clearly see a flow chain. The generation power of the knowledge chain is driven by the subjective demand of the knowledge flow and the knowledge potential difference, and the object of the knowledge chain is the knowledge flow itself. In this process, due to the weakening of organizational boundaries and the development of network technology, knowledge will flow out at every stage of the chain. It mainly includes two parts. One part is the knowledge that cannot be identified and discovered in time during the knowledge acquisition stage and cannot meet the innovation requirements, and the other part is the knowledge loss caused by the phased knowledge output.

In the stage of knowledge acquisition and sharing, enterprises focus on the acquisition and absorption of external knowledge sources. The risk factors of the knowledge flow process in this process lie in the knowledge object, the knowledge subject, and the internal and external environment of knowledge. In the stage of knowledge transfer and integration, companies pay attention to knowledge classification, knowledge transportation and integration of acquired knowledge. The flowing risks of this process are reflected in the paradox of knowledge value, the influence of organizational structure, and the formalization and informalization of internal communication channels within the organization. Influence. In the output stage of knowledge innovation, that is, the stage of knowledge creation and application, the risk of knowledge flow comes from the influence of the organization's control and coordination mechanism, corporate culture and external environment.

## 3  Knowledge Flow and Commercialization of OSS

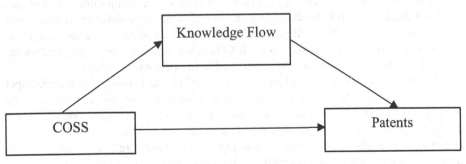

**Fig. 1.** A theoretical model

### 3.1  Open Source

In order for commercial companies to better benefit from the open source community, we need to first clarify the characteristics of open source. First, it can reduce transaction costs by licensing agreements. Second, open source contributes to indirect returns investment of firms on different vertical positions. For instance, companies downstream in the supply chain (middleware, applications, hardware, and services) often have access to resources that were previously protected in part by the applicability regime through open source systems. In addition, companies upstream in the supply chain can benefit from complementary products by increasing the speed of diffusion of industry standards through open source for non-core Technologies [8, 20]. Third, open-source system enables firms to obtain expert skills according to its needs (Fig. 1).

The disadvantage of open source communities mainly comes from the lack of binding contracts between participants. First of all, this leads to unstable innovation output. The output of the open source community depends largely on the experience and skill set of potential contributors and the activity of the contributors. In addition, when a project's major contributors are hired by closed source firms, turning the public outcome of open source into a private product, it may put the project, its members and users at risk.

## 3.2  OSS and COSS

OSS has reemerged as a mode for developing and organizing software innovation. Firms can respond to such a change in the software development process in different ways: by adjusting to, resisting, or supporting it [20]. Currently, more and more profitable companies choose to publish source code and release open source projects on open source hosting platforms, which is a profitable strategy. First, profitable companies can enhance their innovation efficiency by reducing R&D risk. Second, open source can guarantee a certain level of R&D investment recovery. For situations without considering the participation of commercial companies in the open source community, the success factors depend on the severity of the license, the attractiveness of the community, and the quality of the software. The main differences between commercial companies involved in open source projects are the R&D effort, organizational goals and management mechanisms.

R&D mastery can affect the attractiveness of open source communities. Companies need to make a trade-off between relying on external developers and internal developers, and develop a relevant community attractiveness strategy. In addition, because companies rely to some extent on employees as the R&D anchor, this can lead to projects backed by a stable R&D force that guarantees the quality of open source software.

Organizational goals can influence the severity of the license. Commercial open source projects need to choose the right license both to ensure the open status of the project and to seek revenue streams as well as to maintain the unique competitiveness of the enterprise. In addition. Organizational goals can also have an impact on the attractiveness of the open source community. Furthermore, organizational goals can have a significant impact on the quality of the open source community. Companies will certainly promote the proliferation and visibility of open source projects first in order to make profits.

The governance mechanism first has a great impact on the severity of the license. Commercial companies choose their licenses based on their strategy, and at the same time need to consider the level of acceptance of their licenses by users and volunteer developers in the community. Second, governance mechanisms can have an impact on the attractiveness of open source communities. Companies cannot control the community by means of power, and they cannot make the community resistant to users and volunteers. Finally, governance mechanisms have a significant impact on the quality factor of open source software. Companies control open source projects and can therefore position them for high quality output.

## 3.3   COSS, Knowledge Flow and Patents

According to the knowledge-based theory of the firm, when a commercial firm participates in an open source community, there is a high probability that the knowledge absorbed from the community will affect the firm's patent output by increasing the firm's ability to innovate.

Patent rights transfer the rights to exclude others from using the technology but do not transfer the usage rights of the technology to the patent holder [21]. It has been argued that a large portfolio of software patents can be a complementary asset that favors the commercialization It has been argued that a large portfolio of software patents can be a complementary asset that favors the commercialization of OSS products [20]. However, little research has been done to examine how commercial firms influence their patent portfolios through participation in the open source community and what factors influence this relationship.

When we combine the knowledge flow process with the contributors involved in the open source projects distributed by the enterprise in the hosting platform, we are able to identify a number of factors within the enterprise related to R&D output that may be influenced by the open source community. First, when employees of a commercial enterprise interact with development engineers outside the enterprise through projects distributed by the enterprise in an open source hosting platform, they gain knowledge related to open source projects in addition to other tacit knowledge. The process of tacit knowledge manifestation can have an impact on technical knowledge management process other than the current open source project. Secondly, programmers involved in open source projects generally develop better communication skills and are therefore able to facilitate knowledge absorption through iterative confirmation when integrating knowledge acquired from external sources. Finally, programmers who participate in open source projects generally develop a better sense of cooperation, and therefore partially increase the frequency of knowledge sharing in a particular department within the enterprise.

The knowledge acquired by software companies from the open source community is technical knowledge. Technical knowledge from outside the enterprise is imported into the enterprise and influences the innovation activities of the enterprise. The technical knowledge outside the enterprise can be divided into two types, explicit technical and invisible technical knowledge, according to the degree of coding. Explicit technical knowledge mainly includes published scientific and technical literature, technical standards, patents and unpublished scientific and technical literature, and internal company reports; tacit technical knowledge includes individual invisible technical knowledge, such as judgment and intuition, and organizational invisible technical knowledge. The acquisition of explicit technical knowledge and tacit technical knowledge is crucial to enterprise technology innovation and can cause a new round of technical knowledge flow within the enterprise.

The generation and acquisition of technical knowledge in the process of enterprise technology innovation is the starting point of technical knowledge flow, which provides intellectual support for enterprise technology innovation activities. The process of acquiring external tacit technical knowledge and explicit technical knowledge in the process of enterprise technology innovation is the process of inputting external technical knowledge about new products and new processes into the enterprise, and the input technical knowledge is objective. Therefore, the acquisition of technical knowledge in the process of technological innovation of enterprises is not generated, but relies on the internal absorption ability of enterprises to transform external technical knowledge into internal technical knowledge of enterprises under the joint action of various external factors, which is a conditional transformation process. Therefore, the generation and acquisition of technological knowledge have different impacts on enterprise technological innovation, which are manifested in the following two aspects.

### Impact on the Cycle of Enterprise Technology Innovation

Technological innovation derived from the acquisition of technical knowledge from the open source community shortens the cycle of enterprise technological innovation because a large amount of R&D time is eliminated in the R&D phase of enterprise technological innovation. Relying on external acquisition to drive technological innovation is a shortcut. By acquiring external knowledge of new technologies in a paid or unpaid way, it saves the time of the enterprise in the process of research and development, reduces the risk of the enterprise in the process of research and development of new products and processes, improves the success rate of the enterprise's technological innovation, and helps the enterprise to produce marketable goods in accordance with the needs of the times. Therefore, promoting enterprise technological innovation activities by acquiring external knowledge of new technologies is conducive to shortening the enterprise technological innovation cycle.

### Impact on Technology Innovation Mode

Although relying on the acquisition of external technological knowledge to promote enterprise technological innovation activities can shorten the enterprise technological innovation cycle, it is impossible to promote enterprises to master the most advanced technological knowledge due to the stickiness of the new technological knowledge obtained from external sources. The technical knowledge obtained by enterprises from outside in the process of technological innovation has a certain background dependence, and can only function effectively in a specific market atmosphere and working environment, and it is difficult to transfer the core technical know-how, technical secrets and other hidden technical knowledge with strong personal attachment in the process of technical knowledge input, which often causes enterprises to obtain external technical knowledge in the process of acquiring external technical knowledge, and cannot fully obtain all the New technical knowledge. In addition, the technical knowledge obtained from the outside is not the most advanced technical knowledge at that time, therefore, the technological innovation activities of enterprises can only be imitated and followed by innovation, and sometimes it may cause the failure of technological innovation of enterprises.

# 4  Conclusions

Innovation in open-source projects is achieved through active interaction between innovation actors, and knowledge flow explicitly considers these interactions. The subsequent research may focus on empirically testing the theory presented in this paper that a commercial firm's participation in an open-source community can affect a firm's technological innovation through knowledge flow, and thus affect patents. This impact on patents can be either in terms of the number of patent citations or patents, or in terms of the patent portfolio since only some of a firm's personnel participate in the open source community, it is likely to increase only the size of the patent portfolio related to the technology of the open source project.

## References

1. Lerner, J., Tirole, J.: The economics of technology sharing: Open source and beyond. J. Econ. Perspect. **19**, 99–120 (2005). https://doi.org/10.1257/0895330054048678
2. Lakhani, K.R., von Hippel, E.: How open source software works: Free user-to-user assistance. Res. Policy **32**, 923–943 (2003). https://doi.org/10.1007/978-3-322-84540-5_13
3. Shah, S.K.: Motivation, governance, and the viability of hybrid forms in open source software development. Manage. Sci. **52**, 1000–1014 (2006). https://doi.org/10.1287/mnsc.1060.0553
4. Koenig, J.: Seven open source business strategies for competitive advantage. IT Manager's J. **5**, 14 (2004)
5. Fitzgerald, B.: The transformation of open source software. MIS Q. **30**, 587–598 (2006). https://doi.org/10.2307/25148740
6. Bonaccorsi, A., Giannangeli, S., Rossi, C.: Entry strategies under competing standards: Hybrid business models in the opensource software industry. Manage. Sci. **52**(7), 1085–1098 (2006). https://doi.org/10.1287/mnsc.1060.0547
7. Dahlander, L., Gann, D.M.: How open is innovation? Res. Policy **39**, 699–709 (2010). https://doi.org/10.1016/j.respol.2010.01.013
8. Joachim, H.: Selective revealing in open innovation processes: The case of embedded linux. Res. Policy **35**, 953–969 (2006). https://doi.org/10.1016/j.respol.2006.04.010
9. Bonaccorsi, A., Rossi, C.: Why open source software can succeed. Res. Policy **32**, 1243–1258 (2003). https://doi.org/10.1016/S0048-7333(03)00051-9
10. Chesbrough, H.: Open innovation: Where we've been and where we're going. Res. Technol. Manag. **55**, 20–27 (2012). https://doi.org/10.5437/08956308X5504085
11. Chesbrough, H.: The logic of open innovation: Managing intellectual property. Calif. Manag. Rev. **45**, 33–58 (2003)
12. Love, J.H., Roper, S.: Organizing the innovation process: Complementarities in innovation networking. Ind. Innov. **16**, 273–290 (2009). https://doi.org/10.1080/13662710902923776
13. West, J., Gallagher, S.: Challenges of open innovation: the paradox of firm investment in open-source software. R D Manag. **36**, 319–331 (2006). https://doi.org/10.1111/j.1467-9310.2006.00436.x
14. Nelson, R., Winter, S.G.: An Evolutionary Theory of Technical Change. Belknap Press of Harvard University Press, Cambridge, MA (1982)
15. Chesbrough, H.W.: Open Business Models: How to Thrive in the New Innovation Landscape. Harvard Business School Press, Boston, MA (2006)
16. Kessler, E.H., Bierly, P.E., Gopalakrishnan, S.: Internal vs external learning in new product development: Effects on speed, costs and competitive advantage. R D Manag. **30**, 213–224 (2000). https://doi.org/10.1111/1467-9310.00172

17. Alavi, M., Leidner, D.: Knowledge management and knowledge management systems: Conceptual foundations and research issues. MIS Q. **10**, 53–60 (2001). https://doi.org/10.2307/3250961

18. West, J., Bogers, M.: Leveraging external sources of innovation: A review of research on open innovation. J. Prod. Innov. Manage. **31**, 814–831 (2013). https://doi.org/10.1111/jpim.12125

19. Al-Laham, A., Tzabbar, D., Amburgey, T.L.: The dynamics of knowledge stocks and knowledge flows: Innovation consequences of recruitment and collaboration in biotech. Ind. Corp. Chang. **20**, 555–583 (2011). https://doi.org/10.1093/icc/dtr001

20. Fosfuri, A., Giarratana, M.S., Luzzi, A.: The penguin has entered the building: The commercialization of open source software products. Organ. Sci. **19**, 292–305 (2008). https://doi.org/10.1287/orsc.1070.0321

21. Gans, J.S., Stern, S.: Is there a market for ideas? Ind. Corp. Chang. **19**, 805–837 (2010). https://doi.org/10.1093/icc/dtq023

# Author Index